B7

CW00971673

lacks title-page,
o/w as new.

ABOUT
THE AUTHOR

DANIEL P. McLOUGHLIN has been a real estate and business attorney since 1978. During that time, he has represented buyers, sellers, lenders, title insurance companies, developers and agents respecting a wide variety of real estate transactions. He is a member of the Real Property and Business Law Sections of the State Bar of California and is a licensed real estate broker. He is a member of the faculty at San Francisco State University and is certified by the California Department of Real Estate to teach Continuing Education courses.

To My Mother and Father

CONTENTS

SECTION IX   REGULATION OF THE USE OF LAND   353

20 Eminent Domain: The Condemnation Power   355

21 Zoning and Other Public Land Use Controls   371

PREFACE

This book is an introduction to real estate law for undergraduate and graduate students. Business schools usually offer a course in real estate law and departments of architectural and urban planning often include the course in their curricula. A course on the principles of real estate is advised as a prerequisite and a course in business law that covers contracts and agency would be helpful, although not a necessary prerequisite.

In preparing this text, certain goals were kept in mind to distinguish this book from the others in the field. The text is intended to be comprehensive in both the classical and modern sense and to serve as a tool for the effective presentation of the material. It is national in its scope and presents both the general law and significant minority positions. The approach adopted by a particular state or states is identified only for purposes of illustration or if it suggests a significant emerging trend.

Throughout the text, an effort has been made to include material that will enable the student to appreciate the historical context of property law. The other fields of law with which students are most likely to become acquainted are contracts, agency, and business organizations. Unlike these, property law is often more steeped in history than in logic, and material has been included to provide a historical context to help the student better understand the law in its present state.

The sheer mass of necessary material dictates that the case book approach is nearly indispensable to an effective presentation. The cases in this text were selected on the basis of their tendency to serve a useful pedagogic function. The cases have been heavily edited to delete procedural and secondary issues and, for the most part, the facts have been rewritten and reorganized in the interest of clarity. An effort was made to obtain the leading cases and those that contain a particularly careful discussion of the issues. Most cases in the text are followed by additional material to clarify the issues presented, suggest alternative approaches, and pose discussion questions.

At the end of the chapters are a series of questions. These have been developed to promote discussion, emphasize certain material, or clarify items that may warrant additional examination.

The text is divided into nine major sections that can best be presented consecutively. However, some might choose to introduce the materials on noncontractual transfers (Chapter 10) and deeds (Chapter 14) at an earlier stage in the text. The material on landlord and tenant (Chapter 19) and public regulation (Chapters 20 through 22) can probably be presented at any time during the course.

Section I consists of one chapter and provides a broad overview of the nature of legal thinking and the nature of property. Section II introduces the student to the permissible present and future interests in land and, to a large extent, is essential to a comprehensive understanding of the remainder of the text.

Section III consists of Chapter 4 which examines direct restraints on alienation, an issue which recurs, particularly in the material on mortgages and landlord tenant. Chapter 4 also considers the rule against perpetuities. This esoteric subject was included with the idea that it probably will be deleted by all but the most ambitious of professors.

Section IV is concerned with co-ownership of land. Chapter 5 introduces the various forms of co-ownership and Chapter 6 extends the discussion into the area of condominiums and related forms.

Section V examines private land use limitations. Chapter 7 considers so-called inherent limitations, primarily the doctrine of nuisance. Chapter 8 covers the creation, scope, and termination of easements and Chapter 9 addresses convenants and equitable servitudes.

Section VI consists of seven chapters which, for the most part, examine the modern real estate conveyance. Chapter 10 is a survey of noncontractual transfers, particularly intervivos and testamentary gifts and adverse possession. Two chapters are devoted to the role of real estate agents. Chapter 11 considers the nature of the agency relation, particularly the scope of an agent's authority and the fiduciary obligation. Chapter 12 introduces the licensing and regulatory requirements of the brokerage industry and examines the expanding area of civil liability.

Chapter 13 contains a detailed discussion of real estate contracts, including sections on marketable title, performance of conditions, disclosure requirements, and the liability of housing suppliers. Chapters 14 and 15 are respectively devoted to the use of deeds and the operation of recording statutes. Finally, Chapter 16 examines the responsibilities of the escrow holder and the role of title insurance.

Section VII considers security interests in real estate and is composed of two chapters. Chapter 17 examines real estate finance, particularly the creation, operation, foreclosure, and discharge of a mortgage and its equivalents. Chapter 18 considers involuntary liens, with emphasis upon the judgment lien and the mechanic's lien.

Section VIII is comprised of one chapter which discusses, at some length, the commerical and residential landlord-tenant relationship.

The text concludes with Section IX, which examines public regulation of real property. Chapter 20 addresses the scope and operation of the condemnation power and includes sections on inverse condemnation and valuation. Chapter 21 contains an extensive discussion of the subject of zoning. Included in the chapter are sections on the regulatory taking and the administration of the zoning plan through the techniques of the nonconforming use, conditional use, and variance. Exclusionary zoning and examples of the regional approach to zoning are also discussed.

Chapter 22 examines subdivision regulations including dedications and impact fees. Chapter 23 concludes the text with a discussion of environmental protection statutes.

The National Environmental Quality Act (NEPA) and the preparation of the Environmental Impact Statement receive particular attention.

This text is intended to be comprehensive and to afford the professor the opportunity to delete material because of time and other constraints. Case material has been selected and edited to facilitate the students' interest and learning. The text has been class-tested during two semesters at San Francisco State University and modifications have been made on the basis of that experience. We have found that all the material can be covered in a fifteen week semester and that student interest and participation remains high throughout the course. It has been our experience and continues to be our hope that at the end of the semester, the student will emerge with a thorough and enjoyably obtained understanding of this relatively difficult subject.

McGraw-Hill and I would like to thank the following reviewers for their many helpful comments and suggestions: Jerry Belloit, University of North Florida; Richard L. Coffinberger, George Mason University; Judith A. Craven, Attorney-at-Law; Deborah A. Ford, University of Baltimore; Veronica Free, University of North Alabama; Forrest E. Huffman, Temple University; Arthur F. Stelley, Baylor University; Bill W. West, Attorney-at-Law; and Lois J. Yoder, Kent State University.

Daniel P. McLoughlin

PRINCIPLES OF REAL ESTATE LAW

INTRODUCTION TO THE STUDY OF REAL ESTATE LAW

THE NATURE OF LAW AND PROPERTY

TOPICS CONSIDERED IN THE CHAPTER:

1 INTRODUCTION

In its broadest sense, law is simply any recurring mode of interaction among individuals and groups coupled with an expectation that certain conduct will either be approved or disapproved. In primitive societies, the "laws" of the group are little more than customs. At a fairly early stage, the idea that laws should be reduced to a written form developed. The Code of Hammurabi, dating from the eighteenth century B.C., is probably the most well known of the ancient codes.

The western philosophy of law, referred to as jurisprudence, has its origin in Plato's dialogues. The discussions between Plato and Aristotle have continued to create the framework in which the modern question, "What is law?" is addressed.

Most modern legal philosophers consider the role of law to be that of a regulator of human relations operating in much the same fashion as morals and customs. In fact, law adequately performs its function only when it is suited to the expectations and way of life of a people. Thus, the law must be capable of changing in response to social and economic changes. In this sense, the law must reconcile often conflicting demands and have both continuity with the past and adaptability to the present and the future.

2 JURISPRUDENCE: "THE NATURE OF LAW"

Ancient Law

All people and nations of the world have, to some extent, formed certain ideas about the nature of law. Discussion of the subject usually begins with the early Greeks. Plato (427–347 B.C.) believed deeply in the establishment of a class system of rulers, military guardians, and workers, and he believed that a rigorous division of labor among the three classes should prevail in society. Yet even in such a rigid society, Plato acknowledged that disputes would arise between citizens which public authorities would have to resolve.

Aristotle (384–322 B.C.) was strongly influenced by the ideas of Plato, but he differed from Plato in numerous respects. Aristotle believed that a society based upon the rule of law was the only practical means of achieving social and political organization. "Man," he said, "when perfected is the best of animals, but if he be isolated from law and justice he is the worst of all." (Aristotle, *The Politics Book I,* page 1253A)

The Stoic philosophers, who originated in Greece during the third century B.C. believed that reason was a universal force and provided the bases of social law and justice. Cicero (106–43 B.C.), a great Roman lawyer and statesman, was strongly influenced by the Stoic philosophers and believed that nature and reason were the dominating forces in the universe.

Law in the Middle Ages

The Middle Ages are generally considered as the period between the fall of Rome in 476 and the Renaissance in about 1450. During this time, legal philosophy, like other branches of science and thought, was dominated by the Church and its doctrines. Perhaps the most influential of religious philosophers was St. Augustine (A.D. 354–430). It was his conviction that prior to Adam and Eve's fall, a golden age had occurred in which the "law of nature" had been realized. People lived in a state of purity and justice without slavery or other forms of domination. Original sin undermined this state and the nature of people became corrupted by greed and the lust for power.

Attempts to reconcile human law with Christian theology was most carefully accomplished by St. Thomas Aquinas (A.D. 1226–1274). Like Aristotle, Aquinas believed that law was largely based upon reason; laws that were unjust, unreasonable, or contrary to the law of nature were not law at all and need not be observed.

Origins of Modern Legal Thought

During the seventeenth and eighteenth centuries, the rise of science exerted an impact on legal theory. The philosophies of Thomas Hobbes (1588–1679) and Spinoza (1632–1677) sought to reconcile and balance the often competing claims of the law of nature and the need of the central government to maintain order.

The theories of John Locke (1632–1704) and Montesquieu (1689–1755) viewed the law as a product of human reason but also saw it as a means to protect individual liberty against governmental intrusion by limiting the power of a government. Emphasis was placed upon individual liberty and law was conceived, in part, as an instrument to prevent despotism and to enlarge individual freedom.

The philosophies of Locke and Montesquieu formed the philosophical breakground for the United States form of government, particularly for the Declaration of Independence and the Bill of Rights.

3 SOURCES OF LAW IN THE UNITED STATES

The most direct source of U.S. law is the common law of England. All states except Louisiana have adopted the English common law as the rule of law where no conflicting law exists.

Under the democratic form of government in the United States, the people are considered the ultimate source of all power including the power to establish law. The United States has a representative form of democracy in which elected officials exercise their authority on behalf of the people. Central to the operation of the United States government is the concept of Federalism: At the national level, the federal government adopts and enforces laws binding upon all citizens. In addition, each of the states within the United States also has the power to enact laws that govern the conduct of citizens within each state.

At both the federal and state levels, the doctrine of *separation of powers* causes the authority of the government to be divided among three separate branches. The *legislative branch* adopts written laws called statutes which are enforced by the *executive branch* of government and interpreted and enforced by the *judicial branch.*

For many years it was customary to conclude that constitutions, statutes, and the common law as decided by the courts constituted the three sources of law. In addition, the authority given to administrative agencies has led to an additional source for the creation and implementation of law. For example, Congress enacts a statute establishing an administrative agency such as the Internal Revenue Service or the Securities and Exchange Commission and gives the agency the authority to issue rules and regulations. These rules and regulations become an additional source of law.

Constitutions

A constitution establishes the basic principles and authority of a governmental structure. The U.S. Constitution consists of seven articles adopted in 1887 and twenty-six amendments adopted between 1791 and 1971. The U.S. Constitution limits the powers of the states, enumerates the powers of the three branches of the federal government, and delineates the rights that are guaranteed to all American citizens. Among these rights are the freedom of speech and religion, freedom from unreasonable searches and seizures, the right to a jury trial, and so on.

In addition to the federal Constitution, each state has adopted its own constitution. These constitutions generally outline the nature and organization of the state's government, the rights guaranteed to citizens within the state and, like the federal Constitution, apportions the power of government among the executive, legislative and judicial branches of government.

Statutes

Statutes are written laws enacted by a legislative body. At the federal level, the U.S. Congress enacts federal statutes and each state has an equivalent body authorized to enact laws for purposes of governing within the state. Most states also permit lesser governmental units such as counties, cities, towns, or special districts to enact laws, commonly referred to as ordinances, which affect matters of peculiarly local concern. Building codes, zoning laws, and rent control provisions are examples of laws often enacted at the local level, although such provisions may be the subject of regulation by the state.

The Common Law

The third source of law in the United States consists of that body of cases previously decided by appellate level courts. When resolving a controversy, courts will consult first the Constitution and then statutory provisions. If neither of these are sufficient to resolve the matter, the court then looks at prior cases to determine the rule of law that should apply in a particular case.

Marbury v. Madison, 5 U.S. 137 (1803)

In the election of 1800, Thomas Jefferson, a Republican, defeated the incumbent president John Adams, a Federalist. Following the election, President Adams appointed Federalists to fill forty-two vacancies as federal justices of the peace and initiated the formal appointment procedure that required the Secretary of State to deliver sealed commissions to the appointees. Not all of the commissions, however, were delivered prior to the inauguration of Jefferson. The new secretary of state, James Madison, refused to deliver the remaining commissions. William Marbury, an appointee who had not received his commission, filed suit in the Supreme Court asking the Court to order Madison to deliver the commissions. Marbury asserted his right to bring his suit in the Supreme Court based on the Judiciary Act of 1789, a federal statute that authorized the Supreme Court "to issue commands . . . to persons holding office under the authority of the United States."

Although the case was fraught with political issues, the Supreme Court focused on a narrow question: whether or not the provisions of the Judiciary Act of 1789 violated the Constitution. The Constitution enumerates the types of cases that may be brought to the Supreme Court, and these cases do not include disputes seeking to direct the activities of federal officials. The Supreme Court concluded that Congress's attempt to expand the types of cases that the Court may hear to include those cases not listed in the Constitution was "repugnant" to the Constitution. The Court then considered whether it should follow the law established by the Judiciary Act of 1789.

Chief Justice Marshall stated the opinion of the Court:

> . . . The question, whether a statute, repugnant to the Constitution can become the law of the land, is a question deeply interesting to the United States. . . .
>
> The powers of the legislature are defined and limited; and that those limits may not be mistaken, or forgotten, the Constitution is written. To what purpose are powers limited, and to what purpose is that limitation committed to writing, if these limits may, at any time, be passed by those intended to be restrained? . . .
>
> The Constitution is either a superior paramount law, unchangeable by ordinary means, or it is on a level with ordinary legislative acts, and, like other acts, is alterable when the legislature shall please to alter it.
>
> In our view, the Constitution, and since the Constitution is superior to any ordinary act of the legislature, so that the Constitution, and not such ordinary act, must govern the case to which they both apply.
>
> Thus, the particular phraseology of the Constitution of the United States confirms and strengthens the principle, supposed to be essential to all written constitutions, that a law repugnant to the Constitution is void; and that courts, as well as other departments, are bound by that instrument.

The statute must be discharged.

NOTES AND QUESTIONS

Marbury v. Madison is still the leading case for the proposition that a statute which conflicts with the Constitution is void. Suppose a federal statute conflicts not with the U.S. Constitution but with the constitution of a state. Is such an occurrence possible? Would the statute be enforceable?

4 THE AMERICAN COURT SYSTEM

We have seen that the judicial branch of government is responsible for applying and interpreting the law. Consistent with the concept of federalism, the United States has a system of federal courts and each state has a court system of its own.

A The Federal Court System

Article 3 section 1 of the U.S. Constitution provides:

> The judicial power of the United States, shall be vested in one Supreme Court, and in such inferior courts as the Congress may from time to time ordain and establish.

Congress has exercised its authority under Article 3 and has established a three tiered federal court system consisting of the trial level courts called *district courts, circuit courts of appeal* and the *Supreme Court*. In addition, Congress has also established certain specialized federal courts such as the tax courts and bankruptcy courts.

U.S. district courts are the trial courts of the federal judicial system. Congress has enacted a statute which divides the country into *ninety-six judicial districts,* each of which has at least one district court.

In addition, federal law divides the country into *twelve judicial circuits,* plus the District of Columbia. The court of appeals for each circuit is authorized to review district court decisions from districts within the circuit.

The ultimate appellate court in this country is the U.S. Supreme Court. The court is composed of a Chief Justice and eight associate justices who are appointed by the President and confirmed by the Senate.

B State Court Systems

Most state court systems are similar to the federal system. Although the terminology varies from state to state, each state has a court of original jurisdiction, often referred to as the trial court, which has the power to take evidence and apply the law of the state to determine the outcome of a controversy.

Appeals from trial court decisions are usually made to an intermediate level appellate court which has the power to review the trial court's findings and conclusions. In addition, there is usually a final level appellate court often called the supreme court of the state, which hears appeals of the decisions of appellate courts.

5 JURISDICTION

The concept of jurisdiction involves the power or authority of a court to hear a certain kind of controversy. The concept of jurisdiction also helps to delineate the relationship between state and federal courts.

A Subject Matter Jurisdiction

There are two kinds of jurisdiction. The first is *subject matter jurisdiction* that concerns the authority of the court to hear a certain kind of dispute. For example, the subject matter jurisdiction of the federal courts is limited to questions arising under the federal Constitution or federal statutes and disputes between residents of different states. Thus, actions involving federal anti-trust or securities laws are properly filed in federal courts because federal courts have subject matter jurisdiction to hear such cases. In addition, an action between residents of New York and California, for instance, is properly filed in federal court based on diversity of citizenship because the plaintiff and defendant are domiciled in different states.

The subject matter jurisdiction of the federal courts is exclusive. This means that the federal courts, and only federal courts, may hear cases over which they have jurisdiction. For instance, a state court does not have the power to determine a question arising under federal statutes. Similarly, questions involving only the interpretation of a question of state law cannot be heard in federal court because the federal court does not have subject matter jurisdiction to determine such cases.

B   Personal Jurisdiction

In addition to subject matter jurisdiction, a court must have *personal jurisdiction* before it can hear the case. The requirement of personal jurisdiction is based upon the due process clause contained in the U.S. Constitution and requires that persons be given adequate *notice* of a claim pending against them before they will be bound by its outcome.

Issues concerning personal jurisdiction often arose with the enactment by state legislatures of so-called *long arm statutes*. Long arm statutes attempt to give personal jurisdiction to a state court over residents outside the state who were involved in a transaction within the boundaries of the state. Perhaps the most common example involves a vacationing motorist from New York who is involved in an automobile accident in California and who then returns to New York. The California long arm statute would permit the California state court to assert personal jurisdiction over the New York resident based upon the California long arm statute. Such statutes were attacked on various grounds and ultimately the U.S. Supreme Court upheld their use, *provided that* the application of the long arm statute was ''consistent with contemporary notions of fair play and substantial justice''.

6   INTRODUCTION TO THE NATURE OF PROPERTY

The law of real estate is more complicated than most areas of law, because many principles of property law were developed in an age that is far different than our own. Much of the terminology of land law has remained unchanged for hundreds of years. For this reason, a brief explanation of the historical background of property law is presented in this chapter.

Nearly two centuries ago, Sir William Blackstone summarized the nature of private property in the following terms:

> There is nothing which so generally strikes the imagination, and engages the affections of mankind, as the right of property; or that sole and despotic dominion which one man claims

and exercises over the external things of the world, in total exclusion of the right of any other individual in the universe.[1]

The owner of real estate is considered to own not only the surface ground but everything attached to the surface and everything above and below it. This includes timber, crops, and buildings that are attached to the land. It also includes minerals below the surface such as coal, ores, and gravel. In addition, the owner of land owns everything above the land, although this doctrine has been modified by the advent of aircraft.

The rights inherent in ownership of land can be separated. For instance, the owner of land may transfer the mineral rights to one person and the air rights to someone else while retaining ownership of the surface of the land.

In a related example, *A* died, leaving his property to *B,* provided that *C* could ''continue to live in the property at a rent not to exceed $100 per month for as long as she wants.'' *C* has a life estate, subject only to the conditions that she live in the property and pay rent.

Perhaps the most significant change in property law has been the recognition that certain private property rights must be adjusted in the interests of the community. The idea that the general public has a direct and protectable interest in property that is privately owned is a relatively recent development but is now firmly established. Although the topic of public rights in land is deferred to the end of this text, the idea is introduced in this chapter and should be kept in mind as the study of real estate law proceeds.

7 HISTORICAL BACKGROUND

The following quote is from *Introduction to the Law of Real Property,* by Cornelius J. Moynihan, West Publishing Co., 1962, p. 1–7.

It would be economical in terms of time and effort if we could begin the study of the law of real property by proceeding directly to a consideration of that law as it is in our own day and place. Unfortunately, such a short cut is not practical. A thorough understanding of the modern land law is impossible without a knowledge of its historical background. That law has been a millennium in the making. During this long period great changes have been effected by means of legislation and decisions, as well as by the development of new social systems and customs, but the process of change has been one of evolution not revolution. The imprint of the past is still discernible in the present. In this branch of the law more than any other we can time and again invoke the often quoted statement of Mr. Justice Holmes: ''Upon this point a page of history is worth a volume of logic.'' And if the aridity of legal history tends to be irksome we might recall Mr. Justice Cardozo's statement that this is a field ''where there can be no progress without history.''

A The Norman Settlement

And so we begin with the England of William the Conqueror the Norman Conquest (1066). The Norman arrow, shot perhaps at random, that pierced the eye socket of Harold, the Saxon

---

[1] William Blackstone, *Commentaries on the Laws of England, Book II,* 15th ed., 1809, chap. 1, p. 2.

king, decided not only the Battle of Hastings but affected the course of development of English law for centuries to come. The conquest, while preserving the framework of the old English state, gave to England a new dynasty, a new ruling class, and a new system of land holding.

William the Conqueror operated on the principle of political legitimacy. Tenuous as his claim to the English throne may have been, his successes in battle put beyond dispute his assertion that he was the legitimate successor of Edward the Confessor and, therefore, entitled to the rights and prerogatives of an English king. Consequently, those who had opposed him at Hastings and in the later uprisings forfeited their lands. Most of the Saxon nobility, who had formed the backbone of the opposition, were wiped out or driven into exile. Their lands became available for distribution to William's men as a reward for services, and the distribution itself served as a means of establishing a new Norman aristocracy on a solid foundation.

It is a tribute to the extraordinary administrative ability of William that this vast redistribution of English lands was carried out in an orderly manner. The whole process was controlled by the firm hand of the king. Immense holdings were granted, as might be expected, to his kinsmen and to his closest associates in the great project of the Conquest. To ten of his principal followers he gave almost one-fourth of England. To lesser barons he made grants of the smaller fiefs or holdings of English earls. Normally, the grants were not compact territorial units but consisted of manors scattered through several counties.

The larger baronial estates, or honours as they came to be called, were normally created out of the holdings of numerous Englishmen. As many as eighty English estates, situated in different regions, might be combined to compose a single lord's honour. In the course of the Norman settlement, several thousand smaller estates were compressed into fewer than two hundred major honours. The lords of these honours were the men who, with William, established the new English state.

B   The Introduction of Feudal Tenure

From a legal standpoint, one of the significant aspects of the Norman plantation was the introduction into England of the most highly organized type of feudal tenure—military tenure. Feudalism is a generic term that may be used to describe the social structure of Western Europe in the Middle Ages. At its core was the relationship of lord and vassal (not then a word of opprobrium) bound together by a bond of personal loyalty and owing mutual aid and assistance. The relationship was usually sealed by the solemn ceremony of homage wherein the vassal knelt before the lord, acknowledged himself to be his man, and swore fealty to him. The ceremony was frequently accompanied by a grant of land that was to be held by the lord for the vassal as tenant. Ordinally, by the terms of the grant, the tenant was to perform specific services, and these services were considered to be a burden on the land itself.

Military tenure was known in Normandy and William the Conqueror used it in England to build a military organization adequate to maintain the Crown against rebellion from within and invasion from without. Most of the lords and barons to whom William granted English lands held them under an obligation to supply a specific quota of knights for the royal host whenever they should be required. The number of knights to be furnished was in each case fixed by the terms of the charter evidencing the grant and, therefore, initially depended on the will and necessities of the king.

C The Creation of Subtenures

The expense to the tenants of maintaining as part of their households the prescribed quota of knights must have been considerable. Moreover, the constant presence in the household of a number of armed men, inclined to be disorderly at times, was a matter of concern. Slowly at first, but with increasing frequency, the tenants in chief made allotments of lands to their knights who thereupon themselves became tenants of their lords. The amount of land given in return for the obligation to supply the service of one knight varied. It depended on the bargain made by the lord and his prospective tenant. A particular tract might be made up of a number of knights' fees and, in later times, might be subdivided into fractional parts of one knight's fee. In some cases the number of knights enfeoffed, that is, given land, by the tenant in chief exceeded the quota owed for the king's service and in other cases the number was less.

All tenure implied services due from the tenant, but the service fixed at the creation of the tenure might be, and often was, nonmilitary in nature. The king made provision in land for his important administrative and household officials and to such tenures was attached the duty of rendering specific services necessary to the functioning of the royal household. The service prescribed might be that of marshal, steward, butler, or chamberlain. These were tenants with dignity and rank; but this type of tenure also embraced tenants who served the king in his chamber, his pantry, and his kitchen. William the Conqueror, for example, gave half a hide of land (about sixty acres) in Gloucestershire to his cook. The greater tenants in chief, whose households were often royal establishments in miniature, also gave lands to some of their retainers. Those receiving these lands also were subject to the obligation to render a prescribed personal service to the lord.

Moreover, many a small landholder found it advisable in an unruly age to place himself under the protection of some powerful earl or abbot by becoming his ally. The small landholder temporarily surrendered his lands to the lord. Lands would be returned after the duty of rendering military or other service was performed. By this process of commendation the tenurial system was further expanded.

8 THE ROLE OF EQUITY

As the preceding paragraphs indicate, the early common law period evolved a system of landholding that included a series of obligations owed by the lesser lords to the greater ones. These obligations involved the lesser lord providing crops, armaments and able-bodied men to the greater lord. The lesser lord could, and often did, continue this system down the line so he could satisfy his feudal obligations. Failure to satisfy the feudal obligations could result in one's interest in the land being forfeited. In light of the often heavy burden imposed by feudal obligations and the often dire consequences of failing to satisfy them, it is not surprising that efforts gradually were undertaken to avoid the imposition of these obligations.

In addition, there evolved in England a separate court called the Court of Chancery which was designed to provide a remedy where none had existed under the rigid and formal common law courts. The early chancellors were often members of the clergy who sought to dispense justice based upon a moral order and were thereby able to provide a remedy where none existed under the rigid doctrines of the common law. In time, the Courts of Chancery became integrated into a system of jurisprudence that was and is referred as ''Equity.'' The law of real estate today is a result of the application of both common law and equitable doctrines.

An example may help bring the interplay of law and equity into sharper focus. Suppose that Alice, an elderly widow in poor health, owns property in which she lives. Fearing that she may not survive her illness, she makes out a deed to her property and gives it to Bob, her friend, telling him to return the deed to her if she recovers from her illness. Who ''owns'' the property at this point? Bob has the deed so he is considered the legal owner of the property. However because, ''in equity and good conscience,'' Alice is the true owner, she is considered the equitable owner of the property. Suppose further that Bob sells the property to Chad just before Alice recovers from her illness. Now who owns the property? Equitable concepts again come into play. If Chad knew, or had reason to know, of Alice's interest, he will be forced to return the deed to her.

As the study of real estate law continues, you will have ample opportunity to examine the interaction between law and equity further.

9 THE POWER TO EXCLUDE

Common law has long recognized that the right of an owner to use his or her land is not unlimited. For the most part, however, an owner would not be restrained unless the use of the property caused harm to a neighbor's property. For instance, owners have traditionally not been permitted to pollute streams or cause noxious gases to be released from their property if such activities tended to harm another's property. Such interference with the property of another was considered a *nuisance* and is treated in Chapter 9.

However the right of an owner to *exclude* others from entering property was, until recently, nearly absolute. As indicated by the following material, the right to exclude others from private property is subject to various qualifications. When studying this material, try to determine the conditions which must exist before an owner loses the right to deny others access to his or her property.

Pruneyard Shopping Center v. Robins, 447 U.S. 74 (1979)

Facts of the case.

Defendant Pruneyard is a privately owned shopping center in the city of Campbell, California. It covers approximately twenty-one acres—five devoted to parking and sixteen occupied by walkways, plazas, sidewalks, and buildings that contain more than sixty-five specialty shops, ten restaurants, and a movie theater. The Pruneyard is open to the public for people to patronize its commercial establishments. It has a policy of not permitting any visitor or tenant to engage in any publicly expressive activity, including the circulation of petitions, not directly related to its commercial purposes.

Plaintiffs are high school students who sought to solicit support for their opposition to a United Nations resolution against Zionism. On a Saturday afternoon they set up a card table in a corner of Pruneyard's central courtyard. They distributed pamphlets and asked passers-by to sign petitions, which were to be sent to the President and members of Congress. Their activity was peaceful and orderly and, as far as the record indicates, was not objected to by Pruneyard's patrons.

Soon after plaintiffs had begun soliciting signatures, a security guard informed them that they would have to leave because their activity violated Pruneyard regulations. The guard suggested that they move to the public sidewalk at Pruneyard's perimeter. Plaintiffs immediately left the premises and later filed this lawsuit in the California Superior Court seeking to enjoin defendants from denying them access to Pruneyard for the purpose of circulating their petitions.

The superior court held that plaintiffs were not entitled under either the federal or the California Constitution to exercise their asserted rights on the shopping center property and the California Court of Appeal affirmed. The California Supreme Court reversed, holding that the California Constitution protects "speech and petitioning, reasonably exercised, in shopping centers even when the centers are privately owned."

OPINION

It is true that one of the essential sticks in the bundle of property rights is the right to exclude others. And here there has literally been a "taking" of that right to the extent that the California Supreme Court has interpreted the State Constitution to entitle its citizens to exercise free expression and petition rights on shopping center property. But it is well established that not every destruction or injury to property by governmental action has been held to be a "taking" in the constitutional sense.

Here the requirement that defendants permit plaintiffs to exercise state-protected rights of free expression and petition on shopping center property clearly does not amount to an unconstitutional infringement of defendant's property rights. There is nothing to suggest that preventing appellants from prohibiting this sort of activity will unreasonably impair the value or use of their property as a shopping center. The Pruneyard is a large commercial complex that covers several city blocks, contains numerous separate business establishments, and is open to the public at large. The decision of the California Supreme Court makes it clear that the Pruneyard may restrict expressive activity by adopting regulations that will minimize any interference with its commercial functions. Plaintiffs were orderly, and they limited their activity to the common areas of the shopping center. In these circumstances, the fact that they may have "physically invaded" appellants' property cannot be viewed as determinative.

Defendant finally contends that a private property owner has a First Amendment right not to be forced by the State to use his or her property as a forum for the speech of others.

We conclude that neither Pruneyard's property rights nor its amendment rights

have been infringed by the California Supreme Court's decision recognizing a right of plaintiffs to exercise rights of expression and petition on Pruneyard's property. The judgment of the Supreme Court of California is therefore
  Affirmed.

NOTES AND QUESTIONS

1 Did the court conclude that the plaintiff's constitutional rights were violated? What other rights are "too fundamental to be violated on the basis of an interest in real property"?

2 *Lloyd Corp. v. Tanner,* 407 U.S. 551 (1972), involved a situation very similar to Pruneyard. In Lloyd, a shopping center owner adopted a strict policy against distributing handbills that were unrelated to the shopping center's commercial activities. The Supreme Court upheld the right of the shopping center to forbid the handbill distribution noting that "property does not lose its private character merely because the public is generally invited to use it for designated purpose." The Court further noted that a contrary result would be "an unwarranted infringement of property rights." Is the Lloyd case inconsistent with the ruling in Pruneyard? Would *Lloyd v. Tanner* be upheld in light of the ruling in Pruneyard?

3 In *State of New Jersey v. Shack,* 277 A2d 369 (N.J. 1971), the defendants were charged with criminal trespass when they entered the owner's farm to provide medical and legal assistance to migrant workers employed on the farm. The farm owner had previously denied the defendants' request to enter unless they agreed to meet the farmworkers in the presence of the owner. Defendants refused to accept this condition, entered upon the farm, and were arrested for trespass. The New Jersey Supreme Court ordered the charges dismissed with the following observations:

> Property rights serve human values. They are recognized to that end, and are limited by it. Title to real property cannot include dominion over the destiny of persons the owner permits to come upon the premises. Their well-being must remain the paramount concern of a system of law.
>
> A man's right in his real property is not absolute. It was a maxim of the common law that one should so use his property as not to injure the rights of others. Although hardly a precise solvent of actual controversies, the maxim does express the proposition that rights are relative and there must be an accommodation when they meet.
>
> It is not our purpose to open the employer's premises to the general public if in fact the employer himself has not done so. And we are mindful of the employer's interest in his own and in his employee's security. But the employer may not deny the worker his privacy or interfere with his opportunity to live with dignity and to enjoy associations customary among our citizens. These rights are too fundamental to be denied on the basis of an interest in real property and too fragile to be left to the unequal bargaining strength of the parties.

4 Compare Pruneyard with *State of New Jersey v. Shack.* In both cases the court acknowledged the importance of an owner's right to exclude others and in both cases, this right was limited. Do you think that the owner in *State of New Jersey v. Shack* would be required to open his property to the students in the Pruneyard case?

5 In *Savage v. Trammel Crow,* Cal. App., Sept. 24, 1990, the California Court of Appeal decided that the owner of a shopping center could not prohibit an individual from distributing religious pamphlets in the shopping center. The pamphlets themselves were vitriolic diatribes directed at the Roman Catholic Church. In relying on the Pruneyard decision, the court observed that unpopular religious expression created no greater burden on the owner than the burden created by unpopular political expression.

10 PROPERTY AND SOCIAL POLICY

Shelley v. Kraemer, 334 U.S. 1 (1947)

These cases present for our consideration questions relating to the validity of court enforcement of private agreements, generally described as restrictive covenants. These restrictive covenants have as their purpose the exclusion of persons of designated race or color from the ownership or occupancy of real property. Basic constitutional issues of obvious importance have been raised.

Pertinent facts of the case.

On February 16, 1911, thirty out of a total of thirty-nine owners of property fronting both sides of Labadie Avenue between Taylor Avenue and Cora Avenue in the city of St. Louis signed an agreement, which was subsequently recorded, providing in part:

> . . . The said property is hereby restricted to the use and occupancy for the term of fifty (50) years from this date, so that it shall be a condition all the time and shall attach to the land as a condition to the sale of the same, that no part of said property shall be occupied by any person not of the Caucasian race. . . .

On August 11, 1945, pursuant to a contract of sale, petitioners Shelley, who are Negroes, received from one Fitzgerald a warranty deed to the parcel in question.

On October 9, 1945, respondents, as owners of other property subject to the terms of the restrictive covenant, brought suit in the Circuit Court of the city of St. Louis asking that petitioners Shelley be restrained from taking possession of the property and that judgment be entered divesting title out of Shelley and revesting title in the immediate grantor or in such other person as the court should direct. The trial court denied the requested relief on the ground that the restrictive agreement was not signed by all property owners in the district.

The Supreme Court of Missouri reversed and directed the trial court to grant the relief which respondents had requested. That court held the agreement effective and concluded that enforcement of its provisions violated no rights guaranteed by the federal Constitution. At the time the court rendered its decision, the Shelley's were occupying the property in question.

OPINION

Whether the equal protection clause of the Fourteenth Amendment inhibits judicial enforcement by state courts of restrictive covenants based on race or color is a question which this court has not heretofore been called upon to consider.

It is clear that restrictions on the right of occupancy of the sort sought to be created by the private agreements in these cases could not be squared with the requirements of the constitutions if imposed by state statute or local ordinance.

However, the restrictive agreements standing alone cannot be regarded as violating of any rights guaranteed by the Constitution. So long as the purposes of those agreements are accomplished by voluntary adherence to their terms, it would appear clear that there has been no action by the state and the provisions of the Fourteenth Amendment have not been violated.

But here there was more. This is a case in which the purpose of the agreement was secured only by judicial enforcement by state courts of the restrictive terms of the agreements. Respondents urge that judicial enforcement of private agreements does not amount to state action; or, in any event, the participation of the State is so limited as not to amount to state action.

We have no doubt that there has been state action in this case in the full and complete sense of the phrase. It is clear that but for the active intervention of the state courts, supported by the full panoply of state power, petitioners would have been free to occupy the properties in question without restraint.

We hold that in granting judicial enforcement of the restrictive agreements in these cases, the States have denied petitioners the equal protection of the laws and that, therefore, the action of the state courts cannot stand.

For the reasons stated, the judgment of the Supreme Court of Missouri must be reversed.

NOTES AND QUESTIONS

1 The overt racial discrimination presented in *Shelley v. Kraemer* is now prohibited by virtue of the Civil Rights Act. However, the principle of Shelley v. Kraemer retains its vitality and private land use restrictions will not be enforced if they violate some important aspect of public policy.

2 Suppose that a subdivision or condominium project adopts a rule that no one under the age of eighteen may live in the development. Would such a restriction be upheld? What are the arguments for and against the validity of such a rule?

11   SUMMARY

Law is basically a means of regulating human interaction and exists in some form in all societies.

The American system of law is based upon the concepts of federalism and the separation of powers. Federalism provides that certain limited powers are inherent in the federal government while all others are reserved to the states. The doctrine of separation of powers holds that the separate branches of government are vested with certain limited powers and may not intrude upon the authority of the other branches of government. The legislative branch enacts the laws, the executive branch enforces them, and the judicial branch interprets them.

Federal and state constitutions are the supreme law and will prevail over a conflicting statute. It is the responsibility of the judicial branch to determine when a law conflicts with a constitution.

American property law owes much of its complexity to the fact that much of it has been shaped more by history than by logic. This will become more apparent as the study of real estate law proceeds.

The ownership of property is generally thought to comprise a "bundle of rights," among the most important of which is the right to absolute possession of the property owned. Although the right to exclude others remains an important right inherent in ownership of property, this right and others are subject to modification if they undermine an important aspect of public policy.

PRIVATE ESTATES
IN LAND

CHAPTER 2

PRESENT ESTATES IN LAND

TOPICS CONSIDERED IN THIS CHAPTER:

1 INTRODUCTION

The most distinctive feature of property law as it evolved in England and as it now exists in the United States is the doctrine of estates. The theory of estates is based upon the idea that ownership of land is measured in terms of time. An *estate* in land means an interest in which the owner is, or may become, entitled to possession and where ownership is measured in terms of duration. The term estate signifies the degrees, quantity, and extent of the interest that a person has in real property.

This definition might be clarified by a few examples. Suppose that *A* dies leaving a will which transfers a house ''to *B*, provided that *C* may live in the house until *C* dies.'' Who ''owns'' the property? *C* is entitled to possession but certainly *B* has an interest in the property as well. Upon the death of *C, B* will be entitled to immediate possession of the house. *B*'s right will be absolute because nothing can happen which will defeat *B*'s right other than his own actions in transferring the property to another. Let's try another example: suppose *A* transfers the property ''to *B* for her life and then to *C* provided that *C* is twenty-five years old and living when *B* dies.'' *B*'s interest is the same, but *C*'s right to possession is conditioned upon two things, namely his surviving *B* and his reaching the age of twenty-five before *B* dies. Suppose further that *C* dies before *B:* Who owns the property then? A final example: ''To *B* so long as the property is used as a church and then to *C*.'' In this case *B* clearly has an ownership interest but it is capable of being cut short or divested based upon the use that is made of the property. *C* also has something but it may never become possessory. After reading this chapter, and the one which follows, the respective interests of *A, B,* and *C* in each of the preceding examples will be apparent.

The primary classification of estates in land is between present and future interests on the one hand and freehold estates and nonfreehold estates on the other. Present estates are those in which the owner is entitled to present possession of the property. The term *freehold estates* is of purely historical origin and implies ownership in the practical sense and for an indefinite duration. The present freehold estates are considered in this chapter. The future freehold estates are considered in Chapter 4. The nonfreehold estates will be mentioned in order to present a complete picture of the permissible estates in land as they evolved in England and as they now exist in this country. However, modern law pertaining to nonfreehold estates is typically addressed under the topic of landlord and tenant, and these topics will be considered more fully in Chapter 19.

2 THE FREEHOLD ESTATES

When we refer to the fee simple or even to the fee, we typically mean the fee simple absolute, which is the largest estate known to the law. It is the greatest aggregate of rights and privileges that one may have in land. However, a fee simple may be qualified or limited so that it may terminate upon the happening or nonhappening of some event. Such a qualified fee estate is known as the fee simple defeasible.

A The Fee Simple Absolute

''To *A*''

The fee simple absolute was, and still is, the largest estate known to the law. This estate is of potentially infinite duration and is not subject to being defeated for any reason contained within the instrument which creates the estate.

It is commonly understood that a fee simple is the highest right, title and interest that one can have in land. It is the full and absolute estate in all that can be granted. *Masheter v. Davis,* 253 N.E.2d 780, 783 (Ohio 1969)

The magnitude or the quantum of ownership implicit in the fee simple absolute will be clearer when the more limited fee simple interests are understood. In fact, the Restatement of Property defines the fee simple absolute in somewhat negative terms as follows:

> An estate in fee simple absolute is an estate in fee simple which is not subject to a special limitation or a condition subsequent or an executory limitation.
>
> Restatement of Property, section 15

Nearly all states have enacted statutes which create a presumption in favor of the fee simple absolute. In other words, a deed or will transfers a fee simple absolute unless the instrument clearly expresses an intent to transfer a lesser interest. The Restatement of Property embodies this approach in the following terms:

> In determining whether a conveyance expresses an intent to create an estate other than a fee simple absolute, every reasonable doubt as to the existence of such an intent is resolved against the finding of such an intent. . . .
>
> Restatement of Property, section 39, comment b

B The Fee Simple Defeasible

Unlike the fee simple absolute, the fee simple defeasible contains restrictions that may cause the estate to expire or terminate. The fee simple defeasible may be of infinite duration but the interest conveyed may also terminate upon the happening or nonhappening of certain events. There are three subcategories of defeasible fees, the fee simple determinable, the fee simple subject to a condition subsequent, and the fee simple subject to an executory limitation.

Fee Simple Determinable

''To *A* so long as alcohol is not sold on the premises.''

An estate in fee simple determinable creates a fee simple and provides that an estate will automatically expire upon the occurrence of a stated event. In the example above, *A*'s estate automatically expires when alcoholic beverages are sold on the premises and the grantor or grantor's heirs become immediately entitled to possession of the property.

Williamson v. Grizzard, 387 S.W.2d 807 (Tenn. 1965)

Facts of the case.

Many years ago, Mr. and Mrs. R. W. Grizzard conveyed certain property to the Cumberland Presbyterian Church. A provision in the deed reads as follows:

To have and hold said property to the said church forever, provided the following conditions are complied with; said property is to be used by the church as a parsonage and to be known as The Grizzard Memorial Parsonage. Should the property be used for any other purpose than above specified for a period of five consecutive years, then this conveyance to said church will be null and void and title to the property will become vested in the heirs of the said L. Hinton Grizzard.

The complaint alleges that the property in question was used for a church parsonage for many years. The parsonage had previously been located in a residential area, but it is now surrounded by purely commercial property which makes it unsuited for the intended use.

Plaintiffs are the trustees of the Cumberland Presbyterian Church and defendants are the heirs of L. Hinton Gizzard. Plaintiffs seek to have the property sold free of the provision mentioned above and with the express understanding that the proceeds of the sale be re-invested in another parsonage for the Cumberland Presbyterian Church to be known as the Grizzard Memorial Parsonage, which would be located in a more desirable residential district. The deed to the new parsonage to contain the same provisions as to reversion as does the deed in question.

The trial court held as follows:

1 the court has no jurisdiction to divest the defendants of their rights in and to the property described and to create for them the same rights in other property without their consent.

2 The original deed creates the rights of the parties, and the interest of these defendants cannot be divested without their consent and approval.

OPINION

We think it is clear that the intention of the grantors in this case was to give their property to the church so long as it was used for church purposes and, then, when not so used, the property was to revert to the grantors, or their heirs.

Thus, it appears that the deed by which the property was conveyed did not create an absolute title in fee simple. The provisions of the deed clearly show that the church's estate was and is limited, and might be termed a determinable fee or fee simple on condition subsequent, both of which estates are recognized by the property law of this State.

It is the contention of the church that their proposal is merely to substitute a new parcel of land which would have the same conditions and reversionary interests as the original deed. Thus, so the church maintains, the grantors' charitable purpose could be fulfilled and at the same time the appellants would retain their reversionary interests in a tract of land of equal value.

The church's position is untenable. The practical effect of such a plan would be to severely limit the reversionary rights of the heirs. The reversionary interest of the heirs was created in the particular tract of land described in the deed.

The intention of the grantors is clear and should not be changed by this court. If the property ceases to be used for the purposes set forth in the deed, then the property reverts to the heirs of the grantors as expressly provided in the deed.
Affirmed.

Fee Simple Subject to a Condition Subsequent

"To *A* on condition that if liquor is sold on the premises, *A*'s estate will be subject to the grantor's right to reenter the premises."

An estate in fee simple subject to a condition subsequent creates a fee simple estate and provides that upon the occurrence of a stated event, the grantor or his successor shall have the right to enter and terminate the interest which has been granted.

The fee simple subject to a condition subsequent will not automatically defeat the estate of the grantee as in the case of the fee simple determinable. Rather, the grantor, or grantor's heirs, must affirmatively reenter and terminate the interest of the grantee for breach of the condition stated.

Forsgren v. LaFleur, 659 P.2d 1068 (Utah 1983)

This appeal concerns the effect of a condition in a deed. After a trial, the district court held that the deed created a fee simple subject to a condition subsequent, and that the grantor had reacquired the fee by reentry when the condition, was unfulfilled. We affirmed.

Facts of the case.

In February, 1960, the plaintiff Forsgren conveyed 1.4 acres of unimproved property to James H. Sollie. The deed contained the following provisions:

This property is conveyed on the condition that the grantee will build a partition fence along the South side of the above described property; that he will have the above described property surveyed at his own expense, and that the survey must have been made, and the fence erected before any construction or placement of improvements on said property.
This property is conveyed to be used as and for a church or residence purposes only.

Sollie never built the fence, completed the survey, or built anything on the property. He paid no taxes. He left the state some time in the early 1960's. Shortly thereafter, the grantor reentered the property, which remained unimproved. She mowed the weeds annually, did some fencing, and paid some real estate taxes.

In 1978, the defendant, LaFleur, located Sollie in Georgia. LaFleur paid him $1,500 and Sollie and his wife deeded their interest in the property to LaFleur.

In 1979 and 1980, Forsgren excavated and poured concrete for footings in order to build a small building on the property. Observing this, the defendants drove a tractor on the property and knocked over the foundations. Forsgren then brought this action to have her declared the owner of the property.

The trial court held that conditions subsequent for which no time of performance was specified were performable within a reasonable time, failing which the grantor could enforce the right of reentry. Holding that the specified conditions were not performed within a reasonable time and that the grantor had exercised the right of reentry in 1967, the court decreed fee simple ownership in the plaintiff grantor. LaFleur appeals.

OPINION

A fee simple subject to a condition subsequent is an interest in which, upon the occurrence or nonoccurrence of a stated event, the grantor or grantor's successor has the power, at the grantor's option, to terminate the estate and reacquire the property. When an estate is conveyed on contingency (condition subsequent or determinable) and no time is specified for the contingency, the law will imply a reasonable time for the event.

A condition subsequent is normally created by words like "on condition that," "provided that," or phrases of like import, coupled with a provision that if the stated event occurs or does not occur, the grantor "may enter and terminate the estate hereby conveyed" or a phrase of like import. *Restatement of Property* Section 45, Comment j (1936). However, the *Restatement* further states that "the phrase 'upon express condition that' usually indicates an intent to create an estate in fee simple subject to a condition subsequent, even when no express clause for reentry, termination, or reverter accompanies it."

Consistent with the *Restatement,* there are many cases where a deed provision using the word "condition" has been interpreted as creating a fee simple subject to a condition subsequent even though there was no express provision for reentry or revesting of the estate.

All that is necessary is that the language clearly shows the intent of the grantor to make the estate conditional, and where this is the case, a clause of reentry is unnecessary.

The condition not having been fulfilled within a reasonable time, the grantor exercised her power of termination by reentering the premises and thereby reacquired the property in fee simple. The judgment vesting title in the plaintiff is affirmed.

NOTES AND QUESTIONS

1 What was the condition most persuasive to the court in reaching its decision?

2 A dissenting opinion in the *LaFleur* case contained the following statement:

There was no provision in the deed giving the grantor the right of reentry and revesting title in her. Moreover, with regard to the use to be put to the property, all we have here is one terse sentence: "This property is conveyed to be used as and for a church or residence purposes only." This could be nothing more than an attempt on the part of the grantor to prevent the property from being used for commercial or industrial purposes which would interfere with her enjoyment in residing on her remaining property. It does not appear to affirmatively require that a church or residence ever be built.

No condition having been clearly expressed, and recognizing the fact that conditions controlling the use of deeded property are strictly construed against the grantor, and that forfeitures are not favored, I am led to conclude that the judgment below should be reversed.

3 Do you agree with the majority or the dissenting opinion?

Fee Simple Subject to an Executory Limitation

"To A but if A dies without children surviving, then to B."

The fee simple subject to an executory limitation creates a fee simple in the grantee and provides that, upon the occurrence of a stated event, the grantee's estate may be defeated in favor of a person other than the grantor or his successors.

The occurrence of the event that triggers an executory limitation automatically terminates the grantee's estate. Thus, it operates like the fee simple determinable and unlike the condition subsequent. However, unlike both of these estates, the fee simple subject to an executory interest cannot create future rights in the grantor, but rather vests those rights in a third party.

Hall v. Hall, 604 S.W.2d 851 (Tenn. 1980)

This case involves the interpretation and legal effect of a deed in which the grantor gave the grantee an estate in land with an apparent unlimited power of disposition yet conversely placed a condition upon her right of ownership.

Facts of the case.

On December 20, 1920, T. A. Hall conveyed three tracts of land by deed to his wife, Ms. Betty Hall, the plaintiff. In the granting clause of this deed, the grantor stated:

I do this day give and bequeath my entire right and title to the following described tracts of land to wit (property described).

In a later clause, he states:

[t]he condition of this deed is as follows:
In case I, T. A. Hall should die before my wife and leave her a widow then she shall have full control and full power to handle or do just as she should see fit with the above described property just so long as she lives my widow but if she should ever remarry, then this deed becomes void to her and the above described property shall fall to my children.

T. A. Hall died in 1957 and on August 16, 1978, the plaintiff, still a widow and numerous family members including children, daughters-in-law and grandchildren, conveyed the land by deed to Ronnie and Randall Dixon, also plaintiffs in the present action. The validity of this conveyance was questioned by the defendant, Opal Hall, one of the plaintiff's daughters-in-law and several grandchildren. Thereafter, the plaintiffs brought this suit to determine the nature and extent of their estate alleging that Ms. Hall held a fee simple absolute estate and that the Dixons derivatively held a similar estate. The defendants answered alleging that Ms. Hall held the land in a fee simple subject to a conditional limitation or executory interest and not in a fee simple absolute. They contend that the Dixon's ownership of the property is subject to the condition that Ms. Hall not remarry.

In a memorandum opinion, the Chancellor held that the defendants failed to overcome the presumption that T. A. Hall had given Ms. Hall a fee simple absolute, as set forth in Tennessee Statute 64-501, which provides:

> Every grant of real estate shall pass all the estate or interest of the grantor unless the intent to pass a less estate or interest shall appear by express terms, or be necessarily implied in the terms of the instrument.

OPINION

The overriding purpose of any deed interpretation is the determination of the grantor's intent in making the conveyance. In this case, as in many cases where the grantor is not trained in the law and the deed is handwritten, it is difficult to determine the subjective intent of the grantor. For reasons stated below, we are of the opinion that the chancellor and the court of appeals erred in their interpretation of the present deed.

While it is true that the courts have a general attitude of disfavor toward restrictions on the fee and are slow to imply a construction from ambiguous language, such restrictions or conditions are valid and, where legal, will be enforced.

The grantor's intent in the present case is clear and unequivocal. The estate is subject to a condition, the happening of which will forfeit the holder's estate.

We are, therefore, of the opinion that Ms. Hall acquired the estate of fee simple subject to a conditional limitation or executory interest in the deed from her husband. When she sold the real property to the Dixons, she could convey no more of an estate than she possessed. The Dixons, therefore, acquired the property subject to their forfeiture upon the remarriage of Ms. Hall.

Reversed.

NOTES AND QUESTIONS

1 As the preceding cases indicate, the critical factor in determining the kind of estate that has been created is the intent of the transferor. Because deeds and wills are often prepared by people untrained in the area and because many years often elapse before a dispute arises, determination of the transferor's intention can be difficult.

2 Ordinarily, a *fee simple determinable* will be found where the limitation contains the terms "so long as," "until" or "during" or where it provides that the property will revert to the transferor upon the happening of a stated event.

3 A *fee simple subject to a condition subsequent* will be found where the transfer is made upon an express condition and where the transferor retains the right to reenter upon breach of the condition. Courts generally held that "conditions subsequent in a deed will be construed most strongly against the transferor and forfeiture will not be enforced unless clearly established." (*Koonz v. Joint School District,* 41 N.W.2d 616 (Wis. 1950) The *Restatement* provides that a condition subsequent will be created only in the following situations:

1 some one of the following phrases, namely, "upon express condition that," or "upon condition that," or "provided that," or a phrase of like import; and also

2 a provision that if the stated event occurs, the conveyor "may enter and terminate the estate hereby conveyed," or a phrase of like import. (*Restatement, Property Section 45,* comment v)

4 The estate in fee simple followed by an *executory limitation* usually includes language specifying that if a stated event occurs then the property is to go to a person other than the transferor. In *Jenkins v. Shuften,* 575 E.2d 283 (Georgia 1950), a will contained the following provisions:

to my wife free from all charge and limitation whatever, to her own proper use and benefit forever. . . . Provided, however, should she not dispose of the same during her lifetime, the property shall pass to my daughter.

This language was construed as creating a fee simple subject to an executory limitation.

3   THE LIFE ESTATE

"To *A* for life."

A life estate is one which is specifically limited to the life or lives of one or more human beings. It has the shortest duration of the freehold estates.

Unlike the fee simple interests, a life estate cannot be transferred by a will although it is otherwise transferable. A life estate can be measured by the duration of the life of someone other than the owner and is then referred to as a *life estates per autre vie,* for instance, a grant "to *A* for the life of *B.*" A similar situation arises when the owner of a life estate transfers her interest to another. For instance, *A,* the owner of a life estate, transfers the interest to *B. A* can convey no more than she has. *B* has a life estate measured by the life of *A.*

A life estate can be created subject to a special limitation, a condition subsequent, or an executory limitation in the same manner that a fee interest can be so restricted.

A life estate is usually created by language such as the following: "to *A* for *A*'s life." However it is not uncommon for the transfer to convey property while reserving a life estate. For example "*A* to *B,* provided that *A* shall have the right to live in the premises for the rest of his life."

A life estate may also be created where the language of the grant appears at first to create a fee but is followed by a qualification which indicates that only a life estate was contemplated. For example: "to *A* and upon *A*'s death, to *B.*"

A life estate can also be created by operation of law. For instance, various American cities have enacted tenant protection statutes as part of their ordinances governing the conversion of apartment buildings to cooperatives or condominiums. A typical provision might permit a tenant (usually over the age of sixty-five) to continue to occupy the apartment, at a fixed rent, for the rest of the tenant's life. Such an ordinance creates the equivalent of a life estate, contingent upon the payment of rent.

In a related example, *A* died, leaving his property to *B,* provided that *C* could "continue to live in the property at a rent not to exceed $100 per month for as long as she wants." *C* has a life estate, subject only to the conditions that she live in the property and pay rent.

4 RIGHTS AND DUTIES OF THE LIFE TENANT

The holder of a life estate has the right to possess the land and to receive the rents and profits generated by the land. However, the life tenant may not do anything which will unreasonably diminish the value of future interest which follows the life estate. The life tenant is obligated to maintain the property in a state of reasonable repair, but is not obligated to make extraordinary repairs or to make improvements to the property. The life tenant is obligated to pay current taxes and interest payments on outstanding mortgages but is not required to make payments on principal.

The case of *Williams v. Southern Bell Telephone,* 266 S.E.2d 700 (N.C. 1980), illustrates the limited nature of the interest held under a life estate. Ola White had a life estate in property. She gave a permit to Southern Bell permitting it to construct and maintain power lines across the property. It appeared that neither Ola White nor Southern Bell was aware that White had only a life estate.

After White died, a dispute arose between the fee owner of the property and Southern Bell regarding the companies' rights and responsibilities for maintaining the telephone lines. The court ruled as follows:

> It is settled law that a grantor cannot convey an estate of greater dignity than the one he has. The general permit executed by Ola White conveyed to Southern Bell an interest for and during her lifetime and no longer. As a life tenant, she could not create an estate or interest to endure beyond the term of her own estate. As between the parties to this action, there are no rights or obligations of any kind based on the permit.

NOTES AND QUESTIONS

1 There is clearly a degree of tension between the rights of the life tenant and the rights of those who follow. Suppose *A* has a life estate in property used for cutting timber. Is *A* allowed to cut timber during *A*'s life? Can *A* remove all the timber? Suppose that the trees become infected by some pest but *A* refuses to have the trees treated. Could the holders of the future interests intervene to protect the value of their interest?

5 THE NONFREEHOLD ESTATES

The nonfreehold estates, also known as leasehold estates, are significantly different from the freehold estates. The nonfreehold estates are of limited duration and usually involve a continuing relationship between the grantor and the grantee, such as the grantee's obligation to pay rent to the grantor. The law of nonfreehold estates is actually the law of landlord and tenant which will be considered in detail in Chapter 19. However, in order to complete the picture as it relates to estates in land, the nonfreehold estates are briefly listed and described in this chapter.

A The Estate for Years

"To *A* for five years."

An estate for years, also known as the term of years or lease for years, contains as its most salient feature a duration which is fixed and definite, regardless of the length of the period. The estate ends automatically upon the expiration of the term.

The term estate for years is something of a misnomer because a fixed period of less than one year is sufficiently definite and will qualify the grantee's interest as an estate for years. A grant "to *A* for six months" is an estate for years because its duration is fixed. Similarly, a grant to *A* until a specified date is an estate for years, regardless of when the lease was entered into. However, a grant "to *A* so long as she is president of the University" is not an estate for years because the duration of the estate cannot be precisely determined.

An estate for years can be created subject to a special limitation, a condition subsequent, or an executory limitation in the same manner that a fee interest or a life estate can be subject to those restrictions.

B The Estate from Period to Period: The Periodic Tenancy

"To *A* from year to year."

The estate from period to period, also known as the periodic tenancy is an estate which continues for successive periods of a year or less until it is terminated by notice of either party.

There are various kinds of periodic tenancies. They can be from year to year, month to month, week to week, or any other definite period of one year or less. Periodic tenancies often arise by implication based upon the period during which rent is paid. Thus, in the absence of an agreement, if the tenant pays rent on a monthly basis, the tenancy will probably be considered a periodic tenancy from month to month. The periodic tenancy is of indefinite duration and its general characteristics are similar to those of the estate for years. However, unlike the estate for years, periodic tenancy continues indefinitely until it is terminated by notice from either the landlord or tenant. Most states have enacted statutes that regulate the manner in which notice terminating a periodic tenancy must be given.

C The Estate at Will

"To *A* at the will of *B*."

An estate at will is one that may be terminated at the will of either landlord or tenant and that has no other specified period of duration. At the common law, the estate at will could be terminated by either party without notice. This harsh rule has been changed in most states by statutes requiring the giving of notice, typically based upon the period for which the tenant pays rent. As a result, many state statutes have modified the tenancy at will so that it closely resembles the periodic tenancy.

A grant "To *B* at the will of *A*" creates an estate at will because *A,* the lessor, may terminate the estate at any time and *B* may do the same. However, a grant to *B* at the will of *B* may create a significantly different interest.

D   Tenancy at Sufferance

The estate at sufferance is surely the most limited interest in land. It exists when a person who originally had an estate in land wrongfully continues in possession after the termination of that estate. A tenancy at sufferance may arise after the termination of an estate when the tenant, after expiration of the term, continues in possession against the owner's wishes.

The status of a tenant at sufferance is extremely tenuous and differs from that of a trespasser only because the original possession of the property was not wrongful. A tenant at sufferance has no estate or title but only bare possession, and the continued occupancy is due simply to the forbearance of the person entitled to the possession in not proceeding to evict.

6   SUMMARY

The present freehold estates in land form the basic building blocks in the study of modern real estate law. The various freehold estates in land are distinguished by their potential duration. The fee simple absolute has the longest duration because nothing contained in the granting instrument can intervene to cut short or terminate the estate. The life estate is the estate of shortest duration because there is no doubt but that it will end at some point.

In addition, there are three estates which are of potentially infinite duration but which may end sooner depending upon the happening or nonhappening of some event. These are known as the defeasible fee simple estates. All estates, except the fee simple absolute have a future interest attached. The future interests are considered in Chapter 4.

Finally, the law recognizes a series of estates known as nonfreehold estates which, unlike the freehold estate, involves some degree of interaction between the grantor and grantee. The nonfreehold estates have become absorbed by the law of landlord and tenant and they will be treated in a subsequent chapter.

7   QUESTIONS

1 Ewing Hill died, leaving a will which provided that all of his property should go equally to his children, Daniel Hill and Kathryn Hill Holmes. Daniel died before Ewing, leaving a will which gave all his property to his children, Franklin and Daniel Jr. Kathryn claimed that

since Daniel predeceased Ewing she should take all of Ewing's property. Franklin and Daniel Jr. claimed they should take their father's share of Ewing's estate. Who wins?

2 Rodeo Land Company sold property to the Berkeley Hall Foundation by a deed that stated if liquor was sold on the premises, Rodeo could reenter the property and declare Berkeley's interest forfeited. Berkeley Hall sold the property to Agnes Perry by a deed that did not contain the restriction. Agnes opened a liquor store. Can Rodeo enforce the restriction against Agnes?

3 Joseph left a will with the following provision:

> To my wife, Edith, I give and bequeath all my estate, to be and remain hers, with full power, right, and authority to dispose of the same as to her shall seem most proper, so long as she shall remain my widow; upon the express condition, however, that if she should marry again, then it is my will that all of the estate herein bequeathed, or whatever may remain, should go to my surviving children, share and share alike.

Edith sought to convey a fee simple absolute to Roberts. Could she do so?

4 Emily left a will giving property to her two sons and providing that:

> Fee simple title shall not vest until the death of one of the beneficiaries, at which time fee simple title shall vest in the survivor.

What are the interests of the sons?

5 Andrew transferred property as follows:

> to Phyllis for the term of her natural life only, subject, however, to this condition and limitation, that if she and her family move away or vacate the property for as long as three months, the property reverts to Andrew.

What is the nature of Phyllis' interest in the property?

6 Tom left a will giving his property to his daughter Margaret for life and provided that if Margaret sold the life estate, her interest would be forfeited and it would be divided between Tom's sons. Margaret sells her life estate to Carol. What are the interests of Margaret and the sons?

7 A owns property and transfers it to "B so long as the town of C remains unincorporated." What is the nature of B's interest?

8 A owns property and transfers it "to B so long as the cheese factory continues to operate on the property, but if B dies without living children, then to C." What is the nature of A's, B's, and C's interests?

CHAPTER 3

FUTURE ESTATES IN LAND

TOPICS CONSIDERED IN THIS CHAPTER:

1 INTRODUCTION

Chapter 2 introduced the concept of estates in land which delineate the quantum of ownership based upon the potential duration of the interest. Of the various estates, only the fee simple absolute has absolutely unlimited duration. The defeasible fees, on the other hand, contain the possibility that something will happen that will terminate the estate. In the case of the life estate, something certainly will happen to terminate the estate. Who becomes the "owner" of the property after defeasance of the fee simple or the death of the life tenant? An interest following a present estate is known as a future estate or interest, and this species of ownership of property forms the subject matter of this chapter.

34

A future estate is an interest in property in which the privilege of possession or enjoyment is deferred until the future. Whereas the present estates discussed in Chapter 2 are characterized by the owner's immediate right to enjoy the benefits of ownership, the owner of a future interest is not entitled to the benefits of ownership until the termination of the present estate. Future interests are very common, particularly in wills and trusts, and are useful estate planning devices.

2   CLASSIFICATION OF FUTURE INTERESTS

There are five types of future interests: the first three, known collectively as reversionary interests are interests retained by the transferor. These are the following:

1 The reversion;
2 The possibility of reverter; and
3 The power of termination, also known as a right of entry for condition broken.

In addition, there are two types of future interests that are created in persons other than the transferor. These follow:

1 Remainders; and
2 Executory interests

3   THE REVERSION

A reversion is the residue of an estate retained by the transferor. In other words, a reversion is merely the undisposed portion of an estate that the transferor has not conveyed. Suppose the grantor of a fee interest transfers the property "To *A* for life." What happens to the property upon the termination of *A*'s life estate? Because the transfer is not complete, in other words because the grantor has transferred less than her entire interest, the law implies a reversion to the grantor, or her heirs, of the fee simple interest upon termination of *A*'s life estate.

Suppose that *A* makes a will with the following provision: from *A* "to *B* for life then to the children of *B* who are living at *B*'s death." At the time of the transfer, it is unknown whether *B*'s children will survive *B*. If they do survive *B*, their interests will vest in fee simple absolute. If, however, *B* dies with no surviving children, *A* has an implied reversion and the property will go back to *A* or her heirs.

Reversions can also be created by specific language. For instance, *A* transfers property "to *B* for life and then to *C* for life and then to revert to *A*." Again, the residue of *A*'s estate, namely that portion that was not transferred by the grant to *B* and *C* is a reversion to *A*, the original grantor.

4   THE POSSIBILITY OF REVERTER

The Restatement of Property, Section 154(2) defines a possibility of reverter as a reversionary interest subject to a condition precedent. A possibility of reverter typically accompanies the transfer of a fee simple determinable. For instance, grantor, owner of a fee simple absolute, transfers the property ''To *A* for so long as the property is used as a church.'' In this case, the grantor, or his heirs, retain the possibility of regaining the property in the event the property is no longer used as a church. The future interest retained by the grantor is a possibility of reverter which takes effect in possession immediately and automatically upon the happening of the named event.

5 THE POWER OF TERMINATION OR RIGHT OF ENTRY FOR BREACH OF CONDITION

The future interest known as a power of termination or a right of entry is a future interest created in the transferor or his successors upon a transfer of an interest in property subject to a condition subsequent. (*Restatement, Property Section 155*).

The *Restatement* defines the term ''condition subsequent'' as follows:

> Whenever an estate subject to a condition subsequent is created, some person has the power to terminate this estate upon the occurrence of the stipulated event. Thus, such an estate does not end automatically and by expiration as does an estate subject to a special limitation. On the contrary, it is cut short, or divested, if, but only if, the person having the power chooses to exercise it. This option to terminate an estate upon breach of a condition subsequent is referred to in this *Restatement* as a ''power of termination.'' (*Restatement, Property Section 24,* Comment B)

A right of entry or power of termination arises when the transferor conveys an estate of the same quantum as his own but provides that the grantor shall retain the right to terminate the transferee's estate upon the occurrence or nonoccurrence of some stated event. The future interest retained by the transferor is called a right of entry for breach of a condition or a power of termination. The essential elements of a right of entry include a conveyance which contains a condition subsequent giving the grantor or his heirs the right and power to terminate the grantee's estate upon fulfillment of the condition.

Almost any condition can be included as the designated condition subsequent, provided that it is not against public policy. For instance, a conveyance ''to *A* provided that liquor not be sold on the premises and, if liquor is sold, grantor or his heirs shall have the right to enter and terminate the grantee's estate.'' Other such conditions have involved erecting a house, paying the grantor a specific sum of money for the grantor's life, building and maintaining a fence, and the divorce or separation of the grantor and grantee. All these have been upheld as conditions subsequent authorizing the grantor's right of entry upon their breach.

Mahrenholz v. School Trustees of Lawrence County, 417 N.E. 2d (Ill. App. 1981)

Facts of the case.

On March 18, 1941, W. E. and Jennie Hutton executed a deed in which they conveyed certain land, to be known here as the Hutton School grounds, to the

Trustees of School District No. 1, the predecessors of the defendants in this action. The deed provided that "this land to be used for school purpose only; otherwise to revert to Grantors herein." W. E. Hutton died without a will on July 18, 1951, and Jennie Hutton died without a will on February 18, 1969. The Huttons have one heir, their son Harry E. Hutton.

The property conveyed by the Huttons became the site of the Hutton School. Community School District No. 20 succeeded to the Hutton School and classes were held in the building constructed upon the land until May 30, 1973. After that date, the District has used the property for storage purposes only.

Harry E. Hutton executed a deed October 9, 1959, conveying to the plaintiffs over 390 acres of land in Lawrence County. The deed included the forty acre tract from which the Hutton School grounds were taken. The deed from Hutton to the plaintiffs excluded the Hutton School grounds, but purported to convey the disputed future interest to the plaintiffs.

OPINION

The parties are in agreement that the 1941 deed from the Huttons conveyed a defeasible fee simple estate to the grantee and gave rise to a future interest in the grantors.

The future interest remaining in this grantor or his estate can only be a possibility of reverter or a right of re-entry for condition broken.

Consequently this court must determine whether the plaintiffs could have acquired an interest in the Hutton School grounds from Harry E. Hutton. The resolution of this issue depends on the construction of the language of the 1941 deed of the Huttons to the school district. As urged by the defendants, and as the trial court found, that deed conveyed a fee simple subject to a condition subsequent followed by a right of re-entry for condition broken. As argued by the plaintiffs, on the other hand, the deed conveyed a fee simple determinable followed by a possibility of reverter. In either case, the grantor and his heirs retain an interest in the property which may become possessory if the condition is broken. If the grantor had a possibility of reverter, he or his heirs become the owner of the property by operation of law as soon as the condition is broken. If he has a right of re-entry for condition broken, he or his heirs become the owner of the property only after they act to retake the property.

The trial court concluded that the interest created by the 1941 deed was a fee simple subject to a condition subsequent followed by a right of entry for a condition broken and that since Harry E. Hutton failed to re-enter the property, the future interest lapsed and defendant owned the property in fee simple absolute.

The difference between a fee simple determinable (or, determinable fee) and a fee simple subject to a condition subsequent, is solely a matter of judicial interpretation of words of a grant.

We believe that a close analysis of the wording of the original grant shows that the grantors intended to create a fee simple determinable followed by a possibility of reverter.

The terms used in the 1941 deed, although imprecise, were designed to allow the property to be used for a single purpose, namely, for "school purpose." The Huttons intended to have the land back if it were ever used otherwise. Upon a grant of exclusive use followed by an express provision for reverter when that use ceases, courts and commentators have agreed that a fee simple determinable, rather than a fee simple subject to a condition subsequent, is created.

Accordingly, the trial court erred in dismissing plaintiffs' complaint which followed its holding that the plaintiffs could not have acquired any interest in the Hutton School property from Harry E. Hutton. We must therefore reverse and remand this cause to the trial court for further proceedings.

Reversed.

Summary of Future Interests Retained by the Transferor

There are three types of future interests which can be retained by a transferor. The first of these is the *reversion* which usually arises by operation of law when the transferor conveys less than his entire interest in the land. A reversion takes place automatically upon the expiration of the prior possessory estate. For instance, landlord transfers property to tenant for a term of ten years. Landlord retains a reversion which will take effect automatically upon the expiration of the tenant's leasehold estate.

A *possibility of reverter* arises where the transferor creates a fee simple determinable. A possibility of reverter tends to give the transferor some control over the conduct of the transferee. For instance, a transfer, "to A so long as the property is used as a school" reserves an interest in the transferor, or his heirs, which may become possessory in the event the condition is breached. When the condition is breached, when the property is no longer used as a school, the transferee's interest ends and a present possessory interest automatically reverts in the transferor or his heirs.

The *right of entry or power of termination* is based upon a specifically retained power in the transferor which gives the transferor the election to enter and terminate a prior estate upon the occurrence or nonoccurrence of some stated event. The right of entry differs from a reversion because it may arise even though the estate conveyed is of the same quantum as that held by the transferor. The right of entry differs from both the reversion and the possibility of reverter because the transferor's estate does not automatically become possessory upon the termination of the proceeding estate but requires the affirmative election and entry by the transferor.

6   STATUTORY LIMITATIONS UPON THE POSSIBILITY OF REVERTER AND THE RIGHT OF ENTRY

Future interests retained by the grantor, in particular the possibility of reverter and the right of entry for breach of a condition, have the obvious tendency of clogging title to property and thereby interfering with the free use and transferability of the property. Because of this, some states have enacted legislation which limits the enforceability of rights under a right of entry or possibility of reverter.

For example, an Illinois statute provides that neither possibilities of reverter nor rights of entry for breach of a condition subsequent shall be valid for a period longer than forty years from the date of the creation of the condition or possibility of reverter. The statute also provides that if the possibility of reverter or right of entry is created to endure for a period longer than forty years it shall, nevertheless, be valid for only forty years. Most jurisdictions that include statutes limiting these interests contain similar language limiting the interest to forty or, in some cases, thirty years from the date of its creation.

Approximately twenty states have enacted such statutes. These states include Arizona, California, Connecticut, Florida, Michigan, Illinois, Massachusetts, Minnesota, New York, and Wisconsin. These statutes vary significantly in their operation. Some, such as the New York statute, require the holder of a possibility of reverter or right of entry periodically to record a notice of intention to preserve their interest and provides further that such interests will be barred unless notice is served upon the possessor within ten years after the breach of the condition. However, the following case of *Central School District v. Miles* indicates that there are constitutional limitations to a state's ability to restrict these future interests.

Board of Education of Central School District v. Miles, 207 N.E. 2d 181 (N.Y.App. 1965)

Facts of the case.

On May 11, 1854, a deed from John Townsend and wife to the trustees of the Walton Academy was recorded in the Delaware County Clerk's office. The deed was subject to this provision:

> Provided that the lot and the building thereon shall be used for the purposes of an Academy and no other, then this deed shall remain in full force and effect otherwise it shall become Void and the premises herein conveyed shall revert to the said John Townsend party of the first part and to his heirs.

The property was used for educational purposes by the Walton Academy, its successors or assigns, until April 1, 1962, when its use for such purposes was discontinued.

Eugenia T. Miles is the sole heir of the now deceased grantor. The Board of Education has succeeded to the rights of the Walton Academy.

This action has been instituted to obtain a judicial determination of Miles's claim that she has been entitled to possession of the premises, vested with title in fee simple absolute since April 1, 1962, when use for school purposes was discontinued.

The trial court ruled in favor of the Board of Education holding that Miles's reversionary interest was extinguished and that the Board was the owner in fee simple absolute. This appeal followed.

OPINION

Unless their reversionary interest has been extinguished by Section 345 of the *Real Property Law,* Miles's contention is correct. This statute was designed to limit or extinguish nonsubstantial restrictions on the use of land such as possibilities of reverter, rights of entry on failure of conditions subsequent, and similar interests in real property. Its purpose is to provide for recording of a "declaration of intention" to preserve certain interests in land arising from ancient restrictions on the use of land and to extinguish such interests if such declarations of intention are not recorded within the time provided.

The constitutionally of Section 345 of the *Real Property Law* is challenged on this appeal on the grounds that it impairs the obligation of a contract and deprives appellants of property without due process of law. No such question could arise in regard to conveyances delivered after the adoption of this statute; however, it is a familiar rule that retrospective legislation, unless adopted pursuant to the police power, cannot impair vested rights.

In this case, Subdivision 4 of Section 345 provides that the declaration to preserve the reverter must be recorded on or before September 1, 1961, if the date when the special limitation was created was prior to September 1, 1931. In this instance, as has been stated, the deed to the trustees of the Walton Academy containing the reverter clause was recorded prior to 1931, and the property continued to be used for school purposes until 1962. That is to say, the reverter had not matured at the time when the statute prescribed that it became barred, nor could anyone have known prior to the cut-off date who would be parties in interest at the time when the reverter took effect. If Subdivision 4 of Section 345 of the *Real Property Law* be valid under these circumstances, at least, it would be necessary for unascertained persons, not even in being, to have recorded a declaration of intention to preserve a reverter which would not take effect in enjoyment until an indefinite future time. This makes the case resemble more nearly *Biltmore Village v. Royal,* 71 S. 2d 727 (Fla.), decided by the Florida Supreme Court in 1954, which concerned a statute canceling all reverter provisions in deeds in effect for more than twenty-one years but giving to the holder of the reverter interest one year from the date of the act to institute suit to enforce the right. That statute was held to be unconstitutional as impairing the obligation of the contract contained in the deed, and depriving the reversioner of property without due process of law, in a case where the event actuating the reverter occurred after the expiration of the statutory year's limitation. We agree with the analysis of the Florida Supreme Court.

The judgment appealed from should be reversed, and the matter remitted to the trial court for the entry of a judgment declaring that Miles is vested with title in fee to the property free from any claim of the Board of Education.

Future Interests Created in Persons Other Than the Transferor

Just as the transferor may retain a future interest, an equivalent form of future interest may be created in favor of third parties. These future interests are known as *remainders* and *executory interests*.

Remainders and executory interests often operate the same way. A few jurisdictions have even abolished the executory interest, preferring to treat it as a type of remainder. The distinction between remainders and executory interests is largely of historical origin. However, since the prevailing view among the states is to adhere to the distinction and because it is adopted by the *Restatement of Property,* the distinction between remainders and executory interests will be adhered to in this text.

7 THE REMAINDER

The *Restatement of Property,* Section 156, defines a remainder as "any future interest limited in favor of a transferee in such a manner that it can become a present interest upon the expiration of all prior interests simultaneously created, and cannot divest any interest except an interest left in the transferor."

A remainder takes effect upon the expiration of a prior estate and does not act to terminate or cut off the prior estate. For instance, a conveyance "to A for life and then to B" creates a life estate in favor of A and a remainder in favor of B. Similarly, the transfer "to A for ten years and then to B" creates a term of years in favor of A followed by a remainder in favor of B. In both cases, the remainder interest follows naturally upon the conclusion of the prior estate which terminates by its own terms. However a transfer "to A so long as the property is used as a church and then to B" is not a remainder because B's interest has the effect of divesting or terminating the prior interest.

Remainders may exist for life, or in fee. Thus, "to A for life, and then to B for life, and then to C" creates a life estate in A, a remainder life estate in B, and a remainder in fee simple in favor of C. As in the case of other freehold estates, a remainder may be made subject to defeasance or subject to some other limitation. For instance, "to A for life and then to B so long as the property is used as a school." A has a defeasible life estate, B has a remainder in fee simple determinable, and the grantor retains a reversion.

Types of Remainders

Most authorities distinguish remainders into two broad classes, namely vested remainders and contingent remainders. Vested remainders are of three types:

1 Indefeasibly vested;
2 Vested subject to open;
3 Vested subject to complete divestment

Contingent remainders are those not vested because they are subject to a condition precedent. The four categories of remainders tend to indicate the level of probability that the remainder will become and remain a present interest.

The Indefeasibly Vested Remainder

"To A for life and then to B."

When a remainder is indefeasibly vested, the holder of the remainder is certain to acquire, at some time in the future, and from that moment to retain permanently, a present possessory interest in the property. Such a remainder is not subject to any condition or limitation which could defeat or qualify the holder's interest upon the termination of any prior interests. This is true regardless of the number of prior interests which may delay the interest from becoming a present one. For example, "to A for life, then to B for life, then to C for ten years, and then to D." D or his successors, will certainly and unavoidably obtain the present interest in the property and this certainty is not affected by the fact that the interests of A, B, and C may delay D's interest in becoming a present one. If D dies before the interest becomes present, the property will descend to D's heirs subject, of course, to the expiration of the prior estates. D's interest is therefore indefeasibly vested.

Remainder Vested Subject to Open

"To A for life and then to the children of B."

This type of remainder occurs in a gift to a class. In the example above, the remainder becomes vested when the first child of B is born. However, the share of the remainder taken by B's first child is uncertain and will diminish in the event that additional children are born to B. The remainder interest is said to be vested in the children of B as they are born but is subject to "open" when additional children are born.

One court construed a deed which transferred property "to A for life and at his death to his children, if any, and if there are no children, then to B." The court stated that "when the deed is executed, the remainder is contingent as to such child or children until they are born, but the moment a child is born to the life tenant, the remainder vests in such child, subject to open and make room for any child or children who might thereafter be born within the class." (*Blanchard v. Ward*, 92 S.E. 2d 776 (N.C. 1956)

Vested Remainder Subject to Complete Defeasance or Divestment

"To B for life, remainder to C, but if C dies without children living at the time of his death, then to D."

This remainder bears some similarity to the contingent remainder and the executory interest which are discussed next. Nevertheless, because the person who may take possession is presently identified, and because their interest follows the natural termination of a prior estate, the remainder interest is considered vested. Events may arise, however, that defeat the interest; therefore, it is considered to be vested but subject to complete defeasance. In the case mentioned, C's remainder interest is vested but will be defeated if he dies without living children. Similarly, a conveyance "to A for life and then to B for life" creates a vested interest in B which is subject to complete defeasance because it will not become a present interest if B dies before A.

The Contingent Remainder:

"To A for life, remainder to B provided that B attains the age of twenty-one years."

The term *contingent remainder,* although commonly used by courts and commentators, has been abandoned by the *Restatement of Property* that, instead, uses the term *remainder subject to a condition precedent.* Either term denotes an interest subject to greater uncertainty than those involved in a vested remainder. In the case of a contingent remainder, it is not possible to identify with certainty the person who will take possession.

One court discussed the difference between the vested and contingent remainder in the following terms:

> The fundamental distinction between the two kinds of remainders is that in the case of vested remainder, the right to the estate is fixed and certain, although the right to possession is deferred to some future period. In the case of a contingent remainder, the right to the estate as well as the right to the possession of such estate is not only deferred to a future period, but is dependent on the happening of some future contingency. The broad distinction between vested and contingent remainders is this: In the first there is some person in existence known and ascertained who, by the will or deed creating the estate, is to take and enjoy the estate, and whose right to such remainder no contingency can defeat. In the second it depends upon the happening of a contingent event, whether the estate limited as a remainder shall ever take effect at all. The event may either never happen, or it may not happen until after the particular estate upon which it depended shall have been determined, so that the estate in remainder will never take effect. *Fletcher v. Hurdel,* 536 S.W. 2d 109 (Ark. 1976)

NOTES AND QUESTIONS

In the example given above, when will B's interest become vested? Is the answer different if the grant provides: "to A for life and then to B provided that B is at least twenty-one years old when A dies"?

8 THE EXECUTORY INTERESTS

"To A, for life, remainder to C, but if C dies without children living at the time of his death, then to D."

An executory interest, sometimes referred to as an executory limitation, is an interest that will vest an estate in the holder of the interest upon the happening of a condition or event. Unlike a remainder, an executory interest tends to terminate or cut short a prior estate rather than to follow upon the natural expiration of a prior estate.

You will note that the example given is the same one used to illustrate the third type of vested remainder subject to complete defeasance. In fact, in this example, C has a vested remainder subject to complete defeasance and D has an executory limitation that will cut short or terminate C's interest in the event or upon the condition that C dies without leaving surviving children. Similarly, a conveyance in fee to A so long as the property is used as a church, and then to *B*, creates an executory interest in favor of *B*. Upon the happening of an event, namely the discontinuance of the use of the property as a church, *B*'s interest vests and becomes a present interest. In this example, the executory interest is similar in operation to a reversion although, of course, the executory interest is held by someone other than the transferor. In addition, an executory interest can operate like a contingent remainder because, in both interests, a contingency must occur before the future interest will vest.

Dover v. Order of Odd Fellows, 206 N.W. 2d 845 (Neb. 1973)

This case involves the construction of the last will and testament of Nettie M. Dover, deceased. The District Court held that defendant had not acquired any interest in the property of the estate. We affirm that judgment.

Facts of the case.
   The relevant portion of the will provided:

> I give and devise my real estate, to my daughter Edna, to have and to hold during her lifetime, and at her death to her children in equal shares, or if she shall leave no children, then to the Odd Fellows Home at York, Nebraska. Provided, if my daughter Edna shall be left a widow, then upon her becoming a widow, I give and devise all my said real estate to her, by absolute title, believing she may need the same for her maintenance.

Nettie Dover died on January 10, 1942. She was the mother of Edna. The husband of Edna died on January 7, 1969. She never remarried but died a widow on December 5, 1970, without issue.

OPINION

The cardinal rule in construing a will is to ascertain and effectuate the intention of the testator when it can be done consistent with the rules of law.
   The intent of Nettie Dover appears to be clear. The real estate described in the third paragraph of the will is left to the daughter for life, with a provision that if the daughter should become a widow, the remainder interest should immediately vest in the daughter. This is an executory interest that abridged and terminated the life estate and vested the fee simple title in the daughter Edna Dover Miller. The contingent interest of defendant Odd Fellows, which could take effect only in the event the daughter failed to become a widow and failed to leave issue, was thereby terminated.

The judgment of the District Court is affirmed.

Federal Land Bank v. Wood, 334 F. Supp. 1124 (U.S. Dst.Ct., S.C. 1971)

Facts of the case.

Edward Charles Wood died on April 2, 1966, leaving a will that provided as follows:

> I give all my real estate to my beloved wife, Ida Walker Wood, to be hers for and during the term of her natural life; and upon the death of my said wife I will and devise said real estate to my two children, Charles Kenneth Wood and Jewell Wood Hall, share and share alike, PROVIDED, HOWEVER, that if either of my two children should predecease my wife, without leaving a child or children, then and in such event, I will and direct that the share of my said real estate which would have gone to such predeceased child shall go directly to my surviving child, absolutely and in fee; PROVIDED, FURTHER, HOWEVER, That if either of my said children should predecease my wife leaving a child or children, then and in such event, the share that such child or children would have taken, had such child or children survived my wife, shall go in fee to such natural child or children of either of my children who might predecease my wife.

OPINION

In construing the provisions of a Will every effort must be made to determine the intention of the Testator and to carry out such intention. This requires examination of the language used in the instrument. Where the language of the Will is vague or ambiguous the circumstances surrounding the execution of the Will are considered in determining the intention.

The provision of the Will of Edward Charles Wood as above set forth unquestionably gives Ida Walker Wood a life estate in the property. The language "upon the death of my said wife I will and devise said real estate unto my two children, Charles Kenneth Wood and Jewell Wood Hall, share and share alike" would give Charles Kenneth Wood and Jewell Wood Hall the remainder in fee simple. However, the item contains two further provisos. The effect of those provisos must be determined. This court is of the opinion that the unborn children of Charles Kenneth Wood and Jewell Wood Hall in fact have a legally recognizable interest in the property which must be protected by this court.

A vested remainder is one which is limited to an ascertained person in being, whose right to the estate is fixed and certain, and does not depend upon the happening of any future event, but whose enjoyment in possession is postponed to some future time. A contingent remainder, on the other hand, is one which is limited to a person not in being or not ascertained, or, if limited to an ascertained person, it is so limited that his right to the estate depends upon some contingency in the future. The most marked distinction between the two kinds of remainders is that in one case the right to the estate is fixed and certain, though the right to the possession is deferred to some future period; while in the other right to the estate as well as the right to possession of such estate is not only deferred to a future period, but is dependent upon the happening of some future contingency.

Under this test it would appear that the remainder possessed by Charles Kenneth Wood and Jewell Wood Hall is vested. It is limited to ascertained persons in being whose right to the estate is fixed and certain. It is clear that this right to the estate does not depend upon the happening of any future event. While it is true that a future event such as the death of either remainderman could deprive that remainderman of the right of possession and further ownership of the remainder interest such an event has no effect on the remainderman's right to his interest in the estate at this time. That right is already fixed and it in no way depends on his surviving the life tenant. Therefore, the remainder interest possessed by Charles Kenneth Wood and Jewell Wood Hall is vested and not contingent on the happening of any future event.

Therefore, it appears that the state of the title of the real estate devised to Ida Walker Wood and her two named children is a life estate in Ida Walker Wood and a vested remainder subject to divestment in Charles Kenneth Wood and Jewell Wood Hall with executory interests in the unborn children and in Charles Kenneth Wood and Jewell Wood Hall.

NOTES AND QUESTIONS

1 In the preceding case, the court indicates that each of the children of the deceased have both a vested remainder and an executory interest. Is this correct? How can they have two future interests in the same property at the same time?

2 Was the court correct in concluding that the unborn children had executory interests? What is the effect of this ruling?

9   SUMMARY

Future estates are interests in land which will not take effect in possession until the conclusion or termination of a prior estate or estates. Future interests may be reserved in the transferor or in third parties. Future interests reserved in the grantor are collectively known as reversionary interests. Future interests that are created in third persons are known as remainders or executory interests. A remainder tends to follow naturally upon the expiration of the preceding estate, whereas an executory interest tends to terminate or cut short the prior estate.

10   QUESTIONS

1 Fletcher died, leaving a will that gave a life estate to his son, remainder to his son's children. Do Fletcher and his estate have any future interest in the property?

2 Wilson transferred an apartment building by deed to Stanley for life. Wilson then died, leaving all his property to Helen, his wife. Does Helen have an interest in the apartment building?

3 Willis transferred property to a municipality ''for street purposes and upon cessation of such use, the same shall revert to the grantor, his heirs, and assigns forever.'' What interests were created by this instrument?

4 Alfred owns an apartment building and transfers it to ''Betty for life but upon express condition that if Betty ceases to live in the building then Alfred and his heirs may enter and terminate Betty's interest.'' What is the nature of Betty's interest? What is the nature of Alfred's interest?

5 Susan died, leaving a will that left her property to ''Charles for life, remainder at his death to Susan's daughters, provided that if Charles left a surviving spouse, the widow should share equally with Susan's daughters.'' Describe the interests of the daughters.

6 Thomas dies leaving a will which provides as follows: ''to Samuel for life, remainder to Victor, but only if Victor attains the age of twenty-one years.'' What is the nature of Victor's interest? Suppose that Samuel dies when Victor is only fifteen. What is the nature of Victor's interest in that event? Do Thomas's heirs have any interest in the property?

7 Morgan dies leaving a will which provides as follows: ''to Nancy for life, remainder to Oscar but if Oscar dies before Nancy and without children, then to Paulette. What are the interests of Oscar and Paulette?

8 A will left property to ''Helen for ten years, then to her absolutely provided however that if she should remarry during the ten-year period, then to Irving.'' What is the nature of Helen's estate?

LIMITATIONS ON
THE RIGHT TO CREATE
INTERESTS IN LAND

CHAPTER 4

RESTRAINTS UPON ALIENATION

TOPICS CONSIDERED IN THIS CHAPTER:

1   INTRODUCTION

Chapters 2 and 3 identified the primary estates that can be created in property. It should be apparent that one who transfers property, by will, deed, or some other instrument, has the power to restrict ownership of the property and to restrict the manner in which the property is used in the future. This chapter and the next one address the limits of a transferor's right to restrict the ability of subsequent owners to use or further transfer the property.

Limitations imposed by one who transfers real estate are known as restraints on alienation. Such restraints fall into two categories: direct restraints and indirect restraints.

Indirect restraints upon alienation involve the vesting of a future interest in property at a time the law considers too remote. Such indirect restraints are curbed by the rule against perpetuities that is briefly considered in this chapter.

This chapter is primarily concerned with the problem of direct restraints. Direct restraints do not give rise to problems of the vesting of future interests but rather are concerned with present interests that, by virtue of the deed, will, contract, or other instrument creating the interest, purport to restrict the grantees ability to again transfer the property. An obvious example of a direct restraint is a transfer "to *A* but if *A* attempts to transfer the property, then to *B*." The effect of this provision is to deny to *A* the right to convey her interest in the property because, if she tries to do so, the property vests in *B*. Most modern direct restraints upon alienation are considerably more subtle in their operation than the one just mentioned. Of necessity, the law pertaining to direct restraints has attempted to become sufficiently refined to accommodate contemporary transactions while furthering the basic policy objective of promoting the unfettered transfer of interests in property. Issues involving restraints on alienation are pervasive in the law of real estate and arise in the context of contracts, wills, deeds, mortgages, condominiums, and leases.

2   DIRECT RESTRAINTS: DEFINITIONS AND CONSEQUENCES

One of the incidents of ownership is the right to convey the property, and the law will not permit the rights of ownership to be hampered by the imposition of unreasonable restraints. The modern policy against restraints upon alienation derives from the belief that such restraints tend to favor the concentration of wealth and inhibit the productive use of property. The following quote, although an expression of a bygone era, states the problem as well as any:

> A man has a natural right to enjoy his property during his life and to leave it to his child at his death, but the liberty to determine how property shall be enjoyed when he who was once the owner of it, is in his grave, and to destine it in perpetuity to any purposes however fantastical, useless or ludicrous. . . . is a right and liberty which, I think, cannot be claimed by any natural or divine law, and which I think by human law ought to be strictly watched and regulated. *Jeffries v. Alexander,* 8 H.L.C. 584, 648 (1860)

Modern statutes tend to state the principle more directly. For instance, the *California Civil Code* provides: "Conditions restraining alienation, when repugnant to the interest created, are void." (*California Civil Code,* Section 711)

The policy against restraints upon alienation is not part of the early common law that encouraged restraints as a way of enforcing feudal servitudes. Originally, and particularly in the twelfth through fourteenth centuries, restraints upon the alienation of land were an inherent aspect of medieval thinking and the feudal system. During the fourteenth and fifteenth centuries, this thinking began to change and common law courts began gradually to espouse a policy in favor of the free alienability of land. The trend has continued up to the present day.

The Illinois court summarized the policy considerations as follows:

> Restraints on alienation keep property out of commerce, they tend to concentrate wealth, they may prevent the owner consuming the property except as to the income from it, they may deter the improvement of the property and they may prevent creditors from satisfying their claims. Against these and other social and economic disadvantages to the public, the only benefit that would often accrue from such restraints is the satisfaction of the capricious whims of the conveyor. Thus, as a general rule, restraints on alienation are void even though they are limited in time. (Gale v. York, 171 N.E.2d 30 (Ill. 1961)

Harvey v. Harvey, 524 P.2d 1187 (Kan. 1974)

Facts of the case.

Lulu Harvey died on August 4, 1956, leaving a will which provided as follows:

> I hereby give and devise my real estate to my son, Verl Harvey, for the term of his natural life.
>
> Upon the death of my son Verl Harvey said real estate shall go to and become the property of the children of Verl Harvey who are living at the time of this death provided however, that no such child shall mortgage or sell, or attempt to mortgage or sell his or her interest in said real property prior to attaining the age of twenty-five years; in the event any such child shall violate this provision against alienation then immediately upon such violation his or her interest in and to such property shall immediately pass to and become the property of the remaining children then living of the said Verl Harvey, share and share alike.

The will finally left the "rest, residue and remainder of my estate to Verl Harvey."

OPINION

The controversy here is between Verl Harvey, Lulu's son, and Verl Harvey's children who are Lulu Harvey's grandchildren. The trial court held that the provisions against alienation of each remainderman's interest violate the common law rule against unreasonable restraints on alienation and are illegal and void as against public policy. It is clear to us that the findings of the trial court are correct and that under our cases the restraints imposed on the grandchildren as remaindermen, which prohibit them from selling or mortgaging their interest in the property until they attain the age of twenty-five years after the death of their parent as life tenant, are unreasonable restraints on alienation and are therefore void.

The issue presented on this appeal has to do with the legal consequences which follow the determination that the restraints against alienation placed upon the grandchildren are invalid and unenforceable. The trial court held that the provisions restraining alienation may be excised from the will and that the balance of each of those items may be enforced. Verl Harvey takes the position that the remainder interests are invalid in their entirety and hence the property should pass to him under the residuary clause contained in the will. There is ample authority in Kansas to authorize the striking out of a provision of a will which violates the rule against unreasonable restraints on alienation and then to carry out the will as otherwise written. It all depends on whether or not the invalid portion can be excised without destroying the testamentary plan contained in the will. If the testamentary scheme of the testatrix can be determined and carried out regardless of the void provision, that provision will be stricken out and the testamentary plan given effect. We believe that the trial court was correct in concluding that under the factual circumstances presented in this case the invalid restrictions on alienation should be excised and that the balance of the will should be enforced to devise a remainder interest in fee simple to Mrs. Harvey's grandchildren.

For the reasons set forth above the judgment of the district court is affirmed.

NOTES AND QUESTIONS

Restrictions on transfer are often contained in the governing documents of condominiums and cooperatives. In *Aquarian Foundation v. Shalom House,* 448 S.2d 1166 (Fla. 1984), the Florida court examined a provision requiring a condominium owner to obtain written consent from the condominium's Board of Directors prior to selling or leasing a unit in the building. The court analyzed the restriction in the following terms:

> It is well settled that increased controls and limitations upon the rights of unit owners to transfer their property are necessary concomitants of condominium living. Condominium unit owners comprise a little democratic subsociety of necessity more restrictive as it pertains to use of condominium property than may exist outside the condominium organization.

However, condominium associations are not immune from the requirement that the restraint be reasonable. In this manner the balance between the right of the association to maintain its homogeneity and the right of the individual to alienate his property is struck. The basic premise of the public policy rule against unreasonable restraints on alienation is that free alienability of property fosters economic growth and commercial development.

The declaration of condominium in the present case permits the association to reject perpetually any unit owner's prospective purchaser for any or no reason. Such a provision, so obviously an absolute restraint on alienation, can be saved from invalidity only if the association has a corresponding obligation to purchase or procure a purchaser for the property from the unit owner at its fair market value. Otherwise stated, if, as here, the association is empowered to act arbitrarily in rejecting a unit owner's prospective purchaser, it must in turn be accountable to the unit owner by offering payment or a substitute market for the property. When this accountability exists, even an absolute and perpetual restraint on the unit owner's ability to select a purchaser is lawful.

3 CLASSIFICATIONS OF DIRECT RESTRAINTS

Direct restraints on alienation are classified in various ways, and the results of the classification usually determine whether a court will give effect to the restraint or conclude that it is void. If the restraint is void, the remainder of the grant is usually considered valid; the restraint is simply stricken as unenforceable.

A Disabling Restraint on Alienation

A disabling restraint is one that seeks to nullify or make void a later transfer of an interest in the property. For instance, *A* makes a transfer in fee simple to *B* providing that "any transfer of an interest in the property shall be null and void." Such a restraint attempts to "disable" the grantee from transferring the property by making any transfer void.

B Forfeiture Restraint

A forfeiture restraint is one that attempts to terminate or divest the interest created in the event of a later transfer. For instance, *A* transfers property in fee simple to *B* by an instrument providing that "if *B* ever attempts to transfer the property, the property shall pass to *C*." Forfeiture restraints always involve the attempt to create a future interest.

C Promissory Restraint

A promissory restraint is one that seeks to impose contractual liability in the event of a subsequent transfer. An example of a promissory restraint is one in which *A* conveys property to *B* and the instrument of transfer provides that *B* promises and covenants not to transfer the property to a third party. If such a restraint is valid, *A* would have a claim for damages or perhaps injunctive relief against *B* in the event of a transfer. However, unlike a disabling restraint, *B* has the power, if not the right, to transfer the property. Unlike a forfeiture restraint, *B*'s interest is not terminated upon the subsequent transfer; *A* merely has rights either to enjoin it or to obtain damages because of it.

4 LIMITED OR QUALIFIED RESTRAINTS

The examples that have been given are all examples of unlimited or unqualified restraints because they seek to completely forbid subsequent transfers. In addition, one may seek to impose a qualified or limited restraint upon the future right to transfer. For example, *A* transfers to *B* with a limitation that "*B* will not transfer the property for a period of ten years." This is an example of a limited promissory restraint because the restriction purports to prohibit *B* from further transfers only for a limited period of time.

Limited restraints may also specify a certain class of persons to whom the property may or may not be transferred. For instance, *A* conveys to *B* with language providing that "in the event that *B* transfers the property to persons other than *C* and *D* (for example her siblings) then *B*'s interest shall terminate and the property shall revert to *A*." This is an example of a forfeiture restraint limited as to particular persons.

In addition, it is important to identify the character of the interest made subject to the restraint. The previous examples refer to restraints upon fee interests although future interests also may be restrained. In addition, it is quite common for leases to contain restrictions upon the tenant's ability to transfer their interest under the lease. Restrictions in the landlord tenant field are considered in greater detail in Chapter 17.

NOTES AND QUESTIONS

Not all restraints on alienation are invalid. Only "unreasonable" restraints are prohibited. Determination of which restraints are reasonable and which are unreasonable involves balancing the degree or quantum of restraint against the justification for the restraint.

In one case, a city rent control ordinance provided that when a mobile home park owner wished to sell, he must first offer to sell the park to the residents. The court held this restriction invalid because it denied to the owner the fundamental property right to sell to the buyer of his choosing. (*Gregory v. San Juan Capistrano,* Cal. App., 142 Cal. App. 3d 72 (1983)

In another case, however, the seller's contract with the buyer provided that if the buyer resold the property to a certain neighbor within ten years, the buyer would pay the seller $20,000. This provision was upheld because the restriction was minimal; the buyer could resell to anyone except the neighbor.

5 USE RESTRAINTS

For the most part, restrictions pertaining to the use of the property are not considered under the topic of restraints upon alienation. Such restrictions tend to be analyzed either through contract provisions or through doctrines relative to the promises affecting the use of land. These are considered in Chapter 9. For instance, a grant from *A* to *B* "so long as the premises are used as a church" is not a restraint on alienation but a use restraint. *Mountain Brow Lodge v. Toscano,* 64 Cal.Rpt. 816 (Cal. 1968); *Baptist Church v. Parker,* 27 N.E.2d 522 (Ill. 1940) However, as the following case illustrates, even use restraints may be voided by the courts if the restraint is considered unreasonable under the circumstances.

Mutual Housing Cooperative, Inc. v. Sandow, 270 N.Y.S.2d 829 (N.Y. 1966)

Facts of the case.

The plaintiff is a cooperative housing corporation which operates and maintains a cooperative apartment building. The defendants are shareholder-tenants of the plaintiff who, together with their two daughters, reside in a three bedroom apartment in the plaintiff's building.

At issue is the right and power of the board of directors to adopt the following regulation:

BE IT RESOLVED, that the playing of musical instruments shall be prohibited except during the following hours:

a Between the hours of 10:00 A.M. to 8:00 P.M. during weekdays.
b Between the hours of 11:00 A.M. to 8:00 P.M. during Saturdays, Sundays, and legal holidays.

BE IT RESOLVED that the playing of musical instruments in excess of an hour and one-half per day by any one person is prohibited unless special approval is requested and received in writing by the Board of Directors.

The facts are not in dispute. The defendants' two daughters are musical artists. One plays the violin and the other the flute. In furtherance of their training, these girls practice their respective instruments at least three and one-half hours a day. The defendants moved into this building in 1959. Until April 29, 1965, the girls were allowed to practice without interference. On that date, following complaints by the tenants of adjoining apartment units, the rule and regulation set forth above was adopted, the plaintiff's Board of Directors apparently agreeing with Keats that "heard melodies are sweet but those unheard are sweeter."

The neighbors particularly complained about the flute which, by its nature, makes a loud piercing sound. The defendants refused to comply with the rule and regulation.

OPINION

The issue is whether the instant rule and regulation is reasonable.

All the cases cited by the plaintiff are distinguishable since they involved the right of a cooperative housing corporation to ban or restrict dogs or other animals or to outlaw the use of washing machines or food freezers. Regulations dealing with animals or mechanical devices which are attached to the property are essentially regulations pertaining to the use of the land. The instant regulation is basically different since it attempts to regulate the mode of living of the occupants of the building.

Spinoza once said that "one and the same thing can at the same time be good, bad, and indifferent." That applies here with full force. To their neighbors the emanations from the defendant's apartment may sound like discordant ululations, while the defendants may well feel with Nietzsche that "without music life would be a mistake." But whether "music is the most sublime noise that has ever penetrated into the ear of man" is not a matter for judicial determination. It suffices for present purposes to hold that a regulation which would mandate a ban upon the exercise of the musical art, or the enjoyment of music, clearly would be arbitrary and unreasonable. If the plaintiff's regulation restricting the playing of musical instruments to one and one-half hours per day were strictly enforced, it is doubtful that any of its tenants could ever acquire or maintain expertise as a musician.

The one and a half hour provision of the regulation bears internal evidence of its arbitrary character. To take as an example the very defendants in this case and their two daughters. Together they constitute four occupants of the apartment. If each one of them individually availed himself or herself of the right to play a musical instrument for one and a half hours a day, the total playing time thus consumed would be six hours. That would not be prohibited because the regulation provides only that "the playing of musical instruments in excess of an hour and a half per day by one person is prohibited." It is obvious that the plaintiff's other tenants would not be less disturbed if the musical playing over a period of six hours were accomplished by four people instead of by two or by one. Under the circumstances, the limitation to one and one-half hours bears no reasonable relationship to the alleged mischief sought to be met. The Court therefore finds the hour and a half regulation to be arbitrary and unreasonable.

The other portion of the regulation prohibits the playing of "musical instruments" after 8:00 P.M. It is just about that hour that most city dwellers, after having returned from work or school, finish their dinner and have an opportunity for the first time during the day to engage in avocational pursuits. Under the circumstances, to ban the playing of a musical instrument after 8:00 P.M. is in effect tantamount to banning its use completely. To uphold this 8:00 P.M. regulation would mean that no tenant could have a party or social gathering accompanied by piano playing and singing in the evening. So, too, under the broad category of "musical instruments," the playing of stereophonic equipment might well be banned. And if this "musical instrument" regulation were to be held valid, it would necessarily follow that a similar regulation prohibiting the playing of a television set or a radio after 8:00 P.M. would be valid.

While sympathizing with the desire of the plaintiff to secure peace and quiet for its tenants, and recognizing that the daily continuous playing even of a Van Cliburn can be too much of a good thing, the Court is constrained to conclude that neighbors and noise are one of the penalties of a modern civilization. The 8:00 P.M. regulation is therefore held void as being arbitrary and unreasonable.

The Court expresses the hope that the defendants will not so avail themselves of the rights here accorded them as to conclude with Longfellow that "the night shall be filled with music."

However, the cooperative has no right to enforce the rules and regulations adopted by it with respect to the playing of musical instruments, since such rules and regulations, under the circumstances here present, are arbitrary and unreasonable.

NOTES AND QUESTIONS

Do you agree with the court's conclusion in this case? Would a different result obtain if the offending music was the practicing of rap music or heavy metal rock? Can the cooperative association make any rules designed to ensure that the complex is reasonably quiet?

6   VALIDITY OF RESTRAINTS ON ALIENATION

The overwhelming majority rule is that all unqualified restraints upon a fee simple interest are simply invalid and that the grantee of the interest takes possession without regard to the restriction. In addition, most qualified restraints on a fee interest are also invalid. For instance, restraints which are qualified as to duration are invalid in most jurisdictions. The justification for this rule tends to be that suspending all power of alienation, even for a short period of time, will run counter to the policy of freedom of alienation and are void as a result. Thus, in *Ierrobno v. Megaro*, 262 A.2d 17 (N.J. 1970), a will transferred property in fee simple and provided that the beneficiary would not sell the property until his youngest child reached the age of twenty-one years. The court held that because unlimited power of alienation is an inseparable incident of a fee estate, the will could not restrain the fee even for a limited period of time. Similarly, in *Hankins v. Mathews*, 425 S.W. 2d 608 (Tenn. 1968), the court held that a forfeiture restraint which precluded the owner from selling for a ten year period was void.

The *Restatement of Property* (*2d*) (Donative Transfers, Section 4.1 and 4.2) follows the majority rule and concludes that any restraints upon a fee interest is invalid if the restraint would make it impossible for any period of time to transfer the interest. A few jurisdictions, permit restraints that are qualified as to time provided the restraint is "reasonable." In these few jurisdictions, restraints qualified as to time are decided on a case by case basis and, if reasonable under the circumstances, will be upheld.

Where the restraint on alienation of a fee interest seeks to limit the persons to whom the property may be transferred, the restraint will be upheld only if it is reasonable. Many such restraints take the form of limiting potential transferee's to family members. For instance, a will provided that the beneficiaries would have the right to sell "only to each other." This limitation was held invalid. However a restraint which provides that "the property may not be transferred to any member of my immediate family" would probably be valid because the effect of the limitation is slight.

In the case of *Franklin v. Spadafora*, 447 N.E. 2d 124 (1983), the Massachusetts court upheld a condominium association's provision which limited to two the number of units in the building which could be owned by any one individual. Relying on the *Restatement of Property* (*2d*), the court said:

> Reasonable restraints on alienation may be enforced. The following factors, if found, tend to support a conclusion that the restraint is reasonable:
>
> **1** The one imposing the restraint has some interest in land which he is seeking to protect by the enforcement of the restraint;
>
> **2** The restraint is limited in duration;
>
> **3** The enforcement of the restraint accomplishes a worthwhile purpose;
>
> **4** The type of conveyances prohibited are ones not likely to be employed to any substantial degree by the one restrained;
>
> **5** The number of persons to whom alienation is prohibited is small. . . .
>
> *Restatement of Property,* Section 406, Comment i(1944)

None of these factors is wholly determinative, nor is the list exhaustive. Each case must be examined in light of all the circumstances.

7 THE RULE AGAINST PERPETUITIES

This section presents a brief introduction of the second instance in which the law intervenes to restrain a transferor's intent in order to facilitate the larger policy objective of making interests in property more freely transferable.

The rule against perpetuities is a separate rule of property law which is to be distinguished from the rule against restraints on alienation. Although the rule against perpetuities and the rule against restraints on alienation have the same fundamental purpose, the rule against perpetuities is concerned solely with the vesting of future interests in property. The rule does not apply to vested interests but only to contingent estates. It is the primary device which the Anglo-American system of property law has devised to limit the power of an individual to control the disposition of their property after death.

The rule is extremely complicated and is introduced simply to complete the picture as it relates to legal limitations on a transferor's ability to control the subsequent disposition of property. The rule has led to fantastic amounts of litigation and a continuing stream of scholarly efforts to explain its operation. One knowledgeable writer has called the rule "a technicality-ridden legal nightmare" which . . . is a dangerous instrumentality in the hands of most members of the bar." (Leach 67, Harv. Law. Rev. 1349 (1954). Another writer introduced an analysis of the rule by comparing it to the mythical labyrinth of Daedalus which was "according to legend, so artfully constructed that no person enclosed in it could find a way out unassisted." (Dukeminier 74, Cal. Law. Rev. 1867 (1986). In an embarrassing case, the California Supreme Court ruled that an attorney who drafted a will that violated the Rule Against Perpetuities was not negligent, noting that "an attorney of ordinary skill acting under the same circumstances might well have fallen into the net which the rule spreads for the unwary and failed to recognize the danger." (*Lucas v. Hamm,* 364 P.2d 685, 690 (Cal. 1961)

Nevertheless, the rule against perpetuities in its common law form and, with statutory modifications in some jurisdictions, is in effect in all American states and for that reason, an admittedly superficial treatment of the rule is undertaken in this text.

8 STATEMENT OF THE RULE AGAINST PERPETUITIES

The classic statement of the rule formulated by John Chipman Gray in 1885 is as follows:

No interest is good unless it must vest, if at all, not later than twenty-one years after some life in being at the creation of the interest.'' Gray, *Rule Against Perpetuities,* Section 201 (Fourth Ed. 1942). Various authorities have challenged Gray's statement of the rule as hopelessly oversimplified, while other modern writers continued to support and defend Gray's definition.

The New York Estates, *Powers and Trust Law,* Section 9–1.1(a2) contains the following statement of the rule:

Every present or future estate shall be void in its creation which shall suspend the absolute power of alienation by any limitation or condition for a longer period than lives in being at the creation of the estate and a term of not more than twenty-one years.

9 RATIONALE FOR THE RULE AGAINST PERPETUITIES

If the rule against perpetuities is a labyrinth, a ''dangerous instrumentality,'' and a creation of law which, in the view of at least one court, is beyond the understanding of the average practicing attorney, why has society failed to find a substitute for it? Consider the following situation. *A* has considerable wealth when he prepares his will and provides that his property should be transferred, on his death, as follows: To my children for life, then to their children for life, then to my great grandchildren for their life, then to my great great grandchildren for their lives, . . .'' By this will, *A* has managed to tie up the property, render it essentially unmarketable for at least four generations or for a period in the range of 150 years. It is this possibility, namely the reach of the ''dead hand'' to remove property from the stream of commerce ''in perpetuity'' that is the basis for the rule.

The *Restatement of Property* (2d) (Donative Transfers) suggests three justifications for the rule against perpetuities. The first of these involves adjusting the rights between the current owner to prolong control over the property into the future against the rights of the current owner to ''be free from the dead hand.'' This aspect of the rule ''embodies one of the compromises prerequisite to the maintenance of a going society controlled primarily by its living members.'' Second, the rule against perpetuities is considered to contribute to the ''increased use of the wealth of society'' by prohibiting categories of future interests that would otherwise hamper the sale or use of property for long periods of time. Finally, the rule makes property more responsive to the needs of the current owner by making the property presently available for sale, use as security for a loan or for the satisfaction of obligations by creditors. (See *Restatement of Property* (2d) Donative Transfers Introduction, Part I, pages 8–9)

10 OPERATION OF THE RULE

A Interests Subject to the Rule

The rule against perpetuities is a rule which invalidates interests which vest too remotely. In other words, interests that are vested are not subject to the rule. An example is a conveyance "to A for life, then to B for life, and remainder to C." All interests are good under the rule. The remainder to C will not become possessory until some time in the future but the interest is vested and is not subject to the rule.

In addition, and seemingly inconsistent with the general purpose of the rule, interests retained by the grantor are generally not subject to the rule against perpetuities. In other words, reversionary interests, possibilities of reverter, and rights of entry are simply not subject to the limitations imposed by the rule. This exemption is largely of historical origin and is sometimes defended on the ground that such interests in the grantor are "vested." However, the exemption of future interests retained by the grantor is difficult to justify because these interests can tie up land for extraordinary periods of time. See 6 ALP Section 24.62 (A. Casner Ed. 1952).

Nevertheless, the only interests that are subject to the rule are contingent remainders and executory interests. Consider the following conveyances:

1 "to A for so long as the property is used as a church but if it is not used as a church then the property shall revert to the grantor."

2 "To A for so long as the property is used as a church and, if it is not used as a church, then to B and her heirs."

The first of these transfers involves a fee simple determinable with a reversionary interest in the grantor which, as noted, is not subject to the rule against perpetuities. The second example involves a fee simple determinable to A with an executory interest in B. The executory interest is subject to the rule against perpetuities and, in the example given, violates the rule and is void.

The failure of the rule against perpetuities to reach future interests retained by the grantor has been addressed by statutes in various jurisdictions. California, Connecticut, Florida, Illinois, Kentucky, Massachusetts, Michigan, New York, and Rhode Island, among others, have enacted statutes which provide that reversionary interests, rights of entry, and possibilities of reverter are subject to a fixed term limitation, most typically thirty years. Under such statutes, reversionary interests in the grantor expire at the end of the statutory period and no longer constitute a future interest or any interest in the property conveyed. The statutory enactments are not part of the rule against perpetuities but are rather a response to the limitations of the rule.

B The Period of Perpetuities

The period within which an interest must vest is twenty-one years after a life or lives in being at the creation of the interest.

According to Gray, the perpetuities period begins to run "at the creation of the interest." For our purposes, this means that an interest under a deed is created when the deed is delivered to the grantee and that interest under a will is created when the testator dies. This is certainly the simplest aspect of the rule against perpetuities.

Interests are valid if they must vest, if at all, within twenty-one years after the creation of the interest or, within twenty-one years after the death of persons in being at the creation of the interest. Actual periods of gestation are permissible as additions to the twenty-one year period. This particular time limitation originally evolved to accommodate the desire to restrict transfers to persons who had reached the age of majority. For instance, a grant "to my children for life and then to my grandchildren provided they reach the age of twenty-one years" is good under the rule. This transfer is good under the rule although a conveyance "to my children for life and then to my grandchildren provided they reach the age of twenty-two" would violate the rule and the remainder interests to the grandchildren would be void.

C "Lives In Being": The Measuring Lives

In order to be valid, an interest must vest within twenty-one years of a life in being at the creation of the interest. The "life in being" is often referred to as the measuring life. The concept involves locating either by the express terms of the instrument or by implication, some person who will be alive, (or in gestation) at the creation of the interest. For instance, if a will provides that property is to be given to "my grand-children, provided they reach the age of twenty-one," the interest is valid because the testator's children are used as measuring lives. Because all such children are certain to be alive (or born within the period of gestation) upon the death of the testator, the interest in the grandchildren will vest, if at all, within twenty-one years after lives in being at the creation of the interest. However, if this is taken a step further to provide "and then to my great children," the interest in the great grandchildren would be void under the rule.

It is important to note that the measuring lives need not be persons who will take anything under the instrument. In fact, the measuring lives may be completely unre-lated to the persons intended to take possession by the instrument; they may even be selected at random. An English court sustained a gift to "my descendants who shall be living twenty-one years after the death of all lineal descendants of Queen Victoria now living." In re Villar 1 CH. 243 (1929). This remarkable decision required a search as to the lives of 120 descendants of Queen Victoria who were alive at the creation of the interest. Commentators have speculated on the practice which would involve selecting a dozen or so healthy babies at random and using them as measuring lives. Adding twenty-one years would enable the grantor to control the disposition of the property for approximately a century. Nevertheless, this practice would not, strictly speaking, violate the rule against perpetuities.

D The Requirement Of Vesting

As just indicated, the rule against perpetuities is a rule invalidating certain future interests that vest too remotely. The rule does not require that future interests vest in possession within a certain time but only that they vest in interest. Thus a transfer from "*A* for life and then to *B* for life and then to *C* when she reaches the age of forty" does not violate the rule because *C*'s interest is vested although her right to enjoy the property, either through possession or the receipt of income from it, may be postponed for a period beyond that specified by the rule against perpetuities.

If an interest is to satisfy the rule against perpetuities it must be absolutely certain to vest within the period of the rule. Extreme probability of vesting and the fact that the interest does in fact vest in time is not enough. It must be certain that the interests will vest at the creation of the interest. It is in this respect that the rule leads to its most extraordinary and hypertechnical results. Thus a conveyance limited on the condition of "the termination of the present war" would violate the rule because it is possible that the war would last for more than twenty-one years. A similar case involved a testator who owned gravel pits that, if worked at a normal pace, would be exhausted in four years. He died leaving a will that devised the gravel pits to *A* until they were exhausted at which point the property was to be sold and the proceeds divided among *B* and *C*. The pits were actually exhausted in six years but the gift was held invalid on the ground that they might not have been exhausted within twenty-one years.

NOTES AND QUESTIONS

1 In *Seal v. First Bank & Trust,* 295 S.E. 2d 367 (Ga. 1982), the Georgia court held that an option to purchase lots, exercisable for four months after the city accepted a subdivision plan, was held void because the city might not have accepted the subdivision for more than twenty-one years. Does this result make sense?

2 Landlord and tenant entered into an agreement to lease a building that had not yet been built. The lease provided that the building "shall be completed within ninety (90) days after a building permit has been secured by the City and County of San Francisco." The landlord later sought to avoid the lease, claiming that the lease was invalid under the rule against perpetuities because it was possible that the building permit might not be issued for more than twenty-one years. The court ruled simply that the agreement implied that the building would be built within a reasonable time, that a reasonable time is far less than twenty-one years and that the contract was enforceable. (*Wong v. Digrazia,* 386 P2d 817 (Cal. 1963) The case states the emerging trend that the rule against perpetuities does not apply to commercial transactions. Can you think of a simple provision that would avoid a problem in the case of an "on completion" agreement?

11 MODIFICATIONS TO THE RULE AGAINST PERPETUITIES

A The "Wait and See" Doctrine

Recently there has been a movement to modify the Rule Against Perpetuities which permits interests to be validated, if, as measured by actual rather than by possible events, they vest within the period of perpetuities.

Under the so-called "wait and see" rule a court is permitted to wait and see if an otherwise invalid interest can be cured based upon subsequent events that actually transpire. For instance, an example already given involved an interest declared void because it was possible that the removal of gravel from a gravel pit could take more than twenty-one years. Under the traditional approach, it was irrelevant that, in fact, the gravel was mined in only six years. Under the "wait and see" rule, a court would be precluded from passing on the validity of the grant until twenty-one years had elapsed or until the condition had been met. In this case, the condition was met after six years and the interest would become valid at that time. If, on the other hand, after twenty-one years the gravel had not been mined the interest would be declared void at that time.

The "wait and see" rule has generated some controversy as to its wisdom. On the one hand, the doctrine creates uncertainty because the validity of interests cannot be determined until some time after the interest was created. This tends to frustrate the purpose for which the rule was originally adopted. On the other hand, application of the "wait and see" doctrine tends to give effect to a transferor's desires and avoids some of the hypertechnical consequences that can arise under strict application of the rule. Pennsylvania was the first state to enact a statute embodying the "wait and see" philosophy. Since then, statutes enacting some form of the "wait and see" rule have been adopted in Alaska, Connecticut, Kentucky, Illinois, Massachusetts, Maine, Nevada, New Mexico, Ohio, Virginia, and Washington. In addition, courts in Mississippi and New Hampshire have adopted the "wait and see" principle without the benefit of legislative authority. Finally, the *Restatement (2d)* (Donative Transfers) supports the "wait and see" rule and encourages its adoption. At this time, it continues to be a minority position.

B Equitable Reformation

The Cy Pres Doctrine involves the power of a court to reform an invalid transfer so as to conform, as nearly as possible, to the grantor's intent. The doctrine has long been used to reform gifts made to charitable institutions that, for any number of reasons, cannot be accomplished in precisely the terms provided by the donor. Only recently has Cy Pres been applied in the context of the Rule Against Perpetuities.

A few state courts have adopted Cy Pres to validate interests which run afoul of the Rule Against Perpetuities. These are Hawaii, Mississippi, New Hampshire, and West Virginia. In addition, statutes in California, Idaho, Missouri, Oklahoma, and Texas have specifically given courts the authority to use Cy Pres in this regard. Most states that have adopted the "wait and see" rule by statute have also provided that, if necessary, the Cy Pres Doctrine can also be used to reform an interest so as to validate the interest.

12 CONSEQUENCES OF VIOLATING THE RULE

The effect of a violation of the rule against perpetuities usually makes the entire future interest void, but the remaining portions of the grant do take effect. However, valid transfers cannot be enlarged because future interests may be void under the rule. For instance, a transfer to "*A* for life and then to *A*'s children provided they reach the age of twenty-five," violates the rule and the remainder to *A*'s children is void. *A*, however, continues to take only a life estate and the remainder becomes a reversion and transfers back to the original grantor and his or her heirs. A slight exception to this rule may obtain in the case of a will that contains a residuary clause leaving the balance of the testator's property to certain individuals. In this case, the void future interests return to the testator's estate and are distributed pursuant to that paragraph in the will.

13 SUMMARY

A restraint against alienation is a provision in an instrument that purports to limit the owner's right to transfer an interest in the property. Such restraints can be included in wills, deeds, leases, mortgages, and a variety of other instruments. Restraints against alienation are disfavored as tending to render property unmarketable and to impede its productive use.

For the most part, unqualified restraints upon a fee interest are considered repugnant to the nature of a fee and are simply void. The interest in the transferee takes effect without regard to the restraint. Qualified restraints which temporarily suspend the owner's power to transfer are also void as inconsistent with a fee interest. However, restraints that are qualified so as to minimize the extent of the restraint are more likely to be upheld. However, even qualified restraints must be reasonable, must not impose too great a burden upon the ability to transfer the property, and must not offend any other aspect of public policy.

While the doctrine of restraints against alienation forbids unreasonable efforts to limit a transferee's power to convey, the rule against perpetuities forbids the creation of interests that vest too remotely. It does this by requiring that contingent interests, namely executory interests and contingent remainders, must vest, if at all, within twenty-one years of a life in being at the creation of the interest. If an interest violates the rule, it is void at its creation and usually reverts to the transferor.

The common law rule continues to be followed in the majority of American jurisdictions. However, modifications of relatively recent origin are beginning to be encountered in some states. In the first place, a growing minority of jurisdictions apply time limits to the operation of interests retained by a transferor. The so-called "wait and see" approach enables some offending interests to be saved if they vest, in fact, within the time limitations of the rule. Other jurisdictions have utilized the doctrine of equitable approximation or Cy Pres to reform a transfer so that it complies with the rule and to validate the interest as reformed. Finally, courts are becoming increasingly willing to refuse to apply the rule to invalidate purely contractual arrangements.

14 QUESTIONS

1 Northwest transferred a parcel to Carl Einbrod by a deed that provided that "no owner of the land conveyed shall have the right to sell or rent the same without the written consent

of the grantor.'' One year later Einbrod entered into a contract to sell without having first obtained Northwest's consent. May Northwest block the sale?

2 Virgil made a will leaving property to Jim Grubb that provided as follows:

> The said Jim Grubb is to keep this property in his possession ten years before he is able to sell, mortgage, or dispose of the same, and if he should attempt to do so, then in this event the said tracts of land shall revert to Hankins.

Grubb sought to sell the property before ten years elapsed. May he do so?

3 Cynthia gave a mortgage to Bank of America, which stated that if the property were sold, the Bank had the right to declare the entire unpaid principal immediately due and payable. The interest rate that Cynthia paid the Bank was 8 percent and the current market rate for such mortgages was 15 percent. Cynthia transferred the property and the Bank declared the loan due and proceeded to foreclose. Cynthia and the buyer tried to restrain the foreclosure claiming that the due on sale clause was an unreasonable restraint on alienation. Who wins?

4 Smedley donated property to the City of Waldron, Arkansas, for use as a reservoir by a deed that provided as follows:

> The City of Waldron shall never sell, transfer, convey, lease, rent, or otherwise dispose of the lands herein above described to other persons, firms, groups, and/or corporations, except successors and/or assigns of itself, and if it attempts to do so, the lands immediately revert to Hannah Smedley and her heirs[.]

The City sought to lease the mineral rights to the property and Smedley intervened claiming ownership under the reverter clause. Who wins?

5 Thompson made a will leaving property to his wife as follows:

> with full and complete power to her to use, consume and dispose of the same absolutely as she shall see fit,

followed by a provision that,

> After the death of my wife I bequeath and devise whatever of my estate shall remain unconsumed and undisposed of by my said wife to my wife's nephew, Briggs Thornton. . . .

A dispute arose between the wife and the wife's nephew concerning their respective interests in the property. What are their respective interests?

6 A condominium association is formed that contains the following limitation:

> It is intended that this be a retirement community and no one under the age of fifty-five shall be permitted to purchase or live in the complex.

Is the restraint valid?

7 Which of the following interests violate the common law rule against perpetuities?
   a. ''to such of my grandchildren born within ten years after my death as shall attain the age of twenty-one years of age.''
   b. ''to my son John, his wife, and their children for life, remainder to my grandchildren.''
   c. ''to Able, Betty, and Charles, one year after the settlement of my estate.''
   d. David prepares a deed which conveys property ''to my children for life, then to my grandchildren who reach the age of twenty-one years.''
   e. ''to the Church, for use as a Church and, when such use ceases, to revert to grantor or her heirs.''

8 Fred gave an option to Grace providing that Grace may elect to purchase certain property for one year and that the option would automatically be renewed each year. Does the option offend the rule against perpetuities?

9 Finch died in 1956, leaving a will permitting that the property be distributed to three children as follows: "one-third in 1980, one-half in 1992, and the balance in 2005." Does this arrangement offend the rule?

10 Stroelker gave Hanson a perpetual option to purchase property. The law of the State adopted the "wait and see" approach. What is the status of the option?

11 Consider the facts in Problem 4. Suppose the law of the State had adopted the Cy Pres or equitable approximation. What would be the result?

CO-OWNERSHIP
OF INTERESTS
IN REAL ESTATE

CHAPTER 5

CONCURRENT OWNERSHIP

TOPICS CONSIDERED IN THIS CHAPTER:

1 INTRODUCTION

Concurrent ownership refers to circumstances in which equivalent interests in real estate are simultaneously owned by two or more persons. The idea itself is very old and forms of co-ownership are known to have existed as early as the thirteenth century.

Unfortunately, 700 years of progress have managed to complicate the field of concurrent ownership rather than render it more understandable. There is also wide variety among the approaches taken by the various states. Some jurisdictions do not even recognize forms of co-ownership which are popular and well developed in other states. In addition, many instruments creating concurrent interests are drafted by lay people with little understanding of the consequences which can result from their well intentioned but mistaken choice of words. The New Hampshire Supreme Court when attempting to construe a deed given by a husband to himself and his wife in an apparent effort to create a joint tenancy was moved to quote the famous dictum of Oliver Wendell Holmes as follows:

> It is revolting to have no better reason for a rule of law than that it was laid down in the time of Henry IV. It is still more revolting if the grounds upon which it was laid down have vanished long since, and the rule simply persists from blind imitation of the past.

Holmes, *Collected Legal Papers* 187 (1920) (cited in *Dover v. Robin's Estate,* 166 A 247,248 (N. H.)

It is important to emphasize that, while co-ownership can exist with respect to almost any interest in land, the concept assumes a simultaneous and equivalent interest in the same property. In other words, in the grant to A for life and then to B, A has a life estate and B has a remainder. These are not concurrent estates but rather a present interest in A and a future interest in B. By the same token, a grant to A and B for life remainder to C and D would create concurrent interests in A and B as to the life estate and in C and D as to the remainder.

Because of price inflation in the housing market over the past fifteen years, many parts of the country have experienced an ''affordability crisis,'' that has placed home ownership beyond the reach of many. This problem has caused renewed interest in a variety of common ownership arrangements. First of all, an increasing number of people are turning to condominiums and cooperatives to meet their housing needs. These ownership forms are covered in the next chapter.

Less formal arrangements are also being used to help satisfy the goal of home ownership. In urbanized areas, families and individuals have begun to pool their cash resources and credit opportunities to purchase apartment buildings. For example, six people purchase a six unit apartment building, each of whom then moves into the building. A comparable condominium or cooperative would usually cost considerably more.

Another development in the housing market is equity sharing which usually involves two parties, one of whom invests cash, while the other lives in the property and pays all expenses. At the end of the term, the property is usually sold and the proceeds split between the parties. Equity sharing has been in existence for as long as parents, siblings and friends have helped each other purchase property by contributing to the down payment. In some areas the concept has become more formalized and entrepreneurs have assembled groups of investors who participate in equity share arrangements purely as a business arrangement. The advantage to the investor is a relatively safe and trouble-free investment. The advantage to the occupant is that they can build equity in a home without having to wait to save the money otherwise necessary to make the down payment. The nature of relationship between the parties in such a case is the subject of this chapter.

2 OVERVIEW OF MAJOR FORMS OF CONCURRENT OWNERSHIP

Three forms of concurrent ownership, namely the joint tenancy, tenancy in common and tenancy by the entirety have their roots in early English common law. The community property system in America has existed since about 1800 and is derived from the Spanish civil law. Tenancy in partnership, condominium, cooperative, and time-share are relatively recent developments which have their origins in the twentieth century and are rapidly evolving at the present time.

"To A and B as joint tenants" is an example of joint tenancy. The most distinctive feature of a joint tenancy is the right of survivorship. Upon the death of one joint tenant, the remaining joint tenants acquire the interest of the deceased joint tenant. In the example given above, upon the death of A, A's interest in the property is extinguished and B becomes the sole owner of the property to the exclusion of A's heirs. However, either joint tenant may sever or terminate the joint tenancy in various ways that will be discussed later. Upon severance of the joint tenancy, a tenancy in common is created. In our example, if B delivers a deed to C, then A and C become concurrent owners of the property holding title as tenants in common.

"To A and B" is an example of tenancy in common. Unlike the joint tenancy, the tenancy in common does not include the right of survivorship. Upon the death of a tenant in common, his interest passes pursuant to his will or to his heirs. Tenancy in common is the favored form of concurrent ownership and, in the case of ambiguity, a tenancy in common will be favored over a joint tenancy.

"To A and B, husband and wife" is tenancy by the entirety. The tenancy by the entirety is similar to the joint tenancy in that it includes the right of survivorship. However, this form of co-ownership can only exist between a husband and wife, and unlike the joint tenancy, it cannot be severed by the unilateral act of either co-owner. Approximately twenty-two states recognize the tenancy by the entirety in some form and it continues to be a popular form of ownership in certain jurisdictions.

The consequences of holding property in the form of a partnership is best treated under the subject of business organizations and is generally outside the scope of this text. However, the Uniform Partnership Act now in force in almost all states permits partnerships to hold title to real property in the name of the partnership. Each partner becomes a co-owner with the other partners holding title as a tenant in partnership. However the rights between and among the partners are governed by the law of partnership rather than by the law of real property.

The community property system exists in eight states and was brought to the American southwest when this area was under the dominion of Spain. The community property system applies to legally married persons and provides that each spouse owns a one-half interest in all property acquired through and during the course of the marriage, regardless of which spouse produces the income to acquire the property.

To a large extent, the modern forms of ownership interests such as the cooperative, the condominium, and the time-share rely heavily upon concurrent ownership concepts, at least for the common areas within the structure. These specialized forms of ownership and the extent to which elements of concurrent ownership apply to them are treated more fully in the next chapter.

3 THE JOINT TENANCY

The joint tenancy has existed for several hundred years and continues to have the right of survivorship as its distinguishing feature.

Under the common law of England, joint tenancies were favored over other forms of co-ownership. A conveyance to two or more persons was construed to create a joint tenancy unless the contrary intent was apparent from the wording of the instrument. This common law preference was the result of the feudal system that simplified the collection of taxes by concentrating land holdings in the hands of a few. One early case expressed this preference as follows, ''Joint tenancies are favored, for the law loves not fractions of estates, nor to divide and multiply tenures.'' (*Fisher v. Wigg*, 91 Eng.Rep. 340 (1700) The right of survivorship tended to accomplish this end.

With the decline of feudalism, joint tenancies became disfavored. Today a transfer to more than one person will be construed as a tenancy in common unless the intention to create a joint tenancy is clearly expressed in the language of the grant. A few states even require that the right of survivorship be specified in the transferring instrument. Joint tenancies may be created by a deed or by a will but, because of the presumption of tenancy in common, will not be created if property transfers under the laws of intestate succession.

A   The Four Unities

Deslauriers v. Senesac, 163 N.E. 327 (Ill. 1928)

Facts of the case.

Ida Deslauriers owned property in Kankakee County, Illinois. In 1908 she married Homer Deslauriers. In 1910 she and her husband executed a deed attempting to transfer the property to themselves as joint tenants. The deed contained the following language:

> ''Said grantors intend and declare that their title shall and does hereby pass to grantees not in tenancy in common but in joint tenancy.''

On February 22, 1919, Ida Deslauriers died without a will, leaving her husband, and brothers and sisters as her heirs.

A dispute arose between Ida's husband and her siblings. Mr. Deslauriers claims ownership of the entire parcel based upon the survivorship feature of a joint tenancy. Ida's brothers and sisters claim that Ida and her husband owned the property as tenants in common and that, upon Ida's death, her interest passed to them as her heirs. The trial court found that a joint tenancy had been created and that upon Ida's death, Homer became the owner in fee simple.

OPINION

The properties of a joint estate are derived from its unity, which is fourfold; the unity of interest, the unity of title, the unity of time, and the unity of possession;

or, in other words, joint tenants have one and the same interest, accruing by one and the same conveyance, commencing at one and the same time, and held by one and the same undivided possession.

Ida Deslauriers was the sole owner of the property prior to the execution of the deed from herself and husband to themselves. She could not by that deed convey an interest in the property to herself. It is manifest from the deed that she did not intend to convey the whole and entire interest to her husband, for she retained an equal share or interest. Hence the interests of Ida Deslauriers and her husband were neither acquired by one and the same conveyance, nor did they vest at one and the same time. Two of the essential properties of a joint estate—the unity of title and the unity of time—were therefore lacking. Where two or more persons acquire individual interests in a parcel of property by different times, there is neither unity of title nor unity of time, and in such a situation a tenancy in common, and not a joint tenancy, is created.

Homer argues, the deed expressly stated that the conveyance was made to the grantees as joint tenants and that this intention should control. However, the intention of the parties to a deed will be given effect if it can be done consistently with the rules of law. It was not for failure to ascertain the intention of the grantors that the grantees did not take title in joint tenancy, but because, under the law, a joint tenancy could not be created in the manner attempted here. Ida Deslauriers failed to convey any interest to herself as a joint tenant, and for that reason she also failed to convey to her husband in joint tenancy. She could, however, convey, and did convey, to her husband an undivided half interest in the property. The other half she retained, and upon her death it descended to her heirs.

Reversed.

NOTES AND QUESTIONS

1 How could Mrs. Deslauriers have structured the transaction in order to preserve the four unities and thereby create a joint tenancy?

2 The right of survivorship is based upon the concept that the property is owned by an entity which consists of all of the co-tenants and which continues to exist so long as any of them survive. Each joint tenant is considered to have UNDIVIDED INTEREST as an individual which is equal to the interest of every other co-tenant.

3 The *Deslauriers* case states the common law rule which continues to be the majority view in this country. Joint tenancy requires the four unities of time, title, interest, and possession. The unities of time and title require that the joint tenant's interests accrue at the same time by the same instrument. By unity of interest it is meant that the joint tenants shares are all equal and the duration and the quality of their interests are identical. Unity of possession means that each joint tenant has the right to the whole estate and that each is also entitled to enjoy and reap the benefits of the property to the same extent as the other co-tenants.

B Statutory Modifications of the Joint Tenancy

In addition to reversing the common law by creating a preference in favor of tenancy in common and against joint tenancy, other statutory modifications to the common law rule have been made. At least two states, Georgia and Oregon, have abolished the joint tenancy altogether and approximately 10 others, have either abolished the survivorship feature or required explicit language indicating an intent that the parties intended to create a right of survivorship. In addition, various statutory efforts have been made to modify the requirement of the four unities in an effort to effectuate the grantor's purpose when the intent to create a joint tenancy is clearly expressed. This tendency is most noticeable in statutes which permit a grantor who already owns an interest in the property to create a joint tenancy by making a direct conveyance herself and to another. An example of the operation of a statute which modifies the requirement of the four unities is found in the following case.

Riddle v. Harmon, 161 Cal.Rptr. 530 at 532 (Cal. 1980)

At common law, one could not create a joint tenancy in himself and another by a direct conveyance. It was necessary for joint tenants to acquire their interests at the same time (unity of time) and by the same instrument (unity of title). So, in order to create a valid joint tenancy where one of the proposed joint tenants already owned an interest in the property, it was first necessary to convey the property to a disinterested third person, a "strawman," who then conveyed the title to the ultimate grantees as joint tenants. This remains the prevailing practice in some jurisdictions. Other states, including California, have disregarded this application of the unities requirement as one of the obsolete subtle and arbitrary distinctions and niceties of the feudal common law.

By amendment to its Civil Code, California became a pioneer in allowing the creation of a joint tenancy by direct transfer. Under authority of Civil Code Section 683, a joint tenancy conveyance may be made from a "sole owner to himself and others," or from joint owners to themselves and others as specified in the code. The purpose of the amendment was to "avoid the necessity of making a conveyance through a dummy." Accordingly, in California, it is no longer necessary to use a strawman to create a joint tenancy.

C Severance of the Joint Tenancy

Various actions undertaken by individual joint tenants can cause a conversion of the joint tenancy into a tenancy in common with a destruction of the right of survivorship. This is known as severance. For the most part, each joint tenant has the right to sever the joint tenancy either by transferring their interest in the property, or, in some cases, by encumbering it with a mortgage or even executing a lease. Ordinarily, any act that undermines the existence of the four unities will destroy the joint tenancy.

The interests of joint tenants will only be severed to the extent that they no longer hold title to the property in accordance with the unities of time, title, interest, and possession. For example, if *A* and *B* own as joint tenants and *B* gives a deed to *C*, *A* and *C* are now the owners of the property; the unities of time and title do not exist between them; and they hold title as tenants in common with no right of survivorship. However, if *A*, *B*, and *C* own property in joint tenancy, and *C* conveys to *D* then *A*, *B*, and *D* hold as tenants in common of a one-third interest because, among the three of them, there is no unity of time or title. However, as between *A* and *B*, the four unities are still intact and they hold as joint tenants as between themselves. When *A* dies, *B* will survive to *A*'s interest and will then own two-thirds of the property as a tenant in common with *D*.

Tenhet v. Boswell, 554 P.2d 331 (Cal. 1976)

Facts of the case.

Raymond Johnson and plaintiff Hazel Tenhet owned a parcel of property as joint tenants. Without plaintiff's knowledge or consent, Johnson leased the property to defendant Boswell for a period of ten years at a rental of $150 per year. Johnson died some three months after execution of the lease, and plaintiff sought to establish her sole right to possession of the property as the surviving joint tenant. After an unsuccessful demand upon defendant to vacate the premises, plaintiff brought this action to have the lease declared invalid. The trial court ruled in favor of defendant and plaintiff appeals.

OPINION

Our initial inquiry is whether Johnson's creation of a leasehold interest in the property effected a severance of the joint tenancy. It could be argued that a lease destroys the unities of interest and possession because the leasing joint tenant transfers to the lessee his present possessory interest and retains a mere reversion. Moreover, the possibility that the term of the lease may continue beyond the lifetime of the lessor is inconsistent with a complete right of survivorship.

On the other hand, if the lease entered into here by Johnson and defendant is valid only during Johnson's life, then the conveyance is more a variety of life estate pur autre vie than a term of years. Such a result is inconsistent with Johnson's freedom to alienate his interest during his lifetime.

As we shall explain, it is our opinion that a lease is not so inherently inconsistent with joint tenancy as to create a severance, either temporary or permanent.

Under Civil Code sections 683 and 686 a joint tenancy must be expressly declared in the creating instrument, or a tenancy in common results. This is a statutory departure from the common law preference in favor of joint tenancy. Inasmuch as the estate arises only upon express intent, and in many cases such intent will be the intent of the joint tenants themselves, we decline to find a severance in circumstances which do not clearly and unambiguously establish that either of the joint tenants desired to terminate the estate.

If plaintiff and Johnson did not choose to continue the joint tenancy, they might have converted it into a tenancy in common by written mutual agreement. They might also have jointly conveyed the property to a third person and divided the proceeds. Even if they could not agree to act in concert, either plaintiff or Johnson might have severed the joint tenancy, with or without the consent of the other, by an act which was clearly indicative of an intent to terminate, such as a conveyance of her or his entire interest. Because a joint tenancy may be created only by express intent, and because there are alternative and unambiguous means of altering the nature of that estate, we hold that the lease here in issue did not operate to sever the joint tenancy.

By the very nature of joint tenancy, the interest of the nonsurviving joint tenant is extinguished upon his death. And as the lease is valid only in so far as the interest of the lessor in the joint property is concerned, it follows that the lease of the joint tenancy property also expires when the lessor dies.

The estate of joint tenancy is firmly embedded in centuries of real property law and in the California statute books. Its crucial element is the right of survivorship, a right that would be more illusory than real if a joint tenant were permitted to lease for a term continuing after his death. Accordingly, we hold that under these facts, the lease herein is no longer valid.

Reversed.

4   TENANCY IN COMMON

The chief characteristic of a tenancy in common is the unity of possession by two or more owners. All co-owners of a tenancy in common have the right to possession of the entire parcel because the fractional shares of the co-owners are undivided and are not assigned to any particular portion of the property.

For example, A, B, and C own a fifty acre unimproved parcel as tenants in common, each of them owning a one-third interest in the entire parcel. Each co-tenant, regardless of the extent of his interest in the property has the right to possess the whole of the property subject to the rights of the other co-tenants. However, when the land is subdivided into three properties and the co-owners are assigned separate and distinct portions of the property then the unity of possession is destroyed and the tenancy in common no longer exists.

In the case of *Lockler v. Martin*, 96 S.E.2d 24 (N.C. 1957), the court had occasion to determine the existence of a tenancy in common under the following facts:

Charles Baker died leaving a will that left a 120 acre parcel to his children as follows:

> To Minnie Lockler [plaintiff in this action], a fee simple, 100 acres of land, being the northern portion of the land adjoining the lands of R. C. Mitchell. To Ebby Martin, 20 acres of land, being the balance of my parcel adjoining the lands of R. C. Mitchell.

A dispute arose as to the location of the boundary line between the parcels. During the course of the dispute, plaintiff contended that the parties owned the entire parcel as tenants in common. The court addressed the issue in the following terms:

> It is certainly open to question whether the parties were ever tenants in common. Tenancy in common is characterized by a single essential unity—that of possession, or the right to possession of the common property. Tenancy in common does not arise when several persons own distinct portions of the same tract of land. The general rule seems to be that when the will locates the lands devised . . . with such certainty that a surveyor can take the will and locate them without other aid, then the devises would hold individually and not as tenants in common.

As indicated in the preceding example, tenancies in common do not include the right of survivorship. When a co-tenant dies, the surviving co-tenants do not succeed to the interest that is administered as a part of the estate. The tenancy in common is recognized in all American jurisdictions.

Because of the often unanticipated consequences that can flow from the joint tenancy, tenancies in common are preferred by the law and are presumed in the absence of language to the contrary. As a result, a transfer ''to A and B'' is presumed to create a tenancy in common. Tenancies in common will also result when a joint tenant severs his or her interest or when property is inherited under the laws of intestate succession.

Tenants in common may own unequal shares. Thus, A may own one half, B one third, and C and D each one sixth of the property. However, if the instrument creating the tenancy in common does not specify unequal shares, it is presumed that each co-owner has an equal interest in the property. Thus, a grant ''to A, B, C, and D'' is presumed to transfer a one-quarter interest to each co-tenant.

5 TENANCY BY THE ENTIRETY

The tenancy by the entirety is the third relatively ancient form of concurrent ownership that still exists. It resembles the joint tenancy with its emphasis upon the unities of time, title, interest, and possession and has the additional unity that is created by a valid marriage. Unlike the joint tenancy, the tenancy by entirety ends upon the termination of the marriage; it is not subject to severance by the act of one co-tenant.

This tenancy was originally based upon the fictional unity of spouses that, under the common law, gave to the husband the sole and exclusive right to manage the property. The tenancy by the entirety was abolished in England in 1925. The various married women's property acts enacted in the American states that recognized distinct property rights in the husband and wife have caused many jurisdictions to abolish or restrict the tenancy by the entirety. Nevertheless, it prevails in approximately half of the American states including Florida, Massachusetts, New Jersey, New York, and Pennsylvania.

Knight v. Knight, 458 S.W.2d. 803 (Tenn. 1970)

Facts of the case.

Lloyd and Grace Knight were married in 1932 and divorced in 1950. The divorce decree was based upon misrepresentations by Lloyd and, under Tennessee law, was therefore invalid. Lloyd married Ina Knight in 1955. Lloyd and Ina acquired several parcels of real estate taking title as "tenants by the entirety." Lloyd Knight died in 1968 without a will. Bobby Joe Knight, the son of Grace and Lloyd Knight, sought to set aside the divorce decree, have the marriage between Lloyd and Ina declared invalid, and have himself declared the owner of Lloyd's interest in the real estate as his sole heir.

The trial court set aside the divorce decree between Grace and Lloyd Knight and ruled that the subsequent marriage of Lloyd Knight to Ina Knight was invalid. The trial court further held that Lloyd and Ina owned the real estate as tenants in common and that Bobby Joe Knight, as Lloyd's heir, inherited Lloyd's one-half interest in the real estate owned by Lloyd and Ina at the time of Ina's death. Ina appealed.

[The appeals court affirmed the ruling that the divorce decree was invalid and therefore the subsequent marriage of Lloyd Knight and Ina Knight was also invalid. The court then addressed the nature of the interests in the real estate that had been acquired by Lloyd and Ina.]

OPINION

Since Lloyd's subsequent marriage to Ina is invalid the deeds conveying real estate to "Lloyd C. Knight and wife Ina T. Knight, as tenants by the entireties" were not effective to create such an estate.

At common law a simple conveyance to husband and wife made under the essential unities, would create an estate by the entirety, and this result followed where the estate was to husband and wife expressly by the entireties. But since an existing marriage is essential to such an estate, it is clear that no estate by the entirety is created where the grantees are not legally married.

The estate that is created is dependent upon the intention of the grantor, as evidenced by the language of the deed read in the light of the relevant surrounding circumstances.

The intent of Lloyd C. Knight and Ina T. Knight in accepting deeds to the properties that are the subject to this suit is clear if we accept the words of the conveyances as representing the intention of the parties. This must necessarily be done where, as here, no contrary evidence of intention exists. The words used, "tenants by the entirety," mean in law that the parties wanted the property to be inalienable during their joint lives, and on the death of one they wished the survivor to take all. Because they were not legally married and because inalienability is an incident only of estates by the entireties, the law denies them the first of these wishes. It does not follow, however, that the law must deny them the second as well.

Giving effect to the recognized rule of construction that conveyances "should operate, as nearly as possible to produce the effect intended by the parties," in the instant case we hold that the conveyances to Lloyd C. Knight and wife Ina T. Knight, as tenants by the entirety, created "a tenancy in common with a right of survivorship"; and, that Ina T. Knight, having survived Lloyd C. Knight, is the sole owner of the properties.

The decree of the Chancellor so far as it pertains to title to the real property involved in this suit is reversed, and a decree will be entered in this Court showing title to the properties to be in Ina T. Knight.

Reversed in part and affirmed in part.

NOTES AND QUESTIONS

1 Why did the court not conclude that Lloyd and Ina held as joint tenants? Such a holding would have avoided the need to create the anomalous interest of a tenancy in common with a right of survivorship.

2 In the case of *Margarite v. Ewald,* 381 A.2d. 480 (1977), the Supreme Court of Pennsylvania was faced with the following deed: "to John Ewald and Mary Ewald, husband and wife as tenants in common with right of survivorship." The trial court held that a tenancy in common was created. The Court noted that the right of survivorship is not associated with a tenancy in common and that the deed "creates a legal impossibility." The court treated the interest as a tenancy by the entireties. Is this consistent with the holding in the Knight case?

6   RIGHTS AND DUTIES OF CO-OWNERS

A   The Power of a Co-tenant to Convey.

The power of a co-tenant to convey his or her interests in the property depends upon the type of co-tenancy in which the property is held. An individual tenant by the entirety is customarily precluded from transferring his or her property without the consent of the co-tenant spouse. An individual joint tenant, however, is free to transfer his or her interest in the property to a third party and, to that extent, work a severance and destroy the joint tenancy. However, because of the right of survivorship, joint tenancy cannot be conveyed by a will. Property held as tenants in common may be freely transferred by individual co-tenants and will pass through the will or the heirs of a co-tenant who dies without a will.

B   The Duty to Account for Rents, Profits, and Use

The economic relations between and among co-tenants are basically the same regardless of the kind of tenancy by which title is held. We have seen that each co-tenant is entitled to possession of the entire property and owns an undivided interest in the entire property. As a practical matter, of course, property is not owned so that it can lie fallow. Rather it is put to some beneficial use either by improving it, renting it, farming it, extracting minerals from it, or the like. In addition, in most cases, there are taxes, insurance, mortgage payments, and expenses incurred maintaining the condition of the property. Problems often arise in which a co-tenant claims that she or he is entitled to rents or other income generated by the property or that she or he is entitled to a credit for payments either for ongoing expenses, such as insurance and taxes, or for special expenses, such as repairs or improvements.

The best means of resolving such potential disputes is by having an agreement between and among the various co-tenants. Ordinarily such agreements will be enforceable pursuant to their terms. In the absence of such an agreement, various rules have evolved to regulate the relations between and among co-tenants. The basic idea is that each co-tenant is entitled to share the benefits and is liable for the obligations incurred in connection with the property based on their respective interests. The following specific rules tend to advance this basic principle.

1 A co-tenant is accountable for rents received from a person who has leased the property to all other co-tenants. In other words, a co-tenant who receives rental income ordinarily must share that income with the other co-tenants.

2 A co-tenant is accountable for profits derived from the use of the land when that use has depleted the value of the land. An example of such depletion might be harvesting timber, extracting minerals, and the like.

3 Ordinarily a co-tenant is not required to account for use and occupation of the property or for other benefits derived from the use of the land so long as such use does not reduce the value of the property. In other words, if *A, B,* and *C* own a single-family home and *A* lives in the home, *A* is ordinarily not accountable for the rental value of the property. However, the rule stated in this paragraph does not apply if the co-tenant *ousts* or excludes the co-tenants by preventing them from sharing in the benefits of the property. In our example, if *B* or *C* confront *A,* demand that he or she pay rent or vacate the property so that it can be rented to a third party and if *A* refuses to comply, an ouster will have occurred and *A* will be held accountable for the rental value of the premises from the time that the ouster has occurred.

4 A co-tenant who has paid taxes, insurance, or interest on a mortgage may compel the others to contribute their share where he or she is not in sole possession and enjoyment of the property.

5 If the tenant who has paid taxes, interest, or insurance has been in sole possession of the property and the value of the use and enjoyment which he or she has had equals or exceeds such payments, no action for contribution will lie against the other co-tenants.

6 Where a co-tenant makes necessary repairs to maintain the property, she or he is generally entitled to receive contribution from the co-tenants.

7 In the absence of an agreement to the contrary, improvements (as distinguished from repairs) made to the property ordinarily cannot be made the subject of contribution by co-tenants unless or until the property is sold. The reason for this rule is that co-tenants should not be involuntarily made to be debtors but, upon sale of the property, they should not reap a windfall benefit at the expense of the co-tenant who made the improvements.

8 A co-tenant in possession cannot recover against the others for personal services in caring for the property unless there is an agreement to that effect.

7   PARTITION OF CO-OWNED INTERESTS

Partition involves the division of land held in co-tenancy into the co-tenant's respective fractional shares. Tenants in common and joint tenants, but not tenants by the entirety, have an inherent right to seek partition of the property.

Partition may be either voluntary, by mutual agreement of the co-tenants or involuntary through the assistance of the court. In either case, the ultimate result is the same.

To take a simple case, assume *A* and *B* own a ten-acre parcel that can be divided into two five-acre parcels of roughly equal value. Partition by division of the land can be made either voluntarily or by the court. Each co-tenant then becomes the sole owner of a particular parcel. More commonly, the property cannot be divided because, for instance, subdivision regulations may preclude its division or, as in the obvious case of a single-family home, division is not economically feasible. In this case, partition is made by selling the property at the highest price obtainable and distributing the proceeds to the owners pursuant to their respective shares. Typically, partition actions also include an action for accounting that would adjust the contributions of the co-tenants pursuant to the principles outlined in the preceding section.

All of the states have enacted statutes permitting partition either through voluntary action of the co-tenants or under judicial supervision. Costs and expenses of partition are ordinarily allocated among the co-tenants according to their respective shares.

Partition has long been an element of co-ownership and the first statute establishing the right was enacted in 1539, during the reign of Henry VIII. All American states have partition statutes; the vast majority of which consider the action an "equitable" one, giving the court considerable latitude in adjusting the respective rights of the co-tenants.

8 MARITAL INTERESTS: THE COMMUNITY PROPERTY SYSTEM

The community property system provides that property acquired by the labor of legally married persons is owned equally by each spouse who has equal management rights as to the property regardless of which spouse produced the income to acquire the property. Community property has gained wide acceptance in continental western Europe, most of Central and South America, and in certain Canadian provinces. It is, however, foreign to the ownership concepts that were evolved by the English Common Law.

The community property system exists in the states of Arizona, California, Idaho, Louisiana, Nevada, New Mexico, Texas, and Washington. Other states have experimented with forms of community property for the particular purpose of protecting particularly a nonearning spouse in the event of divorce or death of the earning spouse. However, the central premise of community property—namely, that all community property acquired during the marriage belongs equally to each spouse—is only recognized in the states just mentioned.

Under the community property system, a married couple can have two kinds of property, community property and separate property. Community property, as indicated, is that which is acquired by the efforts of either or both spouses during the course of the marriage. Separate property, on the other hand, is property that either husband or wife owned prior to the marriage or property which is acquired after the marriage by either spouse by gift or inheritance. Separate property tends to retain its character as separate property. For instance, if a spouse inherits an apartment building during marriage and does not use community property to maintain the building, the appreciated value of the building and any income that it generates remains the separate property of that spouse. Taken a step further, if the income from separate property is used to acquire additional property, it too is considered the separate property of that spouse.

However, if the husband and wife acquire the apartment building with community funds, the building is owned equally by each, regardless of the manner in which title is taken. Each spouse is considered owning one half, and either spouse may convey their one half or transfer it at their death in whatever manner they choose.

Under the community property system, each spouse is entitled to joint and equal management and control of community property during the course of the marriage. This contrasts to the common law approach that is followed in the noncommunity property states. For instance, if A and B are married in a common law state and A works for a salary while B manages the home, A is considered the sole owner of the property and retains the right to manage or transfer the property. Many states have adopted legislation commonly known as equitable distribution statutes that reserve for the nonearning spouse a certain percentage of the earning spouse's property in the event of divorce or death of the earning spouse. To this extent, such statutes resemble the community property system. However community property is fundamentally different. Under equitable distribution statutes, the nonearning spouse has certain rights to share in property otherwise considered to be owned by the earning spouse. Under the community property approach, the nonearning spouse is actually considered to own one half of the martial property with equivalent rights to manage and transfer the property. The community property system in other words, constitutes a significant departure from the common law and from the majority approach in this country.

9   SUMMARY

Concurrent ownership or co-ownership refers to those situations in which two or more persons simultaneously own equivalent interests in real estate. Almost any interest in property can be co-owned.

The most recurring form of co-ownership is the tenancy in common. It implies only a unity of possession and any co-owner may convey their interest during their life or pursuant to a will. Tenancy in common is the preferred form of co-ownership and is presumed in the absence of specific language to the contrary in the transferring instrument.

The joint tenancy differs from the tenancy in common because it includes the right of survivorship and generally requires the existence of the unities of time, title, interest, and possession as a condition to its existence. Statutes in many jurisdictions have altered the common law characteristics of the joint tenancy either by eliminating the requirements of time and title or by eliminating the survivorship feature. The slight majority rule continues to recognize the joint tenancy in its common law form. Joint tenants may sever the joint tenancy by transferring their interest to third parties and the grantees of the interest become tenants in common with the other owners. However, because of the survivorship feature, joint tenants cannot transfer their interest at their death.

The tenancy by entirety operates like a joint tenancy but requires the additional unity of a valid marriage. Tenancy by the entirety includes the right of survivorship but cannot be severed by the unilateral act of either owner. Because marriage is a prerequisite, the tenancy by the entireties is terminated by divorce, and the tenancy is converted into a tenancy in common.

The community property system is a doctrine creating a form of co-ownership between married persons of property acquired as a product of the labors of the marriage. Each spouse is considered to have equal rights to manage and share the benefits of the property, and either may freely dispose of their community property at death.

The rights and responsibilities of co-owners are roughly the same regardless of the form of co-ownership that is used. Each co-owner is entitled to share in the benefits and burdens of property ownership in proportion to their ownership interest in the property. In the event that one co-owner either spends more or receives less in connection with the property, that party is usually entitled to contribution from the other co-tenants. The right of contribution is usually enforced through an action seeking partition of the property and for an accounting.

10 QUESTIONS

1 Alvin and Baker own an office building as joint tenants. A serious disagreement arises between them and they are no longer on speaking terms. A management company collects rent from the building and pays Alvin and Baker. Alvin dies, leaving a will providing that the property should go to Cathy, Alvin's wife. Who gets the property?

2 David dies, leaving a will providing that a parking garage shall be given to Ellen, Francis, and George. What kind of co-ownership has been created by David's will?

3 Suppose that David's will provides that his property should go "two thirds to Ellen, one sixth to Francisco and George, all as joint tenants." What kind of co-ownership has been created?

4 Smith gave a deed to her husband and son "as joint tenants and provided further that neither would transfer the property without the written consent of the other." The father gave a deed of his interest to his girlfriend and died. Who owns the property, the son or the girlfriend?

5 A will left property as follows: "to Ames and Cheryl as joint tenants and not as tenants in common *and to the survivor of them.* Ames sought to have the property partitioned and distributed one half to each. Cheryl objected. Who wins?

6 Margaret Holt and her husband Horton owned their home as tenants in common. Horton died, leaving his interest in the property to their son Henry. Six months after Horton's death, Henry advised Margaret that she should begin to pay rent on the property. She refused. Henry sues for partition and an accounting. What is the result?

7 Maxwell owned a house in which he lived. He later married Georgia and executed a deed to himself and her as tenants by the entireties. Georgia prepared a will leaving her property to her friend Norman. Georgia dies. Maxwell contests Norman's claim that he owns one half of the property. Who wins?

8 Ward and June were married in 1950. In 1955 Ward inherited an office building. He collected the rents and used the money to buy shares of stock. Ward never held a job, and the family was supported by June's salary as a waitress. In 1990, Ward and June have a falling out. Their only asset is their home worth $100,000. The office building is worth $2,000,000, and the shares of stock are worth $500,000. How will the assets of the couple be divided in a community property state?

CHAPTER 6

THE CONDOMINIUM
AND RELATED FORMS
OF OWNERSHIP

TOPICS CONSIDERED IN THIS CHAPTER:

1   INTRODUCTION

One of the most significant trends in real estate ownership has been the dramatic increase in the use of common interest ownership. Most important of these are the condominium and cooperative. These developments have been attributed to a variety of factors including the increased cost of land, the inability of many and even most American families to afford a traditional single-family dwelling, the desire on the part of certain segments of the population to minimize the time and expense involved in maintaining a single-family dwelling, and the economies of scale that can be achieved in a multi-unit development. The U.S. Department of Housing and Urban Development has estimated that one half of the population of the United States will live in condominiums and related ownership forms by the year 2000.

Although we tend to think of condominiums or cooperatives as residential dwellings in a multi-story building, these forms can also accommodate the development of single-family homes in a subdivision as well as commercial uses. In some areas, developers have begun to create office condominiums in which floors or portions of a floor of an office building are owned in the form of a condominium. Given the advantages of ownership, it is anticipated that the commercial use of the condominium form will continue to increase. In fact, the condominium has already given rise to a relatively novel form of ownership known as the time-share.

2 BASIC DEFINITIONS

A condominium consists of individual or separate ownership of a portion of a multi-unit development coupled with a tenancy in common interest in the common areas of the development. In the simple case of a high-rise residential building, the individual condominium owner owns a fee simple to a unit separately and also owns the common areas of the building in tenancy in common along with all other unit owners. The common areas typically include the building's lobby, elevators, roof, swimming pools, and so on.

A cooperative, while it is the economic equivalent of a condominium, is created in a significantly different manner. A cooperative involves the creation of a business entity, typically a corporation, that owns the fee simple in the entire complex. The corporation then issues shares of stock representing ownership in the corporation and a proprietary lease that entitles the owner to exclusive possession of the individual unit.

A time-share is typically a condominium involving an additional division of ownership of the condominium unit into a number of fixed time periods during which each owner has the exclusive right to use and occupy that unit.

This chapter will emphasize the condominium form of ownership, although the management and maintenance of the complex as a whole are similar in both the condominium and the cooperative.

3 BRIEF HISTORY OF THE CONDOMINIUM

The idea that a building could be subdivided and certain portions of the building separately owned was slow to take hold in England, although the practice was common in various parts of continental Europe as early as the twelfth century. The French code of 1804 expressly regulated separate ownership of portions of a building, but it did so with such brevity that it became customary to delineate the rights of co-owners through private agreements. (See generally Layser, "The Ownership of Flats—A Comparative Study," 7 Int'l and Comp. L.Q. 31, 1958.)

In 1938 France became the first country to enact a modern condominium law. Italy, Spain, and the Netherlands followed. Condominiums have been used extensively in

Latin America, and modern legislative schemes were enacted in Brazil, Cuba, Mexico, and Venezuela in the 1940's and 1950's. The condominium form has achieved wide acceptance in continental Europe and in Latin America as well as the United States.

4   FORMATION OF THE CONDOMINIUM: THE ESSENTIAL DOCUMENTS

Condominium legislation throughout the world is essentially similar and seeks to address problems related to the management of the complex. All American jurisdictions have enacted condominium statutes that attempt to specify the documentation required in order to establish the condominium. The primary objectives of these statutes are to create an association or some other mechanism so that the project can be successfully managed for the benefit of unit owners and to provide for the easy transfer of individual units.

For the most part, three basic documents are required to establish a condominium. These are (1) the Declaration of the condominium, which includes the condominium map; (2) the management documents, which might include Articles of Incorporation, Bylaws, or similar documents; and (3) deeds to the individual units.

A   The Declaration or Master Deed

The declaration for a condominium, also known as the master deed, involves recording a document that describes the entire parcel and gives a legal description of each of the units in the complex and of the common areas.

The master deed is usually prepared by an architect and/or engineer and shows the floor plan of each unit and of the entire project. Common areas are designated and often the location of the project's major systems (electrical, heating, plumbing) are also shown. This document is particularly important because it forms the basis upon which subsequent deeds to individual units will be prepared, and it will often constitute the basis for determining each unit owner's pro rata share of the common area. The unit owner's share often establishes the extent of the homeowner's voting rights and his or her share of common area expenses.

In addition to information locating the units, the declaration must set forth any restrictions that are placed upon the use, occupancy, or transfer of the units. Condominium use restrictions come in a wide variety. The following cases illustrate examples of restrictions commonly found in condominium declarations and indicate a common judicial attitude toward their enforcement.

> Daily in this state thousands of citizens are investing millions of dollars in condominium property and the Articles or Declaration of Condominiums provided for thereunder ought to be construed strictly to assure these investors that what the buyer sees the buyer gets. Every man may justly consider his home his castle and himself as the king thereof; nonetheless his sovereign fiat to use his property as he pleases must yield, at least in degree, where ownership is in common or cooperation with others. The benefits of condominium living and ownership demand no less.
>
> (*Sterling Village v. Breitenbach,* 251 S.2d 685 (Fla. 1971)

In *Hidden Harbour Estates, Inc. v. Horman,* 309 S.2d 180 (Fla. 1975), the Florida court upheld condominium documents and said the following, in part:

> It appears to us that inherent in the condominium concept is the principle that to promote the health, happiness, and peace of mind of the majority of the unit owners since they are living in such close proximity and using facilities in common, each unit owner must give up a certain degree of freedom of choice which he might otherwise enjoy in separate, privately owned property. Condominium unit owners comprise a little democratic subsociety of necessity more restrictive as it pertains to use of condominium property than may be existent outside the condominium organization. The Declaration of Condominium involved herein is replete with examples of the curtailment of individual rights usually associated with the private ownership of property. It provides, for example, that no sale may be effectuated without approval; no minors may be permanent residents; no pets are allowed. It is not necessary that conduct be so offensive as to constitute a nuisance in order to justify regulation thereof by private agreement.

Constellation Condominium Association v. Harrington, 467 S.2d 378 (Fla. 1985)

Facts of the case.

This case involves the enforceability of a condominium age restriction. Appellant, Constellation Condominium Association, Inc. (the Association), appeals from a final judgment denying its request for injunctive relief, court costs, and attorney's fees. The Association sought to enjoin the appellees, Daniel J. Harrington and his wife Sandra (the Harringtons), from residing with their infant child as permanent residents in their condominium unit.

The Harringtons completed the purchase of their unit on January 15, 1981, and have resided there since. When the Harringtons purchased their unit, Rule 26 of the Condominium Declaration provided:

> Children twelve years of age and older are allowed as permanent residents. However, they should not cause disturbances and their conduct while on any condominium property is the direct responsibility of their parents or guardians at all times. Children under the age of twelve years are allowed as temporary residents during vacations, holidays, weekends, etc.

The day after the closing, Mrs. Harrington's doctor told her that she was pregnant. Since the child's birth on August 30 of that year, the child has permanently resided with his parents in their unit.

In November 1982, the Association filed suit. The trial court ruled in favor of the Harringtons concluding that Rule 26 did not specifically prohibit children under twelve years of age from residing as permanent residents at the condominium and, therefore, the Harringtons had the right to reside in their unit with their child.

This appeal followed.

OPINION

We agree with the Association that the trial judge failed to properly construe Rule 26, the age restriction. Rule 26 was recorded as part of the Condominium Documents. The rule, therefore, is clothed with a very strong presumption of validity because each purchaser has adequate notice of the restrictions to be imposed and thereafter purchases a unit knowing of and accepting the restrictions. Accordingly, courts will not invalidate a restriction found in the recorded condominium documents absent a showing that it is clearly ambiguous, wholly arbitrary or unreasonable in its application, violates public policy, or abrogates some fundamental constitutional right.

The age restriction is a mutual agreement entered into by all condominium apartment owners of the complex. With this type of land use restriction, an individual can choose at the time of purchase whether to sign an agreement with these restrictions or limitations. Reasonable restrictions concerning use, occupancy, and transfer of condominium units are necessary for operation and protection of the owners in the condominium concept.

A condominium restriction or limitation does not inherently violate a fundamental right and may be enforced if it serves a legitimate purpose and is reasonably applied. Age restrictions are a "reasonable means to accomplish the lawful purpose of providing appropriate facilities for the differing housing needs and desires of the varying age groups."

Because the age restriction is unambiguous, valid, and enforceable, the Harringtons were required to then demonstrate that the restriction was being enforced selectively or arbitrarily. They have failed to do so. There was no testimony or evidence in the record before us that the restriction had been enforced selectively or arbitrarily by the Association after it took control from the developer. In fact, the Association, as evidenced by its successful eviction proceedings against violators, has consistently enforced and precluded any further violations of the age restriction relating to permanent residency. The enforcement of the rule does not constitute selective and arbitrary conduct.

Reversed.

NOTES AND QUESTIONS

In a multi-unit condominium project, the boundaries of an individual unit are the interior unfinished surfaces of walls, floors, and ceilings located within the unit. The owner owns the interior of the unit and is responsible for its care and maintenance.

The common area is the entire project *except* for the individual units. The boundary walls of a unit and all bearing walls, utility lines, halls, stairways, elevators, driveways, and recreation areas are common areas. Common areas are usually owned by all unit-owners as tenants in common. For example, in a twenty unit complex, each owner might own five percent of the common area, as a tenant in common with other owners.

In addition to ownership of the individual unit, the owner often has exclusive rights to parking and storage spaces. Such exclusive rights can be created either by a fee interest in the space or by an exclusive easement appurtenant to the individual unit.

B   Management Documents

The second major type of document used in creating a condominium is that body of documents that pertain to the management of the project, usually known as the bylaws. The bylaws create the ''house rules'' governing the condominium project. Most condominium projects have bylaws that create an executive board or board of directors, elected by the members of the association and given authority to manage the condominium for the benefit of the owners. The extent of the board's authority and the manner in which it will be elected by the association should be set forth in the bylaws. In addition, bylaws must set forth the authority of members of the association, usually acting through the board of directors, to amend bylaws, hire and fire managing agents and other employees, enter into contracts on behalf of the association, impose and receive payments known as assessments or dues from the members of the association to pay for costs incurred in managing the project, and to otherwise exercise those powers necessary for the operation of the association. You may wish to review the case of *Mutual Housing Coop. v. Sandow,* in chapter 5, that examines the authority of a cooperative's management board to establish regulations intended to limit noise at the project.

The bylaws of a condominium have been referred to as a form of private law whereby individual owners agree to subordinate certain of the rights traditionally associated with the ownership of property. One case upheld the Board of Directors decision to install doors between common area passageways as a legitimate means of deterring vandalism and theft. The court noted,

> [T]he Board of Managers of Burtonwood is the designated decision-making body of the condominium association and exercises broad discretion in the maintenance and operation of the development. Nevertheless, the Board is not at liberty to promulgate arbitrary and capricious rules which bear no relationship to the health, happiness, and enjoyment of life of the unit owners. Thus, in reviewing the action of the Board in this case, we believe the standard to be applied is whether the action of the board is reasonable.
>
> (*Ryan v. Baptiste,* 565 S.W.2d 198 (Mo. 1978)

A set of house rules and regulations is fundamental to the successful operation of any multi-unit project, particularly in light of the shared ownership feature of common areas. In addition, most projects impose use restrictions in an effort to preserve the character of the project in a manner consistent with the desires of a majority of the unit owners. Finally, all projects must have a mechanism whereby fees can be collected from unit owners and the project's structures can be maintained and repaired in an orderly way.

Dues, Assessments, and Enforcement Devices   All common ownership projects require the authority to levy assessments for the maintenance of common areas. This, in turn, creates a need for enforcement devices to give unit owners an incentive to pay the accessments when they become due and to give the managers of the project a simple and relatively inexpensive means of enforcing delinquent obligations. In the case of the cooperative, the unit owners periodic payments are considered rent. Failure to make the payments is considered a breach of the rental obligation that will entitle the corporate owner to initiate proceedings to evict and recover damages for unpaid rent.

In the case of a condominium, periodic payments by the unit owner are considered dues or assessments and are typically enforced by creating a right in the association, acting through its board of directors, to impose a lien against the owner's unit. This lien usually can be enforced through proceedings similar to foreclosure proceedings under a mortgage. In the case of both cooperatives and condominiums, the project documents should provide for an award of reasonable attorney's fees in the event it becomes necessary to initiate proceedings to enforce the collection of the unit owners periodic payments.

Homeowner's dues fall into two broad categories. The first involves payments for ongoing obligations of the complex. These would include items such as garbage removal, payments for ongoing services such as landscaping, pool service, and security guards, and insurance payments. The second category of assessment is for capital expenditures such as exterior painting, roof repair, and upgrading utility systems. The governing board of the complex might decide that a new roof should be installed. Bids to do the work would be obtained and a *special assessment* then levied against the individual homeowners. In an effort to avoid the shock of a special assessment, many homeowners associations establish a *contingency reserve* out of regular assessments in anticipation of the need for capital improvements. Anyone purchasing a condominium unit should carefully examine the Association's financial statements to determine whether there are reserves sufficient to pay for anticipated capital improvements. Many state statutes require that prospective purchasers be furnished with information concerning the Association's financial condition.

The following case illustrates a typical condominium plan concerning assessments.

Association of Unit Owners v. Gruenfeld, 560 P.2d 641 (Ore. 1976)

Facts of the case.

Plaintiff, an association of unit owners under the Oregon Unit Ownership Law, brought this action to recover charges assessed by it against defendant while she was the owner of a condominium at The Inn at the Seventh Mountain and a member of the plaintiff association. The trial court, sitting without a jury, found defendant liable for the full amount of the assessments and entered judgment in favor of plaintiff. Defendant appeals.

Defendant took title to her condominium by deed dated January 3, 1973. As a unit owner, defendant automatically became a member of the plaintiff Association and was subject to its declarations and bylaws.

In accordance with the Association's bylaws, plaintiff's unit owners are liable for assessments charged in accordance with Article VI of plaintiff's amended bylaws. Article VI provides:

> 1 Expenses and Assessment. Each unit owner shall contribute pro rata toward the common condominium expenses of The Inn, including (but without being limited to), the cost of operation, maintenance, repair and replacement of all common elements and the cost of insurance, in the proportion to his interest in the general common areas. The Board of Directors shall fix a monthly assessment for each unit in an amount sufficient to provide for all current expenses, and such other expenses as the Board of Directors may deem necessary. Such monthly assessments shall be due and payable quarterly in advance on the first (1st) day of every calendar quarter without demand, and delinquent accounts shall bear interest at the rate of ten percent (10%) per annum from the due date until paid. The amounts received shall be held by the Treasurer in trust until expended for the purposes for which they were assessed.

OPINION

In its simplest analysis, the association of owners acts as agent for the individual apartment owners in making necessary contracts pertaining to the management and upkeep of the common areas and facilities. The extent of this authority will ordinarily be found in the declaration and in the bylaws.

It is clear that it was the intention of the parties that the Board of Directors of plaintiff be given discretion to determine what expenses were necessary to achieve a uniform plan for the development and operation of the condominium project and to assess the unit owners pro rata for such common expenses. Defendant, in purchasing her condominium unit, agreed to pay a monthly assessment in an amount sufficient to provide for all current expenses, a reasonable reserve for future expenses, and such other expenses as the plaintiff's Board of Directors might deem necessary.

All of the items and services assessed can be reasonably identified as necessary to accomplish the plaintiff's purpose of "creating a uniform plan for the development and operation of the condominium project." The assessment of contingency reserves is specifically provided for in Article VI of plaintiff's bylaws. Such reserves assure available capital to meet emergency expenses such as storm damage or unanticipated problems.

We conclude that the charges, which the court included in the judgment, as assessed by the Board of Directors, were within the discretionary powers granted to plaintiff's Board of Directors by the bylaws, recorded declaration, and statutory law. The evidence supports the court's findings.

Affirmed.

NOTES AND QUESTIONS

What is the difference between the type of authority given to the Association's Board of Directors in this case and the Board's authority to expel owners who violate the age restrictions of a condominium? What are the standards for determining whether the Board's action will be upheld?

C   Deeds to Individual Units

The third type of document necessary to create a condominium is the deed to the individual unit. It is the individual unit deed that enables the owner to sell or encumber the individual unit as distinct from the entire condominium project.

The individual unit deed typically contains a description of the apartment or unit number so that it may be identified as distinct from other units in the complex. The percentage of the unit owner's undivided interest in the common area should also be identified. In addition, the deed should refer to and specifically incorporate all of the terms and conditions of the declaration or any other recorded instrument that may affect or limit an owner's use to the property. As indicated, a typical declaration may contain many pages of restrictions; and it would be an unnecessary burden upon the recorder's office and an unnecessary expense upon the party seeking recordation if the voluminous declaration were rerecorded every time a unit was sold or made subject to a mortgage. As a result, it is common to refer, in the individual unit deed, to the declaration by mentioning the recording information of the declaration so that an interested party may obtain it and review it before deciding to acquire an interest in the unit.

5   LIABILITY OF THE ASSOCIATION AND INDIVIDUAL UNIT OWNERS

We have seen that the unit owner is liable to the Association for the payment of dues and assessments for maintenance and upkeep of the project. The unit owner is also responsible for maintaining the individual unit in a safe condition and will be liable to anyone injured because of the negligence of the unit owner.

In addition, each individual unit owner is jointly responsible for maintaining the common areas in a safe condition. Therefore, if someone is injured in the common area because of a dangerous condition both the Association and each unit owner is jointly liable to the person injured. The owners' liability is based upon their status as owners and the Association's liability is based upon its assumption of management responsibility for the common area. However the unit owners can usually insulate themselves from liability if title to the common area is held by the Association itself. Many state statutes require that condominium associations procure liability insurance for the benefit of the Association and its individual members. The following case, while reviewing many of the elements of a condominium, contains a typical examination of the liability of the Association and the individual homeowners for negligent maintenance of the common area.

Dutcher v. Owens, 647 S.W.2d 948 (Tex. 1983)

Facts of the case.

J. A. Dutcher owned a condominium apartment in the Eastridge Terrace Condominiums, located in Dallas County, which he leased to Ted and Christine Owens. Ownership of the apartment includes a 1.572 percent pro rata undivided ownership in the common elements of the project. The Owenses suffered substantial property loss in a fire, which began in an external light fixture in a common area.

The Owenses filed suit against Dutcher, the Eastridge Terrace Condominium Association, IHS–8 Ltd. (the developer), and a class of co-owners of condominiums in Eastridge Terrace represented by the officers of the homeowners' association. The case was tried before a jury, which found the following:

1 The fire was proximately caused by the lack of an insulating box behind the light fixture in the exterior wall air space;

2 The homeowners' association knew of this defect;

3 The homeowners' association alone was negligent in failing to install an insulating box with knowledge of the defect; and

4 The negligence of homeowners' association resulted in damage to the Owens' property in the amount of $69,150.00.

The trial court rendered judgment against Dutcher on the jury's verdict in the amount of $1,087.04. The award represents the amount of damages multiplied by Dutcher's 1.572 percent pro rata undivided ownership in the common elements of the Eastridge Terrace Condominium project.

By an agreed statement of facts filed with the court of appeals, the parties stipulated that the sole issue for determination on appeal was whether a condominium co-owner is jointly and severally liable or is liable only for a pro rata portion of the damages.

OPINION

In enacting the Texas Condominium Act (the Act), Tex. Rev. Civ. Stat. Ann. Art. 1301a, the Texas Legislature intended to create "a new method of property ownership." A condominium is an estate in real property consisting of an undivided interest in a portion of a parcel of real property, together with a separate fee simple interest in another portion of the same parcel. In essence, condominium ownership is the merger of two estates in land into one: the fee simple ownership of an apartment or unit in a condominium of an apartment or unit in a condominium project and a tenancy in common with other co-owners in the common elements.

"General common elements" consist of the land upon which the building stands, the "foundations, bearing walls and columns, roofs, halls, lobbies, stairways, and entrances and exits or communication ways; . . . and [a]ll other elements of the building necessary to the existence, upkeep, and safety of the condominium regime." An individual apartment cannot be conveyed separately from the undivided interest in the common elements and vice versa.

A condominium regime must be established according to the Act. The declaration must be filed with the county clerk, who must record the instrument in the Condominium Records. Once the declarant has complied with the provisions of the Act, each apartment in the project is treated as an interest in real property. Administration of the regime is established by the Act.

The condominium association or council is a legislatively created unincorporated association of co-owners, having as their common purpose a convenient method of ownership of real property that combines both the concepts of separateness of tenure and commonality of ownership. The California Supreme Court has concluded that "the concept of separateness in the condominium project carries over to any management body or association formed to handle the common affairs of the project, and that both the condominium project and the condominium association must be considered separate legal entities from its units owners and association members" (*White v. Cox,* 95 Cal. Rptr. at 262).

Given the uniqueness of the type of ownership involved in condominiums, the onus of liability for injuries arising from the management of condominium projects should reflect the degree of control exercised by the defendants. We agree with the California court's conclusion that to rule that a condominium co-owner had any effective control over the operation of the common areas would be to sacrifice "reality to theoretical formalism," for, in fact, a co-owner has no more control over operations than he would have as a stockholder in a corporation which owned and operated the project. This does not limit the plaintiff's right of action. The efficiency found in a suit directed at the homeowners' association and its board of directors representing the various individual homeowners, as well as any co-owner casually or directly responsible for the injuries sustained, benefits both sides of the docket, as well as the judicial system as a whole.

Such a result is not inconsistent with the legislative intent. While the Act creates a new form of real property ownership, it does not address the issue of the allocation of tort liability among co-owners. Nevertheless, we are guided in our decision by the other provisions in the Act that proportionately allocate various financial responsibilities. For example, the Act provides for pro rata contributions by co-owners toward expenses of administration and maintenance, insurance, taxes, and assessments.

We hold, therefore, that because of the limited control afforded a unit owner by the statutory condominium regime, the creation of the regime effects a reallocation of tort liability. The liability of a condominium co-owner is limited to his pro rata interest in the regime as a whole, where such liability arises from those areas held in tenancy-in-common. The judgment of the trial court is affirmed.

NOTES AND QUESTIONS

Do you agree with the court's analysis of this case? Does it mean that the Owenses can recover for only 1.572 percent of their damages? What relief, if any could the owner, Mr. Dutcher have recovered if he were living in the unit and sustained the damage? Would the result have been the same if the electrical box that started the fire were located within the unit rather than in the common area?

6 TIME-SHARE PROJECTS

A time-share project is a fairly novel estate in land that gives the owner the right of exclusive use on a periodic basis. For instance, suppose one owns a time-share in a project in Hawaii for two weeks per year. The owner owns the interest in the *unit* along with all owners of the time-share. In addition, the unit owners also own a portion of the common area along with the other unit owners in the complex.

The management documents for a time-share must contemplate the relationship among the various units in the project as well as the rights and obligations among the owners of time-share interests in a particular unit. As a result, the governing documents for a time-share tend to concentrate upon the standards for use of the interior of the unit as well as for the common areas.

7 SUMMARY

The idea of common interest ownership is an old one, but one that has only recently gained wide acceptance in this country. The condominium has become the most prevalent form of such ownership, but others, most notably the cooperative, are common in certain areas.

All states now have enacted statutes pertaining to the creation and management of condominiums. Central to these legislative arrangements is the identification of each individual unit and establishment of a unit owner's relative ownership of the common areas of the project.

Management of the project is vested in an Association of Owners who, in turn, elect a governing body to manage the project on a day-to-day basis. The Association and the governing board are vested with discretion, and so long as their actions are not arbitrary, they will not be set aside by a court.

8 QUESTIONS

1 Suppose four individuals pool their resources and purchase a four-unit apartment building. Each owner moves into one of the units and signs an agreement with the other owners that creates a committee to collect assessments, pay bills, and otherwise manage the project. Has a condominium been created?

2 A cooperative's managing board adopted a regulation that if any tenant at the cooperative failed to pay rent due to cooperative for a period of two months, they would forfeit their rights in the coop. Is this provision enforceable?

3 The Declaration of Restrictions of a condominium project consisting of sixty single-family homes along the Pacific Coast in Northern California provide that no fences would be built, no additions to the exterior of the buildings would be made, no trees or shrubbery would be

planted except those on a list of plants indigenous to the area, and only certain colors of paint could be used on the exterior of the individual buildings. An individual homeowner challenges these restrictions. Will he or she succeed?

4 Assume that the owners of a newly constructed condominium complex discover the existence of numerous construction defects at the property. Who has authority to sue the builder?

5 Suppose that you are retained as a legislative analyst to help draft time-share statutes in your state. In addition to the provisions of state law pertaining to condominiums, what matters do you think should be included to address problems particular to time-share projects?

PRIVATE RIGHTS IN THE LAND OF ANOTHER

CHAPTER 7

INHERENT RIGHTS AND LIMITATIONS IN THE USE OF LAND OF ANOTHER

TOPICS CONSIDERED IN THIS CHAPTER:

1 INTRODUCTION

There are three general ways in which one's right to use land can be limited. The most recent of these involves public land use controls, such as zoning and environmental regulation. These are considered in Section IX of this text. In addition, land use limitations can be imposed by private agreements between owners and, under appropriate circumstances, will run to bind successors in interest to the original contracting parties. Private use restrictions were considered in the context of condominiums and will be examined in detail in chapters 8 and 9.

Long before the appearance of the relatively recent forms of land use control just mentioned, the law recognized certain inherent limits imposed upon a land owner in connection with the use of property. These ''inherent'' limitations are considered in this chapter. The most pervasive of these limitations is the law of nuisance. To a lesser extent, a landowner is limited by the doctrines of lateral and subjacent support. These fairly ancient doctrines continue to have significance in the modern era, in spite of the evolution of more comprehensive efforts to control the use land.

2 THE DOCTRINE OF NUISANCE

Amphitheaters, Inc. v. Portland Meadows, 198 P.2d 858 (Ore. 1948)

Facts of the case.

Plaintiff Amphitheaters operates a drive-in movie theater adjacent to the land of defendant, Portland Meadows, who operates an automobile race track. Both facilities were built at about the same time at considerable expense to both parties. While plaintiff constructed fences along the property to protect against light interference, defendant installed flood lights on eighty-foot poles at intervals around its race track. The floodlights spilled onto plaintiff's property causing serious interference with the quality of pictures shown on plaintiff's screen. Plaintiff sued, claiming defendant was committing trespass and causing a nuisance and asked both for the court to enjoin defendant's use of the lights and for damages.

[On the question of trespass, the court stated: "While the dividing line between trespass and nuisance is not always a sharp one, we think it clear that the case at bar is governed by the law of nuisance and not by the law of trespass." The court then addressed the questions of nuisance.]

OPINION

Since there is no Oregon precedent to support plaintiff's contention, we must go back to fundamental principles. A private nuisance is defined as "anything done to the detriment of the lands of another, and not amounting to a trespass." Definitions in such general terms are of little practical assistance. It has been said that the term *nuisance* is incapable of an exact and exhaustive definition that will fit all cases, because the controlling facts are seldom alike, and each case stands on its own footing.

It is established law that an intentional interference with the use and enjoyment of land is not actionable unless that interference is both substantial and unreasonable. Again it is held that whether a particular annoyance or inconvenience is sufficient to constitute a nuisance depends on its effect upon an ordinarily reasonable person—that is, a normal person of ordinary habits and sensibilities.

In addition, no action can find a nuisance is the cause of damage which, even though substantial, is due solely to the fact that the plaintiff is abnormally sensitive to deleterious influences or uses the land for some purpose requiring exceptional freedom from any such influences.

In *Bradbury Marble Co. v. Laclede Gas Light Co.,* 106 S.W. 594, 599 (Mo.), the court said: ". . . Plaintiff had the legal right to stack its marble on its yard, and to leave it uncovered. Defendant had the legal right to operate its gas machines in a careful and skillful manner, and to discharge such substances therefrom as were not injurious to the neighboring property when used in the usual way. Therefore, if plaintiff is making an unusual use of its yard, in view of the fact that it is located in a district largely devoted to manufacturing purposes, or if the marble it stacks in its yard is of such a delicate nature as to become stained and injured from substances discharged from the smokestacks of factories by which it is surrounded, it ought not recover."

The only case brought to our attention in which light unaccompanied by any other element of an offensive character has been held to constitute a nuisance, is the case of *The Shelburne, Inc. v. Crossan Corporation,* 122 A. 750 (N.J.). The plaintiff was the owner of a large hotel on the boardwalk in Atlantic City, which had been operated in the same location for many years. Sixty of its bedrooms had a southerly or southwesterly exposure. The defendant was the owner of an apartment house located immediately to the southwest. On the roof of the apartment house defendants erected a sign sixty-six feet high and seventy-two feet long on which there were 1084 fifteen-watt lights, 6 one hundred-watt lights and 28 seventy-five watt lights. The sign was parallel to the wing of the hotel and about one hundred ten feet away. The evidence disclosed that the sign "lights upon . . . forty or forty-five rooms of the new wing of the hotel," disturbs the guests and lowers the value of the rooms. The court held that light "may become a nuisance if it (the light) materially interferes with the ordinary comfort of human existence." The trial judge held that the complainant was entitled to a decree restricting the operation of the electric lights during each night after the hour of twelve o'clock midnight. The plaintiff's hotel was located on the famous boardwalk at Atlantic City, where the primary activity appears to be the entertainment of luxury-loving people. We suspect that the court was moved by a comparison of the utility of plaintiff's hotel in that district with the utility of an advertising sign. In any event, the interference was with the normal and ordinary sensibilities of dwellers in the hotel and with the ordinary use of property.

It is not our intention to decide the case upon authority alone, divorced from reason or public policy. The photographic evidence discloses that the properties of the respective parties are not in a residential district and, in fact, are outside the city limits of Portland, and lie adjacent to a considerable amount of unimproved land. Neither party can claim any greater social utility than the other. Both were in process of construction at the same time, and the case should not be decided upon the basis of the priority of occupation. This case differs fundamentally from other nuisance cases, because light is not a noxious but is, in general, a highly beneficial element. The development of parks and playgrounds equipped for the enjoyment of the working public, whose recreation is necessarily taken after working hours and frequently after dark, is a significant phenomenon in thousands of urban communities. Many lighted parks and fields are located adjacent to residential property and must to some extent interfere with the full enjoyment of darkness (if desired), by the residents.

We do not say that the shedding of light upon another's property may never under any conditions become a nuisance, but we do say that extreme caution must be employed in applying any such legal theory. The conditions of modern city life impose upon the city dweller and his property many burdens more severe than that of light reflected upon him or it.

We limit our decision to the specific facts of this case and hold as a matter of law that the loss sustained by the plaintiff by the spilled light which has been reflected onto the highly sensitized moving picture screen from the defendant's property is not a nuisance.

The judgment is affirmed.

NOTES AND QUESTIONS

1 Would the court have concluded differently if the racetrack had been built in a residential area? Would it matter if the movie theater had been built first?

2 As the *Portland Meadows* case suggests, the concept of nuisance is a difficult one to define. It has been said that "there is perhaps no more impenetrable jungle in the entire law than that which surrounds the word *nuisance*. It has meant all things to all people, and has been applied indiscriminately to everything from an alarming advertisement to a cockroach baked in a pie. There is general agreement that it is incapable of any exact or comprehensive definition" (Prosser and Keaton on Torts, 5th Ed. p. 516 (1984).

3 The *Restatement of Torts* includes the following description of the doctrine of nuisance. "It is an obvious truth that each individual in a community must put up with a certain amount of annoyance, inconvenience, and interference and must take a certain amount of risk in order that all may get on together. The very existence of organized society depends upon the principle of 'give and take, live and let live.' The law of torts does not attempt to impose liability or shift the loss in every case in which one person's conduct has had some detrimental affect on another. Liability for damages is imposed in most cases in which the harm or risk to one is greater than he ought to be required to bear under the circumstances, at least without compensation" (*Restatement (2d) Torts*, Section 822, Comment G).

4 In *Lee v. Rolla Speedway*, 494 S.W.2d 349 (Missouri, 1973), neighboring property owners sought to enjoin construction of an automobile racetrack. The court stated that "Interference with the use and enjoyment of their property is not the only question to be decided in determining whether or not plaintiffs are entitled to relief. That determination requires a weighing of the utility of the actor's conduct against 'the gravity of the harm.' "

The *Restatement of Torts* adopts the balancing test which attempts to weigh the extent of the harm caused by the defendant's activity against the utility of that activity.

According to the *Restatement of Torts,* (Section 827, p. 244) the following factors are important in measuring the gravity of the harm:

a. the extent of the harm involved;
b. the character of the harm involved;
c. the social value which the law attaches to the type of use or enjoyment invaded;
d. the suitability of the particular use or enjoyment invaded to the character of the locality;
e. the burden on the person harmed of avoiding the harm.

Concerning the utility of the defendant's conduct, the following factors are significant (Section 828, p. 250):

a. social value which the law attaches to the primary purpose of the conduct;
b. suitability of the conduct to the character of the locality;
c. impracticability of preventing or avoiding the invasion.

Nuisance or Trespass?   A distinction must be drawn between a nuisance and a trespass. A trespass requires a physical invasion of the land that interferes with the owner's exclusive possession. A nuisance is an interference with an owner's use and enjoyment of the property.

For example, in *Wilson v. Interlake Steel Co.* 322 C3d 229, 232 (1982), the plaintiffs alleged that the loud noises from the twenty-four-hour-a-day operation of a steel mill constituted a trespass of their nearby residential property. The court held that there is a distinction "between noise-caused vibrations resulting in damage or injury, and noise waves that are merely bothersome and not damaging." The former would constitute a trespass, but the latter would constitute only a nuisance and not a trespass. "Noise alone, without damage to the property, will not support a tort action for trespass. Recovery is predicated on the deposit of particular matter on the plaintiff's property or on actual physical damage thereto. All intangible intrusions, such as noise, odor, or light alone, are dealt with as nuisance cases, not trespass."

3 MODERN APPLICATIONS OF THE DOCTRINE OF NUISANCE

Prah v. Maretti, 321 N.W.2d 182 (Wis. 1982)

Facts of the case.

Plaintiff owned a residence equipped with a solar heating system. Defendant owns property adjacent to plaintiff and proposes to construct a dwelling that conforms to all applicable building codes but which would, if built, interfere with plaintiff's access to an unobstructed path for sunlight across the neighbor's property.

Plaintiff sought to enjoin construction by defendant in order to preserve unobstructed access to light across defendant's property.

The trial court concluded that the plaintiff presented no claim upon which relief could be granted and entered judgment for the defendant.

OPINION

The rights of neighboring landowners are relative; the uses by one must not unreasonably impair the uses or enjoyment of the other. When one landowner's use of his or her property unreasonably interferes with another's enjoyment of his or her property, that use is said to be a private nuisance.

The private nuisance doctrine has traditionally been employed in this state to balance the conflicting rights of landowners, and this court has recently adopted the analysis of private nuisance set forth in the *Restatement (2d) of Torts,* which defines private nuisance as "a nontrespassory invasion of another's interest in private use and enjoyment of land."

The defendant is not completely correct in asserting that the common law did not protect a landowner's access to sunlight across adjoining property. At English common law a landowner could acquire a right to receive sunlight across adjoining land by both express agreement and under the judge-made doctrine of "ancient lights." Under the doctrine of ancient lights, if the landowner had received sunlight across adjoining property for a specified period of time, the landowner was entitled to continue to receive unobstructed access to sunlight across the adjoining property.

While American courts have not been as receptive to protecting a landowner's access to sunlight as the English courts, American courts have afforded some protection to a landowner's interest in access to sunlight. American courts honor express easements for sunlight and initially enforced the English common law doctrine of ancient lights. It was later that American courts in every state repudiated the doctrine of ancient lights as inconsistent with the needs of a developing country.

Societies' reluctance in the nineteenth and early part of the twentieth century to provide broader protection for a landowner's access to sunlight was premised on three policy considerations. First, the right of landowners to use their property as they wished, as long as they did not cause physical damage to a neighbor, was jealously guarded. Second, sunlight was valued only for aesthetic enjoyment or as illumination. Since artificial light could be used for illumination, loss of sunlight was at most a personal annoyance, given little, if any, weight by society. Third, society had a significant interest in not restricting or impeding land development.

We believe these three policies are no longer fully accepted or applicable. They reflect factual circumstances and social priorities that are now obsolete. First, society has increasingly regulated the use of land by the landowner for the general welfare. Second, access to sunlight has taken on a new significance in recent years. In this case the plaintiff seeks to protect access to sunlight, not for aesthetic reasons or as a source of illumination but as a source of energy. Access to sunlight as an energy source is of significance both to the landowner who invests in solar collectors and to a society that has an interest in developing alternative sources of energy.

Third, the policy of favoring unhindered private development in an expanding economy is no longer in harmony with the realities of our society. The need for easy and rapid development is not as great today as it once was, while our perception of the value of sunlight as a source of energy has increased significantly.

The defendant would have us ignore the flexible private nuisance law as a means of resolving the dispute between the landowners in this case and would have us adopt an approach of favoring the unrestricted development of land and of applying a rigid and inflexible rule protecting his right to build on his land, disregarding any interest of the plaintiff in the use and enjoyment of his land. This we refuse to do.

We therefore hold that private nuisance law—that is, the reasonable use doctrine as set forth in the *Restatement*—is applicable to the instant case. Recognition of a nuisance claim for unreasonable obstruction of access to sunlight will not prevent land development or unduly hinder the use of adjoining land. It will promote the reasonable use and enjoyment of land in a manner suitable to the 1980's and beyond. That obstruction of access to light might be found to constitute a nuisance in certain circumstances does not mean that it will be or must be found to constitute a nuisance under all circumstances. The result in each case depends on whether the conduct complained of is unreasonable.

For reasons set forth, we reverse the judgment of the circuit court dismissing the complaint and remand the matter to circuit court for further proceedings not inconsistent with this opinion.

NOTES AND QUESTIONS

1 The Wisconsin Supreme Court remanded the case to the trial court for a determination of the utility of defendant's conduct in light of the gravity of the harm to plaintiff. Who do you think should win? What factors should the trial court consider?

2 In *Fontainbleau Hotel v. Fortyfive Inc.,* 114 S.2d 357 (1959), the Florida court rejected an attempt to restrain an owner from constructing a building that caused a shadow on a neighboring hotel's swimming pool. The court held there was no legally protected right to access to sunlight. Can the Florida case be reconciled with the position taken by the Wisconsin court?

3 Suppose the plaintiff in *Prah v. Maretti* complained because defendant's proposed structure would block his views? Would the court have given equal weight to this claim?

4   REMEDIES FOR NUISANCE

Boomer v. Atlantic Cement, 257 N.E.2d 870 (N.Y. 1970)

Facts of the case.

Defendant operates a large cement plant near Albany. These are actions for injunction and damages by neighboring land owners alleging injury to property from dirt, smoke, and vibration emanating from the plant. A nuisance has been found after trial; temporary damages have been allowed; but an injunction closing the plant has been denied.

OPINION

The public concern with air pollution arising from many sources in industry and in transportation is currently accorded ever wider recognition accompanied by a growing sense of responsibility of State and Federal Governments to control it. Cement plants are obvious sources of air pollution in the neighborhoods where they operate.

The cement making operations of defendant have been found by the court to have damaged the nearby properties because of the dust, noise, and vibrations, which emanated from the plant. That court, as it has been noted, accordingly found defendant maintained a nuisance. The total damage to plaintiffs' properties is, however, relatively small in comparison with the value of defendant's operation and with the consequences of the injunction that plaintiffs seek.

The ground for the denial of an injunction, notwithstanding the finding both that there is a nuisance and that plaintiffs have been damaged substantially, is the large disparity in economic consequences of the nuisance and of the injunction. This theory cannot, however, be sustained without overruling a doctrine which has been consistently reaffirmed in this state.

The rule in New York has been that a nuisance will be enjoined, although marked disparity be shown in economic consequences between the effect of the injunction and the effect of the nuisance.

The problem of disparity in economic consequences was sharply in focus in *Whalen v. Union Bag & Paper Co.,* 101 N.E. 805. In that case, a pulp mill entailing an investment of more than a million dollars polluted a stream in which plaintiff, who owned a farm, was "a lower riparian owner." The economic loss to plaintiff from this pollution was small. This court, reversing the Appellate Division, reinstated the injunction granted by the trial court against the argument of the mill owner that in view of "the slight advantage to plaintiff and the great loss that will be inflicted on defendant" an injunction should not be granted. "Such a balancing of injuries," the court held, "cannot be justified by the circumstances of this case. Although the damage to the plaintiff may be slight as compared with the defendant's expense of abating the condition, that is not a good reason for refusing an injunction." This rule has been followed in the state of New York with marked consistency.

However, to follow our precedents in this case would require us to close down the plant at once. We note that defendant's investment in the plant is in excess of $45,000,000 and there are over 300 people employed there. This court is fully agreed to avoid the immediately drastic remedy of closing the plant; the difference in view is how best to avoid it.

One alternative is to grant the injunction but postpone its effect to a specified future date to give opportunity for technical advances to permit defendant to eliminate the nuisance; another is to grant the injunction conditioned on the payment of permanent damages to plaintiffs, which would compensate them for the total economic loss to their property present and future caused by defendant's operations. For reasons that will be developed the court chooses the latter alternative.

If the injunction were to be granted unless within a short period—e.g., 18 months—the nuisance be abated by improved methods, there would be no assurance that any significant technical improvement would occur.

The parties could settle this private litigation at any time if defendant paid enough money, and the imminent threat of closing the plant would build up the pressure on defendant. If there were no improved techniques found, there would inevitably be applications to the court for extensions of time to find such techniques on showing of good faith efforts.

Moreover, techniques to eliminate dust and other annoying by-products of cement making are unlikely to be developed by any research the defendant can undertake within any short period, but will depend on the total resources of the cement industry nationwide and throughout the world. The problem is universal wherever cement is made.

On the other hand, to grant the injunction unless defendant pays plaintiffs such permanent damages as may be fixed by the court seems to do justice between the contending parties. All of the attributions of economic loss to the properties on which plaintiffs' complaints are based will have been redressed.

It seems reasonable to think that the risk of being required to pay permanent damages to injured property owners by cement plant owners would itself be a reasonably effective spur to research for improved techniques to minimize the nuisance caused by their operation.

The present cases and the remedy here proposed are in a number of other respects rather similar to *Northern Indiana Public Service Co. v. W. J. & M. S. Vesey,* 200 N.E. 620, decided by the Supreme Court of Indiana. The gases, odors, ammonia, and smoke from the Northern Indiana company's gas plant damaged the nearby Vesey greenhouse operation. An injunction and damages were sought, but an injunction was denied and the relief granted was limited to permanent damages "present, past, and future."

Denial of an injunction in that case was grounded on a public interest in the operation of the gas plant and on the court's conclusion "that less injury would be occasioned by requiring the appellant [Public Service] to pay the appellee [Vesey] all damages suffered by it . . . than by enjoining the operation of the gas plant."

The judgment, by allowance of permanent damages imposing a servitude on land, would preclude future recovery by plaintiffs or their successors. This should be placed beyond debate by a provision of the judgment that the payment by defendant and the acceptance by plaintiffs of permanent damages found by the court shall be in compensation for a servitude on the land.

The orders should be reversed, and the cases remitted to the trial court to grant an injunction, which shall be vacated upon payment by defendant of such amounts of permanent damage to the respective plaintiffs as shall for this purpose be determined by the court.

JASEN, Judge (dissenting)

I do not subscribe to the newly enunciated doctrine of assessment of permanent damages, in lieu of an injunction, where substantial property rights have been impaired by the creation of a nuisance.

It has long been the rule in this State, as the majority acknowledges, that a nuisance that results in substantial continuing damage to neighbors must be enjoined. To now change the rule to permit the cement company to continue polluting the air indefinitely upon the payment of permanent damages is, in my opinion, compounding the magnitude of a very serious problem in our State and Nation today.

In recognition of this problem, the Legislature of this State has enacted the Air Pollution Control Act declaring that it is the State policy to require the use of all available and reasonable methods to prevent and control air pollution.

I see grave dangers in overruling our long-established rule of granting an injunction where a nuisance results in substantial continuing damage. In permitting the injunction to become inoperative upon the payment of permanent damages, the majority is, in effect, licensing a continuing wrong. It is the same as saying to the cement company, you may continue to do harm to your neighbors so long as you pay a fee for it. Furthermore, once such permanent damages are assessed and paid, the incentive to alleviate the wrong would be eliminated, thereby continuing air pollution of an area without abatement.

I would enjoin the defendant cement company from continuing the discharge of dust particles upon its neighbors' properties unless, within eighteen months, the cement company abated this nuisance.

It is not my intention to cause the removal of the cement plant from the Albany area, but to recognize the urgency of the problem stemming from this stationary source of air pollution, and to allow the company a specified period of time to develop a means to alleviate this nuisance.

In a day when there is a growing concern for clean air, highly developed industry should not expect acquiescence by the courts but should, instead, plan its operations to eliminate contamination of our air and damage to its neighbors.

NOTES AND QUESTIONS

1 At the trial of the *Boomer* case, the court found that damages to the plaintiffs are $185,000. What does this sum represent? How was it calculated? Suppose that an owner who had been paid by the cement company later developed a respiratory ailment caused by the cement dust. Would that person be precluded from recovering because of the prior payment? The majority and dissenting opinions disagree on the effect of a damage award in creating an incentive to eliminate the nuisance through technological improvements. Which opinion makes the stronger case?

2 Courts often look to the social value of a defendant's conduct, its suitability to the locale, and whether the defendant can take practical steps to avoid the harm being caused in determining whether or not a nuisance exists. Were these factors relevant in the court's analysis in the *Boomer* case?

3 Would it be relevant if the cement company had been in existence before the development of residences in the area? Early cases held that the one who "moved to the nuisance" would not be heard to complain of it, although the modern trend is to the contrary. The case of *Spur Industries v. Del Webb,* 494 P.2d 700 (Ariz. 1978), adopted a middle ground by permitting a residential developer to enjoin operation of a previously existing meat packing plant on the grounds of a nuisance but only on the condition that the developer pay for the costs incurred by the packing plant in relocating its business. What is the social utility behind requiring a previously existing use to be declared a nuisance for the benefit of newcomers?

5   NUISANCE AND THE EFFECT OF A STATUTE

Two issues arise where a statute either prohibits a certain conduct or specifically authorizes it. In the first case, where a defendant's activity violates a state or local statute, it is likely that defendant's conduct will be deemed a nuisance per se. For example, where statutes limit the location of dog kennels or require the use of pollution controls in connection with a manufacturing process, violation of the statutes will be deemed to constitute a nuisance per se entitling the affected property owner to an injunction without proof of injury.

On the other hand, where an ordinance specifically authorizes a certain use, the question becomes whether an adversely affected neighbor is precluded from claiming that a nuisance has been created. Generally speaking, statutory authorization is not sufficient to justify maintaining a continuous or ongoing nuisance, although such authorization is usually sufficient to justify a nuisance of a temporary nature. For instance, a New York case held that a municipality's burning of trash pursuant to an ordinance did not entitle it to maintain a nuisance *Shering v. City of Rochester,* 273 N.Y.S.2d 464 (N.Y. 1966). However, various cases have held that the construction of a transit system pursuant to statutory authorization precluded a finding of a private nuisance. (See e.g. *Orphum v. San Francisco Bay Area Rapid Transit,* 146 Cal.Rptr. 5 (Cal 1978); *Downside Risk, Inc. v. Metropolitan Atlanta Rapid Transit Authority,* 274 S.E.2d 653 (Ga 1980). In other words, statutory authorization will usually preclude the finding of a temporary nuisance but will not allow the maintenance of a permanent nuisance.

6   LATERAL AND SUBJACENT SUPPORT

Lateral support refers to the support given by adjacent land. Subjacent support refers to the support of surface land by the land underneath it. By definition, questions concerning subjacent support can only exist where there is a separation of ownership between surface and subsurface rights in the land. This occurs for instance, in a transfer of mineral rights by the owner of land to another.

The law of subjacent support has evolved by analogy to the better developed principle concerning lateral support. The rules regarding each are essentially similar and are illustrated in the case that follows.

Spall v. Janota, 406 N.E.2d 378 (Ind. 1980)

Facts of the case.

Spall owns a residence on property that is adjacent to a vacant parcel owned by Janota. Both properties were located on a small hill—the Janota property at the top of the hill, the Spall property at the bottom. In order to build a residence, Spall made excavations on his property for the purpose of installing a concrete foundation.

After the excavation on the Spall lot, Janota noticed cracks appearing in his house, and these cracks have become worse resulting in substantial damage to the house. The cracks and damage to Janota's house were caused by slope failure resulting from the cut or excavation made in the hillside on the Spall property.

Janota testified that, in his opinion, the value of his house if it were not damaged would be $35,000. There was no evidence of its value in its damaged condition and there was no evidence of the cost of restoring Janota's house to its prior condition.

The trial court concluded that Spall's excavations deprived the Janota property of its lateral support and awarded damages of $35,000. Spall appeals.

OPINION

A landowner has an absolute right to have her or his land in its natural state laterally supported by the lands of an adjoining landowner, and if the adjoining landowner excavates on her or his land, thereby depriving the lands of a neighbor of lateral support and damaging said land in its natural state, the adjoining landowner is absolutely liable for such damage even though she or he is free from any negligence.

However, the rule is different when the case involves injury to buildings caused by the withdrawal of lateral support, for there is no absolute right to lateral support of buildings. Liability for damage to buildings resulting from the loss of lateral support must be based upon the negligence of the adjoining landowner in carrying on the activity that occasioned the loss of lateral support. The law is also settled that when a party is about to endanger the land to his or her neighbor by improvements on his or her own land, the party must give notice and use ordinary skill in conducting such improvements; the party is liable for damages caused by willful, or negligent, acts.

There are two viewpoints concerning the effect of the failure to give notice in a case where the notice requirement would be applicable. One view regards the lack of notice as negligence per se, while the other holds that the failure to notify is evidence of negligence for the consideration of the trier of fact. The better view is that failure to give notice is evidence of negligence and this appears to be the general rule.

Since this action seeks damages for injury to Janota's house resulting from the deprivation of lateral support by the excavation on the Spall land, it is clear that the rule of absolute liability is not applicable. Janota can only recover if the loss of lateral support was occasioned by Spall's negligence. Therefore, we must consider what constitutes negligence in such a case. The standard of care required is that common to all negligence actions—that is, the duty to use reasonable or ordinary care under the circumstances.

We see nothing in the evidence in this case that would support a finding of negligence in making the excavation on the Spall property. There is no evidence that the excavation was made in an unskillful or dangerous manner. There is no evidence supportive of a finding that damage to Janota's house reasonably should have been anticipated by the making of the excavation. We perceive no evidence of any of the criteria listed previously, other than a failure to give notice to Janota. However, in view of the facts of this case, the distance separating the cut in the hillside from Janota's house, and the lack of evidence of foreseeability of such consequences, we do not believe that lack of notice, standing alone, is sufficient to support a finding of negligence which was the proximate cause of the injury, and thus impose liability on the basis of negligence.

While we are uncertain whether the court found Spall liable on a theory of absolute liability or upon a negligence basis, neither can be supported. For reasons previously stated, the absolute liability standard is not applicable in cases of damage to buildings, and there is no evidence to support liability predicated upon negligence.

We believe the judgment against Spall is contrary to law if predicated upon absolute liability, and unsupported by sufficient evidence if based on negligence.

Since we reverse on the issue of liability, we need not discuss of damage. Nevertheless, we deem it appropriate to comment upon this issue.

The measure of damages for injury to a building caused by negligent withdrawal of lateral support is either the diminution in its value or the cost of restoration, whichever is less. The evidence in this case was that the value of Janota's house at the time of trial, if it had not been damaged, was $35,000. There was no evidence as to its value in its damaged condition and no evidence as to cost of restoration. There was no evidence upon which the court could have found the proper damages. Thus, the award of damages was improper.

For all the reasons herein stated, the judgment is reversed.

NOTES AND QUESTIONS

The above mentioned case states the general rule that indicates that an adjacent owner is strictly liable when excavation of property damages adjacent property that is "in its natural state"; however, where property has been improved by the addition of a building or otherwise, an adjacent owner who causes damage to the land or the building through excavation is usually liable only where such excavation was negligently conducted.

7 SUMMARY

The law of nuisance is the oldest doctrine that places limits upon one's right to use their land. A nuisance involves an unreasonable interference with the use and possession of the land of another. This involves balancing the utility of the defendant's conduct against the harm caused to the plaintiff.

Even when an activity is characterized as a nuisance, many courts will not enjoin the activity, particularly if the harm caused by a defendant by enjoining the activity is considered to greatly outweigh the benefit to the plaintiff.

Although modern zoning and environmental legislation have displaced the law of nuisance in some instances, the law of nuisance continues to have relevance in modern property law.

The related doctrines of lateral and subjacent support are the other doctrines which impose inherent limitations on the way one uses their property. The rules here are relatively simple: One has an absolute right to the lateral and subjacent support of land that is in its natural state. When the land is improved with a structure, the right to support is less expansive and liability will be imposed only in the case of negligent removal of that support.

8 QUESTIONS

1 Mills burns rubbish on his land which causes smoke, ash, and soot to travel onto Norma's property, which is used as a residence. Norma claims that Mills is causing a trespass and a nuisance. Is she correct?

2 The city of Lafayette maintained a landfill adjacent to a residential subdivision. The landfill was approximately thirty feet high, was unsightly, but did not pose any health or safety risks to the residential owners. The owners sued claiming the city was maintaining a nuisance. Are they correct?

3 Boris seeks to open a mortuary in a residential neighborhood. The neighbors object, claiming that the mortuary will create a "morbid atmosphere" and should not be permitted because it will constitute a nuisance. Who wins?

4 Evans discharged raw sewage onto a nearby beach in violation of a town's sewer ordinance. A neighbor sues. What remedies are available?

5 Chaiken installed a windmill in his backyard to generate electricity for his home. A neighbor objected to the noise of the windmill and sought an injunction against its use. What factors will the court look at in deciding whether a nuisance exists, and what remedy is appropriate?

6 A state law authorized municipalities to construct sewage treatment facilities. One such facility was constructed by a city adjacent to property owned by the plaintiffs. The facility caused foul odors to linger on plaintiffs' property. Can plaintiffs prevail on a nuisance theory? If so, what remedy is available?

CHAPTER **8**

EASEMENTS AND RELATED INTERESTS

TOPICS CONSIDERED IN THIS CHAPTER:

1 INTRODUCTION

An easement is a property interest that entitles the owner of the easement to use the property of another in a limited way. While an easement is an interest in land, it does not entitle the owner of the easement to possession and so an easement is never

115

considered an estate in land. However since the easement is a property right, the owner of the land burdened by the easement may do nothing to interfere with the easement. To that extent, easements constitute another type of limitation upon an owner's right to use her or his property.

Easements can be created for a wide range of purposes, including but not limited to a right to pasture animals, to fish from a pond, to have a right of way across a neighbor's property, to run power lines over or under property, to take water or minerals from property, to receive light, air, or heat over and across neighboring property, and more. None of these interests give the easement owner a right to possession, but all of them give the easement owner a right to use the property of another for a limited purpose.

2 BASIC TERMINOLOGY

Before proceeding to questions concerning the creation, scope, and termination of easements, it may be helpful to define certain terms that will recur throughout the chapter. Easements may be classified in several ways: an *affirmative easement* is one that allows the owner of the easement to perform an act on another's land. An example would be to use a portion of another's land for a roadway. Easements may also be classified as *negative easements*. An example might be a view easement that would entitle the owner of the easement to prevent a neighbor from building on the property in such a way as to interfere with the easement for view. Easements are also classified as appurtenant and in gross. An *appurtenant easement* benefits the land of the easement owner. Either a right-of-way easement or an easement for view benefit the land of the owner and are considered appurtenant easements. An easement *in gross,* however, benefits the owner of the easement in his or her personal capacity rather than conferring a separate benefit on the land of the owner of the easement. A right to extract minerals, cut timber, take fish from a pond, or run power lines are examples of easements in gross.

Easements are also classified in relation to dominant and servient tenements or estates. The *dominant estate* is the land that obtains the benefit of the easement whereas the *servient estate* is the land that is burdened by the easement. There is no dominant estate where the easement is in gross because no particular land is benefited by the easement.

Shingleton v. State of North Carolina, 133 S.E. 2d 183 (N.C. 1963)

Whether an easement is appurtenant or in gross is controlled mainly by the nature of the right and the intention of the parties creating it, and must be determined by the fair interpretation of the grant creating the easement, aided if necessary by the situation of the property and the surrounding circumstances. If it appears from such construction of the grant that the parties intended to create a right in the nature of an easement in property retained for the benefit of the property granted, such right would be deemed an easement appurtenant and not in gross, regardless of the form in which such intention is expressed. On the other hand, if it appears from such construction that the parties intended to create a right to be attached to the person to whom it was granted, it would be deemed to be an easement in gross. In case of doubt, the easement is presumed to be appurtenant and not in gross.

QUESTION

Why is it that in cases of doubt, an easement will be presumed to be appurtenant and not in gross?

3   CREATION OF EASEMENTS

The manner in which the easement is created can be important in determining both the scope of the easement and the manner in which the easement can or will be terminated.

Easements can be created in three general ways: expressly, by implication, and by adverse use. An express easement is usually created by a deed or in a will, in which case the formalities of those instruments must be satisfied. Express easements are divided into two kinds, the first is where an owner conveys an easement to someone against the owner's property. This is known as an express grant of an easement. In the second situation, the owner transfers the entire interest in the property to another but reserves the right to an easement in the property transferred. This is known as express reservation. For instance, owner and neighbor own adjacent parcels. Neighbor wants to lay a drain pipe across owner's property. They reach an agreement and owner gives to neighbor a deed describing the easement. This is an express grant of an easement. Suppose instead that seller owns both parcels and sells one to neighbor but excludes for seller's benefit, the right to an easement to maintain a drain pipe across the property transferred. This is an express reservation of an easement.

Easements can also be created by implication. This usually arises where an owner transfers a portion of a parcel and does not expressly grant or reserve an easement. If an easement across either parcel had been previously used, or if such an easement is necessary for the use of either parcel, the law may imply that the parties intended to grant or reserve an easement. An easement by implication involves construing the implied or apparent intention of the parties in light of their conduct, and the public policy that encourages the productive use of land. For example, owner sells a portion of a lot, failing to grant an easement across the retained parcel. If the only means of access to the transferred parcel is across the owner's retained parcel, an easement will probably be implied. Easements by implication are of two kinds—those that arise from prior use, known as quasi-easements, and those that arise from necessity.

Finally, easements may be created by prescription. This is analogous to adverse possession and requires that the use be open and notorious, continuous, hostile to the owner, exclusive, and under a claim of right. Adverse possession is examined in Chapter 12, Section 8.

A Creation by Express Grant

Easement or Fee? Probably the most common way that an easement is created is by an express grant in which the grantor of the easement prepares and executes a deed conveying the easement and delivers it to the grantee. Nevertheless, even this seemingly simple transaction can cause problems, resulting in uncertainty and disputes, particularly between successors in interest of the original grantor and grantee. The following cases illustrate the nature of the problem and the significant consequences that can flow from a determination that the interest conveyed was either an easement or a fee.

In *Minneapolis Club v. Cohler,* 177 N.W. 2d 786 (Minn. 1970), plaintiff's predecessor conveyed to defendant's predecessor a "right-of-way over and the privilege of the free use as a private alley of an eight-foot wide strip. . . ." Approximately sixty years after the grant, plaintiff sought to expand their facilities and build a walkway sixteen feet above ground level over the alley. Defendants contended that the right-of-way transferred was a fee and that hence it owned the air rights over and above the eight-foot strip in question. The court concluded that the interest transferred was an easement and that plaintiff's proposed construction would not interfere with the defendant's use of the easement.

In the case of *Midland Valley Railroad v. Arrow Industrial Co.,* 297 P. 2d 410 (Okl. 1956), the Oklahoma Supreme Court construed a deed that conveyed "a strip of land thirty feet wide for a right-of-way over and across" certain described property. The court concluded in this case that the interest conveyed was a fee and that the grantor's successors in interest had no remaining claim or interest to the property.

The Supreme Court of Kansas in the case of *Harvest Queen Mill v. Sanders,* 370 P. 2d 419 (Kan. 1962), construed a deed that granted an interest described as "a strip of land one hundred and fifty feet wide" across described property. The interest was originally conveyed in 1887, and in 1958 the grantee's successor in interest executed a mineral rights agreement authorizing a third party to extract oil and gas from beneath the surface of the strip conveyed. If a fee interest had been conveyed, then the owner would clearly have the right to sell the mineral rights; if only an easement were conveyed, then just as clearly they would have no such right. The Kansas Supreme Court held that only an easement was conveyed.

B Easement by Express Reservation

We have seen that one may create an easement across property in favor of another by virtue of an express grant. Similarly, where one conveys property to another he may reserve to himself an easement across the property conveyed. Thus, were *A* to sell property to *B* and deliver a deed to *B* that said: "reserving unto *A* and for the benefit of *A*'s property (described) a right of ingress and egress to the county road over and across the land conveyed,'' *A*, the grantor, has reserved an easement for the benefit of his property. This is known as an easement by express reservation.

Willard v. First Church, 102 Cal. Rpt. 739 (Cal. 1972)

Facts of the case.

Genevieve McGuigan owned two abutting lots in Pacifica known as lots 19 and 20. There was a building on lot 19, and lot 20 was vacant. McGuigan was a member of The First Church of Christ, Scientist (The Church), which was located across the street from her lots, and she permitted it to use lot 20 for parking during church services.

Petersen approached McGuigan with an offer to purchase lot 20. She was willing to sell the lot provided the church could continue to use it for parking. She therefore referred the matter to the Church's attorney, who drew up a provision for the deed that stated the conveyance was "subject to an easement for automobile parking during church hours for the benefit of the Church on the property at the southwest corner of the intersection of Hilton Way and Francisco Boulevard . . . such easement to run with the land only so long as the property for whose benefit the easement is given is used for Church purposes." Once this clause was inserted in the deed, McGuigan sold the property to Petersen, and he recorded the deed.

Ten days later, Petersen sold lot 20 to Willard, the plaintiff herein. The deed from Peterson to Willard did not mention an easement for parking by the church. While Petersen did mention to Willard that the church would want to use lot 20 for parking, it does not appear that he told him of the easement clause contained in the deed he received from McGuigan.

Willard became aware of the easement clause several months after purchasing the property. He then commenced this action to quiet title against the Church. The court found that McGuigan and Petersen intended to convey an easement to the Church, but that the clause they employed was ineffective for that purpose because it was invalidated by the common law rule that one cannot "reserve" an interest in property to a stranger to the title.

OPINION

This rule derives from common law notions and is based on feudal considerations. A reservation allows a grantor's whole interest in the property to pass to the grantee, but revests a newly created interest in the grantor. While a reservation could theoretically vest an interest in a third party, the early common law courts vigorously rejected this possibility.

California early adhered to this common law rule. In considering our continued adherence to it, we must realize that our courts no longer feel constricted by feudal forms of conveyancing. Rather, our primary objective in construing a conveyance is to try to give effect to the intent of the grantor. In general, therefore, grants are to be interpreted in the same way as other contracts and not according to rigid feudal standards. The common law rule conflicts with the modern approach to construing deeds because it can frustrate the grantor's intent.

The highest courts of two states have already eliminated the rule altogether. In *Townsend v. Cable*, 378 S.W. 2d 806 (Ky. 1964), the Court of Appeals of Kentucky abandoned the rule. It said: "We have no hesitancy in abandoning this archaic and technical rule. It is entirely inconsistent with the basic principle followed in the construction of deeds, which is to determine the intention of grantor as gathered from the four corners of the instrument." Relying on Townsend, the Supreme Court of Oregon, in *Garza v. Grayson*, 467 P. 2d 960 (Ore. 1970), rejected the rule because it was "derived from a narrow and highly technical interpretation of the meaning of the terms 'reservation' and 'exception' when employed in a deed" and did not sufficiently justify frustrating the grantor's intention. Since the rule that a grantor may not reserve an easement to a stranger in title may frustrate the grantor's intention and appears to use a useless vestige of the feudal era, we follow the lead of Kentucky and Oregon and abandon it entirely.

The judgment is reversed.

NOTES AND QUESTIONS

1 Until fairly recently, American courts almost invariably followed the common law approach and forbade the reservation of an easement to a third party. As indicated by the California court, the reason for this rule is largely lost in the cobwebs of history and has little to recommend it. The *Restatement of Property*, Section 472, specifically rejects the common law approach and state courts have gradually been adopting the *Restatement's* view. A slight majority of states, however, have yet to specifically reject the common law approach and practice in those states is uncertain.

2 Under the facts of the *Willard* case, how can the transaction be structured in a jurisdiction that continues to follow the common law rule?

C   Easement by Implication

A transfer of an interest in land sometimes gives rise to an implication that the parties intended an easement be created, even though they failed expressly to provide for one. Implied easements always involve a situation where a common grantor has transferred a portion of the land or an adjacent parcel. Implied easements may be considered to be granted or reserved by implication.

Easements by implication arise under one of two situations. The first involves some prior use that gives rise to the doctrine of an implied easement based on a "quasi-easement." The second kind of implied easement is based upon the theory of necessity. The following case excerpts from Illinois illustrate the difference between implication based on quasi-easement and implication based on necessity.

Finn v. Williams, 33 N.E. 2d 226 (III. 1941)

Where an owner of land conveys a parcel thereof which has no outlet to a highway except over the remaining lands of the grantor or over the land of strangers, a way by necessity exists over the remaining land of the grantor. If, at one time, there has been a unity of title, as here, the right to a way by necessity may lay dormant through several transfers of title and yet pass with each transfer as appurtenant to the dominant estate and be exercised at any time by the holder of the title thereto. Plaintiff's land is entirely surrounded by property of strangers and by the land of the Defendant from which it was originally severed. A right-of-way easement by necessity is implied in the conveyance which originally severed the two tracts in 1885, and it passed by several conveyances to plaintiffs in 1937. The fact that the original grantee and his successors in interest have been permitted ingress to and egress from their land over the land owned by surrounding strangers is immaterial when such permission is denied, as in the present case. The subsequent grantees may avail themselves of the dormant easement implied in the deed, which originally severed the dominant and servient estates.

Deisenroth v. Dodge, 131 N.E. 2d 17, 21 (III. 1955)

As to an easement by necessity, one may be implied where the land is surrounded by the land of the grantor or others. If there is a way into and out of the land sold, no way of necessity is implied. In the instant case, no way of necessity can be implied because the Plaintiff does have a means of ingress or egress to her property if she chooses to build such way.

However, the question must still be answered as to whether or not Plaintiff acquired by implication an easement corresponding to the pre-existing "quasi-easement." Such an easement can arise only upon the severance of unity of title, wherein an obvious servitude is imposed on one part of an estate. The general rule may be expressed that where, during the unity of title an apparent and obvious, permanent, continuous, and actual servitude or use is imposed on one part of an estate in favor of another, which at the time of severance of unity is in use and is reasonably necessary for the fair enjoyment of the other, then upon a severance of such unity of ownership there arises by implication of law a grant of the right to continue such use even though such grant is not reserved or specified in the deed.

In such cases it is not necessary that the claimed easement be absolutely necessary for the enjoyment of the estate granted, but it is sufficient that it is reasonably necessary.

NOTES AND QUESTIONS

1 Both the *Finn* case and the *Deisenroth* case refer to the concept of necessity. How is the notion of necessity different in the case of a quasi-easement then in an easement implied by necessity?

2 The analysis of implied easements used by the Illinois courts is the over-whelming majority view in American jurisdictions. Nevertheless, the *Restatement of Property* arguably abandons the distinction substituting a series of eight factors that courts should use in determining whether an easement should be implied. Section 476 of the *Restatement of Property* provides as follows:

Restatement of Property, Section 476

In determining whether the circumstances under which a conveyance of land is made imply an easement, the following factors are important:

a. whether the claimant is the conveyor or the conveyee,
b. the terms of the conveyance,
c. the consideration given for it,
d. whether the claim is made against a simultaneous conveyee,
e. the extent of necessity of easement to the claimant,
f. whether reciprocal benefits result to the conveyor and the conveyee,
g. the manner in which the land was used prior to its conveyance, and
h. the extent to which the manner of prior use was or might have been known to the parties.

The following is taken from *Implied Easements of Necessity Contrasted with Those Based on Quasi-easement,* 40 Kentucky Law Journal 324 by Ernest W. Rivers.

Implied easements include the easement of necessity and the easement implied from a quasi-easement. These two types are similar, and for either to arise, the title to the land must have been in a common owner, and he or she must have conveyed a part of the land by deed in such a way as to create a need for an easement to benefit the land conveyed or the land retained. Also, both types are based fundamentally on implied intention as determined from a construction of the deed. In spite of their similarity, however, implied easements of necessity and implied easements based on quasi-easements are clearly distinguishable, both as to the nature of the implication underlying each and as to the circumstances surrounding the execution of the deed that supports the implication.

An easement of necessity usually arises where there is a landlocked situation. The grantor conveys land in such a manner as to render the land conveyed or retained inaccessible except over the land of the grantor or that of a stranger. If the easement is to arise by implication, it must be over the land conveyed or over the land retained because an easement will not be implied over the land of a stranger.

Before a way of necessity will be implied, it must be a way of absolute necessity.

A quasi-easement exists when a person utilizes one part of his land for the benefit of another part. As long as the land remains in the person subjecting it to such use, an easement does not exist because one cannot have an easement in his own land. The implication giving rise to the intent in an easement based on quasi-easement is the pre-existing condition of the land.

D   Easement by Prescription

The doctrines of adverse possession and prescription involve the use of property in a manner adverse to that of the actual owner. That use, over time, may have the effect of creating or extinguishing property interests. The doctrine of adverse possession is more fully explained in Chapter 12.

In *Masid v. First State Bank,* 329 N.W. 2d 560, 563 (Neb. 1983) the court said:

> The use and enjoyment which will give title by prescription to an easement is substantially the same in quality and characteristic of the adverse possession which will give title to real estate. It must be exclusive, adverse, under a claim of right, continuous and uninterrupted and open and notorious for the full prescriptive period. While some of our earlier opinions have included a requirement that the use also be with "the knowledge and acquiescent of the owner of the serviant tenement" upon further reflection we now determine that such requirement is neither necessary nor proper and is now specifically deleted as a requirement for establishing a prescriptive easement.

In *RKO Stanley v. Mellon National Bank,* 436 F. 2d 1297 (Penn. 1970), the plaintiff operated a motion picture theater and claimed an easement by prescription above the sidewalk to maintain a marquee located in front of an adjacent building and to change the signs on the marquee. Defendant Mellon Bank proposed to construct a building that would physically block one side of the marquee and thereby prevent RKO from changing the signs on it. The Bank claimed that since the land under the marquee was a public sidewalk, RKO's use of the sidewalk was not adverse to the Bank. The court made the following observations:

> The basic question is whether easements can be acquired by prescription in property constituting a public sidewalk, which is "for all intents and purposes a part of the owner's premises subject only to the public's easement of passage." Easements by prescription are created by adverse, open, notorious, continuous, and uninterrupted use of land for twenty-one years.
>
> The difficulty posed by this case is the presence of the public easement. Any use of the sidewalk within the scope of the public easement is not adverse to Mellon Bank and cannot serve as the basis for the acquisition of a prescriptive easement.
>
> While the public's lawful use of a sidewalk is restricted to uses within the scope of the public easement, the abutting fee owner is not so restricted in his use of the sidewalk. The abutting owner has the right to use the sidewalk in any manner not inconsistent with the public easement.
>
> No use outside the scope of the public easement may be made of a sidewalk in opposition to or over the objection of the abutting fee owner. The abutting fee owner's private right is superior to any other private right, and any private use of a sidewalk constitutes a trespass to the property rights of the abutting fee owner. The Pennsylvania decisions have long made clear that the abutting owner can prevent such uses of the public way.

NOTES AND QUESTIONS

Suppose that RKO ultimately prevailed against Mellon Bank. What would be RKO's rights? To what extent would these rights interfere with Mellon's ability to use its property?

4 SCOPE OF THE EASEMENT

The scope or extent of an easement refers both to its potential duration and to the manner in which the easement may be used by the owner of the dominant estate. The passage of time, changes in technology, and intensified use of land often lead to claims that the owner of the dominant estate is exceeding the scope of the easement. Various rules of construction have evolved to remedy such problems, and the application of these rules is often dependent upon the manner in which the easement was originally created.

Scope of Easements Created by Express Grant or Reservation The *Restatement of Property*, Section 482, provides simply that "the extent of an easement created by a conveyance is fixed by the conveyance." It is also generally held, in the absence of a contrary intent evidenced by the agreement, that the uses of the dominant and servient owners are subject to adjustment consistent with the normal development of their respective lands. See e.g. *Bernards v. Link*, 248 P.2d 341 (Ore. 1952). The idea is that the parties to the original grant are presumed to have intended to provide for a reasonably convenient use of the easement in the future. In other words, and particularly in the case of an appurtenant easement, it is generally assumed that the parties intended the easement to accommodate the needs of the dominant estate at the time of its creation and as measured by reasonably anticipated development of the dominant estate. This assumption may, of course, be rebutted by specific language in the grant. For example, an easement granted "for purposes of ingress and egress by horse drawn carriage" will be construed to include ingress and egress by automobiles and may be construed to include ingress and egress by automobiles when the property is subdivided and developed. However, where the easement provides for ingress and egress two times per day, the terms of the grant will control, and use by the dominant owner which exceeds the terms of the grant will not be permitted.

A slightly different problem occurs when the grant is expressed in general terms, but the subsequent conduct of the parties tends to establish their intention when the original grant was made. Thus, when an easement is created by a deed that gave "a right to connect with a sewer outlet now on the property," use of the outlet for sewage from a second house built later on the property constituted an undue burden on the servient estate and exceeded the permissible scope of the easement *Loughman v. Couchman*, 47 N.W.2d 152 (Iowa 1951). Similarly, when a pipeline easement did not state the location or size of a pipe, the scope of the easement became fixed when the pipe was laid and the grantee was not permitted to dig up an eighteen-inch pipeline and replace it with a thirty-inch pipe *Dwyer v. Houston Pipe Line Co.*, 364 S.W.2d 736 (Texas 1963).

Krieger v. Pacific Gas and Electric, 173 Cal. Rprt. 751 (Cal. 1981)

Facts of the case.

Krieger owns property burdened by an easement in favor of Pacific Gas and Electric Company (PG&E), which consists of a ditch for transporting water from the Stanislaus River to a reservoir. The ditch was originally constructed in 1914 and since that time has consisted simply of an open and earthen ditch. The easement was originally created by an act of the U.S. Congress permitting PG&E's predecessor to construct the ditch across the land which, at the time, was owned by the federal government.

During 1975 PG&E began lining the ditch with a clay-type material known as gunite in order to prevent leakage. Krieger filed his complaint seeking a restraining order and asked that PG&E be required to remove the gunite it had installed and restore the affected stretch of the ditch to its prior earthen condition.

The trial court concluded that "the repair of the canal by guniting was within the scope of the easement owned by PG&E, does not alter its mode of operation, and does not increase the burden to Krieger's land."

OPINION

The California courts have consistently held the scope of the easement to be fixed by the location, character, and use in existence at the time the land became subject to the easement, which, in the instant case, is the time the property was patented.

California Civil Code, Section 806, provides: "The extent of a servitude is determined by the terms of the grant, or the nature of the enjoyment by which it was acquired."

When Krieger's land was burdened by the easement, the character and method of use of the easement was an open, earthen ditch for the conveyance of water. This character and method of use fixed the extent of the servitude on Krieger's property under the law. Once fixed, the scope of the easement cannot be changed without the consent of the servient owner.

Both parties have the right to insist that so long as the easement is enjoyed it shall remain substantially the same as it was at the time of the right accrued, entirely regardless of the question as to the relative benefit and damage that would ensue to the parties by reason of a change in the mode and manner of its enjoyment.

Respondent contends the guniting of the ditch falls within the ambit of its "secondary easement" to make necessary repairs. However, a secondary easement is no more than the right to make repairs and to do such things as are necessary to the exercise of the right and to do them only when necessary and in such manner as not to increase the burden needlessly on the servient estate.

The guniting of the earthen ditch enlarges the easement by alteration in the mode of operation and is not merely a repair. "The word *repair* in its ordinary sense relates to the preservation of property in its original condition, and does not carry the connotation that a new thing should be made or a distinct entity created." The easement owner "may make repairs, improvements, or changes that do not affect its substance." Here the repair affects the substance of the easement.

The trial court found that "[g]uniting the earthen stretch of the ditch crossing Krieger's land does not increase the burden to such land" and stated in its intended decision that "there would be no detriment to Krieger's property which can be legally recognized." But the court also found that the riparian vegetation which flourishes in the soil moistened by water percolating through the earthen walls of the ditch would recede and eventually be supplanted by otherwise indigenous vegetation. Presumably, the riparian vegetation has flourished throughout the 120-year history of the earthen water ditch, and is enjoyed by appellant as a benefit of the easement. *Burden* and *benefit* may be understood as two aspects of one concept such that a decrease in benefit achieves a corresponding increase in burden. Thus the court's finding that guniting does not increase the burden to appellant's land is inconsistent with the finding that riparian vegetation would be lost.

PG&E argues, and the trial court agreed, that because Krieger cannot acquire a vested right to seepage he cannot claim a detriment from guniting. PG&E is free to abandon the easement, thereby extinguishing it. However, so long as the easement burdens Krieger's land, he is entitled to the benefit running therewith. Accordingly, the court's finding of no detriment is unsupported by the evidence, and its determination that there would be no detriment legally recognizable is erroneous.

Reversed.

NOTES AND QUESTIONS

1 The *Restatement of Property,* Section 483, provides that the important factors in ascertaining the extent of an express easement are the circumstances under which the grant was made, whether or not the conveyance was gratuitous, and the use made of the servient tenement before and after the conveyance.

In addition, Section 484 of the *Restatement of Property* provides as follows:

> In ascertaining, in the case of an easement appurtenant created by conveyance, whether additional or different uses of the servient tenement required by changes in the character of the use of the dominant tenement are permitted, the interpreter is warranted in assuming that the parties to the conveyance contemplated a normal development in the use of the dominant estate.

Is the *Krieger* case consistent with the approach taken by the restatement?

2 The Utah Supreme Court in *Cottonwood Tanner Ditch Co. v. Moyle,* 174 P. 2d 148 (Utah 1946), faced almost identical facts as in the *Krieger* case but reached the opposite result. The court noted the historically arid conditions in Utah and explained: [T]he common law of Utah presumes that during the time of the creation of this easement all parties concerned knowing the arid nature of this country, contemplated that at some future time the owner of the water would . . . undertake to prevent waste as the need arise for more efficient use of the limited water available.

Secondary Easements   The Krieger case introduces the concept of the secondary easement. Secondary easements are implied in all easements to the extent they are reasonably necessary to maintain the easement. See *Ware v. Public Service,* 412 A.2d (NH). Another court described secondary easement as follows:

> Every easement includes what are termed ''secondary easements''; that is, the right to do such things as are necessary for the full enjoyment of the easement itself. But this right is limited, and must be exercised in such manner as not to injuriously increase the burden upon the servient tenement. The burden of the dominant tenement cannot by enlarged to the manifest injury of the servient estate by any alteration in the mode of enjoying the former. The owner cannot commit a trespass upon the servient tenement beyond the limits fixed by the grant or use (*North Forkwater Co. v. Edwards,* 54 p. 69 (Cal.).

In *Sun Pipeline v. Kirkpatrick,* 514 S.W. 2d 789 (Texas 1974), the Texas court held that the removal of overhead tree branches to permit inspection by air of a pipeline was necessary to the reasonable use of the pipeline easement and therefore was a secondary easement.

Scope of Easements Created by Prescription or Implication   Determining the scope of easements created by implication or by prescription has proven particularly troublesome. On the one hand, such easements are not created by a written instrument, so the intention of the parties is much more difficult to ascertain. In addition, easements by implication and prescription often impose an uncompensated burden upon the servient estate so that courts are more reluctant to increase that burden than in the case of easements that are expressly created. The following cases illustrate the judicial approach to determining the scope of nonexpress easements.

In *Ghen v. Piasecki,* 410 A.2d 708 (N.J. 1980), plaintiff sought an easement by necessity to a seven-acre parcel across defendant's twenty-three-acre parcel to reach the county road. Plaintiff's predecessor left the parcel undeveloped. Plaintiff sought to develop a residential subdivision and obtain a right of way fifty feet wide across defendant's parcel to provide access to the proposed subdivision. The court granted the easement by necessity but limited the scope of it based upon the following explanation:

> The duration and extent of easements by necessity are influenced by the fact that ''necessity'' is basic to their creation. When ''necessity'' no longer exists, the easement terminates. The necessity for the easement is determined as of the time the parcels were originally separated, even though application for establishment of the easement is made by subsequent owners of the landlocked parcel. The dimensions and the rights to be exercised within the easement are determined by the court after a hearing as to what are the needs of the parties. Although

a court may take into account changes from the time of the original severance, such as travel by automobile replacing travel by horse, and may recognize some increase in activity on the landlocked parcel in determining rights, it is the condition and size of the parcels at the time of severance that control.

In *Traders, Inc. v. Partholomew,* 459 A. 2d 974 (Vt. 1983), the Vermont Court, faced with similar factual circumstances, adopted the following standard:

A way of necessity arises out of public policy concerns that land not be left inaccessible and unproductive. Therefore such a way exists only so long as the necessity which creates it: if, at some point in the future accesses to plaintiff's land over a public way becomes available, the way of necessity will cease. While this Court has not had occasion to pass on the scope of a way of necessity, we adopt what appears to be the sounder, majority rule on this issue. That is, since the easement is based on social considerations encouraging land use, its scope ought to be sufficient for the dominant owner to have the reasonable enjoyment of his land for all lawful purposes.

While the way of necessity is thus expansive, it may not grow to such proportions as to interfere materially with the reasonable uses of the servient estate. Thus, it would seem to be coextensive with the reasonable needs, present and future, of the dominant estate for such right or easement, and to vary with the necessity, in so far as may be consistent with the full reasonable enjoyment of the servient tenement.

NOTES AND QUESTIONS

1 Is the assessment of the scope of an easement by necessity consistent in the two cases just discussed?

2 Compare the permissible scope of the easement by implication with that of an easement by prescription set forth next. Are different policy considerations evident between the permissible scope of the two types of easements?

Scope of Easement by Prescription In *Wright v. Horse Creek Ranches,* 697 P. 2d 384 (Colo. 1985), the Colorado court was asked if an easement by prescription could be enlarged from a dirt road, which afforded seasonal access for sightseeing and hunting, to one which provided year-round access to ten residential dwellings. The court made the following observations:

Judicial delineation of the extent of an easement by prescription should be undertaken with great caution.

Section 477 of the *Restatement of Property* offers the following principles as a reasonable standard for determining the extent of easements established by prescription: "[t]he extent of an easement created by prescription is fixed by the use through which it was created." One justification for the principle that a nonowner may establish a legally protected right to burden property possessed by another is the theory that by not protesting the adverse use to which the nonowner has put the property, the property owner can be presumed to have agreed to burden the servient estate to that degree.

Section 478 of the *Restatement of Property* states as follows:

In ascertaining whether a particular use is permissible under an easement created by prescription, a comparison must be made between such use and the use by which the easement was created with respect to (a) their physical character, (b) their purpose, (c) the relative burden caused by them upon the servient tenement.

This rule recognizes that human behavior and the circumstances that influence it inevitably change. Thus, the beneficiary of an easement established by prescription will be permitted to vary the use of the easement to a reasonable extent. This flexibility of use is limited, however, by concern for the degree to which the variance further burdens the servient estate.

5 BURDEN OF REPAIR AND MAINTENANCE

Ordinarily the obligation to repair and maintain an easement rests upon the one who is entitled to the benefit of the easement. This is true regardless of the manner in which the easement was created except that the parties to an express easement may provide that the owner of the servient estate has all or a portion of the duty to repair and maintain the easement. In the absence of an agreement to the contrary, the privilege and the duty to maintain and repair the easement rests with the owner of the dominant estate.

For instance, in *Walsh v. U.S.,* plaintiff granted a highway easement to the United States ''for purposes of a highway to be operated and maintained by the Secretary of Agriculture.'' The servient land was used to pasture cattle. Plaintiff alleged that defendant failed to maintain cattleguards so that plaintiff's livestock strayed causing damage to plaintiff's livestock operation. In holding for plaintiffs, the court stated the general rule as follows:

> The *Restatement of Property* concerns itself with such problems. Section 485 of the *Restatement of the Law of Property,* provides:
> ''In the case of an easement created by conveyance, the existence and the extent of any privilege and any duty of the owner of the easement to maintain, repair and improve the condition of the servient tenement for the purpose of increasing the effective uses of the easement are determined by the conveyance.''
> The *Restatement* comment under the foregoing section makes it clear that the problem has two aspects—who has the privilege of repairing and maintaining the easement, and who has the duty to do so. Both aspects are controllable by the terms of the conveyance, but in the absence of such terms the law grants to the owner of the easement the privilege of entering upon the easement to make reasonable repairs and the law also imposes upon the owner of the easement the duty for the benefit of the owner of the servient tenement to so maintain and repair the easement as to prevent unreasonable interference with the use of the servient tenement.

6 TRANSFER OF EASEMENTS

Although the parties to an express easement may impose limitations on the manner of transfer, for the most part, the transferability of an easement is dependent not upon the manner of its creation but upon whether it is classified as an easement appurtenant or an easement in gross.

A   Appurtenant Easements

An appurtenant easement is, for purposes of transfer, an incident of the ownership of the dominant estate. Thus, transfer of the dominant estate whether by conveyance, descent, operation of law, or any other method including even adverse possession, transfers to the new owner the rights to use the easement appurtenant. The *Restatement of Property,* Section 487, provides as follows:

> Except as prevented by the terms of its transfer or by the manner of the terms of the creation of the easement appurtenant thereto, one who succeeds to the possession of a dominant estate thereby succeeds to the privileges of use of the servient estate authorized by the easement.

NOTES AND QUESTIONS

1 Suppose the owner of the dominant estate wishes to convey the dominant estate without transferring title to the appurtenant easement attached to the dominant estate. Although there seems to be no case law directly on this point, there would seem to be no reason why the grantor could not achieve this result, although the intent to sever the easement from the dominant estate would have to be clearly stated. The *Restatement of Property,* Section 487, Comment B recognizes this right. See also *Anne Arundel v. Litz,* 12 A.2d 1256 (Maryland 1984).

2 Suppose the dominant estate is subdivided. If the dominant estate is subdivided between two or more owners and, provided, that this subdivision does not inpermissibly increase the burden upon the servient estate or violate the terms of the conveyance, the appurtenant easement also becomes subdivided and attaches to each of the new parcels that have been created.

B   Easements in Gross

We have seen that an easement in gross tends to be personal to the owner to the extent that it does not benefit any particular parcel of property. And, as in the case of appurtenant easements, the language of the grant of an easement in gross may limit its transferability.

There has been considerable inconsistency among American and English courts concerning the transferability of easements in gross. As a general rule, courts tend to distinguish between so-called commercial and noncommercial easements in gross concluding that the former but not the later are freely transferable. Thus, an easement permitting *A* to fish in *B*'s pond is likely to be considered personal to *A* and therefore not transferable. However, an easement in favor of *A* to remove timber from *B*'s property would probably be considered a commercial easement and hence more likely to be considered transferable. An easement permitting a telephone company to run wires over the land of *A*, while an easement in gross, would certainly be considered commercial and thus freely transferable.

7 TERMINATION OF EASEMENTS

Easements may terminate in a variety of ways, some involving actions by the owner of the dominant estate, some involving actions by the owner of the servient estate, some involving actions by both, and some involving actions by third parties. The methods by which easements may be extinguished also depend, to some extent, upon the manner in which the easement was created.

Termination by the Express Terms of the Grant Easements, like other interests in property, can be made defeasible on the happening of a certain event. For example, an easement for a right-of-way to *A,* for so long as the dominant estate is used as a church. Easements can be made for a limited period of time (to *A* for ten years) or they can be granted for a specific purpose and will lapse upon completion of the purpose. See e.g. *Maw v. Weber Basin Water District,* 391 P.2d 300 (Utah 1964), holding that privileges to hunt granted in exchange for use of a road was extinguished when the road was flooded by construction of a dam.

Other Means of Extinguishing Easements

Merger Acquisition of the dominant and servient estates by one person will result in extinguishment of the easement through the doctrine of merger.

Release The owner of the dominant estate can release his or her interests to the owner of the serviant estate. Because such a release involves the transfer of an interest in land, the general requirements pertaining to deeds should be followed in order to make the release effective.

Non-use and Abandonment Non-use is insufficient to terminate an easement, although a minority of jurisdictions hold that non-use may terminate a prescriptive easement. The majority rule and the position adopted by the *Restatement of Property* provide that all easements, regardless of the method of their creation, will not be extinguished by non-use alone.

Abandonment, however, involves conduct in respect to the use of an easement that indicates an intention never to make use of the easement again. If this rigorous test is satisfied, then the easement will be extinguished.

Prescription Easements can be extinguished by prescription. Thus if the owner of the servient tenement were to construct fences and plant grass and trees over a right-of-way easement, if the improvements were inconsistent with the express purpose of the easement, and if they continued for the statutory period, they would have the effect of extinguishing the express easement. See *Shelton v. Boydstun Beach Association,* 641 P.2d 1005 (Idaho 1982).

Sale to a Bona Fide Purchaser Pursuant to the operation of the recording statutes, an easement may be extinguished by sale to a good faith purchaser for value and without notice of the existence of the easement. (See generally Chapter 15 for the operation of recording statutes.) The basic idea is that if *A* gives an easement to *B,* and *B* does not record the deed of easement, and *C* purchases from *A* without notice or knowledge of the easement, *C* takes the property free of the easement.

Estoppel Under limited circumstances, easements may be extinguished by estoppel. Estoppel involves statements or conduct by a party that are reasonably relied upon by another and that create a situation in which serious harm can only be avoided by requiring a party to be bound by their words or conduct. Thus if the owner of the dominant tenement tells the owner of the servant tenement that the easement is no longer needed and, in reliance on the statement, the owner of the servient tenement erects a building across the easement, the owner of the dominant estate may be estopped to complain about the encroachment upon the easement. This position is adopted by the *Restatement,* Section 505.

Easement by Necessity   An easement by necessity is typically terminated when the necessity comes to an end. For instance, where the grantee's predecessor acquired an easement by necessity across the serviant estate for access to a beach, the easement was extinguished when a public road was built even though the road was a less convenient way to reach the beach. *Rhoto v. Rollins,* 42 S.E.2d 323 (Vir. 1948).

Excessive Use   Ordinarily an easement is not terminated by virtue of the dominant tenement's excess use of the easement. The reason for this rule is that the owner of the servant estate has redress by way of an injunction to restrain the additional use or for damages caused by the excess use. However, in the rare case where it is impossible to sever the increased burden so as to preserve for the dominant and servient tenements the rights and burdens they are entitled to, the easement may be extinguished.

Mortgage Foreclosure and Eminent Domain Proceedings   An easement may be extinguished by a mortgage foreclosure, provided that the mortgage was recorded before the holder of the mortgage had actual notice of the easement. (See generally Chapter 17 regarding mortgage foreclosure.) In addition, the exercise of the condemnation power will, under appropriate circumstances, extinguish an easement through eminent domain proceedings. (The eminent domain power is considered in Chapter 20.)

8   THE LICENSE

A license is an interest in the land of another that consists of the privilege to use the land but that does not rise to the level of an easement. For example, *A* asks *B* if *A* may put his ladder on *B*'s property for the purpose of painting *A*'s house. If *B* agrees, *A* has a license from *B* for that limited purpose. In other words, a license merely makes lawful an act that would otherwise constitute a trespass.

The general definition and rule with regard to licenses is contained in the case of *Fairbanks v. Power Oil Company,* 77 N.E. 2d 499 (Ohio 1945), that states that a license is ''a permission to do some act or series of acts on the land of the licenser without having any permanent interest in it: it is founded on personal confidence and it may not be transferred. It may be given in writing or orally: it may be with or without consideration, but in either case it is usually subject to revocation, though constituting a protection of the party acting under it until the revocation takes place.''

The *Restatement of Property* elevates the status of a license somewhat by defining it as ''an interest in land in the possession of another which is consensual and which entitles the owner of the interest to use the land of another but which is not an easement'' (*Restatement,* Section 512). The *Restatement* also provides that a license may be assignable ''insofar as it was intended in its creation to be assignable.''

Baseball Pub Company v. Bruton, 18 N.E. 2d 361 (Mass. 1938)

Facts of the case.

Plaintiff obtained from defendant a contract whereby the defendant ''in consideration of twenty-five dollars . . . agrees to give'' plaintiff ''the exclusive right and privilege to maintain an advertising sign ten feet by twenty-five feet on the wall of a building'' in Boston, owned by the defendant, ''for a period of one year with the privilege to renew from year to year for four years more at the same consideration.'' It was provided that ''all signs placed on the premises remain the personal property of the plaintiff.''

On November 10, 1934, plaintiff sent the defendant a check for $25, the agreed consideration for the first year. The defendant returned the check. The plaintiff nevertheless erected the sign, and maintained it until February 23, 1937, sending the defendant early in November of the years 1935 and 1936 checks for $25, which were returned. On February 23, 1937, the defendant caused the sign to be removed. On February 26, 1937, plaintiff brought this action for specific performance, contending that the agreement was a lease. The judge ruled that the agreement was a contract to give a license, and entered a final decree for specific performance, with damages and costs. The defendant appealed.

OPINION

The distinction between a lease and a license is plain, although at times it is hard to classify a particular instrument. A lease of land conveys an interest in land, requires a writing to comply with the statute of frauds. A license merely excuses acts done by one on land in possession of another that without the license would be a trespass. It conveys no interest in land, and may be contracted for or given orally. A lease of a roof or a wall for advertising purposes is possible. The writing in question, however, giving the plaintiff the ''exclusive right and privilege to maintain an advertising sign . . . on the wall of a building,'' but leaving the wall in the possession of the owner with the right to use it for all purposes not forbidden by the contract and with all the responsibilities of ownership and control, is not a lease. The fact that in one corner of the writing are found the words, ''Lease No. ____,'' does not convert it into a lease. Those words are merely a misdescription of the writing.

Subject to the right of a licensee to be on the land of another for a reasonable time after the revocation of a license, for the purpose of removing his or her property, it is of the essence of a license that it is revocable at the will of the possessor of the land. The revocation of a license may constitute a breach of contract and give rise to an action for damages. But it is none the less effective to deprive the licensee of all justification for entering or remaining upon the land.

If what the plaintiff bargained for and received was a license, and nothing more, then specific performance would be futile and for that reason should not be granted. Any judicial decree that might render the license irrevocable for the term of the contract would convert it into an equitable estate in land, and give the plaintiff more than the contract gave. There can be no specific performance of a contract to give a license, at least in the absence of fraud or estoppel.

The writing in the present case, however, seems to us to go beyond a mere license. It purports to give "the exclusive right and privilege to maintain" a certain sign on the defendant's wall. So far as the law permits, it should be so construed as to vest in the plaintiff the right that it purports to give. That right is in the nature of an easement in gross, which is recognized in Massachusetts. We see no objection to treating the writing as a grant for one year and a contract to grant for four more years an easement in gross thus limited to five years.

There is no err in the final decree granting specific performance. The affirmance of this decree will not prevent an assessment of the damages as of the date of the final decree after rescript.

Affirmed.

NOTES AND QUESTIONS

1 Why did the court conclude that the interest transferred was not a license? Why was it not a lease?

2 Are there situations in which a license will not be revocable by the owner of the property?

9 SUMMARY

An easement is an interest in the land of another that entitles the owner of the easement to limited use, but not possession, of another's land.

Easements may be created by an express grant or reservation, and the scope and transferability and termination of the easement will be controlled by the terms of the grant.

Easements may be created by implication. Implied easements arise in two situations but always require common ownership, at some point, of both the dominant and servient estates. In the case of an implied easement by necessity, a portion of land is transferred, leaving the other portion landlocked or essentially unusable unless an easement is implied. The easement must be strictly necessary for the beneficial use of the land. The second kind of implied easement arises from prior use as an easement, where such use is reasonably apparent by inspection of the property. An implied easement based on prior use, also known as a quasi-easement, requires only that the easement be reasonably necessary.

In the case of implied easements, the scope of the easement is measured as of the time the property was divided, subject to adjustment for normal development. Easements by necessity, however, are said to terminate when the necessity terminates. Implied easements are freely transferable.

Easements may be created by adverse use, known in the context of easements as prescription. The scope of such easements tends to be established by the extent of the use that created the easement. Easements by prescription are freely transferable and are terminated in the same manner as an express easement.

Although the initial scope of an easement depends upon the manner of its creation, all easements are deemed to anticipate reasonable changes in the use of the dominate estate.

Easements are further classified as appurtenant or in gross. An appurtenant easement is one that directly benefits a parcel of land, known as the dominant estate. In the case of an easement in gross, there is no dominant estate. Easements in gross are further delineated on the basis of whether they are commercial or noncommercial. Only commercial easements in gross are transferable.

Related to the easement is the privilege to use the land of another that is known as a license. A license is usually considered to be revocable at the will of the grantor of the license.

10 QUESTIONS

1 Alfred owns two tracts of land, tract 1 and tract 2. Only tract 1 has access to the highway. He sells tract 2 to Betty under a contract that provides "no right of way is conveyed, it being understood that Betty will obtain access to the highway through other land." Betty is unable to obtain access across other land. Is Betty entitled to an implied easement across tract 1?

2 Calvin owns property from which he extracts gravel. Calvin sells the property to Dorothy, retaining the gravel rights but without mentioning an access easement to reach the gravel. Can Calvin claim an implied easement? Would it matter if an alternative means of access were available but at considerable cost to Calvin?

3 Evelyn owns property next door to Frank. For the statutory period, Evelyn has been using a walkway on Frank's property to transport her garbage cans from her backyard to the front sidewalk. After the cans are empty, she returns them to her backyard by crossing Frank's walkway. Suddenly Frank puts up a fence that prevents Evelyn from using the passage on Frank's property. Evelyn claims she has an easement. Is she correct?

4 Assume the same facts as in Problem 3. Evelyn now builds a four-unit apartment building on the rear portion of her lot. May the occupants of the apartment house use Frank's sidewalk to get to and from the apartment?

5 Grace operates a windmill that depends upon the free flow of air across property owned by Harry. If Harry seeks to develop his property so that it interferes with Grace's windmill, is such use wrongful?

6 Irving gives an easement to Jennifer with the following limitation: "for use as a footpath to and from Jennifer's property." At the time of the transfer, Jennifer owned a five-room cottage. Many years later, the owner of Jennifer's property seeks to subdivide the property into thirty lots for single-family homes. May the new owner use the easement for a footpath

for all thirty units? May the new owner use the easement for the purpose of driving cars to the individual homes?

7 Kevin lives next to Linda. He asks Linda if he can hunt quail on her property during the hunting season, and they execute an agreement to this affect. Kevin then loses interest in hunting and sells his right to Mary. Linda objects to Mary's hunting on Linda's property. Who wins?

8 Nancy gives an easement for parking on weekend evenings to the Opera Society so long as the premises are used for opera performances. Many years later the Opera Society moves to different quarters and sells the property to a fastfood store. May patrons of the fastfood store use the parking lot on the weekend?

9 Phyllis owns property with an easement for a drain pipe across property owned by Robert. Both Phyllis and Robert die and their property goes to Sandy and Tracy respectively. Does the easement pass to the benefit of Sandy and the burden of Tracy?

10 On your next trip to Hawaii, you make reservations at the finest hotel on the Islands. What is your legal status?

CHAPTER 9

PROMISES AFFECTING THE USE OF LAND

TOPICS CONSIDERED IN THIS CHAPTER:

1 INTRODUCTION

It should be clear by now that the right to use one's property may be limited in a variety of ways. Chapter 7 considered inherent limitations on land use, based on the policy that forbids a landowner from causing unreasonable interference with a neighbor's use and enjoyment of his or her property. Chapter 8 considered the operation of easements, involving a limited right to use the land of another and to preclude the owner of the servient estate from using his or her property in a way that is inconsistent with the easement.

This chapter is concerned with the creation of property rights in the form of a promise, known as a covenant. A covenant is simply a promise to do or refrain from doing something. Rights created by a covenant typically do not permit the owner of the right to use the land of another and are different from easements in this fundamental respect.

A brief introduction to the subject of land covenants is contained in the material on condominiums in Chapter 6. We have seen that a condominium association may limit occupancy of a unit to persons of a certain age, may limit use to residential purposes, and may impose and collect assessments for the benefit of all owners of the condominium project.

This chapter examines the nature, consequences, and enforceability of covenants respecting the use of land.

It should be noted at the outset that the law as it pertains to covenants is technical and often obscure. Professor Rabin summarized the subject in the following terms:

> Although the factual situations involving promises respecting land are usually not complicated, the law in this area is an unspeakable quagmire. The intrepid soul who ventures into this formidable wilderness never emerges unscarred. Some, the smarter ones, quickly turn back to take up something easier like the income taxation of trust and estates. Others, having lost their way, plunge on and after weeks of effort emerge not far from where they began, clearly the worst for wear. On looking back they see the trail they thought they broke obscured with foul smelling waters and noxious weeds. Few willingly take up the challenge again. (Rabin, *Fundamentals of Modern Real Property Law,* 2d Edition, 1982, page 480).

Unfortunately, it is not possible to turn back or to skip ahead because private use restrictions are a pervasive aspect of modern property development and their use is increasing all the time. Virtually all modern subdivisions, condominium projects, planned unit developments, shopping centers, and industrial parks include extensive covenants, which limit and regulate the rights of occupants in their use of the property.

The confusion in this area stems from various sources. The two leading cases, *Spencer's case* (1583) and *Tulk v. Moxhay* (1848) continue to be the leading cases but, in the modern context, generate as many questions as they answer. The field has evolved into two separate but related doctrines, one known as the Doctrine of Covenants Running With the Land at Law and the other known as Equitable Servitudes, which rely, in part, upon the ability of a court of equity to fashion a flexible remedy. The American Law Institute entered the field in 1940 issuing the *Restatement of Property* as it pertains to promises affecting the use of land. The approach adopted by the *Restatement* was not without controversy and led to a series of irreverent and often highly amusing exchanges by noted legal scholars either attacking or defending the *Restatement's* approach. In the end, a coherent consensus has only vaguely emerged as the student and practitioner must make their way as best they can in the face of considerable obstacles.

2   BASIC TERMINOLOGY

Suppose that *A* owns a parcel of land, subdivides it into two parcels, selling the second parcel to *B*. Included within the deed is a covenant whereby *B* and his successors agree to furnish water and heat to the building retained by *A* for the benefit of *A* and *A*'s successors. As between *A* and *B* the promise to supply utilities is enforceable as a simple contract. However, when *A* and/or *B* die or otherwise transfer their interests in the property to *C* and *D* respectively, can *C* enforce the promise against *D?*

Before attempting to answer this question, a note on terminology may be helpful. *A* and *A*'s property have the benefit of the covenant and *B* and *B*'s property have the burden of the covenant. The person making the promise is known as the "covenantor," and the person to whom the promise is made is known as the "covenantee." There are two kinds of covenants, affirmative ones and negative ones. In our example, an affirmative covenant is involved because *B* must undertake an affirmative act, namely furnishing utilities, in order to satisfy the covenant.

When *A* and *B* die or otherwise transfer their interests in the property to *C* and *D* respectively, the ultimate question is: Can *C* (*A*'s successor) enforce the benefit of the promise against *D* (*B*'s successor)? In other words, does the benefit run with the land? Similarly, does the burden of the promise bind *D* (the successor of *B*)? In other words, does the burden of the promise run with the land?

For purposes of analysis, it is essential that one distinguish carefully between the running of the *benefit* on the one hand and the running of the *burden* on the other. If the "quagmire" suggested by Professor Rabin is to be avoided, the benefit and the burden of the promise must be evaluated separately. The law has traditionally been more willing to permit a benefit rather than a burden to run with the land. This perspective relates directly to the policy favoring the free alienation of land, as discussed in Chapter 4. A benefit, in our case the receipt of utilities, enhances the value of the property and hence, enhances the ability of the owner to transfer the property. The burden, on the other hand, is a restriction that decreases the value of the land and, according to the weight of authority, diminishes the owner's ability to alienate the property.

3 ELEMENTS REQUIRED FOR A COVENANT TO RUN WITH THE LAND

Eagle Enterprises, Inc. v. Gross, 349 N.E. 2d 816 (N.Y. 1976)

Facts of the case.

In 1951, Orchard Hill Realties, Inc., a subdivider and developer, conveyed certain property in the subdivision of Orchard Hill to William and Pauline Baum. The deed to the Baums contained the following provisions:

> The Orchard Hill shall supply to the Baums water for domestic use only, from the well located on Orchard Hill's property and the Baums agree to take said water and to pay thirty-five ($35.00) dollars per year, for water so supplied.

In addition, the deed also contained the following:

It is expressly provided that the covenants herein contained shall run with the land . . . and shall enure to the benefit of the heirs, and successors, of the respective parties hereto.

Eagle Enterprises is the successor of Orchard Hill, and Gross is the successor of the Baums. The deed from Baum to Gross does not contain the covenant to purchase water.

Gross has refused to accept and pay for water offered by Eagle Enterprises because Gross has constructed his own well to service his property. Eagle instituted this action to collect the fee specified in the covenant (contained only in the original deed to Baum) for the supply of water that, Eagle contends, Gross is bound to accept. The trial court found that the covenant ran with the land and therefore was binding upon Gross as successor to the Baums. We must now decide whether the promise of the original grantees to accept and make payment for a seasonal water supply from the well of their grantor is enforceable against subsequent grantees and may be said to run with the land.

OPINION

Regardless of the language in a deed, a promise to do an affirmative act contained in a deed is generally not binding upon subsequent grantees of the promisor unless certain well-defined and long-established requirements are satisfied. In order for a covenant to run with the land, the following must be shown:

1. The original grantee and grantor must have intended that the covenant run with the land.

2. There must exist privity of estate between the party claiming the benefit of the covenant and the right to enforce it and the party upon whom the burden of the covenant is to be imposed.

3. The covenant must be deemed to touch and concern the land with which it runs.

It is the third prong of this test that presents the obstacle to Eagle's position.

A close examination of the covenant in the case before us leads to the conclusion that it does not substantially affect the ownership interest of landowners in the Orchard Hill subdivision. The covenant provides for the supplying of water but no claim has been advanced by Eagle that the lands in the subdivision would be waterless without the water it supplies. Indeed, the facts here point to the opposite conclusion since respondent has obtained his own source of water. The record does not demonstrate that other property owners in the subdivision would be deprived of water or that the price of water would become prohibitive for other property owners if Gross were allowed to terminate the service. Thus, the agreement for the supply of water does not seem to relate in any significant degree to the ownership rights of the property owners in the subdivision of Orchard Hill. The obligation to receive water from Eagle resembles a personal, contractual promise to purchase water rather than a significant interest attaching to the property itself. It should be emphasized that the question of whether a covenant is so closely related to the use of the land that it should be deemed to run with the land is one of degree, dependent on the particular circumstances of a case. Here, the record before us is insufficient to establish that the covenant touches and concerns the land, as we have interpreted that requirement.

There is an additional reason why we are reluctant to enforce this covenant for the supply of water. The affirmative covenant is disfavored in the law because of the fear that this type of obligation imposes an undue restriction on alienation. Thus, the covenant falls prey to the criticism that it creates a burden in perpetuity and purports to bind all future owners, regardless of the use to which the land is put. Such a result militates strongly against its enforcement. On this ground also, we are of the opinion that the covenant should not be enforced as an exception to the general rule prohibiting the running of affirmative covenants.

Reversed

NOTES AND QUESTIONS

1 Is a promise to accept and pay for water any different than a promise by a condominium owner to pay for common area expenses? Under the reasoning of *Eagle Enterprises,* could a condominium unit owner refuse to pay for maintenance costs of a swimming pool by showing they did not use the pool? Does the court in *Eagle Enterprises* address this prospect?

2 In *Bremmeyer v. McKenna,* 721 P. 2d 567 (Wash. 1986), the Washington court addressed the touch and concern requirement as follows:

> A covenant is said to run with the land when it touches or concerns the land granted. As the term implies, the covenant must concern the occupation or enjoyment of the land granted and the liability to perform it, and the right to take advantage of it must pass to the successor. Conversely, if the covenant does not touch or concern the occupation or enjoyment of the land, it is a collateral and personal obligation of the grantor and does not run with the land.

3 The consequence of a covenant running with the land is that successors in interest of a promise are treated as if they had made the promise themselves. Is this a desirable social result? Would it matter if the successor did not know of the promise?

4 As indicated in the *Eagle Enterprises* case, before the benefit and burden of a covenant will run with the land certain conditions must be satisfied. (1) the promise must be enforceable as between the original parties; (2) the original parties must have intended the promise to bind successors in interest; (3) the promise must touch and concern the land; and (4) there must be privity of estate.

These requirements are more closely analyzed next.

A Enforceable Promise

This element is usually not in controversy. However, the more important question is whether the covenant must comply with the Statute of Frauds in order to be enforceable. The majority rule, endorsed by the *Restatement of Property,* Section 522, holds that real estate covenants are interests in land and must be created in conformity with the Statute of Frauds. However, a number of jurisdictions have concluded that covenants are not interests in land and hence can be created without the necessity of a writing. As a practical matter, most covenants are created in a writing of some kind, such as a deed or lease, so that in practice the application of the Statute of Fraud seldom will defeat the covenant. See, *Sims, The Law of Real Covenants,* 30 Cornell LQ1 (1944).

B Intent to Bind Successors

As in other contexts, courts have tended to determine the intention of the parties from the language of their transaction in light of the circumstances surrounding it. Technical words are not essential but certainly words such as "successors and assigns" can be persuasive evidence that the original parties intended the covenant to run with the land.

The *Restatement of Property,* Section 531, Comment A states the following rationale for the requirement of intent in order for the burden to run: "A promise respecting the use of land may be intended to be purely personal. It may be intended to be performed by the promisor only and to be binding upon him alone. There is no rule of law that will prevent such an intention from being effective. On the other hand, it may be intended that the successors of the promisor shall be bound as he was bound. Though it is possible that they may not become bound even though it was intended that they should be, since intention alone is not enough to cause them to be bound, they will not be bound unless it was intended that they should be."

C Touch and Concern

The requirement that a promise to touch and concern the land originated in the early English decision of *Spencer's case* (1583). The touch and concern requirement continues to be a part of modern law. A majority of jurisdictions use a form of economic analysis to determine whether the touch and concern requirement is met. If the burden of the covenant renders the covenantor's land less valuable, the burden touches and concerns the land. If, in turn, the benefit of the covenant renders the covenantee's land more valuable, the benefit will be deemed to touch and concern an interest in land. A promise that touches and concerns an interest in land is contrasted with a promise that is merely personal. For instance, *A* conveys property to *B* specifying in the deed that *B* shall furnish water for irrigation purposes from *B*'s land to *A*'s land. Both the benefit and the burden touch and concern the respective interests in the land. On the other hand, suppose *A* conveys property to *B* providing in the deed that, one evening per month, *B* shall prepare and serve dinner to *A*. In this example, neither the benefit nor burden of the promise has anything to do with the parties' respective interests in the property, and therefore the promise does not satisfy the touch and concern requirement, as to either the benefit or the burden. The covenant will not run to successors of either *A* or *B*.

Neponsit Property Owners Asso. v. Emigrant Industrial Bank, 15 N.E. 2d 793 (N.Y. 1938)

Facts of the case.

In 1911 Neponsit Realty subdivided land for the purpose of developing a residential community. Lots were sold to individual purchasers, each deed referring to the subdivisions map, which included a covenant providing that each purchaser agreed to pay an annual fee for the maintenance of roads, parks, and sewers in the subdivision. The covenant stated that it was binding on successors and that it should be construed as a covenant running with the land.

Plaintiff is an Association of owners that is the successor of Neponsit Realty, the original subdivider. Defendant is the successor of one of the original purchasers, who now refuses to pay the annual assessment. The trial court ruled in favor of plaintiff. Defendant appeals.

OPINION

There can be no doubt that Neponsit Realty Company intended that the covenant should run with the land and should be enforceable by a property owners' association against every owner of property in the residential tract. The language of the covenant admits of no other construction. Regardless of the intention of the parties, a covenant will run with the land and will be enforceable against a subsequent purchaser only if the covenant complies with certain legal requirements. These requirements rest upon ancient rules and precedents. The age-old essentials of a real covenant, aside from the form of the covenant, may be summarily formulated as follows: (1) It must appear that grantor and grantee intended that the covenant should run with the land; (2) it must appear that the covenant is one "touching" or "concerning" the land with which it runs; (3) it must appear that there is "privity of estate" between the party claiming the benefit of the covenant and the or party who has the burden of the covenant. Although the deeds of Neponsit Realty Company conveying lots in the tract it developed contained a provision to the effect that the covenants ran with the land, such provision in the absence of the other legal requirements is insufficient to accomplish such a purpose. The question in this case is whether the covenant can be said to "touch" or "concern" the land?

It has been often said that a covenant to pay a sum of money is a personal affirmative covenant, which usually does not concern or touch the land. Such statements are based upon English decisions that hold in effect that only covenants that compel the covenantor to submit to some restrictions on the use of his property touch or concern the land, and that the burden of a covenant that requires the covenantor to do an affirmative act, even on his own land, for the benefit of the owner of a "dominant" estate, does not run with his land. In many jurisdictions of this country the narrow English rule has been criticized, and a more liberal and flexible rule has been substituted. In this State the courts have not gone so far. We have not abandoned the historic distinction drawn by the English courts.

However, some promises to pay money have been enforced as covenants running with the land, against subsequent holders of the land who took with notice of the covenant. The distinction between covenants that run with the land and covenants that are personal must depend upon the effect of the covenant on the legal rights that otherwise would flow from ownership of land and that are connected with the land. The problem then is this: Does this covenant in purpose and effect substantially alter these rights?

Looking at the problem presented in this case and stressing the intent and substantial effect of the covenant rather than its form, it seems clear that the covenant may properly be said to touch and concern the land of the defendant and its burden should run with the land.

Affirmed.

NOTES AND QUESTIONS

The *Neponsit* case indicates the general rule that now permits any burden, either affirmative or negative, to run at law when the benefit runs. Where, however, the burden touches and concerns the land, but the benefit is personal to the grantor, some jurisdictions will enforce the burden while others refuse to enforce it. The latter view is endorsed by the *Restatement of Property,* Section 537, although this view has been subject to considerable criticism.

D   Privity of Estate

In order for the burdens and benefits of a covenant to run with successors in interest, there must be privity of estate. The *Bremmeyer* and *Neponsit* cases have alluded to this requirement.

Horizontal Privity of Estate   Although courts often fail to recognize the distinction, there are clearly two kinds of privity. The first and most difficult is known as horizontal privity. It refers to the grantor-grantee relationship of the original parties. For example, where *A* owns a parcel, subdivides it into two parcels, and sells one half to *B*, *A* and *B* are considered to have horizontal privity of estate between them because of the former unity of title. There are three generally recognized approaches with regard to the existence of horizontal privity for purposes of the running of the covenants with the land.

The most restrictive form of horizontal privity is known as ''Massachusetts privity'' based on a famous decision in 1837, which established a peculiar approach to the problem. The Massachusetts doctrine, which has been followed in modified form only by the State of Nevada, holds that the covenanting parties must hold simultaneous interests in the same parcel of property before horizontal privity will be deemed to exist. In other words, where *A* subdivides and conveys half of a parcel to *B,* no horizontal privity exists under the Massachusetts rule because the grantor and grantee do not hold continuous interests in the same parcel. Under this rule, only a landlord-tenant relationship and the relationship between the grantor and grantee of an easement will suffice to satisfy horizontal privity because only then do the parties have a continuous and simultaneous interest in the property.

A second form of horizontal privity, adopted by the *Restatement of Property,* Section 534, contains what is probably the slight majority rule among American jurisdictions. This form of horizontal privity requires simply a transfer of some interest in the land between parties to the covenant. In other words, in our previous example, where *A* subdivides and transfers to *B,* horizontal privity would be considered to exist.

The third view favored by most legal writers and probably the modern trend, simply abolishes the requirement of horizontal privity. This view would provide that *A* and *B,* simply neighbors with no common ownership in the land, may create covenants that, provided they satisfy the other requirements, will run with the land.

There is considerable confusion among the cases as to whether horizontal privity is, in fact, required. As indicated, a slight majority of jurisdictions require the common ownership form of vertical privity although, even in some of these states, covenants have been permitted to run with land in the absence of horizontal privity or without a useful discussion of the requirement.

Some commentators suggest that the question ultimately boils down to whether the social utility of a particular restrictive covenant outweighs the burden it may impose upon interests in land. If it does, the covenant should be encouraged and allowed to run without undue interference of technical rules such as privity. On the other hand, if a particular restrictive covenant is considered to unduly burden the marketability of property, its enforceability against successors should be limited, and one of the ways to accomplish this is through strict application of the privity requirements.

Vertical Privity of Estate   Vertical privity of estate is somewhat easier to comprehend and apply. Vertical privity refers simply to the interests in the property obtained by successors to the original parties. Thus, where *A* and *B* enter into a covenant, *A* conveys to *C* and *B* conveys to *D. C,* having acquired the interest or estate of *A,* is in vertical privity with *A.* And *D,* having acquired the interest or estate of *B,* has vertical privity of estate with *C.* The primary complication involving vertical privity is that the successors must succeed to an estate of equal dignity to that of the original parties. In other words if *A,* the owner of a fee, transfers a life estate or a leasehold interest, the majority rule is that there is no horizontal privity of estate because the ownership interests of *A* and his successor are not the same.

The doctrine of privity of estate is an area in which the law has been largely unable to modify the rigid formalism of the common law. Statutes in a few states have been enacted to clarify the situation, and such efforts are to be encouraged. The California statute that follows makes certain modifications to the common law rule. What are these changes? Are they desirable? Should the statute have gone further?

California Civil Code Section 1468

Each covenant, made by an owner of land with the owner of other land or made by a grantor of land with the grantee of land conveyed, to do or refrain from doing some act on his own land, which is expressed to be for the benefit of the land of the covenantee, runs with both the land owned by or granted to the covenantor and the land owned by or granted to the covenantee and shall, except as specifically provided in the instrument creating such covenant, benefit or be binding upon each successive owner, during his ownership, of any portion of such land affected thereby and upon each person having any interest therein derived through any owner thereof where all of the following requirements are met:

a. The land of the covenantor which is to be affected by such covenants, and the land of covenantee to be benefited, are particularly described in the instrument containing such covenants;

b. Such successive owners of the land are in such instrument expressed to be bound thereby for the benefit of the land owned by, granted by, or granted to the covenantee;

c. Each such act relates to the use, repair, maintenance, or improvement of, or payment of taxes and assessments on, such land or some part thereof, for a period which is reasonable in relation to the purpose of the covenant;

d. The instrument containing such covenants is recorded in the office of the recorder of each county in which such land or some part thereof is situated.

Malley v. Hanna, 480 N.E. 2d 1068 (N.Y. 1985)

Facts of the case.

Plaintiffs brought this action to enforce a restrictive covenant against defendants that prohibits the construction of two-family dwellings.

Browncroft Extension, a residential neighborhood in the City of Rochester was originally assembled by Brown Brothers Company. Defendants' parcel derives directly from a deed conveyed by Brown Brothers in 1916 in which nine lots, including defendants' four, were transferred to Browncroft Realty Corporation. The conveyance was subject to the following restrictions: "each lot in the [Browncroft] tract . . . shall be used for residence purposes only and no double house, Boston flat, or apartment house, shall ever be built upon any lot in said tract." Subsequently, the property was conveyed in part several times, including in 1983 when four lots were purchased by defendants. Each conveyance, including the transfer to defendants, explicitly provided that title was taken subject to the covenants of record and specifically referred to the Browncroft Extension.

Plaintiff Malley's property, consisting of one lot located three lots east of defendants' parcel, was originally conveyed by Brown Brothers in 1929 and contains the same restriction that was inserted in defendant's deed.

OPINION

In order to establish the privity requisite to enforce a restrictive covenant, a party need only show that his property derives from the original grantor who imposed the covenant and whose property was benefited thereby, and concomitantly, that the party to be burdened derives his property from the original grantee who took the property subject to the restrictive covenant. This "vertical privity" arises wherever the party seeking to enforce the covenant has derived his title through a continuous lawful succession from the original grantor.

The facts establish the requisite vertical privity. Plaintiff Malley derives title to his property from Brown Brothers. The latter burdened the property conveyed to defendants' predecessor by subjecting the conveyance to the restrictive covenant in question, and this covenant, in turn, accrued to the benefit of the property retained by Brown Brothers, including that lot ultimately obtained by Malley. Each transfer was subject to the covenant in question originally imposed by Brown Brothers upon defendants' predecessor in title. Vertical privity requires nothing more.

Finally, contrary to defendants' contention, plaintiff Malley's right to enforce the restrictive covenant does not depend upon his demonstrating a common plan or scheme. Indeed, once the requisite vertical privity has been established, the existence of a plan or scheme need not be determined. Rather, it is sufficient that the surrounding circumstances manifest the original grantor's intent that the covenant run with the land.

Here, the nature of the covenant as one running with the land is clearly revealed by the following; the language of the covenant in defendants' chain of title speaks in terms of perpetuity—i.e., "no double house . . . shall ever be built" on the land originally retained—i.e., including that now owned by Malley—necessarily benefited from the covenant; every conveyance and other relevant instrument of Brown Brothers, the original grantor, included in the record contains an identical or similar covenant; and, indeed, every conveyance in each of the parties' chain of title contains the same either explicitly or by unmistakable reference. There is no requirement to establish that, in addition to the foregoing, there existed a common scheme or plan covering every deed from the original grantor of the originally entitled Browncroft Extension.

Affirmed.

NOTES AND QUESTIONS

1 The *Restatement* approach requires the existence either of mutual privity or "co-ownership" privity and vertical privity in order for the burden to run. However, only vertical privity is necessary for the benefit to run with the land.

2 In the light of Civil Code Section 1468, what is the California rule with regard to the privity requirement?

E A Brief Review

Recall the example given earlier in this chapter in which *A* owns a parcel of land, divides it into two parcels and sells one of them to *B*. The deed from *A* to *B* contains a covenant providing that *B* and his successors agree to furnish water and heat to the building retained by *A* for the benefit of *A* and *A*'s successors and assigns. *A* transfers her interest to *C* and *B* transfers her interest to *D*. Is the covenant enforceable between *C* and *D?*

In the first place, it appears that the original agreement between *A* and *B* was an enforceable contract as there is nothing in our example to suggest otherwise. *A* and *B*, by the language they used, have indicated an intent that the promise run to successors in interest. This is particularly evidenced by their use of the words ''successors and assigns.'' In addition, the benefit touches and concerns the land because it involves furnishing a service to be used on *A*'s land and thereby benefits the land itself. Under the majority view, this is enough for both the benefit and the burden to run. Even under the minority view, it appears that the burden would run, particularly if the utility services are being furnished from parcel *B*. In this case, the burden would be an economic detriment to the land itself and would be considered to touch and concern the burdened parcel. Finally, except in Massachusetts and Nevada, there is horizontal privity of estate because *A* was originally the common owner of the entire parcel who severed a portion of the land and transferred it to *B*. *C*, having succeeded to *A*'s interest, is in vertical privity of estate with *A*. *D*, having succeeded to *B*'s interest, is in vertical privity of estate with *B*. In those jurisdictions following what is probably still the minority but emerging rule, no horizontal privity is necessary although vertical privity continues to be a requirement. In either case, it appears that the requirements have been met in this case and, in nearly all jurisdictions, the covenant between *A* and *B* will run with the land at law and run to the benefit and burden of successors of the original covenantor and covenantee.

4 EQUITABLE SERVITUDES

Tulk v. Moxhay, Eng. Rep. 1143 (1848)

Facts of the case.

In the year 1808 the Plaintiff, being then the owner in fee of a vacant piece of ground in Leicester Square, as well as of several of the houses forming the Square, sold the property by the description of "Leicester Square garden or pleasure ground, with the equestrian statue then standing in the centre thereof, and the iron railing and stone work round the same," to one Elms in fee: the deed of conveyance contained a covenant by Elms, for himself, his heirs, and assigns, with the plaintiff, his heirs, and assigns, "that Elms, his heirs, and assigns should, and would from time to time, and at all times thereafter at his and their own cost and charge, keep and maintain the said piece of ground and square garden, and the iron railing round the same in its then form, and in sufficient and proper repair as a square garden and pleasure ground, in an open state, uncovered with any buildings, in neat and ornamental order."

The piece of land so conveyed passed by after various conveyances into the hands of the Defendant, whose purchase deed contained no similar covenant with his seller; but he admitted that he knew of the covenant in the deed of 1808 when he purchased the property.

The Defendant having manifested an intention to alter the character of the square garden, and asserted a right, if he thought fit, to build upon it, the Plaintiff, who still remained owner of several houses in the square, filed this bill for an injunction; and an injunction was granted to restrain the Defendant from converting or using the piece of ground and square garden, and the iron railing round the same, to or for any other purpose than as a square garden and pleasure ground in an open state, and uncovered with buildings.

Defendant appealed.

OPINION

Defendant contends that the covenant did not run with the land so as to be binding at law upon a purchaser from the covenantor.

That this court has jurisdiction to enforce a contract between the owner of land and his neighbor purchasing a part of it, that the latter shall either use or abstain from using the land purchased in a particular way, is not disputed. Here there is no question about the contract: the owner of certain houses in the square sells the land adjoining, with a covenant from the purchaser not to use it for any other purpose than as a square garden. And it is now contended, not that the original buyer could violate that contract, but that he might sell the piece of land, and that the purchaser from him may violate it without this Court having any power to interfere. If that were so, it would be impossible for an owner of land to sell part of it without incurring the risk of rendering what he retains worthless. It is said that, the covenant being one which does not run with the land, this Court cannot enforce it; but the question is, not whether the covenant runs with the land, but whether a party shall be permitted to use the land in a manner inconsistent with the contract entered into by his seller, and with notice of which he purchased. Of course, the price would be affected by the covenant, and nothing could be more inequitable than that the original purchaser should be able to sell the property the next day for a greater price, in consideration of the assignee being allowed to escape from the liability which he had himself undertaken.

Affirmed.

NOTES AND QUESTIONS

Tulk v. Moxhay was the answer fashioned by the English courts of equity to circumvent the rigid and technical rules applied by courts in the case of covenants running with the land at law. It is from this case that the Doctrine of

Equitable Servitudes has been developed in America. Under the Doctrine of Equitable Servitudes, an agreement may be enforced as an equitable servitude against the burdened land even in cases where the agreement is unenforceable as a covenant running with the land.

5 ELEMENTS OF EQUITABLE SERVITUDES

1 An agreement binding between the original parties

As in the case of covenants running with the land at law, whatever agreement was made by the original parties must have been enforceable between them. This is a contract question and requires that the agreement be sufficiently definite, that it be supported by consideration and, in most states, that the agreement be in writing.

2 Touch and concern

As in the case of covenants at law, an equitable servitude must touch and concern the land in order for successors to be bound. The requirement in this regard is essentially identical to that pertaining to covenants at law.

3 Intent to bind successors in interest

As in the case of covenants at law, an equitable servitude will only bind successors in interest if both original parties to the agreement intended that it bind successors in interest. For all practical purposes, the necessary intent is established in the same way as it is established in the case of covenants at law. The intent to bind successors is ordinarily evidenced by express language in the grant pertaining to successors, assigns, and so forth. However, the context in which the restrictions were made is also relevant in determining the required intent. For instance, one court examined a grant containing restrictions that specified that they were to run to the benefit and burden of heirs and assigns. However, the grantors retained the right to release the restrictions as to other lots they owned and to sell the remaining land without the restrictions. The covenant was held personal because of the grantors right to release the restriction. See *Maples v. Horton,* 80 S.E.2d 38 (N.C. 1954).

Privity

Horizontal Privity A major difference between covenants at law and equitable restrictions is that horizontal privity is not necessary in the case of an equitable servitude. Equitable servitudes apply, in effect, the minority doctrine as it relates to horizontal privity of estate and allow two land owners who are strangers in title to one another to enter into a binding agreement, and under appropriate circumstances, make the agreement binding upon their successors.

Vertical Privity The requirement of vertical privity is also modified in the case of equitable servitudes. Some commentators have suggested that equitable restrictions "sink their tentacles into the soil." This apparently means that the servitude runs with the land itself as opposed to a covenant at law which runs with an estate in land. An equitable servitude will run to a successor who has a lesser estate than the grantor, while this is usually not the case with a covenant at law. Assume that *A* owns property burdened by a covenant and leases the property to *B*. There is no vertical privity of estate between *A* and *B,* because *B* has a lesser estate than *A.* However, this fact alone will not prevent the running of the burden to *B* as an equitable servitude.

The *Restatement of Property* states the issue as follows:

> The equitable obligation has as a corollary to it an equitable interest in the land of the promisor which is affected by the promise. The burden of this equitable interest binds all those having an interest in the land subordinate to or arising after that of the promisor who possesses the land without defense to it, regardless of whether they have the same estate the promisor had or whether they succeeded him in anything other than possession. (*Restatement of Property,* Section 539, Illustration 3, 1944).

Notice In *Tulk v. Moxhay,* the court established the rule that equity will enforce a covenant against subsequent purchasers with notice independently of the question of whether the covenant will run with the land at law. The subject of notice is more fully discussed in Chapter 15, which examines the operation of the recording statutes. At this juncture, a brief summary will suffice: There are three kinds of notice. The first is actual notice, which is similar to knowledge or awareness induced by the actual receipt of information. This was the kind of notice that existed in the case of *Tulk v. Moxhay* because the defendant actually knew of the restriction. The second kind of notice is constructive notice, the kind which is imparted by virtue of compliance with the recording statutes. In other words, if an instrument is properly recorded, a subsequent purchaser is deemed to know of the restriction, even if he or she had no actual notice of it. Finally, there is inquiry notice, which is notice that is obtained from the condition of the land itself. In other words, if the condition of the land or the circumstances surrounding the transaction would make a reasonably prudent person conduct further investigation, he or she will be deemed to know everything such an investigation would have disclosed.

Sandborn v. McLean, 206 N.W. 496 (Mich. 1925)

Facts of the case.

Defendant Christina McLean owns lot 86 of Green Lawn subdivision, located on Collingwood Avenue in the City of Detroit. Mr. and Mrs. McLean started to erect a gasoline filling station at the rear end of their lot, and they were enjoined by decree from doing so, and bring the issues before us by appeal.

Collingwood Avenue is a residential street with single, double, and apartment houses. Plaintiffs are owners of land adjoining and in the vicinity of defendants' land and who claim that the proposed gasoline station will be a nuisance and is in violation of the general plan fixed for use of all lots on the street for residence purposes only. Defendants insist that no restrictions appear in their chain of title, and they purchased without notice of any restriction limiting the use of their property. The subdivision consists of ninety-eight lots, which trace their common ownership to Robert J. and Joseph R. McLaughlin. The deeds conveying approximately seventy of the lots contained the following restriction.

> No residence shall be erected upon said premises which shall cost less than $2,500.00 and nothing but residences shall be erected on said premises.

It appears that the original deed from the McLaughlins to defendant's predecessor did not contain the restriction.

OPINION

If the owner of two or more lots, so situated as to bear the relation, sells one with restrictions of benefit to the land retained, the servitude becomes mutual, and, during the period of restraint, the owner of the lot or lots retained can do nothing forbidden to the owner of the lot sold. For want of a better descriptive term, this is styled a reciprocal negative easement. It runs with the land sold by virtue of express fastening to the land and abides with the land retained until loosened by expiration of its period of service or by events working its destruction. It is not personal to owners, but operates upon use of the land by any owner having actual or constructive notice of it.

In this case, the original plan was repeatedly declared in subsequent sales of lots by restrictions in the deeds, and, while some lots sold were not so restricted, the purchasers thereof, in every instance, observed the general plan and purpose of the restrictions in building residences. For upward of thirty years, the united efforts of all persons interested have carried out the common purpose of making and keeping all the lots strictly for residences, and defendants are the first to depart therefrom.

When Mr. McLean purchased on contract in 1910 or 1911, there was a partly built dwelling house on lot 86, which he completed and now occupies. He had an abstract of title, which he examined and claims he was told by the grantor that the lot was unrestricted. Considering the character of use made of all the lots open to a view of Mr. McLean when he purchased, we think, he was put thereby to inquiry, beyond asking his grantor, whether there were restrictions. He could not avoid noticing the strictly uniform residence character given the lots by the expensive dwellings thereon, and the least inquiry would have quickly developed the fact that lot 86 was subjected to a reciprocal negative easement, and he could finish his house, and, like the others, enjoy the benefits of the easement. We do not say Mr. McLean should have asked his neighbors about restrictions, but we do say that with the notice he had from a view of the premises on the street, clearly indicating the residences were built and the lots occupied in strict accordance with a general plan, he was put to inquiry, and, had he inquired, he would have found of record the reason for such general conformation, and the benefits thereof serving the owners of lot 86 and the obligations running with such service and available to adjacent lot owners to prevent a departure from the general plan by an owner of lot 86.

Affirmed.

NOTES AND QUESTIONS

1 What sort of inquiry should McLean have undertaken? Would the outcome be different if there was a gas station across the street from the McLean property?

2 To summarize, an equitable servitude will arise to bind successors in interest where an enforceable obligation was created by parties having an intent that successors be bound, where the agreement touches and concerns the land, and where the owner of the burdened property acquired his or her interest with notice of the restriction.

3 The *Restatement of Property*, Section 539, summarizes the Doctrine of Equitable Servitudes as follows:

> The equitable interest resulting solely from the enforceability in equity of a promise respecting the use of land is effective against the successors in title or possession of the promisor, except as they are entitled to the protection of the recording acts or the defense of a bona fide purchaser for value.

Under the *Restatement* view, even those who do not have notice of the restriction will be bound by it if they did not pay value for their interest. In other words, people who acquire by gift or through a will, having not parted with consideration, are bound by the restriction even if they did not have notice of it.

6 TERMINATION OF COVENANTS

A restrictive covenant can be terminated in a variety of ways, some of which have been encountered in connection with the termination of other interests in real estate.

1 A covenant can expire pursuant to the terms of its creation. In other words, if the original document creating the covenant or equitable servitude provides that it is to continue in force for a certain period of time or until the happening of some event, then the occurrence of this event will have the effect of terminating the covenant. For instance, a covenant can be created to last ''until the benefited parcel is further subdivided.''

2 Merger, or unity of ownership, of both the benefited and burdened parcels extinguishes the covenant. This is consistent with the termination of an easement by merger although, in the case of covenants, the covenant will not be revived in the event that the unity of ownership is severed. Finally, where the unity of ownership is only partial, the covenant remains in force as to the area or interest that is not merged. (See *Restatement of Property*, Section 555, Comment D).

3 Termination can be by subsequent agreement. The party deriving the benefit of the covenant may agree to release the burdened property from the effects of the covenant. Ordinarily, such a release must comply with the Statute of Frauds in order to be effective.

4 Abandonment of a covenant is analogous to termination of an easement by abandonment. Abandonment involves conduct by the owner of the benefited land clearly showing an intent to relinquish the benefit of the servitude. See *Thodus v. Shirk*, 79 N.W.2d 733 (Iowa 1956).

5 Estoppel can terminate a covenant. As we have seen in other contexts, estoppel involves conduct by a party indicating an intention that certain rights will not be enforced coupled with reasonable reliance by the second party and serious prejudice if the first party were allowed to enforce their rights. For instance, a Texas case involved a situation where an employee of the Homeowners' Association assisted in preparing an incorrect survey and concealed from both the Homeowners' Association and the individual homeowner the fact that the homeowner's proposed construction plans violated a setback requirement contained in the projects restrictive covenants. After construction was completed, the Homeowners' Association learned of the error and sought to compel the owner to remove the offending portion of the structure. This relief was denied because the Association was estopped to complain of the violation. See *Sugarcreek Homes Assn. v. Berry,* 590 S.W.2d 590 (Tex. Civ. App. 1979).

6 Equitable defenses can terminate a covenant. The owner of the burdened land may, under appropriate circumstances, assert various equitable defenses to enforcement of the covenant. For instance, where the complaining party has himself breached the covenant, they may not be permitted to enforce it for their benefit by virtue of the doctrine of unclean hands. For example, in a residential subdivision where one owner violates setback requirements, that owner may be precluded from enforcing the restriction as against other owners. Similar to unclean hands is the *defense of acquiescence,* which arises where owners knowingly permit covenants to be violated. They will be precluded from enforcing the covenant against subsequent grantees. For instance, where a homeowners' association has permitted some owners to violate restrictive covenants, the association may not be permitted to enforce those same covenants against other parties.

7 Change of neighborhood conditions can terminate a covenant. This method of terminating covenants is related to the doctrines of abandonment and acquiescence and is based upon equitable considerations. For example, in *El Di, Inc. v. Bethany Beach,* 477 A. 2d 1066 (Del. 1984), plaintiff owned property burdened by a restrictive covenant that prohibited the sale of alcoholic beverages and provided for residential use only. The restrictions were imposed in 1901 when the Town was first developed. Since that time, numerous commercial uses had intruded into the restricted area and several establishments sold alcohol. In permitting the plaintiff to sell liquor, the court stated the general rule:

> A court will not enforce a restrictive covenant where a fundamental change has occurred in the intended character of the neighborhood that renders the benefits underlying imposition of the restrictions incapable of enjoyment. Review of all the facts and circumstances convinces us that the change, since 1901, in the character of that area of the old Town section now zoned C-1 is so substantial as to justify modification of the deed restriction.

8 Termination can be by the act of a public authority. Condemnation can proceed so as to extinguish restrictive covenants, although compensation typically must be paid. See Chapter 20, section 5.

9 A zoning ordinance will only supersede a restrictive covenant in the somewhat unusual case that the zoning ordinance is more restrictive than the covenant. This rule applies regardless of whether the covenant or the zoning ordinance was enacted first. For example, if the zoning ordinance contains a thirty-foot height limitation but a restrictive covenant contain a twenty-foot height limitation, the covenant will prevail. On the other hand, if the zoning ordinance provides for a twenty-foot height limitation but the restrictive covenant provides for a thirty-foot height limitation then the zoning ordinance prevails to that extent.

7 SUMMARY

Promises that affect the use of land are of two kinds. The first are known as covenants that run with the land. The second are less formal and are known as equitable servitudes. Both have the effect of precluding a use of land that is inconsistent with the restriction.

In order to run with the land at law, a covenant or promise must be made that is, or would have been, enforceable between the original parties who made the promise. The original parties must have indicated an intent that the burden and benefit of the promise run to successors of the original parties. This intent can be ascertained by the language used or by the circumstances surrounding the transaction or both. In addition, a promise must touch and concern the land. This usually involves an economic analysis as to whether the benefit and burden affect the value of the respective parcels. Finally, there must be privity of estate in order for a covenant to run with the land. Privity of estate is of two types: horizontal privity and vertical privity. Horizontal privity refers to the existence of a mutual interest in the land of the original parties to the covenant. Two jurisdictions require a continuing mutual interest in the land, such as that created by an easement. The slight majority approach requires only a momentary mutual interest such as where a common owner sells a portion of the property. A growing minority of jurisdictions dispense with the requirement of horizontal privity altogether. Vertical privity of estate is that which obtains by virtue of the grantor-grantee relationship.

Where the technical requirements of running covenants at law are not satisfied, the benefit and burden of the promise may still be enforced as an equitable servitude. The most important difference between covenants at law and equitable servitudes is that servitudes do not require horizontal privity of estate and require a modified type of vertical privity. In addition, an equitable servitude will usually be enforced against one who has notice of the restriction.

8 QUESTIONS

1 Alice sells her adjacent parcel to Bob with a covenant that Bob will furnish Alice and her successors heat from a boiler on the property conveyed. Alice transfers the property to Carl. May Carl enforce the covenant against Bob?
2 Dorothy transferred an easement for a sewer line to Elston with a covenant that Elston, and his successors, agree to pay for damage to Dorothy's land caused by the easement. Elston transfers to Francis. The sewer line then explodes causing damage to Dorothy's property. Can she enforce the promise against Francis?

3 George purchases property with the restriction that it be used as a "single-family residence." George then used the property as a group home for retarded adults. A neighbor seeks to restrain the use. Assume that all necessary elements for a covenant at law and/or an equitable servitude are met. Who wins?

4 Happy Homes is a residential subdivision, with restrictive covenants limiting use to single-family homes. Just across the street from Happy Homes, a shopping center is being built. Irma owns a lot in Happy Homes and wants to devote it to retail use. She claims that the shopping center indicates that the neighborhood has changed. Is she correct?

5 The subdivision of Forest Hill had a restriction that said "no nuisance shall be maintained on any lot hereby conveyed." Defendant collected eight wrecked automobiles on the property. Has the restriction been violated?

6 Johnson owns parcel A and Katherine owns parcel B. Their properties have a common border. They enter into an agreement whereby they agree that no structure in excess of twenty-five feet will be built on either parcel. Is there privity of estate between Johnson and Katherine?

TRANSFER OF INTERESTS IN REAL ESTATE

CHAPTER 10

TRANSFER OF INTERESTS IN LAND WITHOUT A LAND CONTRACT

TOPICS CONSIDERED IN THIS CHAPTER:

1 INTRODUCTION

Prior chapters considered the interests that can be created in land along with the limitations that may be imposed upon the creation of those interests. Chapters 11 through 16 will examine, in some detail, the modern real estate transaction, which contemplates a voluntary transfer of ownership under a contract of sale. The present chapter describes the other methods by which interests in real estate may be transferred from one person to another.

2 TRANSFER BY GIFT

A gift is a voluntary transfer of an interest in property by the owner (known as the donor) to another (known as the donee). A gift is not accompanied by consideration or compensation, and this feature distinguishes a gift from a transfer by a contract of sale. Gifts can be made during the life of the donor, in which case they are known as intervivos gifts. Gifts which take effect upon the death of the donor are known as testamentary gifts and are treated in this chapter under the topic of Wills.

Hayes v. Hayes, 148 N.W. 125 (Minn. 1914)

Facts of the case.

Timothy Hayes was a prosperous farmer with five sons. As each son came of age, he would purchase a farm for that son to live on and work. For the two oldest boys, the father made a deed out. However, the second son proved improvident and mortgaged the farm. Thereafter title to the farms for the three younger sons remained with the father.

Matthew Hayes was Timothy's fourth son. In 1892 Timothy purchased a farm for him, and Matthew took possession of it that year. In May 1903, Matthew and the defendant Susie Hayes were married. On March 15, 1909, Matthew died. On April 13, 1909, Timothy, the owner of record, executed a deed to his eldest son, Richard Hayes, the plaintiff in this action. Richard recorded the deed and on April 29, 1909, Richard wrote and mailed to Susie, Matthew's widow, the following letter:

Lebannon, April 29, 1909

Mrs. Susie Hayes:

I suppose that you are aware that we own that place now; you have no more to do with it. There is no use in you bothering yourself about the crop, as we are entitled to the share of it. I want you to vacate our place as soon as you can, May 10th at latest.

Yours respectfully,

Richard Hayes

Susie Hayes, the defendant in this action, claimed to own the farm as the sole heir of her husband, Matthew, and refused to vacate. The present action was then commenced. The complaint was in the usual form, alleging title in plaintiffs, and wrongful withholding of possession by defendant. The trial court ruled in favor of Susie Hayes and found that Timothy made a gift of the farm to Matthew. This appeal followed.

OPINION

It appears with little dispute that Matthew Hayes, at all times during the seventeen years that he lived on the farm, treated it as his own. He added to the land by purchases of adjoining parcels, constructed buildings, paid taxes and insurance, and put in and took off crops each year. His relations with his father and brothers were entirely friendly. There is evidence that the father considered the farm as Matt's. Indeed, the evidence is persuasive, considering the entire situation, that but for the accident that caused the son's death there would have been no claim that Matthew did not own the land. The father admitted that he put Matt on the farm, but denied that he gave it to him. He testified:

> I did not exactly put him on it. I told him he might go on. He wanted to go West. I told him he could make a start, and go anytime he had a mind to. I told him, if he wanted, he could live a few years on it until he got started.

There was some testimony of a like purport by brothers of Matthew. But the facts are not quite consistent with this claim of a temporary loan of the place until Matt could "make a start." His marriage, the purchase of additional land, the building of a new barn and other improvements, and preparations, stopped by his death, to build a new house, are circumstances that indicate at least the son's belief that he owned the land and his intention to make it the permanent home of himself and wife. There is evidence, also, of declarations of Timothy Hayes to the effect that the farm was Matt's.

Without further stating here the evidence bearing on the question, our conclusion from the entire record is that there was enough reasonably tending to show a parol gift of the land from Timothy Hayes to his son Matthew to make the question one for the jury.

Affirmed.

NOTES AND QUESTIONS

1 Most cases on the issue hold that three elements are necessary in order to make a valid gift. These are the following:

a The intention of the grantor to make a present gift;
b Delivery of the gift to the donee;
c Acceptance of the gift by the donee.

Were these elements satisfied in the *Hayes* case? How does one make a delivery of real estate?

2 The *Hayes* case is another example of the separation of legal and equitable title to the same parcel of land. Prior to the judgment in this case, who had legal title? Who had equitable title?

3 TRANSFER BY WILL

A will is a written document executed in compliance with specific legal formalities that contains instructions as to the manner in which the owner's property will be distributed at death. A will can dispose only of property which the deceased owns at the time of his or her death. Accordingly, property held in joint tenancy passes, at the moment of death, to the surviving joint tenant and is not subject to the provisions of a will.

The most common issues arising in connection to wills involve challenges that the maker of the will lacked ''testamentary capacity'' or failed to comply with the statutory formalities in preparing the will. *The Estate of Kern* case that follows represents a typical analysis as to the existence of testamentary capacity.

In the Matter of Estate of Kern, 716 P. 2d 528 (Kan. 1986)

Facts of the case.

Birdie Kern was eighty-three years old when she was diagnosed as terminally ill. She had an attorney draw up her will leaving all of her property to two friends, William and Doris Stowell, and excluding her only living relations, two sisters, one brother, and a large number of nephews and nieces. One of the nieces challenged the will claiming that the beneficiaries exercised undue influence over Ms. Kern.

OPINION

The court addressed these issues as follows:

It is the established rule that the deceased possesses testamentary capacity if, on the date she executes the will certain conditions are present. She must know and understand the nature and extent of her property, have an intelligent understanding concerning the disposition she desires to make of it, realize who her relatives are and who the natural objects of her bounty are, and comprehend the nature of the claims of those whom she desires to include and exclude in and from participation in her worldly effects after she has no further need for them.

Here, there is no question that Birdie Kern knew the nature and extent of her property. She knew how she wanted it to go at her death; she knew the names of her brothers and sisters; she knew which of them were deceased; she knew that she wanted to leave nothing to her surviving brother and sisters. We conclude that the trial court's disposition of this issue is well reasoned and should be affirmed.

We turn next to the contention that Birdie Kern was unduly influenced by the Stowells, and that the trial court erred in finding no undue influence.

Undue influence to invalidate a will must amount to such coercion, compulsion, or constraint that the testator's free agency is destroyed, and by overcoming his power of resistance, the testator is obliged to adopt the will of another rather than exercise his own.

In this case it is true that the Stowells were friends of Ms. Kern and that she relied upon their judgement in conducting her personal and business affairs. She was, in other words, in a confidential relationship with the Stowells. However, the mere existence of a confidential relationship between Birdie Kern and the Stowells does not raise a presumption that they exercised undue influence over her. Birdie Kern stated emphatically, at the time of the signing of the will, that the Stowells made no suggestion to her that she leave her property to them. There is no evidence that the Stowells exercised undue influence over her.

In addition, there was clear and undisputed evidence that Birdie Kern was afforded independent advice by her attorney. The evidence before the trial court supports its finding that the will was free of any undue influence.

Affirmed.

NOTE ON FORMALITIES

All jurisdictions require that two, or sometimes three, persons witness the signing of the will. This process usually requires that the maker sign the will in the presence of the witness who then signs the will, attesting to the fact that he ''witnessed'' the maker's signature. Why does the law insist upon such formalities? What are the consequences of failing to satisfy them?

4   TRANSFER AT DEATH WITHOUT A WILL (INTESTATE SUCCESSION)

A person who dies without having left a valid will is said to die ''intestate.'' When this happens, the decedent's property will be distributed to his or her heirs if there are any, according to the state's law on intestate succession.

Intestacy may be partial or total. In other words, if one dies without a will or if the will is declared totally invalid, for whatever reason, all of the decedent's estate passes by virtue of the laws of intestate succession. However, a decedent may die partially intestate. For instance, if the testator's will directs only that the ''house goes to *A* and the car to *B*.'' This intent will be carried out and the balance of the estate will be distributed according to the laws of intestate succession. The problem of partial intestacy illustrates the need for careful drafting of wills. Ordinarily, the problem is resolved through the use of a residuary clause specifying the person or persons who is to take the rest ''residue and remainder'' of the decedent's estate.

Statutes of descent and distribution vary from state to state, but they usually seek to distribute a decedent's property to his or her ''natural objects of bounty'' based upon the heir's ''degree of kinship'' with the decedent. Accordingly, the surviving spouse and children are the first to take. If there are both a surviving spouse and children, they usually divide the estate—for instance, one-half to the surviving spouse, one-half to all of the surviving children. If there is no surviving spouse or children, the property is then distributed to the decedent's parents, brothers and sisters, and nieces and nephews. If there are no survivors in this class, the property is distributed to the decedent's grandparents and their descendants, namely the uncles, aunts, and cousins of the decedent.

It should be apparent that the laws of intestate succession have the effect of making a will for the decedent. It should also be apparent that this scheme of distribution may bear little relationship to the decedent's actual intentions.

5 ESCHEAT

Escheat consists of a body of rules under which the state becomes the owner of property because there is no one in existence who can assert a superior claim. For example, when someone dies intestate and has no heirs, the property will escheat or go to the state who will then become the owner of it. Escheat may also arise in cases where a property is "abandoned." State statutes typically provide for procedures that attempt to notify heirs and potential creditors of the decedent before the state asserts ownership of the property.

6 DEDICATION

Dedication is the term applied to a transfer of private property for a public purpose. In other words, dedication involves the transfer of private property to a public entity for the benefit of the public. For example, a developer subdivides land for housing and agrees to sever a portion of the property for use as a public school; this land would be dedicated to the municipality for this purpose. Because dedications arise most commonly in the context of zoning, and particularly in the creation of subdivisions, material on dedication is deferred until Chapter 22.

7 EMINENT DOMAIN

Eminent domain is the power and procedure of an agency of the government to appropriate private property for a public purpose upon the payment to the owner of just compensation. Because eminent domain, also known as the condemnation power, is an integral aspect of the right of the government to regulate the use of land for a public purpose, the subject is treated more fully in Chapter 20.

8 ADVERSE POSSESSION

All American states have statutory provisions specifying the time after which certain rights must be asserted or be lost. For instance, statutes limit the period during which a claim for personal injury or breach of a contract may be brought, and the failure to bring the claim within that time will result in the claim being extinguished. These provisions are known as statutes of limitations.

In the context of real estate, all states have a statute of limitation barring a record owner's action to recover possession of land where certain conditions are present and when the owner has delayed too long. The consequences of this delay may result in the transfer of interests in land without the consent of the owner and is known as adverse possession. The operation of this concept in connection with the creation and termination of easements was considered in Chapter 10.

Title by adverse possession sounds, at first blush, like title by theft or robbery, a primitive method of acquiring land without paying for it. When the novice is told that by the weight of authority not even good faith is a requisite, the doctrine apparently affords an anomalous instance of maturing a wrong into a right contrary to one of the most fundamental axioms of the law. [However] the policy of statutes of limitation is something not always clearly appreciated. . . . The statute has not for its object to reward the diligent trespasser for his wrong nor yet to penalize the negligent and dormant owner for sleeping upon his rights; the great purpose is automatically to quiet all titles which are openly and consistently asserted, to provide proof of meritorious titles, and correct errors in conveyancing.

Ballantine, Title by Adverse Possession 32 Harv. L. Rev. 135 (1918)

A similar rationale for the philosophy and purpose of the doctrine of adverse possession is found in most modern cases. For instance, the California court described adverse possession in the following terms:

[Adverse possession] is now largely justified on the theory that the intent is not to reward the taker or punish the person dispossessed, but to reduce litigation and preserve the peace by protecting a possession that has been maintained for a statutorily sufficient period of time. Therefore, the present provisions for adverse possession are usually termed statutes of repose.

Finley v. Yuba County Water Dist., 60 Cal. Rptr. 423 (Cal. 1979)

A Elements of Adverse Possession

In order to be successful, one claiming title by adverse possession must show that possession was:

1 Actual, open, and notorious occupation;
2 Hostile or adverse to the interests of the true owner;
3 Exclusive;
4 Continuous for the full statutory period.

In addition, approximately ten states require that the adverse possessor pay accrued property taxes during the term of his or her possession.

It is important to note that both possessory and nonpossessory interests can be acquired by adverse possession. Accordingly, when one satisfies the requirements, a fee interest may be obtained in the property. However, cases arise in which one adversely acquires an easement by virtue of adverse use. In the case of an easement, the elements are essentially the same although the exclusiveness of the use is less than in the acquisition of a fee interest.

In *Jones v. Cagle,* 5091 S.W. 2d 156 (Mo. 1979), the Missouri court had an opportunity carefully to review the elements of a successful claim for adverse possession. The facts of the case are that plaintiff used property in the front of her house for seventeen years. Defendant, a neighbor, had a survey performed that indicated the property was his. The question was whether plaintiff or defendant owned the property in question.

In seeking to establish title by adverse possession, one has the burden of establishing possession that is (1) hostile; (2) actual; (3) open and notorious; (4) exclusive; and (5) continuous, over the statutory period. Whether the burden has been met depends upon the facts of each particular case, and consideration is given to the nature and location of the property, the uses to which it is put, the intent of the parties, and all other facts and circumstances of the possession and use.

"Hostile possession" means possession opposed to the claims of all others and imports the occupation of land by the possessor with the intent to possess the land as her own. To be hostile, it is not necessary to have actual malice, hostility, indifference, or intent to take the property which belongs to another. The intent to possess, occupy, control, use, and exercise dominion over the property is sufficient.

The acts that will characterize possession as "actual" depend on the nature and location of the property, the uses to which it can be applied, and all the facts and circumstances of a particular case. Plaintiff exercised the normal incidence of possession to a residential front yard. She arranged for having it mowed, planted trees, and used it to travel across. No one else, for at least seventeen years, exercised any rights of possession over the premises. We believe that under the circumstances here, the use of the property showed that she had actual possession from 1954 until 1971.

The third element is whether the possession was open and notorious. Numerous witnesses testified that plaintiff cared for the property as a lawn and that residents in the community considered it a part of her yard. Photographs introduced in evidence show that it appears to be what normally would be considered the front yard of her residence. To be open and notorious possession, there need not be a fence, building, or other improvements. It suffices that visible and notorious acts of ownership are exercised over the premises for the time required by the statute. We believe the evidence established that plaintiff's claim was open and notorious.

We next decide if her evidence showed exclusive possession. "Exclusive possession," for the purpose of establishing adverse possession, means that the claimant holds the possession of the land for herself as her own and not for another. All of plaintiff's acts were for herself and she considered the property a part of her front yard. She was not intending to hold possession for anyone else. Exclusive possession was sufficiently shown.

The last element is that plaintiff's possession must be continuous. Again, there was no dispute here. Her acts continued from 1954 through 1971. This exceeded the ten-year minimum set forth in the Missouri statute. Other evidence showed possession by her and her predecessors for fifty years or more. We believe this element to be satisfied.

Plaintiff has established ownership of the property through adverse possession.

Marengo Cave v. Ross, 10 N.E. 2d 917 (Ind. 1937)

Facts of the case.

In 1883, a cavern was discovered that later became known as the Marengo Cave. The entrance to the cave was located on land owned by defendant and his predecessors, while most of the cave itself was located under the land of the plaintiff. For almost fifty years, defendant and his predecessors advertised the existence of the cave and charged admission to it, denying the right to enter to all others.

The fact that part of the cave was located under land owned by plaintiff was not ascertained until 1932, when the boundary line between the respective tracts through the cave was established by means of a survey. Previous to this survey, neither of the parties, nor any of their predecessors in title, knew that any part of the cave was, in fact, beneath the surface of a portion of the land now owned by plaintiff. There is no evidence of, and dispute as to, ownership of the cave, or any portion thereof, prior to the survey, which was approximately forty-nine years after discovery of the cave and the exercise of complete dominion thereover by defendant and its predecessors in title.

It is defendant's contention that it has a fee-simple title to all of the cave, that it owns that part underlying plaintiffs' land by adverse possession. The statute of limitations in this state for the recovery of the possession of real estate is twenty years.

The trial court found in favor of plaintiff.

OPINION

All the authorities agree that, before the owner of the legal title can be deprived of his land by another's possession, through the operation of the statute of limitation, the possession must be actual, visible, notorious, exclusive, under claim of ownership, and hostile to the owner of the legal title and to the world at large (except only the government), and continuous for the full period prescribed by the statute. The rule is not always stated in exactly the same words in the many cases dealing with the subject of adverse possession, yet the rule is so thoroughly settled that there is no doubt as to what elements are essential to establish a title by adverse possession. Let us examine the various elements that are essential to establish title by adverse possession and apply them to the facts that are established by this case.

(1) The possession must be actual. It must be conceded that defendant in the operation of the Marengo Cave used not only the cavern under its own land but also that part of the cavern that underlaid plaintiff's land, and assumed dominion over all of it.

(2) The possession must be visible. The owner of land who, having notice of the fact that it is occupied by another who is claiming dominion over it, nevertheless stands by during the entire statutory period and makes no effort to eject the claimant or otherwise protect his title, ought not to be permitted, for reasons of public policy, thereafter to maintain an action for the recovery of his land. But, the authorities assert, in order that the possession of the occupying claimant may constitute notice in law, it must be visible and open to the common observer so that the owner or his agent on visiting the premises might readily see that the owner's rights are being invaded. It has been declared that the one in possession "must unfurl his flag" on the land, and "keep it flying, so that the owner may see, if he will, that an enemy has invaded his domains, and planted the standard of conquest."

(3) The possession must be open and notorious. The mere possession of the land is not enough. It is knowledge, either actual or imputed, of the possession of his lands by another, claiming to own them bona fide and openly, that affects the legal owner thereof. Where there has been no actual notice, it is necessary to show that the possession was so open, notorious, and visible as to warrant the inference that the owner must or should have known of it.

The purpose of this requirement is to support the principle that a legal title will not be extinguished on flimsy and uncertain evidence. Hence, where there has been no actual notice, the possession must have been so notorious as to warrant the inference that the owner ought to have known that a stranger was asserting dominion over his land. Insidious, desultory, and fugitive acts will not serve that purpose.

(4) The possession must be exclusive. It is evident that two or more persons cannot hold one tract of land adversely to each other at the same time. It is essential that the possession of one who claims adversely must be of such an exclusive character that it will operate as an ouster of the owner of the legal title; because, in the absence of ouster, the legal title draws to itself the constructive possession of the land. A possession which does not amount to an ouster is not sufficient.

The facts as set out above show that plaintiff and his predecessors in title have been in actual and continuous possession of his real estate since the cave was discovered in 1883. It seems to us that the following excerpt from *Lewey v. H. C. Frick Coke Co.,* 31 A. 261 (Penn. 1895), is peculiarly applicable to the situation here presented.

> The title of the plaintiff extends from the surface to the center, but actual possession is confined to the surface. Upon the surface he must be held to know all that the most careful observation by himself and his employees could reveal. But in the coal veins, deep down in the earth, he cannot see. Neither in person nor by his servants nor employees can he explore their recesses in search for an intruder. Nothing short of an accurate survey of the interior of his neighbor's mines would enable him to ascertain the fact. To require an owner, under such circumstances to take notice of a trespass upon his underlying coal at the time it takes place, is to require an impossibility; and to hold that the statute begins to run at the date of the trespass is in most cases to take away the remedy of the injured party before he can know that an injury has been done him. A result so absurd and so unjust ought not to be possible. . . . The reason for this distinction exists in the nature of things. The owner of land is held to be constructively present wherever his title extends. But he cannot be present in the interior of the earth. His senses cannot inform him of the encroachment by such trespasser. He cannot reasonably be held to be present where his presence is, in the nature of things, impossible.

Even though it can be said that defendant's possession has been actual, exclusive, and continuous all these years, we would still be of the opinion that plaintiff has not lost his land.

In this case defendant pretended to use the Marengo Cave as his property, and all the time he was committing a trespass upon plaintiff's land. After twenty years of secret use, he now urges the statute of limitation, as a bar to plaintiff's action. Plaintiff did not know of the trespass and had no reasonable means of discovering the fact. We are of the opinion that possession for twenty years or more of that part of Marengo Cave underlying plaintiff's land was not open, notorious, or exclusive, as required by the law applicable to obtaining title to land by adverse possession.

Affirmed.

B Color of Title

Often an adverse possessor occupies the property without any claim to actual title prior to the expiration of the statutory period. However, in some cases, the possessor occupies the land under ''color of title.'' This arises where the possessor claims the land by virtue of some written instrument that the possessor believes is effective, but which, for whatever reason, is invalid. For example, a forged deed, or a deed mistakenly describing the land, or a deed signed by one who does not have the right or capacity to make a deed to the property are invalid instruments which may create the appearance of a validity.

Where color of title is present, many statutes shorten the period of limitations and may permit the possessor to acquire ownership of an entire parcel even where she actually possessed only a portion of it.

C Tacking

Separate possessions of different parties who succeed each other may sometimes be *tacked* together to make-up the full period of the statute of limitations. There must be continuous and uninterrupted possession by all of the successive owners.

9 SUMMARY

There are various ways in which interests in real estate can be transferred from one person to another. The most common method is through the use of a real estate purchase contract, which is covered in chapters 13 through 18. Another method involves transfer of the right to possession from landlord to tenant, which is the subject of Chapter 19. In addition, interests in property may be acquired by governmental entities, principally by dedication, or through the use of the power of eminent domain. These methods of transferring ownership are taken up in Chapter 24 and Chapter 21, respectively.

The remaining means of transferring interests in real estate are briefly treated in this chapter. Transfer can be made by way of an inter vivos gift, which is a gift during the lifetime of the donor and which requires an intent by the donor, delivery of the gift, and acceptance by the donee. Transfers of property may also become effective upon death, either pursuant to a validly executed will, or, in the absence of a will, by virtue of the laws of intestate succession. If one dies without a will and with no heirs, his or her property will escheat to, and become the property of, the state.

The final method of transferring interests in real estate involves the doctrine of adverse possession. This doctrine is of ancient origin and is a vital aspect of modern property law. It is invoked under appropriate circumstances to vest title and ownership of property as against the actual or prior owner in favor or one who has been in possession for a period of time as set forth in the applicable statute of limitations.

10   QUESTIONS

1 Romeo and Juliet are madly in love. Romeo gives Juliet an expensive engagement ring. Sadly they have a falling out and Juliet elopes with Balthasar. Romeo demands the return of the ring. May Juliet keep it?

2 Shortly before her death, after a six-month illness, Marilyn Sheets, age seventy-two, revoked her prior will that had left all her property to one of her two sons. She had no other heirs. Her new will left all her property to the people who took care of her prior to her death. The son claimed that the will was invalid because the mother lacked testamentary capacity and was subjected to the undue influence of the caregivers. Is he correct?

3 In the prior case, if it is determined that the will is invalid, who will receive the property?

4 Wainwright began farming activities on land owned by Chuck. He cultivated the soil and planted and harvested the crops each year. No structure was built on the property, it was not fenced, and it was allowed to lay dormant during the winter. After the period of limitations has passed, does Wainwright become the owner by adverse possession?

5 Mike and Ilene were friends. Mike needs a place to live and Ilene lets him stay in a house she owns without paying rent. After the statute of limitations has run, Mike sends Ilene a letter saying ''Thanks, the house is now mine!'' Has Mike adversely possessed against Ilene?

6 Upton built a fence around property owned by Victor and used the property as his own. After five years, Upton sold the property, including the fenced area, to Wilbur. Wilbur acted as if he owned the property for another five years. The period of limitations in this state is ten years. Can Wilbur claim ownership by adverse possession or must he wait another five years?

CHAPTER 11

REAL ESTATE AGENTS AND BROKERS: AUTHORITY AND RESPONSIBILITIES

TOPICS CONSIDERED IN THIS CHAPTER:

1 INTRODUCTION

The law of agency is concerned with the legal rights and responsibilities that arise when persons act on behalf of others in commercial transactions. The agency relationship is a fundamental and essential aspect of the conduct of business in the United States. The active involvement of real estate agents in the sale, purchase, rental, and financing of interests in real estate is a common and pervasive feature in contemporary real estate transactions. Particularly in urban areas, the parties to a transaction, be they seller and buyer, landlord and tenant, borrower and lender, may never even meet. Instead, the entire transaction is conducted through agents.

Agency is a consensual and fiduciary relationship in which one party, known as the agent, agrees to act on behalf of another, known as the principal. (*Restatement of Agency,* Section 1) In other words, an agency relationship exists when contractual dealings between two parties are carried on by one or both of them by and through another. The primary characteristic of an agency involves the agent's authority to represent the principal in creating contractual rights with third parties. Although the agency relationship is governed by the agreement between the principal and agent, a whole new set of rules, known collectively as the Law of Agency, are also brought into play.

This chapter will consider the creation of the agency relationship and the rights and duties that are incidental to it. Chapter 12 will address the licensing requirements and regulatory aspects peculiar to agents and brokers practicing in the real estate industry.

2 CREATION OF THE AGENCY RELATIONSHIP: LISTING AGREEMENTS

The relationship between an agent and a principal is a consensual one and is usually based upon a contract, either expressed or implied. In the real estate industry, the most common and standardized agency contract arises between a seller or lessor of property and his or her broker and is known as a listing agreement. Approximately one half of the states require listing agreements to be in writing. The requirement of a writing is most commonly embodied in the state's Statute of Frauds, although in some states, the requirement of the writing is found in a licensing statute or administrative regulations governing real estate agents and brokers. (See generally Powell, *Law of Real Property,* Section 938.16[3].)

Listing agreements should be in writing and should specify the material terms of the contract, in particular the names of the parties, the identity of the property, the terms and conditions of the anticipated sale or lease, the commission to be paid, the expiration date, and the signatures of all parties concerned.

There are various types of listing agreements, and the terminology used to designate them varies somewhat from state to state. Four kinds of listing agreements are most commonly used: (1) the open listing, (2) the exclusive agency listing, (3) the exclusive right to sell listing, and (4) the net listing. In addition, real estate trade associations in most areas of the country provide a service known as the multiple listing, which is not a listing agreement at all but is a mechanism allowing information about listed properties to be disseminated among a wide group of real estate agents.

Open Listing An open listing is the most informal of the four principal kinds of listing agreements and is distinguished by the fact that, although the property is listed for sale with an agent, the owner retains the right either to sell the property herself or to list the property with another agent or agents. Open listings often generate questions regarding an agent's claim to a commission, because sale of the property by either the owner or any subsequently hired agent will defeat the original agent's right to a commission.

Exclusive Agency An exclusive agency is an agreement by which the owner agrees to employ a particular broker and no other. Under an exclusive agency listing, the broker's right to a commission is protected against other brokers for the duration of the listing agreement. However, under an exclusive agency agreement, the owner retains the right to sell the property on his own and, in that event, the owner can terminate the agency agreement and defeat the agent's claim to a commission. Many states require that exclusive agency agreements contain a specified termination date, and failure to include such a provision may defeat an agent's claim to a commission or subject the agent to disciplinary proceedings by the licensing authority.

Exclusive Right to Sell   The exclusive right to sell listing affords the agent the greatest protection and makes that person the sole agent for the sale of the property. Under such an agreement, the agent is entitled to a commission provided only that the property is sold during the listing period, regardless of who procures the buyer. In other words, under an exclusive right to sell agreement, the owner relinquishes both the right to list the property with other agents and the right to defeat the broker's claim for a commission by selling the property herself or himself.

Net Listing   A net listing is one that contemplates the seller realizing a specific net price with the agent's commission consisting of any sum that is realized in excess of the seller's net proceeds. For example, if the seller enters into a net listing with an agent with a $100,000 net price, the broker receives no commission if the net proceeds of the sale are $100,000 or less. However, if the proceeds of the sale are $125,000, the agent is entitled to a commission of $25,000. Because of the potential for creating a conflict of interest between the agent and principal, some jurisdictions limit or prohibit the use of net agency agreements. (See e.g. MASS ANNL, Chp. 12:85 AAA(1) and Title 19 NYCRR Section 175.19(b).)

Hamel v. Ruby, 487 N.E. 2d 409 (Ill. 1985)

Facts of the case.

Defendants entered into a real estate listing contract with plaintiff. In this contract, defendants granted plaintiff the exclusive right to sell their home during the period from February 26, 1983, until August 28, 1983. This contract provides in pertinent part:

> The [defendants] hereby agree to pay [plaintiff] for services rendered a commission of 6% of the agreed sale price [$62,000], subject to a minimum commission of $500.00, on procurement of a buyer who is "ready, willing and able" to purchase the premises on terms herein contained or otherwise approved by the [defendants]. The commission is due and payable if the property is sold by anyone during the time this agreement is in force. The undersigned agrees to pay [plaintiff] the above commission, based upon the last listed price, should the property be withdrawn from the market prior to expiration of this agreement.

By a deed executed on August 30, 1983, and recorded on August 31, 1983, defendants conveyed the real estate in question to the Degenhardts, who are the parents of one of the defendants. In consideration for this conveyance, the Degenhardts extinguished a debt owed to them by defendants and assumed the defendants' mortgage.

The parties stipulated at trial that (1) plaintiff did not procure a "ready, willing and able" purchaser for the real estate, and (2) defendants did not withdraw the real estate from the market prior to the expiration of the listing contract. However, plaintiff maintained that she was entitled to a brokerage commission because defendants had sold the property to the Degenhardts.

At the conclusion of the trial, the trial court entered an order finding that defendants were obligated to pay a brokerage commission to plaintiff because defendants had "sold the real estate . . . to the [Degenhardts]" during the period of the listing contract. Applying the contractual commission rate of 6% of the agreed sale price of $62,000, the trial court ordered defendants to pay the sum of $3720 to plaintiff.

OPINION

On appeal, defendants concede that the listing contract executed by the parties created an exclusive right to sell, which stated in part that plaintiff was entitled to a commission if defendants' property was sold "by defendants, another broker, or anyone else during the time the contract was in force." We conclude, therefore, that plaintiff was entitled to a commission pursuant to her exclusive right to sell if defendants agreed to sell their property to the Degenhardts during the exclusive listing period, in spite of the fact that (1) plaintiff was not the procuring cause of the sale, and (2) defendants and the Degenhardts did not transform their agreement into writing until after the exclusive listing period expired.

Defendants argue that they neither agreed to sell their property to the Degenhardts nor even discussed the sale of the property with the Degenhardts during the exclusive listing period. However, the record establishes that the Degenhardts completed the necessary loan applications concerning the property one day after the expiration of the exclusive listing period and that the warranty deed conveying the property to the Degenhardts was executed two days after the expiration of that period. Accordingly, after consideration of all evidence contained in the record, we conclude that the trial court's finding that defendants sold their property to the Degenhardts before the expiration of the listing agreement, was not contrary to the weight of the evidence.

The language of the listing contract in the case at bar is not ambiguous. The contract provides, in pertinent part, that plaintiff is entitled to a commission if the property in question was "sold by [defendants], another broker or anyone else." A sale of real property is ordinarily defined as a "contract whereby property is transferred from one person to another for a consideration of value," *Black's Law Dictionary*, 1503 (4th ed. 1968). It is undisputed by the parties that (1) defendants' property was in fact transferred to the Degenhardts by a warranty deed, and (2) in consideration for this conveyance, the Degenhardts canceled the debt owed to them by defendants and assumed the remaining outstanding indebtedness on the property.

Affirmed.

NOTES AND QUESTIONS

It appears from this case that the agent was unable to procure a buyer during the listing period. What could the sellers have done to protect themselves under these circumstances?

Multiple Listing   The multiple listing and the multiple listing service (MLS) creates a means by which information concerning individual listings is distributed to all participants of the MLS. For example, a seller lists property for sale with a broker. The broker then transmits a memorandum of the listing including information such as the type of property, its size, location, the purchase price, and other relevant information. This memorandum is transmitted to the MLS, which in turn publishes, either in a booklet or computerized data sharing format, the information submitted by the original listing broker. Other brokers throughout the region are thereby made aware of the existence of the listing and can contact the listing agent with prospective purchasers for the property. When this is done, it is common that the listing broker will split any commission received with the broker who procures the buyer for the property.

3 AUTHORITY OF AN AGENT TO BIND THE PRINCIPAL

A detailed examination of the nature and consequences of the agent's authority to bind a principal is more appropriately treated in a course on Business Law and is outside the scope of this text. However, because of the prevalent use of agents and brokers in conducting real estate transactions, a brief review of an agent's authority to bind the principal is included in this chapter.

General and Special Agents   A general agent is one "authorized to conduct a series of transactions involving a continuity of service," *Restatement of Agency,* Section 3(1). General agents tend to be an integral part of a business enterprise and do not require additional authorization for each transaction that they conduct on behalf of their principal.

A special agent is one who conducts "a single transaction or series of transactions not involving continuity of service," *Restatement of Agency,* Section 3(2). A real estate broker is usually a special agent although, in appropriate circumstances, a form of general agency can arise. The distinction between a general and special agent is important when determining the extent of an agent's authority to bind the principal to contracts made by the agent with third parties.

Agent's Authority to Bind the Principal to Contracts   A principal is liable to third parties upon contracts of an agent having actual authority or apparent authority to make such contracts. In other words, if a principal authorizes an agent to buy, sell, lease, or mortgage real estate, the principal typically will be bound by contracts entered into on the principal's behalf by the agent to the same extent as if the principal had directly entered into the contract himself or herself.

Actual Authority   There are two kinds of actual authority: express authority and implied authority. Express authority is created by the contract with the principal that completely and precisely delineates those activities the agent is authorized to undertake. Thus, if the principal authorizes the agent to acquire a particular single-family residence for the price of $100,000, the agent has express authority to do precisely that and nothing else. The agent would not have express authority to purchase the house for $105,000 or to purchase a different house.

Implied authority exists because it is often impractical or even impossible for the principal to specifically delineate the agent's authority. Implied authority is derived from express authority and will extend to the degree that it is reasonably necessary to accomplish the overall objectives of the agency. In the example just given, an agent may have implied authority to set the time limits for performance of the contract, receive notifications from the seller, wave conditions in the contract, and possibly undertake efforts to obtain a financing for the benefit of the buyer. Implied authority cannot conflict with expressed authority, but it may exist where there is no relevant grant of express authority. The determination of whether implied authority has been given usually involves determining the custom and practice of the business and determining whether the specific act was reasonably necessary for achieving the objectives for which the agency relationship was created.

Apparent Authority   Apparent authority is distinctly different from actual authority, because its existence depends not upon the express or implied agreement between the principal and the agent but upon the reasonable expectations of third parties who have been led to believe that the agent is authorized to act on behalf of the principal. Apparent authority, sometimes referred to as ostensible authority or agency by estoppel, arises when the principal, by words or conduct, leads a third party to believe that another person is his or her agent. In other words, apparent authority will arise and the principal will be "estopped" to deny the existence of the agency or the scope of the agent's authority when the principal's actions have created the appearance of authority in the agent, and a third party reasonably relies to his or her detriment upon this authority. The most common way in which questions concerning apparent authority arise is when the principal has placed a limitation upon the normal and ordinary authority of the agent and fails to communicate this limitation to a third party dealing with the agent. In most cases, the third party will not be bound by this special limitation.

Ratification   The final method by which an agent may acquire authority to bind a principal to contracts involves the doctrine of ratification. Ratification arises when an agent's actions were not authorized, yet the principal, upon receiving notice of the agent's actions, acts in such a manner as to accept the benefits of the agent's conduct. Ratification may be either express or implied. For example, an agent may agree to lease the principal's property to a third party on terms beyond the scope of the agent's authority. Upon learning of the agent's actions, the principal may act to disaffirm the lease and will not be liable because the agent did not have express, implied, or apparent authority to enter into it. However, if the principal informs the agent or the third party that the lease is acceptable to her or him, the principal will have expressly ratified the lease and will be bound by its terms. Somewhat more subtle is the doctrine of implied ratification. In our example, if the principal learns of the agent's purported lease yet fails promptly to disaffirm the lease he or she may be bound by its terms by virtue of the doctrine of implied ratification.

Ripani v. Liberty Loan Corporation, 157 Cal. Rptr. 272 (Cal. App. 1979)

Defendant Liberty Loan of San Jose appeals from a judgment in favor of plaintiff Joseph A. Ripani, on his complaint for money due under a lease of office space. Defendant contends the evidence is insufficient to support a finding that its agent had either actual authority or ostensible authority to bind defendant and that the evidence is insufficient to establish that defendant ratified the acts of the agent.

Facts of the case.

Plaintiff is the owner of commercial property located in Sacramento, California. In 1966 he leased office space to defendant for five years pursuant to a written lease that defendant prepared. In December 1970 plaintiff and defendant entered into a new written lease to commence March 1, 1971, and to terminate on February 28, 1974. Under the terms of that lease, defendant had the option to renew the lease for an additional two years for $3600 per year, by giving written notice to plaintiff at least thirty days prior to the expiration.

On January 3, 1974, plaintiff went to defendant's offices to collect the rent and remind defendant that the lease would soon expire and of defendant's option rights. Michael D. Anderson, who was then the branch manager of the office, prepared and signed a notice that defendant was exercising its option to renew the lease for two years. Plaintiff accepted the renewal. Anderson later informed his supervisors that he had executed the notice exercising the lease option.

Defendant, by letter dated March 28, 1974, notified plaintiff that it would not renew the lease and would vacate the premises on or before April 30, 1974. This was the first notice to plaintiff of defendant's desire not to renew the lease. Defendant paid the rent through April 1974, and vacated the premises by April 4, 1974. Plaintiff made various efforts to relet the premises after defendant vacated but was unsuccessful, and the premises remained vacant throughout the remaining period of the lease.

Plaintiff brought this action to recover the amount of the unpaid rent under the lease. At trial the sole issue was whether the attempted exercise of the option to renew the lease by Anderson was valid. Defendant contended that Anderson was without authority to exercise the option and the company did not ratify his action. The trial court found in plaintiff's favor and entered judgment in the amount of the unpaid rent for the two-year renewal period less the amounts he had been paid in March and April 1974.

OPINION

An agent has such authority as a principal actually or ostensibly confers upon him. Actual authority is that which a principal intentionally confers upon an agent or that which the principal allows the agent to believe herself or himself to possess. Ostensible authority is that which a principal causes or allows a third person to believe the agent possesses. An agent will normally have the authority to do everything necessary or proper and usual in the ordinary course of business for effecting the purpose of his or her agency. Authority may be granted to an agent either by prior authorization or by subsequent ratification.

Anderson was the branch manager of the office. As branch manager, his duties included approving loans, supervising personnel, handling collections, hiring and terminating employees, and signing checks on behalf of the company. The rent under the terms of the lease was paid to plaintiff by check signed by Anderson. Anderson signed the exercise of the lease option because he believed defendant intended to retain the office, and he had the authority to exercise the option as branch manager of the office. The evidence supports a finding that Anderson had the actual authority to exercise the option in the lease.

The evidence further supports a finding that Anderson had ostensible authority to exercise the option. All dealings plaintiff ever had with the company were with the branch manager. Rent was paid by the branch manager by check signed by the branch manager. Any maintenance problem or duty plaintiff had under the lease was reported to him by the branch manager. Throughout the eight years plaintiff leased the premises to defendants, defendants always dealt with plaintiff through branch managers. Defendant placed a branch manager in the office with the express authority to operate the business and the apparent authority to deal with matters under the lease. These facts could properly indicate to plaintiff that the branch manager had the authority to exercise the option in the lease.

We also find that the evidence is sufficient to support the judgment on the theory that defendant ratified the exercise of the option by Anderson. When Anderson signed the statement purporting to exercise the option he informed his superior, the regional manager, that he had done so, and was told that defendant intended to retain the premises. Defendant, although aware that Anderson had purported to exercise the option in the lease and that plaintiff was relying thereon, took no action to communicate to plaintiff that Anderson was without authority to do so and, in fact, remained in the premises beyond the termination of the original lease. When an oral authorization is sufficient for an agent to act, the principal ratifies the agent's act by accepting or retaining the benefits with notice of the agent's act. Defendant's continued occupation of the premises, with knowledge that Anderson had executed the exercise of the option and with the knowledge that plaintiff was relying upon the exercise of the option, constitutes a ratification of the acts of Anderson.

Affirmed.

QUESTION

Suppose Anderson had been told by his superior that he had no authority to enter into a lease with Ripani. Would that change the result in this case? What if the superior told Ripani that Anderson had no authority?

4 DUTIES OF THE AGENT TO THE PRINCIPAL, PARTICULARLY THE FIDUCIARY DUTY

Most agency relationships are created by contract and the rights and obligations of the principal and agent are often determined by the language of the contract. Failure of either party to perform may result in liability for breach of the contract.

In addition, the law of agency imposes various duties upon the agent to act on behalf of the principal. These extracontractual obligations are collectively known as the fiduciary duty. The fiduciary duty consist of various elements.

Duty of Service   A basic characteristic of the agency relationship is that the agent acts under the direction under the control, and for the benefit of the principal. Various specific duties are imposed by the law of agency to advance this purpose.

Duty of Obedience   An agent has the duty to obey all reasonable instructions from the principal.

Duty to Account   The agent must keep and render accurate accounts of money or property received or distributed on the principal's behalf.

Duty to Notify the Principal   The agent is required to keep the principal informed of material facts acquired during the course of the agency that may affect the principal's interests. The duty to notify the principal is particularly important because the principal will be deemed to have knowledge of information that is given to the agent, even if the agent fails to communicate this information. For instance, if the agent for the buyer of property is told by the seller that the property being sold has experienced water damage because of roof leaks, the principal is deemed to have acquired this knowledge and will be precluded from making a claim against the seller for roof leak damage, even if the buyer's agent fails to notify the buyer of this fact. This ''imputed'' knowledge is one of the principal reasons for requiring an agent to notify the principal of material information acquired in connection with the agency.

Duty of Care and Skill   An agent has the duty to possess and exercise the degree of care and skill that is standard in the locality for the kind of work the agent is employed to perform. As discussed in the next chapter, real estate licensing requirements often establish the duty of care and skill required of a real estate agent or broker, and typically establish that the agent possess a requisite degree of skill with regard to real estate contracts, zoning ordinances, financial instruments, and market values. A principal may recover from the agent for the agent's negligent failure to act with appropriate care and skill.

Agent's Duty of Loyalty   Perhaps the most important feature of the fiduciary obligation is the duty of loyalty. The aspect of the fiduciary relationship imposes upon the agent the duty of utmost trust and confidence in dealing with the principal. As the following cases indicate, the agent (1) must act solely for the benefit of the principal, (2) may not compete with the principal in matters within the scope of the agency, (3) may not use confidential information acquired during the course of the agency to the principal's detriment, and (4) must avoid and, if necessary disclose to the principal, the existence of a conflict of interest.

Ward v. Taggart, 336 P. 2d 534 (Cal. 1959)

Facts of the case.

At plaintiff William R. Ward's request in February 1955, LeRoy Thomsen, a real estate broker, undertook to look for properties that might be of interest to Ward for purchase. During a conversation about unrelated matters, defendant Marshall W. Taggart, a real estate broker, told Thomsen that as exclusive agent for Sunset Oil Company he had several acres of land in Los Angeles County for sale. Thomsen said that he had a client who might be interested in acquiring this property. With Ward's authorization, Thomsen submitted an offer on his behalf to Taggart of $4,000 an acre. Taggart promised to take the offer to Sunset. Taggart later told Thomsen that Sunset had refused the offer and would not take less for the property than $5,000 an acre. Thomsen conveyed this information to Ward, who directed Thomsen to make an offer on those terms. Thomsen did so in writing. Subsequently, Taggart told Thomsen that Sunset had accepted Ward's offer and presented to him proposed escrow instructions. Plaintiff paid $360,246 for the 72.0492 acres conveyed to him.

Plaintiff did not learn until after he had purchased the property that Taggart had never been given a listing by Sunset and that he had never presented to Sunset, and had never intended to present plaintiff's offers of $4,000 and $5,000 per acre. Instead, he presented his own offer of $4,000 per acre, which Sunset accepted. He falsely represented to plaintiffs that the least Sunset would take for the property was $5,000 per acre, because he intended to purchase the property from Sunset himself and resell it to plaintiffs at a profit of $1,000 per acre. All of the money he used to pay Sunset the purchase price came from the Ward escrow.

Plaintiff brought an action in tort charging fraud on the part of Taggart. The case was tried without a jury, and the court entered judgment against defendant for $72,049.20 compensatory damages, and for $36,000 exemplary damages. Defendant appeals.

OPINION

Defendant contends that the judgment must be reversed on the ground that there can be no recovery in a tort action for fraud without proof of the actual or "out-of-pocket" losses sustained by the plaintiff and that in the present case there was no evidence that the property was worth less than plaintiff paid for it.

Plaintiff contends, however, that his recovery is not limited to actual damages because he is seeking to recover secret profits. Ward relies on a long line of California cases. These cases all involved situations in which the defendant was the agent of the defrauded person or in which a confidential or fiduciary relationship existed between the parties. They rest on the theory that the principal's right to recover does not depend upon any deceit of the agent, but is based upon the duties incident to the agency relationship and upon the fact that all profits resulting from the relationship belong to the principal. In the present case, however, there is no evidence of an agency or other fiduciary relationship between plaintiff and defendant Taggart. Plaintiff dealt at arms length with Taggart through his agent Thomsen. At no time did Taggart purport to act for plaintiff. There is no evidence of any prior dealings between the parties or any acquaintanceship or special relationship that would create a fiduciary duty of defendant to plaintiff. In the absence of a fiduciary relationship, recovery in a tort action for fraud is limited to the actual damages suffered by the plaintiff.

Even though Taggart was not plaintiff's agent, the public policy of this state does not permit one to take advantage of his own wrong, and the law provides a quasi-contractual remedy to prevent one from being unjustly enriched at the expense of another. The Civil Code provides that one "who gains a thing by fraud . . . or other wrongful act, is, unless he has some other and better right thereto, an involuntary trustee of the thing gained, for the benefit of the person who would otherwise have had it." As a real estate broker, Taggart had the duty to be honest and truthful in his dealings. The evidence is clearly sufficient to support a finding that Taggart violated this duty. Through fraudulent misrepresentations, he received money that plaintiffs would otherwise have had. Thus, Taggart is an involuntary trustee for the benefit of plaintiffs on the secret profit of $1,000 per acre that he made from his dealings with them.

Accordingly, the judgment of $72,092.20, representing the $1,000 per acre secret profit, against defendant Taggart must be affirmed.

Taggart contends that, if recovery is based on the theory of unjust enrichment, the judgment for exemplary damages must be reversed.

Courts award exemplary damages to discourage oppression, fraud, or malice by punishing the wrongdoer. Such damages are appropriate in cases like the present one, where restitution would have little or no deterrent effect, for wrongdoers would run no risk of liability to their victims beyond that of returning what they wrongfully obtained.

The judgment is affirmed.

NOTES AND QUESTIONS

1 As the preceding case demonstrates, the fiduciary duties are inherent in the agency relationship and exist regardless of whether they are included in the contract creating the agency. Suppose the agency contract specifically deletes the fiduciary responsibilities. Would such a provision be enforceable? Does the principal also owe fiduciary responsibilities to the agent?

2 Is *Ward v. Taggart* too severe? After all, the seller was willing to sell for $4,000 per acre, and the buyer was willing to buy for $5,000 per acre. Has not the buyer obtained a windfall? What if the seller, Taggart's principal, now seeks damages against him?

Sub Agency: The Role of the "Cooperating" Broker   The marketing of real estate involves the efforts of a variety of people to give the property wide exposure. For instance, after the seller signs a listing agreement with a broker, the broker advertises the property for sale and usually enters information concerning the property in the M.L.S. (Multiple Listing Service) so that all agents in the vicinity know the property is for sale. Agents can then contact the listing broker, obtain additional information, and possibly preview the property in the hope of locating an interested purchaser. At some point a buyer is found, and buyer and seller, through their respective agents, negotiate the terms of the transaction. Assuming that everything goes well, a purchase contract is entered into by the buyer and seller, and the sale ultimately closes. Who pays the agents? What recourse does an agent have if he or she has not been paid?

The listing agent is usually well protected by virtue of the listing agreement with the seller. In addition, most purchase contracts contain provisions intended to assure that both the listing and cooperating agent are paid. Finally, the information entered into the M.L.S. usually contains a stipulation that the listing broker will pay the cooperating broker a certain commission in return for procuring a qualified buyer.

Unfortunately, there has been considerable confusion concerning the legal statutes of the cooperating broker. Strictly speaking, the listing broker is working on behalf of the seller while the cooperating broker is working on behalf of the buyer. Each agent owes the full panoply of fiduciary obligations to his or her respective client. However, a slight majority of jurisdictions hold that the cooperating broker is a sub agent of the seller and owes fiduciary obligations to the seller as well. This rule is usually justified on the grounds that the cooperating broker is considered a *sub agent* retained by the listing agent on behalf of the seller. Some courts also note that the cooperating agent should be considered a sub agent of the seller, because the agent is paid from the proceeds of the sale—funds that would otherwise pass to the seller.

The rule of sub agency has been criticized for a number of reasons and has periodically led to ridiculous results.

For example, in one case, the cooperating broker made certain misrepresentations about the property to a prospective purchaser procured by him. Since the listing broker had express authority under her exclusive listing agreement to employ the services of the cooperating broker, the court held that the listing broker and the cooperating broker were jointly acting as the agents of the seller. Therefore, the seller was held liable to the buyer for the fraudulent misrepresentations of the cooperating broker, even though it was established that the seller did not even know of the agent's participation in the transaction. (*Johnson v. Seargeants* 152 CA2d 180 (1957)

The emerging trend is to recognize that the cooperating agent is exclusively the agent of the buyer. This approach seems more consistent with the expectations of both buyers and sellers. In most cases, the seller and listing agent have no control over the actions of the cooperating agent. The fact that both agents may take their commission out of proceeds otherwise payable to the seller simply reflects the mutual efforts needed to efficiently market property.

Suppose you are an agent in a state that recognizes sub agency or whose law on the subject is unclear. Is there anything you can do to protect your client and yourself from unanticipated liability?

Dual Agency   It is generally accepted that an agent may not represent adverse parties in the same transaction, absent the consent of both parties. An agent who acts as a dual agent without such consent will usually forfeit any commission. Some jurisdictions even hold that a contract arranged by an unauthorized agent is not enforceable between the parties. The reasons underlying these rules are of ancient origin: ''No man can serve two masters; for either he will hate the one and love the other; or else he will hold to the one and despise the other. . . .'' (*Gospel of Matthew*, 6:24 quoted in *Nahn-Beberer v. Schrader*, 89 S.W. 2d 142 (Mo. App. 1936).

Although dual agency is not forbidden, a broker who represents both parties must act with extreme care. One court formed the issue as follows:

A broker so unwise as to place himself in the anomalous position of representing adverse parties must scrupulously observe and fulfill his duties to both.
(*Martin v. Heiken* 34 S.W. 2d 161, 165 (Mo. App. 1960)

A dual agency can also arise when an agent represents two purchasers, each of whom want to purchase a particular piece of property. In that case, the agent owes a duty to negotiate on behalf of two purchasers to obtain the best terms for both of them. The seller might be required to disclose the terms of one purchaser's offer to the other purchaser and thus create a nearly impossible conflict of interest. The many complications of dual agency are compounded by the growth of large real estate firms with many salespersons. In such firms, it is essential to develop internal procedures to ensure that adverse parties are treated fairly and carefully when represented by different agents within the company.

5   AGENT'S RIGHT TO A COMMISSION

As a general rule, a real estate broker earns a commission when the broker has brought to the seller a purchaser who is ready, willing, and able to buy the property upon the terms for which the agent has authority to sell. Under the rule in a majority of American jurisdictions, the listing broker is entitled to a commission from the principal even if the buyer refuses to complete the transaction through no fault of the seller.

This sometimes harsh rule has recently been overturned in several jurisdictions. The case of *Ellsworth Dobbs, Inc. v. Johnson*, 236 A. 2d 843 (N.J. 1967) denied the broker's commission where the buyer refused to close the transaction. The court's opinion contained the following language:

> In a practical world, the true test of a willing buyer is not met when he signs an agreement to purchase; it is demonstrated at the time of closing of title, and if he unjustifiably refuses or is unable financially to perform then the broker has not produced a willing buyer.

However, the general majority view is that a broker is entitled to a commission if the seller enters into a contract of sale with the buyer, and the broker may receive the commission from the seller even if the purchaser later refuses to conclude the transaction, even if the purchaser is later found to be financially unable to complete the transaction. However, the modern trend as embodied in the *Ellsworth Dobbs* case and the following *Tristam's Landing* case indicate a growing trend in favor of the "no close–no commission" rule. This rule has been adopted by the case law in the states of Connecticut, Idaho, Iowa, Kansas, Massachusetts, Nebraska, North Dakota, Oregon, and Vermont, and the state of Colorado has adopted this rule by statute. (See generally Powell, *Law of Real Property,* Section 938.17(i), Note 16.)

Tristam's Landing, Inc. v. Wait, 327 N.E. 2d 727 (Mass. 1975)

Facts of the case.

The plaintiffs are real estate brokers doing business in Nantucket. The defendant owned real estate on the island that she desired to sell. Defendant entered into a listing agreement with plaintiffs authorizing them to sell her property for $110,000 and agreeing to pay a commission of five percent.

Plaintiffs located a prospective buyer, Louise L. Cashman (Cashman). A contract was entered into, and Cashman gave a deposit of $10,500.

On the date set for closing, the defendant appeared at the registry of deeds with a deed to the property. Cashman did not appear for the closing and thereafter refused to go through with the purchase. No formal action has been taken by the defendant to enforce the agreement or to recover damages for its breach, although the defendant has retained the down payment.

Plaintiff presented the defendant with a bill for commission in the amount of $5,250, five per cent of the agreed sales price. The defendant refused to pay, stating that "[t]here has been no sale and consequently the five percent commission has not been earned." The plaintiffs then brought this action to recover the commission.

OPINION

The general rule regarding whether a broker is entitled to a commission from one attempting to sell real estate is that, absent special circumstances, the broker is entitled to a commission if he or she produces a customer ready, able, and willing to buy upon the terms and for the price given the broker by the owner. In the past, this rule has been construed to mean that once a customer is produced by the broker and accepted by the seller, the commission is earned, whether or not the sale is actually consummated. Furthermore, execution of a purchase and sales agreement is usually seen as conclusive evidence of the seller's acceptance of the buyer.

In the application of these rules to the instant case, we believe that the broker here is not entitled to a commission.

Although what we have said to this point is determinative of the rights of the parties, we note that the relationship and obligations of real estate owners and brokers has been the subject of frequent litigation. In two recent cases where we were faced with this issue, we declined to follow the developing trend in this area, holding that the cases presented were inappropriate for that purpose. We believe, however, that it is both appropriate and necessary at this time to clarify the law, and we now join the growing minority of States who have adopted the rule of *Ellsworth Dobbs, Inc. v. Johnson,* 236 A. 2d 843 (N.J. 1967).

Thus, we adopt the following rules: When a broker is engaged by an owner of property to find a purchaser for it, the broker earns his commission when (a) he or she produces a purchaser ready, willing and able to buy on the terms fixed by the owner, (b) the purchaser enters into a binding contract with the owner to do so, and (c) the purchaser completes the transaction by closing the title in accordance with the provisions of the contract. If the contract is not consummated because of lack of financial ability of the buyer to perform or because of any other default of his or hers there is no right to commission against the seller. On the other hand, if the failure of completion of the contract results from the wrongful act or interference of the seller, the broker's claim is valid and must be paid.

Accordingly, we hold that a real estate broker, under a brokerage agreement hereafter made, is entitled to a commission from the seller only if the requirements stated above are met. This rule provides necessary protection for the seller and places the burden with the broker, where it belongs.

Reversed.

NOTES AND QUESTIONS

Suppose that in light of the holding in *Tristam,* certain brokers insert language in their listing agreements stating that a commission has been earned when the seller signs the contract. Would such a provision dictate a result different than *Tristam's Landing?*

Requirement That The Broker Be "Procuring Cause" In addition to showing that the broker has produced a ready, willing, and able buyer, the broker must sometimes show that she or he was the "procuring and efficient cause" of the transaction before being entitled to a commission. This definition is particularly important in the case of an open listing where more than one broker may be competing for the commission. One case which has addressed this issue defined the term "procuring cause" to be "a cause originating or setting in motion a series of events which, without breaking their continuity, results in the accomplishment of the prime object of the employment of the broker, which may variously be a sale or exchange of the principal's property, an ultimate agreement between the principal and a prospective contracting party or the procurement of a purchaser who is ready, willing, and able to buy on the principal's terms. See *Hecht Realty, Inc. v. Whisnant,* 255 S.E.2d 647 (N.C. 1979).

6 SUMMARY

An agent is someone who is authorized to act on behalf of another, known as the principal, in dealings with third persons. The relationship may be created by express agreement, by implication, or by estoppel. When an agent has authority to act, the principal will be bound by contracts entered into by the agent.

Real estate brokers are considered special agents because their authority is typically limited to a single transaction or series of transactions. The authority of a real estate agent is usually defined by the broker's listing agreement with the principal. As with all agents, real estate brokers owe fiduciary obligations to the principal in addition to the duties specified in the contract. The fiduciary obligation includes the duty of loyalty, the duty to notify the principal, the duty to account to the principal, and others.

The principal's duties to the agent are much more limited. The principal's most important obligation is to pay the agent as agreed. In real estate transactions, compensation usually takes the form of a commission and is usually established in the agreement between the agent and principal. The longstanding rule is that the broker is entitled to a commission when the contract is signed or when all conditions to the contract are removed. The modern trend, at least in consumer transactions, is that a claim to a commission will be defeated if the transaction does not close through no fault of the principal.

7 QUESTIONS

1 Seller entered into a brokerage contract with agent to sell property. Agent procured a buyer. Seller then fired the agent and negotiated directly with the buyer and closed the transaction. Is seller liable to broker for a commission?

2 Richards listed property for sale with Dynamic Real Estate Brokers, Inc. Dynamic located a

buyer who turned out to be an employee of Dynamic. This was not disclosed to Richards. After the transaction closed and Dynamic's commission was paid, Richards learns of the identity of the buyer. Does Richards have a remedy?

3 Seller retains broker to sell property for ''$100,000 all cash.'' Broker procures a buyer, a contract is entered into with a thirty-day condition permitting the buyer to avoid the contract if buyer was unable to procure adequate financing. Buyer could not obtain financing and backed out of the deal. Does the seller owe a commission to the broker?

4 Morgan is the acquisitions manager of Commercial Realty Corp. and regularly purchases property for development on behalf of the corporation. Morgan is told not to purchase any parcels larger than ten acres or that cost more than $1,000,000. Nevertheless, Morgan signs a contract to purchase a twenty-acre parcel for $2,000,000. Is Commercial bound by the contract?

5 Norbert hires Oscar as his agent to sell a parcel of land. Meanwhile, Paula hires Quinten to act as her agent to purchase a parcel of land. Oscar and Quinten meet, discuss a proposed transaction, report to their respective principals, and a contract is signed. Does Oscar owe fiduciary duties to Paula? Does Quinten owe such duties to Norbert?

CHAPTER 12

REAL ESTATE AGENTS AND BROKERS: LICENSING REQUIREMENTS AND SPECIAL CONSIDERATIONS

TOPICS CONSIDERED IN THIS CHAPTER:

1 INTRODUCTION

All of the states have enacted statutes which establish administrative agencies entrusted with the power and responsibility to regulate the practice and conduct of persons engaged in the business of real estate brokerage. The purpose of these licensing statutes is to protect members of the public from dishonest or incompetent persons and, through continuing education requirements, to maintain and elevate the standards of professionalism in the industry.

In keeping with these purposes, licensing agencies have the authority to establish civil and criminal penalties against one who practices without a license, require minimum educational and experience levels as a condition of obtaining the license and vest in the agency continuing jurisdiction over the licensee by giving the agency authority to suspend or revoke a license upon proof of misconduct by the licensee.

2 PENALTIES FOR FAILURE TO OBTAIN A LICENSE

Most states make it a criminal offense to act as a real estate agent or broker without having procured the requisite license. In addition, licensing statutes typically preclude one from obtaining a commission or other compensation for real estate services rendered in the absence of compliance with the licensing statutes.

For example, New York law provides that one who receives compensation without being properly licensed is guilty of a misdemeanor and ''shall also be liable to a penalty of not less than the amount of the sum of money received by him as such commission, compensation or profit and not more than four times the sum so received by him, as may be determined by the court, which penalty may be sued for and recovered by any person aggrieved. . .'' (N.Y. Real Property Law, Section 442–e [3])

Many jurisdictions take the point a step further and prohibit not only the receipt of compensation but also the payment of compensation to an unlicensed person. For example, a California statute makes it a misdemeanor for anyone to pay compensation for services requiring a license, (California Business and Professions Code, Section 10138). Under this statute, one who pays a commission must take steps to verify or document that the person being paid is licensed. Prudent business practice would dictate that the person paying the commission ask to see a copy of a person's license before paying a commission for services requiring a license.

Licensing statutes tend to be broadly construed in favor of the regulatory purpose for which they are enacted. For example, a recent New York case, involved a broker who was licensed in New Jersey and could have become licensed in New York simply by filing an application with the New York Licensing Authority in accordance with New York's reciprocity statutes. No licensing examination or other conditions were necessary for the New Jersey broker to obtain the New York license. However, the broker failed to obtain a New York license and he was denied the right to recover from his principal an agreed upon commission with respect to the sale of real estate located in New York, *NFS Services, Inc. v. West 73rd Street Association*, 102 A.2d 388 (N.Y. 1985).

3 CLASSIFICATION OF LICENSEES

Licensing statutes tend to create classes of licensees with varying degrees of education and experience required of each. Most states have a two tiered system which permits a licensee to practice as a real estate salesperson or as a real estate broker. Ordinarily a salesperson is permitted to practice only under the supervision and under the license of a real estate broker. In other words, while a broker may act generally on behalf of principals in facilitating real estate transactions, a salesperson's license is more limited. The salesperson must be employed by a broker and can receive compensation only from the broker. Commissions can only be received by and paid to the broker who may then pay them to the salesperson. The broker is responsible for supervising the agent and failure to exercise reasonable supervision may result in disciplinary action against the broker. One case examined the relationship between the broker and salesperson in the following terms: "The broker, having met specified experience and training qualifications is authorized . . . to deal with the public, contract with its members and collect money from them; the salesman . . . is strictly the agent of the broker. He cannot contract in his own name nor accept compensation from any person other than the broker under whom he is licensed; it is a misdemeanor for anyone to pay or deliver to anyone other than the broker compensation for services within the scope of the act," *People v. Asucion,* 199 Cal. Rptr. 519 (Cal. 1984).

4 EXEMPTIONS FROM LICENSING REQUIREMENTS: THE ROLE OF "FINDERS"

State licensing requirements do not apply to all persons who act as intermediaries in real estate transactions. Persons representing themselves, lenders extending credit, attorneys performing legal services, and accountants providing accounting services are exempt. Also exempt from licensing requirements is one who acts as merely a "middleman," "middle-person," or "finder," in helping to bring together the principals to the transaction. A person acts as a mere finder when his or her entire activity in the transaction is limited to making an *introduction* of two principals or a principal and a broker. For example, assume a broker is seeking to locate property for a client. You know of qualified property and offer to introduce the owner to the broker, provided the parties agree to pay you a finders fee if an agreement is ultimately reached between the buyer and the owner. State licensing provisions do not prohibit the payment of the fee.

The critical feature is that the finder may do nothing more than make an introduction. The distinction between a broker and a finder is fairly clear. A broker negotiates on behalf of a principal in an effort to enable them to reach an agreement. A finder, on the other hand, does nothing more than make an introduction and leaves it to the parties to negotiate their own transaction.

One who claims the status of a finder must be very careful to refrain from doing anything beyond introducing the parties. Once one participates in negotiations or exercises any discretion on behalf of the principal, the finder becomes an agent and is subject to the licensing requirements and fiduciary obligations of an agent.

5 PROCEDURE FOR OBTAINING A LICENSE

In order to qualify for a license, the applicant must pass an examination that requires a demonstration of competence in the area of real estate transactions in general. Various conditions must also be met before an applicant will even be permitted to take the examination.

For instance, an applicant typically must be at least eighteen years old, may not recently have been convicted of a crime involving untrustworthy conduct, and must have practical experience to some extent. In addition, the applicant for a license must furnish proof that certain educational requirements have been met.

The degree of difficulty of the licensing examination, along with the stringency of the requirements for educational background and practical experience, depend upon the license that is sought. The salesperson's exam is easier and the broker's examination is more comprehensive and difficult.

Most licenses are issued for a term of between two and six years and usually can be renewed only upon the licensee's submitting proof of having successfully completed a certain number of hours of continuing education courses in the field of real estate.

6 ADMINISTRATIVE AUTHORITY TO SUSPEND OR REVOKE A LICENSE

Once a license has been issued to a real estate broker or salesperson, the administrative agency retains authority to revoke or suspend it or to issue various other forms of disciplinary action.

Although state statutes vary widely in the degree to which they specify the conduct for which a licensee may be disciplined, the most common kinds of conduct that disciplinary statutes seek to deter are the following:

1 Any conduct that constitutes fraud or dishonest dealing;

2 Failure to account for money or other property that the licensee holds for the benefit of another, including commingling client funds with funds of the licensee;

3 Any conduct that would have been grounds to deny issuing a license to the applicant, including making a false statement on the application;

4 Conviction of a crime involving moral turpitude;

5 False advertising;

6 Willfully disregarding or violating any provisions of the real estate law;

7 Habitual negligence or incompetence.

In addition, many state statutes delineate specific conduct which may result in disciplinary proceedings. For instance, New Jersey makes it an offense for a licensee to sell property in which they have an interest without disclosing this ownership interest (*N.J. Stat ANN*, Section 45:15–17) and California makes it an offense to represent more than one party to a real estate transaction without the knowledge and informed consent of all parties to it. (*Cal. Bus. and Prof. Codes*, Section 10176d)

LaRossa v. Department of Professional Regulation, 474 S. 2d 322 (Fla. 1985)

Facts of the case.

A two-count administrative complaint was filed against LaRossa seeking to revoke his real estate license based upon violations of the Florida licensing statute. The matter was set for hearing before a hearing officer. The evidence presented indicated that LaRossa had entered into a business deal with his nephew to purchase certain rental property in Coconut Grove. Pursuant to this "partnership" agreement, the nephew turned over $18,000 to LaRossa to be used in the acquisition of the property. LaRossa initially deposited the money in his trust account but subsequently withdrew it and used it for personal purposes. The property that was the subject of the original agreement was never acquired. Following the hearing, the hearing officer entered an order recommending that LaRossa be found guilty of violating the fraud and trust account provisions of the Florida statute and that the appropriate penalty would be a license suspension for ninety days.

The hearing officer's recommended order was accepted by the Commission as to the findings of fact and conclusions of law therein. After reviewing the entire record before it, however, the Commission increased the recommended penalty from a ninety-day suspension to revocation. This appeal followed.

OPINION

A registered real estate broker may be disciplined not only for dishonest conduct in transactions in which his only interest is as a broker, but also for such conduct in his own personal business affairs. We find that there was substantial competent evidence presented to support the finding of the hearing officer that LaRossa was guilty of dishonest dealing with regard to his personal use of his nephew's money. Thus, the Commission's adoption of the hearing officer's finding in this regard was not only proper but also necessary. See *Kibler v. Department of Professional Regulation,* 418 So.2d 1081 (Fla. 1982).

With regard to the finding of a trust account violation, we reach a different conclusion. The applicable provision provides for discipline when a broker fails "to place money entrusted to him by any person dealing with him as a broker in a trust or escrow account to be kept therein until disbursement is properly authorized. . . ." This provision, by its very terms, applies only when a broker accepts money from a party in his professional capacity as a licensed real estate broker. In the present case, the evidence before the hearing officer established that LaRossa was not acting in his professional capacity as a broker when he accepted the $18,000 from his nephew. Rather, it was established that LaRossa was acting in an individual, personal capacity when he accepted the money pursuant to the agreement with his nephew to jointly acquire rental property in Coconut Grove. Since there is a total lack of evidence to support a finding that LaRossa was acting in a professional capacity as a licensed real estate broker, the finding and recommendation of the hearing officer, adopted by the Commission, must be reversed.

It is apparent that in increasing the hearing officer's recommended penalty of a ninety-day suspension to revocation of the broker's license, the Commission was relying in part on its finding that LaRossa's actions violated the trust fund provisions. Since we have reversed the Commission's finding we must remand this cause to the Commission for reconsideration of the penalty imposed. Accordingly, we affirm in part, reverse in part, and remand for further proceedings.

NOTES AND QUESTIONS

1 Why was the nephew not considered a client for purposes of the trust account statute?

2 What do you think happened upon remand to the agency? Would it matter when or if LaRossa repaid the money to the nephew?

Sanctions for Failure to Disclose Material Information   In view of the fiduciary duty owned by a real estate salesperson or broker to her or his principal, the principal is entitled to full and complete disclosure of all material facts and, in particular, to have disclosed any interest of the agent that may conflict with that of the client.

Santaniello v. Department of Professional Regulation, 432 S. 2d 84 (Fla. 1983)

Facts of the case.

Bernard Santaniello is an active broker for Sunair Realty Corporation. He wrote to Mr. and Mrs. Long on a Sunair letterhead suggesting that they might wish to sell their two lots in Port Charlotte. He enclosed an offer to purchase at a stated price and included a ten percent commission. The offer was signed by a prospective purchaser named Anna Czaplinski. The Longs were not aware that Ms. Czaplinski was Santaniello's mother-in-law, and he did not disclose this fact to them.

An administrative complaint was filed against Santaniello by the Board of Real Estate. The hearing officer concluded that the relationship between Santaniello and the proposed buyer was a material fact that the sellers were entitled to know and concluded that Santaniello had violated Section 475.25(1)(b), Florida Statutes (1979) that provide that the board may discipline anyone under its jurisdiction who has:

(b) Been guilty of fraud, misrepresentation, concealment, false promises, false pretenses, dishonest dealing by trick, scheme, or device, culpable negligence, or breach of trust in any business transaction. . . .

The statute further specifies that one may be punished for misconduct without a showing of actual damage. The board fined Santaniello $500.

OPINION

A real estate broker must disclose to his principal all facts within his knowledge that may be material in connection with his employment. In *Macgregor v. Florida*

Real Estate Commission, 99 S. 2d 709 (Fla. 1985), a broker was disciplined for failing to disclose that the purchaser of certain property was an employee of the broker. The court stated that the broker "was under the duty of informing his principal of any circumstances that might reasonably be expected to influence the complete loyalty of the agent to the interest of his principal, or that might reasonably be expected to influence his principal in the negotiation."

Santaniello does not quarrel with the foregoing principles. He simply contends that the existence of the mother-in-law relationship cannot be deemed a material fact. We disagree.

Even though they had never met, by submitting a contract in which a commission would be paid from the proceeds of the sale, Santaniello owed his allegiance to the Longs. Therefore, he was obligated to inform them of anything that might influence their decision to sell. Superficially, the failure to point out the mother-in-law relationship may appear to be of little consequence. Yet, the board is best qualified to decide whether it was a material fact, which should have been disclosed. Agency determination is entitled to increased weight when it is infused by policy considerations for which the agency has special responsibility. The board was entitled to conclude that Santaniello was obligated to tell the Longs that Ms. Czaplinski was his mother-in-law.

Affirmed.

NOTES AND QUESTIONS

Would the result have been different if the buyer rather than the seller was paying the commission? Why was the identity of the mother-in-law material?

7   UNAUTHORIZED PRACTICE OF LAW

A particularly troublesome area for real estate professionals involves allegations that they have rendered advice constituting the unlawful practice of law. This is a particularly difficult area because real estate professionals routinely are called upon to advise their clients with respect to contracts, leases, mortgages, methods of holding title, and other matters requiring a legal interpretation. In discussing this problem, one court noted that "the line between acts permitted by real estate brokers and the unauthorized practice of law has been recognized as thin and difficult to define and, at times, to discern," *Duncan and Hill Realty, Inc. v. Department of State,* 405 N.Y.S. 2d 339, 343 (N.Y. App. 1978). In addition, a licensee who crosses the line may find himself or herself besieged on three fronts. First of all, one who renders legal advice without a license to practice law may be charged with violating criminal statutes intended to deter such conduct. In addition, the real estate licensing agency has authority to initiate disciplinary proceedings against a broker or salesperson found to be engaging in the practice of law. Finally, a licensee may be exposed to civil damage claims by a client, particularly if the agent's interpretation proves to be incorrect and the client suffers a loss as a result.

Given the fine line between permissible advice and the unauthorized practice of law and the substantial consequences that may flow when a licensee crosses the line, prudent licensees tend to use only form contracts approved by the local Real Estate Board and often reviewed by the local Bar Association. In addition, form contracts should clearly state that certain legal rights and obligations are created even by virtue of a form contract, and the client should be encouraged and given the opportunity to seek legal advice. One effective way this can be done is to make an offer or acceptance of a contract contingent upon review by the principal's attorney.

8 CIVIL LIABILITY

Real estate salespersons and brokers are, like all other professionals, under a duty to exercise the degree of diligence, judgment, and care ordinarily used by persons similarly situated. Breach of that duty will cause the broker to be liable to the principal for any harm suffered by the principal as a result of the broker's negligence. In addition, most jurisdictions now provide that an agent's breach of fiduciary obligations will give rise to an independent claim against the licensee.

Expanding the Basis of Liability

Easton v. Strassburger, 199 Cal. Rptr. 383 (Cal. 1985)

Facts of the case.

The property that is the subject of this appeal is a one-acre parcel of land located in the City of Diablo. The property is improved with a 3,000 square foot home, a swimming pool, and a large guest house. Easton purchased the property for $170,000 from the Strassburgers in May of 1976 and escrow closed in July of that year. Valley Realty was the listing broker in the transaction.

Shortly after Easton purchased the property, there was massive earth movement on the parcel. Subsequent slides destroyed a portion of the driveway in 1977. Expert testimony indicated that the slides occurred because a portion of the property was on landfill that had not been properly engineered and compacted. The slides caused the foundation of the house to settle, which in turn caused cracks in the walls. Damage to the property was so severe that, although experts appraised the value of the property at $170,000 in an undamaged condition, the value of the damaged property was estimated to be as low as $20,000. Estimates of the cost to repair the damage caused by the slides and avoid recurrence ranged as high as $213,000.

Valley was represented in the sale of the property by its agents Simkin and Mourning. It is uncontested that these agents conducted several inspections of the property prior to sale. There is also evidence they were aware of certain "red flags" that should have indicated to them that there were soil problems. Despite this, the agents did not request that the soil stability of the property be tested and did not inform respondent that there were potential soil problems.

During the time the property was owned by the Strassburgers, there was a minor slide in 1973 involving about ten to twelve feet of the filled slope and a major slide in 1975 in which the fill dropped about eight to ten feet in a circular shape fifty to sixty feet across. However, the Strassburgers did not tell Simkin or Mourning anything about the slides or the corrective action they had taken. Respondent purchased the property without being aware of the soil problems or the past history of slides.

In December 1976, respondent filed suit against Valley, the Strassburgers, and the builders of the home. Easton alleged causes of action for negligent misrepresentation against Valley.

The action was tried before a jury. The jury returned a verdict finding that all named defendants had been negligent and assessed damages of $197,000. Negligence was apportioned among the parties under the principals of comparative negligence in the following percentages: Valley–5%; Strassburgers–65%; the builders–25%. The jury also found a nonparty (a cooperating broker) five percent responsible.

Valley is the only party to pursue an appeal.

OPINION

Valley's primary contention is that the trial judge committed error by giving the jury an instruction specifying a real estate broker's duty to investigate and disclose defects in property he or she lists for sale. In analyzing the validity of this contention, it must be kept in mind that the judgment against was for simple negligence only. To establish liability for such negligence, respondent was not required to show that appellant had actual knowledge of the soil problems (as would have been required to prove intentional misrepresentation or fraudulent concealment) or that a misrepresentation had been made as to the soil condition of the property (as is required to establish negligent misrepresentation). We are concerned here only with the elements of a simple negligence action; that is, whether Valley owed a legal duty to the buyers to use due care, whether this legal duty was breached, and finally whether the breach was a proximate cause of the Easton's injury.

Valley challenges the following instruction: "A real estate broker is a licensed person or entity who holds himself out to the public as having particular skills and knowledge in the real estate field. He is under a duty to disclose facts materially affecting the value or desirability of the property that are known to him or which through reasonable diligence should be known to him."

Valley argues that a broker is only obliged to disclose known facts and has no duty to disclose facts which "should" be known to him "through reasonable diligence." In effect, Valley maintains that a broker has no legal duty to carry out a reasonable investigation of the property he undertakes to sell in order to discover defects for the benefit of the buyer.

Stated another way, we must determine whether the broker's duty of due care in a residential real estate transaction includes a duty to conduct a reasonably competent and diligent inspection of property he has listed for sale in order to discover defects for the benefit of the buyer.

The theory that a seller's broker cannot be held accountable for what he does not know but could discover without great difficulty would inevitably produce a disincentive for a seller's broker to make a diligent inspection. Such a disincentive would be most unfortunate, since in residential sales transactions the seller's broker is most frequently the best situated to obtain and provide the most reliable information on the property and is ordinarily counted on to do so.

In sum, we hold that the duty of a real estate broker, representing the seller, to disclose known facts includes the affirmative duty to conduct a reasonably competent and diligent inspection of the residential property listed for sale and to disclose to prospective purchasers all facts materially affecting the value or desirability of the property that such an investigation would reveal.

Affirmed.

NOTES AND QUESTIONS

1 The *Easton* case significantly expanded the brokers duty to disclose by expanding it beyond what the broker actually knows about the property to all the information the broker should know about the property. Courts in New Mexico and Kansas have followed the Easton rationale.

2 Would the same result have been obtained if the plaintiff purchased property to build a shopping center?

3 In response to the *Easton* case, the California Legislature enacted Civil Code Sections 2079 through 2079.5, a portion of which is set forth below. Has the California legislature changed the rule in the Easton case?

Civil Code Section 2079

> It is the duty of a real estate broker, licensed in this state, to a prospective purchaser of residential real property comprising one to four dwelling units, to conduct a reasonably competent and diligent visual inspection of the property offered for sale and to disclose to that prospective purchaser all facts materially affecting the value or desirability of the property that such an investigation would reveal, if that broker has a written contract with the seller to find or obtain a buyer or is a broker who acts in cooperation with such a broker to find and obtain a buyer.

Civil Code Section 2079.3

> The inspection to be performed pursuant to this article does not include or involve an inspection of areas that are reasonably and normally inaccessible to such an inspection, and, if the property comprises a unit in a planned development, a condominium, or a stock cooperative, does not include an inspection of more than the unit offered for sale.

Civil Code Section 2079.5

> Nothing in this article relieves a buyer or prospective buyer of the duty to exercise reasonable care to protect himself or herself, including those facts which are known to, or within the diligent attention and observation of the buyer or prospective buyer.

9 SUMMARY

All states have established administrative agencies to license and regulate real estate agents. The purpose of such regulation is to protect the public by establishing education and experience requirements for licensees and by giving the administrative agency continuing jurisdiction over the licensee.

Most regulatory schemes create two classes of real estate agents: the first is known as a salesperson, and the second is the broker. A salesperson can only act under the authority and on behalf of a broker. Only a broker may enter into a listing agreement with a principal and only a broker may receive a commission.

After receiving a license, a real estate agent may be subject to disciplinary proceedings by the agency. State real estate boards have wide discretion in this regard.

In recent years the scope of an agent's civil liability to a client has been expanding. In most states an agent is bound to disclose to a buyer only that information that is material and known by the agent. A few jurisdictions have adopted a rule requiring the agent to make a diligent inspection of residential property in order to meet the agent's duty of care. It remains to be seen whether this stricter approach will become the general law.

10 QUESTIONS

1 Relocation Services, Inc., headquartered in Minnesota, was engaged in the business of assisting employers in finding housing for employees who were being transferred by the employer anywhere in the United States. Does this activity require a real estate license? In which state?

2 A dispute arose between a real estate salesperson and his broker concerning a commission which the salesperson claimed was due. A complaint was filed with the local Real Estate Commission, which refused to hear the case. The salesperson appeals. Who is correct?

3 Alfred Agent was employed by Betty Broker. Betty was hired by Calvin to help buy industrial property and assigned Alfred to undertake the task. Alfred took a deposit from Calvin and deposited it into his personal account, quickly using the funds to cover his personal gambling debts. The Real Estate Commission seeks to discipline both Alfred and Betty. Can the Commission discipline Betty?

4 Long, a broker, represented Clay in connection with the sale of an apartment. At the close of escrow, Clay refused to pay the commission to Long. Long sued and Clay defended, claiming that Long failed to adequately explain the sales contract to him. Does the broker have a duty to explain the sales contract to the seller?

5 Tim makes an application to the State Real Estate Board for a real estate license. He passes the test. As a condition to taking the exam, Tim needed two years of related experience in the real estate business. Tim stated that he had this experience when, in fact, he did not. Three years later it is brought to the attention of the Real Estate Board that Tim made

misstatements on his application, and the Board initiates disciplinary proceedings. Tim defends, saying "no harm, no foul" and that since he now has the required two-years experience that the administrative proceeding should be dismissed. Who is correct?

6 George is a real estate broker who also develops property for his own account. He has built a ten-unit condominium project and tells prospective purchasers that a swimming pool will be built and that extensive landscaping will be undertaken. Because of financial difficulties, George is unable to complete work on the swimming pool or finish the landscaping. Buyers at the project notify the Real Estate Commission, who initiates disciplinary proceedings against George. Will George be disciplined?

CHAPTER 13

TRANSFER OF INTERESTS BY CONTRACT OF SALE

TOPICS CONSIDERED IN THIS CHAPTER:

1   INTRODUCTION

We have seen that real estate law is a diverse and relatively complicated area, which owes many of its principles to historical rather than logical precedents. Property law also tends to be particularly local in character with only periodic efforts toward national uniformity. This is true concerning contracts for the sale of real property, which tend to be more intricate and less uniform than the law as it pertains to the sale of personal property of equivalent value.

Although the sale of land is largely a matter of state law, efforts have been made by the National Conference of Commissions on Uniform State Laws to simplify, standardize, and improve the law as it relates to modern real estate transactions. Two significant acts have been prepared by the national conference. These are

1 The Uniform Land Transactions Act, and
2 The Uniform Simplification of Land Transfers Act.

Although these acts were approved by the commissioners in the mid-1970's, they have not been adopted by state legislatures and hence their authority is limited. Nevertheless, because these acts represent a diligent and concrete effort to state and improve upon present law, it is anticipated that their importance will grow in the future.

2   TRANSFERS AT COMMON LAW

Evidence of written documents to transfer interests precede the Roman Empire. However, during the early medieval period, transfers in England were accomplished not with a writing but by a ceremony. At that time, a transfer of ownership implied a transfer of possession. And, since all but the clergy and the most noble were illiterate, it is not surprising that a substitute for a writing was developed. This became known as the enfeoffment ceremony. The grantor and grantee would go on to the land in the presence of as many neighbors as could be found. There assembled, the grantor would hand to the grantee a twig or clump of sod, defining or identifying the boundaries of the property and the intent of the interest transferred. This was accompanied by words of grant such as "does hereby grant to *A* and his heirs." The assembled neighbors became the witnesses who could testify if the transfer were later challenged.

During the fifteenth century, writing became more common but was not a requirement for transferring land. Parliament was particularly active during the reign of Henry VIII and, in 1535, passed the statute of uses and the statute of enrollments. The statute of uses ultimately led to the creation of many of the equitable interests in property that are a familiar part of the landscape of real estate. The statute of enrollments was a primitive effort to document land transfers. Although the statute was largely ignored at the time, it formed the basis for the enactment of recording statutes, which followed some three centuries later. Finally, in 1677 parliament passed the statute of frauds, which made necessary the use of written documents to transfer interests in land. The enfeoffment ceremony fell into disuse, and land transactions began to assume the character they retain to this day.

3   THE MODERN REAL ESTATE TRANSACTION

Although the scope of this chapter is limited to the formation and performance of the contract between the buyer and seller of real property, even the most simple real estate transaction involves a series of transactions beyond the purchase contract itself. These topics are considered more fully in other chapters but should be kept in mind as the study of this chapter proceeds. Even simple real estate transactions typically require consideration of the following items:

1 The arrangements, if any, with real estate brokers (Chapters 11 and 12);

2 The contract of sale and the terms and conditions that are a part of it (this chapter);

3 Financing arrangements, particularly the documentation and effect of the promissory note and mortgage (Chapter 18);

4 The deed and its dual functions of transferring the seller's title and creating certain warranties in favor of the buyer (Chapter 14);

5 The operation of the recording system, both as it enables buyers and lenders to protect their interests in the property and as it affords a means of evaluating the condition of title to the property (Chapter 15);

6 "Closing" the transaction, usually by means of an escrow (Chapter 16);

7 Title insurance as a means of indemnifying parties in the case of defective title (Chapter 16).

In other words, a real estate transaction involves a series of documents and the involvement of various professionals in addition to the buyer and seller. However, the purchase contract is usually the central and most important document, and its most salient features are addressed in this chapter.

4 THE REQUIREMENT OF A WRITING

We have seen that transfers under the feudal law were accomplished by virtue of an effeoffment ceremony in which the parties and witnesses went to the land itself and transferred a physical piece of the land to symbolize the transfer. When the statute of uses was enacted in 1535, it became possible, although not mandatory, to transfer property by means of a writing instead of through the effeoffment ceremony.

The statute of frauds, enacted in 1677, created the requirement that land transfers be accompanied by a writing. The statute of frauds set the groundwork for a workable system of land title examination.

The English statute of frauds has been adopted with minor variations in every state. It provides as follows:

> No action shall be brought . . . upon any contract or for the sale of lands . . . unless the agreement upon which such action shall be brought, or some memorandum or note thereof, shall be in writing, and signed by the party to be charged therewith, or some other person thereunto by him lawfully authorized."

General contract principles require that the parties agree on all essential terms before formation of the contract can occur. Under the statute of frauds, it is generally required that these essential terms also be in writing. Even if the parties have agreed upon the essential terms of the contract, failure to satisfy the statute of frauds will usually bar enforcement of the agreement. With the exception of leases for less than one year, the statute of frauds applies to the transfer of any interest in real estate. As a result, the essential terms may vary significantly from case to case.

In the case of the ordinary purchase and sale contract, it is usually stated that the document must identify the parties to the transaction, describe the location of the land, state the price and other essential financial terms of the sale, and contain the signature of the party to be charged. In other words, the document must include all the required information. The important point is that a contract may still be formed without satisfying the statute of frauds. However, failure to satisfy the requirement of a writing means that the contract will not be enforceable by a court.

The Uniform Land Transactions Act, Section 2–201(a), provides that an agreement to convey real estate is not enforceable unless there is a writing signed by the party against whom enforcement is sought and which:

1 Contains a description of the real estate that is sufficiently definite to make possible an identification of the real estate with reasonable certainty;

2 Except as to an option to renew a lease, states the price or a method of fixing a price; and

3 Is sufficiently definite to indicate with reasonable certainty that a contract to convey has been made by the parties.

In *Balboa v. Golden,* 639 P. 2d 589 (N.M. 1981), the New Mexico court had an opportunity to discuss the requirement of a writing and the difference between a formal written contract and a memorandum sufficient to satisfy the statute of frauds.

To satisfy the statute of frauds, the contract itself must be in writing; or if verbal, then there must have been some writing subsequently made however informal, signed by the person to be charged, or by his authorized agent acting for him.

There is a difference between a contract in writing and a memorandum of a parol contract as contemplated by the statute of frauds. The former may be made up of letters and telegrams or any other kind of writing or writings, which together will constitute a contract, or it may be a formal contract. But if the contract made is oral, it is written evidence that will prove the particular contract was made that must be produced. The writings need not in themselves amount to a contract or be addressed to the other party. It is sufficient as evidence if the person to be bound signs any statement or document in which he or she admits that parties made the oral contract, sufficiently stating therein its essential terms, no matter what may be his purpose in making the writing, or to whom it is addressed.

All the writings relied upon to evidence the existence of the purported contract between the parties must be signed by the party to be charged, or if only one is signed, it must appear that it was signed with reference to the others.

Vitally significant is the requirement that the essential or material terms of the contract between the parties be set forth in the writings relied upon, and the terms of the purported contract must be ascertainable from the writing or by reference to another writing, and cannot be proved by parol proof. The "essential" terms of unperformed promises must be stated; "details or particulars" need not. What is essential depends on the agreement and its context and also on the subsequent conduct of the parties, including the dispute which arises and the remedy sought.

Another case stated the operation of the statute of frauds as follows:

Oral contracts to convey land are not void, but unenforceable if the party against whom enforcement is sought raises the Statute of Frauds as a defense. A memorandum is required, not for the purpose of obtaining a written contract, but merely to furnish written evidence, signed by the party to be charged, of the obligation to be enforced against him. The writing may consist of correspondence, receipts, telegrams, or a combination of documents. The writing does not need to contain all of the stipulations on which the parties have agreed.

(*Joiner v. Elrod*, 716 S.W. 2d 606 (Tex. 1986)

5 EXCEPTIONS TO THE STATUTE OF FRAUDS

The purpose of the statute of frauds is to prevent spurious claims by requiring that certain kinds of contracts, including real estate contracts, be in writing before they will be enforceable. However, there are situations where a writing will not be required as a condition to enforcement of the contract. Exceptions to the requirement of a writing usually involve situations where application of the statute of frauds would itself tend to perpetuate a fraud or where there is sufficient evidence, independent of a writing, to prove the existence of the contract.

The Doctrines of Equitable Estoppel And Part Performance

Recker v. Gustafson, 279 N.W. 2d 744 (Iowa, 1979)

Facts of the case.

Defendants Alvin and Irene Gustafson, husband and wife, are owners as tenants in common of a 160-acre farm in Fayette County, Iowa. Plaintiffs Loran and Mary Recker, also husband and wife, have been interested in purchasing the farm.

After some preliminary negotiations, the parties met on August 30, 1976, in the office of the Gustafsons' attorney, John W. D. Hofmeyer.

As supported by the testimony of both Loran Recker and attorney Hofmeyer, the parties reached an oral agreement on various specific terms of sale: a 155-acre tract, not including the five acre site on which the buildings were located, was to be sold for $290,000 with a $40,000 down payment on date of possession, which was to be March 1, 1977; annual payments were to be $28,000, including principal and interest, based on a ten-year contract with one final balloon payment at the end of the contract by March 1, 1987; interest was to be $7\frac{1}{2}\%$ per annum on the unpaid balance; and there was to be no deficiency in the event of forfeiture of the contract.

Settlement was to be made at the Oelwein State Bank. It was agreed that the contract would be drafted for execution on an Iowa State Bar Association form, which called for a warranty deed and certified abstract of title showing merchantable title in the sellers. Reckers were to receive clear title to the land as tenants in common.

At the close of the August 30 meeting, Loran, in the presence of Irene, tendered to Alvin a check for $5,000 bearing the notation "earnest money for farm." Alvin accepted the check and deposited it in a joint bank account to which both he and Irene had access.

Upon conclusion of the August 30 meeting, the parties agreed to reduce the terms to writing, which was to be signed at a later date. Hofmeyer had begun to work on the written contract when he received a call from Irene Gustafson instructing him not to complete the contract. No written contract was ever completed or signed.

In a letter dated September 28, the Reckers were notified by attorney Hofmeyer that the Gustafsons had "decided not to sell the farm." Enclosed was a cashier's check for $5,000.

On October 21, the Reckers filed a petition seeking specific performance of the August 30 oral agreement. In answer, the Gustafsons alleged that they had not entered into any contract with the Reckers.

The trial court concluded that the Reckers were entitled to specific performance of the modified contract for the purchase of the 155 acres.

The Gustafsons appealed.

OPINION

We believe the following issues are presented for our review in arriving at disposition of the case:

1 Whether the August 30 oral agreement between Gustafsons and Reckers falls within the statute of frauds;

2 Whether the August 30 agreement is taken out of the statute of frauds because Loran Recker paid Alvin Gustafson $5,000 of the purchase money, which Alvin deposited in a joint checking account;

3 Whether an enforceable oral contract was formed between the Gustafsons and Reckers on August 30;

4 Whether specific performance is an appropriate remedy here.

At trial, the Gustafsons objected to evidence concerning the August 30 oral agreement on the ground that such evidence was incompetent under the statute of frauds.

We have long held that contracts for sale of land fall within the bounds of statute of frauds.

Our statute does not forbid oral contracts or render them invalid. It relates merely to the manner of proof. The impact of the statute of frauds, therefore, is not to void the contract but to render incompetent oral proof of its existence.

Determination that the statute of frauds is applicable, however, does not end our inquiry. The statute of frauds is subject to exception where there has been payment of purchase money.

In determining the applicability of this exception we must decide whether the payment of the $5,000 check constitutes payment of a portion of the purchase price.

The statutory exception to the statute of frauds is set out in Section 622.33, which provides in part: "The provisions of section 308 of the statute of frauds do not apply where the purchase money, or any portion thereof, has been received by the vendor. . . ."

The $5,000 payment accepted by Gustafson takes the oral contract out of the statute of frauds.

Having decided that evidence of the August 30 agreement is not subject to objection under the statute of frauds, we must consider whether the oral negotiations resulted in an oral contract for sale.

Where specific performance of an oral agreement affecting real estate is sought, plaintiffs have the burden to prove the contract by a preponderance of clear, satisfactory, and convincing evidence. The terms are sufficiently definite if the court can determine with reasonable certainty the duty of each party and the conditions relative to performance.

Although the Gustafsons now recite a variety of topics not resolved under the alleged oral contract, the terms of an agreement to sell the land were definitely fixed. More precision, perhaps, would have been prudent. However, prudence of the parties does not govern our decision.

We conclude the August 30 oral negotiations resulted in an oral contract for the sale of the land and that the agreement is enforceable.

Affirmed.

NOTES AND QUESTIONS

1 In recent years, courts have been more willing to find exceptions to the statute of frauds and to supply "reasonable terms" where they may be absent from the written memorandum or from the oral agreement itself. However, the debate between "strict" or "flexible" application of the statute of frauds is a recurring one. An older Texas case expresses the traditional view:

> It will be perceived that the statute inhibits all actions upon contracts for the sale of lands unless the agreement, or some memorandum thereof, shall be in writing; and were this law enforced according to its letter, there would be an end to this suit and to litigation upon contracts of this character. . . ." [O]ne result of the relaxation of the statute is beyond doubt: an uncertain and perplexing rule of action has been substituted for one which was plain, easily understood, and the hardships of which could be attributed rather to the negligence of the party than to the doubtful state of the law.
> (*Garner v. Stubbfield,* 5 Tex. 552 (1851)

2 Do you agree with the court's argument for strict application of the statute of frauds? What is the argument in favor of a flexible approach?

3 Some courts, while permitting exceptions to the statute of frauds based upon part performance or equitable estoppel raise the level of proof necessary to establish the oral agreement. For instance: "A party seeking specific performance of an oral agreement based upon part performance must prove an oral contract, the terms of which are clear, satisfactory, and unequivocal, and that the acts done in part performance were referable solely to the contract sought to be enforced and not such as might be referable to some other or different contract and further that nonperformance by the other party would amount to a fraud upon the party seeking specific performance," *Yates v. Grosh,* 328 N. W. 2 200 (Neb. 1982). Does this standard differ from the one set forth in *Recker v. Gustafson?*

6 MARKETABLE TITLE

The buyer is entitled to receive "marketable" or "merchantable title" from the seller. This requirement is one of the most important of the seller's responsibilities under a real estate contract. Unfortunately, a complete understanding of this concept may not emerge until consideration of the material on deeds, recording statutes, and title insurance. However, because nearly all land contracts either expressly or by implication require the seller to transfer a marketable title to the buyer, an effort is made to address the concept in this chapter.

Marketable title has been variously defined and whether a seller has satisfied his or her obligations in this regard depends, in large measure, upon the interest he or she is purporting to convey under the contract. Consider the following examples: *A,* a life tenant, purports to convey a fee simple to *B; A* purports to convey a fee simple to *B,* but the property is burdened by an easement in favor of *C; A* has a contract to buy property from *B* and enters into a contract to sell it to *C.* Each of these examples may or may not cause *A*'s title to be unmarketable.

A marketable or merchantable title is such that a reasonably prudent person, advised as to the facts and their legal consequences, would be willing to accept and pay the fair value. Title will be rendered unmarketable if it is subject to a reasonable doubt or would create a just apprehension of its validity in the mind of a reasonable and intelligent person.

This definition obviously leaves considerable room for flexibility. Examples of defects in title that have resulted in unmarketability include:

1 An outstanding mortgage;
2 Prior transfer of mineral rights;
3 Encroachments from a public roadway or neighboring land;
4 Violation of a building or zoning ordinance; and
5 Deed restrictions that would limit the buyer's ability to use the land.

If the contract is silent as to the seller's title, it is implied that the parties intended that marketable title be transferred. However, the parties may and often do establish in their agreement the extent to which the condition of the seller's title to the property will affect its marketability. For instance, if the contract provides that the seller will take subject to an easement or to a mortgage or to certain use restrictions, then the existence of these outstanding interests will not render title unmarketable. In other words, the question of marketability tends to be determined on a case by case basis based upon the nature of the outstanding interest or encumbrance, in light of the contract entered into by the parties.

In the case of *Fort Dodge v. American Community Stores,* 131 N.W. 2d 515 (Iowa 1964), the Supreme Court of Iowa considered a contract that required the seller to transfer "good and marketable title" to the buyer. The buyer planned to erect a supermarket on the site. The property was located at the intersection of two state highways and contained the following deed restriction:

> *Conditions.* Any sale of land as herein authorized shall be upon the conditions that the tract, parcel, or piece of land so sold shall not be used in any manner so as to interfere with the use of the highway by the public, or to endanger public safety in the use of the highway, or to the material damage of the adjacent owner.

Because of these provisions in the deed, defendant rejected the tendered title as not marketable.

The seller tried to obtain from the State Highway Commission the removal of the restriction or an interpretation that would allow construction of a supermarket but was unable to do so.

The buyer rejected the seller's title as unmarketable. The court agreed:

> A merchantable title, as recognized and accepted in this state, is one which a reasonably prudent man would accept in the ordinary course of business after being fully apprised of the facts and the law applicable thereto. When called upon to determine whether an abstract of title shows a merchantable title, unless the specific objections urged to the title have been definitely determined by the courts, or are so clear as to not generate a doubt, the court need not pass upon the merits thereof. It is sufficient if the court finds the objections urged present a doubtful question which may submit the objector to good faith litigation regarding same. [I]f so found, then under our acceptable standard of title, the same is not merchantable.
>
> The obligation of the seller in a contract for the sale of land to make a good or marketable title free and clear of encumbrances entitles the buyer to a title free from any restrictions upon the use of the land, which either at law or in equity, would bind the land in his hands and affect his full enjoyment thereof. In the absence of anything to the contrary in the contract, any such restriction which lessens the value of the land for general purposes is regarded as a defect in the seller's title, giving the purchaser the right to reject the title and depriving the seller of his right to compel the purchaser to perform.

In another case a Delaware appeals court was faced with a situation where the seller's property was encumbered by a mortgage in favor of Ronald and Sara Beauchamp, husband and wife. The contract provided that title was to be delivered to the buyers "free of encumbrances." The proceeds of the sale were sufficient to satisfy the obligation of the Beauchamps. Prior to the close of escrow, it was learned that Ronald Beauchamp was confined in a hospital for the mentally ill. The buyers backed out of the deal, contending that Ronald did not have capacity to release the mortgage. Although the seller agreed to hold funds in escrow to satisfy the obligation, the court found that the seller's title was not marketable. The court said:

> The seller contends that the buyer was obliged to accept the deed tendered at the settlement and to take whatever steps were necessary to cause the mortgage to be fully discharged. The answer to this, I think, is that under the terms of the contract plaintiffs cannot shift to defendant the burden and risk of clearing a defect brought to their attention prior to the time of settlement.
>
> Seller's title is not presently marketable in the sense required by the contract.
>
> (*Mosley v. West,* 189 A. 2d 667 (Del. 1963)

QUESTION

Suppose the seller had agreed to pay for the appointment of a conservator who would have authority to accept the money and release the mortgage on behalf of Mr. Beauchamp. Would the seller's title have been marketable?

7   PERFORMANCE OF CONDITIONS

The typical real estate contract invariably includes various conditions that must be met before the transaction is in a position to be completed. We have seen that the state of the seller's title to the property may be a condition to the buyer's duty to perform. In addition, the seller may have the responsibility to furnish the buyer with information concerning income from the property or costs of utilities and to make the premises available for physical inspections by the buyer and his agents. The buyer on the other hand will have the responsibility of accepting or rejecting this information within certain time limits. In addition, since most transactions involve financing at least a portion of the sales price, performance of the contract is often made conditional upon the buyer's ability to obtain appropriate financing. Much of this process requires some degree of cooperation between the parties or, more likely, between their agents. In addition, as the following case indicates, parties to a contract are normally required to exercise some degree of diligence in satisfying conditions contained within the contract.

Sechrest v. Safiol, 419 N.E. 2d 1384 (Mass. 1981)

In this action, Robert C. Sechrest seeks to retain a $3,800 deposit made by George E. Safiol as the buyer under a purchase and sales agreement. A District Court judge ordered that the deposit be returned to Safiol.

Facts of the case.

On September 20, 1977, the parties signed a purchase and sale agreement under which Safiol agreed to buy from Sechrest a vacant lot upon which Safiol planned to build a single-family dwelling. Safiol made a deposit of $3,800. At Safiol's request, the date for performance was extended three times, from October 21, 1977, to December 9, 1977; Safiol was told no further extensions would be allowed. On December 9, 1977, Safiol notified Sechrest that he was terminating the agreement in accordance with the provisions of paragraph thirty-one of the purchase and sale agreement. That paragraph provided that "[t]he BUYER's obligations under this agreement are conditioned upon BUYER obtaining from the proper public authorities all permits and other approvals reasonably necessary, in the judgment of BUYER's attorneys, for construction of a single family residence, similar to those in the neighborhood, on the land being purchased under this agreement. If the BUYER has not obtained all such permits and approvals on or before October 14, 1977 [extended, by agreement, to December 9, 1977], then at the BUYER's option all payments made hereunder by the BUYER shall be refunded forthwith and all other obligations of the parties hereto shall cease and this agreement shall be void and without recourse to the parties hereto."

Safiol never submitted any building plans or any application for a building permit, nor did he seek any other approval necessary for the construction of a single-family dwelling. He did have an architect prepare preliminary drawings, which he submitted for a price estimate to the builder he had chosen. In November, 1977, the builder informed Safiol that he would not be available for the construction. Safiol obtained estimates from other builders but did not select a builder and never completed the final plans.

The judge allowed Sechrest's request for a ruling that "[w]here conditions relate to a Buyer's performance under a real estate Purchase and Sale Agreement, Buyer is obliged to use good faith and to take steps to attempt to fulfill such conditions and cannot seize upon his own inaction as the basis for terminating on the ground of nonfulfillment." The judge found that Safiol had acted in good faith, had made all reasonable efforts to obtain final plans, and had taken reasonable steps to comply with the terms of the agreement. He therefore ordered that the deposit be returned to Safiol.

OPINION

At issue here is the effect of the contractual provision conditioning the buyer's performance on his "obtaining from the proper public authorities all [necessary] permits and other approvals." Sechrest contends that this provision requires the buyer to take steps reasonably calculated to obtain the necessary approval.

Safiol urges us to abide by the language of the contractual provision, which does not expressly require the buyer to try to obtain any permit or approval. We reject such a literal interpretation. The apparent purpose of the provision in agreement was to give the buyer the power to terminate the agreement in the event he was unable to obtain the necessary approval from the town. The provision cannot be viewed as creating a mere option in the buyer to purchase without any requirement of affirmative action on his part. Necessarily implied in the provision is an obligation to use reasonable efforts to obtain town approval.

As the evidence is insufficient to warrant a finding that Safiol had made reasonable efforts to obtain approval, the contractual condition allowing the buyer to terminate the agreement was not satisfied, and Sechrest had the right to retain the deposit.

Reversed.

8 TIME OF PERFORMANCE

In order to avoid disputes concerning the time when performance of contractual obligations is due, contracts typically specify the time in which conditions will be performed and specify the date when the transaction is to close. For instance, a contract might require the seller to furnish the buyer with copies of leases, statements of maintenance costs and a preliminary title report within ten days of signing the contract and provide further that buyer shall have ten days to accept or reject them. In addition, it is common for a contract to specify the time within which loan and other applications must be made and set a date within which escrow must close. Questions often center on such time limitations.

Ordinarily, a slight or reasonable delay will not constitute a breach of the contract or render it unenforceable, unless the contract contains a "time is of the essence" clause. When time is made of the essence, the majority rule is that even a slight delay in performing a material condition will enable the other party to avoid the contract, based upon the failure of a condition. For example, if a contract provides that time is of the essence and that the buyer must furnish the seller with proof of a loan commitment within thirty days, the seller will be justified in terminating the contract, even if the buyer is only one day late. However, many courts refuse to give strict application to a time is of the essence clause and are quick to find a waiver of the provision or that the condition was not essential to the contract. For instance, a Florida case held that a delay of seven days in making a deposit into escrow was not a breach even where time was of the essence. See *Lance v. Martinez,* 251 S. 2d 707 (Fla. 1971). A different result would probably have obtained if the seller had failed to close the purchase on the date stipulated.

The Uniform Land Transaction Act addresses the issue of the time of the performance as follows:

Section 2–302. [Time of Performance; Time of Essence]

(a) If the contract does not fix the time for performance;

(1) the time for performance is a reasonable time after the making of the contract and tender must be at a reasonable hour and after reasonable notice to the other party of intention to tender; and;

(2) either party may fix a time for performance if the time is not unreasonable and is fixed in good faith.

(b) Except as provided in subsection (d), even though the contract specifies a particular time for performance, the failure of one of the parties to tender his performance at the specified time does not discharge the other party from his duties under the contract unless;

(1) the failure to perform, under the circumstances, is a material breach, or;

(2) the contract explicitly provides that failure to perform at the time specified discharges the duties of the other party.

(c) The phrase "time is of the essence" or other similar general language does not of itself provide explicitly that failure to perform at the time specified discharges the duties of the other party.

(d) If the contract specifies a particular time for performance, either party, by reasonable and good faith notice to the other before that date, may specify effectively that failure to perform on the specified date will discharge him from his own duties under the contract.

(e) If the contract specifies a particular time for performance, and a failure to tender performance at the specified time does not discharge the other party (subsections (b) and (d):

(1) the time for performance is a reasonable time thereafter, and

(2) the rules of subsection (a) as to time for tender and fixing of time for performance apply.

9 EQUITABLE CONVERSION AND RISK OF LOSS

We have seen that a feature of real estate sales involves a lapse of time between the signing of the contract and its ultimate performance. This delay is caused by a variety of factors, including the need to examine the condition of title, to obtain necessary financing, to perform inspections or satisfy any other conditions of the contract. This time lapse is variable, but even in simple transactions may last from one to two months. What are the respective rights and responsibilities of the buyer and seller during this interval? What if, during this interval, the seller dies, the property is destroyed, or the zoning laws are changed to preclude the use anticipated by the buyer? The answer to these questions often depends upon the application of equitable principles, collectively known as the Doctrine of Equitable Conversion. The Doctrine of Equitable Conversion attempts to define the real interests of the parties during the time between signing of the contract and closing the transaction. Under this doctrine, the buyer is considered to be the owner of the property, subject to the satisfaction of conditions in the contract and payment of the purchase price. The seller, on the other hand is considered to be the owner of the purchase price, again subject to the satisfaction of the conditions in the contract.

The following case of *Payne v. Meller* is well known and may be yet another example of a common law rule that has worked its way into American property law in spite of the fact that the logical basis for the rule has long since passed. Nevertheless, it continues to be the majority view in this country.

Payne v. Meller, 31 Eng. Rptr. 1088 (Eng. 1801)

Facts of the case.

On September 1, 1796, the plaintiffs sold to the defendant some houses in Ratcliffe Highway, upon the usual terms, a deposit of 25 pounds and a proper conveyance to be executed upon payment of the remainder of the purchase money. On December 18, the houses were burnt, the insurance having been suffered to expire. On December 20, the defendant's solicitor wrote a letter observing, that he had taken an objection to the title; he could not advise his client to accept the title; and he should call for a return of the deposit.

The bill was then filed seeking specific performance of the contract. The defendant claims that he could not have the thing bought; for chance had decided against him. But he had the chance, and he must take it each way. In the case of a life it might last fifty years, and might drop the next day. But this is not a purchase of property depending upon the contingency of life. A man purchasing a house is to consider with himself, whether he will insure, or not. Not a word was said about insurance. Therefore notice was not incumbent on the plaintiff; and there was as much negligence in the defendant in not inquiring about that. Such an accident did not occur to either of them. If in the sale of a house nothing is said about insurance, it could not enter into the bargain. As to the mere affect of the accident itself, no solid objection can be founded upon that simply; for if the party by the contract has become in equity the owner of the premises, they are his to all intents and purposes. They are vendible as his, chargeable as his, capable of being encumbered as his; they may be devised as his; they may be assets; and they would descend to his heir. The true answer has been given; that the party has the thing he bought; though no payment may have been made; for he bought subject to contingency. If it is a real estate, he of course has it. Judgment for plaintiff.

Clay v. Landreth, 45 S.E. 2d 875 (Vir. 1948)

The facts of the case are contained in the opinion.

The issue is whether the contract for the sale of the lot should have been enforced, specifically when the agreed purpose for which it was purchased and sold was defeated by the subsequent unanticipated enactment by the city council of a rezoning ordinance, changing the lot from what is known as business property to residential property.

The Plaintiff, the seller, argues here that the doctrine of equitable conversion applies; that this court should consider done what ought to have been done; and that in equity the seller should be considered the owner of the purchase money and the defendants or buyer the owner of the lot as of the date of the contract, namely, March 13, 1946. The resultant loss of the intended use of the property and the loss in value of the lot sustained by the rezoning would fall on the defendants if this theory were applied.

That the doctrine of equitable conversion exists in Virginia cannot be doubted. It is one of the principles of equity that it looks upon things agreed to be done as actually performed.

The rule, however, is limited in its application to cases where the enforcement of the contract is in accord with the intention of the parties, free from fraud, misrepresentation, and the like, and where it will not produce inequitable results. In both cases the equitable doctrines and their limitations are well defined and set from the same equitable source. Neither will specific performance of a contract be decreed, nor equitable conversion applied if, by doing so, hardship and injustice are forced upon one of the parties through a change in circumstances not contemplated by them when the contract was made.

If something has intervened that ought to prevent it, the doctrine of equitable conversion will not be applied. It does not exist as a matter of right and is not applicable to all circumstances. It is a fiction invented by courts of equity to be applied only when necessity and justice require its exercise.

When the facts are considered, it is apparent that, in this case, the legal fiction of equitable conversion should not be applied because to do so would set at naught the intent and purpose of the parties with resultant hardship and injustice to the defendants. The sole intent of the vendor in the contract was to sell to the vendees and the vendees intended to purchase a lot usable for the erection of a storage plant. This intent has been defeated by the supervening act of the council of Roanoke in rezoning the property, which has effected such a substantial change of conditions and loss in value that it would be inequitable to apply the doctrine of equitable conversion.

The intervention of governmental authority, entirely unanticipated, has vitiated the purpose that was the foundation for the contract. It rendered the property useless to the defendant in that they could not use it for the intended purpose. The complainant cannot convey to the defendants what they agreed to purchase and he agreed to convey.

Affirmed.

NOTES AND QUESTIONS

1 The doctrine of *Payne v. Miller* places the risk of loss after signing of the contract but before close of escrow upon the buyer unless the contract provides to the contrary. This continues to be the majority rule in the United States. Approximately eight states have changed the rule judicially, and follow the approach of *Clay v. Landreth*. Approximately nine more states have changed the rule by statute, often based upon the Uniform Vendor-Purchaser Risk Act which will be discussed shortly.

2 The doctrine of equitable conversion arises from that recurring peculiarity in Anglo-American law, namely the interplay between law and equity. The doctrine holds that upon creation of the contract, the buyer becomes the equitable owner of the property because the buyer can specifically enforce the contract and otherwise preclude the seller from transferring the property to anyone else. Equitable conversion has been defined in the following terms:

> [I]t is one of the principles of equity that it looks upon things agreed to be done as actually performed; and consequently, as soon as a valid contract is made for the sale of an estate, equity considers the buyer as owner of the land, and the seller as trustee for him; and, on the other hand, it considers the seller as the owner of the money, and the buyer as trustee for him.
>
> (*Dunnsmore v. Lyle,* 12 S.E. 2d 610, 611 (Va. 1981)

Shifting the Risk of Loss   The parties to a contract can and should specifically allocate the certain risks, specify who shall insure against them, and state whether a certain event, for instance destruction of the premises, will permit the agreement to be rescinded.

In the absence of an agreement to the contrary, most courts hold that the risk of loss is on the buyer. As indicated above, a growing minority of jurisdictions (approximately seventeen) have rejected the rule. An early expression of the minority viewpoint was stated, in a dissenting opinion, by a member of the Nebraska Supreme Court in 1921:

> [The majority rule] has been adopted, not because it appeals to the reason or to the conscience, nor because it is right, but merely because the weight of authority is said to be on that side. The weight of evidence is not determined by counting the witnesses, and by the same token the better rule is not always determined by counting the authorities.
> *McGinley v. Forrest,* 186 N.W. 74, 76 (Neb. 1921) Dissenting opinion.

Uniform Vendor and Purchaser Risk Act

1 Any contract hereafter made in this State for the purchase and sale of realty shall be interpreted as including an agreement that the parties shall have the following rights and duties, unless the contract expressly provides otherwise:

(a) If, when neither the legal title nor the possession of the subject matter of the contract has been transferred, all or a material part thereof is destroyed without fault of the purchaser or is taken by eminent domain, the vendor cannot enforce the contract, and the purchaser is entitled to recover any portion of the price that he has paid;

(b) If, when either the legal title or the possession of the subject matter of the contract has been transferred, all or any part thereof is destroyed without fault of the vendor or is taken by eminent domain, the purchaser is not thereby relieved from a duty to pay the price, nor is he entitled to recover any portion thereof that he has paid.

2 This act shall be so interpreted and construed as to effectuate its general purpose to make uniform the laws of those states which enact it.

3 This act may be cited as the Uniform Vendor and Purchaser Risk Act.

10 DISCLOSURES ON TRANSFER OF REAL ESTATE

Seller's Duty of Disclosure in Residential Sales   A recurring theme in residential real estate transfers involves the extent to which a seller must disclose to a purchaser the existence of physical deficiencies and other conditions affecting the value of the property. For instance, seller transfers the property to purchaser and, after the close of escrow, it is discovered that the roof leaks and must be replaced. Does the purchaser have a remedy against the seller for the costs incurred in replacing the roof?

The answer to this question depends upon a variety of factors including the state law requirements for the disclosure of material facts by a seller to buyer of residential real estate.

The Demise of Caveat Emptor   According to the common law, which was applied in some form in nearly all states until the 1960's, the entire burden for the discovery of defects was placed upon the purchaser. In most states, the seller was even free to misrepresent the condition of property without legal penalty. The doctrine of caveat emptor or ''let the buyer beware'' generally held that the purchaser had no recourse even if the seller knew of the defect or misrepresented the condition of the property to the purchaser.

Beginning in the 1960's, some states began to modify or abandon the doctrine of caveat emptor in residential property transactions. In addition, the rise of consumer protection legislation during the 1970's has been, and is continuing to be, absorbed into real estate contract law. As one court put it, ''caveat emptor is one of the less desirable hand-me-downs of our Anglo-Saxon common-law heritage and is a doctrine that exalts deceit, condemns fair dealings, and scorns the credulous,'' *Beavers vs. Lamplighters Realty,* 556 P 2d. 1328 (Okla. App. 1976). Although there is considerable diversity among the various states, the general trend has been to abandon or to seriously limit the doctrine of caveat emptor and to impose increasingly stringent responsibilities upon sellers to investigate and disclose material conditions of the property to purchasers.

There are three general approaches that have been adopted by various jurisdictions in this regard. The first, and perhaps the most common, requires a seller to disclose to a purchaser material facts that affect the value of the property and that are known to the seller and not reasonably apparent to the purchaser. States that follow this approach include Arizona, Georgia, Illinois, New Jersey, New York, Ohio, and Pennsylvania. Cases in which a seller knows that there is termite damage or that the basement is subject to flooding, have been held to be items the seller must disclose to the purchaser.

The second general category imposes upon the seller an affirmative duty to investigate the condition of the property and to disclose all facts that materially affect the value of the property. California, Florida, and Wisconsin are among the states following this approach. In these jurisdictions, the seller must, at the very least, conduct a careful physical inspection of the property and disclose to the buyer any deficiencies the seller finds. A prudent seller is well advised to obtain an inspection report from a termite inspector or general contractor to make certain that defective conditions are discovered.

A third category retains vestiges of caveat emptor and requires simply that the seller refrain from making any misrepresentations concerning the property. In these jurisdictions, the seller may say nothing at all concerning the property. However, if anything respecting the condition of the property is said, then full, fair, and accurate disclosure must be made. Connecticut, Massachusetts, Michigan, and Texas adhere to some formulation of this third approach.

It is important to emphasize that the law in this regard is in a state of flux and is changing quickly. The trend is clearly in the direction of requiring full disclosure by sellers and of increasing the responsibility of sellers to investigate the condition of the property prior to selling.

NOTES AND QUESTIONS

Suppose you wish to sell property that has been leased for many years or which you have recently inherited, so that you have no personal knowledge of its physical condition. Under each of three approaches mentioned, what precautions might you take to avoid a subsequent claim by a purchaser that you concealed or failed to disclose the condition of the property prior to sale?

11 REMEDIES

It should come as no surprise that the policy of the law is to encourage the performance of contracts by the parties to them. The primary way this policy is implemented is by giving remedies to a party in the event the other contracting party fails to perform the contract. Remedies for breach of contract fall into three categories. The first, and most passive, is rescission of the contract and restitution of benefits conferred. For instance, if the buyer purchases property based upon seller's false representations that new plumbing and electrical systems have been installed, the buyer will probably be entitled to rescind the contract, return the deed to the seller, and receive from the seller any sums paid pursuant to the contract. Because rescission involves an attempt to restore the status quo, it is incumbent upon the party seeking rescission to act promptly to discover the breach and give notice of the election to rescind. If too much time has elapsed, and it is difficult or impossible to restore the parties to their respective positions before the contract was performed, rescission will be denied.

The second important remedy for breach of contract is known as specific performance. Specific performance is considered an equitable remedy because it operates ''on the person'' of the defendant and will compel that person to perform the contract. For example, if a seller breaches a contract to convey, the court may order the seller to sign and deliver a deed to the buyer conditioned upon the buyer's tender of the agreed purchase price. If the seller refuses, the court's order may be enforced through the court's contempt power. The threat of fines or even confinement are usually sufficient inducement to obtain cooperation of even the most reluctant seller. In addition, the court, in an action for specific performance, has the power to effect a transfer of the property by issuing a judgment vesting title to the property in the buyer, again conditioned upon the buyer tendering the purchase price to the seller. Such a judgment has the same effect as a deed and can be recorded and gives good title to the buyer.

A party may also recover damages for breach of contract. Damages are simply a sum of money usually calculated to place the parties in the position they would have been in had there been no breach. In the first example given, suppose the seller breaches the contract by misrepresenting that new plumbing and electrical systems have been installed. The buyer may elect to stand on the contract and recover damages based upon the cost of bringing the property to the condition as represented. In the second example, where the seller breaches by refusing to sell, the buyer may elect to sue for damages rather than specific performance. There are two methods of computing the amount of damage where a party to the transaction fails to perform as agreed. The first of these awards the nonbreaching party the difference between the contract price and the fair market value as of the date scheduled for performance. For example if the contract price is $100,000, and the property is worth $110,000, but the seller fails to perform, the buyer's benefit of the bargain damages are $10,000. Nearly all American jurisdictions will award benefit of the bargain damages where the party's breach is willful or not in good faith. The states are about equally divided when the breach is not willful or is in good faith. About half of the jurisdictions award benefit of the bargain damages regardless of the nature of the party's breach. The other half will award only ''out of pocket'' damages in the case of a good faith breach of the contract.

The out-of-pocket measure of damages gives to the nonbreaching party only his out-of-pocket losses. Such losses tend to be sums spent preparing to perform, such as appraisal fees, financing fees, and so forth.

Finally, there can be rescission and damages or specific performance and damages where this is necessary to give complete relief to the nonbreaching party.

Specific Performance

Centex Homes Corp. v. Boag, 320 A. 2d 194 (N.J. 1974)

Facts of the case.

Plaintiff Centex Homes is engaged in the development and construction of a luxury high-rise condominium project. The project when completed will consist of six 31-story buildings containing in excess of 3600 condominium apartment units, together with recreational buildings and facilities, parking garages and other common elements associated with this form of residential development.

On September 13, 1972, defendants Mr. and Mrs. Eugene Boag executed a contract for the purchase of apartment unit number 2019 in the building under construction known as "Winston Towers 200." The purchase price was $73,700. Prior to signing the contract, defendants had given Centex a deposit in the amount of $525. At or shortly after signing the contract, defendants delivered to Centex a check in the amount of $6,870 which, together with the deposit, represented approximately ten percent of the total purchase price of the apartment unit. Shortly thereafter Boag was notified by his employer that he was to be transferred to the Chicago, Illinois, area. On September 27, 1972, he advised Centex that he "would be unable to complete the purchase agreement" and stopped payment on the $6,870 check. Centex deposited the check for collection approximately two weeks after receiving notice from defendant, but the check was not honored by defendants' bank. Centex then instituted this action for specific performance of the purchase agreement.

OPINION

Both parties acknowledge, and our research has confirmed, that no court in this State or in the United States has determined in any reported decision whether the equitable remedy of specific performance will lie for the enforcement of a contract for the sale of a condominium apartment.

Centex urges that since the subject matter of the contract is the transfer of a fee interest in real estate, the remedy of specific performance is available to enforce the agreement under principles of equity.

The principle underlying the specific performance remedy is equity's jurisdiction to grant relief where the damage remedy at law is inadequate. The text writers generally agree that at the time this branch of equity jurisdiction was evolving in England, the presumed uniqueness of land as well as its importance to the social order of that era, led to the conclusion that damages could never be adequate to compensate for the breach of a contract to transfer an interest in land. Hence, specific performance became a fixed remedy in this class of transactions.

The judicial attitude is expressed as follows: In applying this doctrine the courts of equity have established the further rule that, in general, the legal remedy of damages is inadequate in all agreements for the sale or lease of land, and in such class of contracts specific performance is an appropriate remedy.

While the inadequacy of the damage remedy suffices to explain the origin of the buyer's right to obtain specific performance, it does not provide a rationale for the availability of the remedy at the instance of the seller of real estate. Except upon a showing of unusual circumstances or a change in the seller's position, such as where the buyer has entered into possession, the seller's damages are usually measurable, his remedy at law is adequate, and there is no basis for equitable relief. English precedents suggest that the availability of the remedy in a suit by a seller was an outgrowth of the equitable concept of mutuality—i.e., that equity would not specifically enforce an agreement unless the remedy was available to both parties.

So far as can be determined from our decisional law, the mutuality of remedy concept has been the prop that has supported equitable jurisdiction to grant specific performance in actions by sellers of real estate. No other rationale has been offered by our decisions, and specific performance has been routinely granted to sellers without further discussion.

Our Supreme Court has squarely held, however, that mutuality of remedy is not an appropriate basis for granting or denying specific performance.

It is not necessary, to serve the ends of equal justice, that the parties shall have identical remedies in case of breach. The disappearance of the mutuality of remedy doctrine dictates the conclusion that specific performance should no longer be automatically available to a seller of real estate, but should be confined to those special instances where a seller will otherwise suffer an economic injury for which his damage remedy will not be adequate, or where other equitable considerations require that the relief be granted.

Here the subject matter of the real estate transaction—a condominium apartment unit—has no unique quality but is one of hundreds of virtually identical units being offered by a developer for sale to the public. The units are sold by means of samples, in this case model apartments, in much the same manner as items of personal property are sold in the marketplace. The sales prices for the units are fixed in accordance with schedules filed by Centex as part of its offering plan, and the only variance as between apartments having the same floor plan is the floor level or the building location within the project. In actuality, the condominium apartment units, regardless of their label as real estate, share the same characteristics as personal property.

From the foregoing, one must conclude that the damages sustained by a condominium sponsor resulting from the breach of the sales agreement are readily measurable, and the damage remedy at law is wholly adequate. No compelling reasons have been shown by Centex for the granting of specific performance relief, and its complaint is therefore dismissed as to the first count.

Judgment for Defendant.

NOTES AND QUESTIONS

It is almost a legal cliché that every parcel of real estate is "unique" from all others, so that the remedy of damages was considered inadequate by definition. Do you agree with the court's explanation that a condominium unit is not "unique"? Would not the same rationale hold true for a home in a subdivision? Do you think the buyer in this case could have obtained specific performance if the seller refused to go through with the deal?

Damages for Breach

Smith v. Warr, 564 P. 2d 771 (Utah 1977)

Facts of the case.

On August 20, 1973, buyer contracted with sellers to purchase the property in question. The Uniform Real Estate Contract they executed provided that title was to be passed by special warranty deed upon full payment. Seller was unable to complete the transaction, breached the contract, and buyer sued for damages.

Damages were awarded, however, only in the amount of buyer's out-of-pocket loss, and both attorney's fees and costs were denied. Buyer is appealing from the judgment in his favor claiming that the court erred in awarding him only his out-of-pocket loss, i.e. the sums reasonably spent preparing to perform, rather than the larger amount of the benefit-of-the-bargain damages, i.e., the market value of the property at the time of the breach less the amount specified in the contract.

The issue on appeal, therefore, is whether the correct measure of damages for a breach of contract for the sale of real property in this State is out-of-pocket loss or benefit-of-the-bargain damages.

There is a split of authority among the states as to which measure of damages is appropriate for a breach of contract for the sale of land. Some states award benefit-of-the-bargain damages only if the breach was committed in bad faith. Others consistently award benefit-of-the-bargain damages, whether or not the breaching party had a good faith reason for failing to convey.

The seller argues that Utah adheres to the good faith-bad faith distinction and that only out-of-pocket loss is to be awarded in the case of a good faith breach. Since the trial court made a finding of good faith on seller's part, seller contends it would then follow that out-of-pocket loss would be the correct measure of damages.

Seller's contention that benefit-of-the-bargain damages have only been awarded in this state when the breach was in bad faith, however, is not well-founded. Sellers rely, for example, on *Bunnell v. Bills,* 13 Utah 2d 83, 368 P. 2d 597 (1962). In that case the seller had contracted to sell to the buyer property that he did not yet own, but which he had contracted to buy. The seller was financially unable to proceed with the purchase of the property, and this contract with the owner was consequently rescinded, whereupon the buyer sued for breach of contract. There is no mention of bad faith in this Court's decision in *Bunnell,* nor is bad faith apparent from the facts of the case, yet this Court stated there:

> The measure of damages where the seller has breached a land sale contract is the market value of the property at the time of the breach less the contract price to the buyer.

Other cases cited by sellers in support of their position that Utah has implicitly followed the rule that awards benefit-of-the-bargain damages only in case of a bad faith breach are similarly unconvincing. Sellers also cited good faith cases, in which only out-of-pocket loss was awarded the buyer. In these cases, however, the buyers had only sought out-of-pocket losses, and the court expressly recognized that damages on the contract would also have been an available remedy.

The rule followed by Utah is that benefit-of-the-bargain damages are to be awarded for breach of contract for the sale of real estate, regardless of the good faith of the party in breach. We therefore reverse, and remand to the District Court for a determination of damages consistent with this opinion, for an award of reasonable attorney's fees as required by the contract, and for costs below in the discretion of this Court.

Reversed.

NOTES AND QUESTIONS:

1 The Uniform Land Transactions Act, Section 2–510. (Buyer's Damages for Seller's Failure to Convey)
  (a) Except as provided in subsection (b), the measure of damages for a seller's repudiation or wrongful failure to convey is the difference between the fair market value at the time for conveyance and the contract

price and any incidental and consequential damages (Section 2–154), less expenses avoided because of the seller's breach.

(b) Unless the title defect is an encumbrance securing an obligation to pay money which could be discharged by application of all or a portion of the purchase price, if a seller is unable to convey because of a title defect of which the seller had no knowledge at the time of entering into the contract, the buyer is entitled to restitution of any amounts paid on the contract price and incidental damages.

2 A slight majority of American jurisdictions follow the approach set forth in the Uniform Land Transactions Act, Section 2–510. This rule gives benefit of bargain damages where the seller commits a total breach but only out-of-pocket damages if the breach is caused by ''good faith'' title defect.

3 What is the appropriate damage remedy if the buyer breaches and fails to perform the contract? What if the seller finds another buyer at a higher price?

Liquidated Damages   Parties to a contract may elect to specify the amount of damages payable to either party in the event of a breach of the contract. Such provisions may be useful in avoiding the cost associated with proving damages, particularly when these may be speculative or otherwise difficult to prove. Related to the question of liquidated damages is the right of a seller to retain any deposits that a buyer has made prior to the contract being breached. As a general rule, liquidated damages provisions are enforceable provided they are not considered a ''penalty.'' Unfortunately, the difference between an enforceable provision and a penalty is often difficult to discern. One court, in upholding a ten percent liquidated damage clause recited the two-part test that is typically used in such cases:

> In order for such a clause to be construed as one for liquidated damages, the sum provided, at the time of making the contract, must seem to bear a reasonable relationship to anticipated damages and the actual damages must be difficult or impossible to ascertain.
>
> *Chaffin v. Ramsey*, 555 P. 2d 459 (Ore. 1976)

The test set forth in this case leaves considerable room for uncertainty and there has been substantial litigation concerning the liquidated damage provisions. Some jurisdictions have passed statutes in an effort to regulate the field. For example, *Cal. Civ. Code Section 1671* provides that a three percent liquidated damage provision is presumptively reasonable in the case of residential dwellings. Such statutory provisions are useful because contracting parties may then comply with the statute and use the provision without fear that it will later be considered unreasonable by a court.

12   LIABILITY OF HOUSING SUPPLIERS

Tyrus v. Resta, 476 A. 2d 427 (Penn. 1984)

Facts of the case.

On August 23, 1976, the Seller entered into a contract with Nelson and Frances Tyrus (Buyers) for the sale of a newly constructed house.

On May 12, 1978, the Buyers filed a complaint which alleged, that "various defects . . . occurred in [their] house which were the direct cause of the Seller's poor workmanship in building said premises, the selection of substandard materials with which to build said premises, or both."

The jury rendered a verdict for the Buyers in the amount of $6,750. The Seller appealed.

OPINION

In *Elderkin v. Gaster,* 188, 288 A. 2d 771 (Pa. 1972), Pennsylvania numbered among the first jurisdictions acknowledging an implied warranty of habitability, as well as an implied warranty of reasonable workmanship, in contracts whereby builder-vendors sold newly constructed houses. We are now asked to decide whether in selling new homes, builder-vendors can limit or disclaim the implied warranties.

Compared to the ordinary home purchaser, the builder-vendor possesses superior knowledge and expertise in all aspects of building, including its legal aspects. In the vast majority of cases, the vendor enjoys superior bargaining position. Standard form contracts are generally utilized and express warranties are rarely given, are expensive, and impractical for most buyers to negotiate. Inevitably the buyer is forced to rely on the skills of the seller.

In *Elderkin,* the Pennsylvania Supreme Court recognized that the implied warranties of habitability and reasonable workmanship were necessary to equalize the disparate positions of the builder-vendor and the average home purchaser, by safeguarding the reasonable expectations of the purchaser compelled to depend upon the builder-vendor's greater manufacturing and marketing expertise.

It is our view that one who purchases a development home justifiably relies on the skill of the developer that the house will be a suitable living unit. Not only does a housing developer hold himself out as having the necessary expertise with which to produce an adequate dwelling, but he has by far the better opportunity to examine the suitability of the home site and to determine what measures should be taken to provide a home fit for habitation. As between the builder-vendor and the buyer, the position of the former, even though he exercises reasonable care, dictates that he bear the risk that a home which he has built will be functional and habitable in accordance with contemporary community standards.

Accordingly, we hold that the builder-vendor impliedly warrants that the home he has built and is selling is constructed in a reasonably workmanlike manner and that it is fit for the purposes intended—habitation.

Given the important consumer protection afforded by the implied warranties, we hold that such warranties may be limited or disclaimed only by clear and unambiguous language in a written contract between the builder-vendor and the home purchaser.

To create clear and unambiguous language of disclaimer, the parties' contract must contain language which is both understandable and sufficiently particular to provide the new home purchaser adequate notice of the implied warranty protections that he is waiving by signing the contract.

In the present case paragraph thirteen of the Vendors' contract with the Buyers contains the following disclaimer:

> Buyer has inspected the property or hereby waives the right to do so, and he has agreed to purchase it as a result of such inspection and not because of or in reliance upon any representation made by the Seller . . . and that he has agreed to purchase it in its present condition unless otherwise specified herein.

A reasonable pre-purchase inspection requires examination of the premises by the intended purchaser—not by an expert. Defects which would not be apparent to an ordinary purchaser as a result of a reasonable inspection constitute latent defects covered by the implied warranties.

Furthermore, a reasonable inspection does not necessitate "a minute inspection of every nook and cranny."

We hold that the disclaimer of implied warranties in paragraph thirteen of the parties' contract is not a valid limitation. The disclaimer fails because it does not refer to its impact on specific, potential latent defects and so does not notify the Buyers of the implied warranty protection they are waiving by signing the contract supplied by the Vendors.

Affirmed.

NOTES AND QUESTIONS

1 Various theories have been adopted to impose liability upon a builder for defective construction of a residence. The *Tyrus* case employs the implied warranty of habitability. Some jurisdictions have adopted strict liability, and others have evolved the tort of negligent construction. In addition, some states have extended the statute of limitations, in some cases as long as ten years, in which to file a claim for defective construction.

2 The implied warranty of habitability was first recognized in the English case of *Miller v. Cannon Hill Estates, Ltd.* 2 K.B. 113 (1931). The court said that in the purchase of an unfinished house the builder was aware that his buyer intended to live in the house and therefore impliedly warranted that it would be suitable for that purpose. In 1957 an Ohio court in *Vanderschrier v. Aaron,* 140 N.E. 2d 819 (1957), applied the Hiller rule for the first time in the United States.

By 1980 at least thirty-five state courts had afforded some measure of protection for purchasers of new homes by implying some form of a warranty of habitability. See Sheed, *The Implied Warranty of Habitability: New Implications, New Applications,* 8 Real Estate L.J. 291, 308, 316 (1980). This trend has continued since that time.

3 In 1976 the Supreme Court of Indiana became the first jurisdiction to extend the warranty of habitability to subsequent purchasers, *Barns v. MacGrown Co.,* 342 N.E. 2d 619 (Ind. 1976). A number of states have extended the implied warranty to subsequent buyers and this position is adopted by the ULTA Section 2–312.

4 In deciding to extend the implied warranty to subsequent purchasers, the Supreme Court of Illinois examined the purpose of the warranty and made the following observations:

> The warranty of habitability is a creature of public policy. It is a judicial innovation that has evolved to protect purchasers of new houses upon discovery of latent defects in their homes. While the warranty of habitability has roots in the execution of the contract for sale, we emphasize that it exists independently. Privity of contract is not required. Like the initial purchaser, the subsequent purchaser has little opportunity to inspect the construction methods used in building the home. Like the initial purchaser, the subsequent purchaser is usually not knowledgeable in construction practices and must, to a substantial degree, rely upon the expertise of the person who built the home. If construction of a new house is defective, its repair costs should be borne by the responsible builder-vendor who created the latent defect. The compelling public policies underlying the implied warranty of habitability should not be frustrated because of the short intervening ownership of the first purchaser; in these circumstances the implied warranty of habitability survives a change of hands in the ownership.
>
> *Redarowicz v. Ohlendorf,* 441 N.E. 2d 324 (Ill. 1982)

13 SUMMARY

The requirements of a valid real estate contract are essentially the same as in the case of any other contract. However, certain factors are recurring elements of the land contract. The first is that contracts representing the transfer of an interest in real estate must be in writing in order to be enforceable. The statute of frauds requires that a memorandum identifying the parties, the property, and the essential terms be signed by the party against whom enforcement of the contract is sought. Because of its potential severity, some courts will enforce a real estate contract even in the absence of a writing. In such cases the complaining party must clearly show the existence of an oral agreement and that it was performed, so that injustice can only be avoided by enforcing the agreement.

Nearly all real estate contracts require the seller to deliver marketable title to the buyer. This means that the seller's title must be reasonably free of potential doubt, except to the extent that the parties have expressly contracted to the contrary.

Even the simplest transaction requires the buyer to review title and other information concerning the property, and it is common for real estate contracts to be made conditional upon certain events. The parties have an implied obligation to act in good faith when satisfying conditions under a contract. In addition, the time in which conditions must be performed and the transaction closed is ordinarily considered to be a reasonable time. However, when the parties insert a provision stating that "time is of the essence," then performance, at least of important conditions, must be satisfied on or before the date specified.

Because there is almost always a period of time that elapses between signing the contract and its ultimate performance, questions sometimes arise as to the parties respective interests in the property during this interval. The potential risks during this period can be allocated by contract. If the contract is silent in this regard, a majority of states strictly follow the doctrine of equitable conversion and thereby place the risk of loss, and hence the duty to insure during this interval, upon the buyer. A number of states have changed this rule either by adopting the uniform vender-purchaser risk act or by judicially refusing to apply the doctrine of equitable conversion.

In the event of a breach, the parties have various remedies at their disposal. In all jurisdictions, the buyer may seek to specifically enforce the agreement against the seller. A growing minority of jurisdictions hold that the seller may not specifically enforce the agreement against the buyer. These jurisdictions usually conclude that the seller's remedy of damages is adequate.

Either the buyer or seller may recover damages for breach of the contract. Some jurisdictions limit damages to the expenses incurred by the party attempting to perform the contract. This is referred to as the ''out-of-pocket'' rule. The majority rule gives the nonbreaching party the ''benefit-of-the-bargain.'' In other words, the nonbreaching party is entitled to the difference between the contract price and the fair market value usually measured as of the date the contract should have been performed.

A number of jurisdictions have created special rules of liability between a buyer and the builder of residential property. These rules involve imposing liability on a builder for latent defects, regardless of the provisions in the contract between the parties.

14 QUESTIONS

1 For ten years, Kennedy worked for Jackson at Jackson's gas station. Kennedy received less than the normal wages for his work because of an oral promise by Jackson that he would sell the gas station to Kennedy. Jackson fired Kennedy, who sued for specific performance of the oral agreement. Jackson asserts the statute of frauds as a defense. What result?

2 Able makes an oral agreement with Barker to sell Barker a parcel of land. Pursuant to the oral agreement, Barker hired a surveyor and installed a sewer line at a cost of $7,000. Able did not object to the work being done. Able refused to complete the transaction, and Barker sought specific performance. Will it be granted?

3 Carter gave an option to purchase property to Darnell. The option expired. Darnell sought to exercise the option, claiming that it had been orally extended. Can Darnell exercise the option?

4 Seller entered into a contract to sell a fifty-acre farm to buyer. An abstract of title showed that the seller only owned forty-five acres. Seller obtained a legal opinion that the seller had acquired the remaining five acres by adverse possession. Is the seller's title marketable?

5 Seller agrees to sell property to buyer ''free of all encumbrances,'' but title abstract indicates a road maintenance agreement against the property. Buyer obtains an appraiser's opinion that the encumbrance decreases the value of the property by $10,000. Buyer demands that seller reduce the price by this amount. Seller refuses. Buyer seeks specific performance. Who prevails?

6 Seller and buyer have an agreement to sell land, which provides, among other things, that buyer will increase their deposit to $50,000 within thirty days of signing the agreement. On the thirty-fifth day, buyer makes the deposit. Seller refuses to accept the deposit and terminates the contract. Can buyer get specific performance?

7 Seller and buyer have an agreement to sell a retail shopping strip. Before close of escrow, the property is damaged by a flood. The contract is silent as to the risk of loss prior to closing. Must the buyer pay the full purchase price?

8 Dandy Developers construct a fifty-unit condominium project but are only able to sell ten of the units. Elmer buys a unit for $1,000,000. The remaining units are put up for auction and a unit identical to Elmer's sells for $400,000. Does Elmer have any recourse?

9 Frickel purchases a newly built forty-unit apartment building from Sunnyside Enterprises, the builder. After the purchase, the buyer found various design and construction defects at the property. The buyer sues, claiming the buyer breached the implied warranty of habitability. Does such a warranty exist in this case?

CHAPTER 14

THE DEED AND ITS OPERATION

TOPICS CONSIDERED IN THIS CHAPTER:

1 INTRODUCTION

As the previous chapters indicate, there are several ways in which interests in real property can be transferred. Some transfers are voluntary, others involuntary, and some transfers contain elements of both.

With the possible exception of the lease, the most prevalent method of transferring an interest in land is by use of a deed. As a result, the requirements and consequences flowing from the use of a deed deserve particular attention. This chapter will consider types of deeds that are in common use, the warranties that are implied by the use of a deed, and the formalities necessary to accomplish the transfer of an interest in land through use of a deed.

The term *deed* denotes simply an instrument in writing signed and delivered by the grantor wherein an interest in real estate is transferred from the grantor to the grantee. Additional formalities may be necessary in order to satisfy the requirements of the recording statutes and these are considered in Chapter 17.

Except in the case of transfer by will or intestate succession, the transfer of a fee interest is almost always accomplished through use of a deed. Nearly all transfers of real estate by sale or gift will require the use of a deed. In addition, lesser interests such as easements are typically transferred through use of a deed, and a security interest in property, such as a mortgage, must also comply with the requirements pertaining to deeds.

2 HISTORICAL BACKGROUND

We have seen that transfers of interests in real estate have been accomplished through the use of symbolic gestures since the early feudal period. Between the twelfth and seventeenth century, a conveyance was typically accompanied by a public ceremony known as the enfeoffment ceremony.

After the passage of the Statute of Uses in 1536, new methods of creating and transferring interests in real estate arose. Certain interests in land could then be created without the need of a public ceremony. This created the possibility of secret conveyances and, coupled with the inevitable tendency of the human memory to have lapses and, ultimately, be extinguished altogether, elements of uncertainty became a prevalent feature with respect to land transactions.

Finally, in 1677, the passage of the Statute of Frauds established that transfers of interest in real estate must be made by a written document. Before too long, the idea that land records should be maintained became established and the deed, in roughly the form that we now know it, came into prevalent use.

3 TYPES OF MODERN DEEDS

There are many different kinds of deeds used to accomplish land transfers in the United States. To some extent these differences relate merely to local custom and the terminology that is applied to it. Local customs and statutory provisions often require that certain kinds of deeds be used, depending upon the nature of the interest transferred and the status of the grantor. For example, some jurisdictions use a special form of deed when transferring an interest in a condominium unit, and others require particular forms of deeds when the interest is being transferred by a partnership or a corporation. Nevertheless, the deeds in most common use in the United States fall into one of two categories. The first category, known as warranty deed or, in some jurisdictions, the grant deed, provides that the grantor makes certain express or implied promises with regard to the condition of the title to the property. The second kind of deed is known as the quitclaim deed, or deed without warranties, and is delivered to the grantee without express or implied promises with regard to the grantor's title or ability to transfer good title to the grantee.

The difference between the types of deeds will become more clear after consideration is given to the subject of covenants of title.

4 FORMAL REQUIREMENTS PERTAINING TO THE VALIDITY OF A DEED

The essential elements of a valid deed are relatively simple. A deed must be in writing, must identify the grantor and grantee, must describe the property so that it can be identified, must be signed by the grantor who, in turn, must have the legal capacity to transfer the property, and must be delivered to, and in some cases, accepted by the grantee.

A Capacity and Identity of the Parties

Capacity of the Grantor   The capacity of the grantor to execute a deed is similar to the capacity needed to enter into a contract. Thus, the grantor must be of legal age or be acting through a duly appointed legal guardian, must understand the nature of the transaction, the extent and value of the property, and the manner in which he or she desires to dispose of it. When questions arise concerning the competency of the grantor, further questions pertaining to "undue influence" and the existence of a "confidential relationship" often need to be considered.

The subject of capacity and the doctrine of undue influence have been treated both in the context of capacity to make a gift (Chapter 12) and capacity to enter into a contract (Chapter 15). The capacity necessary to transfer property by a deed is very similar to the capacity necessary to enter into a contract.

Undue Influence   In *Delaney v. Delaney,* 402 N.W. 2d 701 (S.D. 1987), the South Dakota court characterized these issues in the following terms:

Undue influence requires a person susceptible to undue influence; an opportunity to exert undue influence and effect a wrongful purpose; a disposition to do so for an improper purpose; and a result clearly showing the effect of undue influence. A confidential relationship arises when the facts show the parties to be on unequal footing and one in a position of dominance over the other.

Whether undue influence exists often depends upon whether the grantor is in a confidential relationship with the grantee. The Mississippi court analyzed the existence and consequences of a confidential relationship in the following terms:

Whenever there is a relation between two people in which one person is in a position to exercise a dominant influence upon the former, arising either from weakness of mind or body, or through trust, the law does not hesitate to characterize such a relationship as fiduciary in character.

A confidential relationship such as would impose the duties of a fiduciary does not have to be a legal one, but may be moral, domestic, or personal. The relationship arises when a dominant, overmastering influence exercises control over a dependent person.

Mullins v. Ratcliff, 515 S. 2d 1183 (Miss. 1987)

Most courts agree that a confidential relationship imposes duties similar to that of a fiduciary upon the grantee. (The features of a fiduciary relationship were considered in Chapter 12) The existence of a confidential relationship will not necessarily preclude the grantee from receiving a valid deed from the grantor.

In *Land v. Land,* (Ill. 1984), the Illinois court was faced with a case where a deed was executed by an 84-year-old woman to her son. The heirs of the grantor challenged the delivery of the deed. The court found in favor of the son and stated the following rule:

The fact that a deed was made between parties standing in a fiduciary relation does not necessarily require that the transaction be set aside. Where a confidential relation exists and the dominant party is the grantee of a deed executed during the existence of the relationship, the conveyance between the parties is presumptively fraudulent, and the burden rests upon the grantee to show the fairness of the transaction and that it was equitable and just and did not proceed from undue influence. . . . There is no rule of law, however, prohibiting a grantor from making a gift to one standing in a fiduciary relation to him, provided the gift is voluntary and not the result of undue influence.

Identity of the Parties   To be valid, a deed must indicate the names of the parties so that they can be identified. This seemingly obvious feature has been extensively regulated by statute. These statutes are intended to minimize the uncertainty and confusion that can arise, particularly where the parties have common names or the grantor has a different name than when title to the property was originally taken. For instance, Jane Smith acquires property in her name, then gets married, changing her name to Jane Jones or Jane Smith Jones. Statutes typically require that a deed from Jane Smith-Jones, as grantor, indicate her prior name and/or the fact that she took title under her prior name. The failure to comply with such statutes may have serious consequences. For instance, in *Puccetti v. Girola,* 128 P. 2d 13 (Cal. 1942), property was taken in the name of Girola Bros. who changed its name to Mandelay, Inc., later delivering a deed from Mandelay, Inc., as grantor to a relative of the officers of Mandelay, Inc., who did not pay consideration for the transfer. A creditor of the Girola Bros. was permitted to set aside the transfer from Mandelay, Inc., based in part upon the failure to comply with the statute.

B Description of the Property

Before a deed may act as a legal conveyance, it is essential that the subject property be described with sufficient certainty to identify the parcel as distinct from all others.

Courts have developed various rules of construction and will, in appropriate circumstances, resort to information outside the deed itself to assist in giving effect to an otherwise ambiguous description. However, if the land cannot be identified, the deed is ineffective to transfer an interest in property.

Types of Descriptions Broadly speaking, there are two ways to describe property in a deed. One is the common or informal description such as a street address or the "The Jones Farm." The second method is known as a legal description.

Informal Descriptions Informal descriptions are seldom used in deeds, although when they do occur, they are still enforceable if the property referred to is otherwise capable of being identified as distinct from other parcels. For instance a deed purporting to convey "my house in Brooklyn" will probably be effective so long as the grantor owns only one house in Brooklyn.

In *Harlan v. Vetter,* 732 S.W. 2d 390 (Tex. 1987), the Texas court summarized the standards for a legally sufficient description:

> The sole purpose of the description of property, as contained in a deed of conveyance, is to identify the subject matter of the grant. And in construing the deed the court endeavors to carry into effect the intention of the parties as expressed therein. Hence, it is a general rule of law that where the description specifies a property intended to be conveyed, and the instrument furnishes other sufficient means of determining the particular property covered thereby, the description is legally sufficient. In other words, if there appears in the instrument enough to enable one by pursuing an inquiry based upon the information contained in the deed to identify the particular property to the exclusion of others, the description will be held sufficient. It is a familiar rule that even though the description of the property contained in the conveyance, standing alone, would be insufficient, yet if it refers to another instrument which contains a proper description of the property, such other instrument may be looked to in aid of the description.

Legal Descriptions Modern practice rarely resorts to the use of the common or informal descriptions in deeds, and legal descriptions are used in the vast majority of cases. Legal descriptions usually involve the services of a surveyor or engineer and will identify the property without resort to extrinsic evidence. Legal descriptions are of three principal types.

Metes and Bounds The metes and bounds description is the oldest method of description and continues to be used in all American states. A metes and bound description begins from a fixed point and attempts, through the use of distances, angles, and sometimes arcs, to delineate the outer boundaries of the property. An example of a metes and bounds description is given below.

Legal Description for 1314 Spruce Street, Berkeley, California.

Beginning at a point on the western line of Spruce Street, distant thereon northerly 406 feet from the northern line of Rose Street, as said streets are shown on said map; running thence along said line of Spruce Street northerly 40 feet to the northern line of said lot 10; thence along the last named line westerly 135 feet to the western line of said lot 10; thence along the last named line southerly 37 feet, more or less, to a line drawn westerly at right angle to said line of Spruce Street from the point of beginning; and thence along said line so drawn easterly 135 feet to the point of beginning.

NOTES AND QUESTIONS

With a protractor or even a ruler, you should be able to follow the description just given and trace the boundaries of the property described. Do you see a problem with the legal description contained above?

Description by Government Survey   The government survey is a system of land description undertaken by the government of the United States during the early nineteenth century in an effort to survey the vast stretches of unexplored land, which it was then intending to settle. It accomplished this by creating thirty-six square-mile parcels of land, each with its own identification, and known as townships. In turn, each township is subdivided into thirty-six one-square-mile (360 acre) parcels known as sections. In turn, each section is further subdivided in a variety of ways, such as the northern southwest one quarter, which can further be subdivided into east and west one half of the southwest one quarter, which can be further subdivided into the southeast one quarter of the southwest one quarter, which can be further subdivided along the same lines. In addition, metes and bounds descriptions are commonly used to further subdivide a section, particularly where the desired description is irregular.

Reference to a Plat or Subdivision Map   Reference to a plat or subdivision map involves a two-step process. A subdivision is first surveyed, usually by virtue of a metes and bounds description in which each parcel within the subdivision is given a number. The original subdivision map is then recorded and subsequent parcels can then be described simply by their number and with reference to the previously recorded subdivision map. This is a simplified method of describing property once the original subdivision survey has been completed and recorded. For instance, ''lot 28, Michel Tract, being a subdivision of the southerly half of lots 15 and 16, Dohr Tract, filed July 26, 1894, map book 14, page 19, Alameda County Records.''

Reference to Physical Monuments   Property descriptions often establish boundaries with reference to physical objects such as streets, trees, rivers, or fences. Rules of construction have been developed concerning the effect to be given to such descriptions, particularly if the location of the physical monument conflicts with some other aspect of the description. Suppose a description calls for a boundary beginning at a fixed point and ''running thirty feet to the old oak tree.'' This description is probably sufficient; however, if the distance from the point of beginning to the oak tree is say twenty-five or thirty-five feet, a question of construction is presented.

Ordinarily, reference to a natural monument prevails in a conflict with distances or angles. Fences may be used as a monument so long as the fence line is visible and relatively permanent. Finally, where a deed contains reference to a boundary that is a street or road, a conveyance to the middle of the road is implied. In other words, a description, ''running along the northerly boundary of Spruce Street,'' is construed to include the mid-point of the street. This presumption can be overcome by specific language in the deed indicating a contrary intent.

C The Requirements of a Writing

With minor exceptions, contracts pertaining to interests in real estate must be in writing in order to be enforceable. (See Chapter 15.) A deed, by its very nature, is a written document, and questions concerning the deed's validity tend to be limited to whether the deed includes the appropriate words of conveyance and the grantor's signature.

Words of Conveyance   In *Harlan v. Vetter,* 732 S.W. 2d 390 (Tex. 1987), cited earlier in this chapter, the Texas court also considered the effect of the following language to accomplish a transfer:

> It is the wish of Eugene H. Harlan, by execution of this instrument, that his wife be considered to own these Mineral Interests, with him as Joint Tenants, with the right of survivorship. . . .

The court considered this language with the following observation:

> For a deed or instrument to effect conveyance of real property, it is not necessary to have all formal parts of a deed formerly recognized at common law or to contain technical words. If, from the whole instrument, a grantor and grantee can be ascertained, and if there are operative words or words of grant showing an intention of the grantor to convey title to a real property interest to the grantee, and if the instrument is signed and acknowledged by the grantor, it is a deed which is legally effective as a conveyance.
>
> However, we are of the opinion that the phrase ''wish . . . [to] be considered'' to ''own'' or ''have'' are not sufficient operative words to convey title. The word ''wish'' is precatory: a recommendation or advice or the expression of desire, but not a positive command or direction.

NOTES AND QUESTIONS

If the objective of reviewing a deed is to give effect to the grantor's intent, was the Texas court incorrect in the Harlan case? To what extent can the court look outside the language of the instrument to determine the grantor's intent?

Signature of the Grantor   In order for a deed to be effective, it must be signed by the grantor. Until the twentieth century, it was also a required formality that the instrument be under seal. This was usually done by obtaining a wax impression and affixing it to the deed. Most American jurisdictions have abolished the requirement of a seal, and those few which still require a seal tend to find the requirement satisfied by a simple ink stamp impression.

As a condition to recording, all states require some additional form of authentication of the deed. Usually this means that the deed must be acknowledged by a notary public who attests to the validity of the grantor's signature. The absence of an acknowledgment typically does not affect the validity of the deed as between the grantor and grantee but simply is a requirement and condition precedent to the deed's being recorded. The requirements necessary to satisfy the recording statutes are considered in the next chapter.

D   Delivery of the Deed

Before a deed can operate to effectively transfer title it must be delivered and become effective during the lifetime of the grantor. Delivery of the deed signifies the passing of dominion and control over the property from the grantor to the grantee. Delivery of the deed is essential to its validity, because the deed takes effect only from the time it is delivered.

In determining whether delivery has occurred, the intention of the grantor is more important than physical transfer of possession of the deed. For instance, in *Sattler v. Sattler,* 507 N.E. 2d 430 (Ohio 1986), the grantor entered into a contract with the grantee to sell certain property and to deliver the deed to the grantee after all payments under the contract had been made. In addition, the parties also agreed that in the event the grantor died, the grantee would own the property without any further obligation under the contract. Grantor delivered a deed to grantee to be used only if the grantor died before all installments under the contract were made. The grantee then recorded this deed and claimed to be the absolute owner of the property. The grantor then sought to set aside the deed. In holding for the grantor the court said:

> In order for delivery of a deed to be effective, there must be an intent to make a present, immediate, and unconditional conveyance. It is the general rule that there is a presumption of delivery arising from the possession of a deed by the named grantee. . . . But the mere manual transfer of a deed does not constitute delivery unless it is coupled with an intent to make a present, immediate, and unconditional conveyance of title.

Conditional Delivery   Particular problems arise when the grantor delivers a deed subject to conditions. The consequences of such a delivery often depend upon whether the delivery is made directly to the grantee or to a third person. The courts are not in agreement as to the effectiveness of a conditional delivery and tend to examine the nature of the condition as an indication of the grantor's intent. For instance, grantor gives the deed to grantee with instructions that it will only take effect in ten years when the grantee turns thirty-five. Most courts would hold that no delivery has occurred because there is no present intention to transfer an immediately operative interest in the property. However, if the grantor attends the grantees thirty-fifth birthday and acknowledges that the grantee is now the owner of the property, delivery has occurred. The grantor now has a present intent to transfer an interest in the property, regardless of the fact that physical delivery of the deed took place years before.

This example may be contrasted with the situation where the grantor delivers the deed to a third party with instructions to deliver it when the grantee turns thirty-five. Assuming the grantor has not retained the right to recall the deed, this is a valid conditional delivery, and delivery will be complete when the third party ultimately delivers the deed to the grantee.

Delivery conditional upon the grantor's death presents additional problems. Ordinarily, if the grantor delivers a deed to the grantee with instructions that it is not to take effect until the grantor's death, no present delivery has occurred, and the deed is not effective. However, a few courts have construed this situation as a transfer of a future interest with a reservation of a life state to the grantor, and thereby have held the conveyance to be effective. Where the grantor delivers the deed to a third party upon condition that it is to take effect upon the death of the grantor, the validity of the deed typically depends upon the person to whom the deed was delivered and whether the grantor retained the ability to obtain a return of the deed.

Phenneger v. Kendrick, 133 N.E. 637 (Ill. 1921)

Facts of the case.

Anna E. Saylor, was a woman of unusual business experience and ability, managing her farms and attending to considerable business affairs. On January 27, 1914, she went to the office of Edwin Johnston, her attorney, and told him that she wanted to make some deeds but did not want the deeds turned over to the grantees at that time. She gave him directions as to how the lands were to be divided and the deeds to be prepared, and she talked the matter over at considerable length, giving reasons for what she was doing. Johnston wrote drafts of the deeds as Saylor directed, and she signed them. She said she was doing business at the Barry Bank, and she wanted to put the deeds in the custody of John Weber of that bank. The attorney told her that it was better to make a delivery to the grantees at the time to avoid any questions. She said she did not want to do that but wanted to put the deeds with Weber, to be delivered at her death. Johnston explained the law on that subject to her, and told her the deposit must be unconditional, with the distinct understanding that it was beyond her recall, and that Weber would have the right to deny her the custody of the deeds; in other words, the delivery must be irrevocable and could not be recalled, and absolute possession must leave her. Saylor said she would do that and brought her husband to the office. He signed the deeds, and they were acknowledged. Saylor took the deeds to the Barry Bank and delivered them to Weber, the cashier, and they remained in the custody of the bank until after her death.

Certain heirs of Anna Saylor have brought this action, claiming that the deeds in question were not delivered and that the property described in the deeds remains part of Anna Saylor's estate to be distributed according to her will. The trial court agreed, finding that the deeds had not been delivered.

OPINION

Delivery is essential to make a deed operative, but no particular ceremony is necessary. It may be by acts without words, or words without acts, or both. No particular form or ceremony is necessary to constitute a delivery, and anything that clearly manifests the intention of the grantor that the deed shall presently become operative and effectual, and that the grantor loses all control over it, constitutes a sufficient delivery. Intention is the controlling element, determining whether a deed has been delivered, and the question depends in great measure upon the particular circumstances of each case.

Where a grantor executes a deed and places it in the hands of a third person to be delivered to the grantee unconditionally after the death of the grantor, and the grantor loses all control and dominion over the deed, such act constitutes a valid delivery, and the deed takes effect, not at the death of the grantor, but immediately upon being delivered in escrow. If the deeds were delivered the title passed, and nothing that Mrs. Saylor could do or say would divest the title.

Reversed.

NOTES AND QUESTIONS

1 When did delivery to the grantees occur? Was the deposit of the deeds a conditional delivery? Do you think that Mrs. Saylor could have demanded that the bank return the deeds to her? Would it matter? Consider the following:

> Where the grantor in a deed deposits it with a third person, to receive and hold the same for delivery to the grantee after the death of the grantor, with a declared or manifest intention to place it beyond the custody and control of grantor and thereby to give it effect as a present conveyance, it is a sufficient delivery, and in such a case title is deemed to vest at once in the grantee with only the enjoyment of the property being postponed.
>
> *Pizel v. Pizel*, 643 P. 2d 1094 (Kan. 1982)

2 It is common for deeds to be delivered to third parties for ultimate delivery to the grantee upon the satisfaction of conditions. For instance, where a grantor delivers a deed to the grantor's agent with instructions to deliver it to the grantee in ninety days, no delivery has occurred until the agent gives the deed to the grantee. This is because the agent acts under the direction of the grantor and must, at any time before the ninetieth day, return the deed to the grantor upon demand. However, if the deed is delivered to an agent of the grantee with the same instructions, a valid delivery has occurred subject only to the condition that ninety days will elapse. This is because the grantee's agent is not obligated to follow the instructions of the grantor, and the delivery is then considered irrevocable and complete.

The Conditional Delivery into Escrow   The mechanics and responsibilities of an escrow holder are more fully described in Chapter 18. Escrow affords a convenient means of effectuating real estate transactions. The grantor delivers a deed into escrow upon condition, among other things, that the grantee deliver to escrow the purchase price. Upon tender of the purchase price by the grantee, the escrow holder delivers the deed to the grantor.

Acceptance by the Grantee   A slight majority of American jurisdictions require that the deed be accepted by the grantee as a final condition of its effectiveness. The apparent rationale for this rule is that no one should be required to own property against her or his will. States requiring some form of acceptance almost unanimously permit it to occur by implication and require no particular affirmative act or conduct by the grantee other than the failure to affirmatively disclaim the interest in the property.

5   COVENANTS OF TITLE

The term *covenant* is one that recurs throughout the law of real estate. We have seen that a covenant is simply an agreement to do or not to do a particular thing. Leases and mortgages often contain covenants, and these will be discussed in the chapters dealing with those subjects. Covenants entered into with respect to the use of land were treated in Chapter 9. Modern subdivisions and condominiums bristle with covenants, which regulate one's right to use the land. Deeds, as well, contain promises, referred to as covenants, by which the grantor makes promises to the grantee, and in some cases to successors of the grantee, respecting the validity to the title of property being transferred in the deed.

Modern real estate transactions typically involve professional title searches and usually the issuance, by an independent third party, of some form of title insurance. Buyers tend to rely upon these professional services when purchasing property. However, the covenants of title continue to be an important aspect of real estate transfers and afford a grantee an independent source of recovery, if there is a defect in the grantor's title.

The operation of deed covenants is largely based upon the express or implied contractual arrangements of the parties. Thus, whether a title defect constitutes a breach of a deed covenant often depends on whether the grantee knew of the defect and agreed to take the property subject to it. To this extent the subject of deed covenants is analogous to the material on marketable title considered in Chapter 13, Section 6.

In the United States the customary covenants of title contained in a warranty deed or a grant deed are the following: 1) Seisin, 2) Right to Convey, 3) Against Encumbrances, 4) Of Quiet Enjoyment, and 5) Of Warranty. Deed covenants or covenants of title refer to the quality of the title transferred by the grantor. For instance, where a life tenant purports to transfer a fee simple interest or where one conveys property which is subject to claims of adverse possession, the grantor's title is of a lesser quality than was contemplated by the parties.

A   Covenants of Seisin and Right to Convey

The covenants of seisin and right to convey are nearly identical and are considered by some courts to be synonymous. They are covenants whereby the transferor promises that he or she is the owner of the property and has the right to both possess and convey an estate of the quantity and quality that is being represented. For example, if the grantor purports to convey property that is also owned by a co-tenant or is subject to a lease and these limitations are not disclosed, the covenants of seisin and right to convey will be breached.

In *Simpson v. Johnson*, 597 P. 2d 600 (Idaho 1979), Johnson transferred property to Simpson by a warranty deed which described the property as having a street frontage of 327.5 feet. This description was taken directly from records in the county assessor's office. In fact, the property had a street frontage of only 267 feet. Neither party knew of the mistake. The court addressed the issue in the following terms:

> The evidence establishes a breach of the covenants of title. In the warranty deed the Johnsons covenanted "that they are the owners in fee simple of said premises. . . ." By this covenant of seisin the Johnsons assured that at the time of conveyances they were lawfully seized of the estate they purported to convey. Here, it is undisputed that the Johnsons did not have title to all the property encompassed by the description in the deed. Generally, a material deficiency in the quantity of land described in the deed constitutes a breach of that covenant.

In *Bosnic v. Hill*, 731 S.W. 2d 204 (Ark. 1987), the grantor conveyed by warranty deed a twenty-five acre parcel to the grantee. Sometime later a third party claimed to own two and one half acres by adverse possession. The grantee filed an action against the third party and ultimately prevailed. The grantee then sought to recover the costs incurred in the prior action. In holding for the grantee, the court gave the following explanation:

> One can wade in the sea of adjudicated cases in order to discover what is meant by the word *seisin* until he is totally submerged and lost. But it seems clear, as matter of common sense, that a covenant of seisin implies that the convenantor is in possession of the land conveyed and all of it, and that if any one is actually in possession claiming adversely to the covenantor, the covenant of seisin is broken, no matter by what right he so claims, and no matter whether his claim is lawful or unlawful, and in any such case the grantee is as much entitled to recover the cost and expense of ejecting him as he would be entitled to those items in unsuccessfully defending his title if he were himself sued in ejectment. In either case he is endeavoring to vindicate the rights under his warranty. If in its suit the adverse claimant, had prevailed, the plaintiff would be entitled to his costs and attorney's fees herein, under nearly all of the adjudicated cases. It would seem strange, indeed, if it could recover them if it had failed in that suit, but could not recover them if it prevailed.

NOTES AND QUESTIONS

1 The covenants of seisin and the right to convey are considered personal covenants that are breached, if at all, when they are made and they are not considered covenants that can be enforced by successors of the grantee.

2 In *Simpson v. Johnson*, suppose that the property had not been surveyed, and therefore neither party knew the actual size of the parcel being transferred. In such a case, how can a seller avoid the possibility that the grantee will come back and seek a reduction in the purchase price?

B   Covenant Against Encumbrances

The covenant against encumbrances is breached when a lien, such as a mortgage is a charge against the land. For instance, when the grantor agrees to transfer property ''free and clear'' but instead transfers the property subject to a mortgage or other lien, the covenant against encumbrances will be breached.

In *Monti v. Tangora,* 425 N.E. 2d 597 (Ill. 1981), the purchaser claimed that the seller breached the covenants in a warranty deed respecting the sale of a residential apartment building where the city closed the building because of building code violations. The evidence indicated that the seller knew of the code violations, but the buyer did not. The court discussed the issue of deed covenants as follows:

> An encumbrance is any right to, or interest in, land which may subsist in a third party to the diminution of the value of the estate, but which is not inconsistent with the passing of the fee by conveyance. Although the word *encumbrance* is said to have no technical, legal meaning, the covenant is construed broadly to include not merely liens such as mortgages, judgment liens, taxes, or others to which the land may be subjected to sale for their payment, but also leases, water rights, easements, restrictions on use, or any right in a third party that diminishes the value or limits the use of the land granted.
>
> The case law in Illinois does not consider building code violations as encumbrances against title. However, plaintiff cites authority from the state of Wisconsin in support of their position. In *Brunke v. Pharo,* the Wisconsin court held that the sale of a building with undisclosed building code violations constitutes a breach of the covenant against encumbrances.
>
> Plaintiff recognizes a split of authority among the jurisdictions, but urges us, nonetheless, to adopt the Wisconsin rule. We have already noted that Illinois cases express the rule that a building code violation is not of itself an encumbrance. We therefore do not adopt the Brunke view. The problem created by the existence of code violations is not one to be resolved by the courts, but is one that can be handled quite easily by the draftsmen of contracts for sale and of deeds. All that is required of the law on this point is that it be certain. Once certainty is achieved, parties and their draftsmen may place rights and obligations where they will. It is the stability of real estate transactions that is of paramount importance here.

NOTE

1 The Illinois court states the prevailing view that building code violations do not constitute a breach of the covenant against encumbrances.

2 Like the covenant of seisin, the covenant against encumbrances is generally considered a personal covenant, which cannot be asserted against the grantor by successors of the grantee.

C   Covenants of Quiet Enjoyment and Warranty

The covenants of warranty and quiet enjoyment are essentially identical and constitute a continuing promise by the grantor to defend the grantees' possessory interest in the land from all lawful claims existing at the date of the transfer and to compensate the grantee for losses resulting from a breach. These covenants are considered real covenants, which run to the benefit of successors of the grantee. These covenants may be breached when the grantee cannot obtain possession of the property because a tenant occupies under a lease, because of an encroachment, or because of an easement across the property.

Some jurisdictions create a distinction between a general warranty and a special warranty. Under this approach, a general warranty means that the grantor agrees to warrant and defend the grantee and his successors against all claims, regardless of when they arose. Under a special warranty, the grantor is considered to agree to warrant and defend against claims that have arisen to the grantor.

The Illinois court described the covenants of warranty and quiet enjoyment in the following terms:

> The covenant of quiet enjoyment is synonymous with the covenant of warranty. By this covenant, the grantor warrants to the grantee, his heirs and assigns, the possession of the premises and that he will defend the title granted by the terms of the deed against persons who may lawfully claim the same, and that such covenant shall be obligatory upon the grantor, his heirs, personal representatives, and assigns.
>
> *Brown v. Lober,* 389 N.E. 2d 1189 (Ill. 1979)

6 REMEDY FOR BREACH OF COVENANTS

The traditional rule in the case of a breach of a deed covenant distinguishes between situations where the grantee's loss is total and where the loss is partial. If, by virtue of a breach of a covenant, the grantee's loss is total, the grantee is entitled to recover any consideration paid to the grantor. However, the grantee is not entitled to recover anticipated profit as is often the case in a breach of contract. If the loss is partial, such as where there is an encumbrance or where there is an easement, then the grantee is entitled to a reduction in the fair market value of the property caused by the title defect. This is done by subtracting the value of the property after the defect is discovered from its value before the defect existed. See *Yonkers v. Josanth,* 494 N.E.2d 452 (N.Y. 1986).

7 STATUTES AFFECTING DEED COVENANTS

All states have enacted statutes that attempt to codify the use of deed covenants. The Massachusetts statute is a typical example:

Massachusetts General Statute 183–16

In a conveyance of real estate the words *warranty covenants* shall have the full force, meaning and effect of the following words: "The grantor, for himself, his heirs, executors, administrators, and successors, covenants with the grantee, his heirs, successors, and assigns, that he is lawfully seized in fee simple of the granted premises; that they are free from all encumbrances; that he has good right to sell and convey the same, and that he will, and his heirs, executors, administrators, and successors shall warrant and defend the same to the grantee and his heirs, successors, and assigns forever against the lawful claims and demands of all persons.''

Massachusetts General Statute 183–17

In a conveyance of real estate the words *quitclaim covenants* or the words *limited covenants* shall have the full force, meaning, and effect of the following words: ''The grantor, for himself, his heirs, executors, administrators, and successors, covenants with the grantee, his heirs, successors, and assigns, that the granted premises are free from all encumbrances made by the grantor, and that he will, and his heirs, executors, administrators, and successors shall warrant and defend the same to the grantee and his heirs, successors, and assigns forever against the lawful claims and demands of all persons claiming by, through, or under the grantor, but against none other.''

The Uniform Land Transaction Act provides as follows:

A seller who executes a deed that does not provide to the contrary implies that:

   1 The real estate is free from all encumbrances;

   2 The buyer will have quiet and peaceable possession of, or right to enjoy, the real estate conveyed;

   3 The seller has power and right to convey the title which he or she purports to convey; and

   4 The seller will defend the title to the real estate conveyed against all persons lawfully claiming it.

8   SUMMARY

A deed is perhaps the most typical instrument used to transfer interests in real estate. Although a deed is usually used to accomplish a transfer pursuant to a contract, deeds are also effective to transfer property by gift.

The term *deed* denotes an instrument in writing, signed and delivered by the grantor, whereby an interest in real estate is transferred from the grantor to the grantee.

There are a wide variety of deeds in modern use, and the terminology used to designate them depends largely upon local practice and custom. More important is whether or not the deed creates warranties of title. The warranty deed, sometimes known as the grant deed, typically implies that the grantor warrants that certain covenants of title are included. On the other hand, a quitclaim deed does not imply warrants of title but simply transfers whatever interest the grantor may have.

In order to be effective, a deed must satisfy various formalities. The deed must be in writing and signed by the grantor. It must include language indicating the intention to transfer an interest in the property, and the property must be described so that it can be conclusively identified.

The deed must also be delivered and, in some jurisdictions, it must be accepted by the grantee. Delivery is said to be a question of the grantor's intent to transfer a presently operative interest in the property. The grantor may make a conditional delivery of the deed but such delivery is effective only if the grantor relinquishes the right to recall the deed, unless the condition fails.

The covenants of title contained in warranty deeds create assurances in favor of the grantee that the grantor has the right and ability to transfer the interest that the grantor purports to convey. The covenants of seisin, right to convey, and against encumbrances are considered personal to the grantee and are breached, if at all, when the deed is delivered in violation of the deed covenants. The covenants of warranty and quiet enjoyment are considered continuing covenants, which require the grantor to defend the grantee's title if it is challenged and to compensate the grantee for losses suffered.

9 QUESTIONS

1 Grandmother gives a deed to her grandson that is absolute on its face. She imposes the following oral condition: "This deed is to become effective only if you maintain a *B* average during your next three years at college." Has a delivery of the deed been made?
2 Grandmother makes a deed in favor of her granddaughter and delivers it to escrow with instructions that the deed is only to be delivered if granddaughter maintains a *B* average during college. Granddaughter maintains only a *C* average but the escrowholder, feeling sorry for her, gives her the deed anyway. Has delivery occurred?
3 Bob owns a one hundred acre farm and wants to transfer fifty acres to his son. He makes out a deed describing the land as "one half of my farm" and delivers it to the son. Is the deed effective?
4 Euclid makes a deed in favor of Frieda, telling her it is in his desk drawer and that she is to have it when he dies. Frieda can't wait, takes the deed, and sells the property to Gipper. What are the respective rights of Euclid, Frieda, and Gipper?
5 Igor sold investment property to Jantzen. Unknown to Jantzen, the property was leased for ten-year term to Kendel. Has a warranty been breached? What is Jantzen's remedy?

CHAPTER 15

RECORDING STATUTES
AND PRIORITIES

TOPICS CONSIDERED IN THIS CHAPTER:

1 INTRODUCTION

The general purpose of the recording statutes is to provide a public record of transactions affecting title to land, so that interested persons can determine the ownership of land and be reasonably certain that their interests will be protected. For the most part, recording is not essential between the actual parties to a transaction. In other words, if *A* gives a deed or mortgage to *B*, *B*'s failure to record the instrument does not affect the validity of the obligation between *A* and *B*. Recording is important in relation to the rights of third parties. Thus if *A* gives a deed to *B* who records it, and *A* then gives a deed to *C*, *C* has no interest because he or she is deemed to know of the deed to *B* because it was recorded. However, if *B* does not record the deed and

A then gives a deed to *C, B*'s failure to record may invalidate *B*'s interest in the property as against the claims of *C*.

2 HISTORY OF RECORDING ACTS

Recording statutes have existed in America since colonial times but they were not a part of early common law of England. As we have seen, early methods of conveying land were conducted without any written instrument. The Statute of Frauds, enacted in 1677, set the stage for a more orderly system of keeping and maintaining records of ownership to land.

The common law arrangement created a priority between subsequent grantees of the deed. However, the recording statutes are not concerned with delivery of the deed but create priority based upon the time of recording.

3 PERSONS PROTECTED BY RECORDING

The kinds of questions resolved by the recording statutes may be illustrated by the following examples: Suppose that *A* delivers a deed to escrow for the benefit of *B*, to be delivered to *B* in ten days and upon the payment of $100,000. Meanwhile, *A* opens another escrow, on the same terms, this time preparing a deed for the benefit of *C*. Both *B* and *C* pay *A* and their respective deeds are recorded. Who owns the property? In other words, who has priority?

One court has observed that "the recording acts have been enacted in response to a need to provide protection for purchases of real property against the risk of prior secret conveyances by the seller," *Page v. Fees-Krey,* 617 P.2d 1188 (Colo. 1980).

Another court recognized a twofold aspect of recording statutes:

> We proceed from the premise that the recording act was enacted to accomplish a twofold purpose. First, it was intended to protect the rights of innocent purchasers who acquire an interest in property without knowledge of prior transfers. Second, the statute was designed to establish a public record which would furnish potential purchasers with notice, or at least "constructive notice," of previous conveyances and encumbrances that might affect their interests.
>
> *Andy Association v. Bankers Trust,* 399 N.E. 2d 1160 (N.Y. 1979)

All American states have enacted recording statutes. These statutes vary significantly from state to state, and precise determination of the priorities created by them can only be determined by an examination of the law in that particular jurisdiction. Nevertheless, the variations among the states concern the finer points of priorities created by the recording statutes, all of which fall within one of the three categories that are set forth in Section 5 of this chapter. The recording statutes tend only to protect good faith purchasers, namely those who acquire their interest for value, in good faith, and without notice of a prior transfer. As a result, these topics are the first to be considered in this chapter.

Bona Fide Purchaser   As indicated, the protection afforded by the recording statutes usually applies only to a bona fide purchaser or mortgagee, or one who has acquired title from such a party. A bona fide purchaser (B.F.P.) is one who acquires an interest in property in good faith, for a valuable consideration, and without notice of the claims of another.

Value Under most recording systems, the only persons entitled to protection are those who give value for their interest and acquire it without notice of prior claims. As a result, one who acquires their interest by virtue of a gift has parted with nothing of value and is not protected by the recording statutes (Colorado is the only exception based on the peculiar wording of its recording statute).

The value that must be given to obtain protection under the recording statutes is similar to, but not identical to, the notion of consideration in contract law. One need not give full value in order to be protected. However, if one gives substantially less than full value, it is often argued that the bargain price should have put the purchaser on notice of a potential prior claim. The interaction between value and notice are treated next.

4 NOTICE

There is a lack of harmony in the cases and among writers about the manner in which the concept of notice should be identified and delineated. Fortunately, this issue is largely one of terminology. This text adopts the majority view that there are three kinds of notice identified as follows:

1 Actual Notice
2 Constructive Notice
3 Inquiry Notice

We have previously seen the operation of notice in connection with equitable servitudes in Chapter 9.

1 Actual notice is similar to knowledge and, in the context of the recording acts, refers to the actual receipt of information concerning the adverse claim. Thus if *A* gives a deed to *B* and then gives a deed to *C*, while telling *C* of the prior delivery to *B*, *C* has actual notice of *B*'s potential prior claim.

2 Constructive notice occurs when one is deemed to have notice of a particular event, regardless of his or her actual state of mind or knowledge of the event. For instance, the operation of the recording statutes imparts constructive notice of any instrument that is properly recorded. So if *A* delivers a deed to *B* who records it and then delivers a deed to *C*, *C* is charged with constructive notice of *B*'s recorded deed regardless of whether *C* actually knew of the prior deed. The imparting of constructive notice is the most important function of the recording statutes.

3 Inquiry notice involves the existence of information that would make a reasonably prudent person sufficiently suspicious of a prior claim to undertake an investigation to determine its existence. When inquiry notice arises, one is charged with knowledge of all matters that would have been discovered had a reasonable investigation been undertaken. When one acquires an interest in real estate he or she is charged with notice of everything that an inspection of the property would reveal.

The case of *Martinique Realty Corp. v. Hull,* 166 A. 2d 803 (N.J. 1960), described inquiry notice as follows:

> An essential characteristic of the bona fide purchaser is his lack of notice of the interest of the unrecorded or late-recorded party. It is long settled that the purchaser of an interest in property has a duty to make inquiry as to the extent of the rights of any person of the premises; if this duty is not discharged, then notice is imputed to the purchaser of all facts which a reasonably prudent inquiry would have revealed.

In the case of *Jefferson County v. Mosley,* 226 S. 2d 653 (Alabama 1969), Dillard conveyed a roadway easement across his property to Jefferson County, which did not record the instrument. The easement was described as being eighty feet wide and for the purpose of widening a previously existing gravel road, which was visible on the property. Two years later, Dillard conveyed the entire parcel to Mosley without reference to the easement. The deed to Mosley stated that it was ''subject to all public roads or easements and rights of way.'' Mosley claimed he was a bona fide purchaser who took the property free of the easement of the county.

The question presented was whether Mosley was an innocent purchaser for value without notice of Jefferson County's rights under the easement. The court addressed the question in the following terms:

> As far as the record discloses, Mosley, at the time he secured his deed from Dillard, did not have actual knowledge of the deed executed by Dillard to Jefferson County. He was not charged with the constructive notice because Jefferson County did not record its deed until after Mosley secured his deed and after it was recorded.
>
> But it is well settled in this state that whatever is sufficient to excite attention and put the party on his guard and call for inquiry is notice of everything to which the inquiry would have led; that when a person has sufficient information to lead him to a fact, he shall be deemed conversant with it; that one who has knowledge of facts sufficient to put him on inquiry as to the existence of an unrecorded deed is not a purchaser without notice within the protection of the registry statutes.
>
> It has been said that it is difficult, if not impossible, to lay down any general rule as to what facts will in every case be sufficient to charge a party with notice or put him on inquiry.
>
> Cases from other states are authority for the proposition that a person is charged with notice of the contents of the instrument by which he takes title and of all the facts which would be disclosed with a reasonably diligent search.
>
> It seems to us that a reasonably prudent man who obtained a deed containing an exception such as was included in the deed from Dillard to Mosley would have made inquiry from his grantor as to why such an exception was included. If such an inquiry had been made, Mosley would no doubt have been advised of the right-of-way deed executed by Dillard to Jefferson County in 1945.
>
> In addition, the existence of the road at the time Mosley secured his deed from Dillard was apparent, and its presence was such notice as to put Mosley on inquiry, and the notice was not confined to that part of the right-of-way used as a road or highway, but extended to the lands described in the deed from Dillard to Jefferson County.
>
> The established rules of law may operate harshly in this case, but they are well established, and we have no alternative but to apply the law as it is.

In conclusion, we hold that Mosley was not a bona fide purchaser for value without notice of Jefferson County's easement.

NOTES AND QUESTIONS

1 Was it the fact that the road was apparent or the exception in the deed which led to the result in this case?

2 Would the result be different if Dillard had told Mosley that the road was no longer used and that no one had the right to use it?

The following case demonstrates the problems that can arise when a grantor makes multiple conveyances.

Wineberg v. Moore, 194 F. Supp. 12 (N.D. Cal. 1961)

Facts of the case.

Barker sold 880 acres of land to Wineberg. Wineberg did not record the deed for three years. In the interim, Barker sold the timber rights of the same property to Construction Engineers, who recorded their interest. Barker then sold the fee interest in the property to Natural Resources, Inc., who also recorded. Wineberg had paid the taxes on the property since receiving his deed, had posted "no trespassing" signs on the property that listed Wineberg's name, and Wineberg used the only building on the property as a recreational home. The road leading to the property was obstructed by a locked gate. The question in the case was whether the interests of Natural Resources and Construction Engineers was superior to that of Wineberg.

OPINION

The critical factual question for resolution is whether or not Wineberg's possession was sufficient to impart notice to Construction Engineers, Inc., and Natural Resources, Inc., which would prevent them from establishing a superior right to the property.

The common law rule was that once a grantor conveyed all his or her interest in a parcel of real property the grantor could create no further rights in the property in a third person, absent any elements of estoppel. The recording statutes have altered this rule, for it is now possible for a grantor to make a second conveyance divesting the first grantee, as long as the second grantee pays a valuable consideration, records first, and is in good faith. The California recording statute requires the second purchaser to be without notice, actual or constructive, of the interest of the prior purchaser. A deed that is not recorded is nevertheless valid between the parties thereto, and persons who have notice thereof. Section 18 of the Civil Code of the State of California defines notice as follows:

One who purchases property from a title holder of record where a third person is in possession is presumed to purchase "with full notice of all the legal and equitable rights in the premises of such party in possession and in subordination of these rights, and this presumption is only to be overcome or rebutted by clear and explicit proof on the part of such purchaser, of diligent, unavailing effort by the vendee to discover or obtain actual notice of any legal or equitable rights in behalf of the party in possession." In the absence of actual inquiry a person is still chargeable with the notice imparted by possession—such notice is akin to, if not equivalent to, constructive notice.

Thompson in his treatise on real property states that:

It is held that the law will impute to a purchaser all information which would be conveyed to him by an actual view of the premises.
Thompson on Real Property (permanent edition), Vol. 8, Section 4464, page 318.

This "view of the premises" is by actual visit to the property and not by looking at an aerial map of the terrain nor by flying over the property, even if this is customary with some persons who do not conduct themselves in a prudent manner. This approach may be suitable in an inaccessible terrain, but not as here, where the property is readily accessible by automobile.

The acts of dominion exercised by Wineberg do not present the strongest case possible in his favor, but, nevertheless, in viewing all the acts and circumstances surrounding the timber contract from Barker to Construction Engineers, Inc., and the conveyance from Barker to Natural Resources, Inc., these acts were sufficient to prevent these defendants from claiming that they purchased their respective interests "in good faith."

NOTES AND QUESTIONS

Is this a correct resolution of the case? After all, Wineberg need only have recorded his deed and the subsequent grantees could have searched the record and learned of the prior conveyance.

5 TYPES OF RECORDING STATUTES

The recording statutes in American jurisdictions fall into three general categories: (1) a race statute, (2) a notice statute, and (3) a race-notice statute. These are examined next:

Race Statutes Under the pure race statutes, the first party to record their interest prevails. Under a race statute, the concept of notice is largely irrelevant. For example, A conveys to B who does not record, A then conveys to C who records, C prevails over B regardless of whether C had notice of the prior conveyance to B simply because C was the first to record.

Race statutes have the virtue of simplicity and certainty, but they also contain substantial potential for injustice. Only two states, North Carolina and Louisiana, have pure race statutes and, even in those states, courts have tended to intervene and refused to apply the statute in cases involving outright fraud.

Notice Statutes   Under a notice statute, it does not matter who records first and a second purchaser will have priority provided she or he takes without notice of a prior claim, regardless of who first records. For example, if *A* conveys to *B* who does not record, and then *A* conveys to *C*, *C* will prevail provided she did not have notice of the prior conveyances to *B*.

Notice statutes tend to promote an equitable result because a subsequent purchaser, who has notice, will not prevail. In our example, *B* would have been protected simply by recording the instrument and the failure to take advantage of the recording statutes may result in the loss of the property interest in favor of a good faith purchaser without notice. In this case, the equities would tend to lean in favor of *C* who, at least to some extent, was deprived of the opportunity to have notice of the prior conveyances by virtue of *B*'s failure to make use of the recording statutes, which would have afforded constructive notice to *C*. Approximately one half of the states have NOTICE type statutes.

Race-Notice Statutes   Under a race-notice recording statute, a subsequent bona fide purchaser prevails over a prior interest provided they are the first to record. In the prior example, where *A* conveys to *B* and *A* then conveys to *C*, *C* will again prevail if she does not have notice, but only if she records her deed prior to its being recorded by *B*. However, if *B* records first and if *B* is also a good faith purchaser without notice, *B* will prevail over *C*. Race-notice statutes are in affect in approximately half of the American jurisdictions.

Policy Considerations   It may be useful at this point to recall the purposes of the recording statute. An eminent authority summarizes them as follows:

> Their [recording acts'] object has been variously stated as being the original one of securing a prompt recordation of all conveyances by according priority of right to the purchaser who is first to record his conveyance, the equitable one of protecting subsequent purchasers against secret and unknown conveyances and agreements by reason of which they would otherwise be prejudiced, and the constructive one of preserving an accessible history of each title, so that anyone needing the information may reliably ascertain in whom the title is vested and the encumbrances against it.
>
> Patton Land Titles, Section 6, A p. 15

The three basic types of recording acts reflect different emphases among the purposes that Patton describes: Race, giving priority to the first transferee to record; notice, giving priority to the transferee who acquires an interest without notice of a prior transfer; and race-notice, giving priority to the transferee who acquires an interest without notice of a prior transfer only if that subsequent transferee is first to record.

The race statute encourages compliance with the recording statute by rewarding the first person to record. However, it tends to encourage fraudulent practices and, by disregarding the concept of notice, tends to ignore the other policy objectives that the recording statutes seek to advance.

The notice statute tends to achieve more equitable results than a race statute because a subsequent purchaser will only prevail if he or she acquires interest without notice—actual, constructive, or inquiry of the prior conveyance.

The race-notice statute includes attributes of both the race and notice forms of recording statutes. An example of the race-notice statute is found in New York, which provides that:

> Every conveyance not so recorded is void as against any person who subsequently purchases . . . in good faith . . . and whose conveyance . . . is first duly recorded. . . .
>
> *N.Y. Real Property Law,* Section 291

The race-notice statute imposes two requirements upon a subsequent purchaser. First, he or she must acquire the interest without notice of the prior conveyance and, second, he or she must be the first to record it.

It is not always clear from the language of the statute whether a jurisdiction follows a notice or race-notice approach. For example, in the case of *Page v. Fees-Krey,* 617 P. 2d 1188 (Colo. 1980), the court examined the Colorado recording statute, which provides as follows:

> All deeds, or other instruments in writing conveying or affecting the title to real property, . . . may be recorded in the office of the county clerk and recorder and no such instrument or document shall be valid as against any class of persons with any kind of rights, except between the parties thereto and such as have notice thereof, until the same is deposited with such county clerk and recorder. . . ."

The court's opinion contained the following discussion:

> Plaintiff contends that the Colorado Recording Act should be construed as a "race-notice" recording statute, pursuant to which a transferee of an interest in real property can prevail over a prior conflicting interest in that property only if he takes without notice of the prior interest and secures priority of record as against that interest. I disagree with this construction of the statute. Our recording statute is most appropriately characterized as a "pure notice" recording statute, pursuant to which the subsequent transferee, in order to prevail over the prior interest, must take without notice but need not secure priority of record as against that interest.
>
> Because the Colorado recording statute does not explicitly require that the transferee of real property secure priority of record as against a prior transferee, it more closely resembles a "pure notice" statute than a "race-notice" statute.
>
> Among the purposes of the Colorado recording statute is to "render title to real property and every interest therein more secure and marketable." Characterization of the statute as a "pure notice" recording statute best serves this policy. The "pure notice" construction tends toward security and marketability of titles, because it enables a transferee of an interest in real property, when he evaluates the validity of that interest with respect to possible prior transfers, to rely on record title as it exists at the time of the conveyance to him, without regard to the possibility of subsequent recording of a prior transfer. On balance, a "pure notice" statute provides the greater incentive toward prompt recording of documents of conveyance, enhancing the completeness of title records and, hence, the security and marketability of title to real property.

NOTES AND QUESTIONS

1 Do you agree with the court's statement of the advantage of the pure notice statute?

2 Section 3–202 of the Uniform Simplification of Land Transfers Act (USLTA) provides, in part, as follows:

> A purchaser for value who has recorded his conveyance also acquires the real estate free of any subsisting adverse claim, whether or not the transferor had actual authority to convey, unless the adverse claim is:
>
> (1) created or evidenced by a document recorded before the conveyance to the purchaser is recorded;
>
> (2) of a person using or occupying the real estate whose use or occupancy is inconsistent with the record title to the extent the use or occupancy would be revealed by reasonable inspection or inquiry;
>
> (3) one of which the purchaser had knowledge at the time his interest was created.

3 How would you characterize the USLTA recording statute?

6 THE MECHANICS OF RECORDING

The mechanics of recording are relatively simple, although failure to comply with them may have serious consequences. Ordinarily, documents affecting property must be recorded in the Office of the Recorder in the county or counties where the property is situated.

The most important condition to recording is that the document be acknowledged or witnessed. This procedure involves simply signing the document in the presence of a notary public or some other public official, who authenticates the signature and affixes some kind of seal or stamp to the document. The purpose of this requirement is similar to that pertaining to the witnessing of wills and is simply an effort to minimize and reduce the incidence of forgery. Ordinarily the Recorder's Office will not accept an instrument for recording unless it is properly acknowledged.

The Uniform Simplification of Land Transfers Act has deleted the requirement of an acknowledgement as a condition to recording (USLTA Section 2–301 b). This position has not found support in state statutes, which almost invariably require some form of authentication before an instrument can be recorded.

In addition to the recording requirements imposed by state law, local county recorder's offices often impose their own conditions to the recording of documents. Such conditions might include the payment of transfer taxes or the filing of an affidavit or other document relative to the purchase price of the property and almost invariably require that certain recording fees be paid prior to accepting the instrument for recording.

7 METHODS OF INDEXING

The two primary methods of indexing instruments affecting property in the United States are the grantor/grantee index and the tract index. Although the tract index is easier to use and is gradually being implemented in various areas, the grantor/grantee index is still the most prevalent and is likely to remain so for some time.

The grantor/grantee index lists all transfers that have been recorded under the names of both the grantor and the grantee. Using the grantor/grantee index, the recorder keeps two separate sets of books, one for grantors and one for grantees. The books are indexed alphabetically, covering certain periods of time and will enable one to search the title backward to determine the chain of title respecting a particular parcel.

The tract index designates to each parcel in a county a particular number, so that all transactions affecting the parcel can be indexed as against that particular tract. The tract index is simpler to use and maintain and it does not give rise to many of the problems pertaining to the "chain of title" that are illustrated in the following cases.

A document is "in the chain of title" if it can be located by an ordinary examination of the public records. If a prudent examination of the public records does not reveal the existence of a recorded document, it is considered to be "outside the chain of title." The following case illustrates the problems that can arise when a document is recorded outside the chain of title.

Sabo v. Horvath, 559 P. 2d 138 (Alaska 1976)

Facts of the case.

This appeal arises because Grover C. Lowery conveyed the same five-acre piece of land twice—first to William A. Horvath and Barbara J. Horvath and later to William Sabo and Barbara Sabo. Both conveyances were by separate documents entitled "Quitclaim Deeds." Lowery's interest in the land originates in a patent from the United States Government under the Alaska Homesite Law. Lowery's conveyance to the Horvaths was prior to the issuance of the patent, and his subsequent conveyance to the Sabos was after the issuance of the patent. The Horvaths recorded their deed on January 5, 1970; the Sabos recorded their deed on December 13, 1973. The transfer to the Horvaths, however, predated patent and title, and thus the Horvaths' interest in the land was recorded "outside the chain of title." Mr. Horvath brought suit to quiet title, and the Sabos counterclaimed to quiet their title.

The superior court held that Horvath had the superior claim to the land because his prior recording had given the Sabos constructive notice.

OPINION

In this case, the Horvaths recorded their interest from Lowery prior to the time the Sabos recorded their interest. Thus, the issue is whether the Sabos are charged with constructive knowledge because of the Horvaths' prior recordation. Horvath is correct in his assertion that in the usual case a prior recorded deed serves as constructive notice and thus precludes a subsequent recordation from taking precedence. Here, however, the Sabos argue that because Horvath recorded his deed prior to Lowery having obtained his patent, they were not given constructive notice by the recording system. They contend that since Horvaths' recordation was outside the chain of title, the recording should be regarded as a "wild deed."

It is an axiom of law that a purchaser has notice only of recorded instruments that are within his "chain of title." If a grantor (Lowery) transfers prior to obtaining title, and the grantee (Horvath) records prior to title passing, a second grantee who diligently examines all conveyances under the grantor's name from the date that the grantor had secured title would not discover the prior conveyance. The rule in most jurisdictions that have adopted a grantor-grantee index system of recording is that a "wild deed" does not serve as constructive notice to a subsequent purchaser who duly records.

Alaska's recording system utilizes a grantor-grantee index. Had Sabos searched title under both grantor's and grantee's names but limited his search to the chain of title subsequent to patent, he would not be chargeable with discovery of the pre-patent transfer to Horvath.

On one hand, we could require Sabo to check beyond the chain of title to look for pretitle conveyances. While in this particular case, the burden may not have been great, as a general rule, requiring title checks beyond the chain of title could add a significant burden as well as uncertainty to real estate purchases.

It is unfortunate that in this case due to Lowrey's double conveyances, one or the other party to this suit most suffer an undeserved loss. We are cognizant that in this case, the equities are closely balanced between the parties to this appeal. Our decision, however, in addition to resolving the litigants' dispute, must delineate the requirements of Alaska's recording laws.

Because we want to promote simplicity and certainty in title transactions, we choose to follow the majority rule and hold that the Horvaths' deed, recorded outside the chain of title, does not give constructive notice to the Sabos and is not "duly recorded" under the Alaskan Recording Act. Since the Sabos' interest is the first duly recorded interest and was recorded without actual or constructive knowledge of the prior deed, we hold that the Sabos' interest must prevail. The trial court's decision is accordingly.

Reversed.

NOTES AND QUESTIONS

1 The Indiana Court of Appeals in a case similar to that of the Sabo case, made the following observation:

Recording acts are designed to protect subsequent purchasers and encumbrances from a common grantor. They impact constructive notice only to those who claim through or under the grantor in question. However, an otherwise valid instrument which is not entitled to be recorded or is improperly recorded, or recorded out of the chain of title, does not operate as constructive notice but may bind persons having actual notice.

(*Rogers v. City of Evansville*, 437 N.E. 2d 1019 (Ind. 1982)

2 What kind of recording statute is in effect in Alaska? Would a similar result be obtained under a different type of recording statute?

3 Would the same result be obtained in a jurisdiction having a tract system rather than a grantor/grantee index system? Consider the case of *Hanson v. Zeller,* 187 N.W. 2d 47 (Ind. 1971), which provided by statute for a tract index:

> The registers of deeds shall prepare from the records of their offices respectively, and shall hereafter keep a numerical index of the deeds, mortgages, and other instruments of record in their respective offices affecting or relating to the title to real property, in lieu of the indexes by names of grantors and grantees, as now kept.

An issue arose concerning the operation of the Indiana System, and the court made the following observations concerning the tract system:

> The existence of a tract index, which not only makes all instruments equally accessible to reasonable search, and which has its primary focus upon tracts of land rather than upon grantors and grantees, makes the concept of "chain of title," as developed in relation to the old grantor and grantee type index, inapplicable.
>
> Under the tract index system the title is traced by searching the tract index for instruments pertaining to the tract to be searched. The names of the grantor and grantee are not material to this search. We conclude that a prospective purchaser cannot be deemed to have constructive notice of instruments that are not indexed in the tract index under the specific tract of real estate to which they pertain. We conclude that there must be substantial compliance with those sections of the recording laws that pertain to the matter of notice in order to give constructive notice. Failure to index an instrument in the tract index does not constitute such compliance.
>
> Except as the existence of error is apparent on the face of the record, a subsequent purchaser is bound by what appears upon the record only, regardless of the contents of the original instrument. This rule places the loss upon the beneficiary in the instrument in the transcribing of which the error was made. As between him and the subsequent purchaser, he is the only one who had it in his power to make comparison and to have the error corrected, and upon him devolved the duty, not merely of filing his instrument for record, but of having it correctly recorded.

4 Although the tract system is generally considered superior to the grantor/grantee index, the grantor/grantee index is by far the more widely used in this country. Is there a reason for this? And, as the Hanson case illustrates, even the tract index is not free of problems and resulting losses to land purchasers.

8 ERRORS BY THE RECORDING OFFICER

Given the great number of documents submitted for recording, particularly in more populous counties, and the fact that indexing systems, particularly the grantor/grantee index, are only marginally efficient, it is no surprise that errors occur from time to time. For instance, *A* gives a mortgage to *B* who records it. Through error by the recording officer, the mortgage is either not recorded or indexed incorrectly. *A* then sells to *C* without paying the mortgage. Who bears the loss, *B* or *C*?

The state courts that have considered the issue are fairly equally divided as to who must suffer the loss from errors committed by the recording officer. Some courts hold that a grantee, by presenting the instrument to the recorder's office, is absolved of the consequences of the recorder's failure to record it or recording it in the wrong index. These states hold, in essence, that one has no duty to see that an instrument is properly recorded after it has been given to the recording officer. States following this approach include Alabama, Illinois, Massachusetts, Pennsylvania, and Texas. Other states hold that subsequent purchasers are bound only by what is properly recorded and that a grantee of a conveyance bears the responsibility of making certain that the recording was correctly accomplished. Among the states holding this view are California, Georgia, Maryland, Michigan, New York, North Carolina, and Washington.

QUESTION

What are the policy considerations that would be relevant in deciding which approach should be adopted?

9 SUMMARY

The recording statutes provide a means whereby a record of transactions affecting land titles is maintained so that purchasers and lenders can determine the owner of property and the existence of encumbrances against the owner's interest. Recording a document imparts constructive notice of the documents' contents.

The recording statutes are intended to protect parties who have paid value to acquire their interest in the property and who acquire their interest without notice of the prior claims of others. One who meets this standard is often referred to as the bona fide purchaser for value or the B.F.P.

The most difficult aspect of the B.F.P. concept is the requirement that the interest be acquired without notice of prior claims. Notice can be acquired in three ways: the first is actual notice, which implies knowledge of the prior claim. The second form of notice is constructive notice, which is notice implied by law, particularly that notice which is imparted by compliance with the recording statutes. The final form of notice is inquiry notice, which involves the existence of circumstances that would arouse the suspicions of a reasonably prudent person as to the existence of a competing interest in the property. One who is charged with inquiry notice, will be deemed to have knowledge of all facts that a reasonable inquiry would have uncovered.

Recording statutes are of three types. The race statute holds that the first party to record prevails. This type of statute has few adherents and is of little modern significance. American jurisdictions typically follow either the notice or race-notice approach. Under a notice statute, a subsequent purchaser prevails provided he or she does not have notice of the prior conveyance. Under a race-notice statute, a subsequent purchaser prevails if he or she does not have notice and if he or she is the first to record.

Recording a document is usually a routine matter, requiring simply that the document be notarized and that applicable recording fees be paid. However problems still arise, which are beyond the power of the party seeking to record. When a party attempts to record a document but fails to accomplish this end, most jurisdictions attempt to place the loss upon the party who is in the best position to avoid the error.

10 QUESTIONS

1 Adam delivers a deed to Betty who, in turn, gives it to Carl, her agent, with instructions to record it the next day. Carl forgets to record the deed. Does the failure to record affect the transfer from Adam to Betty?

2 Courtney sells a single-family home by delivering a deed to Dalton. Dalton takes possession but does not record. Courtney, short of funds, borrows money and gives a mortgage against the property to Elmira Bank, which records. Prior to recording, Courtney told Elmira that Dalton was a tenant and produced a phony lease. Is Elmira a good faith encumbrancer?

3 Suppose you are contemplating the purchase of a multi-unit apartment building. You are concerned about knowing the terms and duration of the leases by which the tenants occupy. You ask the seller to give you copies of the leases, which the seller does. Have you satisfied your burden of making inquiry? What possible problems might arise if you do nothing more than get copies of the leases? What additional step might you take under the circumstances?

4 Suppose you have just purchased an option on raw land, intending to obtain necessary plans and permits to develop the property. You are wary of the seller and want to protect your rights under the option. What can you do?

5 Suppose Frank transfers property to Gregory by deed with height and building setback limitations. Gregory then transfers the property to Hilda to transfer to Irving. All transfers are duly recorded. Only the deed to Gregory contains the restrictions. Is Irving bound by the restriction? (Assume all requirements of a covenant running with the land have been met.)

CHAPTER 16

CLOSING THE TRANSACTION: ESCROW HOLDERS AND INSURERS OF TITLE

TOPICS CONSIDERED IN THIS CHAPTER:

1 INTRODUCTION

We have seen that the process of transferring real estate by contract tends to be more involved than the sale of personal property. Even the simple sale of a single-family residence usually involves a series of contractual relations between various parties, which must be performed before the transaction is in a position to be finalized. A typical transaction involves a contract between the seller and the seller's agent; another contract between the buyer and the buyer's agent; the contract of sale between the seller and the purchaser; a loan contract between the purchaser and the purchaser's lender; documentation of the status of the seller's title, usually performed by a professional title examiner; the preparation, submission, and signature of escrow instructions by the buyer, seller, and usually the buyer's lender; the delivery of a deed by the seller to the escrow holder; and the delivery by the buyer and the buyer's lender of funds sufficient to complete the transaction. When all this has been done, escrow is prepared to close. This is also know as law day. The escrow holder issues a check in favor of the seller and delivers the funds according to the seller's instructions. The deed in favor of the buyer is then recorded. The buyer's legal and equitable interests merge, and the buyer becomes the owner of the property. Finally, the buyer and the buyer's lender usually require the issuance of some form of title insurance to indemnify both interested parties in the event of a defect in the seller's title.

This chapter examines the roles and responsibilities of the escrow holder and title insurer in the final stages of the transaction.

2 NATURE OF AN ESCROW

Because the transfer of title by a seller and the payment of the purchase price by the buyer are concurrent conditions, most real estate transactions are handled by a neutral escrow holder. The buyer does not want the money transferred to the seller until there is assurance that the seller will convey good title to the property. The seller, in turn, does not want the deed recorded in favor of the buyer without assurances that the purchase price will be paid. An escrow holder is a useful intermediary, because it can act as the repository, simultaneously disbursing funds and recording documents for the benefit of the parties to the transaction.

An escrow holder may be an individual or an institution. An escrow holder is merely a depository, a custodian who receives documents and funds with instructions to deliver, record, or disburse when certain conditions are met. In the simple case, seller delivers a deed to escrow with instructions to deliver it to the buyer when the escrow is able to tender the purchase price to the seller. The buyer, in turn, delivers the purchase price to escrow with instructions to release the funds to the seller when escrow is in a position to record the deed in favor of the buyer. The important point is that neither party can stop the transaction from going forward except upon failure of a condition.

An escrow holder is considered the agent of both the buyer and seller, yet the escrow holder may only act pursuant to the mutual instructions of both parties. An escrow holder is thus a dual agent who acts on behalf of both parties to the escrow but is controlled by neither party.

An early California case described the operation of an escrow in the following terms:

> Delivery of a deed may be absolute, that is, to the grantee himself, or to a third person for him; or it may be conditional, that is, to a third person, with directions to keep it till some condition is performed by the grantee. In the first case, the title presently passes, but in the second case, the instrument is an escrow, and no title passes until the condition is performed, and generally, until the second delivery of the deed. Every act necessary to be performed by either party to the deed, in order that the present title may pass to the grantee, must also be performed, in case of an escrow, except only the delivery of the deed to the grantee. An escrow differs from a deed in one particular only, and that is the delivery.
>
> In this case, because the deed cannot be regarded as an escrow, there was nothing agreed to be done by or on the part of the grantee, as the condition upon the performance of which

the deed was to become absolute, and to be delivered to him by the third person. It is the general rule, that a deed delivered to a third person is viewed as an escrow only in case it is agreed that the deed is to be delivered to the grantee upon the performance by him of the stipulated condition.

Finch v. Bunch, 30 Cal. 208 (Cal. 1866)

The Ohio court in a more recent example, made the following observations concerning the nature of an escrow:

An escrow is a matter of agreement between parties, usually evidenced by a writing placed with a third-party depositary providing certain terms and conditions the parties intend to be fulfilled prior to the termination of the escrow.

* * *

Escrow is controlled by the escrow agreement, placing the deposit beyond the control of the depositor and earmarking the funds to be held in a trust-like arrangement.

Matalka v. Lagemann, 486 N.E. 2d 1220 (Ohio 1985)

An escrow is a useful device for a number of reasons. First of all, in most urban transactions, the buyer and seller do not know each other and often never even meet during the course of the transaction. There is little opportunity to establish trust between the parties. An escrow enables the parties to be more assured that the funds from the seller will clear the bank and that the buyer will have had less opportunity to transfer the property to a third person without the buyer's knowledge. Equally important, a professional escrow is more able to keep track of the documentation and prorations which accompany the usual sale. For instance, a transaction quite often involves either the pay off by the seller or the assumption by the buyer of a mortgage against the property. The precise balance of this obligation must be determined as of the date escrow closes and, in the case of a pay off, instruments sufficient to remove the mortgage from title to the property must be obtained and recorded. Income and expenses associated with the property must also be prorated as of the date escrow closes. For example, property taxes and even insurance may have been paid by the seller and not be due for some period of time after escrow closes. As a result, the seller would be entitled to a credit for the amount of taxes or insurance that was prepaid. Another example is when the property is being rented, and a tenant has paid an entire month's rent to the seller. In this case, the buyer would be entitled to a pro rata credit for rental income for the balance of the month after escrow closes. Finally, professional escrow holders are less likely to make mistakes in the preparation of deeds and other documents necessary to close the transaction.

3 LIABILITY OF THE ESCROW HOLDER

Because an escrow holder is considered an agent of the parties to the transaction, most jurisdictions hold that the escrow holder owes fiduciary obligations to the principals. The escrow holder must act impartially and with reasonable skill and diligence.

One court defined the scope of the escrow holder's obligations in the following terms:

It is well settled that the relation existing between a principal and agent is a fiduciary one demanding conditions of trust and confidence.

In all transactions concerning and affecting the subject matter of his agency, it is the duty of the agent to act with the utmost good faith and loyalty for the furtherance and advancement of the interest of his principal. The agent must give the principal the benefit of all his knowledge and skill and cannot withhold or conceal information from the principal.

Sanders v. Park, 578 P. 2d 1131 (Kan. 1978)

The Supreme Court of Utah described the status of the escrow holder as follows:

It is well established that an escrow agent assumes the role of the agent of both parties to the transaction, and, as a fiduciary, is held to a high standard of care in dealing with its principals.

Freeguard v. First Western, 738 P. 2d 614 (Utah 1987)

However, an escrow holder is also considered a *limited agent* whose fiduciary and other obligations are limited to the faithful performance of the instructions given by the parties.

When the escrow holder receives instructions and deposits of documents and money from each party, it holds the money and documents as the agent of both parties and may deliver or dispose of the money or documents pursuant to the instructions of the parties.

The liability of the escrow holder may be premised upon breach of contract or upon negligence. If the escrow holder fails to comply with the instructions of the parties, or fails to perform an implied promise created by the instructions, the injured party acquires a cause of action for breach of contract. Similarly, if the escrow holder acts negligently, it would ordinarily be liable for any loss occasioned by its breach of duty.

In the case of *Lee v. Title Ins. & Trust Co.,* 264 Cal. App. 2d 160 (Cal. 1968), the California court faced an allegation that the escrow holder was negligent for failing to advise the purchasers that the sellers had conspired to inflate the value and hence the purchase price of the property. There was evidence that the escrow holder knew that the purchase price was inflated but did not participate in the scheme. However, it did not notify the purchasers. The trial court dismissed the action against the escrow holder and the court of appeals affirmed.

Initially, the court noted that the plaintiff had not alleged that the escrow holder colluded with the sellers to defraud him. Nor did the plaintiff allege that the escrow holder negligently failed to comply with the escrow instructions. The court explained: "Put abstractly, the crucial question is whether an escrow holder is under a fiduciary duty to go beyond the escrow instructions and to notify each party to the escrow of any suspicious fact or circumstance, which has come to his attention before or during the life of the escrow, which could conceivably affect such party, even though the fact or circumstance is not related to his specific escrow instructions."

In concluding that no such duty existed the court first explained that an escrow holder was an agent of the parties to the transaction only for the limited purpose of acting in accordance with the escrow instructions. The court then reasoned that if this duty were expanded to include a duty to disclose then "once an escrow holder received information (from whatever source) he would be forced to decide independently whether to believe the information and disclose it or disbelieve it and conceal his knowledge. If he concealed his knowledge, he would risk suit. If he discloses and the information is inaccurate, he may be sued by all the parties to the escrow for interfering with their contract. Establishing a rule, which would create such a dilemma and subject the escrow holder to a high risk of litigation, would damage a valuable business procedure.''

NOTES AND QUESTIONS

Do you agree with the California court's limiting of the duty to disclose information to a party to the escrow? Should the escrow holder have a duty to investigate if it believes that one party to the escrow is defrauding another?

4 REAL ESTATE SETTLEMENT PROCEDURES ACT (RESPA)

The Real Estate Settlement Procedures Act, commonly known as RESPA, was enacted by the U.S. Congress to insure that purchasers and sellers of residential real estate are provided with greater and more timely information concerning the nature and cost of the settlement or closing process. The Act also prohibits certain kinds of kick-backs or referral fees. To accomplish this purpose, the Secretary of Housing and Urban Development has prepared a standard form called the Statement of Settlement Costs, which itemizes all charges to be imposed upon the seller and borrower in connection with certain real estate transfers. This statement must be completed and delivered prior to the close of escrow.

The Act applies only to the sale of residential real estate that is financed by a ''federally related mortgage loan.'' Residential real estate is residential property of one to four units in which the owner intends to occupy the premises. A federally related mortgage loan is a loan secured by a first lien on the residential real estate made by a lender insured or regulated by any federal agency or which is intended to be sold in the federally regulated secondary market. Because the vast majority of residential sales involve the use of institutional financing, very few such transactions fall outside the scope of RESPA.

5 THE ROLE OF TITLE INSURANCE

The practice of protecting a buyer or lender's title through the issuance of a policy of title insurance is customary in most urban and many rural areas of the country. Title insurance is used in all states with the sole exception of Iowa which, for reasons apparently unique to that state, has outlawed the practice. It is safe to say that, with the growing complexity in both the structure and financing of modern real estate transactions, the use of title insurance will become even more common in the future.

Reasons for Using Title Insurance   The prevalence of title insurance in this country is based in large measure upon the inadequacies of the recording system and the inability of the average person to conduct a meaningful title search.

We have seen that the term *title* refers to the manner in which an interest in real estate has been acquired, and the legal evidence by which that interest can be demonstrated. This, in turn, is largely based upon information contained in the public records by virtue of the recording statutes. In simpler times, and in smaller communities today, someone skilled in the operation of the local recording statutes could search the grantor/grantee index and issue an opinion letter for the use of the buyer or lender concerning the status of title to the property.

This practice has its limitations. In the first place many, if not most, public land records are somewhat haphazardly maintained and to search them is time consuming and not particularly cost effective. A professional title company can more economically perform the title search by developing separate sources of land records, commonly known as title plants. These title plants are based upon the information contained in public records but are often more comprehensive, more well indexed, and more automated, and thereby allow the title searcher to more efficiently obtain the information necessary to render an opinion concerning the state of title to the property. In addition, even a thorough and accurate title search may not disclose certain ''off record'' title defects. For instance, the existence of a forgery, unrecorded interest, or a claim against title by adverse use would not appear in the grantor/grantee index unless some memorandum of the interest or claim were recorded. As to these kinds of risks, many buyers and lenders desire the assurance afforded by an insurance company that is in the business of evaluating and protecting against these kinds of risks.

Nature of a Title Insurance Policy   To a large extent, title insurance is much like any other form of insurance, and state regulations governing the insurance industry usually apply to title insurers with equal force. In addition, rules of construction concerning the interpretation of insurance policies generally apply to title insurance policies as well. For instance, in most states, title insurance policies are governed by the rule of construction, which states that ambiguities in the policy are to be resolved against the insurer. This is a general rule of insurance policy interpretation that also applies to policies issued by title insurance companies.

However, title policies differ significantly from other insurance policies such as auto, fire, accident, or life insurance policies. This is because most insurance looks to future events that might trigger a claim under the policy, whereas title insurance constitutes a continuing obligation by the title insurer but is based upon claims against title that existed as of the date of the policy. One New Jersey court stated this distinction in the following terms:

> Unlike fire or accident policies, which are for fixed terms and which are such as contemplate a reappraisal of the risk on the part of the insurer at the end of the term, title policies by nature are without time limit and are not subject to reassessment of risk, for they insure solely on the basis of what is irretrievably cast.
>
> *Sandler v. New Jersey Realty,* 178 A. 2d 1 (N.J. 1962)

6   THE EXTENT OF COVERAGE

As indicated, a standard policy of title insurance is simply a contract to pay for losses that arise because of defects, discrepancies, or other impediments affecting the title or interfering with the right of possession of property described in the policy. As such, it is a form of contract. For the most part, title insurers, like other insurers, are free to accept, reject, and delineate the risks they are willing to assume. Nevertheless, the issuance of title insurance policies has become relatively standard nationwide, and forms promulgated by the American Land Title Association (ALTA) are used in the great majority of cases. A few states—California, New York and Texas in particular—have managed to create forms of their own, but even these are substantially similar to the policies in general use elsewhere.

The two most common forms of title insurance are the owner's policy and the lender's policy. The provisions of a typical owner's policy are reviewed in the following paragraphs. However, it is important to keep in mind that there are a wide variety of special endorsements an insured may obtain, typically at a higher premium and subject to whatever conditions may be imposed by the insurer. A common example involves an endorsement discrepancy concerning the size and boundaries of the property insured. The standard owner's and lender's policy excludes coverage for losses that could have been avoided by performing a survey. For an additional premium, an insured may obtain an endorsement guaranteeing the boundaries of the property. As a condition to the issuance of such a policy, the title company will usually require that the insured, at their expense, obtain a survey of the property.

Summary of Coverages Under the Basic Owner's Policy   The ALTA has promulgated two forms of owner's policy, know as Form A and Form B. The primary difference between the two is that Form B insures the owner as to the marketability of title whereas Form A does not. Since Form B gives the more comprehensive policy and because it is more widely used than form A, particularly in metropolitan areas, the following summary of the coverages is made particularly with reference to ALTA Form B.

The ALTA Form B owner's policy begins "subject to the exclusions from coverage, the exceptions from coverage contained in Schedule B and the conditions and stipulations. . . ." The company insures against loss or damage to the amount of the policy by reason of:

1 Title to the estate or interest described in Schedule A being vested other than as stated therein;
2 Any defect in or lien or encumbrance on the title;
3 Unmarketability of the title;
4 Lack of a right of access to and from the land.

The company will also pay the costs, attorney's fees, and expenses incurred in defense of the title but only to the extent provided in the Conditions and Stipulations.

Schedule A of the policy then sets forth the name of the insured party, the interest that is insured (e.g. fee, life estate, lease, etc.), and a legal description of the property being insured.

Exclusions Contained in Schedule B   Schedule B of the standard ALTA policy lists various matters specifically excluded from coverage.

The Policy does not insure against loss or damage which arise by reason of the following:

1 Any facts, rights, interests, or claims which are not shown by the public records but which could be ascertained by inspection of the land or by making inquiry of persons in possession thereof.

2 Easements, liens or encumbrances, or claims thereof, which are not shown by the public records.

3 Discrepancies, conflicts in boundary lines, shortage in area, encroachments, or any other facts which a correct survey would disclose, and which are not shown by the public records.

4 Any right, title, interest, estate, or easement in land beyond the lines of the area specifically described or referred to in Schedule C, or in abutting streets, roads, avenues, alleys, lanes, ways, or waterways, but nothing in this paragraph shall modify or limit the extent to which the ordinary right of an abutting owner for access to a physically open street or highway is insured by this policy.

5 Any law, ordinance, or governmental regulation (including but not limited to building and zoning ordinances) restricting or regulating or prohibiting the occupancy, use or enjoyment of the land, or regulating the character, dimensions or location of any improvement now or hereafter erected on the land, or prohibiting a separation in ownership or a reduction in the dimensions or area of the land, or the effect of any violation of any such law, ordinance, or governmental regulation.

6 Rights of eminent domain or governmental rights of police power unless notice of the exercise of such rights appears in the public records.

7 Defects, liens, encumbrances, adverse claims, or other matters (a) created, suffered, assumed, or agreed to by the insured claimant; (b) not shown by the public records and not otherwise excluded from coverage but known to the insured claimant either at Date of Policy or at the date such claimant acquired an estate or interest insured by this policy or acquired the insured mortgage and not disclosed in writing by the insured claimant to the Company prior to the date such insured claimant became an insured hereunder; (c) resulting in no loss or damage to the insured claimant; (d) attaching or created subsequent to Date of Policy; or (e) resulting in loss or damage which would not have been sustained if the insured claimant had been a purchaser or encumbrancer for value without knowledge.

In summary, the standard owner's policy insures the record interest of the owner against claims of title except as they relate to zoning and similar governmental regulation. The policy only covers condemnation or similar governmental proceeds if notice of the proceeding has been recorded. Policies generally exclude items which are not shown on the public records but which could be ascertained by an inspection or by making inquiry of the persons in possession of the property and tend to exclude from coverage matters which would otherwise constitute a lien except for the fact that the insured party agreed to take the property subject to the claim. For instance, the insured agrees to purchase subject to an unrecorded agreement to maintain a private road. A neighbor seeking to enforce the agreement against the insured party would not give rise to a claim against title, even though the road maintenance agreement is not recorded and would otherwise constitute a claim against title, because the insured party has agreed to buy the property subject to the road maintenance agreement.

Coverages for Off-Record Defects   The greatest value of title insurance is the partial protection it affords against matters not disclosed by an inspection of the public records. For instance a forged signature or a deed obtained without proper delivery might not be revealed by a title search, yet the title insurer is liable for such defects. In addition, lack of capacity because of minority or insanity might be grounds to set aside a transfer, but the title insurer would be liable for any resulting loss to the purchaser.

7   THE LIABILITY OF THE TITLE INSURER

The liability of a title insurer falls under two categories. The first involves liability pertaining to the abstract of title, and the second concerns liability under the title insurance policy itself. One court expressed the difference between the two in the following terms:

> An abstracter of title is hired because of his professional skill, and when searching the public records on behalf of a client he must use the degree of care commensurate with that professional skill; unlike a title insurer who can define the extent of his liability under the insurance policy, the abstracter must report all matters which could affect his client's interests and which are readily discoverable from those public records ordinarily examined when a reasonably diligent title search is made. It is this kind of protection that a person is entitled to expect from a skilled abstracter of title.
>
> *Contini v. Western Title,* 115 Cal. Rptr. 257 (Cal. 1979)

Insurer's Duty of Good Faith and Fair Dealing   A policy of title insurance obligates the insurer to defend the insured against claims against title to the property and to prosecute any action necessary to remove a title defect. Attorney's fees, court costs, and settlement payments must be paid by the insurer.

Many states, through legislation, court decisions or both, have created rights in favor of insured parties and against insurers for unfair claims settlement procedures. An insurer who engages in unfair practices may be liable to the insured both for breach of the insurance contract and for the tort of unfair claims settlement practices.

The law in this area varies widely among the states. However, to the same extent that a particular jurisdiction recognizes a tort remedy against insurance companies in general, it will recognize the same remedies in the case of title insurance.

8   SUMMARY

Most real estate sales are accomplished through the use of an escrow and professional title company. The reasons for using an escrow revolves around the time that elapses between formation of the contract to convey and the satisfaction of the conditions contained in the contract. An escrow is useful in managing the mass of documents that often accompany a transfer. Often an escrow is better able to prepare documents correctly and otherwise see the transaction to a successful close.

Title insurance is a feature of real estate transactions for two reasons. First, the professional title abstracter is better equipped to determine accurately the status of title to property. In addition, title insurance serves the important function of guaranteeing the state of title and of affording protection against certain kinds of defects beyond the scope of an ordinary title search.

9 QUESTIONS

1 Suppose Saul is selling an office building to Theresa. An escrow is opened with Escrow Services, Inc. An employee of Escrow calls Saul and Theresa asking them to submit escrow instructions. The parties submit instructions, but they do not agree on certain important terms such as contract price, security deposits held by seller, and target date for closing. After some effort, Escrow is unable to obtain mutual instructions from the parties. What should Escrow do?

2 Elmer is selling property to Francine. Escrow Services, Inc., is the escrow holder. Just before close, Gregor visits Escrow's office with an invoice from Elmer and demands that escrow pay Gregor out of the proceeds of escrow. Escrow calls Elmer who admits that he owes the money but tells Escrow not to pay because he (Elmer) would take care of it. What should Escrow do? Would it change the answer if the debt had been reduced to a judgment?

3 Hanson agrees to sell property to Irma, and an escrow is opened to facilitate the sale. Irma deposits $10,000 into escrow pursuant to her contract with Hanson. Irma breaches the contract, and Hanson demands that escrow release the deposit to him as provided in the contract. What should escrow do?

4 Maxwell purchases a building and obtains the standard ALTA owner's policy from Title Insurance Company. Shortly thereafter, the prior spouse of the seller files an action against the buyer seeking to set aside the transaction and claiming that she owned an interest in the property that was sold. Maxwell tenders the claim to the Title Insurance Company. Is this claim covered?

5 After close of escrow and getting the standard ALTA owner's policy, buyer notices neighbor driving across a portion of the property. Buyer confronts neighbor who claims he's "always" used that portion of buyer's property as a shortcut across his property to the county road. The right to cross the property was not listed as an exclusion in buyer's title policy and buyer tenders the matter to the title insurer. Is this covered?

REAL ESTATE AS SECURITY FOR OBLIGATIONS

CHAPTER **17**

REAL ESTATE
FINANCING DEVICES

TOPICS CONSIDERED IN THIS CHAPTER:

1 INTRODUCTION

The material in this chapter examines the use of real estate as security for obligations. Although substantial emphasis is placed on the real estate mortgage, its functional equivalents, primarily the deed of trust, are also considered.

It is evident that the use of real estate as security for land transactions is an important aspect of the American economic system. Very few people have the cash on hand to acquire or build a home or commercial property, and the vast majority of real estate acquisitions are accomplished through the use of credit secured by real estate. As a result, a substantial portion of the national wealth is affected by the law of mortgages.

Ordinarily a real estate mortgage involves the transfer of an interest in real estate by the debtor-mortgagor to the creditor-mortgagee to be held as security for the performance of an obligation, usually the payment of a debt. A mortgage is usually created by an instrument bearing many of the attributes of a deed, and the formalities of transferring interests by deed typically apply in the case of a mortgage. The validity and priority of a mortgage as to third parties often depends upon compliance with local recording statutes.

In the basic situation, *A* is the owner of the property and wants to borrow money from *B*. The loan is made and is conditioned upon *A*'s promise to repay the money to *B* on certain terms and conditions. This promise is evidenced by a promissory note. However *B* is unwilling to make the loan based only upon *A*'s promise to repay it. Instead, *B* insists upon security for the loan. *A* then executes a mortgage or a mortgage substitute in favor of *B*. *A* signs the mortgage, delivers it to *B,* who then records it. If *A* defaults on the mortgage, *B* may exercise his rights of foreclosure *against the property* by causing the property to be sold and the proceeds of sale distributed to satisfy the debt. In the absence of a mortgage, the creditor generally may not proceed directly against the property but must pursue his civil remedies to a judgment and then seek to execute upon the debtor's property wherever it may be found. The operation of judgment liens is discussed in Chapter 20.

2   THE NATURE OF A MORTGAGE

A   The Mortgage at English Common Law

The common law treated the mortgage as a transfer of the fee title by the mortgagor to the mortgagee subject to the condition of repayment of the debt. Upon payment, title was reconveyed by the mortgagee to the mortgagor. Prior to repayment of the debt, the mortgagee was entitled to all the attributes of ownership, including possession and the right to receive rents and profits from the property.

The common law mortgage was particularly severe on the mortgagor. The payment date was called the law day. Under the common law, no excuse justified the failure to pay on that day, and the consequence of failure to pay resulted in the mortgagor forfeiting all of his interest in the property.

B   American Developments Affecting Mortgage Law

In the United States, there are two basic theories that form the foundation of the law of mortgages. Although these theories often overlap and are usually not rigidly applied in practice, they may be denominated as the *title theory,* and the *lien theory.*

Title Theory   The title theory considers the mortgage transaction as a transfer of a fee interest by the debtor to the creditor subject only to a condition subsequent, namely that the debtor pay the creditor as agreed. In its strictest application, the mortgagee is entitled to possession of the property as well as to recover rents and other profits generated by the property during the time the obligation remains unsatisfied.

However, most title theory states have come to recognize, either through judical decision or statute, that the mortgagee holds title for *security purposes only* and that, for practical purposes at least, the mortgagor is to be regarded as the owner of the property.

The Lien Theory   A substantial majority of states now follow the lien theory of mortgages. Under this theory the mortgagor returns legal title to the property and to all of the benefits which legal title implies, particularly the right to possession and rents. The legal title only vests in the mortgagee if the mortgagee purchases the property at a foreclosure sale.

C The Uniform Land Security Interest Act

Like much real estate law, the principles governing the field of mortgages have roots in the English feudal system. In the United States, mortgages are subject to a wide variety of substantive and procedural differences in the law as applied by the various states.

In an effort to lend logic and harmony to the field, the Uniform Land Security Interest Act was approved in 1985 and was recommended for adoption in all states. As of this writing, no state has yet adopted the Act. Nevertheless, the Act provides a detailed and practical analysis that attempts to accommodate the economic realities of contemporary real estate finance while incorporating relatively recent developments in consumer and contract law.

Its purposes as set out in Section 1–102 of the Act are the following:

1 To simplify, clarify, and modernize the law governing real estate transactions;

2 To promote the interstate flow of funds for real estate transactions;

3 To protect consumer buyers and borrowers against practices which may cause unreasonable risk and loss to them; and

4 To make uniform the law with respect to the subject of this Act among states enacting it.

3 PROPERTY WHICH MAY BE SUBJECT TO A MORTGAGE

As a general rule, any interest in real estate that can be transferred can be encumbered by a mortgage. Typically this involves granting a mortgage against the mortgagor's fee interest in the property. However, other interests in real estate such as future interests, leasehold, and mineral rights may also be used for this purpose. In recent times, expanded notions of what constitutes real property have lead to an expansion of the types of property that can be made subject of a mortgage.

Ingram v. Ingram, (Kan. 1974) 521 P.2d 254

Facts of the case.

This case involves a dispute as to the priority of two liens asserted against an oil and gas leasehold interest. The essential facts are as follows: The plaintiff Natalie Ingram is the former wife of the defendant, Billy L. Ingram. On October 8, 1968, plaintiff, was granted a divorce from defendant. As a part of the decree, Billy L. Ingram was ordered to pay alimony and child support and he was awarded an oil and gas lease free and clear of the claims of Natalie Ingram. This lease will be referred to in this opinion as the Solbach lease. On August 18, 1969, Billy L. Ingram, obtained a loan and executed a promissory note in the amount of $12,500 to the Home State Bank. In order to secure the loan, Billy L. Ingram assigned to the Home State Bank his interest in the Solbach lease. At that time Billy L. Ingram and the Home State Bank orally agreed that the Solbach lease was assigned to secure and mortgage all indebtedness incurred or *to be incurred* by Billy L. Ingram by future advances made to him by the bank. This assignment was recorded. On October 11, 1969, the Home State Bank loaned Billy Ingram additional moneys, and the $12,500 note was renewed and incorporated in a new note in the amount of $36,400. Natalie Ingram had no actual knowledge of these financial transactions between Mr. Ingram and the bank.

The controversy arose when Billy Ingram defaulted on his alimony and child support payments. On January 23, 1973, Natalie Ingram levied execution on the Solbach lease in order to collect delinquent alimony and child support payments. All of the delinquencies in alimony and child support payments arose after the execution of the second promissory note of Billy Ingram on October 11, 1969. The attempt of Natalie Ingram to levy execution upon the interest of Billy L. Ingram in the Solbach lease prompted the Home State Bank to attempt to enjoin the sale of the Solbach lease.

The trial court held that the assignment of the Solbach lease secured only the original indebtedness of $12,500 that the Home State Bank has priority only as to the unpaid balance of that indebtedness, and that the judgment lien of Natalie Ingram was superior as to any amount in excess of that figure. Home State Bank appealed.

OPINION

The Kansas courts, like those of other jurisdictions, have found some difficulty in fitting the interest of an oil and gas lessee into the traditional common law classifications relating to ordinary surface interests in land. It is agreed that an oil and gas leasehold interest is a property right, but there still remains wide disagreement among the jurisdictions of this country whether it is real property or personal property.

We have concluded that the legislature has determined that oil and gas lease-hold interests are to be treated as *real property* under the statutes pertaining to the recording of instruments conveying or affecting real estate. We therefore hold that a mortgage or assignment of an oil and gas leasehold interest for security purposes which is recorded in the real estate mortgage records of the county wherein the property is situated fixes a lien upon the oil and gas leasehold effective from the filing of the instrument and that filing imparts notice to all persons of the contents thereof.

We now turn to the question of whether or not the assignment of the Solbach lease for security purposes executed on August 18, 1969, secured future advances made to Billy Ingram by the Home State Bank. It is well settled that a mortgage given to secure future advances is valid and that advances made from time to time under such a mortgage, have priority over liens which attach after the recording of the mortgage but before the making of the advances.

Accordingly, it is clear to us that the assignment of the Solbach leasehold interest to the bank for security purposes secured future advances and may be enforced against plaintiff, an attaching creditor. Therefore the claims of the bank for the indebtedness owed to it by Billy Ingram are prior and superior to the claims of Natalie Ingram as a judgment creditor. Judgment reversed in favor of the bank.

NOTES AND QUESTIONS

1 In this case, the *future advance* was made before plaintiff sought to execute on her judgment. Would the result be different if the future advance was made after the judgment was recorded?

2 Most courts grant priority to later advances only if the creditor was obligated to make them in its agreement with the debtor. In other words, if the creditor is not contractually obligated to make future advances, such advances will not have priority over intervening claims. See generally Skipworth, *Should Construction Lenders Lose Out On Voluntary Advances If The Loan Turns Sour?* 5 Real Estate L.J. 221 (1977).

3 The home equity line of credit is a currently popular device in which credit is extended based upon the owner's equity in property, usually a personal residence. The credit line is secured by a mortgage, usually in second position. The homeowner may draw down the line of credit by writing checks in a total amount which does not exceed the credit line. Under traditional analysis, checks written by the homeowner would be considered future advances and have priority over liens created after the equity line mortgage because the creditor is obligated to extend the credit.

4 A problem related to that posed by the *Ingram* case arises where the mortgagee seeks to impose its lien against improvements subsequently made by the debtor. For example, creditor lends money to debtor, secured by a mortgage against debtor's property. At the time the mortgage is given, the property was improved by a single-family home. Debtor then builds another home on the parcel. May the creditor include the new improvement as part of its collateral?

5 The answer to this question depends upon various factors. First, the mortgage instrument must contain a provision giving the creditor recourse to "after acquired property" of the debtor. Most states have statutes which declare that such provisions are valid. However, where another creditor has lent money to acquire or construct the after acquired property, the second lender will usually prevail as against the original lender. This result is consistent with the priority that is traditionally given to a purchase money lender and is examined more fully in Section 8 of this chapter.

4 THE OBLIGATION

An essential feature of a mortgage is the existence of an *obligation* and there can be no mortgage without a mortgage debt. The obligation may have arisen in the past, it may be created with the execution of the mortgage, or it may arise in the future. Usually the obligation is simply the payment of money, which is evidenced by a promissory note, although other kinds of obligations may be secured by a mortgage. However, it is essential to the validity of the mortgage that the obligation is capable of being reduced to an ascertainable money equivalent.

Walston v. Twiford, 105 S.E. 2d 62 (N.C. 1958)

Facts of the case.

On March 27, 1952, plaintiff borrowed from her mother, Mattie A. Picot, the sum of $6,500. The debt thus created was evidenced by a note and secured by a deed of trust in favor of W. C. Morse, a relative of Mrs. Picot. Mrs. Picot died on April 22, 1957. Mrs. Picot was the owner of the note at her death. Plaintiff paid the interest on the note to March 1953 but made no other payments. Defendant, the executor of the estate of Mrs. Picot, demanded payment of the note and commenced foreclosure when payment was not made.

Plaintiff seeks to enjoin the foreclosure, asserting that the debt has been discharged. Defendants ask for a judgment in the sum of $6,500 with interest from March 1953 and foreclosure of the deed of trust for the purpose of enforcing payment.

The deed of trust is in customary form except that it contains the following provision: "It is agreed and understood by and between the grantors and the said Mattie A. Picot that any balance of either the principal or interest due on the amount herein secured at the time of the death of said Mattie A. Picot, such amount is herewith positively to be treated, deemed, and considered a gift to said grantors by said Mattie A. Picot."

The trial court, being of the opinion that the quoted provisions were ineffectual and void, ruled that plaintiffs were not entitled to enjoin the sale and that defendants could recover the sum of $6,500 with interest and authorized the trustee to foreclose. Plaintiffs appealed.

OPINION

A mortgage is a conveyance by a debtor to his creditor, or to someone in trust for him, as security for a debt. A mortgage which purports to secure the payment of a debt has no validity if the debt has no existence.

Prior decisions of this Court upholding the provisions of contracts similar to the one involved in this case are in accord with the conclusions reached by the majority of the courts in other jurisdictions.

We perceive no sound reasons why we should overrule our prior decisions. The provision is good not as a gift, not as a testamentary disposition, but as a part of the contractual obligation agreed upon by the parties when the loan was negotiated. It appears from the evidence that Mrs. Picot went to live with her daughter and her husband, mortgagors, at or about the time the loan was negotiated. She remained with them until her death. Although she had the right to compel payment of interest or principal during her lifetime, only one payment of interest was made. By express language set out in mortgagors' contract, the note and deed of trust were satisfied upon Mrs. Picot's death.

Reversed.

NOTES AND QUESTIONS

The *Walston* case states the general rule that there can be no mortgage in the absence of an enforceable obligation. However the consideration that creates the debt need not necessarily be paid to the mortgagor.

For example, in *Parr v. Reiner,* 508 N.Y. S. 2d 829 (N.Y. 1986), the owner of the property gave authority to certain persons to obtain a loan, secured by a mortgage against her property. Through no fault of the lender, the owner's agents managed to direct the loan proceeds to their own use. The owner claimed the mortgage as invalid because the loan proceeds did not go to her benefit. The New York court disagreed, citing a long line of authority which held that a mortgage is not invalid because it is given to secure the debt of a third party.

A Alternative Mortgage Instruments

When money is loaned at a fixed rate, both lender and borrower assume the risk that interest rates may fluctuate. If interest rates exceed the borrower's loan rate, the lender may lose money on the loan. If prevailing rates are less than the loan amount, the borrower will often refinance the loan at a lower rate. Most lenders have not forgotten the problems of the early 1980's when prevailing interest rates were often more than double the rates at which these funds had been lent.

Prepayment penalties offset the tendency of borrowers to refinance when interest rates decline. ''Due on Sale'' clauses, notes with shorter terms, and balloon payments tend to enable the lender to adjust interest rates more frequently, thereby diminishing the impact of holding loans that are below current market rates.

The variable interest rate is a device used by lenders to share the risk of interest rate fluctuations with the borrower. There is an ever-growing variety of variable rate mortgages in the marketplace, only the most common of which are mentioned in this text.

B The Adjustable Rate Mortgage (ARM)

The Adjustable Rate Mortgage (ARM) provides for an interest rate that is periodically adjusted according to an index set forth in the note. For instance, the note might be pegged to the prime rate, the Federal Reserve cost of funds index, or the rate paid on jumbo certificates of deposit. In these cases, the note rate usually includes a ''spread'' over the index rate. A note which provides an interest rate of ''prime plus two'' would be two percentage points above the prevailing prime rate. As the prime rate changes, the interest rate in the note also changes. Most states have regulated the extent to which the loan rate and payment amount can be adjusted in an effort to limit the impact of interest rate changes upon a borrower's ability to pay. For example, many statutes provide that the monthly payment amount can only be changed once per year and cannot be increased by more than 7.5 percent in one year. In such case, a loan with a monthly payment of $1,000.00 could only increase to $1,075.00 after one year.

The Graduated Payment Adjustable Mortgage Loan (GPAM) is a loan in which the monthly payments begin at a level lower than necessary to pay off the loan during its term but which increase during the loan term to a level sufficient to eventually amortize the loan. The marketing purpose of such loans is to assist home buyers to qualify for loans by permitting smaller payments in the early years on the assumption that the borrower's income will rise over time; thus permitting payment of the loan at a higher rate in later years.

5 MORTGAGE SUBSTITUTES

For a number of reasons, the lender and borrower may structure their transaction in such a way that it does not comply with the technical requirements of a mortgage. In some states, use of the deed of trust or the installment land sale contract have become common practice. We shall see that, although different in form, courts have tended to examine the economic nature of the transaction and, if it involves the use of security for performance of an obligation, to treat the transaction as if it were a mortgage.

In addition, some lenders, anxious to avoid the potential delay and limitations of a foreclosure proceeding, will induce or require the borrower to deliver a deed to the fee interest in the property subject to having the deed returned upon condition of satisfaction of the obligation. In this case as well, courts will look to the substance of the transaction and apply principles of mortgage law in order to prevent overreaching by one party to the transaction.

A The Deed of Trust

The ordinary device whereby a security interest is created in real property is referred to as a mortgage, and throughout this chapter, the term mortgage will be used. However, for various reasons, other kinds of instruments are often used to create security interests in real estate. The principal of these is the deed of trust or trust deed. The trust deed form is used in approximately twenty states and the District of Columbia. It differs from the mortgage because the borrower transfers an interest *not* to the creditor but to a third party to be held in trust for the benefit of the creditor. The terminology is also different because the debtor is referred to as the *trustor*, the creditor is known as the *beneficiary* and the third party who holds the obligation is known as the *trustee.*

Bank of Italy v. Bentley, 20 P. 2d 940 (Cal. 1933)

Facts of the case.

Bentley executed a promissory note in favor of the Bank of Italy and a deed of trust, which conveyed real property to a named trustee as security for the note. Bentley defaulted on the note, and the trustee proceeded to sell the property under the power of sale contained in the deed of trust. Before the property was sold, the bank filed this action on the promissory note seeking a judgment for the unpaid balance of the note.

California Code of Civil Procedure, Section 726, requires the holder of a *mortgage* to exhaust the security by foreclosure before seeking to impose personal liability against the debtor. The bank maintains that Section 726, because it only refers to mortgages, does not apply to deeds of trust so that the bank is free to proceed directly against the debtor without regard to the security.

OPINION

At common law, and in most states in the absence of statute, a default will permit the mortgagee to sue on the note, or foreclose, or to pursue both remedies at once. The obvious injustice of this rule caused the passage of Section 726 of the Code of Civil Procedure, which requires, in the case of a mortgage, a resort to the security before any personal liability of the mortgagor can be enforced.

It has been generally acknowledged in the United States that a deed of trust, both in legal effect and in theory, differs not at all from a mortgage with a power of sale. The real difficulty is caused by the anomalous nature of deeds of trust in this state. Although this state, at an early date, adopted the "lien" theory of mortgages, it adopted the "title" theory in reference to deeds of trust. Thus it has been held that a deed of trust differs from a mortgage in that title passes to the trustee in the case of a deed of trust, while, in the case of a mortgage, the mortgagor retains title.

However, we do not feel justified in holding, merely because "title" passes by a deed of trust, while only a "lien" is created by a mortgage, that the two instruments should be treated differently in this context. Fundamentally, it cannot be doubted that in both situations the security for an indebtedness is the important and essential thing in the whole transaction. The economic function of the two instruments would seem to be identical. Where there is one and the same object to be accomplished, important rights and duties of the parties should not be made to depend on the more or less accidental form of the security.

Considering all these factors, it must be held that, either by reason of implied agreement or by reason of public policy, the holder of a note secured by a deed of trust must first exhaust the security before resorting to the personal liability of the trustor.

Affirmed.

NOTES AND QUESTIONS

The Bentley case anticipated the discussion of foreclosure and limitations on foreclosure discussed in Section six of this chapter. Does the Bentley case suggest a reason why the bank chose to use a deed of trust rather than a mortgage to secure its debt?

B The Deed Absolute

Every deed which by any other writing appears to have been intended only as security for payment of an indebtedness or performance of an obligation, though expressed as an absolute grant, is considered a mortgage. The person for whose benefit the deed is made may not have any benefit or advantage from the recording of the deed, unless every other writing operating as a defeasance of it, or explanatory of its being intended to have the effect only of a mortgage, also is recorded in the same records at the same time.

Maryland Real Property Law, Section 7–101

Hanson v. Bonner, 661 P. 2d 421 (Mont. 1983)

Facts of the case.

On December 12, 1979, the Hansons executed and delivered a promissory note for $25,000 to the Bonners, payable on or before June 12, 1982.

At the same time, the Hansons executed and delivered to the Bonners a contract that recited the debt and a quitclaim deed to the Bonners for a certain parcel in Kalispell, Montana.

Because of defaults in the payments, the Bonners recorded the quitclaim deed, claiming thereafter to own whatever interest in the real property the Hansons owned. The trial court ruled that the transaction was a mortgage, which must be foreclosed by the Bonners. They appeal.

OPINION

We hold that the transaction between the parties is a mortgage. In this case the contract recited that the quitclaim deed would be recorded without notice if the Hansons defaulted. There can be no question that the delivery of the quit-claim deed was made as security for the performance by the Hansons of the promissory note. Every transfer of an interest in property, other than in trust, made only as a security for the performance of another act is deemed to be a mortgage. When a debt is shown to exist between the parties, a deed absolute on its face delivered in connection with the indebtedness will be construed as a mortgage when it is shown that the instrument was intended to secure the indebtedness. Under our statutes, enforcement of any right secured by a mortgage upon real estate must be in accordance with the foreclosure provisions of the Montana statutes. Montana is a "lien state," and a mortgage of itself does not convey any title of the mortgaged lands to the mortgagee.

Affirmed.

NOTES AND QUESTIONS

Some states have enacted legislation along the lines of the Maryland provision given. These statutes attempt to limit the incentive to use an absolute deed to disguise a security transaction. Massachusetts, New York, and Pennsylvania have provisions very similar to Maryland's. Regardless of the existence of such a stat-ute, the deed absolute is disfavored and will be set aside and treated as a mort-gage if the overall transaction indicates that the parties intended the deed to operate only as a form of security.

C The Installment Land Sale Contract

The following is from *Installment Land Contracts—The National Scene Revisited* by Grant S. Nelson and Dale A. Whitman, from the 1985 Brigham Young Law Review 1, page 3–11.

The installment land contract is the most common substitute for the mortgage or deed of trust. It is also sometimes referred to as a "contract for deed," a "long-term land contract," or a "land sale contract." The installment land contract and the pur-chase money mortgage fulfill the identical economic function: permitting the seller to finance the unpaid portion of the real estate purchase price. Under the installment land contract, the vendee normally takes possession and makes monthly installment pay-ments of principal and interest until the principal is paid off. The vendor retains legal title until the final payment is made, at which time full title is conveyed to the vendee. Such contracts may be amortized over time periods as short as a year or as long as more than twenty years. During the contract period, the vendee normally will be required to pay taxes, maintain casualty insurance, and keep the premises in good repair.

The installment land contract must be distinguished from the ordinary executory contract for the sale of land, variously known as an "earnest money contract" or a "marketing contract." The earnest money contract is used primarily to establish the parties' rights and liabilities during the period between the date of the bargain and the date of closing. This period is usually only a month or two. At the end of the period, title passes to the purchaser and security agreements, if any, are consummated. While the earnest money contract is completed at closing when the purchaser either tenders the full purchase price of the land or enters into a separate security agreement, the installment land contract governs the parties throughout the life of the debt. Indeed, it is not uncommon for parties to agree to enter into an installment land contract at the closing date of the earnest money contract.

Traditionally, the vendor in an installment land contract has relied primarily on a forfeiture clause. The forfeiture clause, found in virtually every installment contract, typically provides that "time is of the essence" and that when a vendee fails to comply with the contract, including the obligation to pay promptly, the vendor has the option to declare the contract terminated. The vendor can then take possession of the premises without legal process and can retain all prior payments as liquidated damages. Generally, the clause also relieves the vendor from all further obligations under the contract.

As one commentator has aptly pointed out, "If the contract is enforceable as written and if title will not be clouded, [the installment land] contract gives the vendor a very favorable remedy, much more advantageous than would be available under a purchase money mortgage or deed of trust." [citation omitted] Indeed, under a mortgage or deed of trust, the defaulting mortgagor has a right to redeem (the equity of redemption) which the mortgagee can eliminate only by a foreclosure proceeding. Furthermore, in many states the mortgagor has postsale statutory redemption rights even after a foreclosure sale. Conversely, the forfeiture clause in an installment land contract appears to give the vendor an efficient remedy unfettered by such equitable and statutory mortgagor protections. . . .

Traditionally, installment land contract forfeiture provisions were routinely enforced in favor of the vendor. The courts presumably based enforcement of such provisions on a desire to carry out the intent of the parties, even though forfeiture often resulted in a substantial loss to the vendee and a windfall gain to the vendor. Enforcement became especially burdensome on the vendee as the contract neared completion and the vendee's cash investment increased. Courts tended to ignore the mortgage substitute aspect of the installment land contract and to treat it instead as an executory contract for the sale of land.

However, during the past several decades, an increasing number of courts and legislatures have focused on the installment land contract and its forfeiture clause with a mortgage law analogy in mind. One court recently asked, "If [the absolute deed] kind of forfeiture may not be enforced by the secured party according to the express terms of the agreement, why, then, should a forfeiture under a land sale contract be so enforced?" The foregoing process, however, has not produced either an analytical or practical consensus. Consequently, the law in this area is not susceptible to orderly analysis. "Not only does the law vary from jurisdiction to jurisdiction, but within any one state results may vary depending upon the type of action brought, the exact terms of the land contract, and the facts of the particular case." *Braunstein v. Trotter,* P. 2d 1379, 1382 (Ore. 1981) The interplay of these factors makes predicting whether the vendee's interest will be forfeited extremely difficult. While forfeitures are still occasionally judicially enforced, no jurisdiction will automatically enforce a forfeiture provision as it is written. This change is the result of legislative and judicial intervention to ameliorate the harsh impact of automatic forfeiture.

Several states have attempted to alleviate some of the harshness in forfeiture clauses by enacting legislation regulating the circumstances under which forfeiture will be permitted. These statutes often incorporate a grace period within which late payments must be accepted.

Absent statutory regulation, numerous state courts have refused to enforce forfeiture clauses deemed unreasonable or inequitable. These courts have employed several approaches to save the vendee from forfeiture. Some courts, for example, have permitted the vendee to tender the remainder of the purchase price, or even his arrearages, in a suit or counterclaim for specific performance of the contract. When the vendee is unable or unwilling to redeem, courts have occasionally ordered the judicial foreclosure of the land contract. Some courts, after determining that a particular forfeiture clause is unfair, have extended to the defaulting vendee the right to restitution—the right to recoup his payments to the extent that they exceed the vendor's damages caused by the vendee's default.

NOTES AND QUESTIONS

As the preceeding material indicates, there are a variety of devices by which real estate can be used to secure the payment of a debt. Nearly all states have enacted statutes that attempt to protect debtors against overreaching by creditors and that restrict the creditor's rights to foreclose upon the property. These limitations, in turn, have inspired creditors to seek ways to avoid the limitations. However, it should be reasonably clear that if the transaction, in fact, involves security for the payment of a debt, courts will disregard the form of the transaction and look to its substance. In short, efforts to disguise a mortgage very seldom hold up when challenged.

6 FORECLOSURE OF MORTGAGE AND LIMITATIONS ON FORECLOSURE

The primary advantage of a creditor's having security by way of a mortgage is that it tends to increase the number and scope of remedies available to the creditor in the event that the debtor defaults on the underlying obligation. In the absence of security, a creditor is generally limited to filing a civil action on the obligation, thereby seeking to reduce the claim to a judgement, which can then be used to execute on the debtor's property wherever it can be found. The time, expense, and additional risk inherent in an unsecured obligation cause many lenders to refuse to extend credit unless it is secured or to demand a substantially higher interest rate to compensate for the additional risk inherent in an unsecured obligation.

The early common law mortgage gave ample protection to the creditor and provided that a mortgagor would forfeit his or her entire interest in the mortgaged property, even in the event of a minor default. Foreclosure proceedings were unnecessary because the mortgagee already held title to the property. To ameliorate the often harsh consequences of this rule, the common law equity courts created the *equity of redemption,* which permitted the defaulting mortgagor to pay the debt at any time after it was due and, upon such payment, regain title to the property.

The equity of redemption protected mortgagors from forfeiture but it tended to limit the marketability of property, because a prospective purchasor or encumbrancer could not be certain whether a prior mortgagor would return and seek to have the property returned upon payment of the debt to the original mortgagee. Both the utility of real estate as security for a debt and the marketability of land titles was undermined.

In response to the problems created by the equity of redemption, common law equity courts developed what came to be known as strict foreclosure. Strict foreclosure was a proceeding which could terminate the mortgagor's equity of redemption. This procedure permitted the mortgagee to petition the court to order the mortgagor to pay the debt at a certain date under penalty of terminating the mortgagor's right to redeem the mortgaged property. Unlike other foreclosure proceedings, strict foreclosure did not result in sale of the property, but rather extinguished the mortgagor's equity of redemption.

Today most foreclosures result in the property being auctioned at public sale to the highest bidder and the proceeds of the sale being distributed to the mortgagor to the extent of the mortgagee's debt. There are two kinds of foreclosure proceedings commonly used in the United States. The first is *judicial foreclosure,* which involves the filing of a civil action and the foreclosure being supervised by the court, the second is *power of sale foreclosure,* which proceeds without court supervision in accordance with the power of sale provision contained in the mortgage. Power of sale foreclosure is widely used in about half the states and is permitted in most. A few states, including Illinois, Missouri, and New York, prohibit power of sale foreclosure. Where it is permitted, power of sale foreclosure is usually preferred by creditors because it is quicker and less cumbersome, although judicial foreclosure may be preferred when there are questions concerning the validity of the mortgage or its priority as against other liens. The Uniform Land Security Interest Act permits either type of foreclosure, at the election of the mortgagee.

Default and Acceleration   An action to foreclosure must be based upon a default by the mortgagor. Default can include the failure to make payments when due, failure to procure insurance, pay taxes, maintain the property, or sale to a third party without the creditor's consent. However the acts constituting the default generally must constitute a breach of either the mortgage or the underlying obligation that the mortgage secures.

An essential provision of the mortgage and its underlying obligation is an acceleration clause. This provision is particularly important in the case of a long-term, installment-obligation mortgage. For instance, borrower agrees to pay lender equal monthly installments for the next thirty years. Borrower defaults on the third payment. Strictly speaking, this is only a partial breach of the agreement to pay the debt, leaving the lender in the absurd position of instituting foreclosure proceedings on each default for the next thirty years.

The acceleration provision however enables the lender to ''accelerate'' the obligation and declare the entire unpaid balance of the loan due and payable upon a default by the borrower.

Prepayment Penalties

George H. Nutman, Inc. v. Aetna Business Credit, Inc., 453 Supp. 2d 586 (N.Y. 1982)

Facts of the case.

On September 6, 1977, Aetna loaned to plaintiff, George Nutman, Inc., the sum of $1,200,000. Aetna received as security for the loan a first mortgage on various commercial property owned by plaintiff located in Brooklyn and Queens. The mortgage agreement provided for monthly installments of principal and interest to be due on the first day of each month, with a five-day grace period before the mortgagor would be deemed to be in default. In addition, the mortgage agreement contained provisions for an interest penalty for late payments, a prepayment penalty, and an acceleration clause.

Plaintiff was continually late and in arrears on its payments. On February 28, 1979, after plaintiff defaulted, Aetna instituted a foreclosure action. A receiver for the property was appointed. On August 31, 1979, the parties entered into a Stipulation of Settlement whereby Aetna agreed to discontinue the foreclosure action upon plaintiff's payment of the mortgage principal, interest, and late charges in full.

On October 18, 1979, plaintiff sold certain of the property to Martin Paint Stores, Inc. Prior to the closing of title, Aetna prepared a "satisfaction letter" setting forth the amounts due and owing, which included a prepayment penalty of $46,501.60. When plaintiff protested the inclusion of the prepayment penalty, plaintiff was notified that a "satisfaction of mortgage" would not be executed until the prepayment penalty was paid. Plaintiff then paid the sum and commenced the present action.

OPINION

Acceleration clauses give the mortgagee the option to declare the entire mortgage debt due and payable upon the happening of a stated condition, such as the default by a mortgagor in payment of principal and interest and the right to foreclose for nonpayment. Prepayment clauses give the mortgagor the option, upon the payment of a premium, to voluntarily terminate the mortgage prematurely.

The question presented in this case is whether the mortgagee, after electing to accelerate the mortgage because of a default, can still exact a prepayment penalty because of the premature termination of the mortgage. The court determines that it cannot.

The election by the mortgagee herein to accelerate the mortgage and to treat the mortgage debt as due was not a voluntary act by the mortgagor sufficient to bring the prepayment penalty into operation.

Since plaintiff was under duress when making the prepayment penalty of $46,501.60, which it was not contractually obligated to do, it is entitled to recover that amount, plus interest.

NOTES AND QUESTIONS

1 In most cases, the Acceleration Clause is essential if the creditor is to have an effective remedy in the event of default. For example a creditor has a mortgage which secures a note, payable in monthly installments for thirty years. Consider the difficulty in foreclosing without an Acceleration Clause. Can you think of a promissory note in which an Acceleration Clause is not necessary?

2 Prepayment penalties are treated in greater detail in Section 9 of this chapter.

Limitations on Acceleration   All states regulate the manner in which a creditor may proceed to foreclosure in the event of default by the debtor. Most states established a two step process. The first occurs when the creditor declares a default and accelerates the entire balance of the obligation. During this period, the debtor may *cure* the default by payment only amount in default. After a period of time, usually ninety days, the debtor may cure the default only by paying the entire accelerated amount of the loan. The procedure adopted by Minnesota, which is examined below, is a typical example.

> In any proceeding for the foreclosure of a real estate mortgage, if, at any time before the sale of the premises under such foreclosure the mortgagor pays to the holder of the mortgage being foreclosed, the amount actually due at the time of the commencement of the foreclosure proceedings, . . . then, and in that event, the mortgage shall be fully reinstated and further proceedings in such foreclosure shall be thereupon abandoned.
>
> Minn. St. 1969, 580.30

Davis v. Davis, 196 N.W. 2d 473 (Minn. 1972)

The issue raised by this appeal is whether an acceleration clause in a mortgage requires the mortgagor to tender the entire principal balance in order to reinstate the mortgage under Minn. St. 580.30. The trial court held such tender necessary, and we reverse.

Facts of the case.

Plaintiff executed a mortgage in favor of defendant in 1967. This mortgage became delinquent in 1970. The mortgagee declared the entire balance of the mortgage payable under an acceleration provision. The mortgagor tendered only the delinquent installments referred to, and the tenders were declined. Thereupon, foreclosure proceedings were commenced. This action seeking to enjoin the foreclosure followed.

The trial court held:

> . . . [O]nce the election to accelerate the entire principal due and payable was exercised by the mortgagee, the amount actually due thereon was the entire balance plus accrued interest. The mortgagor after exercise of the acceleration provision in the mortgage could not avail himself of the provisions of Minn. St. Sec. 580.30.

This statute was adopted in 1923 in response to hardships experienced by mortgagors resulting from the depressed economic conditions of the times. The statute applies to all foreclosures and permits the mortgage to be "reinstated" by the payment of "the amount actually due thereon and constituting the default actually existing at the time of the commencement of the foreclosure proceedings. . . ." We are of the opinion and hold that the use of the words "actually due" and "the default actually existing" was intended by the legislature to permit reinstatement by the payment of only what was delinquent, plus the costs set out in the statute, without requiring the accelerated principal to be tendered.

There is also merit in the argument that to give the acceleration clause effect by requiring the full principal to be tendered in order to reinstate the mortgage would not, as the statute suggests, "reinstate" the mortgage, but would in fact "satisfy" it.

The judgement of the trial court is accordingly reversed.

Default Other Than Failure To Pay A typical mortgage contains numerous provisions ostensibly intended to require the mortgagor to maintain the property so as to protect the security of the mortgagee. For example, an owner is usually required to maintain adequate insurance, keep the property free of liens, pay property taxes when they come due, and see that the property is maintained in good order. Suppose the owner fails to pay taxes or insurance. The mortgage often allows the creditor to pay these amounts and add them to the loan balance. If the owner fails to pay the additional amounts to the lender, the mortgagee can declare a default and accelerate the loan.

Conduct of the Sale The method of conducting a foreclosure sale is largely regulated by state statute. There is considerable variation in the procedures used from state to state. All require that some form of notice of the default be sent to the mortgagor. Many statutes, such as the Minnesota provision just discussed, provide time limitations in which the mortgagor may cure the default by paying *arrearages* or, if the period to cure has passed, to avoid foreclosure by paying the accelerated balance of the mortgage.

Another purpose of the notice provisions is to inform potential buyers of the pendency of the sale. All parties to the mortgage transaction, including junior creditors, have an interest in obtaining the highest price possible at the foreclosure sale. However, it is generally acknowledged that foreclosure sales usually do not generate a price equivalent to the fair market value of the property. This is particularly true during adverse economic cycles. As a result, both courts and state legislatures have attempted to limit the remedies of the foreclosing mortgagee in order to relieve debtors of the often harsh consequences of foreclosure and to prevent the creditor from obtaining a windfall at the debtor's expense.

An example of this tendency is the rule in some jurisdictions that a mortgagee forfeits any deficiency judgment if foreclosure proceeds under a power of sale. And, if the creditor choses judicial foreclosure, some state statutes require the court to condition approval of the sale upon the mortgagee giving credit to the debt of the mortgagor in excess of the amount actually realized at the sale.

In the case of a judicial foreclosure, courts generally will not refuse to confirm a sale merely because the price realized at the sale is inadequate when compared to the market value of the property. There are exceptions to this rule, such as when the price is grossly inadequate. At various times, courts have exercised their equitable authority in ways intended to protect the debtor from the consequences of foreclosure.

Suring State Bank v. Giese, 246 N.W. 556 (Wis. 1933), is a famous depression era case, which illustrates the extent to which a court can go in protecting a debtor while ignoring and modifying the terms of the mortgage contract between the parties.

In the *Suring Bank* case, the foreclosed property had been sold at a sheriff's sale for approximately one third of its pre-depression value and the mortgagee, who was the purchaser at the sale, was demanding a deficiency judgment for the balance. If the sale price had been confirmed, the mortgagee would have had the property and still had a claim for more than four fifths of the original loan. The Wisconsin Supreme Court recognized the existing economic depression and emergency and acknowledged the inadequacy of a judicial sale to establish a fair value for the property because of the absence of competitive bidders. The court established guidelines for trial courts when presented with a motion to confirm a foreclosure sale. The trial court could do any one of the following things:

1 The court may decline to confirm the sale where the sale price is substantially inadequate.

2 The court, in ordering a sale or a resale, may, in its discretion, take notice of the present emergency and, after a proper hearing, fix a minimum price at which the premises must be bid in if the sale is to be confirmed . . .

3 The court may, upon application for the confirmation of a sale, if it has not theretofore fixed a price, conduct a hearing, establish the value of the property, and, as a condition to confirmation, require that the fair value of the property be credited upon the foreclosure judgement.

Distribution of the Proceeds of Sale   A number of events can occur when property is sold at foreclosure. If a bidder at the sale tenders more than the amount owing on the debt, the debt is discharged upon payment, the bidder becomes the owner of the property, and the balance of the bid price is given to the original mortgagor. On the other hand, if the amount bid is less than the amount of the debt, the creditor's obligation is satisfied only to that extent and a deficiency exists. In addition, if no one bids at the sale, or if the creditor does not accept a bid for less than the amount of its debt, the creditor may "credit bid" by bidding the amount of the debt, and thus become the owner of the property.

Suppose however that the property is encumbered by two mortgages, a $100,000 first mortgage and a $50,000 second. In this case, the outcome depends, to a large extent, upon which lender forecloses first. If the second mortgagee forecloses, any purchaser (including the second mortgagee) will take the property subject to the first mortgage. However, if the first mortgagee goes to sale, then the second mortgage is "wiped out" and its lien is extinguished. In this case a purchaser, including the first mortgagee, will own the property without regard to the second mortgage, which was extinguished upon the sale under the first mortgage. When the amount bid on sale under the first mortgage exceeds the amount of the first mortgage debt, the surplus is then applied to satisfy any junior liens. Only if such junior liens are satisfied will the remaining surplus be tendered to the original mortgagor.

QUESTION

Suppose you hold a second mortgage and the first mortgage is in default. What should you do to protect your interest?

Antideficiency Legislation   A deficiency exists where the proceeds of the foreclosure sale are insufficient to satisfy all underlying obligations plus any costs incurred during foreclosure. In the absence of a statutory limitation, a judgment in the amount of the deficiency is entered against the debtor. Such a judgment is enforceable in the same manner as any other judgment.

Approximately half of the states have now enacted legislation intended to limit the creditor's right to obtain a deficiency judgment after foreclosure. Many states prohibit a deficiency if foreclosure proceeds under a power of sale, permitting a deficiency judgment only when the creditor proceeds with judicial foreclosure. Other states require the creditor to reduce the amount of the deficiency by the "fair value" of the property before confirming the sale and entering a deficiency judgment. Finally, some statues create certain classes of transactions such as owner-occupied dwellings, as to which a deficiency judgment is simply prohibited.

A Note on Redemption   Under the common law and in most states today, the mortgagor has the right to *redeem* the property by paying the full amount of the debt at any time before the foreclosure sale takes place. This is known as the *equity of redemption* and it is terminated once the foreclosure sale is held.

About half the states have enacted statutes that give the mortgagor a period of time (usually about one year) to redeem the property *after* the foreclosure sale takes place by paying the amount that was bid for the property at the sale. This is known as *statutory redemption* and is allowed in the states of Arizona, Illinois, Michigan, Minnesota, and Texas, among others.

QUESTION

Does the statutory right of redemption affect the amount likely to be bid at the foreclosure sale? Does your answer depend on whether the creditor or a third party is making the bid? Would it matter if a deficiency judgment was not available?

7 ASSIGNMENT OF MORTGAGE AND OF PROPERTY SECURED BY A MORTGAGE

In the absence of a provision to the contrary, both the mortgagor and mortgagee may transfer their respective interests in the property. Such transfers tend to be known as assignments and are generally governed by the law of contracts. For instance, the owner of mortgaged property may sell the property to a third person, receiving consideration and delivering a deed in recordable form to the buyer. If the mortgagee has complied with recording statutes, the mortgage passes with the property and the obligation is unaffected by the transfer. In the event of default, the mortgagee may proceed with foreclosure to the same extent as if the original mortgagor still owned the property.

In addition, it is common for lenders to assign their notes and mortgages for collection by third parties. In this event, the obligations of the third party are simply to notify the debtor, who then must make payments to the new holder of the note in order to avoid default.

Transfer by Mortgagor

Prudential Savings and Loan Association v. Nadler, 345 N.E. 2d 782 (III. 1976)

Plaintiff Prudential Savings and Loan Association filed this suit in the circuit court of Cook County to collect the balance of the promissory note executed by defendant Eugene Nadler.

Facts of the case.

On June 18, 1962, defendant purchased a one-half interest in improved property at 2200 Division Street in Chicago. To finance the purchase, defendant borrowed $20,400.00 from Prudential, executed a promissory note in that amount, and secured the note with a mortgage on the property. The note was payable to Prudential in monthly installments of $172.00 with interest at six percent per annum. On September 15, 1965, defendant conveyed his interest in the secured property, subject to the indebtedness, to Frances Hannigan. Prudential was not a party to the transaction. Nadler did not notify Prudential when he conveyed the property to Hannigan nor did he attempt to obtain a release from liability on the note. After the conveyance, Hannigan assumed the payment of the note and took over management of the property. Nadler made no further payments on the debt or of taxes on the premises. While Hannigan made some payments on the note, the payments were not regular and the loan became increasingly delinquent.

During this time the building fell into disrepair, and in 1968, the City of Chicago filed suit to have the structure demolished. Prudential did not notify Nadler of the continuing default on the loan and did not advise him of the deterioration of the property. The loan remained in default, and in 1971 Prudential instituted this action against Nadler to collect the entire balance due on defendant's note.

OPINION

As between the mortgagor and his grantee who assumes the payment of an encumbrance, the grantee becomes the principal debtor and the mortgagor becomes his surety. If the mortgagee is not a party to the agreement, its interest is not affected. Upon default, it may disregard the agreement and bring an action against the original debtor, or it may accept the promise made for its benefit and bring the action against the grantee. The contract rights of the mortgagee cannot be changed by any arrangement between the mortgagor and his grantee unless the mortgagee agrees to such change. The mortgagee, by it's dealings with the grantee and mortgagor, may recognize the former as the principal debtor and the latter as a surety towards itself. The mortgagee, then, is bound to respect the relationship between the parties and any material alteration of the mortgage contract has the legal effect of discharging the surety and will operate to release the mortgagor.

In the present case Nadler failed to offer any evidence at trial that Prudential entered into any agreement with Hannigan or that such agreement materially altered the terms of the loan obligation.

Having carefully examined the record, we find that Prudential proved its right to the balance due on the promissory note and that Nadler failed to establish a valid defense.

The Wraparound Mortgage   A wraparound mortgage is a second mortgage which includes or ''wraps around,'' but does not extinguish, the obligation under a prior mortgage, secured by the same property.

The wraparound mortgage, also known as the all inclusive or overlapping mortgage, can be illustrated by the following example:

Suppose a mortgagor owns property worth $300,000 subject to a first mortgage of $100,000 with interest at nine percent. The mortgagor desires to obtain an additional $100,000 secured by the property. A second mortgage lender may be willing to provide a wraparound or all inclusive mortgage for the principal amount of $200,000 (the $100,000 first plus the $100,000 second) at the rate of twelve percent. Under this arrangement, the wraparound mortgagee agrees to pay the first mortgagee out of the proceeds paid to it by the mortgagor. This form of financing is particularly attractive to the wraparound mortgagee because it increases the effective yield on the wraparound note by the difference or ''spread'' between the interest rate in the wraparound note and that in the underlying note. In our example, the wraparound mortgagee has lent $100,000 at twelve percent. However, he is collecting interest at twelve percent on $200,000 while, in effect paying interest at only nine percent on the underlying $100,000.

A second advantage to the wraparound mortgage is the degree of control it can maintain. In the case of an ordinary junior mortgage, the owner makes separate payments to the senior and junior lenders. If the mortgagor fails to pay the senior loan, the junior mortgagee must take steps to learn of the default in order to protect its interests under the junior obligation. In the case of the all inclusive mortgage, the owner makes one payment directly to the holder of the all inclusive note, and a portion of this payment is then used to make the payment to the underlying or senior mortgagee. The holder of the all inclusive knows immediately if there has been a breach and can more quickly act to have the default cured or to otherwise protect its rights.

Transfer by Mortgagee   We have seen that the holder of a mortgage on real estate has both a personal obligation owed to it by the mortgagor and an interest in the property securing that obligation. Both of these property rights may be transferred by the mortgagee and, almost without exception, both must be transferred to the same person.

The practical context in which most of these assignments occur involves the transfer of mortgages in the so-called secondary market. The federal government, state governments, and individual investors, all actively participate in purchasing assignments of mortgages from lenders and these assignments are generally considered to be essential to the efficient operation of the residential mortgage market.

Typically, an institutional lender will receive funds from depositors which it, in turn, will lend to borrowers for the purchase of property secured by mortgages. In the absence of the secondary market, this lending activity will stop when the lender has exhausted its available funds. However, in order to make additional loans, the lender may package a number of mortgages, discount the face value of the promissory notes, and assign them for collection to a purchaser in the secondary market. In return for transferring its assets, namely the secured promissory notes, the lender receives cash with which to make additional loans.

The existence of a national secondary market in mortgages is an important element in national housing policy and many mortgages are purchased by the Federal National Mortgage Association (FNMA) and the Government National Mortgage Association (GNMA). In addition, insurance companies and other financial institutions are engaged in the acquisition of mortgage-backed promissory notes in the secondary market.

8   SATISFACTION AND DISCHARGE OF THE MORTGAGE

The discharge of the obligation, by payment or otherwise, results in the mortgage lien being extinguished. A secured debt is discharged in the same way as an unsecured one and may be accomplished in any number of ways. The methods of discharging obligations are typically governed by the law of contracts. Discharge can be obtained by a compromise and release executed by the parties or pursuant to any condition contained in the contract creating the obligation.

Payment is surely the most common method of obtaining a satisfaction, and full and timely payment results in the obligation being satisfied, and the mortgage lien being discharged.

Typically, when the obligation has been paid, a formal instrument is executed by the mortgagee in form sufficient for recordation indicating that the mortgage has been released, satisfied, or reconveyed. Modern state statutes often provide for a penalty and liability for damages in the event the mortgagee refuses to execute the forms necessary to effect a release of the mortgage so that title to the mortgagor's property can be cleared.

Prepayment and the Prepayment Penalty Conventional mortgage loans obligate the borrower to make monthly payments of interest and principal in an amount sufficient to gradually amortize or payoff the loan. The amortization period is highly variable, but many mortgage loans contemplate a thirty-year payoff schedule, and periods of forty years are beginning to become more common. Suppose the owner wishes to sell the property or refinance the loan or, for whatever reason, to pay it off other than pursuant to the terms of the note. Must the lender accept prepayment? If it accepts prepayment may it charge a fee for the privilege?

The common law rule viewed the situation in purely contractual terms and held that the lender was not obligated to accept payment other than as specified in the agreement. This is still the general rule, although current practice tends to permit prepayment upon condition that the borrower pay a fee, known as a prepayment penalty. The operation of a prepayment penalty provision is considered in the following case.

Lazzareschi Investment Company v. San Francisco Federal Savings and Loan Association, 99 Cal. Rptr. 417 (Cal. 1972)

Facts of the case.

On February 21, 1967, Frank A. Marshall borrowed $300,000 from defendant San Francisco Federal Savings and Loan Association, for which he executed a promissory note secured by a deed of trust on property used for commercial purposes. In the note Marshall reserved the right to prepay the $300,000 obligation in whole or in part at any time prior to maturity. This privilege, however, was subject to a prepayment fee provision.

On November 17, 1967, plaintiff purchased the real property securing San Francisco Federal's loan from Frank Marshall. The purchase price was $570,000. In order to consummate the purchase, plaintiff had to procure new financing. Immediately before the close of escrow, San Francisco Federal submitted a demand in the sum of $9,130.02, which constituted the prepayment fee computed in accordance with the provisions of the note. This sum was in addition to the price and other payments, including accrued interest, which plaintiff had agreed to pay for the property. Plaintiff paid and defendants received the amount demanded, but plaintiff noted in the buyer's instruments that it did so under protest.

Plaintiff declares that the interest rate of defendant's loan was then $7^3/_4$ percent, substantially less than that which defendants could obtain by a new loan of the recovered funds; wherefore defendants actually profited from the early prepayment rather than being prejudiced thereby. On the basis of these circumstances, plaintiff alleges in its complaint that the amount of the prepayment charge bears no reasonable relationship to any damage allegedly sustained by the defendants by virtue of the prepayment. Plaintiff also alleges that the prepayment fee constitutes an unreasonable restraint on alienation.

OPINION

For the purpose of this appeal, we proceed to examine the contract, which is the promissory note. It is necessary, however, to examine it not as an isolated transaction, but as a transaction existing with a multitude of others which the lender must enter in order to stay in business. If interest rates increase sharply, the lender has no option to renegotiate the loan. Of course, if a prepayment is made at the borrower's choice when interest rates have increased, the lender may gain from the repayment. But in the whole portfolio there may be many loans which will not be repaid although some of the borrowers have become well able to repay. The borrowers can use the money more advantageously. On the other hand, if interest rates decline, borrowers will be able to refinance at lower rates, and if there were not adequate charge for repayment, they could discharge the note, giving the original lender funds which could be put out only at a lower rate.

Plaintiff contends that because the loan was secured by a deed of trust which could not be lifted without satisfying the promissory note, it partakes of the nature of a restraint on alienation. But it has been held that reasonable restraints made in protection of justifiable interests of the parties are sustainable. The prepayment charge by no means constitutes an absolute restraint and because we do not regard it as an exorbitant burden and because there are legitimate interests of the lender to be protected, we do not discern an unlawful restraint on alienation.

Finally, we remark that the control of charges, if it be desirable, is better accomplished by statute or by regulation authorized by statute than by ad hoc decisions of the courts. Legislative committees and an administrative officer charged with regulating an industry have better sources of gathering information and assessing its value than do courts in isolated cases. Besides, institutions which lend vast sums of money should be informed, not by judgments after the facts on a case-to-case basis, but by laws or regulations which are in existence in advance of the undertaking to execute loans.

Judgment for Defendant.

NOTES AND QUESTIONS

Many states have enacted statutes to regulate the operation of prepayment penalties. This legislation varies considerably in substance but tends to be limited to loans secured by owner-occupied residential real estate. Some statutes flatly prohibit prepayment penalties in this class of loan and others limit the amount that can be charged as a prepayment penalty, usually as a percentage of the outstanding principal balance of the loan.

In addition, various states, either by statute or by judicial decision, prohibit the enforcement of a prepayment penalty if it is triggered by the mortgagee's enforcement of a due on sale clause or similar provision. In this context, you may wish to review *Nutman v. Aetna* included in Section 6 of this chapter.

9 PRIORITY PROBLEMS

As indicated at the beginning of this chapter, many of the formalities with respect to the creation of a mortgage are dependent upon the principles applicable to deeds and, as against third parties, upon compliance with the recording statutes.

A mortgage, if not recorded, is invalid against a subsequent purchaser or mortgagee who gives value and takes without notice, provided, in some states, that the conveyance to a subsequent purchaser is recorded before the prior mortgage is recorded. Similarly, a subsequent purchaser or mortgagee takes subject to a recorded mortgage, even in the absence of actual knowledge because of the constructive notice that is imparted by virtue of recording statutes.

Subordination Agreements   It is well established that a mortgagee may, without relinquishing her or his lien, give priority to one who would otherwise be a junior mortgagee. Such agreements are particularly common in the construction industry and involve an agreement by the mortgagor, first mortgagee, and the construction lender that the construction loan will have priority, notwithstanding the priority that would otherwise be established by virtue of recording statutes.

The Purchase Money Mortgage   An exception to the rule that priority of a mortgage is determined by virtue of the time of recording is found in the so-called purchase money mortgage. A purchase money mortgage is usually one that is executed at the same time as the deed of conveyence and in order to finance the purchase of the property. Generally speaking, a purchase money mortgage has priority over previously recorded liens of the buyer/mortgagor. This priority extends to a seller who takes back a mortgage as a portion of the purchase price and, in many states, applies equally to a third party lender of the purchase price. An example of a statute that embodies this principal is the following:

> If property is sold and granted, and at the same time the purchaser gives a mortgage or deed of trust to secure total or partial payment of the purchase money, the mortgage or deed of trust shall be preferred to any previous judgment or decree for the payment of money which

is obtained against the purchaser if it recites that the sum received is all or part of the purchase money of the property. This section is applicable regardless of whether the mortgage or deed of trust is given to the vendor of the property or to a third party who advances all or part of the purchase money.

(Maryland Annotated Code, Section 7–104)

Citizens National Bank v. Smith, 284 S.E. 770 (S.C. 1981)

Facts of the case.

In 1973 LaBorde, owned three parcels of undeveloped land in Richland County. The parcels consisted of 133, 489 and 490 acres, respectively. LaBorde sold this land to developers Smith and Williams receiving only purchase money mortgages in return. He agreed to subordinate these purchase money mortgages in order for the developers to obtain money to develop the land. This subordination provision read in part:

Seller agrees to execute such documents as may from time to time, be required to perfect such subordination.

The precise meaning of this provision is in dispute. Construction loans were placed on each of the parcels, and subsequently, LaBorde was informed that the developers had placed additional mortgages on the land without advising him or obtaining his consent.

Upon contacting the developers a new agreement was entered into in March 1974 in which they agreed as follows:

1 The purchase money mortgages would be satisfied.

2 New mortgages were to be executed in place of the purchase money mortgages.

3 LaBorde would, in writing, subordinate these new mortgages to any other mortgages provided the developers would satisfy the outstanding mortgages within three months and would pay to LaBorde $4,000.00.

Pursuant to this agreement, LaBorde executed a complete release to Smith and Williams, and fully complied with the terms of the new (March 1974) agreement. Smith and Williams agreed to pay off the mortgages. Instead they extended the mortgages without the knowledge of LaBorde. LaBorde has not been paid anything by Smith and Williams on any mortgage, new or old.

While there are numerous foreclosures relating to this financial debacle, here we are only concerned with the foreclosure by LaBorde, and others, on the 490-acre tract. Citizens Bank is involved because it loaned the developers two hundred and fifty thousand ($250,000.00) dollars, took a mortgage on the 490 acres, and later extended the due date of this mortgage by one year.

OPINION

At common law and in equity, a purchase money mortgage will ordinarily be given priority over other security instruments in realty, but it may be subordinated by agreement of the parties. Because it alters the normal priority of the mortgages, priority under a subordination agreement is strictly limited by the express terms of the agreement.

Here, LaBorde consented to the subordination of his mortgage to Citizens Bank and acknowledged in writing that his mortgage would be subordinate to the bank's until the latter had been satisfied, at which time LaBorde's mortgage would become a "first mortgage." This agreement was drafted by LaBorde's attorney and signed by LaBorde with full knowledge of the facts and circumstances.

Subsequently, Citizens Bank extended the time for payment of the $250,000.00 mortgage for one year without LaBorde's knowledge and consent. We hold that Citizens Bank lost its priority vis-a-vis LaBorde by doing this. A lender and a borrower may not bilaterally make a material modification of the loan to which the seller has subordinated without the knowledge and consent of the seller to that modification, if the modification materially affects the seller's rights.

If the terms of the debt are materially altered without the subordinated mortgagee's consent, the priority of the mortgages will be reserved in favor of the subordinated purchase money mortgage. The trial court held that the bank's extension of time past June 7, 1974, prejudiced LaBorde. This finding is supported by evidence that LaBorde considered repayment of the debt of June 7, 1974, a material inducement for subordinating his mortgage to the bank. We hold on the particular facts of this case, the bank lost its priority by modifying the terms of the loan to Smith and Williams in a manner that prejudicially affected LaBorde's rights without his knowledge or consent.

NOTES AND QUESTIONS

Do you agree that LaBorde was prejudiced by the extension? What would La-Borde's position have been if the bank proceeded to foreclose? Delays are a common feature of construction projects, and most banks would rather give a developer an extension than foreclose on a partially completed project. What should the bank have done in this case to avoid losing its priority? How could the bank have anticipated the need for an extension?

10 SUMMARY

A mortgage is an interest in real property that is given in order to secure an obligation or promise. Most often, the secured promise is one to repay money, although other forms of obligations can be secured by a mortgage. The secured promise, whatever it may be, must be capable of being reduced to a money equivalent of a definite sum.

For the most part, any interest in real estate that can be transferred can be made subject to a mortgage. Most mortgages involve encumbering the owner's fee interest although interests in mineral rights, leases, air rights, and the like may also be encumbered by a mortgage.

Under the common law, a mortgage was considered to be a transfer of the fee interest to the mortgagee, which the mortgagor could redeem upon satisfaction of the underlying obligation. Modern practice tends to consider a mortgage to be simply a security interest and a transfer for security purposes only, so that possession, rents, and the other attributes of ownership are retained by the mortgagor.

The primary advantage to a creditor of holding security in the form of a mortgage involves the power to foreclose in the event of a default in performance of the underlying obligation. Foreclosures are usually conducted either by virtue of a power of sale provision contained in the mortgage or through a judicial foreclosure proceeding in which the foreclosure is subject to judicial supervision. The mechanics of the foreclosure proceeding are largely dependent upon local practice and procedure. However, modern notions of consumer and debtor protection have worked their way into the law governing mortgage foreclosures, particularly as they relate to owner-occupied residential dwellings. Although these debtor protection statutes vary widely, they tend to relieve a debtor from the consequences of a default and limit the consequences of foreclosure in the event that a default cannot be cured. Some statutes permit the debtor to reinstate an obligation that is in default and thereby to avoid the consequences of acceleration. Others limit the creditor's remedy to foreclosure only and limit or abolish a creditor's right to obtain a deficiency judgment against the debtor in the event that the proceeds from the foreclosure sale are insufficient to satisfy the debt.

As a general rule, and in the absence of a provision to the contrary contained within the mortgage or other contract between the parties, either the mortgagor or mortgagee may transfer their respective interests to third parties. Such assignments are usually governed by the law of contracts.

Because there can be no mortgage in the absence of an obligation, satisfaction of the obligation will discharge or release the mortgage. Most states require a mortgagee to execute documents necessary to clear title to the mortgage when the obligation is satisfied.

As between two valid mortgages, the first to be recorded will usually have priority although a mortgagee may subordinate this priority by agreement with the mortgagor and/or the otherwise junior mortgagee.

At common law and under modern practice, a seller and, in most cases, a lender who lends money toward the purchase price take precedence over any other lien which attaches to the property through the buyer/mortgagor. Numerous reasons have been advanced to justify the preferred status that is given to a purchase money mortgagee, most of which revolve around the idea that a lien claimant should not be permitted to obtain a windfall at the expense of a seller who has parted with property in reliance upon the existence of security sufficient to satisfy the obligation in the event the buyer defaults.

11 QUESTIONS

1 Albert entered into an agreement with Betty in which Albert agreed to furnish labor and materials to construct a building on land Betty owned. Betty agreed to make periodic payments as the work progressed. The contract price was $100,000. Albert and Betty executed a mortgage to secure Betty's performance of the contract, and Betty failed to pay as agreed. Does Albert have an enforceable mortgage?

2 What are the factors a court might consider when deciding whether a deed absolute is really a mortgage?

3 Assume that your state legislature is considering enacting a statute that provides as follows: "In the case of all purchase money mortgages only the security can be looked to for recovery of the debt in the event of default by the mortgagor." What purposes would such a statute serve and what are the arguments against it?

4 Mr. and Mrs. Barattini purchased a house from John McKenna for $50,000. They paid $12,500 down, borrowed $22,500 from a bank secured by a first mortgage, and gave a note in the amount of $15,000 secured by a second mortgage to Mr. McKenna for the balance of the purchase price. Barattini defaulted on the note to McKenna who foreclosed the second mortgage and bid $4,000 at the foreclosure sale, subject to the first mortgage balance of $19,000. McKenna then filed a petition seeking a decree for the $11,000 deficiency. Barattini claimed that since McKenna promptly resold the property for a $10,000 gain that any deficiency against Barattini should be reduced accordingly. The trial court agreed with Barattini and McKenna appeals. What result?

5 Jones borrowed money from Smith evidenced by a promissory note secured by a mortgage against Jones's property. Jones paid the obligation in full but Smith has refused to execute a release of the mortgage. As a result, Jones was unable to complete a contract to sell the property to Wilson. Does Jones have a remedy against Smith?

CHAPTER 18

INVOLUNTARY LIENS ON REAL PROPERTY

TOPICS CONSIDERED IN THIS CHAPTER:

1 INTRODUCTION

We have seen that a lien against real estate involves the creation of an interest in the property for the purpose of securing performance of an obligation, usually the payment of money. For instance, a lien may be created in favor of a condominium association to secure and enforce payment of homeowner's dues and assessments (Chapter 8). In the preceding chapter we examined the lien created by a mortgage and the mechanics for enforcing the mortgage through foreclosure proceedings. Such liens, since they arise by agreement between the parties, are considered voluntary liens.

This chapter considers situations in which a creditor may impose a lien or charge against real estate owned by the debtor. Because the debtor does not expressly authorize use of the property as security for the lien, such liens are considered to be involuntary. However, once the lien attaches to the property, the consequences are roughly the same in either case.

An involuntary lien has two important consequences: first, it constitutes a burden or cloud upon title to the property making it nearly impossible for the owner to sell or encumber the property without removing the lien, typically by paying it off. Second, the creditor need not wait for the obligation to be paid but may initiate proceedings to force a sale of the property and direct that the proceeds of sale be used to satisfy the obligation represented by the lien.

There are three types of liens that will be considered in this chapter. The first is known as the equitable lien that, as its name suggests, arises in order to prevent unjust enrichment and to enforce a debt which the landowner, in good conscience, should not be permitted to avoid. The second kind of lien is referred to as the statutory lien. The statutory lien enables certain types of creditors to have resort to the debtor's property in order to obtain payment of a debt. Finally, governmental entities have the power to impose a lien against property in order to assist in the collection of revenue, particularly the payment of property taxes.

2 EQUITABLE LIENS

An equitable lien arises in situations where equity and good conscious dictate that particular property should be burdened by a lien in order to enforce an obligation that the landowner should not be permitted to avoid. For example, A in a will, devises real estate to B providing further that B should make monthly payments to C. Upon A's death, B may of course, reject the property by disclaiming his interest under the will. However, if B accepts the property, C's right to receive payments will be secured in the form of an equitable lien against the property in the event that B does not make payments as stipulated. The rationale is that B should not be permitted to receive the benefits of A's will unless he is also willing to honor the condition that A imposed. In order to help guarantee B's compliance, the law will impose an equitable lien against the property in favor of C.

In *Ross v. Gerund*, 69 S. 2d 650 (Fla. 1954), the pastor and deacon of a Baptist church hired a contractor to make repairs to property owned by the church. Unknown to the contractor, the pastor and deacon did not have authority to enter into contracts on behalf of the church, which refused to pay the contractor for the work performed. Although the contract was not enforceable, the court imposed an equitable lien against the church's property and described the creation of the lien in the following terms:

> Such liens may arise from written contracts which show an intention to charge some particular property with a debt or obligation, or they may be declared by a court of equity out of general consideration of right and justice as applied to the relations of the parties and the circumstances of their dealings.

In *Marback v. Gnadl*, 219 N.E. 2d 572 (Ill. 1966), plaintiff sold a building to defendant under an installment contract. Plaintiff retained title pending payment by defendant of installments for five years. Defendant was obligated to insure the property. During the term of the contract, a fire destroyed the building. Defendant collected the insurance proceeds and defaulted on the contract. Plaintiff sought to impose an equitable lien against the insurance proceeds to the extent of the unpaid purchase price of the contract. The court agreed with plaintiff and imposed the lien. The court said:

> Equity recognizes, in addition to the personal obligation, in some cases, a peculiar right over the thing concerning which a contract deals, which it calls a ''lien,'' and which, though not property, is analogous to property, by means of which the plaintiff is enabled to follow the identical thing and to enforce the defendant's obligation by a remedy which operates directly upon that thing. The essential elements of an equitable lien include a debt, duty, or obligation owing by one person to another, and property to which that obligation fastens, identified or described with reasonable certainty.

Being a creature of equity, the equitable lien is capable of great flexibility and is somewhat difficult to define. As the preceding excerpts indicate, there are three things usually required before an equitable lien will be imposed. First, there must be a debt or other obligation running from the defendant to the plaintiff. Second, there must be specific and identifiable property of the defendant, which is closely related to debt or obligation. Finally, the overall context must be such that the defendant would be unjustly enriched if its property were not made available to the plaintiff to secure payment of the debt.

3 STATUTORY LIENS

There are two types of statutory liens. The first of these is the judgment lien, which enables one who has obtained a court judgment for money to impose a lien against any property owned by the judgment debtor. A second and relatively more recent statutory lien is known as the mechanic's lien. The mechanic's lien enables one who has furnished labor or materials for the benefit of a construction project to impose a lien against the improved property in order to secure payment for the labor or materials rendered.

A Judgment Liens

The judgment lien was first made possible in England by virtue of a statute enacted in the year 1285. According to that statute, one who had obtained a final judgment could then obtain an order from the court commanding the Sheriff to deliver to the creditor one half of the judgment debtor's land, the income of which was then to be used by the creditor until the amount of the judgment was satisfied. Perhaps the most remarkable feature of this statute is that, 700 years later, the requirements and procedure for obtaining a judgment lien have changed very little.

All American states have enacted statutes authorizing and regulating the creation of judgment liens against real property. In addition, Congress has enacted a statute allowing judgment liens to be issued pursuant to federal court judgments.

There is wide variety among the various judgment lien statutes, although two characteristics are fundamental to all of them. First of all, there must be a valid and final judgment rendered against the judgment creditor. It is not enough that a creditor has a claim against the debtor. The claim must have resulted in the filing of a lawsuit and the rendition of a judgment against the debtor. The judgment may arise after a trial, by default or by stipulation. The judgment must be "final," which means that it is no longer subject to a right of appeal. In addition to having a final judgment, the judgment creditor must comply with the applicable state statute concerning the filing or recording of some memorandum of the judgment.

The federal judgment lien statute seeks to maintain consistency between federal and local law and reads as follows:

> Every judgment rendered by a District Court within a State shall be a lien on the property located in such State in the same manner to the same extent and under the same conditions as a judgment of a court of general jurisdiction in such State, and shall cease to be a lien in the same manner and time. Whenever the law of any State requires a judgment of a State court to be registered, recorded, docketed or indexed, or any other act to be done, in a particular manner or in a certain office or county or parish before such lien attaches, such requirements shall apply only if the law of such State authorizes the judgment of a court of the United States to be registered, recorded, docketed, indexed or otherwise conformed to rules and requirements relating to judgments of the court of the State.
>
> 28 U.S.C. Section 1962

Citibanc of Alabama v. Potter, 379 S. 2d 553 (Ala. 1980)

Facts of the case.

April 27, 1976: Citibanc obtained a judgment against Guy and Hazel Potter for $19,363.25 and costs of $27.50. The judgment was recorded the same day.

November 1, 1976: The Potters received a deed to the lot in question from their son, reciting $10 consideration. The deed was duly recorded. The same day the Potters executed a construction mortgage for $15,000 to Alabama Exchange Bank, which was also duly recorded.

December 1976: The Potters entered into a construction contract with Tuskegee Lumber Company, Inc., to construct the house for $38,000.

February 22, 1978: The Potters executed a mortgage to Tuskegee Federal Savings and Loan Association to cover $30,000 of the construction contract, including the $15,000 mortgage to Alabama Exchange. On this same date, the Potters executed a second mortgage to Tuskegee Lumber Company for $8,000 to cover the balance of the construction contract.

July 12, 1978: Citibanc brought its action for declaratory judgment.

April 18, 1979: A final judgment was entered in which the court held that Tuskegee Federal Savings and Loan Association had a first mortgage on the property, and that Citibanc had a judgment lien on the equity of the Potter's interest. The court refused to grant priority to Citibanc's lien because such a result "abhors justice and is rejected because the plaintiff (Citibanc) would be unjustly enriched." Citibanc then appealed.

OPINION

The issue, plainly stated, is whether the judgment lien should be given priority over subsequently created construction mortgages. As the trial court noted, there is no case law covering this exact point in Alabama. The question is therefore one of first impression. We hold that a duly registered judgment lien must be given priority over subsequently created construction mortgages.

Here, appellant Citibanc obtained a judgment against the Potters. It recorded that certificate of judgment in the court of their home county. A duly registered judgment lien, filed in accordance with the code is superior to any rights acquired under a mortgage on the debtor's property executed subsequently.

The fact that the mortgages are construction mortgages makes no difference. The statutory lien attaches to the Potters' interest in the property acquired after registration of the lien, and all subsequent mortgagees are charged with notice of the statutory lien. The facts make it unmistakably clear that Citibanc complied with the statutory requirements to perfect its judgment lien. It could do no more.

It is true that Citibanc waited until the construction mortgages were executed and construction began before it sought a declaration of its rights. However, the statute does not place a duty upon the judgment lienholder to notify lending institutions of the judgment lien. Rather, the statute places prospective subsequent mortgages on notice of the judgment lien against the debtor's property. The subsequent mortgagees can protect themselves by a check of judgment records to determine whether there are outstanding liens against the debtor or his property.

Thus, we hold that the trial court erred in granting the subsequent mortgagees priority over the prior judgment lien. The judgment lien attached to the Potters' property immediately upon transfer from their son. Appellees were given statutory notice of the lien. They acted in disregard of such notice and are therefore subordinated to the prior judgment lien.

Reversed.

NOTES

1 The proper filing of the judgment creates a lien against all property owned by the debtor within a certain area. This is usually done on a county by county basis so that the filing of the judgment will impress a lien against all property owned by the debtor within the county. Accordingly, it is common practice to file or record the judgment in all counties where the debtor is believed to own real property.

2 The duration of a judgment varies among the states but is usually between five and ten years. For instance, if the statute says the lien lasts for eight years, the judgment creditor has that long to execute upon the judgment, after which time it expires and the lien is no longer valid.

B Mechanic's Liens

The mechanic's lien is of relatively recent origin and was not part of the English common law. The first such statute was enacted in Maryland in 1791. By 1850, most American states had enacted some form of mechanic's lien statutes and all jurisdictions have mechanic's liens statutes today. The purpose of the mechanic's lien laws are to assist persons who furnish labor, materials, or services to a building project by giving such persons lien rights in the property that is being improved. Typically, anyone whose efforts directly result in enhancing the value of the land may obtain the benefits of the mechanic's lien statutes. Contractors, laborers, suppliers, and design professionals such as architects and engineers are usually covered. Because mechanic's liens are statutory creations, one seeking to obtain such a lien and the rights afforded the holder of a mechanic's lien, are entirely dependent upon compliance with the state statute pertaining to such liens.

As usual, there are considerable differences in the terminology and operation of the statutes of the various states, and efforts to promulgate a uniform mechanic's lien law have been notably unsuccessful. Nevertheless, there are certain features or attributes of a mechanic's lien that tend to be consistent among the various jurisdictions.

The operation of the mechanic's lien statutes may be illustrated by a typical example. Suppose an owner wants to construct a building on property which she owns. She will retain design professionals, namely architects and engineers, and will hire a general contractor to do the job. The general contractor will usually hire various subcontractors, such as electricians, plumbers, and so on. These subcontractors, may in turn, hire additional subcontractors and, along with the general contractor, will enter into agreement so that materials are delivered to the site. Except for the design professionals and the general contractor, none of the suppliers and subcontractors has an agreement directly with the owner. As the work progresses, the subcontractors and suppliers submit invoices to the general contractor who reviews them and submits them to the owner for payment. If the owner does not pay or even if the owner does pay the general contractor, but the general contractor fails to use the proceeds to pay subcontractors, the absence of a contractual arrangement with the owner leaves the subcontractor and supplier with only a breach of contract claim against the general contractor. This may be a relatively expensive and time consuming alternative, which the mechanic's lien statutes are intended to both simplify and expedite.

Provisions for mechanic's lien statutes are often embodied in state constitutions and authorize and direct the state legislature to enact a statutory scheme for such the enforcement of such liens. The Texas Constitution, Article XVI, Section 37 is a typical example. This section states:

> Mechanics, artisans and material men, of every class, shall have a lien upon the buildings and articles made or repaired by them for the value of their labor done thereon, or material furnished therefore; and the Legislature shall provide by law for the speedy and efficient enforcement of said liens.

The case of *Barry Properties v. Fick Bros. Roofing,* 353 A. 2d 222 (MD 1976), involved a constitutional challenge to the Maryland mechanic's statute. In upholding the overall validity of the statute, the court took the opportunity to review the purpose and operation of the Maryland statute which is essentially similar to those in effect in the other American states.

> Generally speaking, mechanic's liens statutes, in an endeavor to provide for the public welfare, are designed to encourage construction by ensuring that those who contribute to a project are compensated for their efforts. Maryland's law, in furtherance of this purpose, grants to those who have supplied labor or materials to the creation, erection, improvement, or repair of specified property (principally buildings) a lien, enforceable by foreclosure, on the structure and the immediately adjacent land.

> Under the terms of the Maryland statute, a lien is created and attaches to the property as soon as work is performed or materials are supplied, and lasts until "the expiration of 180 days after the work has been finished or the materials furnished, although no claim has been filed for them [with the clerk of the court]." However, if a laborer or materialman is a subcontractor, meaning he did not directly contract with the property owner, he "is not entitled to a lien unless, within ninety days after furnishing the work or material, he or his agent gives notice in writing, . . . to the owner . . . of his intention to claim a lien." The purpose of this notice is to inform the property owner that a lien may be claimed so that he, "may retain from the costs of the building the amount which he ascertains to be due to the party giving notice." The statute further provides that if either a subcontractor who gives the required notice or a general contractor has not been fully paid and desires to retain his mechanic's lien, he must within 180 days, file a claim containing specified information concerning the claim with the clerk of the circuit court of the county where the property is located, at which time the lien will be recorded on a special "Mechanics' Lien Docket." Once filed with the clerk the lien subsists for one year from the date of its filing unless within that period the claimant commences a proceeding to enforce it, in which case the lien is "stayed until the conclusion of the proceeding." During that one-year period, however, "the owner of the property subject of the lien, or any other person interested in it, may bring proceedings to compel the claimant to prove the validity of the lien or have it declared void," or, with court approval, the owner may release his property from the lien by substituting a bond. An action to enforce a mechanic's lien is an equity proceeding of which all interested parties are entitled to notice. If, in such a proceeding, the claimant establishes that he is entitled to the lien, the court will order a sale of the property to pay the claimant unless the amount found to be due is paid on or before a specified date.

Procedure for Perfecting a Mechanic's Lien As indicated, the procedures that relate to creating a mechanic's lien are of considerable variety and are often relatively technical. Failure to comply with the requirements of the local statute usually results in the invalidity of the mechanic's lien leaving the contractor, subcontractor, or supplier to pursue their contractual remedies.

Most mechanic's liens statutes distinguish between parties who have a direct contractual relationship with the property owner and those who do not. This distinction is based upon the fact that an owner's property may be subject to a lien by someone whom the owner would not otherwise know is furnishing labor or materials to the project. As a result, persons who do not have a contractual relationship with the owner are usually required to give notice to the owner, often by registered mail, prior to furnishing labor or materials to the construction site. Because the owner will be aware of the lien rights of the general contractor and others with whom the owner has a direct contractual relationship, such persons are not required to give notice to the owner.

A second requirement, applicable to all lien claimants, involves the filing and typically the recording of a document usually known as a "claim of lien." This claim of lien must be filed and/or recorded within a certain time after the labor or materials were furnished, must state the nature of the work that was done, and the amount which is being claimed. At this point, the contractor or supplier has a lien against the property to the same extent as a judgment creditor who has filed or recorded an abstract of judgment. The lien is a burden or cloud upon the title to the property and the owner is effectively precluded from selling or encumbering the property without removing the lien.

Finally, if the contractor or supplier is not paid within a certain time, he may file an action in the appropriate court to foreclose the mechanic's lien. If the lawsuit to foreclose the lien is not filed within the statutory time limits, the lien expires and will be lost. A mechanic's lien foreclosure action proceeds in much the same fashion as an action to judicially foreclose a mortgage and will result in the property being sold and proceeds sufficient to satisfy the lien being directed to the lien claimant.

Priority of Mechanic's Liens   An important aspect of mechanic's liens is whether and to what extent the lien claimant has priority over other liens against the property. A typical example may help to illustrate the problem.

Suppose owner hires general contractor to construct a building. Owner obtains construction financing secured by a mortgage against the property. The general contractor hires subcontractors to build foundations, install electrical, plumbing and heating systems and, let us suppose, to install a sprinkler system and to landscape the grounds around the building site. Clearly the subcontractors will furnish labor and materials to the job site at different times, the foundation work being first, the landscaping last. If none of the subcontractors are paid in full, what are their respective priorities as against each other, as against the construction lender, and as against judgment creditors whose liens are perfected during the course of construction?

The answers to these questions usually depend upon the time that the mechanic's lien is considered to attach to the owner's property. The time a mechanic's lien attaches, is dependent upon the language of the state's mechanic's lien statute and on this point there are four different views.

The majority rule fixes the critical time as the beginning of actual construction at the site. Under this rule, which is followed in Alabama, California, Kansas, Minnesota, Ohio, Tennessee, and others, the lien of any claimant relates back to the moment when work first began. This rule tends to treat all mechanic's lien claimants as having equal priority regardless of the time the particular claimant furnished labor or materials to the site.

A second approach, followed in Arkansas, Virginia, and a few others, creates priority based upon the time the lien claimant itself furnished labor or material to the site. This rule clearly favors lien claimants whose work is needed earlier in the course of construction.

A third rule, followed in Illinois and a few other jurisdictions, holds that the mechanic's lien relates back to the time the contract to furnish labor or materials was entered into. In our example, the lien claimant's priority would not depend upon the commencement of work or the time the claimant furnished labor or materials but rather upon the date of the contract by which the claimant agreed to furnish labor or material to the site.

Finally, a few jurisdictions, most notably New York, hold that the claimant has no lien until it is perfected. Under this rule, commencement of construction, date of the contract, and actual furnishing of labor or materials by the contractor are not directly relevant. Rather, the lien claimant has priority only to the extent that it perfects its lien as provided in the statute. This approach would also tend to favor claimants whose services are required earlier in the construction process because such claimants will be the first to have the right to perfect their liens.

NOTES AND QUESTIONS

1 In *Summer v. DCR Corp.*, 351 N.E. 2d 485 (Ohio, 1976), construction began on August 9, and the property was encumbered by a mortgage two months later. A dispute as to priority arose between the mortgagee and various mechanic's lien claimants. In holding for the mechanic's lien claimants, the court, applying the majority approach noted that:

> It is incumbent upon the lender who desires to secure priority over mechanic's liens . . . to record his purchase money mortgage promptly, and before the visible commencement of work upon the mortgaged premises, in the case of intervening mechanic's lienors. Having failed to avail itself of this means of securing priority over mechanic's liens, the mortgagee must be held subsequent in priority thereto.

2 Do you see any problems inherent in the majority approach? Suppose the bank learns that grading work has commenced just before it is prepared to fund its loan and record the construction mortgage. What will probably happen next?

4 LIENS IN FAVOR OF GOVERNMENTAL ENTITIES

Governmental entities at the federal, state, and local level are typically vested with authority to impose liens against real property to enforce the collection of taxes, fees, or other assessments. Generally, the power of an agency to impose a lien on property is considered an aspect of the power to levy a tax. As a result, local governments have lien rights to facilitate the collection of property taxes and other municipal assessments. Local departments and even private corporations may be given the power to impose liens for the collection of water and sewer service charges, garbage collection, and other essential municipal services. In addition, state and federal income tax authorities may impose liens on a taxpayer's real estate for unpaid income taxes. Government liens may also be imposed to expedite the collection of unemployment insurance contributions, social security payments, or other similar contributions.

For example, the Internal Revenue Code contains various provisions which enable the I.R.S. to levy against property of the taxpayer. One such provision provides as follows:

> If any person liable to pay any tax neglects or refuses to pay the same within ten days after notice and demand, it shall be lawful for the Secretary [or his delegate] to collect such tax (and such further sum as shall be sufficient to cover the expense of the levy) by levy upon all property and rights to property . . . belonging to such person or on which there is a lien provided in this chapter for the payment of such tax . . . 26 U.S.C. Section 6331(a)

In *U.S. v. Rodgers,* 461 U.S. 677 (1983), the Supreme Court examined Section 6331(a) in the following terms:

> Administrative levy, unlike an ordinary lawsuit, does not require any judicial intervention, and it is up to the taxpayer, if he so chooses, to go to court if he claims that the assessed amount was not legally owing.
> The common purpose of this formidable arsenal of collection tools is to ensure the prompt and certain enforcement of the tax laws in a system relying primarily on self-reporting.

5   SUMMARY

A lien is a charge against property that enables the holder of the lien to satisfy it and obtain payment out of the proceeds of the sale of the property encumbered by the lien. Unlike a mortgage, which is considered a consensual or voluntary lien, an involuntary lien is created by operation of law to assist a creditor in obtaining satisfaction of a debt. A lien survives the transfer of the property, and one may not transfer good title to property subject to a lien. In addition, if the lien is not satisfied, the creditor may initiate proceedings which will result in the property being sold and the proceeds distributed to the creditor to the extent of the value of the lien. Such a forced sale operates like a mortgage foreclosure sale.

There are three kinds of involuntary liens. The equitable lien arises when specific property is made subject to a lien to secure performance of an obligation which the debtor, in equity and good conscience, should not be permitted to avoid.

The statutory lien, as its name suggests, exists by virtue of legislation that enables the lien to be created and that specifies the procedures necessary to perfect the lien. The judgment lien permits a creditor who has obtained a final judgment against a debtor to impose a lien against any property owned by the judgment debtor. Judgment liens are perfected by following the provisions of the state statute and usually involve filing and/or recording a memorandum of the judgment in the county where the property is located.

The second type of statutory lien is the mechanic's lien. Such a lien is created in favor of persons who furnish labor or materials to a construction project. One who perfects a mechanic's lien is entitled to foreclose the lien and thereby obtain payment out of the proceeds of the sale of the property.

Finally, certain governmental entities are authorized to impose liens against real estate. Governmental liens differ from other liens because they are imposed by administrative action and without judicial supervision. The burden of contesting a governmental lien is upon the debtor who must file an action in order to have the lien invalidated.

6 QUESTIONS

1 Angelica owns property and enters into a contract with Basic Hauling to remove rocks and debris from the property. In the meantime, Capital Bank forecloses on their delinquent loan and becomes the owner of the property. Basic is unaware of this and, the day after the foreclosure, performs the contract. Angelica is bankrupt and Capital refuses to pay. Does Basic have a lien against the property. What kind?

2 Dorothy sues Ellen for specific performance of a contract to sell a parcel of land and prevails. May Dorothy impose a lien against the parcel or against other property owned by Ellen?

3 Frank has a judgment against Grace for personal injuries sustained in an auto accident. Frank complies with all statutory formalities and obtains a lien in a county where Grace owns several parcels of property. Grace's equity in each of the parcels exceeds the amount of Frank's judgment. Which parcel is subject to the lien? Who decides?

4 Henry has a lien against Ira. Ira takes a deed from Joan, records it and sells the property to Kevin. The deeds to Ira and from Ira to Kevin were consecutive so that Ira only owned the property for a moment. Did Henry's lien attach? If it attached, did it survive the transfer to Kevin?

5 Lamont owns property upon which a hotel is being built. Lamont hires Master Builders as a general contractor who, in turn, hires subcontractors, including Novice Electric. Novice has a contract with Master for $50,000. Novice finishes the work but it was done late and poorly, costing Lamont an additional $40,000 in delays and additional charges. Lamont refuses to pay Novice anything. Assuming Novice has complied with the mechanic's lien statutes, can Novice file a lien for $50,000?

LANDLORD AND TENANT

CHAPTER 19

LANDLORD AND TENANT

TOPICS CONSIDERED IN THIS CHAPTER:

1 INTRODUCTION

With the possible exception of zoning, no area of real estate law has changed as dramatically or as quickly as the landlord and tenant relationship. The English common law evolved to meet the needs of an agrarian society in which the land itself, rather than the buildings upon the land, was of primary importance and in which the law itself placed very few responsibilities upon the landlord.

In the United States, the common law was adhered to, for the most part, until approximately 1970. Since that time, first through court decisions then through legislation in most of the states, the law, particularly as it pertains to the residential landlord and tenant relationship, has undergone profound change.

The landlord and tenant relationship has a long history and covers many situations. In the modern context, a rental may involve a furnished room in a private residence, a single-family residence, an apartment in a multi-unit building, a suite of offices in an office building, a retail store in a shopping center, space in a warehouse, an industrial complex, agricultural land, and so forth. In reviewing the materials that follow, it is important to distinguish between a residential rental and a commercial one. A residential rental involves premises leased as a primary or secondary dwelling, and a commercial rental includes everything else.

In the case of a commercial rental, many of the common law principles continue to control the relationship, although often in modified form. The perception of courts and legislatures is that in the commercial context, the parties are of relatively equal bargaining power and sophistication and are therefore able to freely negotiate the terms of a lease to the mutual satisfaction of both parties.

In the residential context, the recognition of the existence of a serious housing shortage in many parts of the country, along with the rise of consumerism generally, have combined to impose upon residential landlords various responsibilities entirely foreign to the common law.

The National Conference of Commissioners on Uniform State Laws has produced a document known as the Uniform Residential Landlord and Tenant Act (URLTA), and the American Law Institute has drafted the *Restatement (2d) of Property* (Landlord and Tenant). Both of these documents attempt to restate much of the entire field of landlord/tenant law, primarily as it relates to the residential landlord and tenant relationship. Because both the URLTA and the *Restatement* have had a significant impact upon the development of the law in this area, they will be referred to periodically in this chapter.

2 LANDLORD AND TENANT: THE BASICS

Where an owner of property grants possession to another and retains a reversion, the transaction is known as the lease. Possession is usually fundamental to the nature of a lease, although there are a few exceptions. For instance, an owner may lease to another a side of a building for the placement of a sign. In this case, the lease gives exclusive use or occupation of the side of the building but not possession of it. For the most part, however, a lease confers possession, usually exclusive possession, to the tenant.

A   Classification of the Common Law Estates

The Term of Years   The term of years is a possessory estate in real property, which lasts for a fixed or computable period, even if the duration of the estate is less than one year. A term for a week, a month, a year, or ten years are all considered periodic tenancies because they have a fixed and definite term. Generally speaking, a term of years ends automatically upon the expiration of the term without notice to or from either party.

The Periodic Tenancy   The periodic tenancy continues for successive periods of not more than one year. Termination of the periodic tenancy must be accompanied by notice. The periodic tenancy is considered a continuing interest subject to termination at appropriate intervals. A lease ''from year to year'' or ''from month to month'' are considered periodic tenancies.

Where the period is not specified, an inference usually arises based upon the payment of rent. For instance, if rent is paid on a semi-annual basis, then the term will be considered to be a semi-annual term. However, the ULRTA, Section 1.401(d) provides that where there is no term, a month-to-month periodic tenancy is implied, regardless of the timing of the rental payments.

The periodic tenancy requires notice in order to terminate the estate. At common law, the notice was based upon the length of the term. Statutes in most states have changed this rule and most of those specify a thirty-day notice, although some statutes specify sixty days, others ninety days, and a few one hundred and twenty days. The *Restatement 2d,* Section 1.5, provides that a thirty-day notice is required in order to terminate a periodic tenancy.

The Tenancy At Will   The tenancy at will is an estate, which terminates at the will of either party and which has no other period of duration. In other words, a tenancy at will lasts only so long as both parties desire it to continue. There was no notice requirement under the common law, although most states now have statutory requirements of notice to terminate a tenancy at will usually requiring thirty-days notice. The effect of notice statutes is to give to the tenancy at will many of the attributes of a thirty-day periodic tenancy.

The Tenancy at Sufferance   The tenancy at sufferance is really not an estate in land and is not really a tenancy in the usual sense. It arises where a tenant holds over and continues in possession after termination of a previously valid interest in the property—for instance, when a tenant holds over after termination of a periodic or other tenancy or where the seller of property wrongfully holds over and remains in possession after the close of escrow. The only difference between a tenant at sufferance and a mere trespasser is that the tenant at sufferance originally took possession rightfully.

3   TYPICAL PROVISIONS OF A LEASE

A   Essential Terms

Most jurisdictions and the *Restatement 2d* hold that the statute of frauds requires that a lease for a term in excess of one year must be in writing in order to be enforceable.

A writing sufficient to satisfy the Statute of Frauds requires that (1) the parties be identified, (2) the premises be described, (3) the duration of the lease be specified, (4) the amount and due date of the payment of rent be set forth, and (5) the agreement be signed by the parties. The rules of construction with regard to the statute of frauds generally apply in the case of leases. (Recall the discussion in Chapter 13, Section 4.) For example, if the parties fail to describe the premises, the defect will be cured if the lessee takes occupancy of the premises, and when the amount of rent is omitted from an otherwise enforceable lease, a court may imply that the parties intended to provide for the reasonable rental value of the premises. However, when the agreement is silent as to duration, the agreement will probably be construed as merely at tenancy at will.

B   Provisions for the Payment of Rent

The Gross Lease   The gross lease is the most common form of residential arrangement whereby the tenant pays a fixed amount of rent, and the landlord pays insurance, taxes, and certain other costs associated with owning the property. A gross lease can also be used in a commercial rental, although it is less commonly found in the commercial context.

The Net Lease   The net lease is common in commercial rentals and provides that, in addition to paying a fixed or flat periodic rent, the tenant also pays all or a portion of property taxes, insurance, and similar assessments. For instance, in a multi-tenant building, each tenant would be assigned a pro-rata share of certain expenses based upon the percentage of the building they occupy. When bills for insurance, taxes, special assessments, and possibly utilities are received by the owner, an accounting is rendered and each tenant is billed accordingly; this amount then being added to the base rent.

Percentage Lease   A percentage lease is used exclusively in commercial situations and provides that rent payable is based upon a percentage of the sales or income generated by the tenant. Percentage leases afford some protection to the tenant in the case of business fluctuations and usually require considerable interaction between the landlord and tenant. Obviously, the landlord must have the right to examine a tenant's financial statements, and a covenant in this regard will be implied even if it is not included in the lease. Drafting of such leases requires great care in defining the sales activity that will be used to determine the amount of rent and in specifying the accounting methods that are to be used.

The case of *Elfstrom v. Brown,* 366 P. 2d 728 (Ore. 1961), is a typical example of a percentage lease. The lease provided, in part, as follows:

> In addition to the minimum base rent provided for above ($600.00 per month), the Lessee agrees to pay one per cent (1%) annually on all gross sales in excess of $620,000.00 per year. . . . In determining the amount of gross sales for the purpose of computing the rent hereunder, the Lessee agrees to report to the Lessors and include in the amount of said sales the gross business from all of the various departments, concessions, and activities of the Lessee's business. Gross sales are not intended to cover or be affected by any branch business which may be established by the Lessee in the future in other trading areas, but the Lessee agrees that it will not discriminate against the Lessor's interest in said gross sales for the Salem trading area in favor of any branch which the Lessee may establish.

During the lease term, the tenant acquired interests in two other businesses within the Salem trading area. The landlord demanded that the gross sales of the tenant included sales made by the two other businesses. The court concluded that the affiliated companies were ''departments'' or ''concessions'' of the tenant within the meaning of those terms as used in the lease so that sales by those companies should be included when determining the tenant's gross sales.

In *Dover Shopping Center v. Cushman,* 164 A. 2d 785 (N.J. 1960), the New Jersey court was presented with a percentage lease containing the following provision:

> Tenant agrees, during the entire term of this lease, to operate its business in the demised premises; to keep its store open daily for the regular conduct of its business during the same hours at least as are customarily employed by other similar stores in the neighborhood and to keep and maintain the show window displays in an attractive and dignified manner. Tenant hereby agrees to join with the other tenants in the shopping center in any endeavor to formulate a common plan of store hours and business days; and if Tenant and said other tenants shall arrange such a common plan, then the store hours and business days of Tenant's store on the demised premises, in lieu of the store hours and business days hereinabove set forth in this Article, shall be those prescribed by said common plan during the continuance thereof.

The lease provided for a minimum annual rental of $7,000 plus a shifting percentage of gross sales in excess of the minimum rent.

Defendant took possession and began business on September 15, 1957. On May 1, 1959, defendant wrote plaintiff that it was permanently ceasing operations, indicating that it had found the enterprise unprofitable and had decided it would be less costly to pay the minimum rent than to resume operations.

The landlord instituted an action seeking a mandatory injunction to require defendant to reopen and resume its retail bakery business, to display the name of ''Cushman's'' on the outside of the premises, to keep the store open as required by the lease, and to maintain a manager or salesperson in charge.

The trial court granted this relief and the Court of Appeals affirmed noting that:

Courts have recognized the uniqueness of a percentage lease and have generally implied therefrom an obligation on the part of the lessee to occupy the property and to use reasonable diligence in operating the business in a productive manner.

NOTES AND QUESTIONS

Do you agree with the relief given by the New Jersey court? Do you foresee problems with requiring the tenant to stay in business apparently against its will? Is there a less onerous alternative?

Reappraisal Provisions   Long-term leases that provide that at least a portion of the obligation is in the form of a fixed rent typically provide that the amount will be re-assessed periodically. The important aspect of such provisions is that the reappraisal provision provides a definite formula for the periodic adjustment of rent. Provisions that increase the rent based upon the ''fair rental value'' of the property are generally enforceable, particularly if a method of determining the fair value is also contained within the lease. Provisions that peg rent increases to the rate of inflation or the consumer price index (CPI) are more definite and preferable for that reason. Provisions that provide for a ''reasonable adjustment'' or that provide that the rental adjustment will be negotiated in the future are typically unenforceable for lack of certainty and should be avoided for that reason.

In *Karamanos v. Hamm,* 513 P. 2d 761 (Ore. 1973), the Oregon Supreme Court considered a lease renewal provision that provided the following:

As further consideration for the acceptance of this lease, lessors hereby extend the above described lease for a period of two years from June 1, 1972, to June 1, 1974, under the same terms and conditions as to said lease contained, except that the monthly rental during the extension period of said lease is to be negotiable.

The parties were unable to agree upon the rental amount during the extension period and the landlord gave notice terminating the lease. In holding for the landlord, the court stated the general rule as follows:

There are three essential elements of a lease: a description of the property, the duration of the term, and the rental consideration. Lacking such definiteness of time and rent, there is no contract to extend or renew. The exact terms may be left for future arbitration provided the method is fixed, but if there is no such certain method, the agreement is void for uncertainty. The rule, in essence, is that a provision for the extension or renewal of a lease must specify the time the lease is to extend and the rate of rent to be paid with such a degree of certainty and definiteness that nothing is left to future determination. If it falls short of this requirement, it is not enforceable. Since the essential element of monthly rental is lacking in the consent to the assignment and there is no method providing for fixing the amount of rental, the agreement to extend the lease is fatally defective and unenforceable.

The Destruction of the Leased Premises   According to the common law, and in the absence of an agreement to the contrary, a landlord had no duty to rebuild damaged or destroyed premises, but the tenant's rental obligation continued for the duration of the lease term.

> At common law the obligation of a landlord to repair or rebuild leased premises rested solely on an express covenant or understanding. Without such, he was not bound to repair or to pay for repairs made by the tenant. Similarly, the lessee was held by the obligation of his express covenant to pay rent, although the premises had been actually destroyed.
>
> To ameliorate the harsh effect of this rule, we have enacted, as many states have done, legislation that states as follows: "The lessee of a building which, without fault or neglect on the part of the lessee, is destroyed or so injured by the elements or any other cause as to be untenantable or unfit for occupancy, is not liable thereafter to pay rent to the lessor owner unless expressly provided by written agreement, and the lessee may thereupon quit and surrender possession of the premises.
>
> *General Assurance Corp. v. Traders,* 104 P. 2d 157 (Ariz. 1965)

A majority of states have abrogated the common law rule either by statute or by court decision. Some states continue to follow the common law rule. Georgia, for instance, provides by statute that in the event the commercial premises are damaged or destroyed, the tenant is not entitled to a rent abatement and cannot terminate the lease.

In the modern commercial context, the issue of who bears the risk of loss if the property is destroyed is often allocated based upon who has the duty to insure the premises. This question should be addressed in any commercial lease.

4 RIGHTS AND DUTIES OF THE PARTIES

A The Duty to Deliver Possession

In the typical case, the tenant finds the leased premises available and unoccupied on the day the lease term begins. Occasionally, however, another person, usually a prior tenant with or without a rightful claim to possession, continues to occupy the premises. The question then becomes, "What is the incoming tenant's remedies as against the landlord and the prior tenant in possession?"

Adrian v. Rabinowitz, 186 A. 29 (N.J. 1936)

Facts of the case.

Adrian leased from Rabinowitz a commercial building in Paterson, New Jersey. The premises were to be used to conduct a shoe business. The lease was to commence on June 15.

When the lease was signed, the premises were occupied by another who failed to vacate upon notice by the landlord. Plaintiff was not able to take possession until July 9. Plaintiff filed this action claiming damages for lost business during the time he was unable to use the premises. The trial court ruled in favor of plaintiff and this appeal followed.

OPINION

The question is whether the lessor, in the absence of an express understanding to that effect, is under a duty to put the lessee in actual, as well as legal, possession of the demised premises at the commencement of the term. We are of the view that he is. There seems to be no dissent from the doctrine that the lessor implied covenants that the lessee shall have the legal right of possession at the beginning of the term. But there are different views to whether this implied obligation extends as well to actual possession, especially where, as here, the prior tenant wrongfully holds over.

In some of our American jurisdictions, the rule obtains that while the lessee is entitled to have the legal right of possession, there is no implied covenant to protect the lessee against wrongful acts of strangers. The English rule is that, where the term is to commence in the future, there is an implied undertaking by the lessor that the premises shall be open to the lessee's entry, legally and actually, when the time for possession under the lease arrives.

The English rule, so-called, is on principle much the better one. It has the virtue, ordinarily, of effectuating the common intention of the parties—to give premises to the lessee on the day fixed for the commencement of the term. This is what the lessee generally bargains for; and it is the thing the lessor undertakes to give.

Affirmed.

NOTES AND QUESTIONS

1 The Rabinowitz case states the so-called "English Rule" which is the majority view in this country. It is the rule in the states of Alabama, Arizona, Georgia, Iowa, North Carolina, Ohio, and Texas, among others.

2 *Restatement of Property (2d),* Section 6.2 provides, in part, as follows:

> Except to the extent that the parties to lease validly agree otherwise, there is a breach of the landlord's obligation if a third person is improperly in possession of the leased property on the date the tenant is entitled to possession and the landlord does not act promptly to remove the person and does not in fact remove him within a reasonable period of time.

The *Restatement* goes on to provide that, for the breach, a tenant may either terminate the lease or affirm the lease and recover damages, obtain an abatement in rent and recover from the landlord, or the tenant in possession, costs incurred by the incoming tenant if he chooses to initiate eviction proceeding against the prior tenant.

3 The Uniform Residential Landlord Tenant Act, Section 2–307 is essentially in agreement with the *Restatement.*

4 The so-called "American Rule," which is a minority view in this country, provides that, absent a provision in the lease to the contrary, the landlord has no implied duty to deliver actual possession and the incoming tenant cannot terminate the lease or get damages against the landlord where a third party wrongfully holds over. Under this approach, the landlord must give the tenant the right to possession but not necessarily actual possession. The American Rule, unlike the English Rule, places the risk of a holdover on the incoming tenant rather than the landlord. The rationale for the American Rule is that the incoming tenant is entitled to possession and may seek possession or damages or both against the holdover tenant. Some American Rule jurisdictions also base their position on the general rule that an innocent party (in this case the landlord) is not liable for the torts of a third party (in this case the tenant who wrongfully retains possession). Jurisdictions adhering to the minority American Rule are, among others, California, Illinois, Maryland, Massachusetts, New Hampshire, New York, Pennsylvania, and Wisconsin.

B Interference with Possession During the Tenancy

As noted above, there is split of authority as to whether the landlord or the tenant is responsible for obtaining actual possession for the tenant at the commencement of the lease although the majority rule holds that this responsibility is placed upon the landlord. Once possession has been established, however, it is generally the tenant's responsibility to maintain that possession against third parties, unless there is a covenant to the contrary in the lease. Thus, a tenant of farm land whose crops were damaged by the crop dusting of a neighbor had no claim against the landlord, and his remedy was limited to a claim against the negligent neighbor. See *Binder v. Perkins,* 516 P. 2d 1012 (Kan. 1973).

A slightly different problem is presented when the actions complained of are those of another tenant of the lessor. Most American cases hold that the landlord is not liable for the acts of other tenants, although there is modern authority to the contrary. See *Gottdiner v. Mailhot,* 431 A. 2d 851 (N.J. 1981).

If the tenant is actually evicted by the landlord or through the fault of the landlord then the tenant may terminate the lease and seek damages against the landlord. An obvious example of an actual eviction would be when the landlord changes the locks on the doors, although there are numerous more subtle ways in which the tenant's right to possession can be defeated by action of the landlord or one acting by or through the landlord.

An actual eviction should be contrasted with a constructive eviction. In an actual eviction the tenant is physically excluded by the landlord from all or a part of the premises. A constructive eviction, however, refers to conduct by the landlord that interferes with the tenant's enjoyment of the premises but that does not amount to physical exclusion of the tenant. These will be more fully explored next.

Partial Actual Eviction Another curiosity of the common law is the doctrine of partial actual eviction. Under this rule, when a tenant is partially evicted—in other words, evicted from a portion of the premises—the tenant may remain on the premises but the duty to pay rent is completely suspended so long as the partial actual eviction continues. This rule is difficult to rationalize except with reference to common law concepts, although it continues to be the majority approach in this country.

In *Smith v. McEnany,* 48 N.E. 781 (Mass. 1873), Justice Holmes was faced with the situation where a brick wall was built upon adjoining land with the lessor's permission that encroached upon a narrow strip of the leased premises. The court said:

> ["I]t is settled in this state, in accordance with the law of England, that a wrongful eviction of the tenant by the landlord from a part of the premise suspends the lease. The main reason which is given for the decisions is that the enjoyment of the whole consideration is the foundation of the debt and the condition of the covenant, and that the obligation to pay rent cannot be apportioned. . . . the land is hired as one whole. If by his own fault the landlord withdraws a part of it, he cannot recover on the lease or outside of it for the occupation of the residue.

A minority of courts have rejected the doctrine of partial actual eviction and permit the landlord to recover rent subject to a tenant's right to an abatement reflecting the loss of value caused by the partial eviction and provided that the tenant has not been evicted from a "substantial" portion of the premises.

In *Dussin Investment Co. v. Bloxham,* 157 Cal. Rptr. 646 (Cal.1979), the tenant, Bloxham leased a 14,000 square-foot warehouse from Dussin. Dussin apparently believed it was entitled to use a portion of the leased premises, and it built a wall enabling it to take possession of 335 square feet of the leased premises, which it used as a storage area. Bloxham stopped paying rent, and Dussin filed an action to evict Bloxham. Bloxham's contention was that Dussin's enlarging and taking possession of the enlarged storage area amounted to an actual, partial eviction of Bloxham and constitutes a full defense to Dussin's eviction proceeding. Dussin contends that its conduct did not constitute an actual eviction of Broxham from a "substantial" portion of the premises.

> Bloxham is correct that in appropriate circumstances an actual, partial eviction of a tenant by a landlord will relieve the tenant from liability for future rents so long as the eviction continues, even though the tenant remains in possession of the balance of the premises. However, the tenant's obligation to pay rent is not thus suspended unless the tenant has been actually evicted from a substantial portion of the demised premises. A tenant is not relieved entirely of the obligation to pay rent by an actual partial eviction unless the eviction is from a substantial portion of the premises and in determining the question of substantiality, the court may and should consider the extent of the interference with the tenant's use and enjoyment of the property. These conclusions are particularly appropriate where, as here, the eviction was not malicious or in bad faith but, rather, resulted from an honest, though mistaken, interpretation of an ambiguous lease provision.

NOTES AND QUESTIONS

1 The *Restatement 2d Property,* Section 6.1, follows the approach adopted by the California courts.

2 What is the justification for the majority rule as set forth in Smith v. Mc-

Enany? Which rule do you think makes more sense? Should the motivation of the lessor be relevant?

3 In the case of *Brash v. Pennsylvania Terminal Real Estate Corp.,* 256 N.E. 2d 707 (N.Y. 1970), the New York court affirmed the traditional rule in the following terms:

> In the case of an actual eviction, even where the tenant is only partially evicted, liability for all rent is suspended although the tenant remains in possession of the portion of the premises from which he was not evicted. In the leading case of *Fifth Ave. Bldg. Co. v. Kernochan,* 117 N.E. 579, 580, the court stated: "We are dealing now with an eviction which is actual and not constructive. If such an eviction, though partial only, is the act of the landlord, it suspends the entire rent because the landlord is not permitted to apportion his own wrong."

Constructive Eviction

Blackett v. Olanoff, 358 N.E. 2d 817 (Mass. 1977)

Facts of the case.

Tenant leased an apartment in an apartment building from landlord. Next door to the apartment building was another building, which landlord owned and which was later leased as a cocktail lounge. The lounge produced substantial noise particularly between the hours of 9:30 P.M. and 2:00 A.M. This noise could be heard through the walls of the tenants' apartments. The tenants vacated the premises and refused to pay rent for the balance of the lease term. The landlord filed an action claiming breach of the lease, seeking to recover the unpaid rent. The trial judge found that, although the landlord did not intend to create the conditions, the landlord "had it within his control to correct the conditions which . . . amounted to a constructive eviction of the tenant." He also found that the landlord promised each tenant to correct the situation, that the landlord made some attempt to remedy the problem, but was unsuccessful, and that each tenant vacated his apartment within a reasonable time.

OPINION

Our opinions concerning a constructive eviction by a breach of the implied covenant of quiet enjoyment sometimes have stated that the landlord must perform some act with the intent of depriving the tenant of the enjoyment and occupation of the whole or part of the leased premises. There are occasions, however, where a landlord has not intended to violate a tenant's rights, but there was still a breach of the landlord's covenant of quiet enjoyment which flowed as the natural and probable consequence of what the landlord did, what he failed to do, or what he permitted to be done. This court has sustained findings of a breach of the covenant of quiet enjoyment in the following situations: failure to supply light, heat, power, and elevator services; intrusions of smoke and soot over a substantial period of time due to a defective boiler; failure to install a necessary heating system; landlord authorizing another lessee to obstruct the tenant's light and air. Although some of our opinions have spoken of particular action or inaction by a landlord as showing a presumed intention to evict, the landlord's conduct, and not his intentions, is controlling.

The judge was warranted in ruling that the landlords had it within their control to correct the condition which caused the tenants to vacate their apartments. The landlords introduced a commercial activity into an area where they leased premises for residential purposes. We conclude that, as matter of law, the landlords had a right to control the objectionable noise coming from the lounge and that the judge was warranted in finding that the landlords could control the objectionable conditions.

This situation is different from the usual annoyance of one residential tenant by another, where traditionally the landlord has not been chargeable with the annoyance. Here we have a case more like *Case v. Minot,* 33 N.E. 700 (Mass. 1893), where the landlord entered into a lease with one tenant, who the landlord specifically permitted to engage in activity that would interfere with the rights of another tenant. There, to be sure, the clash of tenants' rights was inevitable, if each pressed those rights. Here, although the clash of tenants' interests was only a known potentiality initially, experience demonstrated that a decibel level for the entertainment at the lounge, acoustically acceptable to its patrons and hence commercially desirable to its proprietors, was intolerable for the residential tenants.

Because the disturbing condition was the natural and probable consequence of the landlords' permitting the lounge to operate where it did and because the landlords could control the actions at the lounge, they should not be entitled to collect rent for residential premises which were not reasonable habitable.

Judgments affirmed.

NOTES AND QUESTIONS

1 Would the result have been the same if someone other than the landlord had leased premises which created the noise problem complained of in the Olanoff case?

2 The related doctrines of quiet enjoyment and constructive eviction have been recognized in the United States since the early nineteenth century, and they are the overwhelming majority view in the United States. The covenant of quiet enjoyment obligates the landlord to refrain from conduct that substantially interferes with the tenant's enjoyment of the premises. Such interference, which causes the tenant to vacate, is actionable by the tenant as "constructive" eviction.

3 The Illinois case of *Agni Motor Fuel v. Scene Corp.,* 172 N.E. 35 (Ill. 1930), contains the following discussion of the nature of a constructive eviction as distinct from an actual eviction.

The eviction which will discharge the liability of the tenant to pay rent is not necessarily an actual physical expulsion from the premises or some part of them. Any act of the landlord which deprives the tenant of the beneficial enjoyment of the premises constitutes a constructive eviction of the tenant, which exonerates him from the terms and conditions of the lease and he may abandon it.

Not every act of a landlord in violation of his covenants or of the tenant's enjoyment of the premises under the lease will amount to a constructive eviction. Some acts of interference may be mere acts of trespass to which the term *eviction* is not applicable. To constitute an eviction there must be something of a grave and permanent character done by the landlord clearly indicating the intention of the landlord to deprive the tenant of the beneficial enjoyment of the premises in accordance with the terms of the lease. There can be no constructive eviction, however, without the vacating of the premises. Where a tenant fails to surrender possession after the landlord's commission of acts justifying the abandonment of the premises, the liability for rent will continue so long as possession of the premises is continued. Whether the acts of the landlord amount to a constructive eviction is ordinarily a question of fact for the decision of a jury, depending upon the circumstances of the particular case.

4 As the prior case suggests, the doctrine of constructive eviction leaves the tenant with a somewhat hazardous remedy because the tenant must vacate the premises with the risk that a court may later decide that the activity complained of was not a substantial interference and therefore is not a breach of the landlord's covenant of quiet enjoyment. In response to this dilemma, a few courts, most notably in the Commonwealth of Massachusetts, have evolved a rule permitting the tenant to remain in possession while filing an action to cancel the lease claiming that he or she has been constructively evicted by the landlord's breach of the covenant of quiet enjoyment. Such a procedure said the court "is more nearly adequate than the incomplete and hazardous remedy at law which requires that the lessee (a) determine at its peril that the circumstances amount to a constructive eviction and (b) vacate the demised premises, possibly at some expense, while remaining subject to the risk that a court may decide that the lessor's breaches do not go to the essence of the lessor's obligation," *Charles E. Burt Inc. v. Seven Grand Corp.,* 163 N.E. 2d 4, 7 (Mass. 1959).

5 However most jurisdictions continue to require the tenant to vacate before having the right to claim a constructive eviction. Both the *Restatement 2d of Property* (Section 6.1) and the URLTA (Section 4.105 a) provide that the tenant may retain possession and sue for an abatement in rent. However, this position has not been widely followed by state courts or legislatures. In the residential context, the impetus for change has largely been supplemented by the development of the warranty of habitability.

5   DEVELOPMENTS IN RESIDENTIAL HOUSING

A   The Implied Warranty of Habitability

Under the common law, a landlord made no warranty and was not liable for the condition of the leased premises. This immunity reflected the largely rural nature of the landlord-tenant relationship, which emphasized the transfer of the land rather than the buildings on the land. The tenant was expected to inspect the premises and, if they were unsuitable, to get an agreement with the landlord to repair. In the alternative, the tenant was considered free to decline to enter into the lease. This rule prevailed for hundreds of years.

The first indications of change came in 1892 when the Massachusetts court held that, in the case of a short-term furnished rental, the landlord had an implied warranty that the premises would be fit for occupancy. The "vacation rental" exception was followed by some other jurisdictions, but, for the most part, the doctrine of caveat emptor prevailed and the landlord was considered to have no duty to provide livable premises at the commencement of the lease and had no duty to repair the premises during the term of the lease.

Then, in 1961, the Supreme Court of Wisconsin ruled that the common law rule could not stand in light of the enactment of modern housing codes. Finally during the 1970's, the dam burst and the implied warranty of habitability quickly became the overwhelming majority view as it relates to the residential landlord and tenant relationship.

Javins v. First National Realty, 428 F. 2d 1071 (1970)

These cases present the question whether housing code violations, which arise during the term of a lease, have any effect upon the tenant's obligation to pay rent. The trial court ruled proof of such violations inadmissible when offered as a defense to an eviction action for nonpayment of rent.

Because of the importance of the question presented, we granted appellants' petitions for leave to appeal. We now reverse and hold that a warranty of habitability, measured by the standards set out in the Housing Regulations for the District of Columbia, is implied by operation of law into leases of urban dwelling units covered by those Regulations and that breach of this warranty gives rise to the usual remedies for breach of contract.

Facts of the case.

The facts revealed by the record are simple. By separate written leases, each of the appellants rented an apartment in a three-building apartment complex in Northwest Washington known as Clifton Terrace. The landlord, First National Realty Corporation, filed separate actions seeking possession on the ground that each of the appellants had defaulted in the payment of rent due for the month of April. The tenants, appellants here, admitted that they had not paid the landlord any rent for April. However, they claimed that numerous violations of the Housing Regulations were "an equitable defense or [a] claim by way of set-off in an amount equal to the rent claim."

The Trial Court and The District of Columbia Court of Appeals rejected the argument made by appellants that the landlord was under a duty to maintain the premises in compliance with the Housing Regulations.

OPINION

Since, in traditional analysis, a lease was the conveyance of an interest in land, courts have usually utilized the special rules governing real property transactions to resolve controversies involving leases. However, as the Supreme Court has noted in another context, "the body of private property law . . . , more than almost any other branch of law, has been shaped by distinctions whose validity is largely historical." Courts have a duty to reappraise old doctrines in the light of the facts and values of contemporary life—particularly old common law doctrines which the courts themselves created and developed. As we have said before, "[T]he continued vitality of the common law . . . depends upon its ability to reflect contemporary community values and ethics."

The assumption of landlord-tenant law, derived from feudal property law, that a lease primarily conveyed to the tenant an interest in land, may have been reasonable in a rural, agrarian society; it may continue to be reasonable in some leases involving farming or commercial land. In these cases, the value of the lease to the tenant is the land itself. But in the case of the modern apartment dweller, the value of the lease is that it gives him a place to live. When American city dwellers, both rich and poor, seek shelter today, they seek a well known package of goods and services—a package which includes not merely walls and ceilings, but also adequate heat, light, and ventilation, serviceable plumbing facilities, secure windows and doors, proper sanitation, and proper maintenance.

In our judgment the common law itself must recognize the landlord's obligation to keep his premises in a habitable condition. This conclusion is compelled by three separate considerations. First, we believe that the old rule was based on certain factual assumptions which are no longer true and can no longer be justified. Second, we believe that consumer protection requires that the old rule be abandoned in order to bring residential landlord-tenant law into harmony with contemporary principles. Third, we think that the nature of today's urban housing market also dictates abandonment of the old rule.

Court decisions in the late 1800's began to recognize that the factual assumptions of the common law were no longer accurate in some cases. For example, the common law, since it assumed that the land was the most important part of the leasehold, required a tenant to pay rent even if any building on the land was destroyed. Faced with such a rule and the ludicrous results it produced, in 1863 the New York Court of Appeals declined to hold that an upper story tenant was obliged to continue paying rent after his apartment building burned down. The court simply pointed out that the urban tenant had no interests in the land, only in the attached building.

Another line of cases created an exception to the no-repair rule for short term leases of furnished dwellings. The Massachusetts Supreme Judicial Court, a court not known for its willingness to depart from the common law, supported this exception, pointing out:

> . . . [A] different rule should apply to one who hires a furnished room, or a furnished house, for a few days, or a few weeks or months. Its fitness for immediate use of a

particular kind, as indicated by its appointments, is a far more important element entering into the contract than when there is a mere lease of real estate.

Thus we are led to the conclusion that the old common law rule imposing an obligation upon the lessee to repair during the lease term was really never intended to apply to residential urban leaseholds. Contract principles established in other areas of the law provide a more rational framework for the appointment of landlord-tenant responsibilities; they strongly suggest that a warranty of habitability be implied into all contracts for urban dwellings.

We also believe that the District's housing code requires that a warranty of habitability be implied in the leases of all housing it covers. Official enforcement of the housing code has been far from uniformly effective. Innumerable studies have documented the desperate condition of rental housing in the District of Columbia and in the nation. In view of these circumstances, we think the conclusion reached by the Supreme Court of Wisconsin as to the effect of a housing code on the old common law rule cannot be avoided.

> [T]he legislature has made a policy judgment—that it is socially (and politically) desirable to impose these duties on a property owner—which has rendered old common law rule obsolete. To follow the old rule of no implied warranty of habitability in leases would, in our opinion, be inconsistent with the current legislative policy concerning housing standards. . . .

We therefore hold that the Housing Regulations imply a warranty of habitability, measured by the standards which they set out, into leases of all housing that they cover.

In the present cases, the landlord sued for possession for nonpayment of rent. Under contract principles, however, the tenant's obligation to pay rent is dependent upon the landlord's performance of his obligations, including his warranty to maintain the premises in habitable condition. In order to determine whether any rent is owed to the landlord, the tenants must be given an opportunity to prove the housing code violations alleged as breach of the landlord's warranty.

At trial, the finder of fact must make two findings: (1) whether the alleged violations existed during the period for which past due rent is claimed, and (2) what portion, if any or all, of the tenant's obligations to pay rent was suspended by the landlord's breach. If no part of the tenant's rental obligation is found to have been suspended, then a judgment for possession may issue forthwith. On the other hand, if the jury determines that the entire rental obligation has been extinguished by the landlord's total breach, then the action for possession on the ground of nonpayment must fail.

The jury may find that part of the tenant's rental obligation has been suspended but that part of the unpaid back rent is indeed owed to the landlord. In these circumstances, no judgment for possession should issue if the tenant agrees to pay the partial rent found to be due. If the tenant refuses to pay the partial amount, a judgment for possession may then be entered.

The judgment of the District of Columbia Court of Appeals is reversed and the cases are remanded for further proceedings consistent with this opinion.

NOTES AND QUESTIONS

1 The courts of approximately twenty states have followed the *Javins'* approach and have judicially adopted some form of warranty of habitability. The courts in only four states have specifically rejected the warranty.

2 In addition, many states have enacted legislation adopting the warranty of habitability. A good example of such a statute is included below. URLTA, Section 2.104,

a A landlord shall

1 Comply with the requirements of applicable building and housing codes materially affecting health and safety;

2 Make all repairs and do whatever is necessary to put and keep the premises in a fit and habitable condition;

3 Keep all common areas of the premises in a clean and safe condition;

4 Maintain in good and safe working order and condition all electrical, plumbing, sanitary, heating, ventilating, air-conditioning, and other facilities and appliances, including elevators, supplied or required to be supplied by him;

5 Provide and maintain appropriate receptacles and conveniences for the removal of ashes, garbage, rubbish, and other waste incidental to the occupancy of the dwelling unit and arrange for their removal; and

6 Supply running water and reasonable amounts of hot water at all times and reasonable heat.

3 This rapid development has had time to run its course to some extent so that a more precise understanding of the warranty of habitability is now possible. The doctrine of the implied warranty of habitability is clearly the majority rule with respect to residential leases and has been adopted by approximately forty states. Under this doctrine, the landlord warrants that the dwelling is habitable and fit for occupancy at the inception of the lease and that it will remain so during the entire term. Some question still exists about whether and to what extent the warranty is based upon the standards set forth in local housing codes. Some jurisdictions hold that if property is in compliance with local housing statutes the warranty of habitability has not been breached. Other jurisdictions suggest that compliance with housing codes is an aspect of the warranty of habitability but is not necessarily controlling.

The warranty of habitability covers all latent and patent defects in the essential facilities of a residential dwelling; the warranty cannot be waived by any provision in the lease. Ordinarily, the tenant must show that he or she has notified the landlord of the deficiency and that the landlord has failed to correct it within a reasonable time. A tenant may assert the defense of habitability in an action by the landlord seeking to oust the tenant for nonpayment of rent. The warranty of habitability may also be asserted as an affirmative claim for damages based on the difference between the fair market value of the premises as warranted and the fair market value following the breach of the warranty.

4 The case of *Academy Spires, Inc. v. Brown,* N.J. 268 A. 2d 556, (1970), gives a good indication of the general scope of the warranty of habitability. In that case, a tenant in a multi-story apartment building complained of a series of defects, including (1) the periodic failure to supply heat and water, (2) the malfunctioning of an incinerator, (3) the failure of the hot water supply, (4) several leaks in the bathroom, (5) defective Venetian blinds, (6) cracks in plaster walls, (7) unpainted condition of walls, and (8) a nonfunctioning elevator. The court reviewed these claims and held the following:

> Some of these clearly go to the bare living requirements. In a modern society one cannot be expected to live in a multi-storied apartment building without heat, hot water, garbage disposal, or elevator service. Failure to supply such things is a breach of the implied covenant of habitability. Malfunction of Venetian blinds, water leaks, wall cracks, lack of painting—at least of the magnitude, presented here—go to what may be called "amenities." Living with lack of painting, water leaks, and defective Venetian blinds may be unpleasant and aesthetically unsatisfying, but do not come within the category of uninhabitability.

5 The problem of measuring the damages flowing from a breach of the warranty of habitability has proven particularly difficult. Some jurisdictions use a standard that seeks to measure the difference between the rental value of the premises if they had been free of habitability violations and the fair value during occupancy by the tenant in the unsafe or unsanitary condition. The court in *Academy Spires* above, after fully acknowledging the difficulty of precisely determining damages resulting from a landlord's breach of an implied warranty of habitability, assessed damages by a "percentage reduction of use" approach, under which the court reduced the tenant's rental obligation by a percentage corresponding to the relative reduction of use of the leased premises caused by the landlord's breach. In applying this approach, the court carefully reviewed both the importance of the particular defects in the premises (including failure to supply heat, hot water, elevator service, and a working incinerator) and the length of time such defects had existed (from one or two days to several weeks), and finally concluded that under all the circumstances "the dimunition of rent of 25 percent is a fair amount."
(268 A. 2d at p. 562.) See also *Samuelson v. Quinones,* 119 N.J. Super. 338, 291 A. 2d 580, 583 (1972); *Morbeth Realty Corp. v. Rosenshine,* 67 Misc. 2d 325 [323 N.Y.S. 2d 363, 366–367] (1971).

6   PROTECTION AGAINST TERMINATION OF THE LEASE

At common law, the periodic tenancy and tenancy at will were terminable at will, provided that notice was given, and the landlord was free to refuse to renew a tenancy of a term of years for any reason or for no reason at all. For the most part, the landlord is still free to terminate or refuse to renew a tenancy for any reason. However, certain inroads have been made that, under certain circumstances, limit the landlord's right to evict a tenant or to refuse to renew a tenant's lease. As the following section indicates, some limitation on a landlord's right to evict was considered necessary to advance the policy considerations embodied in the warranty of habitability.

A Retaliatory Eviction

Edwards v. Habib, 397 F. 2d 687 (D.C. 1969)

Facts of the case.

In March 1965, the appellant, Ms. Yvonne Edwards, rented housing property from Nathan Habib, on a month-to-month basis. Shortly thereafter she complained to the Department of Licenses and Inspections of sanitary code violations, which her landlord had failed to remedy. In the course of ensuing inspections, more than forty such violations were discovered, which the Department ordered the landlord to correct. Habib then gave Ms. Edwards a thirty-day statutory notice to vacate. Ms. Edwards answered the complaint and alleged as a defense that the notice to quit was given in retaliation for her complaints to the housing authorities. At the trial, the judge deemed evidence of retaliatory motive irrelevant and directed a verdict for the landlord.

Ms. Edwards then appealed to the District of Columbia Court of Appeals (DCCA), which affirmed the judgment of the trial court. In reaching its decision the DCCA relied on a series of its earlier decisions holding that a private landlord was not required, under the District of Columbia Code, to give a reason for evicting a month-to-month tenant, and the landlord was free to do so for any reason or for no reason at all.

OPINION

While the landlord may evict for any legal reason or for no reason at all, he is not, we hold, free to evict in retaliation for his tenant's report of housing code violations to the authorities. As a matter of statutory construction and for reasons of public policy, such an eviction cannot be permitted.

The housing and sanitary codes indicate a strong and pervasive congressional concern to secure for the city's apartment dwellers decent, or at least safe and sanitary, places to live. Effective implementation and enforcement of the codes obviously depend in part on private initiative in the reporting of violations. To permit retaliatory evictions would clearly frustrate the effectiveness of the housing code as a means of upgrading the quality of housing in Washington.

As judges, we cannot shut our eyes to matters of public notoriety and general cognizance. When we take our seats on the bench, we are not struck with blindness and forbidden to know as judges what we see as men. In trying to effect the will of Congress and as a court of equity, we have the responsibility to consider the social context in which our decisions will have operational effect. In light of the appalling condition and shortage of housing in Washington, the expense of moving, the inequality of bargaining power between tenant and landlord, and the social and economic importance of assuring at least minimum standards in housing conditions, we do not hesitate to declare that retaliatory eviction cannot be tolerated. There can be no doubt that the apartment dweller, even though his home be marred by housing code violations, will pause long before he complains of them if he fears eviction as a consequence. Hence, an eviction under the circumstances of this case would not only punish appellant for making a complaint which she had a constitutional right to make, but also would stand as a warning to others that they dare not be so bold.

This is not, of course, to say that even if the tenant can prove a retaliatory purpose she is entitled to remain in possession in perpetuity. If this illegal purpose is dissipated, the landlord can, in the absence of legislation or a binding contract, evict his tenants or raise their rents for economic or other legitimate reasons, or even for no reason at all. The question of permissible or impermissible purpose is one of fact for the court or jury, and while such a determination is not easy, it is not significantly different from problems with which the courts must deal in a host of other contexts.

Reversed.

NOTES AND QUESTIONS

1 Prior to the Edwards case, the landlord's right to terminate a tenancy in a manner consistent with the lease was considered absolute. Edwards was followed by a number of jurisdictions that recognized the defense of retaliatory eviction but that differed considerably in the degree of proof required of the landlord and tenant to establish or defend against the charge that an eviction was being pursued for an improper purpose.

2 It is usually essential for a tenant seeking to avoid termination of a lease based on the doctrine of retaliatory eviction to present evidence concerning the motive or state of mind of the landlord. Some jurisdictions, such as Wisconsin, require the tenant to establish that the landlord's action was "exclusively motivated by retaliation," *Dick Hut v. Norton,* 173 N.W. 2d 297 (Wis. 1970). Other states, such as New Jersey, place the burden on the landlord to show that the decision to evict was independent of "any consideration of privileged actions of the tenant."

3 The approach taken by the *Restatement of Property 2d,* Section 14.8, limits the doctrine of retaliatory eviction to landlords "in the business of renting residential property" and provides that the tenant must show that the landlord's *primary* motive was retaliatory. Some jurisdictions, even when the tenant has established a retaliatory motive, will permit the landlord to prevail provided they can establish a substantial nonretaliatory motive for seeking to evict.

4 A majority of states now recognize, in some form, the doctrine of retaliatory eviction. However, there are a few dissenters. In *Lincoln v. Ferrier,* 567 P. 2d 1102 (Utah 1977), the Utah Supreme Court expressly rejected the doctrine of retaliatory eviction. The court said:

> The question that must be confronted and answered is: If the landlord cannot enforce the terms of his lease and proceed under the express provisions of our statutory law to reclaim his property, what has happened to his property rights? If he is compelled to surrender his contractual and statutory rights by being required to furnish an apartment to someone other than he desires as a tenant, that is nothing other than a deprivation of his property.
>
> Upon the basis of what has been said above it is our opinion that the trial court was correct in its analysis and its conclusion that the allegations of the defendant above discussed constitute neither a defense to the plaintiff's complaint for eviction nor a counterclaim related thereto which is cognizable under our law; and that they were thus properly stricken and disregarded.

5 A large number of states have enacted statutes establishing the doctrine of retaliatory eviction. These states include California, Connecticut, Delaware, Illinois, Maine, Massachusetts, Michigan, New Jersey, and New York. The various statutory schemes are similar in that they create a defense to eviction in cases where the landlord's motive for proceeding with eviction has the effect of abridging a protected right of the tenant. These statutes differ considerably in their details, particularly as they relate to the proof requirements of either the landlord or tenant. A fairly typical example of a retaliatory eviction statute is contained in URLTA, Section 5.101, which provides, in part, as follows:

> **(a)** Except as provided in this section, a landlord may not retaliate by increasing rent or decreasing services or by bringing or threatening to bring an action for possession after:
>
> **(1)** the tenant has complained to a governmental agency charged with responsibility for enforcement of a building or housing code of a violation applicable to the premises materially affecting health and safety; or
>
> **(2)** the tenant has complained to the landlord of a violation concerning habitability;
>
> **(3)** the tenant has organized or become a member of a tenant's union or similar organization.
>
> **(b)** If the landlord acts in violation of subsection (a), the tenant . . . has a defense in any retaliatory action against him for possession. In an action by or against the tenant, evidence of a complaint within [one] year before the alleged act of retaliation creates a presumption that the landlord's conduct was in retaliation. The presumption does not arise if the tenant made the complaint after notice of a proposed rent increase or diminution of services.

B Eviction for Cause Only

The notion that a landlord may seek to recover possession only if there is good cause is typically a feature of rent control statutes. New Jersey is the only state that, by state statute, requires a landlord to have "good cause" before terminating or refusing to renew any residential tenancy. Because New Jersey has consistently been in the forefront of the rapid evolution of the concept of tenants' rights, and because most rent control ordinances contain similar limitations upon an owner's right to evict, pertinent provisions of this statute are set forth below:

N.J. Stat. Ann., Section 2 A:18–61

No lessee or tenant . . . may be removed by the county district court or the Superior Court from any dwelling leased for residential purposes, except upon establishment of one of the following grounds as good cause:

a The person fails to pay rent due and owing under the lease whether the same be oral or written;

b The person has continued to be, after written notice to cease, so disorderly as to destroy the peace and quiet of the occupants or other tenants living in said house or neighborhood;

c The person has willfully or by reason of gross negligence caused or allowed destruction, damage, or injury to the premises;

d The person has continued, after written notice to cease, to substantially violate or breach any of the landlord's rules and regulations governing said premises, provided such rules and regulations are reasonable and have been accepted in writing by the tenant or made a part of the lease at the beginning of the lease term;

e The person has continued, after written notice to cease, to substantially violate or breach any of the covenants or agreements contained in the lease for the premises where a right of reentry is reserved to the landlord in the lease for a violation of such covenant or agreement, provided that such covenant or agreement is reasonable and was contained in the lease at the beginning of the lease term;

f The person has failed to pay rent after a valid notice to quit and notice of increase of said rent, provided the increase in rent is not unconscionable and complies with any and all other laws or municipal ordinances governing rent increases;

g The landlord or owner (one) seeks to permanently board up or demolish the premises because he has been cited by local or State housing inspectors for substantial violations affecting the health and safety of tenants, and it is economically unfeasible for the owner to eliminate the violations.

h The landlord or owner proposes, at the termination of the lease, reasonable changes of substance in the terms and conditions of the lease, which the tenant, after written notice, refuses to accept;

i The person, after written notice to cease, has habitually and without legal justification failed to pay rent which is due and owing;

j The landlord or owner of the building is converting from the rental market to a condominium, cooperative, or fee simple ownership.

k The owners of a building of three residential units or less seeks to personally occupy a unit, or has contracted to sell the residential unit to a buyer who wishes to personally occupy it, and the contract for sale calls for the unit to be vacant at the time of closing;

l The landlord or owner conditioned the tenancy upon and in consideration for the tenant's employment by the landlord or owner as superintendent, janitor, or in some other capacity, and such employment is being terminated.

NOTES AND QUESTIONS

1 Does the New Jersey statute regulate the amount an owner can charge for rent?

2 The URLTA provides as follows:

Every duty under this Act and every act which must be performed as a condition precedent to the exercise of a right or remedy under this Act imposes an obligation of good faith in its performance or enforcement.

Does this provision provide for termination of a tenancy only for cause?

7   TENANT'S OBLIGATIONS TO THE LANDLORD

A   Rent

Rent is simply a periodic payment representing the cost of occupying the property. As indicated in Section 3–B, rent can be measured in various ways. In the typical residential rental, rent involves the payment of a fixed amount, usually on a monthly basis. In a commercial lease, rent may include a fixed monthly payment along with payment of all or a portion of insurance premiums, property taxes, and common area maintenance expenses. For instance, when the landlord receives the property tax bill, he or she might prorate the bill among the various tenants and add this additional amount to the next lease payment. The additional amount would then constitute a portion of the *rent* due from the tenant. In the case of a retail tenant, rent might also include an obligation that the tenant pay a certain portion of gross receipts as rent.

B   Deposits and Other Security for Performance

Both residential and commercial leases require that the tenant make an advance deposit of money to the landlord as security for performance of the tenant's obligations under the lease. Tenant deposits are usually classified as either *prepaid rent* or as a *security deposit;* although, in most cases, there is little practical difference between the two. In addition, some leases call for a nonrefundable deposit such as a cleaning deposit.

Prepaid rent is usually intended as a form of security deposit in the event the tenant fails to pay rent during the term of the lease. In residential leases, it is often called a "last month's rent" to be credited by the landlord for that purpose. In commercial leases, prepaid rent often involves greater variety and complexity but the object—security for the payment of future rent—remains basically the same. For instance, the tenant might post a letter of credit equal to six months rent, which the landlord can draw upon if the tenant defaults in the payment of rent. However it is structured, prepaid rent has the basic goal of affording protection to the landlord in the event of a default in the payment of rent by the tenant.

Security deposits are also intended to help guarantee performance by the tenant of other obligations in the lease, most typically maintaining the property in good condition. Upon termination of the lease, the landlord may apply the security deposit toward repairing any damages to the property caused during the term of the lease.

C Limitations on the Use of Security Deposits

Many small controversies arise concerning the landlord's obligation to refund a security deposit. Most of these involve the landlord's effort to keep all or a portion of a security deposit in the face of the tenants claim that there is no damage, or that it was pre-existing, or that it is ordinary "wear and tear" for which the tenant should not be held responsible. Most of these disputes go no farther than small claims court, although tenant organizations have periodically filed class action law suits against landlord's perceived as habitual abusers of tenant security deposits.

Legislatures in many states have intervened in an effort to regulate the use of security deposits, particularly in the residential landlord-tenant context. Some of these statutes limit the amount of the security deposit, establish the reasons for which the landlord may refuse to refund the deposit, and require the landlord to provide a written accounting to the tenant specifically explaining why any portion of the security deposit was not returned. Some statutes also provide that security deposits must bear interest and impose penalties in cases where the landlord fails to comply with the provisions of the security deposit statute. As indicated, these statutes tend not to apply to commercial leases.

8 FAIR HOUSING LEGISLATION

We have seen that during the past twenty years, novel legal doctrines have arisen that limit an owner's right to terminate or refuse to renew a residential tenancy. The tenant protections affirmed by the warranty of habitability and the doctrine of retaliatory eviction do not address the question of whether an owner is under any obligation to enter into the lease in the first place. Historically, the landlord's right to refuse to enter into a lease was absolute.

The case of *Dorsey v. Stuyvesant Town Corporation*, 87 N.E. 2d 541 (N.Y. 1949), illustrates a fairly common fact pattern and a typical judicial response. In *Dorsey*, the defendant was the owner of a large housing project developed with the assistance of state and municipal tax incentives in order to provide housing for low-income persons. The owner adopted an express policy of refusing to rent apartments to African-Americans. Plaintiffs were a group of tenants who had been denied the opportunity to live in the complex because of their race and who sought to require the owner to consider all applicants for housing, regardless of race. The trial court ruled in favor of the landlord and New York's highest court affirmed. The court said that "no statute in

New York recognizes the opportunity to acquire an interest in real property as a civil right. . . .''

The Fair Housing Act of 1968 (42 U.S.C Sections 3601 to 3631) was intended to correct the ruling in cases such as *Dorsey* and to address the problem of discrimination at all levels of the housing industry. The Act prohibits landlords from refusing to rent or from discriminating in a lease on the basis of race, color, religion, or national origin. The extensive legislative record, which accompanied the passage of the Act, indicates that Congress intended to eliminate all forms of prohibited discrimination in the sale or rental of real estate. It is fair to say that overt forms of discrimination, such as the announced policy of the landlord in the *Dorsey* case, have become rare. More common and certainly more difficult to detect are covert or unstated forms of discrimination. Courts continue to struggle with the level of proof needed to establish a discriminatory intent and with the problem presented when a facially neutral policy has a disproportionate impact upon a group protected under the Act.

In *Boyd v. Lefrak,* 502 F. 2d 1110 (2d Cir. 1975), the landlord, who owned or managed over 15,000 apartments in New York City, adopted a policy providing that any proposed tenant must have a weekly net income equal to ninety percent of the monthly rental of the apartment applied for. Plaintiffs sued on behalf of low-income black and Puerto Rican persons who could not qualify for the apartments under the ninety percent rule. The trial court ruled in favor of plaintiffs and enjoined use of the ninety percent rule. The court of appeals reversed making the following observations:

> The Fair Housing Act prohibits discrimination in housing because of ''race, color, religion, or national origin.'' Plaintiffs argue that defendants by utilizing the ninety percent rule have violated this prohibition. They reason that the ninety percent rule excludes all public assistance recipients, that a large majority of public assistance recipients in New York City are black or Puerto Rican, and that therefore the use of the ninety percent rule is racially discriminatory. Despite implicit recognition of the correlation between racial minority and low income, this court has consistently refused to equate the two factors. While blacks and Puerto Ricans do not have the same access to Lefrak apartments as do whites, the reason for this inequality is not racial discrimination but rather the disparity in economic level among these groups. A businessman's differential treatment of different economic groups is not necessarily racial discrimination and is not made so because minorities are statistically overrepresented in the poorer economic groups. The fact that differentiation in eligibility rates for defendants' apartments is correlated with race proves merely that minorities tend to be poorer than is the general population. In order to utilize this correlation to establish a violation of the Fair Housing Act on the part of a private landlord, plaintiffs would have to show that there existed some demonstrable prejudicial treatment of minorities over and above that which is the inevitable result of disparity in income.

The dissent noted that the ninety percent rule excluded a higher percentage of black and Puerto Rican applicants and argued that the trial court should be affirmed based upon the record presented:

> Faced with the discriminatory consequences of their conduct appellants failed to offer any satisfactory nonracial explanation, such as business necessity. There was no showing, for instance, that experience in the rental of apartments of the type here under consideration had demonstrated that the ninety percent rule was reasonably necessary to insure tenants'

payment of rent and that there had been losses, substantial defaults, or failure to collect back rental payments under less stringent rules. Nor was there proof that welfare recipients as tenants have a greater incidence of rent failures or defaults than other tenants.

In *U.S. v. City of Black Jack,* 508 F. 2d 1179 (8th Cir. 1979), the court considered a claim that minority tenants were adversely affected by an otherwise neutral policy. The court concluded as follows:

> To establish a prima facie case of racial discrimination, the plaintiff need prove no more than that the conduct of the defendant actually or predictably results in racial discrimination; in other words, that it has a discriminatory effect. . . . The plaintiff need make no showing whatsoever that the action resulting in racial discrimination in housing was racially motivated. . . . Effect, and not motivation, is the touchstone, in part because clever men may easily conceal their motivation. . . .

Finally, the court in *Williams v. Mathews Co.,* 499 F. 2d 826 (1978), the court stated the general test for an individual claim of racial discrimination as follows:

> [W]here a black rental applicant meets the objective requirements of a landlord, and the rental would likely have been consummated were he or she a white applicant, a prima face inference of discrimination arises as a matter of law. If the inference is not satisfactorily explained away, discrimination is established.

NOTES AND QUESTIONS

1 Is the majority opinion in *Boyd v. Lefrak* consistent with the view given in *City of Black Jack?*

2 The *Williams* case sets forth the rule as it relates to an individual plaintiff who alleges wrongful discrimination. How are the standards of proof different in a case alleging individual discrimination from one alleging impact?

State Statutes Approximately forty states have legislation intended to protect tenants and prospective tenants against certain forms of discrimination. The state statutes all prohibit discrimination on the basis of race, color, religion, or national origin and most prohibit discrimination on the basis of sex.

Beyond this, the state antidiscrimination statutes are exceedingly varied in the scope of activities that are covered and in the extent to which certain classes of landlords and rental transactions are exempt. Most of the state antidiscrimination statutes tend to go further than their federal counterparts, and many also prohibit discrimination against tenants because they have children or on the basis of their age, marital status, receipt of public assistance, or physical handicap.

9 LANDLORD'S TORT LIABILITY

As we have seen, the common law viewed a lease as essentially a sale of the premises for a term with a reversionary interest reserved to the landlord. Generally the landlord had no liability if the tenant or guests of the tenant were injured because of physical defects on the premises. However, at an early stage, courts recognized exceptions to the general rule of landlord immunity.

For its part, the modern law on this subject is in a state of flux. Three different approaches are used to resolve questions concerning the landlord's liability for personal injuries caused because of a defective leased premises. Most states still continue to adhere to the common law approach conferring general tort immunity upon the landlord and abrogating this immunity only in the case of certain specified exceptions. Second, some states have abandoned the landlord immunity rule and substituted general negligence standards in its place. Finally, at least one state has gone so far as to impose strict liability on the landlord for any defective condition on the property that causes injury to a tenant. These three approaches are considered next.

A Common Law Rule

Landlord's Immunity with Exceptions   The common law doctrine, which continues to be the majority rule in this country, is that the landlord is immune from tort liability to a tenant or the tenant's guests unless one of the following conditions are present.

1 The landlord concealed or failed to disclose a dangerous condition which the tenant did not discover;

2 The landlord negligently failed to discover and remedy a defective condition where the property was leased for a purpose involving admission of the public;

3 The landlord negligently failed to discover and remedy a defective condition concerning leased property over which the landlord retained control (for instance, common areas in an apartment building);

4 The landlord breached an obligation of the lease requiring him to make repairs to the premises;

5 The landlord is under a legal duty, such as by statute or more recently, an implied warranty of habitability, to make necessary repairs;

6 The landlord, although not necessarily under a duty to make repairs, makes them in a negligent manner.

A majority of American jurisdictions and the *Restatement of Property* (2d) follow the approach that the landlord is not liable unless the injury flows from one of the situations mentioned above.

NOTES AND QUESTIONS

In *Cuthbert v. Stempin,* 396 N.E. 2d 1197 (Ill. 1979), a tenant was injured when the front steps of the leased premises collapsed. The tenant admitted that she knew that the steps were in poor condition when the house was leased and, as a result, the landlord was held not liable to the tenant (396 N.E. 2d 1197). Do you think that Illinois recognized the implied warranty of habitability at the time the *Cuthbert* case was decided?

B Negligence Liability

Sargent v. Ross, 308 A. 2d 528 (N.H. 1973)

The question in this case is whether the defendant landlord is liable to the plaintiff in tort for the death of plaintiff's four-year-old daughter who fell to her death from an outdoor stairway at a residential building owned by the defendant.

Facts of the case.

There was no apparent cause of the fall except for evidence that the stairs were dangerously steep, and that the railing was insufficient to prevent the child from falling over the side. The jury returned a verdict in favor of the plaintiff in her action against the defendant landlord.

Claiming there was no evidence that the defendant retained control over the stairway, that it was used in common with other tenants, or that it contained a concealed defect, defendant urges that there was accordingly no duty owing to the deceased child for the defendant to breach. This contention rests upon the general rule, which has long obtained in this and most other jurisdictions, that a landlord is not liable, except in certain limited situations, for injuries caused by defective or dangerous conditions in the leased premises. The plaintiff does not directly attack this rule of nonliability but instead attempts to show, rather futilely under the facts, defendant's control of the stairway. The issue as framed by the parties is whether the rule of nonliability should prevail or whether the facts of this case can be squeezed into some exception to the general rule of landlord immunity.

OPINION

General principles of tort law ordinarily impose liability upon persons for injuries caused by their failure to exercise reasonable care under all the circumstances. A person is generally negligent for exposing another to an unreasonable risk of harm, which foreseeably results in an injury. But, except in certain instances, landlords are immune from those simple rules of reasonable conduct which govern other persons in their daily activities. But courts and legislatures alike are beginning to reevaluate the rigid rules of landlord-tenant law in light of current needs and principles of law from related areas.

As is to be expected where exceptions to a rule of law form the only basis of liability, the parties in this action concentrated at trial and on appeal on whether any of the exceptions applied, particularly whether the landlord or the tenant had control of the stairway.

It appears to us that to search for gaps and exceptions in a legal doctrine, which exists only because of the somnolence of the common law and the courts, is to perpetuate further judicial fictions when preferable alternatives exist.

Considerations of human safety within an urban community dictate the landowner's relative immunity, which is primarily supported by values of the agrarian past, be modified in favor of negligence principles of landowner liability.

This conclusion springs naturally and inexorably from our recent decision in *Kline v. Burns,* 276 A. 2d 248 (N.H. 1971). Kline was a suit in which the tenant claimed that the premises were uninhabitable. Following a small vanguard of other jurisdictions, we modernized the landlord-tenant contractual relationship by holding that there is an implied warranty of habitability in an apartment lease transaction.

To the extent that *Kline v. Burns* did not do so, we today discard the rule of "caveat lessee" and the doctrine of landlord nonliability in tort to which it gave birth. We thus bring up to date the other half of landlord-tenant law. Henceforth, landlords as other persons must exercise reasonable care not to subject others to an unreasonable risk of harm. The questions of control, hidden defects, and common or public use will now be relevant only inasmuch as they bear on the basic tort issues such as the foreseeability and unreasonableness of the particular risk of harm.

NOTES AND QUESTIONS

1 The highest courts in a few jurisdictions, in particular the District of Columbia, Florida, Idaho, Massachusetts, Montana, Utah, and Wisconsin have followed the lead of *Sargent v. Ross* although some jurisdictions have rejected it. Intermediate courts in Arizona, Indiana, and New York suggest that those states may adopt the general negligence standard in the near future.

2 In *Webster v. Heim,* 399 N.E. 2d 690 (Ill. 1980), the Illinois Court of Appeals faced a claim by a tenant that her landlord was negligent in failing to provide fire escapes or smoke detectors. A fire broke out and plaintiff was injured when she jumped from a second story window. The trial court dismissed the case. The Court of Appeals concluded that none of the recognized exceptions to the common law immunity rule applied to the case and addressed the tenants claim that the landlord was negligent in the following terms:

> Webster argues that the common law rule of nonliability of landlords for injuries to tenants should be rejected and a rule of reasonable care adopted.
> Webster urges us to make a fundamental change in the well established law of this State. We are not persuaded by her arguments that the present law is so inequitable as to dictate or demand a change and hence will not comply with her request.

C Strict Liability

In *Becker v. IRM Corp.,* 698 P. 2d 116 (Cal. 1985), the California Supreme Court became the only American jurisdiction to hold a landlord strictly liable for personal injuries sustained by a tenant. In that case, plaintiff slipped and fell against a shower door, severely lacerating his arm. The door was made of untempered glass although this fact was not known to the landlord and was not observable upon inspection. The apartment complex contained thirty-six units and was twelve years old when it was purchased by the defendant landlord.

The California Court reviewed cases concerning the strict liability of manufacturers and also reviewed the recent evolution of landlord-tenant law. Turning to the issue at hand, the Court concluded as follows:

> We are satisfied that the rationale of the foregoing cases, establishing the duties of a landlord and the doctrine of strict liability in tort, requires us to conclude that a landlord engaged in the business of leasing dwellings is strictly liable in tort for injuries resulting from a latent defect in the premises when the defect existed at the time the premises were let to the tenant. It is clear that landlords are part of the "overall producing and marketing enterprise" that makes housing accommodations available to renters. A landlord, like defendant owning numerous units, is not engaged in isolated acts within the enterprise but plays a substantial role.
>
> The tenant purchasing housing for a limited period is in no position to inspect for latent defects in the increasingly complex modern apartment buildings or to bear the expense of repair whereas the landlord is in a much better position to inspect for and repair latent defects.
>
> The tenant renting the dwelling is compelled to rely upon the implied assurance of safety made by the landlord. It is also apparent that the landlord by adjustment of price at the time he acquires the property, by rentals, or by insurance is in a better position to bear the costs of injuries due to defects in the premises than the tenants.
>
> In these circumstances, strict liability in tort for latent defects existing at the time of renting must be applied to insure that the landlord who markets the product bears the costs of injuries resulting from the defects rather than the injured persons who are powerless to protect themselves.

A dissenting opinion, relying in part on the New Jersey approach took the following view:

> I concur in that portion of the majority opinion which holds that a landlord may be held liable for dangerous conditions of which he knew or should have known. However, I cannot join in imposing upon landlords strict liability for latent defects in any component of their property no matter who built or installed the defective item.
>
> Taking an unprecedented leap, the majority imposes an unusual and unjust burden on property owners. . . . The landlord will be faced with liability for every injury claim resulting from any untoward condition in every cranny of the building, whether it is reasonably foreseeable or not. Any landlord, even one renting the family home for a year, will now be insurer for defects in any wire, screw, latch, cabinet door, pipe, or other article on and in his premises at the time they are let, despite the fact that he neither installed the item nor had any knowledge or reason to know of the defect. I believe, in conformance with the almost unanimous judgment of other jurisdictions considering this issue, that such imposition of liability is inappropriate. As one authority has remarked, "One problem in analyzing product liability law is our tendency to study rule changes in isolation and not to analyze their aggregate effect on liability costs or primary behavior," Epstein, Commentary 58 N.Y.U. L. Rev. 930, 931 (1983). My colleagues here have taken just such an "isolated" viewpoint.

NOTES AND QUESTIONS

So far, *Becker* has not been followed by other jurisdictions. However, a recent New Jersey case suggests that a landlord may be strictly liable for injuries sustained by a tenant from criminal activity where the landlord breached the warranty of habitability in failing to provide safe premises.

(Trentacot v. Brussel, 412 A. 2d 436 (N.J. 1980)

10 TRANSFER OF LEASED PREMISES (ASSIGNMENT AND THE SUBLEASE)

Suppose you enter into a two-year lease for an apartment in Manhattan. A few weeks later you are notified that your employer plans to transfer you to Los Angeles. You are ready to go but your landlord will not let you out of the lease. You advertise in the paper, find someone willing to "take over" your lease. May your landlord refuse to consent to this transfer? If he does consent but your successor fails to pay rent, or breaches any other provision in the lease are you liable for that breach?

The material which follows addresses two major themes. The first is the extent to which a landlord's efforts to limit the tenant's ability to transfer the lease constitute a restraint on alienation. The second is whether the original tenant remains liable on covenants in the lease after it has been transferred.

Restrictions on the Rights Transfer As in the case of other interests in property, both the landlord and tenant are typically free to transfer their respective interests in the property. By selling the property, the landlord is, in effect, transferring the reversionary interest in the property, and the new owner takes the property subject to all terms, express or implied in the lease between the tenant and original owner. Similarly, in the absence of an agreement to the contrary, the tenant is free to transfer the lease to another who takes the property subject to the obligations incurred by the original tenant.

Many leases attempt to restrict the tenant's right to transfer the leasehold interest either by denying the right altogether or making it subject to the consent of the landlord. The enforceability of such restrictions upon transfer of the lessee's interest is carefully discussed in the following case.

Kendal v. Pestana, 709 P. 2d 837 (Cal. 1985)

Facts of the case.

This case concerns the effect of a provision in a commercial lease that the lessee may not assign the lease or sublet the premises without the lessor's prior written consent. The question we address is whether, in the absence of a provision that such consent will not be unreasonably withheld, a lessor may unreasonably and arbitrarily withhold his or her consent to an assignment. This is a question of first impression in this court.

The lease at issue is for 14,400 square feet of hangar space at the San Jose Municipal Airport. Ernest Pestana, Inc., the lessor, entered the lease with one Robert Bixler to be used by Bixler for the purpose of conducting an airplane maintenance business.

Bixler conducted such a business under the name "Flight Services" for ten years when he agreed to sell the business to appellant Jack Kendall. The proposed sale included the business and the equipment, inventory and improvements on the property, together with the existing lease. The proposed assignees had a stronger financial statement and greater net worth than the current lessee, Bixler, and they were willing to be bound by the terms of the lease.

The lease provided that written consent of the lessor was required before the lessee could assign his interest, and that failure to obtain such consent rendered the lease voidable at the option of the lessor. Accordingly, Bixler requested consent from respondent Ernest Pestana, Inc. Respondent refused to consent to the assignment and maintained that it had an absolute right arbitrarily to refuse any such request. The complaint recites that respondent demanded "increased rent and other more onerous terms" as a condition of consenting to Bixler's transfer of interest.

The proposed assignees brought suit seeking, a declaration "that the refusal of ERNEST PESTANA, INC., to consent to the assignment of the lease is unreasonable and is an unlawful restraint on the freedom of alienation. . . . The trial court dismissed the complaint and this appeal followed.

OPINION

The law generally favors free alienability of property, and California follows the common law rule that a leasehold interest is freely alienable. Contractual restrictions on the alienability of leasehold interests are, however, permitted. Such restrictions are justified as reasonable protection of the interests of the lessor as to who shall possess and manage property in which he has a reversionary interest and from which he is deriving income.

The common law's hostility toward restraints on alienation has caused such restraints on leasehold interests to be strictly construed against the lessor. Nevertheless, a majority of jurisdictions have long adhered to the rule that where a lease contains an approval clause (a clause stating that the lease cannot be assigned without the prior consent of the lessor), the lessor may arbitrarily refuse to approve a proposed assignee no matter how suitable the assignee appears to be and no matter how unreasonable the lessor's objection. The harsh consequences of this rule have often been avoided through application of the doctrines of waiver and estoppel, under which the lessor may be found to have waived (or be estopped from asserting) the right to refuse consent to assignment.

The traditional majority rule has come under steady attack in recent years. A growing minority of jurisdictions now hold that where a lease provides for assignment only with the prior consent of the lessor, such consent may be withheld only where the lessor has a commercially reasonable objection to the assignment, even in the absence of a provision in the lease stating that consent to assignment will not be unreasonably withheld.

The impetus for change in the majority rule also comes from the nature of a lease as a contract. In every contract there is an implied covenant that neither party shall do anything which will have the effect of destroying or injuring the right of the other party to receive the fruits of the contract.

Here the lessor retains the discretionary power to approve or disapprove an assignee proposed by the other party to the contract; this discretionary power, therefore, should be exercised in accordance with commercially reasonable standards.

Under the minority rule, the determination whether a lessor's refusal to consent was reasonable is a question of fact. Some of the factors that the trier of fact may properly consider in applying the standards of good faith and commercial reasonableness are: financial responsibility of the proposed assignee; suitability of the use for the particular property; legality of the proposed use; need for alteration of the premises; and nature of the occupancy, that is, office, factory, clinic, and so on.

Denying consent solely on the basis of personal taste, convenience or sensibility is not commercially reasonable. Nor is it reasonable to deny consent "in order that the landlord may charge a higher rent than originally contracted for." This is because the lessor's desire for a better bargain than contracted for has nothing to do with the permissible purposes of the restraint on alienation—to protect the lessor's interest in the preservation of the property and the performance of the lease covenants.

In conclusion, both the policy against restraints on alienation and the implied contractual duty of good faith and fair dealing militate in favor of adoption of the rule that where a commercial lease provides for assignment only with the prior consent of the lessor, such consent may be withheld only where the lessor has a commercially reasonable objection to the assignee or the proposed use.

Reversed.

NOTES AND QUESTIONS

1 Suppose the lease had simply prohibited any transfer by the tenant. Would such a provision have been upheld by the court under the rationale of *Kendal*? Suppose a landlord wants to retain discretion to review the proposed successor in a way that would be considered "commercially unreasonable." Can you think of a lease provision that would give the landlord more flexibility in this regard?

2 In *Ontel Corp. v. Helasol*, 515 N.Y.S. 2d 567 (N.Y. 1987), The New York Court made the following observation:

The evidence adduced at the hearing demonstrated that, in refusing consent to an assignment of the lease, the defendant's general manager had relied primarily upon his subjective belief that a representative of the proposed assignee should have contacted him to discuss its financial status prior to making the application to assign. Such subjective concerns and personal desires cannot play a role in a landlord's decision to withhold its consent to an assignment of a lease, and the trial court properly held that the defendant had unreasonably withheld its consent.

3 Nevertheless, the majority view continues to be that where the lessor's consent is required, the lessor may withhold consent for any reason, however arbitrary. As indicated in the *Kendal* case, the emerging, although still minority, rule provides that consent may not be unreasonably withheld. This view is adopted by the *Restatement of Property*, which provides as follows:

> A restraint on alienation without the consent of the landlord of a tenant's interest in leased property is valid, but the landlord's consent to an alienation by the tenant cannot be withheld unreasonably, unless a freely negotiated provision in the lease gives the landlord an absolute right to withhold consent.
>
> *Restatement 2d Property,* Section 15.2(2) (1977)

In addition, statutes in a few states prohibit lessors from arbitrarily refusing to consent to a transfer of the lease. These states are Alaska (residential leases only), Delaware (residential and commercial leases), Hawaii (residential only), and New York (residential only). A number of other jurisdictions have adopted the standard of good faith and commercial reasonableness. These states include Alabama, Florida, Illinois, Massachusetts, New Mexico, North Carolina, and Ohio.

11 THE EFFECT OF TRANSFER UPON COVENANTS IN THE LEASE

The famous case of *A.A. Juliard v. American Woolen Co.*, 32 A. 2d 800 (R.I. 1943), involved seven assignments of the lessees' interest between the period of 1899 and 1941. The lease term was to expire in 1955. Defendant was the sixth assignee who then assigned to a successor tenant who failed to pay the rent and who was essentially bankrupt. The landlord sued the defendant claiming that as an assignee the defendant was liable for the unpaid rent even though the defendant did not expressly assume the obligations in the lease. In rejecting plaintiff's claim, the court expressed the general rule regarding the liability of the parties in the event of an assignment:

> The law on this point is well settled. In leases, the lessee being a party to the original contract, continues always liable, notwithstanding any assignment; but the assignee is only liable in respect of his possession of the thing. He bears the burden while he enjoys the benefit, and no longer. Unless fraudulent, a new assignment of the lease terminates the assignee's liability to the lessor for rent subsequently accruing. If such assignee, by a new assignment, fairly relinquishes not only possession of the leased premises but also all benefits therefrom, it is immaterial that the new assignee may be financially irresponsible, or that he gave no consideration, or even that he received a bonus as an inducement to accept the assignment of the lease.

This statement of a transferee's liability is adopted by the *Restatement (2d) of Property,* Section 16.1, which provides in part as follows:

Section 16.1 Obligation Created by an Express Promise-Burden of Performance After Transfer

1 A transferrer of an interest in leased property, who immediately before the transfer is obligated to perform an express promise contained in the lease that touches and concerns the transferred interest, continues to be obligated after the transfer if:

a the obligation rests on privity of contract, and he is not relieved of the obligation by the person entitled to enforce it; or

b the obligation rests solely on privity of estate and the transfer does not terminate his privity of estate with the person entitled to enforce the obligation, and that person does not relieve him of the obligation.

In the case of sublease, the obligation of successors is quite different. In a sublease, the original tenant transfers something other than her entire interest and retains some rights to the property as against the subtenant. In the case of sublease, the obligation of the subtenant run, not to the landlord but the sublessor who, in turn, remains exclusively liable to the landlord. This may seem strange but perhaps a typical example will add clarity: Landlord leases to tenant #1 for ten years at a rent of $10,000 per year. After a few years, tenant #1 transfers to tenant #2 at a rent of $20,000 per year. This is a sublease because tenant #1 has retained an interest in the property, namely the right to receive $20,000 per year. Tenant #2 pays tenant #1 and tenant #1 pays the landlord. If tenant #1 defaults, landlord may regain possession without regard to whether tenant #2 has paid tenant #1. Under these facts, tenant #1 has a valuable interest to protect and will pay landlord even if tenant #2 defaults. In this case, tenant #1 would have the right to evict tenant #2 but, so long as landlord is being paid, it has no right to evict.

NOTES AND QUESTIONS

1 Using the *Restatement* language, the defendant in the Juliard case prevailed because there was neither privity of estate nor privity of contract. Privity of contract was missing because the defendant was not an original party to the lease and did not expressly agree to assume and be bound by the covenants in the lease. Privity of estate was present only during the time the defendant was in possession of the property. When the defendant transferred the lease, privity of estate was terminated within the meaning of *Restatement Second,* Section 16.1 (1.) (b).

2 Generally speaking, a purchaser of the landlord steps into the shoes of the original landlord and takes subject to all rights of the tenant including, for example, the right to renew the lease. (See *Bickford v. Dillion,* 71 N.E. 2d 611.) Similarly, the successor of the original landlord can bring an action against the tenant for breach of an obligation contained in the lease. (*Cortiana v. France,* 208 S.W. 2d 436 (Ark. 1948)

Touch and Concern. The promise by the landlord or the tenant ''touches and concerns'' their respective interests in the leased property if the promise affects the use and enjoyment of the property or if it enhances the reversionary interest of the landlord. Thus, landlord leases to tenant for five years, and tenant promises to keep the property in repair. The performance of this promise enhances the reversionary interest of the landlord and touches and concerns the landlord's interest in the leased property. The touch and concern requirement in the context of leases is essentially the same as in the context of land use covenants (Chapter 9).

12   TERMINATION OF THE LEASE

Notice of Termination   Except for a tendency for a fixed term, either party may terminate a tenancy by giving notice to the other party. Most states provide that a ''thirty-day notice'' is sufficient, although there is wide variety among the jurisdictions in this regard. Provided that a lease does not specify to the contrary, either the landlord or the tenant may terminate the relationship upon notifying the other party. When the notice period has expired, the landlord-tenant relationship is terminated.

When a tenant defaults in the performance of a lease obligation, the landlord must also give notice so that the tenant will have an opportunity to cure the default. Notice to the tenant in the case of default is usually of much shorter duration, typically three to five days. For example, if a tenant fails to pay rent when due, the landlord may elect to terminate the lease but must first give notice to the tenant, specifying the nature of the default, and thereby giving the tenant a chance to cure the default. If the tenant complies the notice, the lease is reinstated. In our example, if the tenant pays the rent, the default is considered cured, and the landlord may not terminate the lease or proceed to evict the tenant.

Lease Provisions Affecting Notice   As indicated, all states have passed statutes that regulate the giving of notice to terminate a tenancy or to declare a default by the tenant. Provisions in a lease may also specify the time limitations and manner of giving notice, although such provisions are only enforceable to the extent they increase the applicable notice periods. For instance, if a state statute provides that the notice period to terminate a lease because of a default by the tenant is five days, the lease could effectively extend the period beyond five days but could not shorten the period to less than five days.

Eviction Procedures   If the landlord gives appropriate notice to the tenant but the tenant fails to cure the default and retains possession of the premises, the landlord may proceed to oust or evict the tenant and recover possession. The procedure to regain possession is usually called unlawful detainer, although different terminology is often used.

Unlawful detainer is considered a *summary procedure* because it moves much more quickly than other civil proceedings and because the primary issue is simply the landlord's right to possession. Although again there is substantial variation among the various states, a typical unlawful detainer would proceed along the following lines.

1 Landlord gives notice of a default or of the election to terminate the tenancy;

2 Upon expiration of the notice period, the landlord files the unlawful detainer action.

3 The summons and complaint are served upon the tenant.

4 The time in which to answer the complaint is significantly shorter than in a typical civil action. A reduction of the time to respond from thirty days to five days is not uncommon. In addition, since the right to possession is the primary issue, the tenant's rights to raise issues other than those which pertain to the right to possession is severely restricted. Habitability and retaliatory eviction are the primary defenses.

5 An unlawful detainer proceeding is usually given trial setting preference over all other civil actions so that the case will proceed to trial much more quickly than other cases.

6 At trial, the issues for decision are usually limited to whether the tenant breached the lease and was given appropriate notice. Assuming this is the case, and that there are no defenses, the court will enter an order that the landlord is entitled to immediate possession. Often the appeal rights of the tenant are also limited.

7 The landlord then takes the Order for Possession, hands it to the Sheriff or other appropriate officer, who will then forcibly remove the tenant from the premises.

13 SUMMARY

The field of landlord and tenant law has undergone profound changes in recent years, particularly as it relates to residential rentals. Nevertheless, the common law doctrines have continuing relevance because the common law classification and many of its other doctrines continue to be followed to this day.

Since a lease is an interest in real estate, the provisions of the statute of frauds must be satisfied if the lease term is in excess of one year. Although a lease may contain extensive and elaborate terms, the statute of frauds will be satisfied if the agreement specifies the parties, the premises, the duration of the lease, the rental payments, and it is signed.

The weight of authority in the United States is that the landlord must deliver possession of the premises to the tenant at the commencement of the lease. A minority of jurisdictions hold that the landlord must simply give the tenant the right to possession. Once in possession, it is usually up to the tenant to retain possession against third parties. However, the landlord may do nothing that substantially interfaces with the tenant's quiet enjoyment of the premises.

Since about 1970, American courts and legislatures have come to believe that the common law approach to the landlord's legal responsibilities to a residential tenant did not conform to modern realities. The shortage of housing, the disparity of bargaining power, the application of housing codes, and the rise of the consumer movement—all pointed to the conclusion that greater responsibility should be placed upon the lessor of residential property. Today nearly all jurisdictions have responded by adopting the warranty of habitability and implying the existence of the warranty into all residential rentals. Coupled with the warranty of habitability is the doctrine of retaliatory eviction. Under this doctrine, a landlord may not evict or refuse to renew a lease if the landlord is motivated by the desire to retaliate against the tenant for exercising rights that the tenant has.

The civil rights statutes and particularly the Fair Housing Act of 1968 have also limited an owner's right to terminate a lease or refuse to enter into one. A landlord may still reject a tenant's application to make a lease but may not do so on the basis of the applicant's race, color, creed, or national origin.

Another aspect of landlord tenant law that has been undergoing some change involves the landlord's liability for injuries sustained on the leased property. The common law held to the doctrine that the landlord was immune from tort liability but began to recognize exceptions to this immunity at a fairly early stage. Some of the harshness and rigidity of the "immunity with exceptions" rule is modified to the extent that liability will often be imposed if the tort arises by virtue of a breach of the warranty of habitability.

A minority of jurisdictions have followed the lead of *Seargent v. Ross* and have substituted general negligence principles in place of the immunity with exceptions doctrine. One state has imposed strict liability upon the landlord, using the analogy to products liability to reach this result.

As in the case of other interests in real estate, interests under a lease are freely transferable. However, efforts are often made to restrict the tenant's ability to assign or sublet the lease. For the most part, the landlord may completely restrict the tenants ability to transfer. And, if the lease requires the landlord to consent to a transfer, the majority rule is that the landlord may refuse to give consent for any reason. A growing minority of jurisdictions hold that the landlord may only refuse to consent if there is a good faith business reason for refusing to consent.

When the tenant's interest is transferred, the original tenant remains bound by the terms of the lease unless the landlord releases the tenant. The successor tenant is bound so long as they are obtaining the benefits of the lease.

14 QUESTIONS

1 Landlord leased two floors of an office building in the Chicago Loop to tenant. Landlord later gave a license to the James Beam Distilling Company to erect signs on the outside walls of the building. Assuming the lease was silent on the owner's rights to the exterior walls, does the tenant have a remedy against landlord and/or Jim Beam?

2 Landlord and tenant enter into a lease, which specifies the premises, and provides for rent to be paid every two months. The lease is signed but does not specify a duration. Is the lease valid? If so, what is the term of the lease?

3 Landlord and tenant have a written lease for a term of five years. Is the landlord required to give notice to the tenant to vacate at the end of the term? What is the status of the tenant if it remains in possession after the end of the term?

4 Landlord leases a warehouse to tenant. In the meantime, bank forecloses on its mortgage against the property because of a default in payments. Bank evicts tenant. Does tenant have a claim against landlord?

5 Landlord and tenant enter into a lease of residential property, which provides, among other things, that tenant is to keep the premises in good repair during the term of the lease. The heating system in the building fails, and landlord refuses to fix it based upon the provision in the lease. Tenant claims a breach of the warranty of habitability. Who is correct?

6 Landlord leases a residential dwelling to tenant. The air conditioning fails to work. Tenant, annoyed, breaks a window trying to open it. Tenant claims that the warranty of habitability

has been breached because of the landlord's failure to replace the window or fix the air conditioning. Is the tenant correct?

7 Landlord was a migrant farm labor contractor who hired seasonal farmworkers and provided simple lodging for them. The tenants were migrant farmworkers who went on strike and filed an action in federal court charging the employer/landlord with violations of the Farm Labor Act. The landlord filed actions to evict the tenants. The tenants claimed this was retaliatory and therefore barred by the state's statute which prohibited eviction for a retaliatory motive. Are the tenant's correct?

8 Tenant was asphyxiated when the exhaust valve on a hot water heater became blocked causing gas to escape. Is the landlord liable?

9 Assume the same facts as in Question 8, but that a guest of the tenant is also injured. May the guest recover?

10 Tenant sustained serious injuries when she was assaulted by an intruder in the common hallway of her apartment building. Is the landlord liable to the tenant?

11 Landlord enters into a ten-year lease with tenant. Tenant later transfers to a second tenant reserving only the right to obtain possession from the first tenant one day before the lease term expires. Is this an assignment or a sublease?

12 Landlord leases to tenant for five years. Tenant promises to put a new roof on the building before the end of the lease term. Tenant assigns to tenant two. Is the promise to build the roof binding on tenant two? What if tenant one makes a sublease with tenant two?

REGULATION OF THE USE OF LAND

CHAPTER 20

EMINENT DOMAIN: THE CONDEMNATION POWER

TOPICS CONSIDERED IN THIS CHAPTER:

1 INTRODUCTION

The final four chapters of this text consider the power of federal and state government, and their agencies, to regulate the use of land. Chapter 23 considers the relatively new field of environmental protection. Chapters 21 and 22 address the government's right to regulate land use by the implementation of zoning. Zoning regulations have been in general use in this country for about fifty years, although recently there have been significant developments in this difficult area.

The present chapter considers a much older power of government and one which is perhaps the ultimate form of land use regulation. The topic of eminent domain, often called the condemnation power, refers to situations in which the government, or an agency of the government, asserts control over private property. The first of these situations involves the well established and inherent right of the government to take private property for a public purpose provided that just compensation is paid to the owner. The power to condemn is inherent in the federal government and in the governments of all states, and it may be delegated by state government to its political subdivisions, such as counties and cities. It is closely related to the power to the government to impose regulations in the public interest. The power to regulate is known as the ''police power'' and its parameters are fully explored in the next chapter.

The second form of condemnation is somewhat more elusive and arises when governmental action has the effect of taking or damaging private property. This is referred to as a de facto taking, or inverse condemnation. There are two general types of inverse condemnation. The first typically involves the situation where a public project gives rise to a private injury because of some form of physical occupation of the property. The second type of inverse condemnation arises when a governmental regulation goes too far and excessively limits an owner's right to use her or his land. The first type of inverse condemnation is considered in this chapter. The second type, the ''regulatory taking,'' is considered under the topic of Zoning.

In situations where the government intentionally exercises its condemnation power, the primary question involves determination of the value of the property for purposes of paying just compensation. In the case of inverse condemnation, the initial question of whether a taking has occurred must first be addressed, before the question of compensation will arise.

2 NATURE AND SOURCE OF THE POWER TO CONDEMN

The power of eminent domain is considered an inherent attribute of sovereignty and is generally considered essential to the operation of government in the interests of the general public. Both the federal government and state governments can, and often do, delegate their power to condemn to designated agencies and may even confer or use this power for the benefit of private persons. For instance, the legislature often will authorize private railroads, irrigation companies, or utilities to condemn property for its use upon payment of just compensation, provided that the use for which the property is condemned is of a public character.

The Fifth Amendment to the United States Constitution has two express limitations upon the exercise of governmental power in relation to private property: ''nor shall any person be . . . deprived of . . . property, without due process of law; nor shall private property be taken for public use without just compensation.'' This limitation is imposed upon the states by virtue of the due process provisions in the Fourteenth Amendment of the Constitution. Nearly all state constitutions contain similar provisions. In other words, the power to condemn is not found in the constitution but is an inherent attribute of government. The condemnation power has constitutional dimensions because of the limitations imposed upon the power by the Fifth Amendment.

As the following material illustrates, courts have tended to give great deference to the legislature's determination that a condemnation is based upon a ''public purpose.''

3 A "PUBLIC PURPOSE"

Hawaii Housing Authority v. Midkiff, 467 U.S. 229 (U.S. 1984)

The Fifth Amendment of the United States Constitution provides, in pertinent part, that "private property [shall not] be taken for public use without just compensation." These cases present the question whether the Public Use Clause of that Amendment, prohibits the State of Hawaii from taking, with just compensation, title in real property from lessors and transferring it to lessees in order to reduce the concentration of ownership of fees simple in the State. We conclude that it does not.

Facts of the case.

The Hawaiian Islands were originally settled by Polynesian immigrants from the western Pacific. These settlers developed an economy around a feudal land tenure system in which one island high chief, the *ali'i nui,* controlled the land and assigned it for development to certain subchiefs. The subchiefs would then reassign the land to other lower ranking chiefs, who would administer the land and govern the farmers and other tenants working it. All land was held at the will of *ali'i nui* and eventually had to be returned to his trust. There was no private ownership of land.

Beginning in the early 1800's, Hawaiian leaders and American settlers repeatedly attempted to divide the lands of the kingdom among the crown, the chiefs, and the common people. These efforts proved largely unsuccessful and the land remained in the hands of a few. In the mid-1960's, after extensive hearings, the Hawaii Legislature discovered that, while the State and Federal Governments owned almost 49% of the State's land, another 47% was in the hands of only 72 private landowners. The legislature further found that 19 landholders, with tracts of 21,000 acres or more, owned more than 40% of this land and that on Oahu, the most urbanized of the islands, 22 landowners owned 72.5% of the fee simple titles. The legislature concluded that concentrated land ownership was responsible for skewing the State's residential fee simple market, inflating land prices, and injuring the public tranquility and welfare.

To redress these problems, the legislature decided to compel the large landowners to break up their estates. The legislature considered requiring large landowners to sell lands which they were leasing to homeowners. However, the landowners strongly resisted this scheme, pointing out the significant federal tax liabilities they would incur. Indeed, the landowners claimed that the federal tax laws were the primary reason they previously had chosen to lease, and not sell, their lands. Therefore, to accommodate the needs of both lessors and lessees, the Hawaii Legislature enacted the Land Reform Act of 1967 (Act), which created a mechanism for condemning residential tracts and for transferring ownership of the condemned fees simple to existing lessees. By condemning the land in question, the Hawaii Legislature intended to make the land sales involuntary, thereby making the federal tax consequences less severe while still facilitating the redistribution of fees simple.

Plaintiffs are landowners who feel they will be adversely affected by the Act. They filed suit in February 1979 asking that the Act be declared unconstitutional and that it's enforcement be enjoined. The District Court found that the Act's goals were within the bounds of the State's police powers and that the means the legislature had chosen to serve those goals were not arbitrary, capricious, or selected in bad faith.

The Court of Appeals for the Ninth Circuit reversed and determined that the Act could not pass the requisite judicial scrutiny of the Public Use Clause. It found that the transfers contemplated by the Act were unlike those of takings previously held to constitute "public uses" by this Court. The Court of Appeals concluded that the Act was simply "a naked attempt on the part of the State of Hawaii to take the private property of A and transfer it to B solely for B's private use and benefit."

OPINION

There is, of course, a role for courts to play in reviewing a legislature's judgment of what constitutes a public use, even when the eminent domain power is equated with the police power. But this role is an extremely narrow one. Any departure from this judicial restraint would result in courts deciding on what is and is not a governmental function and in their invalidating legislation on the basis of their view on that question at the moment of decision, a practice which has proved impractical in other fields. In short, the Court has made clear that it will not substitute its judgment for a legislature's judgment as to what constitutes a public use "unless the use be palpably without reasonable foundation," (*United States v. Gettysburg Electric R. Co.,* 160 U.S. 668, 680 (1896).

To be sure, the Court's cases have repeatedly stated that "one person's property may not be taken for the benefit of another private person without a justifying public purpose, even though compensation be paid," (*Thompson v. Consolidated Gas Corp.,* 300 U.S. 55, 80 (1937). But where the exercise of the eminent domain power is rationally related to a conceivable public purpose, the Court has never held a compensated taking to be proscribed by the Public Use Clause.

On this basis, we have no trouble concluding that the Hawaii Act is constitutional. The people of Hawaii have attempted, much as the settlers of the original thirteen Colonies did, to reduce the perceived social and economic evils of a land oligopoly traceable to their monarchs. The land oligopoly has, according to the Hawaii Legislature, created artificial deterrents to the normal functioning of the State's residential land market and forced thousands of individual homeowners to lease, rather than buy, the land underneath their homes. Regulating oligopoly and the evils associated with it is a classic exercise of a State's police powers. We cannot disapprove of Hawaii's exercise of this power.

Nor can we condemn as irrational the Act's approach to correcting the land oligopoly problem. The Act presumes that when a sufficiently large number of persons declare that they are willing but unable to buy lots at fair prices the land market is malfunctioning. When such a malfunction is signalled, the Act authorizes HHA to condemn lots in the relevant tract. The Act limits the number of lots any one tenant can purchase and authorizes HHA to use public funds to ensure that the market dilution goals will be achieved. This is a comprehensive and rational approach to identifying and correcting market failure.

When the legislature's purpose is legitimate and its means are not irrational, our cases make clear that empirical debates over the wisdom of takings—no less than debates over the wisdom of other kinds of socioeconomic legislation—are not to be carried out in the courts. Redistribution of fees simple to correct deficiencies in the market determined by the state legislature to be attributable to land oligopoly is a rational exercise of the eminent domain power.

The Hawaii Legislature enacted its Land Reform Act not to benefit a particular class of identifiable individuals but to attack certain perceived evils of concentrated property ownership in Hawaii—a legitimate public purpose. Use of the condemnation power to achieve this purpose is not irrational. Since we assume for purposes of these appeals that the weighty demand of just compensation has been met, the requirements of the Fifth and Fourteenth Amendments have been satisfied. Accordingly, we reverse the judgment of the Court of Appeals, and remand these cases for further proceedings in conformity with this opinion.

NOTES AND QUESTIONS

1 In *Midkiff,* the court specifically relied upon the 1954 case of *Berman v. Parker* for its expansive interpretation of the public purpose requirement.

In *Berman,* the Court held constitutional the District of Columbia Redevelopment Act of 1945. That Act provided both for the comprehensive use of the eminent domain power to redevelop slum areas and for the possible sale or lease of the condemned lands to private interests. In discussing whether the takings authorized by that Act were for a "public use," the Court stated:

We deal, in other words, with what traditionally has been known as the police power. An attempt to define its reach or trace its outer limits is fruitless, for each case must turn on its own facts.

Once the object is within the authority of Congress, the right to realize it through the exercise of eminent domain is clear. For the power of eminent domain is merely the means to the end. . . . Once the object is within the authority of Congress, the means by which it will be attained is also for Congress to determine. Here one of the means chosen is the use of private enterprise for redevelopment of the area. Appellants argue that this makes the project a taking from one businessman for the benefit of another businessman. But the means of executing the project are for Congress and Congress alone to determine, once the public purpose has been established.

2 The Court of Appeals' decision, which was reversed by the Supreme Court in *Hawaii Housing v. Midkiff,* reviewed the constitutional history of the public use requirement in eminent domain proceedings and made the following observations:

> If we look to the language of the Federal Constitution, and interpret the protection afforded to property owners, it becomes unmistakably clear that the Hawaii Land Reform Act is unconstitutional. As anticipated by James Madison, the Hawaii Legislature has become the instrument by which private property held by a minority of the persons within that state is to be redistributed to appease the desires of the landless majority to own residential land. The Federal Constitution and the Fifth Amendment were adopted with the express purpose of invalidating the taking of the private property from one person for the private and exclusive enjoyment by another.
>
> The founders of this nation sought to give constitutional protection to minority rights. They wisely foresaw that attempts would be made by the states to take away the private property rights of the landed minority. Our Federal Constitution and the Bill of Rights were designed to prevent such abuses by the majority. That Constitution now compels us to find that the Hawaii Land Reform act violates the public use limitation of the Fifth and Fourteenth Amendments
>
> *Midkiff v. Tom,* 702 F.2d 788 (9th Cir. 1983)

3 Do you think the Supreme Court or the Court of Appeals does the better job of addressing the issues in this case?

After Midkiff, can you think of any action under the eminent domain power that would fail for lack of a public purpose? Suppose that a state legislature, concerned about high housing costs and the plight of the homeless decides to condemn the property of homeowners who own property for investment purposes and give fee interests in the condemned property to the homeless. Would such a scheme be upheld under *Midkiff*?

Poletown Neighborhood Council v. Detroit, 304 N.W. 2d 455 (Mich. 1981)

Facts of the case.

This case arises out of a plan by the Detroit Economic Development Corporation to acquire, by condemnation a large tract of land to be conveyed to General Motors Corporation as a site for construction of an assembly plant. The plaintiffs, a neighborhood association and several individual residents of the affected area, brought suit to challenge the project on a number of grounds.

OPINION

This case raises a question of paramount importance to the future welfare of this state and its residents: Can a municipality use the power of eminent domain granted to it by the Economic Development Corporations Act to condemn property for transfer to a private corporation to build a plant to promote industry and commerce?

The Economic Development Corporations Act is a part of the comprehensive legislation dealing with planning, housing, and zoning whereby the State of Michigan is attempting to provide for the general health, safety, and welfare through alleviating unemployment, providing economic assistance to industry, assisting the rehabilitation of blighted areas, and fostering urban redevelopment.

To further the objectives of this Act, the legislature has authorized municipalities to acquire property by condemnation and to transfer the property from the municipality to private users.

What plaintiffs challenge is the constitutionality of using the power of eminent domain to condemn one person's property to convey it to another private person in order to bolster the economy. They argue that whatever incidental benefit may accrue to the public, assembling land to General Motors' specifications for its convenience and its uncontrolled use in profit making is really a taking for private use and not a public use, because General Motors is the primary beneficiary of the condemnation.

The determination of what constitutes a public purpose is primarily a legislative function, subject to review by the courts when abused. The determination of the legislative body should not be reversed except in instances where determination is manifestly arbitrary and incorrect.

In this case, the benefit to be received by the municipality is a clear and significant one and is sufficient to satisfy this Court that the project is a legitimate object of the Legislature, even though a private party will also receive a benefit.

The power of eminent domain is to be used in this instance primarily to accomplish the essential public purposes of alleviating unemployment and revitalizing the economic base of the community. The benefit to a private interest is merely incidental.

The power of eminent domain is restricted to furthering public uses and purposes and is not to be exercised without substantial proof that the public is primarily to be benefited. Where, as here, the condemnation power is exercised in a way that benefits specific and identifiable private interests, a court inspects with heightened scrutiny the claim that the public interest is the predominant interest being advanced. Such public benefit cannot be speculative or marginal but must be clear and significant if it is to be within the legitimate purpose as stated by the Legislature. We hold this project is warranted on the basis that its significance for the people of Detroit and the state has been demonstrated.

NOTES AND QUESTIONS

Review the last paragraph of the case. Is the public benefit clear and significant? What did the legislature do to demonstrate that the project was warranted? If General Motors wants to build an assembly plant, is there any reason why it should not be expected to purchase the land from its owners and build it? Are there variables which, if known, would lean in favor of the Michigan Legislature's decision to condemn?

4   WHAT CONSTITUTES A "TAKING"? INVERSE CONDEMNATION

In the preceding section we saw that the concept of a public purpose is extremely broad and will seldom be found lacking in the exercise of the condemnation power. In addition, the power of the government to regulate the use of land in the public interest is also broad, and courts are generally reluctant to interfere with that exercise even when the value of the landowner's property is significantly diminished. The question then becomes whether, and at what point, the exercise of governmental authority will be considered the exercise of the power of eminent domain. Certainly the government is free to conduct its business without paying every time the value of someone's property is diminished. However, there is a point at which the government's objectives may only be accomplished through the eminent domain power, the exercise of which requires payment to the affected landowner.

In *Varjabedian v. City of Madera,* 572 P. 2d 43 (Cal. 1977), the California Supreme Court was asked to uphold an award of damages in favor of a property owner against a municipality based on the loss of value to the owner's property caused by the City's operation of a water treatment plant. The plant caused obnoxious odors to pervade plaintiff's property, which consisted of a residence and several acres of vineyards. The trial court awarded damages based on a nuisance but denied plaintiff's claim of inverse condemnation finding that there was no trespass and no physical damage to the plaintiff's property. The Supreme Court reversed.

> Article I, Section 19, of the California Constitution requires that "just compensation" be paid when "private property" is "taken or damaged for public use."
>
> In assessing whether plaintiff's allegations may serve as a basis for inverse liability, we note that physical damage to property is not invariably a prerequisite to compensation. Rather, the determination of the scope of the just compensation clause rests on its construction as a matter of interpretation and policy. The competing policies which guide that construction have often been described as follows: "on the one hand the policy underlying the eminent domain provision in the Constitution is to distribute throughout the community the loss inflicted upon the individual by the making of the public improvements. . . . On the other hand, fears have been expressed that compensation allowed too liberally will seriously impede, if not stop, beneficial public improvements because of the greatly increased cost."
>
> Several factors present militate in favor of a distribution throughout the relevant community of the type of loss involved here. Plaintiffs' claim stems from the recurring violation of their property by a gaseous effluent. As such, the injury is not far removed from those core cases of direct physical invasion which indisputably require compensation. Thus, damage from invasions of water or other liquid effluents often provides the basis for inverse liability. Plaintiff's complaint, which includes the claim that their land was made "untenantable for residential purposes," is clearly sufficient to depict a permanent and "substantial impairment" in their use of the land.
>
> At the same time, fears that "compensation . . . will seriously impede, if not stop" the beneficial construction of sewage treatment plants might be realized if courts were to award compensation for every objectionable odor, however insubstantial or widely dispersed, pro-

duced by such facilities. But the problem of reconciling this consideration with the competing policy of loss-distribution is not presented in its most difficult form by this case, which we feel is within the doctrine of *Richards v. Washington Terminal Cow.,* 233 U.S. 546, 34 S.Ct. 654, 58 L.Ed. 1088 (1914). In *Richards* the plaintiff complained of "inconvenience . . . in the occupation of his property" caused by "gases and smoke" emanating from a nearby railroad. The United States Supreme Court ruled that under the "taking" clause of the Fifth Amendment to the federal Constitution, the plaintiff could not recover for "those consequential damages that are necessarily incident to proximity to the railroad. . . ." Yet the landowner was entitled to compensation for "gases and smoke emitted from locomotive engines while in a tunnel, and forced out of it by means of a fanning system through a portal located so near to plaintiff's property that these gases and smoke materially contributed to render the house less habitable than otherwise. . . ." Construing federal statutes immunizing the railroad from nuisance liability "in light of the Fifth Amendment," the court concluded "they do not authorize the imposition of so direct, peculiar, and substantial a burden upon plaintiff's property without compensation to him."

Of course, *Richards* may be distinguished from this case with respect to the nature of the public facility involved, or on the ground that there is no device here which directs the noxious gases onto plaintiffs' property. However, such factual differences do not render the underlying principle of *Richards* inapplicable to the problem at hand, particularly when it is considered together with the California Constitution, which protects a somewhat broader range of property values from government destruction than does the analogous federal provision. If a plaintiff can establish that his property has suffered a "direct, peculiar, and substantial" burden as a result of recurring odors produced by a sewage facility—that he has, as in Richards, been in effect "singled out" to suffer the detrimental environmental effects of the enterprise—then the policy favoring distribution of the resulting loss of market value is strong and the likelihood that compensation will impede necessary public construction is relatively slight. In these circumstances, the necessity of breathing noxious sewage fumes may be a burden unfairly and unconstitutionally imposed on the individual landowner.

NOTES AND QUESTIONS

The court in Varjabedian took note of the competing policies of compensating owners whose property is harmed by a public improvement without deterring the construction of public works by making them too expensive. Where does one draw the line? For instance, how many of the plaintiff's neighbors will be able to recover? Does the case of *Richards v. Washington,* cited by the court, provide any clue?

In *Loretto v. Teleprompter,* 458 U.S. 419 (1982), the U.S. Supreme Court faced an inverse condemnation claim based upon the following facts.

In order to encourage tenant access to cable television hookups, the State of New York enacted a statute (Section 828) which provided that a landlord "may not interfere with the installation of cable television facilities upon his property or premises," and may not demand payment from a tenant or from any cable television company an amount in excess of $1 as a condition to installation.

Plaintiff and other landlords sued, claiming that the cable installations were a trespass and that Section 828 permitted a taking without just compensation. The New York Court of Appeals determined that Section 828 serves the legitimate public purpose of "rapid development of and maximum penetration by a means of communication which has important educational and community aspects," and thus is within the State's power to regulate in the public interest (the police power). The U.S. Supreme Court disagreed and made the following observations.

> We have no reason to question that the statute (Section 828) is within the scope of the police power. It is a separate question, however, whether an otherwise valid regulation so frustrates property rights that compensation must be paid.
>
> We conclude that a permanent physical occupation authorized by government is a taking without regard to the public interests that it may serve. Our constitutional history confirms the rule, recent cases do not question it, and the purposes of the Takings Clause compel its retention.
>
> When faced with a constitutional challenge to a permanent physical occupation of real property, this Court has invariably found a taking. As early as 1872, in *Pumpelly v. Green Bay Co.,* this Court held that the defendant's construction, pursuant to state authority, of a dam which permanently flooded plaintiff's property constituted a taking. A unanimous Court stated, without qualification, that "where real estate is actually invaded by superinduced additions of water, earth, sand, or other material, or by having any artificial structure placed on it, so as to effectively destroy or impair its usefulness, it is a taking, within the meaning of the Constitution." Seven years later, the Court re-emphasized the importance of a physical occupation by distinguishing a regulation that merely restricted the use of private property. Later cases, relying on the character of a physical occupation, clearly establish that permanent occupations of land by such installations as telegraph and telephone lines, rails, and underground pipes or wires are takings, even if they occupy only relatively insubstantial amounts of space and do not seriously interfere with the landowner's use of the rest of his land.

More recent cases confirm the distinction between a permanent physical occupation, a physical invasion short of an occupation, and a regulation that merely restricts the use of property. In *United States v. Causby,* 328 U.S. 256 (1946), the Court ruled that frequent flights immediately above a landowner's property constituted a taking, comparing such overflights to the quintessential form of a taking:

> If, by reason of the frequency and altitude of the flights, respondents could not use this land for any purpose their loss would be complete. It would be as complete as if the United States had entered upon the surface of the land and taken exclusive possession of it.

In short, when the character of the governmental action is a permanent physical occupation of property, our cases uniformly have found a taking to the extent of the occupation, without regard to whether the action achieves an important public benefit or has only minimal economic impact on the owner.

The judgment of the New York Court of Appeals is reversed, and the case is remanded for further proceedings not inconsistent with this opinion.

NOTES AND QUESTIONS

1 Although the *Loretto* case involves a regulation, it is distinguishable from the zoning cases because of the aspect of physical occupation upon the plaintiff's land. Is this distinction sound? In the *Loretto* case, the installation of cable hook-ups may have increased the value of plaintiffs' property. On the other hand, a regulation that limits the use of property may significantly decrease the value of the property but, since there is no physical occupation, no taking will have occurred. Would it make more sense to focus on economic impact rather than physical occupation?

2 An inverse condemnation action essentially involves a claim by an owner that the court find a taking when the government insists that none was intended and none occurred. The ways in which the interest taken is valued is discussed below.

5 JUST COMPENSATION: METHODS OF VALUATION

We have seen that there are two general ways in which a public entity may take or appropriate private property. The first involves the relatively simple situation in which the public entity initiates formal eminent domain proceedings with the intention of paying "just compensation" for the property.

In this case the usual measure is the fair market value of the property at the time of the taking or the diminished value of the property if the taking is only partial.

A similar measure is used in cases where some action by the government is deemed to have taken private property through inverse condemnation. If the physical occupation is "complete," then the measure of compensation is the fair market value of the land, usually measured as of the time of the taking. In this case, valuation of the interest taken proceeds along lines similar to the case of formal condemnation. In the case of a partial taking, "just compensation" tends to reflect the extent to which the fair market value of the property was diminished at the time the taking occurred.

Compensation Where Eminent Domain Proceedings Are Initiated The general rule is that just compensation requires the payment of the fair market value of the land based upon its highest and best use. One court expressed the idea of fair market value as follow:

> When the Government condemns private property for a public purpose, it must pay just compensation for that property. Just compensation means the monetary equivalent of the property taken, and the federal courts have employed the concept of "fair market value" to determine the owner's loss.
>
> In determining fair market value, courts consider all facts and circumstances that would reasonably influence the price agreed upon by a reasonable seller willing but not obligated to sell and a reasonable buyer willing but not obligated to buy. Accordingly, courts appropriately consider evidence regarding the highest and best use to which the land is put or reasonably may be adapted in the future, as well as any facts which would naturally influence

a person of ordinary prudence desiring to purchase. Further, we assume that buyers or sellers of ordinary prudence are knowledgeable and not motivated by speculation or conjecture.
(*U.S. v. 760 Acres of Land,* 731 F. 2d 1449 (1984, 9th Cir.)

The date upon which the property is valued is usually the date upon which con-demnation proceedings are initiated, although different valuation dates have been used from time to time. For example, *City of St. Louis Park v. Almore Co.,* 313 N.W. 2d 606 (Minn.), held that condemnation damages are to be assessed as of the date of the condemnation award if this is required to fairly compensate the property owner.

The determination of value is based upon an objective standard of fair market value and does not take account of any subjective or personal attachment which the land-owner may have. For instance, *State Highway Commission v. Bredvik,* 268 N.W. 2d 144 (S.D.), involved a case where the landowner was blind and claimed that because he was so familiar with the property, which had been in his family for two generations, he was still able to operate the property as a farm in spite of his blindness. In keeping with the general approach, the court ignored these special circumstances and limited the owner's recovery to the fair market value of the land.

A slightly unusual fact pattern occurred in *U.S. v. 50 Acres of Land,* 469 U.S. 24 (U.S. 1984). In that case the U.S. Government condemned property owned by the City of Duncanville, Texas, which had been using the site as a landfill. The fair market value of the land was $225,000 but the cost of obtaining a substitute facility was $725,000. The Court of Appeals held that since the City had a duty to secure an alternate landfill site that the City's loss was "the amount of money reasonably spent to create a functionally equivalent facility." The court also held that this amount should be adjusted by any material differences in the substitute site. The U.S. Supreme Court reversed with the following explanation:

> The Court has repeatedly held that just compensation normally is to be measured by "the market value of the property at the time of the taking contemporaneously paid in money." Considerations that may not reasonably be held to affect market value are excluded. Devi-ation from this measure of just compensation has been required only when market value has been too difficult to find, or when its application would result in manifest injustice to owner or public.
>
> This case is not one in which an exception to the normal measure of just compensation is required because fair market value is not ascertainable. Such cases, for the most part, involve properties that are seldom, if ever, sold in the open market. Under those circum-stances, we cannot predict whether the prices previously paid, assuming there have been prior sales, would be repeated in a sale of the condemned property. In this case, however, the testimony at trial established a fairly robust market for sanitary landfill properties, and the jury's determination of the fair market value of the condemned landfill facility is ade-quately supported by expert testimony concerning the sale prices of comparable property.
>
> The city contends that in this case an award of compensation measured by market value is fundamentally inconsistent with the basic principles of indemnity embodied in the Just Compensation Clause. If the city were a private party rather than a public entity, however, the possibility that the cost of a substitute facility exceeds the market value of the condemned parcel would not justify a departure from the market value measure. The question, is whether a substitute-facilities measure of compensation is mandated by the Constitution when the

condemnee is a local government entity that has a duty to replace the condemned facility.

The city argues that its responsibility for municipal garbage disposal justifies a departure from the market value measure in this case. This responsibility compels the city to arrange for a suitable replacement facility or substitute garbage disposal services. This obligation to replace a condemned facility, however, is no more compelling than the obligations assumed by private citizens. Even though most private condemnees are not legally obligated to replace property taken by the Government, economic circumstances often force them to do so. When a home is condemned, for example, its owner must find another place to live. The city's legal obligation to maintain public services that are interrupted by a federal condemnation does not justify a distinction between public and private condemnation for the purpose of measuring ''just compensation.''

NOTES AND QUESTIONS

1 Under the standard of *U.S. v. 50 Acres of Land,* would a public or private condemnee be entitled to recover for the cost of relocating a facility?

2 Suppose the condemnee is a retail business that has accumulated considerable good will and anticipates that it will lose business if forced to relocate. Are these items compensable?

Under the traditional fair market value standard, relocation costs are not considered when valuing property for condemnation purposes, although many state condemnation statutes provide compensation for relocation. Concerning good will, the general rule is that loss of good will is not compensable, although this rule has been widely criticized. The Uniform Eminent Domain Code, Section 1016, attempts to reverse the general rule and provides that loss of good will is a compensable item in eminent domain proceedings.

Severance Damages In some cases, the exercise of the Eminent Domain power is directed at only a portion of the owner's property. In the case of a partial taking, *severance damages* may be awarded in addition to compensation for the property taken in order to reflect the diminished value of the remaining portion of the property. Severance damages are awarded only when the property taken and the remainder belong to the same party. For example, when the government condemns ten acres of a forty-acre parcel, and thereby deprives the owner of the street frontage and diminishes the value of the rest of the parcel, the owner would be entitled to compensation for the land taken and for severance damages for the diminished value of the remaining parcel.

Divided Interests Consistent with the constitutional mandate supporting the right of eminent domain, all persons with an interest in the property are entitled to compensation. The owner of an easement is entitled to compensation. The holder of a future interest will be compensated if the interest is extinguished. If a taking impairs the security of a mortgage, the holder has a right to share in the condemnation proceeds with the property owner. Finally, a tenant has a right to compensation based on the unexpired term of the lease, usually based upon the difference between the lease rental and the fair rental value. In other words, everyone with an interest in the property is entitled to share in the condemnation award along with the owner of the fee interest.

Valuation for Taking By Inverse Condemnation   We have seen that a claim for inverse condemnation may lie in favor of a property owner whose property is injured or taken through the operation of a project by government. If it is determined that a taking has occurred, and that the taking is total, the measure of damages is the fair market value of the property as of the date of the taking. If the taking is partial, the measure of damages is the extent to which the value of the property owner's property is diminished.

In *Tibbs v. City of Sandpoint,* 602 P. 2d 1005 (Idaho, 1979), the Idaho Supreme Court considered a situation where a group of property owners sought inverse condemnation based upon the reduction of their property values caused by expansion of the City's airport. The court found that a taking had occurred and that it should be measured by the difference in value before and after the taking.

The problem in the *Tibbs* case involved identifying the time of taking in light of the fact that the increased air traffic and thus the taking itself had occurred gradually. Nevertheless, the court directed the trial court to determine the date upon which the taking occurred:

> The actual date of taking, although not readily susceptible to exact determination, is to be fixed at the point in time at which the impairment, of such a degree and kind as to constitute a substantial interference with plaintiffs' property interest, became apparent.

QUESTION

Do you think the property owners in *Tibbs* will attempt to fix the date of the taking in distant past or more recently? Would it matter whether the local eminent domain law provided for interest from the time of the taking?

6   CONDEMNATION PROCEDURES

Federal and state constitutions require that a landowner be given notice of the condemnation proceedings and an opportunity to present evidence, either to contest the proceeding on its merits by showing no public purpose or, more likely, by presenting evidence concerning the fair market value of the property. Condemnation procedure is regulated by statute and these statutes must be strictly followed by the government if the condemnation is to be valid.

Condemnation usually proceeds on a two-step basis. The first involves an administrative decision to condemn, followed by notifying the owner of the decision. As indicated, in nearly all cases of formal condemnation, the primary issue is valuation. The tendency is for the owner and agency to meet and attempt to negotiate a price for the property. Only if these negotiations fail does the second step of the condemnation process become necessary.

If the parties cannot reach agreement on price or if the owner disputes the "public purpose" of the condemnation, the agency will file an action seeking a judicial determination of the right to condemn and of the value of the property. This action proceeds much like any other lawsuit and ultimately proceeds to trial. The judge will rule on the "public purpose" for the condemnation, nearly always finding that the requirement has been met. The parties are then free to introduce evidence, usually through expert appraisers, concerning the fair market value of the land. Based upon this evidence, the judge makes a ruling as to value and will issue an order that, upon payment of the price, the agency will become owner of the property. Unless either party files an appeal, the agency may then record the order and will then become the legal owner of the property.

7 SUMMARY

The power of eminent domain, or the power to condemn is considered inherent in the exercise of government and allows the government or an authorized agency of it to take private property for a public purpose provided that compensation is paid. Two types of eminent domain are considered in this chapter: the first is where formal condemnation proceedings are undertaken by the government; the second is where the operation of a public project has the effect of occupying or damaging the owner's property.

In the case of the formal condemnation, the government must show the existence of a public purpose. This tends to be an easy burden to meet because of the judicial deference given to the decision to condemn and the broad definition of what constitutes a public purpose. The second feature of formal condemnation involves payment of "just compensation." This usually means payment of the fair market value of the property as of the date that condemnation proceedings are initiated. If the taking is only partial, such as where an easement or only a portion of the property is taken, valuation proceeds on the basis of the difference between the fair market value of the property before and after the taking.

Where a property owner can show that activity of the government has resulted in the physical occupation of private property or that the property owner has suffered a unique and appreciable harm because of some governmental activity, an action in inverse condemnation may be brought. When it is determined that a de facto taking has occurred, the valuation of the loss proceeds along the same lines as in the case of formal eminent domain.

8 QUESTIONS

1 Landowner is a radio station which operates broadcasting towers. The Commissioner of Public Works of the City of Syracuse initiated condemnation proceedings to acquire landowner's property and to remove the towers in order to improve flight access to the City's airport. The landowner claimed the proceeding would destroy its ability to do business, was unconstitutional, and was not for a public purpose. Who prevails?

2 Rose was the owner of a commercial building in the City of Coalinga, which was struck by

an earthquake in 1983. The City maintained that the building was unsafe and must be torn down. Rose obtained reports from an engineer and architect stating that the building could be repaired and brought up to current code. The Director of Public Works, however, insisted that the building be torn down and the City proceeded to tear down the building. Rose claims inverse condemnation. Is she correct?

3 The City of Los Angeles operates electrical transmission lines. Through no fault to the City, the lines caused sparks, which ignited a fire in which several homes were burned. The homeowners bring a claim for damages based on inverse condemnation. Are they correct?

4 Margaret Guyton is a tenant in a commercial building. Her lease has five years remaining and a five-year renewal option. Condemnation proceedings are initiated against the building. Is Margaret entitled to be compensated? How would such compensation be measured?

5 Owner purchased fifty acres of land, which he subdivided into one hundred lots intending to build one hundred single-family homes. Before submitting building plans, the City initiated condemnation plans. Owner introduces persuasive evidence that his profit if he were able to build the homes would be $1,000,000. Is anticipated profit an element of compensation in a condemnation proceeding?

ZONING AND OTHER PUBLIC LAND USE CONTROLS

TOPICS CONSIDERED IN THIS CHAPTER:

1 INTRODUCTION

The idea that the use of land may be limited through government regulation is now well established, although the notion is of relatively recent origin. The first comprehensive zoning ordinance in this country was adopted by New York City in 1916. The general validity of such laws was upheld by the United States Supreme Court in the landmark case of *Euclid v. Amber Realty Co.,* decided in 1926. In response to the Euclid case, the U.S. Department of Commerce passed the Standard State Zoning Enabling Act which became the model for states seeking to enact zoning ordinances.

Before the advent of comprehensive zoning laws, land uses were controlled primarily under the doctrine of nuisance and restrictive covenants. These forms of control were clearly unsuited to the rapid growth that occurred, particularly in the urban regions of the United States. Efforts to control the effect of this growth through zoning spread quickly during the late 1920's. Zoning is now so prevalent throughout the United States that nearly all communities except the most isolated ones have adopted at least some form of zoning. In the urban areas, zoning regulations have become complex and affect many of the decisions made by owners concerning the use of, and development of, their property.

2 SOURCES OF THE ZONING POWER

The power to enact zoning laws derives from the inherent power of the government to adopt and enforce laws necessary to protect the public health, safety, morals, and general welfare. This power is known as the police power. The power of government to zone and control land use is broad and, although not without controversy, is generally considered essential to achieving a satisfactory quality of life in both rural and urban communities.

> Zoning is not just an expansion of the common law of nuisance. It seeks to achieve much more than the removal of obnoxious gases and unsightly uses. Underlying the entire concept of zoning is the assumption that zoning can be a vital tool for maintaining a civilized form of existence only if we employ the insights and the learning of the philosopher, the city planner, the economist, the sociologist, the public health expert, and all the other professionals concerned with urban problems.
>
> *Udell v. Haas,* 235 N.E. 2d 897 (N.Y. 1968)

While the police power is inherent in the federal government and in the states, it is not inherent in political subdivisions such as cities and counties. As a result, this power must be delegated by the states to cities and counties in order for them to have the power to enact zoning regulations.

Although zoning is conducted almost entirely at a local level, local zoning authorities have only those powers expressly provided by the enabling statute. Unlike the federal government or the state governments, counties and municipalities are not vested with the constitutional or common law right to regulate property through the passage of zoning ordinances. Such ordinances are the result of the police power vested in the state legislature, which in turn may delegate to the legislative branch of a municipal government a specified portion of that power. The following Act is typical of state enabling legislation, and many of its provisions have been incorporated into local ordinances.

Although the Standard Act is fairly long and fairly dry, it is recommended reading because it defines the limits of the zoning power and establishes the procedures to be followed when implementing and managing a zoning plan. Reference will be made to the Standard Act throughout the course of this chapter.

U.S. Department of Commerce, A Standard State Enabling Act (1926)

SEC. 1. *Grant of Power.* For the purpose of promoting health, safety, morals, or the general welfare of the community, the legislative body of cities and incorporated villages is hereby empowered to regulate and restrict the height, number of stories, and size of buildings and other structures, the percentage of a lot that may be occupied, the size of yards, courts, and other open spaces, the density of population, and the location and use of buildings, structures, and land for trade, industry, residence, or other purposes.

SEC. 2. *Districts.* For any or all of said purposes the local legislative body may divide the municipality into districts of such number, shape, and area as may be deemed best suited to carry out the purposes of this act; and within such districts it may regulate and restrict the erection, construction, reconstruction, alteration, repair, or use of buildings, structures, or land. All such regulations shall be uniform for each class of kind of building throughout each district, but the regulations in one district may differ from those in other districts.

SEC. 3. *Purposes in View.* Such regulations shall be made in accordance with a comprehensive plan and designed to lessen congestion in the streets; to secure safety from fire, panic, and other dangers; to promote health and the general welfare; to provide adequate light and air; to prevent the overcrowding of land; to avoid undue concentration of population; and to facilitate the adequate provision of transportation, water, sewage, schools, parks, and other public requirements. Such regulations shall be made with reasonable consideration, among other things, to the character of the district and its peculiar suitability for particular uses, and with a view to conserving the value of buildings and encouraging the most appropriate use of land throughout such municipality.

SEC. 4. *Method of Procedure.* The legislative body of such municipality shall provide for the manner in which such regulations and restrictions and the boundaries of such districts shall be determined, established, and enforced, and from time to time amended, supplemented, or changed.

SEC. 5. *Changes.* Such regulations, restrictions, and boundaries may from time to time be amended, supplemented, changed, modified, or repealed. In case, however, of a protest against such change, signed by the owners of twenty percent or more either of the area of the lots included in such proposed change, or of those immediately adjacent in the rear thereof extending _____ feet therefrom, or of those directly opposite thereto extending _____ feet from the street frontage of such opposite lots, such amendment shall not become effective except by the favorable vote of three fourths of all the members of the legislative body of such municipality.

SEC. 6. *Zoning Commission.* In order to avail itself of the powers conferred by this act, such legislative body shall appoint a commission, to be known as the zoning commission, to recommend the boundaries of the various original districts and appropriate regulations to be enforced therein. Such commission shall make a preliminary report and hold public hearings thereon before submitting its final report, and such legislative body shall not hold its public hearings or take action until it has received the final report of such commission. Where a city planning commission already exists, it may be appointed as the zoning commission.

SEC. 7. *Board of Adjustment.* Such local legislative body may provide for the appointment of a board of adjustment, and in the regulations and restrictions adopted pursuant to the authority of this act, may provide that the said board of adjustment may, in appropriate cases and subject to appropriate conditions and safeguards, make special exceptions to the terms of the ordinance in harmony with its general purpose and intent and in accordance with general or specific rules therein contained.

Appeals to the board of adjustment may be taken by any person aggrieved or by any officer, department, board, or bureau of the municipality affected by any decision of the administrative officer. Such appeal shall be taken within a reasonable time, as provided by the rules of the board, by filing with the officer from whom the appeal is taken, and with the board of adjustment, a notice of appeal specifying the grounds thereof. The officer from whom the appeal is taken shall forthwith transmit to the board all the papers constituting the record upon which the action appealed from was taken.

The board of adjustment shall fix a reasonable time for the hearing of the appeal, give public notice thereof, as well as due notice to the parties in interest, and decide the same within a reasonable time. Upon the hearing any party may appear in person or by agent or by attorney.

The board of adjustment shall have the following powers:

1 To hear and decide appeals where it is alleged that there is error in any order, requirement, decision, or determination made by an administrative official in the enforcement of this act or of any ordinance adopted pursuant thereto.

2 To hear and decide special exceptions to the terms of the ordinance upon which the board is required to pass under the ordinance.

3 To authorize, upon appeal in specific cases, such variance from the terms of the ordinance as will not be contrary to the public interest, where, owing to special conditions, a literal enforcement of the provisions of the ordinance will result in unnecessary hardship, and so that the spirit of the ordinance shall be observed and substantial justice done.

In exercising the above-mentioned powers, the board may, in conformity with the provisions of this act, reverse or affirm, wholly or partly, or may modify, the decision or determination appealed from and may make such order or determination as ought to be made, and to that end shall have all the powers of the officer from whom the appeal is taken.

SEC. 8. *Enforcement and Remedies.* The local legislative body may provide by ordinance for the enforcement of this act and of any ordinance or regulation made thereunder. A violation of this act or of such ordinance or regulation is hereby declared to be a misdemeanor, and such local legislative body may provide for the punishment thereof by fine or imprisonment or both. It is also empowered to provide civil penalties for such violation.

In case any building or structure is erected, altered, repaired, or maintained, or any building, structure, or land is used in violation of this act or of any ordinance or other regulation made under authority conferred hereby, the proper local authorities of the municipality may institute any appropriate action or proceedings to prevent such un-lawful construction, alteration, repair, maintenance, or use, to restrain, correct, or abate such violation, to prevent the occupancy of said building, structure, or land, or to prevent any illegal act, conduct, business, or use in or about such premises.

NOTES AND QUESTIONS

1 The Standard State Zoning Enabling Act has been widely followed in all American jurisdictions. Its contents are important because, for the most part, zoning has evolved as a peculiarly local matter. In other words, the vast majority of zoning regulations are passed by counties and cities pursuant to the authority delegated by an enabling statute such as the one given.

2 A zoning ordinance not adopted in accordance with the enabling statute is invalid. See *Borroughs v. Board of Commissioners,* 540 P. 2d 233 (N.M. 1975). A zoning ordinance will also be held invalid if it fails to meet any of the purposes of zoning as set forth in the enabling statute or if it fails to establish sufficiently definite standards to inform property owners of their rights under the zoning ordinance. See e.g., *J. D. Construction Corp. v. Board of Adjustment,* 29 A 2d 452 (N.J. 1972).

3   CONSTITUTIONAL LIMITS ON THE POWER TO ZONE

In the early days of zoning there was considerable opposition to the concept by some property owners and this is true today. Challenges to the constitutional validity of zoning ordinances met with some success, and some state courts invalidated zoning ordinances on the grounds that they were a taking of private property without payment. Although the question of when a regulation becomes a taking is still very much alive, the notion that zoning itself was a taking was resolved in the Euclid case which follows.

Because the effect of a zoning ordinance is to limit private rights in the interest of public welfare, the exercise of municipal zoning power must be carefully guarded and is permitted only when circumstances and conditions disclose the need for it. Municipal power to limit the rights of landowners cannot be imposed unless it bears a substantial relationship to the public health, safety, morals, or general welfare.

Euclid v. Ambler Realty Co., 272 U.S. 365 (U.S. 1926)

Facts of the case.

The Village of Euclid is an Ohio municipal corporation. It adjoins and is a suburb of the City of Cleveland. Its estimated population is between 5,000 and

10,000, and its area from twelve to fourteen square miles, the greater part of which is farm land or unimproved acreage.

Ambler Realty Co. (Ambler) is the owner of a tract of land containing sixty-eight acres, situated in the westerly end of the village.

On November 13, 1922, an ordinance was adopted by the Village Council, establishing a comprehensive zoning plan for regulating and restricting the location of trades, industries, apartment houses, two-family houses, single family houses, the lot area to be built upon, the size and height of buildings, etc. The ordinance would limit Ambler's use of the land to single-family residences.

The ordinance is assailed on the grounds that it violates the federal Constitution in that it deprives Ambler of liberty and property without due process of law and denies it the equal protection of the law. Ambler seeks an injunction restraining the enforcement of the ordinance and all attempts to impose or maintain any of the restrictions, limitations, or conditions set forth in the zoning ordinance. The court below held the ordinance to be unconstitutional and void, and enjoined its enforcement.

Ambler alleges that the tract of land in question is vacant and has been held for years for the purpose of selling and developing it for industrial uses; that for such uses it has a market value of about $10,000 per acre, but if the use be limited to residential purposes the market value is not in excess of $2,500 per acre.

OPINION

Ambler alleges that the effect of the ordinance is to greatly reduce the value of its lands and destroy its marketability. Ambler's attack is directed, not against any specific provision or provisions of the ordinance, but against the ordinance as an entirety.

Building zone laws are of modern origin. They began in this country about twenty-five years ago. Until recent years, urban life was comparatively simple; but with the great increase and concentration of population, problems have developed, and constantly are developing, which require, and will continue to require, additional restrictions in respect of the use and occupation of private lands in urban communities.

The ordinance now under review, and all similar laws and regulations, must find their justification in some aspect of the police power, asserted for the public welfare. The line, which in this field separates the legitimate from the illegitimate assumption of power, is not capable of precise delimitation. It varies with circumstances and conditions. A regulatory zoning ordinance, which would be clearly valid as applied to the great cities, might be clearly invalid as applied to rural communities. In solving doubts, much of the common law of nuisances will furnish a fairly helpful clue. Thus, the question whether the power exists to forbid the erection of a building of a particular kind or for a particular use, like the question whether a particular thing is a nuisance, is to be determined not by an abstract consideration of the building or of the thing considered apart, but by considering it in connection with the circumstances and the locality. A nuisance may be merely a right thing in the wrong place, like a pig in the parlor instead of the barnyard. However, if the validity of the legislative classification for zoning purposes be fairly debatable, the legislative judgment must be allowed to control.

The inclusion of a reasonable margin to insure effective enforcement will not put upon a law, otherwise valid, the stamp of invalidity. Such laws may also find their justification in the fact that, in some fields, the bad fades into the good by such insensible degrees that the two are not capable of being readily distinguished and separated in terms of legislation. In the light of these considerations, we are not prepared to say that the end in view was not sufficient to justify the general rule of the ordinance, although some industries of an innocent character might fall within the proscribed class. It cannot be said that the ordinance in this respect passes the bounds of reason and assumes the character of a merely arbitrary fiat.

The Village has advanced a number of reasons in support of the ordinance. If these reasons do not demonstrate wisdom or sound policy in all respects, at least the reasons are sufficiently cogent to preclude us from saying that such provisions are clearly arbitrary and unreasonable, having no substantial relation to the public health, safety, morals, or general welfare. The decree is reversed.

NOTES AND QUESTIONS

1 In retrospect, the ruling in *Euclid* seems unavoidable but, at the time, the power to zone was subject to considerable limitation and doubt. Prior to *Euclid,* a significant minority of state courts had rejected the practice of zoning as unconstitutional, particularly as it related to restrictions on use. The highest courts of Maryland, New Jersey, and Texas, among others, approved height and area restrictions but rejected zoning ordinances which imposed limitations upon the use of property. The Texas court summarized this widely held view as follows: "It is idle to talk about the lawful business of an ordinary retail store threatening the public health or endangering public safety," *Spann v. City of Dallas,* 235 S.W. 513 (Tex. 1921).

2 In *Necto v. City of Cambridge,* 277 U.S. 183 (1928), the Supreme Court made clear that the power to zone was not without limitation. In *Necto* the ordinance itself was valid but its application to a particular landowner would have rendered a portion of the owner's land nearly worthless. In holding the ordinance unconstitutional as applied, the court noted that "the power to interfere by zoning regulations is not unlimited, and . . . cannot be imposed unless it bears a substantial relation to the public health, safety, morals, or general welfare."

4 ZONING AS A TAKING

A Inverse Condemnation

We have seen that inverse condemnation is the description for a cause of action against the government to recover the lost value of property that has been taken or damaged by the government action even though no formal condemnation proceedings have been initiated. Situations in which government action physically interferes with an owner's property were considered in Chapter 22. This section considers the second type of inverse condemnation, which arises without physical interference but by virtue of a regulation that has the effect of taking an owner's property by denying the owner all reasonable use. As efforts to regulate the use of land, particularly through zoning, have become more pronounced, claims that the regulation constitutes a taking have increased dramatically. Although courts have had much to say on the subject in recent years, the idea of the regulatory taking was first formulated by Justice Holmes in the famous case of *Pennsylvania Coal v. Mahon,* 260 U.S. 393 (1922). This formulation continues to be the basis upon which the issue of the regulatory taking is decided.

> Government hardly could go on if to some extent values incident to property could not be diminished without paying for every such change in the general law. As long recognized, some values are enjoyed under an implied limitation and must yield to the police power. But obviously the implied limitation must have its limits, or the contract and due process clauses are gone. One fact for consideration in determining such limits is the extent of the dimunition. When it reaches a certain magnitude, in most if not in all cases there must be an exercise of eminent domain and compensation to sustain the act. So the question depends upon the particular facts. The greatest weight is given to the judgment of the legislature, but it always is open to interested parties to contend that the legislature has gone beyond its constitutional power. . . .
>
> The general rule, at least, is that while property may be regulated to a certain extent, if regulation goes too far it will be recognized as a taking. . . . We are in danger of forgetting that a strong public desire to improve the public condition is not enough to warrant achieving the desire by a shorter cut than the constitutional way of paying for the change. As we have already said, this is a question of degree.

As Justice Holmes indicates, whether a taking has occurred is "a question of degree." In reviewing the materials that follow try to determine if this standard has become more precise with the passage of time.

The extent of the government's authority to regulate the use of land through zoning is at least as broad as the power to condemn. However, in between a regulation and a condemnation is an area that has proved particularly difficult to isolate or define. The so-called regulatory taking involves a situation where legislation, usually in the form of a limitation upon use, goes so far as to constitute a taking. Efforts to define the point at which an effort to regulate will constitute inverse condemnation have been the subject of considerable confusion. The Supreme Court itself has noted the lack of definition and the absence of precise standards for determining when a regulation "goes too far." Justice Blackman has said that "[T]he attempt to determine when regulation goes too far so that it becomes . . . a 'taking' has been called the lawyer's equivalent of the physicist's hunt for the quark." *Williamson County v. Hamilton Bank,* 473 U.S. 172 (1985). Other Supreme Court opinions have acknowledged the problem: "This court, quite simply, has been unable to develop any 'set formula' for determining when 'justice and fairness' require that economic injuries caused by public action be compensated by government rather than remain disproportionately concentrated on a few persons," *Penn Central City v. New York,* 437 U.S. 104 (1978).

"Rather, it has examined the 'taking' question by engaging in case by case factual inquiries that have identified several factors—such as the economic impact of the regulation, its interference with reasonable investment backed expectations and the character of the governmental action—that have particular significance,'' *Kaiser Aetna v. U.S.,* 444 U.S. 164 (1979).

The state courts that have addressed the issue have tended to impose a stringent standard upon an owner claiming inverse condemnation. For instance, the California courts have consistently held that "a zoning ordinance may be unconstitutional and subject to invalidation only when its effect is to deprive the landowner of substantially all reasonable use of the property,'' *Agins v. City of Tiburon,* 198 P. 2d 29 (Cal. 1980). New York's highest court has said that the test to determine a regulatory taking is whether the regulation "renders the property affected by it so unsuitable for any purpose for which it is reasonably adapted as effectively to destroy its economic value,'' *Northern Westchester Associates v. Town of Bedford,* 453 W.E. 2d 809 (N.Y. 1983). In other words, a reduction in the value of the property, even if substantial, will not be considered a taking so long as there is some remaining economic value to the property. In *Pace Resources v. Schrewsbury Township,* 808 F. 2d 1023 (3rd Cir. 1987), the owner sought damages for inverse condemnation when the municipality changed the zoning of the property from industrial to agricultural. Although the owner claimed that the property declined in value from $495,000 to $52,000, the court did not feel that these figures necessarily established that a taking had occurred.

In *Landmark Land Co. v. City of Denver,* 728 P. 2d 1281 (Colo. 1986), the owner intended to build a twenty-one story office building but had not submitted building plans. In the meantime, the City of Denver passed an ordinance protecting mountain views. The owner claimed the ordinance was a taking because it would limit the height of any structure that could be built on the property. The court quickly dispensed with the owner's claim noting that since some form of development was still allowed that "all reasonable uses" had not been precluded by the ordinance.

In the case of *Nolan v. California Coastal Commission,* 97 L. ed. 2 677 (U.S. 1987), the U.S. Supreme Court made its most recent effort to address the regulatory taking issue. In *Nolan,* the California Coastal Commission granted a permit to the Nolans to replace a small bungalow on their beachfront lot with a larger house but only upon the condition that they allow the public an easement to pass across their beach, which was located between two public beaches. The California courts held that imposition of the condition did not violate the Takings Clause of the Fifth Amendment. The Supreme Court reversed noting that

> the imposition of the access-easement condition cannot be treated as an exercise of land-use regulation power since the condition does not serve a public purpose related to the permit requirement. The Commission's justification for the access requirement . . . is that it is part of a comprehensive program to provide beach access arising from prior coastal permit decisions. . . . But this is simply an expression of the belief that the public interest will be served by a continuous strip of publicly assessable beach. Although the State is free to advance its "comprehensive program" by exercising its eminent domain power and paying for access easements, it cannot compel coastal residents alone to contribute to the realization of that goal.

The court in *Nolan* did not specify any particular test to determine when a regulation will constitute a taking. Instead, the *Nolan* court based its decision on the police power, finding there was no rational basis to support the Coastal Commission's action.

B   Remedies for Inverse Condemnation

In addition to the considerable problem of defining when a regulatory taking occurs, there has been substantial doubt concerning the remedies available to an owner whose property has been the subject of a regulatory taking. As the following case indicates, the Supreme Court has finally taken clear steps to resolve this issue.

First England Evangelical Lutheran Church v. Los Angeles, 96 L. ed 2d, 250 (U.S. 1987)

In this case the California Court of Appeal held that a landowner who claims that his property has been "taken" by a land-use regulation may not recover damages for the time before it is determined that the regulation constitutes a "taking" of his property. We disagree, and conclude that in these circumstances the Fifth and Fourteenth Amendments to the United States Constitution would require compensation for that period.

Facts of the case.

The plaintiff church owned property on which it operated a recreation facility. The property was subject to flooding during 1978 which destroyed the buildings on the property. In response to the flooding, the County of Los Angeles passed an ordinance that provided that nothing shall be built in the area in which the church property was located. The church filed a complaint alleging inverse condemnation and seeking damages from the City of Los Angeles. The trial court dismissed the claim for damages relying on the California Supreme Court decision in *Agins v. Tiburon*.

In *Agins v. Tiburon,* the Supreme Court of California decided that a landowner may not maintain an inverse condemnation suit in the courts of that State based upon a "regulatory" taking. In the court's view, maintenance of such a suit would allow a landowner to force the legislature to exercise its power of eminent domain. Under this decision, then, compensation is not required until the challenged regulation or ordinance has been held excessive in an action and the government nevertheless decides to continue the regulation in effect. Based on this decision, the trial court explained that "a careful re-reading of the Agins case persuades the Court that when an ordinance even a nonzoning ordinance, deprives a person of the total use of his land, his sole remedy is to challenge the ordinance so as to have it invalidated." Because the appellant alleged a regulatory taking and sought only damages, the allegation that the ordinance denied all use of the property was deemed irrelevant.

The California Court of Appeal found itself obligated to follow Agins "because the United States Supreme Court has not yet ruled on the question of whether a state may constitutionally limit the remedy for a taking to nonmonetary relief. . . ." The Supreme Court of California denied review.

OPINION

Appellant asks us to hold that the Supreme Court of California erred in *Agins v. Tiburon* in determining that the Fifth Amendment does not require compensation as a remedy for "temporary" regulatory takings—those regulatory takings which are ultimately invalidated by the courts. Four times this decade, we have considered similar claims and have found ourselves for one reason or another unable to consider the merits of the *Agins* rule. For the reasons explained below, however, we find the constitutional claim properly presented in this case, and hold that on these facts the California courts have decided the compensation questions inconsistently with the requirements of the Fifth Amendment.

The Fifth Amendment provides in relevant part that "private property [shall not] be taken for public use, without just compensation." As its language indicates, and as the Court has frequently noted, this provision does not prohibit the taking of private property, but instead places a condition on the exercise of that power. This basic understanding of the Amendment makes clear that it is designed not to limit the governmental interference with property rights per se, but rather to secure compensation in the event of otherwise proper interferences amounting to a taking. Thus, government action that works a taking of property rights necessarily implicates the "constitutional obligation to pay just compensation."

We have recognized that a landowner is entitled to bring an action in inverse condemnation as a result of the self-executing character of the constitutional provision with respect to compensation.

It has also been established doctrine, at least since Justice Holmes' opinion in *Pennsylvania Coal Co. v. Mahon,* 260 U.S. 393, 43 S.Ct. 158, 67 L.Ed. 322 (1922), that "[t]he general rule at least is, that while property may be regulated to a certain extent, if regulation goes too far it will be recognized as a taking." While the typical taking occurs when the government acts to condemn property in the exercise of its power of eminent domain, the entire doctrine of inverse condemnation is predicated on the proposition that a taking may occur without such formal proceedings. In *Pumpelly v. Green Bay Co.,* (1872), construing a provision in the Wisconsin Constitution identical to the Just Compensation Clause, this Court said:

> It would be a very curious and unsatisfactory result if . . . it shall be held that if the government refrains from the absolute conversion of real property to the uses of the public it can destroy its value entirely, can inflict irreparable and permanent injury to any extent, can, in effect, subject it to total destruction without making any compensation, because, in the narrowest sense of that word, it is not taken for the public use.

Later cases have unhesitatingly applied this principle.

While the Supreme Court of California may not have actually disavowed this general rule in *Agins,* we believe that it has truncated the rule by disallowing damages that occurred prior to the ultimate invalidation of the challenged regulation. The Supreme Court of California justified its conclusion at length in the *Agins* opinion, concluding that:

> In combination, the need for preserving a degree of freedom in the land-use planning function, and the inhibiting financial force which inheres in the inverse condemnation remedy, persuade us that on balance an action to invalidate the regulation rather than inverse condemnation is the appropriate relief under the circumstances.

We, of course, are not unmindful of these considerations, but they must be evaluated in the light of the command of the Just Compensation Clause of the Fifth Amendment. Invalidation of the ordinance after a period of time, though converting the taking into a "temporary" one, is not a sufficient remedy to meet the demands of the Just Compensation Clause.

Nothing we say today is intended to abrogate the principle that the decision to exercise the power of eminent domain is a legislative function, for Congress and Congress alone to determine. Once a court determines that a taking has occurred, the government retains the whole range of options already available— amendment of the regulation, withdrawal of the invalidated regulation, or exercise of eminent domain. Thus we do not permit a court, at the behest of a private person, to require the Government to exercise the power of eminent domain. We merely hold that where the government's activities have already worked a taking of all use of property, no subsequent action by the government can relieve it of the duty to provide compensation for the period during which the taking was effective.

We realize that our present holding will undoubtedly lessen to some extent the freedom and flexibility of land-use planners and governing bodies of municipal corporations when enacting land-use regulations. But such consequences necessarily flow from any decision upholding a claim of constitutional rights; many of the provisions of the Constitution are designed to limit the flexibility and freedom of governmental authorities and the Just Compensation Clause of the Fifth Amendment is one of them. As Justice Holmes aptly noted more than fifty years ago, "a strong public desire to improve the public condition is not enough to warrant achieving the desire by a shorter cut than the constitutional way of paying for the change."

Here we must assume that the Los Angeles County ordinances have denied appellant all use of his property for a considerable period of years, and we hold that invalidation of the ordinance without payment of fair value for the use of the property during this period of time would be a constitutionally insufficient remedy. The judgment of the California Court of Appeals is therefore reversed, and the case is remanded for further proceedings not inconsistent with this opinion.

NOTES AND QUESTIONS

      1 Did the court hold that the Los Angeles ordinance was a taking? Do you think a taking occurred? Assuming that a taking had occurred and that the county rescinded the regulation, how would damages be measured?

      2 The First English Church case was remanded to the California trial court, which concluded that no taking had occurred because the ordinance in question "substantially advanced a preeminent state interest in public safety and did not deny the church all use of its land." This ruling was upheld by the California Court of Appeal. (See 210 Cal. App 3d 1353, 1989.)

5 OBJECTIVES OF ZONING

      Section 3 of the Standard State Zoning Enabling Act sets forth the general purpose under which most zoning ordinances operate. And, as we have seen, zoning ordinances, to be valid, must tend to further public health, safety, morals, or general welfare. This is a flexible limitation, which can expand or contract to meet the new and different conditions constantly coming into the field of operation.

      Zoning ordinances have routinely been upheld which regulate the minimum lot size, the minimum or maximum floor area and front, rear and side yard requirements, and which establish classifications that delineate areas in which only certain kinds of uses will be permitted.

A Aesthetics

      Aesthetic zoning, or zoning for the purpose of maintaining community appearance, first developed from community opposition to billboards. Early cases have tended to invalidate aesthetic zoning as being outside the scope of the police power. Most courts now recognize that aesthetic zoning is a valid aspect of zoning and will sustain such ordinances when they are part of a regulation that also satisfies the more traditional police power objectives of health, safety, and public welfare.

      A few states, including California, Florida, New Jersey, and New York permit aesthetics alone to support the application of a zoning law. The Florida court for instance in the *City of Coral Gables v. Wood*, 305 S. 2d 261 (Fla. 1974), sustained the validity of an ordinance that limited the location and use of camper type vehicles, noting that the ordinance was intended to prevent unsightly appearance and the diminution of property values caused by the parking or storing of such vehicles in residential areas.

B Historic Preservation

      An important aspect of aesthetic zoning is the quickly growing area of zoning law devoted to historic preservation. The use of the police power to require a property owner to maintain a historic building can have significant economic consequences upon the owner with an arguably marginal benefit to society, particularly when measured by the constitutional standard of public health, safety, and general welfare. In response to this, courts and particularly legislatures, intent upon preserving buildings or districts considered to be of historic significance, have developed various forms of compensation which are intended to minimize the taking problems inherent in such regulations. One of the most elaborate of such schemes is the New York Landmarks Preservation Law, which gave rise to one of the most significant of all zoning cases.

Penn Central Transportation Co. v. City of New York, 438 U.S. 104 (U.S. 1978)

The question presented is whether a city may, as part of a comprehensive program to preserve historic landmarks and historic districts, place restrictions on the development of individual historic landmarks—in addition to those imposed by applicable zoning ordinances—without effecting a "taking" requiring the payment of "just compensation." Specifically, we must decide whether the application of New York City's Landmarks Preservation Law to the parcel of land occupied by Grand Central Terminal has "taken" its owners' property in violation of the Fifth and Fourteenth Amendments.

Facts of the case.

Over the past fifty years, all fifty States and over five hundred municipalities have enacted laws to encourage or require the preservation of buildings and areas with historic or aesthetic importances. These nationwide legislative efforts have been precipitated by two concerns. The first is recognition that, in recent years, large numbers of historic structures, landmarks, and areas have been destroyed without adequate consideration of either the values represented therein or the possibility of preserving the destroyed properties for use in economically productive ways. The second is a widely shared belief that structures with special historic, cultural, or architectural significance enhance the quality of life for all. Not only do these buildings and their workmanship represent the lessons of the past and embody precious features of our heritage, but they also serve as examples of quality for today.

New York City, responding to similar concerns and acting pursuant to a New York State enabling Act, adopted its Landmarks Preservation Law in 1965. The city acted from the conviction that "the standing of [New York City] as a worldwide tourist center and world capital of business, culture, and government" would be threatened if legislation were not enacted to protect historic landmarks and neighborhoods from precipitated decisions to destroy or fundamentally alter their character." The city believed that comprehensive measures to safeguard desirable features of the existing urban fabric would benefit its citizens in a variety of ways: for instance, by fostering "civic pride in the beauty and noble accomplishments of the past"; protecting and enhancing "the city's attractions to tourists and visitors"; "supporting and stimulating business and industry";

"strengthening the economy of the city"; and promoting "the use of historic districts, landmarks, interior landmarks, and scenic landmarks for the education, pleasure, and welfare of the people of the city."

The operation of the law can be briefly summarized. The primary responsibility for administering the law is vested in the Landmarks Preservation Commission. If the Commission determines, after giving all interested parties an opportunity to be heard, that a building or area satisfies the ordinance's criteria, it will designate a building to be a "landmark," or will designate an area to be an "historic district."

Final designation as a landmark results in restrictions upon the property owner's options concerning use of the landmark site. First, the law imposes a duty upon the owner to keep the exterior features of the building "in good repair" to assure that the law's objectives not be defeated by the landmark's falling into a state of irremediable disrepair. Second, the Commission must approve in advance any proposal to alter the exterior architectural features of the landmark or to construct any exterior improvement on the landmark site, thus ensuring that decisions concerning construction on the landmark site are made with due consideration of both the public interest in the maintenance of the structure and the landowner's interest in the use of the property.

Although designation of a landmark and landmark site restricts the owner's control over the parcel, designation also enhances the economic position of the landmark owner in one significant respect. Under New York City's zoning laws, owners of real property who have not developed their property to the full extent permitted by the applicable zoning laws are allowed to transfer development rights to contiguous parcels on the same city block.

This case involves the application of New York City's Landmarks Preservation Law to Grand Central Terminal (Terminal). The Terminal, which is owned by the Penn Central Transportation Co. and its affiliates (Penn Central), is one of New York City's most famous buildings. Opened in 1913, it is regarded not only as providing an ingenious engineering solution to the problems presented by urban railroad stations, but also as a magnificent example of the French beaux-arts style.

The Terminal is located in midtown Manhattan. Its south facade faces 42nd Street at that street's intersection with Park Avenue. At street level, the Terminal is bounded on the west by Vanderbilt Avenue, on the east by the Commodore Hotel, and on the north by the Pan-American Building. Although a twenty-story office tower, to have been located above the Terminal, was part of the original design, the planned tower was never constructed. The Terminal itself is an eight-story structure which Penn Central uses as a railroad station and in which it rents space not needed for railroad purposes to a variety of commercial interests.

On January 22, 1968, Penn Central, to increase its income, entered into a renewable fifty-year lease and sublease agreement with UGP Properties, Inc. (UGP), a wholly owned subsidiary of Union General Properties, Ltd., a United Kingdom corporation. Under the terms of the agreement, UGP was to construct a multistory office building above the Terminal. UGP promised to pay Penn Central $1 million annually during construction and at least $3 million annually thereafter. The rentals would be offset partly by a loss of some $700,000 to $1 million in net rentals presently received from concessionaires displaced by the new building.

UGP and Penn Central then applied to the Commission for permission to construct an office building atop the Terminal. Two separate plans, both apparently satisfying the terms of the applicable zoning ordinance, were submitted to the Commission for approval. After four days of hearings at which over eighty witnesses testified, the Commission denied this application as to both proposals.

The Commission's reasons for rejecting certificates respecting Breuer II Revised are summarized in the following statement:

> [We have] no fixed rule against making additions to designated buildings—it all depends on how they are done . . . But to balance a fifty-five story office tower above a flamboyant Beaux-Arts facade seems nothing more than an aesthetic joke. Quite simply, the tower would overwhelm the Terminal by its sheer mass. The "addition" would be four times as high as the existing structure and would reduce the Landmark itself to the status of a curiosity.
>
> Landmarks cannot be divorced from their settings—particularly when the setting is a dramatic and integral part of the original concept. The Terminal, in its setting, is a great example of urban design. Such examples are not so plentiful in New York City that we can afford to lose any of the few we have. And we must preserve them in a meaningful way—with alterations and additions of such character, scale, material, and mass as will protect, enhance, and perpetuate the original design rather than overwhelm it.

Penn Central filed suit in New York Supreme Court, Trial Term, claiming that the application of the Landmarks Preservation Law had "taken" their property without just compensation in violation of the Fifth and Fourteenth Amendments and arbitrarily deprived them of their property without due process of law. The trial court enjoined the city from using the Landmarks Law to impede any lawful construction on the terminal site. The Appellate Division of the New York Supreme Court reversed and the New York Court of Appeals (the state's highest court) affirmed the Appellate Division.

Penn Central appealed to this court. We affirm.

OPINION

The issues presented by Penn Central are whether the restrictions imposed by New York City's law upon appellants' exploitation of the Terminal site effect a "taking" of appellant's property for a public use within the meaning of the Fifth Amendment and, if so, whether the transferable development rights afford Penn Central "just compensation" within the meaning of the Fifth Amendment.

Before considering Penn Central's specific contentions, it will be useful to review the factors that have shaped the jurisprudence of the Fifth Amendment injunction that "nor shall private property be taken for public use, without just compensation."

The question of what constitutes a "taking" for purposes of the Fifth Amendment has proved to be a problem of considerable difficulty. While this Court has recognized that the Fifth Amendment's guarantee is designed to bar Government from forcing some people alone to bear public burdens which, in all fairness and justice, should be borne by the public as a whole, this Court, quite simply, has been unable to develop any "set formula" for determining when "justice and fairness" require that economic injuries caused by public action be compensated by the government, rather than remain disproportionately concentrated on a few persons. Indeed, we have frequently observed that whether a particular restriction will be rendered invalid by the government's failure to pay for any losses proximately caused by it depends largely upon the particular circumstances of that case.

In engaging in these essentially ad hoc, factual inquiries, the Court's decisions have identified several factors that have particular significance. The economic impact of the regulation on the claimant and, particularly, the extent to which the regulation has interfered with distinct investment-backed expectations are, of course, relevant considerations. So, too, is the character of the governmental action. A "taking" may more readily be found when the interference with property can be characterized as a physical invasion by government than when interference arises from some public program adjusting the benefits and burdens of economic life to promote the common good.

"Government hardly could go on if to some extent values incident to property could not be diminished without paying for every such change in the general law," (*Pennsylvania Coal Co. v. Mahon*), and this Court has accordingly recognized, in a wide variety of contexts, that government may execute laws or programs that adversely affect recognized economic values.

The important question, in this case, is whether the interference with Penn Central's property is of such a magnitude that "there must be an exercise of eminent domain and compensation to sustain [it]." That inquiry may be narrowed to the question of the severity of the impact of the law on appellants' parcel, and its resolution in turn requires a careful assessment of the impact of the regulation on the Terminal site.

The New York City law does not interfere in any way with the present uses of the terminal. Its designation as a landmark not only permits but contemplates that appellants may continue to use the property precisely as it has been used for the past sixty-five years: as a railroad terminal containing office space and concessions. So the law does not interfere with what must be regarded as Penn Central's primary expectation concerning the use of the parcel. More importantly, we must regard the New York City law as permitting Penn Central not only to profit from the Terminal but also to obtain a "reasonable return" on its investment.

Appellants exaggerate the effect of the law on their ability to make use of the air rights above the Terminal in two respects. First, it simply cannot be maintained, on this record, that appellants have been prohibited from occupying any portion of the airspace above the Terminal. While the Commission's actions in denying applications to construct an office building in excess of fifty stories above the Terminal may indicate that it will refuse to approve any comparably sized structure, nothing the Commission has said or done suggests an intention to prohibit any construction above the Terminal. The Commission's report emphasized that whether any construction would be allowed depended upon whether the proposed addition "would harmonize in scale, material, and character with [the Terminal]." Since appellants have not sought approval for the construction of a smaller structure, we do not know that appellants will be denied any use of any portion of the airspace above the Terminal.

On this record, we conclude that the application of New York City's Landmark Law has not effected a "taking" of appellants' property. The restrictions imposed are substantially related to the promotion of the general welfare and not only permit reasonable beneficial use of the landmark site but also afford appellants opportunities further to enhance not only the Terminal site property but also other properties.

Affirmed.

NOTES AND QUESTIONS

1 Penn Central is an important decision both because it validates historic preservation efforts and because it is the most detailed statement by the Supreme Court on the question of a regulatory taking. Do you agree that no taking occurred in this case? Would one occur if instead of a fifty-story building, Penn Central unsuccessfully sought to add ten stories to the terminal? Could the Landmarks Commission prevent Penn Central from altering the terminal if the alteration is necessary to continue operating passenger trains?

2 In a footnote to the opinion the court made the following observation:

The consensus is that widespread public ownership of historic properties in urban settings is neither feasible nor wise. Public ownership reduces the tax base, burdens the public budget with costs of acquisitions and maintenance, and results in the preservation of public buildings as museums and similar facilities, rather than as economically productive features of the urban scene.

Are these valid considerations on the issue of a taking?

3 In *Maher v. City of New Orleans,* 516 F. 2d 1051 (5th Cir. 1975), plaintiff was denied permission to demolish a Victorian cottage in the French Quarter of New Orleans based upon an ordinance which required the preservation of buildings having "architectural and historical value." The court upheld the ordinance as an appropriate exercise of the police power.

Nor need the values advanced be solely economic or directed at health and safety in their narrowest senses. The police power inhering in the lawmaker is more generous, comprehending more subtle and ephemeral societal interests. The values that the police power represents are spiritual as well as physical, aesthetic as well as monetary. It is within the domain of the legislature to determine that the community should be beautiful as well as healthy, spacious as well as clean, well-balanced as well as carefully patrolled.

How ephemeral can social interests be and still fall within the public purpose limitation of the police power? Would a limitation which specified the kinds of vegetation that could be planted be upheld?

6 ZONING CLASSIFICATIONS

By its very nature, zoning involves the division of a community into districts and within these districts regulating both the nature of the land uses that may be permitted and the physical dimensions of these uses. After the Supreme Court approved zoning classifications in the case of *Euclid v. Amber Realty,* most municipalities adopted what came to be known as ''Euclidian zoning'' which involved dividing the community into three basic uses: residential, commercial, and industrial. Typical ordinances further subdivide these classifications. For instance, a residential-use zone could include subclassification of single-family, two-family, multiple-dwelling, apartment-house uses, and so forth.

The municipality may also decide whether permissible uses are to be cumulative or exclusive. Under a cumulative zoning arrangement, less intensive uses are permitted in more intensive use districts. For instance, residences may be permitted in a commercial or industrial zone and single-family dwellings may be permitted in an area zoned for multi-family dwellings. The reverse of this is not true under cumulative zoning. For instance, an industrial use, being more intensive, would not be permitted in a commercial zone or residential zone.

Although cumulative zoning was originally the general rule, the modern tendency provides for exclusive use of the zoning classifications. In other words, residential uses are limited to residentially zoned districts and are not permitted in any other zone. Modern zoning plans tend to be considerably more detailed than the early models. For example, the city of Berkeley, California, with a population of about 100,000, has the following zoning districts within its city limits:

DISTRICTS

ES-R	ENVIRONMENTAL SAFETY-RESIDENTIAL	SI	SPECIAL INDUSTRIAL
R-1	SINGLE FAMILY RESIDENTIAL	M	MANUFACTURING
R-1A	LIMITED TWO-FAMILY RESIDENTIAL	U	UNCLASSIFIED
R-2	RESTRICTED TWO-FAMILY RESIDENTIAL	-H	COMBINED HILLSIDE
R-2A	RESTRICTED MULTIPLE-FAMILY RESIDENTIAL	-PS	COMBINED PLANNED SHOPPING
R-3	MULTIPLE-FAMILY RESIDENTIAL	C-1A	COMMUNITY COMMERCIAL
R-4	MULTIPLE-FAMILY RESIDENTIAL	C-1B	RETAIL COMMERCIAL
R-5	HIGH DENSITY RESIDENTIAL	C-1C	NEIGHBORHOOD COMMERCIAL
C-1	GENERAL COMMERCIAL	C-1A(NS)	NORTH SHATTUCK COMMERCIAL
C-2	CENTRAL COMMERCIAL	C-1B(E)	ELMWOOD COMMERCIAL
C-3	COMMERCIAL(NOT IN USE)	C-1(SA)	SOUTH AREA COMMERCIAL

In addition to specifying the kinds of uses permissible within a given district, zoning regulations typically regulate the physical characteristics of structures built within each zone. The right to regulate the size of a structure in a zone has long been recognized as a legitimate goal of zoning laws and limitations concerning the height, bulk, or density of a building are typically upheld as appropriate exercise of the police power.

In *Pierro v. Baxendale,* 118 A. 2d 401 (N.J. 1955), the Supreme Court of New Jersey considered a challenge to a zoning classification of the City of Palisades Park which permitted "boarding and rooming houses" but not hotels or motels. Boarding and rooming houses were defined in the ordinance as "any dwelling in which more than six persons not related to the owner . . . are lodged and boarded for compensation."

Plaintiff owned property within this zone and sought to build a twenty-seven unit motel. The request for a permit was denied and plaintiff filed an action to compel issuance of the permit.

The trial judge ruled in favor of the plaintiff, expressing the view that "a motel is a rooming house" and that there is no "fair and reasonable distinction between a motel as a rooming house and some other type of rooming house" and held that the plaintiff was entitled to a building permit for the erection of a motel provided its manner of construction was in conformity with the borough's building requirements.

The New Jersey Supreme Court reversed.

> Plaintiffs deny the borough's right to permit boarding and rooming houses and at the same time exclude motels. If this classification by the borough has no reasonable basis then it must fall as the plaintiffs contend; if, on the other hand, it has a reasonable basis then it may be permitted to stand and serve to exclude the operation of a motel in the zone.
>
> Legislative bodies may make such classifications as they deem necessary and as long as their classifications are based upon reasonable grounds "so as not to be arbitrary or capricious" they will not be upset by the courts.
>
> We recently upheld a zoning ordinance which permitted public and parochial elementary and high schools, but prohibited colleges and other schools of higher learning, in residential areas. In the course of his opinion, Justice Burling set forth grounds for differentiating schools for the education of community children from institutions of higher learning and quoted approvingly from the *Euclid* case where Justice Sutherland pointedly remarked that "if the validity of the legislative classification for zoning purposes be fairly debatable, the legislative judgment must be allowed to control."
>
> In another case, we have held that the business of selling used cars may properly be distinguished from the selling of new cars. It seems clear to us that motels may without difficulty be differentiated from boarding and rooming houses. Motels are business institutions which cater to members of the general public and by and large are obligated to serve them indiscriminately. On the other hand, boarding and rooming houses may select guests with care and are admittedly "less public in character." They are located in buildings which have the outward appearances of private dwelling houses and their commercial features and incidents are insignificant when compared to those of motels.
>
> The officials of Palisades Park viewed boarding and rooming houses as being consistent with residential areas and motels as being inconsistent therewith; it seems clear to us that their views may not be said to be wholly without reasonable basis and that the lower court's

conclusion to the contrary was wrong. It must always be remembered that the duty of selecting particular uses which are congruous in residential zones was vested by the Legislature in the municipal officials rather than in the courts. Once the selections were made and embodied in the comprehensive zoning ordinance they became presumptively valid and are not to be nullified except upon an affirmative showing that the action taken by the municipal officials was unreasonable, arbitrary, or capricious.

In other words, reasonable restrictions designed to preserve the character of a community and maintain its property values are within the proper objectives of zoning. Justice Douglas has recently stated the broad parameters of the police power as follows:

> The concept of the public welfare is broad and inclusive. The values it represents are spiritual as well as physical, aesthetic as well as monetary. In the present case, the Congress and its authorized agencies have made determinations that take into account a wide variety of values. It is not for us to reappraise them. If those who govern the District of Columbia decide that the Nation's capital should be beautiful as well as sanitary, there is nothing in the Fifth Amendment that stands in the way. (*Berman v. Parker*)

In our own State the general welfare concept has received similarly broad definition. Reversed.

NOTES AND QUESTIONS

1 The *Pierro* case illustrates a fairly typical zoning classification and presents a not uncommon problem in determining which uses are included or excluded from the zone.

2 In *J.D. Construction v. Township of Freehold,* 290 A. 2d 452 (N.J. 1972), the New Jersey Supreme Court faced a challenge to a portion of a zoning ordinance which, in addition to creating various residential use zones, provided as follows:

> The total number of individual apartment units in all apartment projects within the Township of Freehold shall not exceed fifteen (15) percent of the total number of single-family residences situated within the limits of the Township of Freehold.

The court then reviewed the judicial standards commonly employed in reviewing challenges to zoning ordinances:

> Zoning ordinances must be given a reasonable construction and application. They are to be liberally construed in favor of the municipality. Zoning powers, like all police power, must be reasonably exercised. A zoning regulation must not be unreasonable, arbitrary, or capricious. The means selected must have a real and substantial relation to the object sought to be attained. The regulation must be reasonably calculated to meet the evil and not exceed the public need or substantially affect uses which do not have the offensive character of those which caused the problem sought to be ameliorated.
>
> The party attacking the validity of a zoning ordinance has a heavy burden of affirmatively showing it bears no reasonable relationship to public health, morals, safety, or welfare. Proof of unreasonableness must be beyond debate.
>
> The judicial role in reviewing a zoning ordinance is tightly circumscribed. There is

a strong presumption in favor of its validity. A court cannot pass upon the wisdom or lack of wisdom of an ordinance. It may only invalidate a zoning ordinance if the presumption in favor of its validity is overcome by a clear, affirmative showing that it is arbitrary or unreasonable.

A zoning ordinance must be clear and explicit in its terms, setting forth adequate standards to prevent arbitrary and indiscriminate interpretation and application by local officials.

The provision does not fulfill any of the purposes of the New Jersey enabling statute and fails to set forth sufficient standards to govern its application. It is invalid.

3 Do you agree with the New Jersey Court's conclusion? Is the court simply passing on the "wisdom" of the ordinance or is the court legitimately concerned that the ordinance is too vague? What is vague about the ordinance?

7 ZONING BY INITIATIVE OR REFERENDUM

Land use control through voter referendum or initiative has become increasingly popular. The *initiative* involves the introduction of a zoning proposal by the public which is then placed on the ballot to be adopted or refused by vote. A *referendum* is a public vote to approve or disapprove an action taken by a governmental body.

The initiative process is often used to limit development in areas experiencing growth. For example, in *Arnel v. Costa Mesa,* 620 P 2d 565 (Cal. 1980), the City approved development of plaintiff's project to construct 127 single-family homes and 539 apartment units on fifty acres of land. Soon after, a homeowner's association qualified an initiative, which was adopted by the electorate, that rezoned the parcel and two others for single-family dwellings only. The City then refused to issue a building permit and the developer sued. The California Supreme Court, upheld the initiative while noting that such initiatives may be challenged on the same grounds as a zoning ordinance adopted through the legislative process. In other words, an ordinance adopted by referendum still must have a reasonable relationship to public welfare and may not deprive the property owner of substantially all use of their land.

The problems raised by zoning initiatives are similar in the case of a zoning referendum. As indicated, the referendum involves approval by the electorate of action already taken by a governmental body. In many cases, the requirement of a referendum was created by initiative.

In *Eastlake v. Forest City,* 426 U.S. 668 (1976), the City of Eastlake, Ohio, had a requirement that changes in land use adopted by the City Council must also be approved by a fifty-five percent vote in a referendum. The City Council approved a zoning change to permit construction of an apartment house, but the voters rejected the change. The Ohio Supreme Court held that the referendum requirement was unconstitutional because it was a delegation of legislative authority without standards. The U.S. Supreme Court reversed the decision. The Court noted that the results of any referendum are subject to constitutional challenge if they are unreasonable or amount to a taking. In the absence of such an infirmity, a zoning referendum is valid. It is not a delegation of legislative authority but "a means for direct political participation, allowing the people the final decision, amounting to a veto power over enactments of representative bodies.'' On the other hand, some states, such as Arizona, have held that zoning through initiative or referendum is unconstitutional, because it fails to afford due process guarantees to property owners. See *Margolis v. Superior Court,* 439 P 2d 290 (AZ 1968). The New Jersey courts have barred both the initiative and referendum on zoning matters, concluding that land use decisions must be ''comprehensive'' and must not be subject to ''piecemeal'' attacks. See *Sparta v. Spillane,* 312 A 2d 154 (N.J. 1973). Finally, even states that recognize or encourage direct voter participation in land use decisions will invalidate the results of an election if it is inconsistent with a validly adopted general plan. See *de Bottari v. City Council,* 217 C.R. 790 (Cal.App. 1985).

8 ADMINISTRATION OF THE ZONING PLAN

For the most part, the zoning plan is managed and implemented by an administrative agency, often referred to as the zoning commission or planning board. Because the validity of a zoning scheme may depend upon its ability to deal with peculiar situations, a degree of flexibility is needed to implement the zoning plan as it relates to particular parcels within a municipality. The three principal devices used by the zoning commission to accomplish a desired flexibility are the nonconforming use, the variance, and the conditional use.

A The Nonconforming Use

The term nonconforming use refers to any activity or structure that violates a valid zoning ordinance but which was in legal existence before enactment of the ordinance. In other words, a nonconforming use was a lawful use as of the effective date of the zoning ordinance that is permitted to exist, subject to various restrictions, after the enactment of the ordinance. A simple example is a gas station operating in an area recently zoned for residential use only. A new gas station would not be permitted to locate within the zone but an existing one will be permitted to remain. Although constitutional requirements protect certain nonconforming uses from the retroactive effect of a zoning enactment, such uses are not favored by the law. The policy and spirit of zoning laws encourages the gradual elimination of nonconforming uses and tends to hold them within strict limits.

> A nonconforming use is a lawful use existing on the effective date of the zoning restriction and continuing since that time in nonconformance to the ordinance. A provision permitting the continuance of a nonconforming use is ordinarily included in zoning ordinances because of the hardship and doubtful constitutionality of compelling the immediate discontinuance of nonconforming uses. It is generally held that a zoning ordinance may not operate to immediately suppress or remove from a particular district an otherwise lawful business or use already established.
>
> *City of Los Angeles v. Gage,* 274 P. 2d 34 (Cal. 1954)

In the leading case of *Jones v. City of Los Angeles,* 295 P. 14 (Cal. 1930), the California Supreme Court considered a zoning ordinance that sought to prohibit the existence of hospitals for the treatment of nervous disorders. The ordinance was ret-roactive in effect and sought to impose penalties upon hospitals in existence when the ordinance was enacted. Faced with a challenge by a hospital covered by the ordinance the California Supreme Court made the following observation:

> The ordinance in question, in so far as it prohibits the establishment of hospitals for the treatment of nervous diseases in certain districts in the city of Los Angeles, and permits their establishment in other specified district, is valid. The businesses so restricted are proper subjects of such regulation, and hence the ordinance does not result in a denial of due process. This much is clear, we feel, with respect to the establishment of new businesses of this character in the prohibited districts. But does the same result necessarily follow with regard to existing businesses in these districts? In other words, does the broad view of the police power, which justifies the taking away of the right to engage in such businesses in certain territory, also justify the destruction of existing businesses? We do not think it does.

> This case involves a situation materially different from that presented in the usual zoning case. The exercise of power in this instance is, on the whole, far more drastic than in those in which a mere right to engage in a particular business is restricted. We are asked to uphold a municipal ordinance which destroys valuable businesses, built up over a period of years. If we do so on the ground that this is a proper exercise of the police power in the enactment of zoning legislation, then it follows that the same thing may be done to apartment houses, flats, or stores. The establishment of many lawful and not dangerous businesses in a city would then become an extremely hazardous undertaking. At any time, in pursuance of a reasonable plan for its future development, the city could prohibit the continuance of the businesses, and make property valueless, which was previously constructed and devoted to a useful purpose. It may well be that in the course of years one of the outlying permitted districts in the present scheme will become residential in character, and will, by another ordinance, be placed in the prohibited area. If the plaintiffs, at great expense, reestablish themselves in that district, they might be pursued and again eradicated. All this is to be justified under the police power as a proper taking of private property for public use, without compensation. The approval of such a doctrine would be a blow to rights in private property such as this court has never before witnessed. Only a paramount and compelling public necessity could sanction so extraordinary an interference with useful business.

> We do not mean to hold that those engaged in the zoning of cities must always be faced with the impossibility of eradicating nonconforming uses. If the city desires to abolish the nonconforming use, this may be a legitimate object of the police power, but the means of its exercise must not include the destruction of the property interest without compensation. The words of Mr. Justice Holmes in *Pennsylvania Coal Co. v. Mahon*, are very much in point:

>> In general it is not plain that a man's misfortunes or necessities will justify his shifting the damages to his neighbor's shoulders. . . . We are in danger of forgetting that a strong public desire to improve the public condition is not enough to warrant achieving the desire by a shorter cut than the constitutional way of paying for the change.

> Our conclusion is that where, as here, a retroactive ordinance causes substantial injury and the prohibited business is not a nuisance, the ordinance is to that extent an unreasonable and unjustifiable exercise of police power.

> It follows that the present ordinance is valid in so far as it prohibits the further estab-lishment of businesses of this type in the restricted district; and is invalid in its retroactive application to these plaintiffs.

State enabling statutes usually confer upon local government the authority to permit nonconforming uses and define the parameters of that authority. A typical example is Ohio Revised Code, Section 713.15:

> The lawful use of any dwelling, building, or structure and of any land or premises, as existing and lawful at the time of enacting a zoning ordinance or amendment thereto, may be continued, although such use does not conform with the provisions of such ordinance or amendment, . . .

Another example is *Massachusetts Annotated Laws Chp. 40A, Section 5,* which provides:

> This ordinance shall not apply to any building or structure, or to land to the extent to which it is used at the time of adoption of the ordinance or bylaw, but it shall apply to any change of use and to any alteration of a building or structure when the same would amount to reconstruction, extension, or structural change. . . . Such an ordinance or by-law may regulate nonuse of nonconforming buildings and structures so as not to unduly prolong the life of nonconforming uses. . . .

The nonconforming use can take many forms. For instance a single-family home built three feet from the property line before an amendment to the zoning ordinance requiring a four-foot setback. Any new structures built within the zone must satisfy the four-foot requirement. The owner of the property will not be required to remove the nonconforming foot but, if the building is destroyed, the owner will not be permitted to rebuild except in conformity with the current zoning regulations.

In an example provided by a Florida case, the developer built an apartment building which had 172 off-street parking spaces. The city's zoning ordinance was later changed to require 348 parking spaces for an equivalent building. The building was a nonconforming use as to the off-street parking requirements of the ordinance.

In the examples just given, the hardship upon the owners in eliminating the nonconformity would be great when compared to the public benefit that would be obtained. However, if the nonconforming use is, for instance a foundry or other industrial operation in a district zoned for residential use only, the public benefit of eliminating the use is greater, and measures reasonably tailored to that end become more permissible.

B Restrictions on Nonconforming Uses

We have seen that nonconforming uses are entitled to constitutional protection under the takings clause and are subject to the reasonableness standards of the police power. Nevertheless, such uses are considered disfavored because they tend to undermine the integrity of the zoning plan. The policy of the law is that such uses should be discouraged. This policy is advanced in various ways.

It is generally held that a nonconforming use cannot be changed, enlarged, or altered, that it can be lost through abandonment and that efforts seeking to phase out or amortize the use over time will be upheld if they are reasonable.

Change of Use Most zoning ordinances adopt a narrow definition of the term *use* and will not permit one nonconforming use to be transferred into another. For example, a nonconforming use as a penny arcade will not be changed to allow a gift shop. See *Town of Hampton v. Brust,* 446 A. 2d 458 (N.H. 1982). In another case, the owner of a nonconforming medical office in a residential district was not permitted to lease the building for use as a law office. See *Appeal of Schneider,* 521 A. 2d 528 (Penn. 1987).

Whether zoning authorities will permit a change in use often depends upon the precise wording of the zoning ordinance. In an example previously given, the Florida court permitted conversion of an apartment building to condominiums where the building was nonconforming as to the number of off-street parking spaces. The zoning ordinance provided that "if no structural alterations are made, a nonconforming use of a building may be changed to another nonconforming use of the same or a more restricted classification." The court overruled the zoning board and permitted the conversion to condominiums noting that:

> A nonconforming use relates to the use of the property and not to the type of ownership of the property. Changing the type of ownership of real estate upon which a nonconforming use is located will not destroy a valid existing nonconforming use. This is the only significant change in the real property and improvements involved in the instant litigation. Therefore, there was no abandonment of the nonconforming use under the zoning ordinances of the City of Miami Beach.
>
> *City of Miami Beach v. Arlen King Cole Association,* 302 S. 2d 777 (Fla. 1974)

There is also a tendency to permit a change in a nonconforming use when the change tends to decrease the nonconformity. For instance, the owner of a four-family building in a single-family zone might be permitted to convert the building to a two-family residence because this would lessen the extent of the nonconforming use. Conversion to a five-family residence would probably not be permitted, because this would increase the intensity of the nonconforming use.

Enlargement of the Nonconforming Use The general rule is that a nonconforming use cannot be enlarged. For example, a nonconforming restaurant or grocery store will usually not be allowed to expand their hours of operation beyond those in existence when the ordinance was adopted. However, it is also generally held that a "natural expansion" as opposed to a physical expansion to a nonconforming business is a permissible extension of the use. Clearly this is not an easy line to draw. If the zoning ordinance so provides and if the expansion is considered detrimental to public health, safety, and welfare, then the expansion can be restricted. See *Seltzer v. Zoning Board,* 395 A.2d 1041 (Penn. 1979).

The limitations inherent in the policy regulating nonconforming use again come into play. In *Hofforth v. County of St. Clair,* (Ill. 1977), the Illinois court overturned the zoning board's refusal to allow the expansion of a nonconforming archery range:

> While it is true that the plaintiffs will expand their business to some extent when they move from the old building to the new one, there has been presented no evidence that the change will substantially increase traffic or otherwise interfere with enjoyment and use of adjoining

property. From the facts presented, it is apparent that plaintiff's nonconforming use will not be inconsistent with the objective of the applicable zoning ordinance.

Abandonment of the Nonconforming Use   Consistent with the policy against continuation of nonconforming uses, it is generally held that the right to such use may be lost if the owner fails to continue the use for a certain period of time. Most enabling legislation and zoning ordinances provide for termination of such uses by abandonment.

There are two different approaches to finding whether a nonconforming use has been abandoned. The first involves statutes specifying a time period that will cause the right to be terminated when the use is discontinued. A typical statute would provide that the nonconforming use is terminated if the use ceases for the period of one year. Most such ordinances provide a time frame of between six months and two years.

A second approach provides that the use will be terminated only when the owner "intended" to abandon it. The Rhode Island Court stated the test for finding an abandonment as follows:

> To constitute an abandonment, there must be an intention to relinquish and permanently cease to exercise a known right to devote the property to a permitted nonconforming use, evidenced by an overt act or a failure to act sufficient to support an implication of such intent. . . . In most jurisdictions the cessation or discontinuance of a use is merely evidence that is relevant to the issue of the existence of an intent. The decisive test is whether the circumstances surrounding the cessation of use are indicative of an intention to abandon the use and the vested rights therein.
>
> *A.T.&G. Inc. v. Zoning Board of Rhode Island,* 322 A. 2d 294 (1974)

Amortization of a Nonconforming Use   Because of the public policy that nonconforming uses should ultimately be terminated and because of the difficulty in eliminating such uses through attrition or by other means, many jurisdictions have set time limits during which the nonconforming use must be phased out and ended. These periods may range from a few months to several years, depending upon the impact of the nonconforming use upon the integrity of the zoning plan, and the extent of the owner's investment. Although a few states have held that all amortization provisions are unconstitutional, most jurisdictions hold that such provisions are valid if they are reasonable under the particular circumstances. One court phrased the issue in the following terms:

> We believe the critical question which must be asked is whether the public gain achieved by the exercise of the police power outweighs the private loss suffered by owners of nonconforming uses. While an owner need not be given that period of time necessary to permit him to recoup his investment entirely, the amortization period should not be so short as to result in a substantial loss of his investment.
>
> *Modjeska Sign Studios, Inc. v. Berle,* 403 N.Y.S. 2d 359 (N.Y. 1977)

In *Los Angeles v. Gage,* 274 P. 2d 34 (Cal. 1954), the California Supreme Court upheld the validity of an ordinance that required the removal, within five years, of a plumbing supply business from an area zoned residential; the court said:

There is no distinction between requiring the discontinuance of a nonconforming use within a reasonable period and provisions which deny the right to add to or extend buildings devoted to an existing nonconforming use, or which deny the right to resume a nonconforming use, or which deny the right to substitute new buildings for those devoted to an existing nonconforming use—all of which have been held to be valid exercises of the police power.

The New York Court, on similar facts, upheld the amortization schedule with the following explanation:

> When the termination provisions are reasonable in the light of the nature of the business of the property owner, the improvements erected on the land, the character of the neighborhood, and the detriment caused the property owner, we may not hold them constitutionally invalid.
> *Harrison v. Buffalo,* 152 N.E. 2d 42 (N.Y. 1958)

NOTES AND QUESTIONS

Recall the *Jones v. City of Los Angeles* case. Are amortization provisions consistent with the opinion in that case? Would the court have upheld a five-year amortization provision eliminating the hospitals?

C   The Variance

Nearly all enabling acts and zoning ordinances authorize and create an administrative board typically called the Board of Adjustment. (See the Standard Act, Paragraph 7, reprinted above.) Such boards are vested with broad administrative authority to grant relief from the application of a zoning ordinance in cases where particular hardship to the owner would result from enforcement of the ordinance. Such relief is typically known as a variance.

The variance procedure is often considered a constitutional requirement by virtue of the Fifth Amendment's taking clause. A recent New Jersey case discussed the issue as follows:

> Underlying the request for a hardship variance is that without such relief the property will be zoned into inutility . . . so that an exercise in eminent domain will be called for and compensation must be paid. When that occurs, all taxpayers in the municipality share the economic burden of achieving the intent and purpose of the zoning scheme.
> *Paris Enterprises v. Karpf,* 523 A. 2d 137 (N.J. 1987)

Most statutes provide the criteria for granting a variance. The California Government Code is a typical example:

> Variances from the terms of the zoning ordinance shall be granted only when, because of special circumstances applicable to the property, including size, shape, topography, location, or surroundings, the strict application of the zoning ordinance deprives such property of privileges enjoyed by other property in the vicinity and under identical zoning classification.

In addition, the zoning board is usually given authority to impose conditions upon the grant of a variance to "assure that the adjustment thereby authorized shall not constitute a grant of special privileges inconsistent with the limitations upon other properties in the vicinity and zone in which the property is situated,'' *Topanga v. County of Los Angeles,* 522 P. 2d 12 (Cal. 1974).

Most jurisdictions draw a further distinction between a variance affecting the size or construction of a building and one which affects the use of the property. The first kind of variance, usually known as an area variance might permit construction of an otherwise conforming building upon an undersized lot, or permit a structure to be built without satisfying height or setback requirements.

A use variance, on the other hand, permits the property to be used in a manner inconsistent with the zoning ordinance. Authorization of a factory in an agricultural zone or a duplex in a single-family zone are examples of a use variance.

As between the two, most jurisdictions tend to impose a less exacting standard to justify an area variance. This tendency seems to be based upon the perception that the use variance is more detrimental to the integrity of the zone than the area variance.

The standard of ''unnecessary hardship'' in the use variance is often framed in terms of the regulatory taking discussed previously. For instance, in *Gaglione v. DiMuro,* 478 A. 2d 573 (R.I. 1984), the Rhode Island Court refused to permit the granting of a variance where the owner failed to prove ''that the present return on the property is so low that to require its continued devotion to its present use or to other uses permitted under the ordinance would be confiscatory.'' In *Fayetteville v. Jarrold,* 440 N.Y.S. 2d 908 (N.Y. 1981), where an applicant sought a commercial use in a residential zone, and claimed he could not otherwise obtain an adequate return on the property, the court required the owner to present ''dollars and cents'' proof that residential use was unfeasible.

The tendency however is to authorize an area variance based simply upon a showing that compliance with the statute will cause ''practical difficulties'' for the landowner. This approach involves balancing the hardship upon the owner against the adverse impact that may be caused by granting the variance. Under this standard, a variance may be granted, although it is not strictly necessary to enable the owner to obtain an adequate return on the property.

D The Conditional or Special Use

The conditional use, also known as the special use, is an administrative device authorizing a zoning board to impose conditions or limitations upon land uses otherwise permitted in the particular zone. The conditional use is designed to cope with situations where a particular use, although not inherently inconsistent with the use classification of a particular zone, may create special problems and hazards if allowed to develop and locate without some limitation.

The Minnesota Court characterized the conditional use in the following terms:

By this device, certain uses (e.g., gasoline service stations, electric substations, hospitals, schools, churches, country clubs, and the like) which may be considered essentially desirable to the community, but which should not be authorized generally in a particular zone because of considerations such as current and anticipated traffic congestion, population density, noise, effect on adjoining land values, or other considerations involving public health, safety, or general welfare, may be permitted upon a proposed site depending upon the facts and circumstances of the particular use.

Zylka v. Crystal, 167 N.W. 2d 45 (Minn. 1969)

A typical zoning ordinance will specify the uses within a zone that are expressly permitted and provide that certain other uses are permitted, subject to conditional use authorization.

To obtain a conditional use permit, the applicant typically must show (1) that the permit will not cause substantial detriment to the public welfare; (2) that the permit will not substantially impair the purpose of the zoning ordinance; and (3) all conditions enumerated in the ordinance have been satisfied. See *Swimming Club of Rockford v. City of Rockford,* 473 N.E. 2d 1375 (Ill. 1985).

The conditional use procedure is authorized by the states enabling act and implemented by the zoning ordinance and zoning board regulations. Zoning ordinances tend to permit certain types of conditional uses in certain zones and often limit the zoning board's discretion to deny the application, once the owner has demonstrated a willingness and ability to satisfy the conditions set forth in the ordinance.

For instance, an area zoned for residential use only might be made subject to a conditional use ordinance permitting the establishment of schools, churches, utility easements, public parks, hospitals, and libraries. Such uses would be subject to conditions, such as those related to the location of driveways, open space, parking lots, times of operation, and so forth. The following case illustrates the operation of a conditional use ordinance in a commercial zone and the standards which the zoning board must apply in reviewing such applications.

Mobile Oil Corporation v. Oaks, 390 N.Y.S. 2d 276 (N.Y. 1976)

Facts of the case.

Mobil, owner of a gasoline service station in the Town of Henrietta, Monroe County, sought a special permit to construct a gasoline service station upon a parcel of land within a "A" Commercial District. The Henrietta Zoning Ordinance permits gasoline filling stations in "A" Commercial Districts subject to the limitations imposed by the ordinance and provided that the applicant obtain a special permit from the Town Board following a public hearing. The Ordinance contains many restrictions on the issuance of a special use permit for a filling station. It sets forth building setback provisions, approach driveways, signs, lot size, and curb requirements, and fuel and gasoline pump setback requirements.

In addition, the Zoning Ordinance provides certain criteria for the Town Board in making its determination about whether to grant or deny a special permit. Among the standards to be met before a special use permit may be issued, the

Town Board must determine "whether the proposed use will be in harmony with the existing and probable future development of the neighborhood in which the premises is situated."

OPINION

A special use permit differs from a variance in that the former contemplates a use expressly permitted by a particular zoning ordinance, while the latter is authority to use property in a manner which is otherwise forbidden. Thus, when the ordinance sets forth conditions to be met before a special permit will issue, the burden of proof on an applicant requires a showing of compliance with the conditions and the board's power is limited to determining whether an applicant for a special use permit meets the standards recited in the zoning ordinance.

Mobil contends that the inclusion of a permitted use in an ordinance, subject only to a special permit, indicates that the use is in harmony with the neighborhood. However, the Henrietta Zoning Ordinance does not contain a legislative finding that since a gasoline filling station is a permitted use in an "A" Commercial District, provided a special permit be obtained, it is per se in harmony with the general zoning plan. Rather, the legislature left for the Zoning Board to consider whether "the proposed use will be in harmony with the existing and proposed future development of the neighborhood in which the premises is situated." Courts will not generally interfere with the Town Board's determination in a zoning dispute, since these matters are best "resolved by the commonsense judgments of representative citizens doing their best to make accommodations between conflicting community pressures." This rationale is particularly apt in a case such as this where to interfere would be to ignore the important ingredient of flexibility, which the Town Board plainly reserved to itself when it enacted the Henrietta Zoning Ordinance.

The Henrietta Town Board made detailed findings based in part upon a comprehensive although not formally adopted plan. The findings are supported by substantial evidence that demonstrates that moving the gasoline service station to the northeast corner of the intersection would not be in harmony with the present or probable future development of the lands immediately adjoining the proposed site.

Judgment affirmed.

NOTES AND QUESTIONS

Given the court's deference to the Zoning Board's conclusion, is there any case in which a court could rationally disagree with a conclusion so vague as that made by the Henrietta Town Board? If the Board can rest its decision on the basis that the use will not "be in harmony with existing and proposed development," can any meaningful review of the basis of the decision be made? Would a more objective standard impair the Boards flexibility? Is an owner entitled to a greater degree of objectivity and certainty when making decisions for the development of property?

9 EXCLUSIONARY ZONING

It should be obvious that the main feature of zoning is that it excludes certain kinds of uses from a particular area. Somewhat less obvious is the tendency to discourage the creation of low and moderate income housing from many residential zones.

The tendency of zoning ordinances to exclude lower income groups has long been recognized and is well documented. The district court opinion in the *Ambler Realty* case noted that "in the last analysis the result to be accomplished [by zoning] is to classify the population and segregate them according to their income or station in life." (*Ambler Realty v. Village of Euclid,* 297 F. 307 (N.D. Ohio 1924). For example, minimum lot area requirements of two acres, three acres, and even five acres have been sustained as have prohibitions on multiple family dwellings. Regardless of the intention behind such zoning provisions, the obvious effect is to limit or preclude altogether the development of housing for low or moderate income groups. The economic forces behind such zoning efforts have also been well documented.

> The residents of high income suburbs have an incentive to protect their favorable tax base, since a large tax base per family means low tax rates for any chosen spending level. Admitting families into the community who purchase with a value below the community average will lower the tax base per family. Thus, if the community wishes to maintain current spending levels, it will be forced to raise taxes. This increase in tax rates will make the suburbs less attractive to future residents and hence lower the resale value of the remaining residents' property.
>
> 92 Harvard Law Review 1662, 1685 (1979)

In response to this problem, courts in a few jurisdictions have reacted by refusing to recognize the traditional presumption of validity where a zoning ordinance is shown to have an exclusionary effect. In particular, the courts in California, New Jersey, New York, Pennsylvania, and to a lesser extent in Michigan and Illinois have demonstrated an increasing awareness of the exclusionary effect of many types of zoning ordinances and have periodically refused to uphold such ordinances.

Pennsylvania was among the first states to address the exclusionary effect of certain zoning ordinances. In the case of *National Land Investment Co. v. Kohn,* 215 A. 2d 597 (Penn. 1965), the Pennsylvania Supreme Court faced a classic example of "snob zoning" and invalidated a seven-acre minimum lot size requirement in the following terms:

> Zoning is a tool in the hands of governmental bodies which enables them to more effectively meet the demands of evolving and growing communities. It must not and cannot be used by those officials as an instrument by which they may shirk their responsibilities. Zoning is a means by which a governmental body can plan for the future—it may not be used as a means to deny the future. Zoning provisions may not be used to avoid the increased responsibilities and economic burdens which time and natural growth invariably bring.
>
> The Township argues that it wants to maintain the "character" of this area. The pho-

tographic exhibits placed in the record by appellants attest to the fact that this is an area of great beauty containing old homes surrounded by beautiful pasture, farm, and wood land. It is a very desirable and attractive place in which to live.

There is no doubt that many of the residents of this area are highly desirous of keeping it the way it is, preferring, quite naturally, to look out upon land in its natural state rather than on other homes. These desires, however, do not rise to the level of public welfare. This is purely a matter of private desire, which zoning regulations may not be employed to effectuate.

The question posed is whether the Township can stand in the way of the natural forces which send our growing population into hitherto undeveloped areas in search of a comfortable place to live. We have concluded not. A zoning ordinance whose primary purpose is to prevent the entrance of newcomers in order to avoid future burdens, economic and otherwise, upon the administration of public services and facilities cannot be held valid. Of course, we do not mean to imply that a governmental body may not utilize its zoning power in order to insure that the municipal services which the community requires are provided in an orderly and rational manner.

The brief of the Township points up the factors which sometime lurk behind the espoused motives of zoning. What basically appears to bother them is that a small number of lovely old homes will have to start keeping company with a growing number of smaller, less expensive, more densely located houses. It is clear, however, that the general welfare is not fostered or promoted by a zoning ordinance designed to be exclusive and exclusionary.

NOTES AND QUESTIONS

What do you think were the effects of this ruling on the Township of Easttown? Suppose a developer seeks to build low-cost tract housing in the town? Are the citizens powerless to prevent the character of their Township from being undermined? Should they be?

10 THE REQUIREMENT OF A "REGIONAL APPROACH"

Efforts to minimize the exclusionary effect of some zoning ordinances have proven difficult, particularly in light of the fact that most zoning ordinances are adopted at a local level by a single municipality. The Pennsylvania Supreme Court was also among the first to address this problem and, in *Appeal of Girsh,* 263 A. 2d 395 (Penn. 1970), the court invalidated a suburban townships ordinance that prohibited multiple family dwellings. The court noted that the exclusionary problem would, "in an ideal world," be addressed by regional planning and zoning . . . so that a given community would have apartments, while an adjoining community would not. But as long as we allow zoning to be done community by community, it is intolerable to allow one municipality (or many municipalities) to close its doors at the expense of surrounding communities and the central city." (263 A. 2d at 399)

The New Jersey Supreme Court has been the most vigorous proponent of a regional approach to the problem of low- and moderate-income housing. In its landmark decision in the case of *Southern Burlington County NAACP v. Township of Mount Laurel,* 336 A. 2d 713 (N.J. 1975), known as Mt. Laurel I, the New Jersey Supreme

Court broke new ground and held that municipalities would no longer be allowed to disregard regional housing needs through the enactment of local zoning ordinances. The Mt. Laurel zoning ordinances had effectively excluded the development of housing for low- and moderate-income families. The court unanimously concluded that the zoning ordinance was invalid:

> We conclude that every municipality must, by its land use regulations, make realistically possible an appropriate variety and choice of housing. More specifically, it cannot foreclose the opportunity of the development of low- and moderate-income housing and in its regulations must affirmatively afford that opportunity, at least to the extent of the municipality's fair share of the present and prospective regional need therefore. These obligations must be met unless the municipality can sustain the heavy burden of demonstrating peculiar circumstances, which dictate that it should not be required to do so.
>
> It is plain beyond dispute that provision for adequate housing of all categories of people is certainly an absolute essential in promotion of the general welfare required in all local land-use regulation. Further, the universal and constant need for such housing is so important and of such broad public interest that the general welfare, which developing municipalities like Mt. Laurel must consider, extends beyond their boundaries and cannot be parochially confined to the claimed good of the particular municipality. It has to follow that, broadly speaking, the obligation arises for each such municipality affirmatively to plan and provide for in its land-use regulations, the reasonable opportunity for an appropriate variety and choice of housing, including of course low- and moderate-cost housing, to meet the needs, desires, and resources of all categories of people who may desire to live within its boundaries. Negatively, it may not adopt regulations or policies which thwart or preclude that opportunity.

Mt. Laurel II   Eight years later, the New Jersey Supreme Court had occasion to review the implementation of its decision in *Mt. Laurel I.* In *Mt. Laurel II,* 456 A. 2d 390 (N.J. 1983), the court strengthened its earlier opinion and expressed its concern that not a single unit of low-income housing had been built in Mt. Laurel since the court's original opinion.

> This is the return, eight years later, of . . . *Mt. Laurel I.* We set forth in that case, for the first time, the doctrine requiring that a municipality's land-use regulations provide a realistic opportunity for low- and moderate-income housing. The doctrine has become famous. The Mt. Laurel case itself threatens to become infamous. After all this time, ten years after the trial court's initial order invalidating its zoning ordinance, Mt. Laurel remains affected with a blatantly exclusionary ordinance. Papered over with studies, rationalized by hired experts, the ordinance at its core is true to nothing but Mt. Laurel's determination to exclude the poor. Mt. Laurel is not alone; we believe that there is widespread non compliance with the constitutional mandate of our original opinion in this case.
>
> *Mt. Laurel II* 456 A. 2d 390 at 409–410

In *Mt. Laurel II,* the court adopted an extensive procedure which attempted to streamline and standardize the permit approval process, created, in effect, a tribunal of judges who would hear all zoning-related litigation in the State of New Jersey and conferred upon these trial court judges the power to order municipalities to undertake the construction of low- and moderate-income housing. Finally, the court placed the burden upon the municipality to demonstrate that it has met its Mt. Laurel obligations.

Proof of a municipality's bona fide attempt to provide a realistic opportunity to construct its fair share of lower income housing shall no longer suffice. Satisfaction of the Mt. Laurel obligation shall be determined solely on an objective basis. If the municipality has in fact provided a realistic opportunity for the construction of its fair share of low and moderate income housing, it has met the Mt. Laurel obligation to satisfy the constitutional requirement; if it has not, then it has failed to satisfy it.

Impact of Mt. Laurel   The *Mt. Laurel* decisions have had some impact upon the courts in other states and a number of jurisdictions have imposed similar obligations upon municipalities to address regional housing needs in their zoning ordinances. The courts in California, New Hampshire, New York, and Pennsylvania have, to some extent, followed the Mt. Laurel approach. In addition, the states of California and Massachusetts have enacted statutes that specifically require that zoning ordinances must address and accommodate the regional housing needs, both present and future, of all income groups. The practical effect of the Mt. Laurel approach has not been significant as, by all accounts, the shortage of low- and moderate-income housing has become ever more pronounced. For the most part, the concept of exclusionary zoning has been raised to defeat certain restrictive zoning ordinances that probably would have been upheld in the past. However, it is safe to say at this time that the Mt. Laurel approach has failed to impose a meaningful obligation upon municipalities to specifically address the need for affordable housing.

11   ZONING FOR THE CONTROL OF GROWTH

Various communities, in an effort to control, limit, or even halt the growth of their communities, have attempted, in various ways, to obtain these ends through the use of zoning ordinances. Such regulations are often imposed in response to a period of explosive and often uncontrolled development. Boca Raton, Florida, about thirty miles north of Miami approved an initiative petition that provided that only a certain number of additional building units would be approved within the city limits. A state appellate court held that this limitation bore no rational relationship to a valid municipal purpose and was therefore unconstitutional, (*City of Boca Raton v. Boca Villas Corp.*, 371 S. 2d 154 and 160). In Petaluma, California, a community about forty miles north of San Francisco, the city council, in response to rapidly accelerating growth in the early 1970's, passed a measure that limited the issuance of building permits to 500 units per year for a five-year period. This was approximately one third of the number of permits that had been issued in each of the prior three years. The basic objectives of the plan were to ensure orderly growth, protect the city's small town character, and provide for a variety of housing choices and densities. The plan was ultimately upheld by the 9th Circuit Court of Appeals. See *Construction Industry Association v. City of Petaluma*, 522 F. 2d 897 (9th Cir. 1975). Growth control plans are usually upheld if they are reasonable, do not amount to a taking, and are intended to control but not altogether stop land development.

The case of *Golden v. Town of Ramapo*, 285 N.E. 2d 291 (N.Y. 1972), is the leading authority on the subject of growth control plans and illustrates the general acceptance of a carefully drafted plan.

In 1969, the Town of Ramapo amended its zoning ordinance for the stated purpose of eliminating premature subdivisions and urban sprawl. Ramapo, located approximately twenty-five miles north of New York City, had experienced substantial growth, which had changed its character from a rural to a suburban community. The zoning amendment sought to manage residential development so that it would proceed according to the provision of adequate municipal services. It provided that all residential development was subject to special use authorization, which was linked to and made conditional upon the creation of five essential public services. These were:

> (1) public sanitary sewers or approved substitutes; (2) drainage facilities; (3) improved public parks or recreation facilities, including public schools; (4) state, county, or town roads— major, secondary, or collector; and, (5) firehouses.

The establishment of these public services, and hence the ability to build housing under the ordinance, was to be phased over a period of eighteen years.

A group of property owners and developers sought to invalidate the amended ordinance on the grounds that the state enabling statute did not specifically authorize an ordinance intended to limit or defer growth and that, in any case, the ordinance was not a proper exercise of the police power. The court, in a careful review of the nature of zoning and its limitations, adopted an expansive view of the authority of government to plan for and direct the development of land.

The court's opinion is long and often turgid but, even in the relatively short excerpts which follow, it reveals an uncommon breadth of understanding and points out one of the most serious weaknesses of the system of zoning and land use which has evolved in this country.

> Undoubtedly, current zoning enabling legislation is burdened by the largely antiquated notion which deigns that the regulation of land use and development is uniquely a function of local government—that the public interest of the State is exhausted once its political subdivisions have been delegated the authority to zone. While such jurisdictional allocations may well have been consistent with formerly prevailing conditions and assumptions, questions of broader public interest have commonly been ignored.
>
> Experience over the last quarter century, however, with greater technological integration and drastic shifts in population distribution, has pointed up serious defects, and community autonomy in land-use controls has come under increasing attack by legal commentators and students of urban problems alike, because of its pronounced insularism and its correlative role in producing distortions in metropolitan growth patterns, and perhaps more importantly, in crippling efforts toward regional and State-wide problem solving, be it pollution, decent housing, or public transportation.
>
> The obvious purpose of this ordinance is to prevent premature subdivision absent essential municipal facilities and to insure continuous development commensurate with the Town's obligation to provide such facilities. They seek, not to freeze population at present levels, but to maximize growth by the efficient use of land, and in so doing testify to this community's continuing role in population assimilation. We only require that communities confront the challenge of population growth with open doors. Where, in grappling with that problem, the community undertakes, by imposing temporary restrictions upon development, to provide required municipal services in a rational manner, courts are rightfully reluctant to strike down such schemes.

Of course, these problems cannot be solved by Ramapo or any single municipality, but depend upon the accommodation of widely disparate interests for their ultimate resolution. To that end, State-wide or regional control of planning would insure that interests broader than that of the municipality underlie various land-use policies. Nevertheless, that should not be the only context in which growth devices such as these, aimed at population assimilation, not exclusion, will be sustained; especially where, as here, we would have no alternative but to strike the provision down in the wistful hope that the efforts of the State Office of Planning Coordination and the American Law Institute will soon bear fruit. . . .

These considerations, admittedly real, to the extent which they are relevant, bear solely upon the continued viability of "localism" in land-use regulation; obviously, they can neither add nor detract from the initial grant of authority, obsolescent though it may be. The answer which Ramapo has posed can by no means be termed definitive; it is, however, a first practical step toward controlled growth achieved without forsaking broader social purposes.

It is the nature of all land use and development regulations to circumscribe the course of growth within a particular town or district and to that extent such restrictions invariably impede the forces of natural growth.

Perhaps even more importantly, timed growth, unlike the minimum lot requirements recently struck down by the Pennsylvania Supreme Court as exclusionary, does not impose permanent restrictions upon land use.

Without a doubt restrictions upon the property in the present case are substantial in nature and duration. They are not, however, absolute. The amendments contemplate a definite term, as the development points are designed to operate for a maximum period of eighteen years, and during that period the Town is committed to the construction and installation of capital improvements.

While even the best of plans may not always be realized, in the absence of proof to the contrary, we must assume the Town will put its best effort forward in implementing the physical and fiscal timetable outlined under the plan. Should subsequent events prove this assumption unwarranted, or should the Town because of some unforeseen event fail in its primary obligation to these landowners, there will be ample opportunity to undo the restrictions upon default. For the present, at least, we are constrained to proceed upon the assumption that the program will be fully and timely implemented.

NOTES AND QUESTIONS

1 Is the action of the Town Board a temporary taking? Does the Supreme Court's decision in First Lutheran Church limit the ability to municipalities to enact "slow growth ordinances"?

2 A few states, in particular California, New Hampshire, and Oregon have enacted statutes intended to enable municipalities to respond to the problems of rapid growth while meeting their obligations to produce affordable housing. An example of such legislation is found in Section 65302.8 of the California Government Code which provides:

If a county or city adopts or amends a mandatory general plan element which operates to limit the number of housing units which may be constructed on an annual basis, such adoption or amendment shall contain findings which justify reducing the housing opportunities of the region. The findings shall include all the following:

(a) A description of the city's or county's appropriate share of the regional need for housing;

(b) A description of the specific housing programs and activities being undertaken by the local jurisdiction to fulfill the requirements of the mandatory housing element requirements of the general plan;

(c) A description of how the public health, safety, and welfare would be promoted by such adoption or amendment;

(d) The fiscal and environmental resources available to the local jurisdiction.

Would an ordinance drafted pursuant to the California statute pass a constitutional challenge under the Ramapo approach? What factors might a court look at when passing on the validity of such an ordinance?

12   ENFORCEMENT OF ZONING REGULATIONS

Actual enforcement of zoning regulations initially falls to an administrative agency, such as the zoning department or commission. Ordinarily if a proposed project does not comply with zoning ordinances, the agency can preclude the issuance of a building permit.

In addition, zoning regulations may be enforced by the agency through abatement proceedings or through an injunction restraining the owner from building in violation of the ordinance. In *Alexander v. Town of Hamstead,* 525 A. 2d 276 (N.H. 1987), the owner built a two-story house and violated the height limitations in the town's zoning ordinance. The town ordered the offending portion of the structure torn down. The owner applied for a variance, which was denied. The New Hampshire Supreme Court affirmed the order that the owner must tear down the structure in order to comply with the ordinance.

13   SUMMARY

The idea of zoning and land-use regulations generally are relatively recent concepts, which are continuing to evolve at a fairly quick pace.

The power to zone is an aspect of the police power which is inherent in Federal and State but not local government. As a result, all States have passed enabling statutes that authorize local governments to enact and implement zoning regulations.

Zoning is intended to afford local government a flexible system for regulating the use of land in the public interest. The power to zone is the power to limit permissible uses, establish lot size, and building densities, formulate construction requirements, and preserve historic and aesthetic features.

Inherent in zoning is the power of government to restrict an owner's use of land. Much has been written and said in attempting to locate the point at which a regulation goes so far as to constitute a taking of property for which compensation must be paid. When the regulation authorizes some physical intrusion, a finding of inverse condemnation will usually be made. However, when the regulation involves purely a limitation on use, most courts hold that the regulation will be upheld so long as it does not preclude all reasonable economic use of the property.

CHAPTER 21: ZONING AND OTHER PUBLIC LAND USE CONTROLS **409**

The zoning plan is administered by an administrative agency usually known as the zoning board. The board has broad authority to implement the zoning ordinance, consistent with the enabling ordinance and the limitations of the police power.

Recent years have witnessed growing dissatisfaction with aspects of zoning policy. A growing number of jurisdictions have invalidated zoning regulations that tend to exclude development of low- and moderate-income housing. This trend has been furthered in those jurisdictions, which include in their enabling statutes a requirement that regional housing needs be considered in connection with all local ordinances. However, an ordinance intended to limit development, so that it can proceed in more orderly fashion has usually been upheld as valid.

14 QUESTIONS

1 The State of Washington passed a statute giving a state agency the authority to do various things to protect the state's apple industry. Pursuant to that statute, Mr. and Mrs. Miller were ordered to cut down a large number of ornamental cedar trees, because they produced a cedar rust that was fatal to apple trees grown nearby. The state paid the cost of removing the trees but did not pay the diminished value of the land. Is this a proper exercise of the police power?

2 The City enacts a comprehensive zoning plan, which changes the permissible uses of your property in a way that seriously devalues the land. You wish to contest the zoning ordinance. What must you show before the ordinance will be invalidated?

3 Wayne Township passes an ordinance saying that in a certain residential zone one-story dwellings must have at least 800 square feet, two-story dwellings at least 1000 square feet, and corner lots must be at least 1200 square feet. Is the ordinance a proper exercise of the policy power?

4 A state statute provides that all apartment houses built of nonfireproof construction (as defined by the statute) must install sprinkling systems throughout the buildings at considerable cost. An apartment building owner challenges the ordinance. What is the likely result?

5 A zoning ordinance provides that, except for a narrow corridor in the retail district, zoning uses are limited to single-family homes. Is the ordinance valid?

6 Andrew owns a lot 50 feet by 100 feet in the Town of Bradleyville, on which is constructed a duplex. The duplex has been there for many years and before the enactment of any zoning ordinances. Recently, the Town enacted a statute imposing density limits of 50×100 feet (or 5000 square feet) for single-family homes and 75×100 feet (or 7500 square feet) for duplexes. The ordinance also provides that all structures within the zone must be made to comply within two years of the ordinance. Is the ordinance valid as applied to Andrew?

7 Chester operates a topless bar and mudwrestling emporium as a nonconforming use in an area zoned "neighborhood commercial." He wants to change the use to a restaurant without entertainment, where alcohol is only served with meals. Will the zoning board permit the change in use?

8 Danville owns a lot that is 85 feet by 50 feet in a residential zone. (4250 square feet). He wants to build a single-family home but the local zoning ordinance provides for a minimum lot size of 5000 square feet. Danville applies for a variance. What must he show to be entitled to a variance? Will it be granted?

9 Elmira is a builder who constructs a four-plex. Because of an error by her surveyor, she

builds the property six inches too deep, thereby violating the rear yard requirements of the local zoning ordinance. The building inspector issues an order to abatement directing Elmira to remove the encroaching six inches. Must Elmira remove this part of the building?

10 The zoning ordinance of the Town of Harnett provides that automobile garages and gas stations may be located in a particular zone, pursuant to conditional use authorization. Ivan seeks and is issued a conditional use for a carwash. Is this action valid?

CHAPTER 22

REGULATION OF SUBDIVISIONS

TOPICS CONSIDERED IN THIS CHAPTER:

1 INTRODUCTION

A subdivision may be defined as the division of a track of land into smaller parcels. This is accomplished by recording a subdivision map or subdivision plat, which outlines each lot within the larger parcel. Regulations designed to control this process are, like zoning, an aspect of the exercise of the police power and must be aimed at protecting public health, safety, morals, and the general welfare of the community. All American states have regulations pertaining to the creation of subdivisions. These statutes regulate the design and sale of subdivisions and authorize conditions for approval of subdivision maps, such as the payment of fees, dedication of land for public use, and the installation of improvements.

2 THE MASTER PLAN

While zoning is concerned primarily with use regulations, planning is a broader concept, which also includes concern for the location of streets, parks, utility services, and other civic amenities. With the steady and often rapid movement of populations into previously undeveloped areas, the need for long-range planning in the public interest becomes evident.

The Master Plan of Maryland is a typical example. Note how this master plan is phrased in terms of the police power while it goes beyond the typical classifications and concerns of zoning.

> The plan shall be made with the general purpose of guiding and accomplishing the coordinated, adjusted, and harmonious development of the jurisdiction and its environs, which will, in accordance with present and future needs, best promote health, safety, morals, order, convenience, and promote efficiency and economy in the process of development; including among other things, adequate provisions for traffic, the promotion of public safety, adequate provision for light and air, conservation of natural resources, the prevention of the healthful and convenient distribution of population, the promotion of good civic design and arrangement, wise and efficient expenditure of public funds, and the adequate provision of public utilities and other public requirements.
>
> Maryland Planning and Zoning Study Commission, Section 3.06

In *Commissioners of Cecil County v. Gaster,* 401 A. 2d 666 (Maryland 1979), the Maryland appeals court upheld the denial of a proposed subdivision, which satisfied the county's zoning ordinance, but which failed to comply with the Master Plan.

There is, in other words, a close relation between planning, zoning, subdivision control, and the power to employ zoning regulations and master plan concepts in the context of a subdivision.

3   PROCEDURE FOR OBTAINING SUBDIVISION APPROVAL

Like zoning, subdivision regulations are usually adopted at the local level, based upon authority conferred by virtue of an enabling statute enacted by the state legislature. Ordinarily, such enabling statutes delegate authority over subdivisions to a specific municipal planning board and are usually implemented by ordinances which prohibit the recording of the subdivision plat without obtaining the necessary approvals. The Ohio Enabling Legislation is a typical example:

> Whenever a city planning commission adopts a plan for the major streets or thoroughfares and for the parks and other open public grounds of a city or any part thereof . . . then no plat of a subdivision of land within such city or territory shall be recorded until it has been approved by the city planning commission and such approval endorsed in writing on the plat.
>
> *Ohio Revised Code, Section 711.09*

Enabling statutes and local ordinances establish the procedures necessary to subdivide a parcel. As indicated, these statutes are generally implemented at the county or municipal level pursuant to state enabling legislation. However, a few states also impose regulations at the state level and thereby require the subdivider to obtain approval from both state and local administrative agencies.

Obtaining subdivision approval is usually a two-step process. The first step involves obtaining approval by the appropriate agency of a preliminary plat, sometimes referred to as a tentative plat or tentative map. The preliminary plat is a drawing showing the proposed layout of the subdivision. It is not in final form for recording and usually does not have all the details completely computed. The purpose of the preliminary plat is to enable the administrative agency to obtain a general understanding of the proposed subdivision.

Upon approval of the preliminary plat, the subdivider may proceed to the second and final stage of subdivision approval. This involves approval of the final plat, which is a finished drawing of the subdivision showing all information necessary and required by the subdivision regulations. Typically this includes a survey of the property showing the boundary lines of each parcel, the location of streets and public areas, the location of utilities and related services, and all easements.

4 STANDARDS OF REVIEW OF THE PLANNING BOARD

The powers of the Planning Board (or other agency) are limited by the state enabling statute, which tends to vest broad discretion in the local agency. However, this discretion is not unlimited. It must be exercised pursuant to the authority conferred by the enabling ordinance, and it must be consistent with the limitations inherent in the police power.

5 CONDITIONS UPON PLAT APPROVAL: DEDICATIONS AND IMPACT FEES

Inherent in the Planning Board's discretion to approve subdivisions for consistency with the master plan and zoning regulations, is the Board's ability to approve the subdivision subject to certain conditions. For instance, the Planning Board may condition approval upon the developer's making design or density changes, and making contributions of land or money to accommodate anticipated increases in demand for public services caused by the development.

One court addressed the scope of the Planning Board's authority in a case where the subdivider was required to either dedicate land or pay money to the municipality as a condition to receiving approval of the subdivision. The court said:

> The test of reasonableness is always applicable to any attempt to exercise the police power. The basis for upholding a compulsory land dedication requirement in a platting ordinance in the nature of the instant ordinance is this:
>
> The municipality by approval of a proposed subdivision plat enables the subdivider to profit financially by selling the subdivision lots as homebuilding sites and thus realizing a greater price than could have been obtained if he had sold his property as unplatted lands. In return for this benefit the municipality may require him to dedicate part of his land to meet a demand to which the municipality would not have been put but for the influx of people into the community to occupy the subdivision lots.
>
> *Jordan v. Menomonee Falls,* 137 N.W. 2d 442 at 448 (Wis. 1965)

It is generally held that a municipality may require the developer to dedicate land to the municipality for any purpose reasonably related to the creation of a subdivision so long as the state's enabling legislation permits such a dedication, the subdivision ordinance itself authorizes the imposition of such conditions, and the condition itself is reasonable both in terms of its value and its relationship to the subdivision. Conditions are often imposed that require dedications of land for schools, parks, streets, highways, and for other improvements. These are routinely upheld provided they are rationally related to the subdivision itself or relate to an anticipated demand upon public facilities caused by the proposed subdivision.

Many municipalities have become increasingly aggressive and creative in attempting to condition the grant of development rights upon the owner making a contribution of some kind to the municipality. These efforts have met with mixed success when reviewed by the courts.

In *San Telmo Associates v. City of Seattle,* 715 P. 2d 673 (Wash. 1987), an ordinance required that a demolition permit be obtained before low-income housing could be demolished. To obtain the permit an owner was required to assist in relocating the tenants and either replace a percentage of the lost housing with other low-cost housing or make a cash contribution to a fund for the development of low-cost housing. The court invalidated the ordinance on the ground that it was not authorized by the State's Enabling Act.

On the other hand, the California court upheld an ordinance that required the developer to make a $6.00 per square foot contribution to a municipal transportation fund. The court concluded that the payment was authorized by the State's Enabling Statute and was not a tax but rather a fee intended to defray the additional burden imposed on the public transportation system by the development.

If the dedication or impact fee is authorized by state law, it still must satisfy the requirement of the police power before it will be upheld. In *Dunbar v. Toledo Planning Commission,* 367 N.E. 2d 1193 (Ohio 1976), the Ohio Court of Appeals was asked to invalidate the municipal condition that required the developer of a subdivision to dedicate a 100-foot wide road through the proposed subdivision. The developer had already agreed to dedicate internal streets and coordinate them with external thoroughfares. The reason for the additional condition was to preserve the land in the event the city later wished to develop it as a major road. The court attempted to define that elusive point between a regulation and a taking in the context of subdivision restrictions:

> The developer of a subdivision may be required to assume those costs which are specifically and uniquely attributable to his activity and which would otherwise be cast upon the public. However, simply because the requirement that a plat of subdivision be approved affords an appropriate point of control with respect to costs made necessary by the subdivision, it does not follow that communities may use this point of control to solve all of the problems which they can foresee. The distinction between permissible and forbidden requirements is suggested in *Ayres v. City Council of Los Angeles,* 34 Cal. 2d 31, 207 P. 2d 1, which held that the municipality may require the developer to provide the streets which are required by the activity within the subdivision but cannot require him to provide a major thoroughfare, "the need for which stems from the total activity of the community."

In *Jenod v. Village of Scarsdale,* 218 N.E. 2d 673 (N.Y. 1966), the Village of Scarsdale required the developer of subdivisions to dedicate a portion of the property for public parks or, in the alternative, to make a payment to a recreational fund. In upholding this arrangement, the New York court made the following observation:

> Scarsdale and other communities, observing that their vacant lands were being cut up into subdivision lots, and being alert to their responsibilities, saw to it, before it was too late, that the subdivisions make allowance for open park spaces therein. This was merely a kind of zoning, like setback and side yard regulations, minimum size of lots, etc., and akin also to other reasonable requirements for necessary sewer, water mains, lights, sidewalks, etc. If the developers did not provide for parks and playgrounds in their own tracts, the municipality would have to do it, since it would now be required for the benefit of all the inhabitants.
>
> But it was found, in some instances, that the separate subdivisions were too small to permit substantial parklands to be set off, yet the creation of such subdivisions, too, enlarged the demand for more recreational space in the community. In such cases it was just as reasonable to assess the subdividers an amount per lot to go into a fund for more park lands for the village or town. One arrangement is no more of a ''tax'' or ''illegal taking'' than the other.

Finally, the Pennsylvania Court discussed the issue in the following terms:

> It is clear that some of the costs of off-site improvements can fairly be charged to a developer whose plans so burden existing facilities as to necessitate their accelerated improvement or construction. However, conditions placed on tentative approval must be reasonable and economically feasible. The rationale for imposing off-site costs is not to transfer all costs of development from municipalities to private developers. The primary responsibility for providing these services lie with local governments. The purpose of imposing reasonable off-site costs on developers is to cushion municipalities from the effect of rapid, large-scale development.
>
> *Mueller Associates v. Buffalo Board of Supervisors,* 373 A. 2d 1173 (Pa. 1977)

6 SUMMARY

Subdivision regulation is another element of the police power which draws its support both from zoning and the broader notion of urban planning. As in the case of zoning, subdivision regulation must be based upon enabling legislation passed by the state.

A subdivision is simply the division of a tract of land into smaller parcels, typically through the recording of a subdivision map or subdivision plat. All states regulate subdivisions by imposing limitations upon the right to record the subdivision plat.

Because a subdivision usually transforms previously unused land to residential use, it typically results in an increase in the local population and a corresponding increase in the demand for nearly all municipal services. Accordingly, it is well established that subdividers may be expected to bear the cost of the increased demand upon such services caused by the development.

The most common ways that subdividers pay for the cost of increased municipal services is through forced dedications and impact fees. A dedication is a requirement that the subdivider dedicate, to the municipality, land for a public purpose, such as parks, schools, roads, and the like. An impact fee is a requirement that the subdivider pay a sum of money into a specific fund to help pay for certain municipal services. For instance, a subdivision might be required to contribute to a fund for improved public transportation, schools, libraries, low cost housing, and so on. As with any police power regulation, the dedication or impact fee must bear a reasonable relation to a legitimate municipal purpose and be authorized by the state's enabling statute.

7 QUESTIONS

1 Dave Developer proposes to create a subdivision of one hundred homes on a fifty-acre parcel. He applies for tentative plat approval and is told by the planning commissioner that he will be required to dedicate approximately five acres to the municipality as a condition to receiving approval for the subdivision. What is a dedication and what are the consequences of it?

2 Dave Developer goes to an area more eager to attract residential builders. He obtains tentative and final plat approval for a sixteen-acre development without any dedication or impact fee. Then the City enacts a general plan for parks and playgrounds, which reserved 4 and $\frac{1}{2}$ acres of Dave's land to be dedicated to the city. Dave objects and sues. Will he win?

3 A developer wants to build a subdivision and is told, as a condition to final plat approval, that he must bear the entire cost of sewers, fire hydrants, and water systems for the subdivision. Developer balks and sues. Who wins?

4 A state subdivision code provides that the code applies to all subdivisions of more than four parcels. Doris owns a sixteen-acre parcel which she divides into four equal parcels. Must she obtain subdivision plan approval? Suppose she waits one year and further divides each parcel into four parcels. Must she now get subdivision approval?

CHAPTER 23

LAND USE AND ENVIRONMENTAL PROTECTION

TOPICS CONSIDERED IN THIS CHAPTER:

1 INTRODUCTION

For centuries the use and development of property was conducted in an atmosphere in which technological and economic factors were the paramount and even sole considerations. However, a growing awareness that certain physical resources were not infinite gave rise to the idea that environmental consequence should also be considered when reviewing proposals for development of real estate.

In response to these concerns, Congress passed a series of environmental protection statutes in the late 1960's and early 1970's. These include the National Historic Preservation Act, and legislation aimed at controlling air pollution, water pollution, noise pollution, and managing the disposal of hazardous waste. Federal and state pollution control laws are beyond the scope of this text. However, one statute, the National Environmental Policy Act of 1969 (NEPA) (42 U.S.C. Sections 4321 et. seq.) will be introduced in this chapter. NEPA is generally considered the most important federal environmental statute and, along with its state counterparts, has had an important impact on land development in this country.

NEPA is truly a landmark statute and has had a number of important consequences: first of all, it established a national policy concerning environmental protection and altered the decision-making process of federal agencies by requiring them to consider environmental factors when deciding to proceed with certain projects and to integrate environmental values into the decision-making process. The Act created the Council on Environmental Quality (CEQ) to gather information on environmental issues and to advise the President accordingly. Perhaps the most significant aspect of NEPA is the requirement that an environmental impact statement report (EIS) be prepared in connection with proposed federal projects that may significantly affect the environment and the requirement that the EIS must be considered before deciding whether the project should go forward. Finally, NEPA created a model that has been followed by many states so that notions of environmental protection have been introduced into the decision-making process at the state and local level. It is important to note that NEPA only applies to projects undertaken by, or requiring the approval of, an agency of the federal government. However, certain state counterparts to NEPA extend similar oversight to projects requiring the approval of a state or local agency.

2 NEPA STATEMENT OF ENVIRONMENTAL POLICY

NEPA mandates the "creation and maintenance of conditions under which man and nature can exist in productive harmony." This policy statement and the broad environmental mandate that it includes have been instrumental in causing courts to conclude that the provisions of the Act should be broadly construed in an effort to meet the Act's objectives.

The policy statement of NEPA is as follows:

(a) The Congress, recognizing the profound impact of man's activity on the interrelations of all components of the natural environment, particularly the profound influences of population growth, high-density urbanization, industrial expansion, resources exploitation, and new and expanding technological advances and recognizing further the critical importance of restoring and maintaining environmental quality to the overall welfare and development of man, declares that it is the continuing policy of the Federal Government, in cooperation with State and local governments, and other concerned public and private organizations, to use all practicable means and measures, including financial and technical assistance, in a manner calculated to foster and promote the general welfare, to create and maintain conditions under which man and nature can exist in productive harmony, and fulfill the social, economic, and other requirements of present and future generations of Americans.

(b) In order to carry out the policy set forth in this chapter, it is the continuing responsibility of the Federal Government to use all practicable means, consistent with other essential considerations of national policy, to improve and coordinate Federal plans, functions, programs, and resources to the end that the Nation may—

(1) Fulfill the responsibilities of each generation as trustee of the environment for succeeding generations;

(2) Assure for all Americans safe, healthful, productive, and esthetically and culturally pleasing surroundings;

(3) Attain the widest range of beneficial uses of the environment without degradation, risk to health or safety, or other undesirable and unintended consequences;

(4) Preserve important historic, cultural, and natural aspects of our national heritage, and maintain, wherever possible, an environment which supports diversity and variety of individual choice;

(5) Achieve a balance between population and resource use which will permit high standards of living and a wide sharing of life's amenities; and

(6) Enhance the quality of renewable resources and approach the maximum attainable recycling of depletable resources.

(c) The Congress recognizes that each person should enjoy a healthful environment and that each person has a responsibility to contribute to the preservation and enhancement of the environment.

42 U.S.C. Section 4331

NEPA has generated considerable litigation and the federal courts and the Supreme Court in particular have had occasion to review the Act and assess its purpose and scope. In one decision, the Supreme Court said:

NEPA has twin aims. First, it places upon an agency the obligation to consider every significant aspect of the environmental impact of a proposed action. Second, it insures that the agency will inform the public that it has indeed considered the environmental concerns in its decision-making process. NEPA requires that the agency take a "hard look" at the environmental consequences before taking a major action in reviewing an agency's compliance with NEPA, the role of the court is simply to insure that the agency has adequately considered and disclosed the environmental impact of its actions and that its decision is not arbitrary or capricious.

Baltimore Gas and Electric Co. v. Natural Resources Defense Council, Inc.,
462 U.S. 87, (1983) 97–98

3   THE COUNCIL ON ENVIRONMENTAL QUALITY

As indicated, NEPA created the Council on Environmental Quality (CEQ) to gather, analyze, and submit to the President information of environmental significance. The CEQ is required to prepare an annual report on environmental quality. The duties and functions of the Council are set forth in the Act.

It shall be the duty and function of the Council—

(1) To assist and advise the President in the preparation of the Environmental Quality report;

(2) To gather timely and authoritative information concerning the conditions and trends in the quality of the environment both current and prospective, to analyze and interpret such information for the purpose of determining whether such conditions and trends are interfering, or are likely to interfere, with the achievement of the policy set forth in this Act, and to compile and submit to the President studies relating to such conditions and trends;

(3) To review and appraise the various programs and activities of the Federal Government in the light of the policy set forth in the Act for the purpose of determining the extent to which such programs and activities are contributing to the achievement of such policy, and to make recommendations to the President with respect thereto;

(4) To develop and recommend to the President national policies to foster and promote the improvement of environmental quality to meet the conservation, social, economic, health, and other requirements and goals of the Nation;

(5) To conduct investigations, studies, surveys, research, and analyses relating to ecological systems and environmental quality;

(6) To document and define changes in the natural environment, including the plant and animal systems, and to accumulate necessary data and other information for a continuing analysis of these changes or trends and an interpretation of their underlying causes;

(7) To report at least once each year to the President on the state and condition of the environment; and

(8) To make and furnish such studies, reports thereon, and recommendations with respect to matters of policy and legislation as the President may request.

42 U.S.C. Section 4344

NOTES AND QUESTIONS

The CEQ functions much like a public "think tank." It assembles information, issues regulations, and reports to the President. However, its purpose is not regulatory, and it does not issue permits or impose penalities for failure to comply with NEPA. The primary purpose of the Council is to assemble information and coordinate the reporting requirements under NEPA so that Congress, the President, and the public can be more well-informed about issues of environmental significance.

4 THE ENVIRONMENTAL IMPACT STATEMENT (EIS)

NEPA requires federal agencies to consider the environmental consequences of federal projects and to make its assessment of these consequences available to the public. A "federal project" is one sponsored by, or requiring the approval of, an agency of the federal government. The primary means by which NEPA's aims are accomplished is through the Environmental Impact Statement (EIS). The requirement and contents of the EIS are set forth in NEPA. In reading this statute, observe the interdisciplinary approach and the way in which Congress intended to use the EIS as both a decision-making tool and as a document for informing the public about the environmental consequences of a proposed project.

An EIS must be prepared in all cases when a proposal for major federal action may significantly affect the quality of the human environment. The policy behind the EIS and the items which the EIS must address are specifically set forth by Congress:

> The Congress authorizes and directs that, to the fullest extent possible: (1) the policies, regulations, and public laws of the United States shall be interpreted and administered in accordance with the policies set forth in this Chapter, and (2) all agencies of the Federal Government shall—
>
> (a) Utilize a systematic, interdisciplinary approach which will insure the integrated use of the natural and social sciences and the environmental design arts in planning and in decision-making which may have an impact on man's environment;
>
> (b) Identify and develop methods and procedures, in consultation with the Council on Environmental Quality, which will insure that presently unquantified environmental amenities and values may be given appropriate consideration in decision-making along with economic and technical considerations;
>
> (c) Include in every recommendation or report on proposals for legislation and other major Federal actions significantly affecting the quality of the human environment, a detailed statement by the responsible official on—
>
> **(i)** The environmental impact of the proposed action,
>
> **(ii)** Any adverse environmental effects which cannot be avoided should the proposal be implemented,
>
> **(iii)** Alternatives to the proposed action,
>
> **(iv)** The relationship between local short-term uses of man's environment and the maintenance and enhancement of long-term productivity, and
>
> **(v)** Any irreversible and irretrievable commitments of resources which would be involved in the proposed action should it be implemented.
>
> Prior to making any detailed statement, the responsible Federal official shall consult with, and obtain the comments of, any Federal agency which has jurisdiction by law or special expertise with respect to any environmental impact involved. Copies of such statement and the comments and views of the appropriate Federal, State, and local agencies, which are authorized to develop and enforce environmental standards, shall be made available to the President, the Council on Environmental Quality, and to the public, and shall accompany the proposal through the existing agency review processes.
>
> 42 U.S.C., Section 4332

5 "MAJOR FEDERAL ACTION"

Foundation on Economic Trends v. Heckler, 756 F. 2d 143 (9th Cir. 1985)

This appeal presents an important question at the dawn of the genetic engineering age. What is the appropriate level of environmental review required of the National Institute of Health (NIH) before it approves the deliberate release of genetically engineered, recombinant-DNA-containing organisms into the open environment? More precisely, in the context of this case, the question is whether to affirm an injunction temporarily enjoining NIH from approving deliberate release experiments without a greater level of environmental concern than the agency has shown thus far.

Facts of the case.

In September 1983 three environmental groups and two individuals filed suit against the federal officials responsible for genetic engineering decisions. Arguing that NIH had not complied with the requirements of NEPA, plaintiffs sought to enjoin a proposed NIH-approved experiment by University of California scientists that would represent the first deliberate release of genetically engineered organisms into the open environment. They also sought to enjoin NIH's approval of any other deliberate release experiments. On May 18, 1984, the District Court granted the requested relief and enjoined both the University of California experiment and NIH approval of all other deliberate release experiments.

OPINION

A   National Environmental Policy Act

On January 1, 1970, the National Environmental Policy Act (NEPA) became law. Recognizing "the profound impact of man's activity on the interrelation of all components of the natural environment," Congress sought to "fulfill the responsibilities of each generation as trustee of the environment for succeeding generations." The major "action-forcing" provision of NEPA is the requirement that "all agencies of the Federal government" prepare a detailed environmental analysis for "major Federal actions significantly affecting the quality of the human environment." Congress mandated that this detailed statement, long known as an Environmental Impact Statement (EIS), include such considerations as "the environmental impact of the proposed action," "any adverse environmental effects which cannot be avoided should the proposal be implemented," and "alternatives to the proposed action."

Two fundamental principles underlie NEPA's requirements: federal agencies have the responsibility to consider the environmental effects of major actions significantly affecting environment, and the public has the right to review that consideration. NEPA's dual mission is thus to generate federal attention to environmental concerns and to reveal that federal consideration for public scrutiny.

In passing NEPA, Congress emphasized its particular concern with the role of new technologies and their effect on the environment. The statute explicitly enumerates "new and expanding technological advances" as one of the activities with the potential to threaten the environment.

NEPA thus stands as landmark legislation, requiring federal agencies to consider the environmental effects of major federal actions, empowering the public to scrutinize this consideration, and revealing a special concern about the environmental effects of new technology.

B   Genetic Engineering

Genetic engineering is an important development at the very cusp of scientific advances. Broad claims are made about both the potential benefits and the potential hazards of genetically engineered organisms. Use of recombinant DNA may lead to welcome advances in such areas as food production and disease control. At the same time, however, the environmental consequences of dispersion of genetically engineered organisms are far from clear. According to a recent report by a House of Representative subcommittee, "The potential environmental risks associated with the deliberate release of genetically engineered organisms or the translation of any new organism into an ecosystem are best described as a low probability, high consequences risk"; that is, while there is only a small possibility that damage could occur, the damage that could occur is great.

On June 1, 1983, the Director gave final approval to the experiment at issue on appeal—the request by Dr. Nickolas Panopoulos and Dr. Steven Lindow of the University of California at Berkeley to apply genetically altered bacteria to plots of potatoes, tomatoes, and beans in northern California. The goal was to increase the crops' frost resistance. Because of the cancellation of the previous two experiments, the Panopoulos-Lindow experiment would be the first NIH approved deliberate release experiment actually to be conducted.

THE INJUNCTION

In September 1983, three public interest organizations and two individuals filed suit against the three federal officials ultimately responsible for NIH deliberate release decisions; they later added the Regents of the University of California as a defendant. The University of California experiment was scheduled to begin on or about May 25, 1984. On May 18 the District Court issued an injunction enjoining the University of California experiment and NIH approval of other deliberate release experiments. The District Court found that plaintiffs were likely to succeed in showing that NIH should have completed at least a more complete environmental assessment, and perhaps an EIS, before approving the University of California experiment; it also found them likely to succeed in showing that NIH should have completed an Environmental Impact Statement in connection with its imminent "program" of deliberate release approvals.

REVIEW OF AN AGENCY DECISION NOT TO PREPARE AN EIS

That courts must play a cardinal role in the realization of NEPA's mandate is beyond dispute. As the Supreme Court recently emphasized, the critical judicial task is "to ensure that the agency has adequately considered and disclosed the environmental impact of its actions and that its decision is not arbitrary or capricious." Since NEPA requires the agency to "take a 'hard look' at the environmental consequences before taking a major action," the judiciary must see that this legal duty is fulfilled. Although the "agency commencing federal action has the initial and primary responsibility for ascertaining whether an EIS is required," the courts must determine that this decision accords with traditional norms of reasoned decision-making and that the agency has taken the "hard look" required by NEPA.

THE ADEQUACY OF THE ENVIRONMENTAL REVIEW: THE PROPOSED EXPERIMENT

On September 17, 1982, Drs. Lindow and Panopoulos, scientists at Berkeley, submitted a request for NIH approval of an experiment that would involve deliberate release of genetically altered organisms in the open environment. NIH approval was required because the University of California receives NIH funds for recombinant-DNA research. Lindow and Panopoulos proposed to apply the genetically altered bacteria to various crops, including potatoes, tomatoes, and beans. By changing the bacteria's genetic composition, Lindow and Panopoulos hoped that the bacteria would change from frost-triggering bacteria to nonfrost-triggering bacteria; they further hoped that the engineered nonfrost-triggering bacteria would displace the natural frost-triggering bacteria. The ultimate goal was to protect the crops from frost and thus to extend their growing season.

NIH's only environmental impact statement on genetic engineering specifically identified dispersion as one of the major environmental concerns associated with recombinant-DNA research. The consequences of dispersion of genetically altered organisms are uncertain.

Thus the problem of dispersion would seem to be one of the major concerns associated with the Lindow-Panopoulos experiment, the first experiment that would actually release genetically engineered organisms in the open environment. Yet the only statement considering dispersion is the following: "Although some movement of bacteria toward sites near treatment locations by insect or aerial transport is possible, the numbers of viable cells transported has been shown to be very small; and these cells are subject to biological and physical processes limiting their survival." This sentence, was taken almost verbatim from the Lindow-Panopoulos proposal. NIH therefore, completely failed to consider the possible environmental impact from dispersion of genetically altered bacteria, however small the number and however subject to processes limiting survival.

In light of this complete failure to address a major environmental concern, NIH's environmental assessment fails to meet the standard of environmental review necessary before an agency decides not to prepare an EIS. The argument that this consideration would be adequate if contained in a document labelled "Environmental Assessment" simply misconceives the clear requirements of NEPA as articulated by the courts and by the Council on Environmental Quality. An environmental assessment that fails to address a significant environmental concern can hardly be deemed adequate for a reasoned determination that an EIS is not appropriate. NEPA places upon an agency the obligation to consider every significant aspect of the environmental impact of a proposed action.

It should be stressed that this inquiry into the adequacy of an environmental assessment is ultimately relevant to the agency's determination that its proposed federal action will not have a "significant impact" on the environment—and thus no EIS is required. In that connection, it is notable that NIH never directly addressed the question of whether an EIS should be prepared. Such an inquiry is, of course, the ultimate purpose of an environmental assessment.

To reiterate, NIH must first complete a far more adequate environmental assessment of the possible environmental assessment of the possible environmental impact of the deliberate release experiment than it has yet undertaken. That assessment must "provide sufficient evidence and analysis for determining whether to prepare an environmental impact statement or a finding of no significant impact." Ignoring possible environmental consequences will not suffice. Nor will a mere conclusory statement that the number of recombinant-DNA-containing organisms will be small and subject to processes limiting survival. Instead, NIH must attempt to evaluate seriously the risk that emigration of such organisms from the test site will create ecological disruption. Second, until NIH completes such an evaluation the question whether the experiment requires an EIS remains open. The University of California experiment clearly presents the possibility of a potential environmental hazard. This fact weighs heavily in support of the view that an EIS should be completed, unless NIH can demonstrate either that the experiment does not pose the previously identified danger, or that its assessment of the previously identified danger has changed through a process of reasoned decision-making. Nor is it sufficient for the agency merely to state that the environmental effects are currently unknown. Indeed, one of the specific criteria for determining whether an EIS is necessary is the degree to which the possible effects on the human environment are highly uncertain or involve unique or unknown risks.

Affirmed.

NOTES AND QUESTIONS

1 *Economic Trends v. Heckler* indicates compliance with NEPA requires an agency to do more than simply "rubber stamp" a project. Does the case hold that an Environmental Impact Statement is required before the proposal can proceed? Why did NEPA even apply to the proposed experiment? Why was this experiment considered a "major Federal action" within the meaning of NEPA?

2 NEPA has given rise to challenges to an Agency's decision even when no "major Federal action" was *presently* contemplated. This can occur because NEPA requires most federal agencies to prepare and implement regulations to assess the environmental impact of *proposed* projects. The case of *Calvert Cliff's v. U.S.*, (D.C.Cir. 1971), involved a challenge to NEPA regulations drafted by the Atomic Energy Commission (AEC) later changed to the Nuclear Regulatory Commission (NRC). *Calvert Cliff's* was one of the first cases to interpret the provisions of NEPA. Its recognition of the broad reach of the statute has been widely followed. The court ordered the AEC to implement procedures consistent with the broad mandate of NEPA.

Congress did not establish environmental protection as an exclusive goal; rather, it desired a reordering of priorities, so that environmental costs and benefits will assume their proper place along with other considerations.

Thus the general policy of the Act is a flexible one. However, the Act also contains very important "procedural" provisions—provisions which are designed to see that all federal agencies do, in fact, exercise the discretion given them. These provisions are not highly flexible. Indeed, they establish a strict standard of compliance.

NEPA makes environmental protection a part of the mandate of every federal agency and department. The Atomic Energy Commission, for example, had continually asserted, prior to NEPA, that it had no statutory authority to concern itself with the adverse environmental effects of its actions. Now, however, its hands are no longer tied. It is not only permitted, but compelled, to take environmental values into account. Perhaps the greatest importance of NEPA is to require the Atomic Energy Commission and other agencies to consider environmental issues just as they consider other matters within their mandates.

In order to include all possible environmental factors in the decision equation, agencies must identify and develop methods and procedures . . . which will insure that presently unquantified environmental amenities and values may be given appropriate consideration in decision-making along with economic and technical considerations. Environmental amenities will often be in conflict with economic and technical considerations. To consider the former along with the latter must involve a balancing process. In some instances environmental costs may outweigh economic and technical benefits, and in other instances they may not. But NEPA mandates a rather finely tuned and "systematic" balancing analysis in each instance.

To ensure that the balancing analysis is carried out and given full effect, NEPA requires that responsible officials of all agencies prepare a "detail statement" covering the impact of particular actions on the environment, the environmental costs which might be avoided, and alternative measures which might alter the cost-benefit equation. The apparent purpose of the "detailed statement" is to aid in the agencies' own decision-making process and to advise both interested agencies and the public of the environmental consequences of planned federal action. Beyond the "detailed statement," all agencies must specifically "study, develop, and describe appropriate alternatives to recommended courses of action in any proposal which involves unresolved conflicts concerning alternative uses of available resources." This requirement, like the "detailed statement" requirement, seeks to ensure that each agency decision maker has before him and takes into proper account all possible approaches to a particular project (including total abandonment of the project) which would alter the environmental impact and the cost-benefit balance. Only in that fashion is it likely that the most intelligent, optimally beneficial decision will ultimately be made.

6 "SIGNIFICANTLY AFFECTING" THE ENVIRONMENT

As indicated, the fist element that triggers the requirement of an environmental assessment is a proposal for "major federal action." Closely related is the prospect that the proposed action may have a significant affect upon the environment. This aspect of NEPA is also given expansive interpretation but, as the following case indicates, certain potential consequences are considered beyond the scope of NEPA and cannot have a significant environmental impact with the meaning of NEPA.

Metropolitan Edison Co. v. People Against Nuclear Energy (PANE), 460 U.S. 766 (U.S. 1983)

The issue in this case is whether the Nuclear Regulatory Commission (NRC) complied with the National Environmental Policy Act (NEPA), when it considered whether to permit petitioner Metropolitan Edison Co. to resume operation of the Three Mile Island Unit 1 nuclear powerplant (TMI–1). The Court of Appeals for the District of Columbia Circuit held that the NRC improperly failed to consider whether the risk of an accident at TMI–1 might cause harm to the psychological health and community well-being of residents of the surrounding area. We reverse.

Facts of the case.

Metropolitan owns two nuclear powerplants at Three Mile Island near Harrisburg, Pa. Both of these plants were licensed by the NRC after extensive proceedings, which included preparation of Environmental Impact Statements (EIS's). On March 28, 1979, TMI–1 was not operating; it had been shut down for refueling. TMI–2 was operating, and it suffered a serious accident that damaged the reactor. Although, as it turned out, no dangerous radiation was released, the accident caused widespread concern. The Governor of Pennsylvania recommended an evacuation of all pregnant women and small children, and many area residents did leave their homes for several days.

After the accident, the NRC ordered Metropolitan to keep TMI–1 shut down until it had an opportunity to determine whether the plant could be operated safely. The NRC then published a notice of hearing specifying several safety-related issues for consideration.

People Against Nuclear Energy (PANE) is an association of residents of the Harrisburg area, who are opposed to further operation of either TMI reactor. PANE contended that restarting TMI–1 would cause both severe psychological health damage to persons living in the vicinity, and serious damage to the stability, cohesiveness, and well-being of the neighboring communities.

Although these arguments are appealing at first glance, we believe they skip over an essential step in the analysis. They do not consider the closeness of the relationship between the change in the environment and the "effect" at issue.

To paraphrase the requirements of NEPA in light of the facts of this case, where an agency action significantly affects the quality of the human environment, the agency must evaluate the "environmental impact" and any unavoidable adverse environmental effects of its proposal. The theme is sounded by the adjective *environmental;* NEPA does not require the agency to assess every impact or effect of its proposed action, but only the impact or effect on the environment. If we were to seize the word *environmental* out of its context and give it the broadest possible definition, the words *adverse environmental effects* might embrace virtually any consequence of a governmental action that someone thought "adverse." But we think the context of the statute shows that Congress was talking about the physical environment—the world around us, so to speak. NEPA was designed to promote human welfare by alerting governmental actors to the effect of their proposed actions on the physical environment.

The statements of two principal sponsors of NEPA, illustrate this point:

> What is involved [in NEPA] is a congressional declaration that we do not intend, as a government or as a people, to initiate actions which endanger the continued existence or the health of mankind: That we will not intentionally initiate actions which do irreparable damage to the air, land and water which support life on earth.
>
> Remarks of Sen. Jackson

> [W]e can now move forward to preserve and enhance our air, aquatic, terrestrial environments . . . to carry out the policies and goals set forth in the bill to provide each citizen of this country a healthful environment.
>
> Remarks of Rep. Dingell

Thus, although NEPA states its goals in sweeping terms of human health and welfare, these goals are ends that Congress has chosen to pursue by means of protecting the physical environment.

The federal action that affects the environment in this case is permitting renewed operation of TMI–1. The direct effects on the environment of this action include release of low-level radiation, increased fog in the Harrisburg area (caused by operation of the plant's cooling towers), and the release of warm water into the Susquehanna River. The NRC has considered each of these effects in its EIS. Another effect of renewed operation is a risk of a nuclear accident. The NRC has also considered this effect.

PANE argues that the psychological health damage it alleges "will flow directly from the risk of a nuclear accident." But a risk of an accident is not an effect on the physical environment. A risk is, by definition, unrealized in the physical world.

If contentions of psychological health damage caused by risk were cognizable under NEPA, agencies would, at the very least, be obliged to expend considerable resources developing psychiatric expertise that is not otherwise relevant to their congressionally assigned function.

This case bears strong resemblance to other cases in which plaintiffs have sought to require agencies to evaluate the risk of crime from the operation of a jail or other public facility in their neighborhood. The plaintiffs in these cases could have alleged that the risk of crime (or their dislike of the occupants of the facility) would cause severe psychological health damage. The operation of the facility is an event in the physical environment, but the psychological health damage to neighboring residents resulting from unrealized risks of crime is too far removed from that event to be covered by NEPA. The psychological health damage alleged by PANE is no closer to an event in the environment or to environmental concerns.

We do not mean to denigrate the fears of PANE's members, or to suggest that the psychological health damage they fear could not, in fact, occur. Nonetheless, it would be extraordinarily difficult for agencies to differentiate between "genuine" claims of psychological health damage and claims that are grounded solely in disagreement with a democratically adopted policy. Until Congress provides a more explicit statutory instruction than NEPA now contains, we do not think agencies are obliged to undertake the inquiry.

Reversed.

NOTES AND QUESTIONS

1 Does the decision in *PANE* mean that human health, including psychological health is simply outside the scope of NEPA? How is this case different from *Economic Trends v. Heckler?* Was it not the potential or the "risk" of an accident with genetically engineered organisms that the agency failed to address in that case?

2 The opinion in *PANE* notes that the effect of low-level radiation was properly considered in the utility's EIS. Do you think that the health consequences of such radiation is a required consideration under NEPA? How about the psychological health consequences of such radiation?

7 CONTENTS OF THE EIS

Under NEPA, the agency must undertake a two-step process when evaluating environmental consequences. If the proposal does not involve "major federal action which may significantly affect the environment," findings to that effect must be made, but an Environmental Impact Statement (EIS) is not required. The decision not to prepare an EIS cannot be lightly made as the decision in *Economic Trends v. Heckler* indicates. The standards and findings necessary to support such a decision are considered in Section 8 of this chapter.

Courts have consistently held that the EIS must make the decision-making entity and the public fully aware of the environmental ramifications of a proposed project. Proposals for minimizing the environmental effect and alternatives to the project must also be considered.

One court referring to the informational purpose of the EIS stated as follows:

Congress contemplated that the Impact Statement would constitute the environmental source material for the information of the Congress as well as the Executive, in connection with the making of relevant decisions, and would be available to enhance enlightenment of—and by—the public. The impact statement provides a basis for (a) evaluation of the benefits of the proposed project in light of its environmental risks, and (b) comparison of the net balance for the proposed project with the environmental risks presented by alternative courses of action.

A sound construction of NEPA, requires a presentation of the environmental risks incident to reasonable alternative courses of action. The agency may limit its discussion of environmental impact to a brief statement, when that is the case, that the alternative course involves no effect on the environment, or that their effect, briefly described, is simply not significant. A rule of reason is implicit in this aspect of the law as it is in the requirement that the agency provide a statement concerning those opposing views that are responsible.

National Resources Defense Fund v. Morton, 458 F. 2d 872 (D.C.Cir. 1971)

Another aspect of the EIS as a decision-making tool is that it must examine a project in light of related projects in the area and further actions which may be contemplated in the area. For instance, in the case of *Environmental Defense Fund v. Callaway,* 524 F. 2d 79 (2d.Cir. 1975), the Secretary of the Navy prepared an EIS in connection with dredging and dumping operations off the coast of New London Harbor in the State of Connecticut so that the Harbor could accommodate a new class of Navy submarine. The dredging operations were intended to proceed in several phases, although the Navy's EIS considered the ecological impact of the first phase only. The court concluded that the EIS failed to furnish the information essential to environmental decision-making because it failed to assess the cumulative effects of all phases of the proposed project. ''The agency may not,'' said the court,

> treat a project as an isolated single-shot venture in the face of persuasive evidence that it is but one of several substantially similar operations, each of which will have the same polluting effect in the same area. To ignore the prospective cumulative harm under such circumstances could be to risk ecological disaster.
>
> The Navy's failure to consider these and possibly other proposed dredging projects in the New London area is an example of the isolated decision-making sought to be eliminated by NEPA.

The fact that a proposed project may or will cause environmental harm does not mean that the project cannot proceed. Rather NEPA, and its principal tool, the EIS, require that the scope of the harm be identified and the alternatives to the project (including abandonment of the project altogether) be considered before the decision to proceed is made.

Another requirement of the EIS is that it discuss measures that can be undertaken to minimize the environmental consequences of a proposed project. For instance, in *Oregon National Resources Council v. Marsh,* 820 F. 2d 1051 (9th Cir. 1987), the plaintiff sought to enjoin construction of a dam on Elk Creek, a tributary of the Rogue River in southern Oregon. The EIS acknowledged that fish and wildlife along the creek would be affected by the dam. Plaintiffs claimed that the EIS failed to address the ways in which the adverse environmental consequences could be minimized. The court agreed and made the following observations:

> The importance of the mitigation plan cannot be overestimated. It is a determinative factor in evaluating the adequacy of an environmental impact statement. Without a complete mitigation plan, the decision-maker is unable to make an informed judgment as to the environmental impact of the project—one of the main purposes of an environmental impact statement.
>
> As long as significant measures are undertaken to mitigate the project's effects, the measures need not compensate completely for adverse environmental impacts. The mere listing of mitigation measures, however, is insufficient to satisfy the NEPA requirements. Moreover, the EIS must analyze the mitigation measures in detail and explain the effectiveness of the measures.
>
> Here, the mitigation plan for wildlife is not yet fully developed. The mitigation plan, states: ''Measures to compensate project-caused loss of wildlife habitat associated with reservoir construction will be developed, based upon the results of the wildlife compensation plan currently underway.'' No mitigation plan has been finalized. We fail to see how mit-

igation measures can be properly analyzed and their effectiveness explained when they have yet to be developed.

NOTES AND QUESTIONS

What is the purpose of requiring mitigation measures be included in the EIS? In the *Oregon* case, the court issued a preliminary injunction against construction of the dam. What was the government required to do before the project was to go forward?

8 PROCEDURES FOR PREPARING THE EIS

We have seen that an (EIS) is required where a proposal for major federal action may significantly affect the quality of the human environment. The purpose of the EIS is to force federal agencies to evaluate the environmental consequences of their actions and to inform decision-makers and the public about the nature and extent of those consequences.

The preparation of the EIS is usually a two step process. The agency must first prepare a document known as an "environmental assessment." The environmental assessment is intended to provide sufficient evidence and analysis for determining whether it is necessary to prepare an EIS. If the agency finds that the proposal has "no significant impact" upon the environment, then it is not necessary to prepare an EIS. Of course, such a finding must be supported by substantial evidence or, as in the case of *Economic Trends v. Heckler,* a court will restrain the project from going forward until an EIS is prepared. Unless the environmental assessment concludes that there will be "no significant impact," an EIS must be prepared.

Courts have tended to strictly scrutinize an agency's conclusion of no significant impact. The standard of judicial review usually involves a four-part analysis:

(1) Whether the agency took a "hard look" at the problem;

(2) Whether the agency identified all relevant areas of environmental concern;

(3) As to the problems identified, whether the agency made a convincing case that the impact was insignificant; and

(4) If there was an impact of true significance, whether the agency convincingly established that changes in the project reduce it to a minimum.

Mid-Tex v. FERC, 773 F. 2d 327 (D.C.Cir. 1985)

The project may go forward in the absence of an EIS only if all of these requirements have been satisfied.

Preparation of the EIS is itself a two step process. The first step is known as the "draft" environmental impact statement. The draft EIS must include a description of the project and the affected environment, along with the environmental consequences, alternatives, and mitigation measures. The draft EIS is then circulated to interested government agencies and individuals. Because the EIS procedure is designed, in part, to inform the public, almost anyone who wants a copy of the draft EIS may obtain one.

The purpose of the draft EIS is to enable other agencies and the public to review and comment upon the EIS. The agency which prepares the draft EIS is required to solicit comments from any other federal or state agencies which have jurisdiction over the subject matter of the proposed project or which has particular expertise in the field. Federal agencies, in turn, have a duty to comment upon the draft EIS if they have jurisdiction or particular expertise in the area. For example, the Environmental Protection Agency (EPA) is requested to comment on nearly all EIS's and other federal and sometimes state agencies are solicited for comments depending upon their expertise in relation to the proposed project.

The final EIS must respond to comments to the draft and must discuss all responsible opposing views that were raised during the comment period. In other words, the agency must respond to issues raised during the comment period. The final EIS is also circulated to interested agencies and persons and to anyone who responded during the comment period.

Finally, the agency must supplement the EIS if there are substantial changes in the proposed action or if significant new information is brought to the attention of the agency. The supplemental EIS must be circulated and made available for comment in the same manner as the draft EIS.

The judicial response to the EIS requirement has been to recognize the statement as a central and essential element to NEPA and the courts have consistently required agencies to satisfy both the letter and spirit of the EIS requirement. The important early case of *Calvert Cliff's,* mentioned previously discussed the requirement of the EIS in the face of a claim by the Atomic Energy Commission that it was not required to respond to comments concerning its EIS. The court stridently disagreed, emphasizing the importance which Congress attached to the procedural aspects of NEPA.

> The Commission's crabbed interpretation of NEPA makes a mockery of the Act. What possible purpose could there be in requiring the "detailed statement" to be prepared by hearing boards, if the boards are free to ignore entirely the contents of the statement? NEPA was meant to do more than regulate the flow of papers in the federal bureaucracy. The word "accompany" in Section 102(2)(C) must not be read so narrowly as to make the Act ludicrous. It must, rather, be read to indicate a congressional intent that environmental factors, as compiled in the "detailed statement," be considered through agency review processes.
>
> Thus, the EIS duties are not inherently flexible. They must be complied with to the fullest extent, unless there is a clear conflict of statutory authority. Considerations of administrative difficulty, delay, or economic cost will not suffice to strip the section of its fundamental importance.
>
> We conclude, then, that NEPA mandates a particular sort of careful and informed decision-making process and creates judicially enforceable duties. If the decision was reached procedurally without individualized consideration and balancing of environmental factors—conducted fully and in good faith—it is the responsibility of the courts to reverse the agency's decision.
>
> 449 F. 2d at 1115 and 1118

9 POLLUTION CONTROL

There have been extensive efforts at the federal level and by most states, to identify, regulate, and control environmental pollution. The details of these efforts are beyond the scope of this text but are summarized in order to provide a brief overview of this extensive area of regulation.

A   Water Quality

The U.S. Congress and most state legislatures have enacted statutes aimed at controlling water as a natural resource. The Federal Water Pollution Control Act (33 U.S.C. Section 1251 et. seq.), known as the Clean Water Act, establishes a permit system to regulate the discharge of pollutants into navigable waters. Civil and criminal penalties may be imposed for violation of the Act.

B   Air Quality

The Federal Clean Air Act (42 U.S.C. Section 7401) directs the Environmental Protection Agency (EPA) to establish national standards for air quality and requires each state to submit plans for meeting these standards.

C   Hazardous Waste

The control of hazardous waste has been the subject of much legislation and commentary. Historically, the contamination of real property by hazardous substance has been resolved between neighbors under the common law principles of nuisance and trespass. In recent years, public concern about the health and safety consequences of contamination have received considerable attention. Various Federal and State statutes attempt to regulate the disposal and clean-up of hazardous substances. The primary Federal statute is the Comprehensive Environmental Response, Compensation and Liability Act of 1980 (CERCLA) 42 U.S.C. Section 9601.

CERCLA is the most important piece of legislation governing the relationship between hazardous substances and real property. A ''hazardous substance'' is defined as including any substance designated by the Clean Water Act, any hazardous air pollutant listed under the Clean Air Act, any hazardous wastes defined by the Solid Waste Disposal Act, and any hazardous chemical substance or mixture designated as such under the Toxic Substances Control Act. In addition, the administrator of the Environmental Protection Agency (EPA) has the authority to designate additional substances that may pose an imminent and substantial danger to public health or welfare.

CERCLA has three main components. It empowers the Federal government to take corrective action upon the release or threatened release of a hazardous substance. Second, it creates a fund to finance the clean-up of hazardous waste sites by the government. This ''super fund'' was intended to provide funds for cleaning up hazardous waste sites where there is no solvent owner to perform the work. Third, the Act imposes liability upon the ''owners and operators'' and requires them to clean up hazardous substances from their property.

Liability for cleaning up a site under CERCLA attaches to any ''owner or operator'' of a facility that has been contaminated by hazardous substances. Liability to clean up the site applies regardless of fault. For instance, in *U.S. vs. Monsanto Co.,* 858 F

2d. 160 (1988), the owner leased property to a chemical company under an oral month-to-month agreement for a rent of $350 per month. The chemical company deposited more than 7,000 barrels of chemical waste on the site. The government sued the owner under CERCLA to recover governmental clean-up costs of approximately $1.8 million. The court rejected the owners claim that they were innocent, absentee-landlords and held that the owners were strictly liable even though they were unaware of the waste disposal activities on the site. In another case, the lender who acquired contaminated property through a foreclosure sale was held liable for clean-up costs under CERCLA. (*U.S. vs. Maryland Bank & Trust,* 632 F. Supp. 573 (1986). Although the Maryland Bank case is an extreme example, and ''innocent buyers'' may be able to insulate themselves from CERCLA liability, the case illustrates the rigor with which CERCLA is applied, and the limited defenses that are available to the owner of a site polluted with a hazardous substance. The liability provisions under CERCLA are extremely broad. CERCLA imposes strict liability so that a defendant may be liable, regardless of fault, concerning the release of a hazardous substance. In addition, liability is retroactive so that a defendant may be held liable under CERCLA for releases or clean-up efforts that occurred before CERCLA was enacted in 1980. In addition, clean-up liability under CERCLA is perpetual. In other words, the responsible party may be held liable indefinitely as future problems develop and additional clean-up costs are incurred.

NOTES AND QUESTIONS

Suppose that you are contemplating the purchase of one hundred acres of un-developed land upon which you propose to construct a residential subdivision. In view of CERCLA and its state counterparts, what precautions should you take in order to avoid liability for clean-up costs?

10 ENVIRONMENTAL LEGISLATION ENACTED BY THE STATES

Most states have enacted some form of environmental legislation. Many, but not all of these are based upon the federal example set forth in the NEPA legislation.

For instance, California, Connecticut, Hawaii, Indiana, Maryland, Massachusetts, Minnesota, New York, and Washington, among others, have adopted legislation which closely follows the approach of NEPA. These states use the EIS concept for all projects which involve major state action.

Other jurisdictions have adopted more limited environmental statutes. For instance, Delaware has adopted the EIS requirement but only for portions of its coastal zone. Other states require an EIS only for areas considered to be particularly sensitive to environmental harm. Florida and Minnesota have statutes that create zones known as ''critical areas,'' which require a heightened review before a project will be allowed to proceed which may affect those critical areas.

The following case contains a careful examination of one state's effort to address environmental concerns and illustrates the operation of a NEPA-type statute at the state level and the concept of ''major action'' at the state level.

Friends of Mammoth v. Board of Mono County, 502 P. 2d 1049 (Cal. 1972)

This case affords us the first opportunity to construe provisions of the California Environmental Quality Act of 1970 (EQA). As the express legislative intent declares, the EQA was designed to be a milestone in the campaign for "maintenance of a quality environment for the people of this state now and in the future. . . ." The specific question presented here is whether a municipal body is required to submit an environmental impact report pursuant to the code before it issues a conditional use or building permit.

Facts of the case.

International Recreation, Ltd., (International) filed an application for a conditional use permit on April 20, 1971, with defendant Mono County Planning Commission (Commission). The applications described the proposed use as two multi-story structures housing sixty four condominiums with one, two, three, or four bedrooms, plus one hundred and twenty studio-type condominiums, a proposed restaurant, specialty shops, and ample parking and recreational facilities.

Mono County is situated in eastern California and is bordered on the east by the State of Nevada. The boundary on the west generally follows the crest of the Sierra Nevada mountain range. The county is primarily mountainous and open range land, almost all above 5,000 feet. It is California's third smallest county in population. Although historically a county oriented to the economy of cattle and sheep ranching, nature's bountiful gifts of majestic mountains, lakes, streams, trees, and wildlife have produced in the area one of the nation's most spectacularly beautiful and comparatively unspoiled treasures.

OPINION

The principal legal question that arises is whether the EQA applies to private activities for which a permit or other similar entitlement is required, or whether it is limited to projects sponsored by state or local government.

Though recognition of the problem in and out of government is more pervasive today, concern over violation of our environment is not entirely a contemporary phenomenon. Four decades ago Justice Holmes described a river as "more than an amenity, it is a treasure. It offers a necessity of life that must be rationed among those who have power over it," *New Jersey v. New York*, 283 U.S. 336 (1931). Five years ago Justice Douglas spoke for the high court in admonishing the Federal Power Commission that the issue is not "whether the project will be beneficial to the licensee. . . . The test is whether the project will be in the public interest . . . in preserving reaches of wild rivers and wilderness areas . . . and the protection of wildlife," *Udall v. Federal Power Commission*, 387 U.S. 428 (1967). More recently, a circuit court discussed statutes attesting "to the commitment of the government to control, at long last, the destructive engine of material 'progress.' " The duty of the judiciary, it held, is to assure that important environment purposes, heralded in legislative halls, are not lost or misdirected in the vast hallways of administrative bureaucracy, *Calvert Cliffs' v. Atomic Energy Comm., supra.*

California Environmental Quality Act of 1970 requires various state and local governmental entities to submit environmental impact reports before undertaking specified activity. These reports compel state and local agencies to consider the possible adverse consequences to the environment of the proposed activity and to record such impact in writing.

We conclude that the Legislature intended the EQA to be interpreted in such manner as to afford the fullest possible protection to the environment within the reasonable scope of the statutory language. We also conclude that to achieve that maximum protection the Legislature necessarily intended to include within the operation of the act, private activities for which a government permit or other entitlement for use is necessary.

To limit the operation of the EQA solely to what are essentially public works projects would frustrate the effectiveness of the act. It is undisputed that the Legislature intended that environmental considerations play a significant role in governmental decision-making and that such an intent was not to be effectuated by vague or illusory assurances by state and local entities that the effect of a project on the environment had been "taken into consideration."

To exclude all private activity from being covered by the act would be inconsistent with the broad legislative intent appearing therein. More specifically, if private activities for which a permit is required were exempted from the operation of the act, projects with admittedly adverse ecological consequences would be covered only if construction, acquisition, or other development were undertaken by the governmental authority but not if the same authority allowed private enterprise to engage in the identical activity. The incongruity of such interpretation would be most vivid in the less populous counties, such as Mono, which because of limited economic capabilities might never engage in massive public works projects significantly affecting the environment, but could achieve the same result in permitting, licensing, or partially funding similar private activities.

We emphasize that by the terms of the act an environmental impact report is required only for a project "which may have a significant effect on the environment." In the case at bar the issue whether the proposed project of International might have such an effect was not resolved presumably because it was believed the project was not covered by the act in any event.

We recognize that the reach of the statutory phrase, "significant effect on the environment," is not immediately clear. To some extent this is inevitable in a statute which deals, as the EQA must, with questions of degree.

Two general observations, nevertheless, may be made at this time. We stress that the Legislature has mandated an environmental impact report not only when a proposed project will have a significant environmental effect, but also when it "may" or "could" have such an effect. On the other hand, common sense tells us that the majority of private projects for which a government permit or similar entitlement is necessary are minor in scope—e.g., relating only to the construction, improvement, or operation of an individual dwelling or small business—and hence, in the absence of unusual circumstances, have little or no effect on the public environment. Such projects, accordingly, may be approved exactly as before the enactment of the EQA.

The order appealed from is reversed with directors ordering defendants to set aside the issuance of the conditional use and building permits.

NOTES AND QUESTIONS

1 States which follow the NEPA example tend to require an environmental assessment to determine whether an EIS must be prepared and to extend the operation of the statute to all or nearly all projects for which a permit is required. Is this consistent with NEPA? Should NEPA and its state counterparts consider the expense and delay of complying with environmental concerns?

2 Suppose that the project proposed in the *Mono County* case required the issuance of a permit by a federal agency. Would NEPA have applied? Would an EIS be necessary?

11 SUMMARY

In response to the perception that the human environment was being permanently degraded, Congress passed a series of statutes designed to address and modify this process. The National Environmental Policy Act is perhaps the most important environmental protection statute and certainly has had the greatest impact upon land use policies and practice.

NEPA requires that federal agencies carefully consider environmental factors during the course of projects initiated by the federal government or requiring the approval of the federal government. Under NEPA, environmental consequences must be considered along with technological, economic, and other factors in determining whether and in what form, a project should be undertaken.

The primary tool for accomplishing the objectives of NEPA is the Environmental Impact Statement (EIS). The EIS is intended to inform the decision-making agency and the public of the environmental consequences of ''major federal action'' that may have a ''significant affect'' upon the environment. The EIS must address these impacts and discuss the alternatives and ways in which the environmental consequences of the project can be minimized. The federal courts have not been hesitant to enjoin projects from going forward if an EIS is not prepared or if it is carelessly prepared.

Nearly all states have enacted statutes aimed at regulating the environmental consequences of certain projects. Many of these are patterned after NEPA and employ the concept of the EIS along the same lines of the federal model.

12 QUESTIONS

1 A logging company needs a federal permit to harvest timber from land that is included within the national forest. An EIS is prepared which satisfies all procedural aspects of NEPA. The

EIS concludes that some wildlife habitat will be destroyed and that some soil erosion will occur that is likely to interfere with stream beds, fish, and water fowl. A citizen's group contends that on the basis of the EIS, the agency may not approve the project. Are they correct?

2 The City of Atlanta built a new runway for its airport. The runway was not being used because the Federal Aviation Administration had not approved the airport's use of navigational equipment and flight procedures relative to the runway. Is the application to make the runway operational "major federal action" within the meaning of NEPA?

3 The Army Corps of Engineers issued a permit to build a barge docking facility on the Mississippi River. The permit was issued on the basis of an environmental assessment that concluded the facility would have no significant impact upon the environment. Is the Army Corps required to prepare an EIS?

4 Faced with the fact of a large number of suicides by jumping off the Duke Ellington Bridge in Washington, D.C., the U.S. Department of Transportation sought to erect suicide barriers along the span of the bridge. This action was challenged on various grounds, including failure to consider environmental factors under NEPA. Does NEPA apply to this "federal action"?

5 Federal court decisions held that the Alabama prison system was inadequate and must be upgraded. In response to these developments, Alabama planned for the development of a new prison facility. Does NEPA apply to this project?

INDEX

Divided interest in just compensation, 367
Doctrine of Covenants Running with the
    Land at Law, 138
Doctrine of nuisance, 102
Dominant estate, 116
Dual agency, 183

E

Earnest money contract, 281
Easement by express reservation, 117,
    118–119, 124
    Willard v. First Church, 119–120
    scope of easements, 124–126
Easement in gross, 116, 130
Easement by implication, 117, 120, 122
    based on necessity, 120–122, 132
        Deisenroth v. Dodge, 121
    quasi-easements, 117, 120–122
        Finn v. Williams, 121
    scope of easements, 127–128
    secondary easements, 127
Easement by prescription, 117, 123
    scope of easement, 127–129
Easements, 115–134
    burden of repair/maintenance, 129
    creation of, 117–124
    license, 132–134
    scope of, 124–126
    termination of, 131–132
    terminology, 116–117
    transfer of, 129–130
EIS. *see* Environmental impact statement
    (EIS)
Eminent domain, 164, 355, 365, 367
    See also Condemnation power
Enfeoffment ceremony, 201, 202
English common law, 5, 74, 314
    mortgage at, 272
Environmental impact statement (EIS), 418,
    420–421, 423–424
Environmental legislation enacted by states,
    434–435
Environmental protection, 417–437
    contents of EIS, 429–431
    council on environmental quality, 419–420
    environmental impact statement (EIS),
        420–421
    legislation enacted by states, 434–435

Environmental protection (*Cont.*)
    *Friends of Mammoth v. Board of Mono
        County*, 435–437
    "major federal action," 421
        *Foundation on Economic Trends v.
            Heckler*, 421–425
    NEPA statement of environmental policy,
        418–419
    pollution control, 433–434
    procedures for preparing EIS, 431–433
    "significantly affecting," 426–427
        *Metropolitan Edison Co. v. People
            Against Nuclear Energy (PANE)*,
            427–429
Environmental Protection Agency (EPA),
    432, 433
EPA. *see* Environmental Protection Agency
    (EPA)
Equitable conversion and risk loss, 212
    shifting risk of loss, 214–215
    Uniform Vendor and Purchaser Risk Act,
        215
Equitable liens, 301–302
Equitable reformation, 65
Equitable servitudes, 138, 148
    elements of, 150–151
        Sandborn v. McLean, 151–152
        Tulk v. Moxhay, 148–149
Equity, 12–13
Equity of redemption, 284, 289
Escheat, 164
Escrow, nature of, 259–260
Escrow holders, 258–262
    liability of, 260–262
Estate, 21
    definition, 22
    freehold, 22
    future interests, 22
    nonfreehold, 22
    present interests, 22
Estate from period to period, periodic
    tenancy, 31
Estate at will, 31–32
Estate for years, 31
Eviction, 321
    actual, 321
    for cause only, 333–334
    constructive, 323
    partial actual, 321–322